COUNTRY LIVING
MAGAZINE

Guide to Rural England

THE HEART OF ENGLAND

Derbyshire, Herefordshire, Leicestershire, Lincolnshire, Northamptonshire, Nottinghamshire, Rutland, Shropshire, Staffordshire, Warwickshire, West Midlands, Worcestershire

By Peter Long

Published by:
Travel Publishing Ltd
Airport Business Centre, 10 Thornbury Road,
Estover, Plymouth PL6 7PP

ISBN13 9781904434887
© Travel Publishing Ltd
Country Living is a registered trademark of The National
Magazine Company Limited.

First Published: 2001
Second Edition: 2004
Third Edition: 2007
Fourth Edition: 2009

COUNTRY LIVING GUIDES:

East Anglia	Scotland
Heart of England	The South of England
Ireland	The South East of England
The North East of England	The West Country
The North West of England	Wales

PLEASE NOTE:

All advertisements in this publication have been accepted in good faith by Travel Publishing and they have not necessarily been endorsed by *Country Living* Magazine.

All information is included by the publishers in good faith and is believed to be correct at the time of going to press. No responsibility can be accepted for errors.

Editor:	Peter Long
Printing by:	Latimer Trend, Plymouth
Location Maps:	© Maps in Minutes ™ (2009) © Collins Bartholomews 2009 All rights reserved.
Walks:	Walks have been reproduced with kind permission of the internet walking site: www.walkingworld.com
Walk Maps:	Reproduced from Ordnance Survey mapping on behalf of the Controller of Her Majesty's Stationery Office, © Crown Copyright. Licence Number MC 100035812
Cover Design:	Lines & Words, Aldermaston
Cover Photo:	Tredington Green, Tredington, Warwickshire © Britain on View
Text Photos:	Text photos have been kindly supplied by the Pictures of Britain photo library © www.picturesofbritain.co.uk and © Bob Brooks, Weston-super-Mare

Foreword

From a bracing walk across the hills and tarns of The Lake District to a relaxing weekend spent discovering the unspoilt hamlets of East Anglia, nothing quite matches getting off the beaten track and exploring Britain's areas of outstanding beauty.

Each month, *Country Living Magazine* celebrates the richness and diversity of our countryside with features on rural Britain and the traditions that have their roots there. So it is with great pleasure that I introduce you to the *Country Living Magazine Guide to Rural England* series. Packed with information about unusual and unique aspects of our countryside, the guides will point both fair-weather and intrepid travellers in the right direction.

Each chapter provides a fascinating tour of the Heart of England area, with insights into local heritage and history and easy-to-read facts on a wealth of places to visit, stay, eat, drink and shop.

I hope that this guide will help make your visit a rewarding and stimulating experience and that you will return inspired, refreshed and ready to head off on your next countryside adventure.

Susy Smith

Susy Smith
Editor, Country Living magazine

PS To subscribe to *Country Living Magazine* each month, call 01858 438844

Introduction

This is the fourth edition of the *Country Living Guide to Rural England - The Heart of England* and we are sure that it will be as popular as its predecessors.

Peter Long, a very experienced travel writer has, of course, completely updated the contents of the guide and ensured that it is packed with vivid descriptions, historical stories, amusing anecdotes and interesting facts on hundreds of places in Derbyshire, Herefordshire, Leicestershire, Lincolnshire, Northamptonshire, Nottinghamshire, Rutland, Shropshire, Staffordshire, Warwickshire, the West Midlands and Worcestershire. In the introduction to each village or town we have also summarized and categorized the main attractions to be found there, which makes it easy for readers to plan their visit.

The advertising panels within each chapter provide further information on places to see, stay, eat, drink and shop. We have also selected a number of walks from walkingworld.com (full details of this website may be found to the rear of the guide), which we highly recommend if you wish to appreciate fully the dramatic landscapes, rich cultural heritage and rural charm of the varied rural landscapes of the Heart of England.

The guide however is not simply an 'armchair tour'. Its prime aim is to encourage the reader to visit the places described and discover much more about the wonderful towns, villages and countryside of the Heart of England. In this respect we would like to thank all the Tourist Information Centres who helped us to provide you with up-to-date information. Whether you decide to explore this region by wheeled transport or on foot we are sure you will find it a very uplifting experience!

We are always interested in receiving comments on places covered (or not covered) in our guides so please do not hesitate to use the reader reaction forms provided at the rear of this guide to give us your considered comments. This will help us refine and improve the content of the next edition. We also welcome any general comments which will help improve the overall presentation of the guides themselves.

For more information on the full range of travel guides published by Travel Publishing please refer to the order form at the rear of this guide or log on to our website (see below).

Travel Publishing

Did you know that you can also search our website for details of thousands of places to see, stay, eat or drink throughout Britain and Ireland? Our site has become increasingly popular and now receives monthly hundreds of thousands of visits. Try it!

website: www.findsomewhere.co.uk

Contents

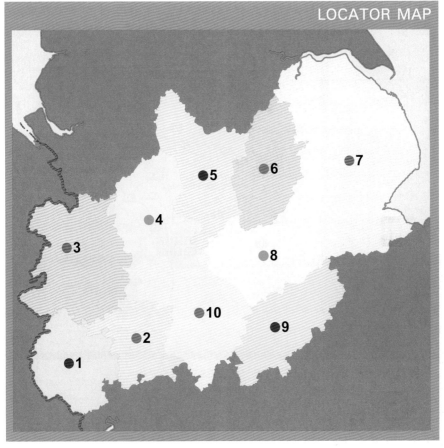

LOCATOR MAP

LOCATOR MAP

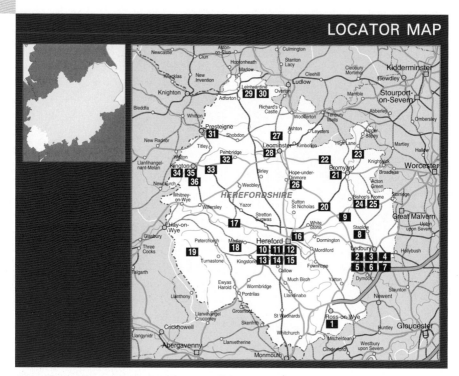

ADVERTISERS AND PLACES OF INTEREST

🏛 historic building   🏛 museum   🏛 historic site   🍃 scenic attraction   🌿 flora and fauna

1 | Herefordshire

"Wherever one goes, there will not be a mile that is visually unrewarding." Sir Nikolaus Pevsner was clearly impressed, and today's visitors will also find delights at every turn in the rolling landscape, the pretty villages and the charming market towns. Herefordshire had few natural resources, so the industrial scars that spoil many counties are mercifully absent; the beauty and peace remain relatively intact, and motorists will generally find traffic-free roads. Apples and hops are the traditional crops of Herefordshire, and the cider industry is still a thriving one. The days when almost every farm produced its own cider are long gone, but many of the old mills are preserved on the farms or in museums. Large areas (over 9,500 acres) of the county are given over to cider orchards, and 63 million gallons of cider are produced here each year - well over half the UK total. The Cider Museum in Hereford is a good starting point for taking the Cider Route, which tours the Herefordshire countryside and includes more than a dozen cider-makers.

In western Herefordshire perry is something of a speciality, It is made in a similar way to cider but with pears instead of apples. Hops have been cultivated in the county since the 16th century and once provided late summer work for thousands of pickers, mainly from the Black Country and south Wales. The industry is considerably smaller now, and mechanisation has greatly reduced the need for manual labour. The poles and wires used to support the hops are a less common sight, but they can still be seen, along with the occasional kiln for drying the hops - the Herefordshire equivalent of Kent's oast houses. Sheep and cattle are a familiar sight; Hereford cattle are found in many parts of the world, particularly on the American continent.

Industry was never developed to any great extent in the county, partly through the remoteness of the location and the poverty of communications, and the visible traces of its heritage are confined largely to castles (this is Border territory) and churches. The castles were mainly of the straightforward motte and bailey variety, the motte being a tower-topped earthen mound surrounded by a small court, the bailey a larger yard with the stables and workshops and accommodation. Skirmishes with the Welsh were a common occurrence for many centuries, and one of the county's best-known landmarks, Offa's Dyke, was built in the 8th century as a defence against the Welsh marauders.

ADVERTISERS AND PLACES OF INTEREST

📖 stories and anecdotes 🦢 famous people ✏ art and craft ✐ entertainment and sport 🚶 walks

South Herefordshire

The River Wye rises in the Plynlimon mountains east of Aberystwyth, near the spot where the Severn also has its source. The Wye enters England by Hay-on-Wye and winds its way through some of the most delightful scenery in the whole land, changing mood and direction from time to time and finally joining its original neighbour at the Severn Estuary. The whole of its length offers great touring and walking country, and the Wye Valley Walk, waymarked with the logo of the leaping salmon, follows the river closely for 112 miles, almost half of which are in Herefordshire. The valley was designated an Area of Outstanding Natural Beauty (AONB) in 1971, and the river itself was the first to be recognised as a Site of Special Scientific Interest (SSSI). The salmon logo is, of course, wholly appropriate, as the Wye is a Mecca for anglers. In the 18th century, artists, poets and the leisured classes enjoyed the Wye Tour, a highly agreeable alternative to the European Grand Tour, and three centuries later the car, train and bicycle have brought the charm of the valley within the reach of all.

SYMONDS YAT
5 miles NE of Monmouth off the A40 and B4164

🏛 Seven Sisters Rock   🏛 Caves

🌿 Jubilee Park   🍃 Amazing Hedge Puzzle

Travelling upstream, a journey through the southern part of the county starts at the beauty spot of Symonds Yat, an inland resort to which visitors flock to enjoy the views, the walks, the river cruises, the wildlife (peregrine falcons nest at Coldwell Rocks), the history and the adventure. Into the last category fall canoeing - rushing down the Wye gorge south of the village - and rock climbing. Symonds Yat (yat means gap) is divided into east and west by the Wye, with no vehicular bridge at that point. Pedestrians can make use of the punt ferry, pulled across the river by chain, but the journey by car is 4.5 miles. Walking in the area is an endless delight and, at The Biblins, a swaying suspension bridge provides vertiginous thrills across the river. Notable landmarks include the **Seven Sisters Rocks**, a collection of oolitic limestone crags; **Merlin's Cave**; **King Arthur's Cave**, where the bones of mammoths and other prehistoric creatures have been found; Coldwell Rocks and Yat Rock itself, rising to 500 feet

The River Wye from Yat Rock

above sea level at a point where the river performs a long and majestic loop. Also on the Symonds Yat walkabout is a massive boulder measuring 60 feet by 40 feet, one of the largest in the country.

Other entertainment in the area is provided by the **Amazing Hedge Puzzle** devised by brothers Lindsay and Edward Heyès to celebrate Queen Elizabeth's 1977 Jubilee. On the same site is a museum of mazes and a puzzle shop with the largest collection of puzzle games in the UK. Also in the **Jubilee Park** is a garden centre with an extensive range of plants plus garden furniture and a gift shop. The church in Symonds Yat, built in the 14th century, is dedicated to St Dubricius, a local who converted the area to Christianity and who, according to legend, crowned King Arthur.

In 1993 Symonds Yat provided the backdrop for the film *Shadowlands* starring Anthony Hopkins and Debra Winger and based on the life of CS Lewis and his wife.

WHITCHURCH
4½ miles NE of Monmouth off the A40

🏚 Goodrich Castle 🌱 Zoo

At Symonds Yat West, close to the village of Whitchurch, the **Wye Valley Butterfly Zoo** gives visitors the chance to experience the warmth of a tropical hothouse with butterflies flitting freely about their heads. See them fly, hatch, court, lay eggs, display their colours and sup nectar from the fragrant tropical plants. Open daily throughout the year. A little further up, just off the A40, is Kerne Bridge, a settlement that grew around a bridge built in 1828, where coracles are still made, and from where the energetic walker can hike to the historic and majestic **Goodrich Castle**,

which stands in a commanding position above the Wye. Built of red sandstone in the 11th century by Godric Mapplestone, the castle is now ruined but still magnificent. It was the last bastion to fall in the Civil War, attacked by 'Roaring Meg', a siege gun cast in Whitchurch that could hurl a 200lb ball and which can now be seen in Hereford. The siege lasted four and a half months and marked the end of the castle's 'working life'. English Heritage maintains the ruins, and the 12th-century keep and elements from the following two centuries are well worth a visit, either to walk the ramparts or just to imagine the glorious sight it once presented. The Castle is open daily from April to 1 November, Wednesday to Sunday at other times.

Torwood, near Whitchurch, is an interesting cottage garden by the village school, specialising in shrubs, conifers and herbaceous plants. Private visits welcome.

GOODRICH
6 miles NE of Monmouth off the A40

Goodrich village is notable for the landmark 14th-century broach spire of its parish church. The vicar at a critical point in the Civil War was one Thomas Swift, grandfather of Jonathan Swift, author of *Gulliver's Travels*. This staunch royalist hid some of the church's treasures, including a superb silver chalice, from the marauders and, it is said, sewed 300 pieces of gold into his waistcoat to take to the king.

WELSH NEWTON
4 miles N of Monmouth on the A466

The village lies right on the A466, and just off it stands Pembridge Castle, now a private house. In the village churchyard of St Mary the Virgin lies the body of John Kemble, a

Roman Catholic who was executed in 1679 for daring to hold a mass in the castle. A plain slab commemorates the martyr, who was 80 years of age when he met his violent end. Several more castles along the River Monmow are further reminders that this pretty part of the world was once a very turbulent one.

ST WEONARDS
9 miles N of Monmouth on the A466

🏛 Violette Szabo GC Museum

This little hilltop village is named after an obscure Welsh saint who is portrayed in early-16th century stained glass in the church named after him. Most of the church is of the same period, but a 13th-century doorway in the porch has survived.

About three miles north of St Weonards, at Wormelow Tump, the **Violette Szabo GC Museum** celebrates the bravery of the young Herefordshire woman who was parachuted into Nazi-occupied France to work with the maquis. While trying to save a key agent, using a sten gun single-handed, she was captured, imprisoned, tortured and shot in January 1945. The 1950s film *Carve Her Name With Pride*, with Virginia McKenna in the title role, tells her dramatic story. The museum, opened in June 2000, contains memorabilia of this remarkable woman and is open on Wednesdays from April to October, other times by appointment (01981 540477/540328).

LLANROTHAL
6 miles NW of Monmouth off the A466

Standing in isolation at the end of a lane by the river is the Church of St John the Baptist, built in the 12th and 13th centuries and restored from almost total ruin in the 1920s.

SKENFRITH
7 miles NW of Monmouth on the B4521

🏛 Skenfrith Castle

A drive or an energetic walk takes in the remains of **Skenfrith Castle** (the round tower is an impressive sight), an ancient mill and the Church of St Bridget, dating, like the castle, from the 12th and 13th centuries. All in the tiny village of Skenfrith!

GARWAY
9 miles NW of Monmouth on a minor road

🏛 Dovecote   🌾 Garway Hill

Marvellous views from the wild and remote **Garway Hill** take in the river valley, the Forest of Dean beyond Symonds Yat to the east, and the Black Mountains. The church at Garway was built by the Knights Templar and the influences from the Holy Sepulchre in Jerusalem can clearly be seen. During the purges of Henry VIII's reign, the Abbot of Monmouth was one of many who sought refuge in the church tower. The most unusual building in Garway is undoubtedly the famous **Dovecote**, the first of several to be mentioned in this guide. Built in the 1300s (probably the work of the same good knights) it stands in a farmyard next to the church and has precisely 666 pigeonholes.

GROSMONT
12 miles NW of Monmouth on the B4347

In the village of Grosmont lies another castle with impressive remains, and another interesting church, this one dedicated to St Nicolas of Myra.

A little way beyond Grosmont is Kentchurch Court, a one-time border castle rebuilt by John Nash around 1800 and featuring some splendid wood carvings by

Grinling Gibbons. The Court has for many centuries been the home of the Scudamore family, one of whose number married Owen Glendower.

Ross-on-Wye

🏠 Market House 🖋 Festival

The lovely old market town of Ross-on-Wye is signalled from some way off by the towering spire of St Mary's Church, surrounded up on its sandstone cliffs by a cluster of attractive houses. Opposite the church is a row of Tudor almshouses, which have an ancient yet ageless look and show off the beauty of the rosy-red sandstone to great effect. The town was visited by the Black Death in 1637, and over 300 victims are buried in the churchyard. A simple stone cross commemorates these hapless souls, who were interred in the dead of night in an effort to avoid panicking the populace. Notable features in the church include 15th-century stained glass figures and a tomb chest with effigies of William Rudhall, Attorney General to Henry Vlll and founder of the almshouses, and his wife. Pride of place in the market square goes to the 17th-century Market House, with an open ground floor and pillars supporting the upper floor, which is a Heritage Centre. Spot the relief of Charles ll on the east wall.

Among the many other interesting buildings in Ross is Thrushes Nest, once the home of Sir Frederick Burrows, a railway porter who rose in life to become the last Governor of Bengal. Opposite **Market House** stands the half-timbered house (now shops) of the town's greatest benefactor, John Kyrle. A wealthy barrister who had studied law at the Middle Temple, Kyrle settled in Ross around

Market House, Ross-on-Wye

each August and grows in stature year by year. In and around Ross are several examples of modern public art, including leaping salmon metal sculptures (Edde Cross Street) and a mural celebrating the life of locally-born playwright Dennis Potter. At Ross-on-Wye Candlemakers in Gloucester Road are a shop and workshop showing the manufacture of all types of candles, with evening demonstrations and group visits by appointment.

Around Ross-on-Wye

WESTON-UNDER-PENYARD
2 miles E of Ross on the A40

🌿 Hope Mansell Valley   🌿 Forest of Dean

Leave the A40 at Weston Cross to Bollitree Castle (a folly), then turn left to Rudhall and you'll come upon Kingstone Cottages, whose delightful informal gardens contain the National Collection of old pinks and carnations. Private visits welcome.

South of Weston lies **Hope Mansell Valley**, tucked away between the River Wye and the Forest of Dean, and certainly one of the loveliest and most fertile valleys in the region. It is an area of wooded hills and spectacular views, of farms and small settlements, with the tiny village of Hope Mansell itself at the far end. **The Forest of Dean**, over the border in Gloucestershire, is a vast and ancient woodland full of beauty and mystery, with signs of an Iron Age settlement. Later a royal hunting ground, and the home of charcoal-burners and shepherds, it became the first National Forest Park.

1660 and dedicated the rest of his life to philanthropic works: he donated the town's main public garden, The Prospect; he repaired St Mary's spire; he provided a constant supply of fresh water; and he paid for food and education for the poor. Alexander Pope was as impressed as anyone by this benefactor, penning these lines some time after the great man died in 1724 at the age of 87:

Rise, honest Muse, and sing the Man of Ross,
Health to the sick and solace to the swain,
Whose causeway parts the vale in shady rows,
Whose seats the weary traveller repose,
Who taught that heav'n directed spire to rise?
'The Man of Ross', each lisping babe replies.

The **Ross International Festival** of music, opera, theatre, comedy and film takes place

🏛 historic building   🏛 museum   🏚 historic site   🌿 scenic attraction   🍃 flora and fauna

YATTON
5 miles NE of Ross on the A449

In a remote farmyard setting off the B4224, Yatton Chapel, disused for many years, is a simple little church with a 12th-century doorway, a wooden belfry, agricultural floor and largely unplastered walls.

MUCH MARCLE
7 miles NE of Ross on the A449

🏛 Church 🏛 Hellens 🐏 Westons Cider Mill

🏛 Cider Museums 🐏 Great Marcle Yew

🐏 Newbridge Farm Park

This is Big Apple Country, with major cider connections in the shape of **Westons Cider Mill** and Lyne Down Farm, where traditional methods of making cider and perry are still employed. Among the many attractions are free cider tasting, the Bottle Museum, a wetland nature reserve, the award-winning Henry Weston Courtyard Garden, a traditional and rare breeds farm park, shire horse dray rides and a tea room. Open daily; tours start every day at 11am, 12.30pm and 2.30pm (free samples for adults!). The **Church of St Bartholomew** is notable for some superb tombs and monuments, amongst them an effigy of Much Marcle's 'Sleeping Beauty'. The well-preserved effigy portrays Blanche Mortimer, daughter of the 1st Earl of March, who died in 1347. As was customary at that time, the effigy depicts her as aged around 30 – the supposed age at which Christ was crucified – suggesting the possibility of marriage to Him in Heaven.

The church contains another striking figure, a rare painted wooden effigy, carved from solid oak, which is thought to be the likeness of a 14th-century landowner called Walter de Helyon. Up until the 1970s he was painted a rather sombre stone colour, but was then loaned for an exhibition of Chaucer's London and was repainted in his original colours. The **Great Marcle Yew** is a talking point among all visitors to the village - its massive trunk has been hollowed out, allowing up to eight people to enjoy cosy comfort on the bench inside.

A short distance north of Much Marcle, **Hellens** is an untouched Tudor/Stuart house set in 15 acres of grounds with coppices, lawns and fishponds. The house contains a wealth of period furnishings and decorations, fine paintings, miniatures and artefacts.

Closer to Ledbury, on the A4172 at Little Marcle, is **Newbridge Farm Park**, where families can enjoy a day out on the farm in the company of a large assortment of friendly farm animals (01531 670780).

LEDBURY
10 miles NE of Ross on the A449

🏛 Barrett Browning Institute 🏛 Market House

🏛 Church 🏛 Eastnor Castle

🏛 How Caple Court 🏛 Butchers Row Museum

🏛 Heritage Centre 🏛 Painted Room

A classic market town filled with timber-framed black-and-white buildings, mentioned in the Domesday Book as Ledeberge and accorded its market status in the 12th century. The centre of the town is dominated by the **Barrett Browning Institute** of 1892, erected in memory of the poet Elizabeth Barrett Browning, whose family lived at nearby Colwall. Alongside it are the almshouses of St Katherine's Hospital, founded in 1232 for wayfarers and the poor. Church Lane, much in demand for calendars and as a location for film scenes, is a cobbled medieval street where some of the buildings seem almost to meet across the street. In the **Heritage Centre**, in a

WYEBRIDGE INTERIORS

26 High Street, Ledbury,
Herefordshire HR8 1DS
Tel: 01531 634102
e-mail: info@presentsR4U.com
website: www.presentsR4U.com

"A wonderful range of designer
led gifts for every occasion at
affordable prices."

Wyebridge Interiors incorporating
Wyebridge 2 and PresentsR4U.com
is situated in our shop in Ledbury
High Street, Herefordshire. Ledbury is in the heart of the beautiful English countryside and central
to the Malvern Hills, Gloucester, the Cotswolds, Hereford, the Wye Valley and the proximate
Welsh Marches and Leominster.

"We specialise in all aspects of Designer led interior furnishings including: furniture, pictures,
lighting, mirrors, soft furnishing, cushions, fabrics, and paints. Our fashion accessories include:
jewellery , handbags, scarves and gloves. A complete range of original and high quality gifts and
presents are to be found on the website as well as in the Ledbury shop. We also offer a
comprehensive wedding list service. The utmost care is taken in obtaining the best quality
products from our diverse range of international craftsmen and suppliers. You can source fabrics
and wallpapers at Chelsea Harbour and then order through us. Our friendly staff are always ready
to assist be it in the shop or on the telephone."

In 1987 Mary Pytel set up Wyebridge interiors in Hereford. With her background in antiques,
decorative textiles and an art school training, the business quickly became Herefords leading
interior design showroom. In 1997, Mary branched out, opening another shop in the thriving
market town of Ledbury in the High Street. Wyebridge 2 is now a successful home interiors,
accessories and gift shop, offering a sophisticated blend of unusual artefacts and attracting a wide
range of customers and clients from many parts of the world.

Walenty Pytel is internationally renowned as Europe's leading metal sculptor of birds & beasts
and his sculptures can be viewed on the shop website. One of his best known public works is the
majestic jubilee fountain standing under Big Ben at the Houses of Parliament.

🏛 historic building   🏛 museum   🏛 historic site   🌳 scenic attraction   🌿 flora and fauna

timber-framed former grammar school, visitors can learn about Ledbury's past, John Masefield and Elizabeth Barrett Browning, and try their hand at timber framing. Opposite the Heritage Museum is the **Butchers Row Museum**, a tiny museum depicting Victorian life. The house used to stand in the middle of the High Street but was demolished in about 1830. It was re-erected in 1979 in Church Lane by the Ledbury & District Society. Also in Church Lane is the 16th-century **Painted Room** with unique Tudor wall paintings.

The town's symbol is the **Market House**, dating from about 1650 and attributed to John Abel, the royal carpenter. Another notable landmark is the Norman parish **Church of St Michael and All Angels**, with a soaring 18th-century spire set on a separate 13th-century tower, a golden weather vane, some magnificent medieval brasses, fine monuments by Westmacott, Flaxman and Thornycroft, and bullet holes in the door - the scars of the Battle of Ledbury. The town's history has in general been fairly placid, but its peace was broken with a vengeance in April 1645, when Royalist troops under Prince Rupert surprised a Roundhead advance from Gloucester. In the fierce fighting that followed there were many deaths, and 400 men were taken prisoner.

Annual events at Ledbury include a poetry festival in July, a street carnival in August and a hop fair in the autumn. Among the famous sons of the town is one of our most distinguished Poets Laureate, John Masefield, born in 1878 in a house called The Knapp. William Langland, who wrote Piers Plowman, was born in 1332 in nearby Colwall. The town is a great place for walking and, on the fringes, nature-lovers will find plenty to delight in Dog Hill Wood, Frith Wood and

THE VELVET BEAN

Church Lane, Ledbury, Herefordshire HR8 1DH
Tel: 01531 634744
e-mail: shop@thevelvetbeanchocolates.co.uk
website: www.thevelvetbeanchocolates.co.uk

Located in the heart of Ledbury lies a treat for chocolate lovers everywhere. Ben and Melissa Boyle's **The Velvet Bean** is a small yet delightful chocolate shop. The first thing you'll notice upon entering the shop is the wonderful comforting aroma of chocolate. You could get your chocolate fix just breathing in the chocolate fumes. Irresistibly delicious chocolate of the finest quality and the most unique flavours are hand-crafted by Ben and Melissa at their home just outside Ledbury.

Using only premium ingredients from around the world, such as the finest Belgium chocolate, local Herefordshire cream and local liquors, Ben and Melissa have created an extensive range of handmade mouth-watering dark, white and milk chocolates, pralines and truffles to choose from. They do like to indulge themselves and their customers, so they are always experimenting with new flavours and fillings, you'll always find something new to try when you visit them in store. The Velvet Bean's chocolates make great gifts for loved ones and you can now order them from the online shop!

JOHN NASH INTERIORS

18 High Street, Ledbury,
Herefordshire HR8 1DS
Tel: 01531 635714
Fax: 01531 635050
e-mail: enquiries@johnnash.co.uk
website: www.johnnash.co.uk

John Nash Interiors specialise in antiques and bespoke interior design for commercial and private property. Owners John Nash & Louis Calleja are known all over Great Britain and Europe for their high standard of workmanship and unrivalled knowledge of antiques. John's specialist knowledge and contacts contribute to the unique selection of antiques and collector's items that can be found in the shop. John also sources individual pieces for clients, shipping both large and small items abroad on a regular basis. Louis and his design team work closely with their clients, carefully interpreting clients instructions, and at the same time, providing innovative working solutions for required criteria on both domestic and commercial projects.

The fabric showroom houses from over seventy different designers/suppliers, in addition, an extensive range of flooring and lighting products guarantee that every aspect of a project has access to the most comprehensive and current range of products and materials. John Nash Interiors is the oldest business in Ledbury and offers the most stylish and contemporary interior design service outside of London.

CELEBRATIONS

1 High Street, Ledbury, Herefordshire HR8 1DS
Tel: 01531 634566
e-mail: celebrations@ledbury.hotmail.com

Situated in the heart of Ledbury town centre, **Celebrations** is an Aladdin's Cave of gifts, local crafts and greetings cards. It is owned and run by Melissa and Ben Boyle, who moved to Ledbury from the Home Counties after falling in love with the area while visiting relatives. They have revamped the shop and introduced many new lines, with an amazing variety of gifts for all the family to suit every pocket. There's a fabulous range of toiletries from Norfolk Lavender, collectable mugs and plates, toys, games, gizmos and teddies, and locally made craftware includes baskets and blankets, picture frames, preserves, cards for all occasions and much, much more. **The shop also stocks a wide selection of souvenirs with a Ledbury, Malvern & Herefordshire theme.** Celebrations is open from 9 to 5 Monday to Saturday

Melissa and Ben also own the **Velvet Bean**, a delightful shop in the same building (just round the corner in Church Lane) selling a mouthwatering selection of chocolates made by hand not far from the shop. The Velvet Bean (Tel: 01531 634744) is open from 10 to 5 Monday to Friday and from 10 to 4 on Saturday.

🏠 historic building   🏛 museum   🏚 historic site   🔱 scenic attraction   🌿 flora and fauna

Conigree Wood, as well as on Wellington Heath and along the Old Railway Line.

Two-and-a-half miles outside Ledbury on the A438 towards Tewkesbury stands **Eastnor Castle**, overlooking the Malvern Hills. This fairytale castle, surrounded by a deer park, arboretum and lake, has the look of a medieval fortress but was actually built between 1812 and 1824 and is a major example of the great Norman and Gothic architectural revival of the time. The first Earl Somers wanted a magnificent baronial castle and, with the young and inspired architect Robert Smirke in charge, that's exactly what he got. The combination of inherited wealth and a judicious marriage enabled the Earl to build a family home to impress all his contemporaries. The interior is excitingly beautiful on a massive scale: a vast 60ft hall leads into a series of state rooms including a library in Italian Renaissance style containing a treasure house of paintings and tapestries, and a spectacular Gothic drawing room designed by Pugin. The grounds, part of which are a Site of Special Scientific Interest, are home to a wonderful variety of flora and fauna, and throughout the year the castle is the scene of special events. The arboretum contains the finest collection of cedars in Britain.

The Edwardian gardens at **How Caple Court**, set high above the Wye in park and woodland, are magnificent indeed, with formal terraces, yew hedges, statues, pools, a sunken Florentine water garden and woodland walks. How Caple's medieval Church of St Andrew and St Mary contains a priceless 16th-century German diptych depicting, among other subjects, the martyrdom of St Clare and St Francis, and

🎭 stories and anecdotes   🦜 famous people   🎨 art and craft   🎟 entertainment and sport   🚶 walks

GURNEYS BUTCHERS

12 High Street, Ledbury, Herefordshire HR8 1DS
Tel: 01531 632526

Ledbury is a fine old market town with some interesting buildings and some excellent shops. It's well worth taking time for a stroll around the town, and for many of the locals a regular visit to **Gurneys Butchers** is high on the agenda. Paul Gurney has been working in the shop since he was 14, learning the traditional values of his trade, and now as the owner he still holds to the essentials of good produce and great customer service. Paul and his staff know their trade and they also know their customers, and the people of

Ledbury and the surrounding area have responded with their loyal custom over the years.

All the meat in Paul's spotless shop is sourced locally, including prime cuts and joints of beef, lamb and pork, free-range chickens and seasonal game. The beef is hung for 21 days to ensure maximum flavour and tenderness, and Gurneys cures its own bacon and produces sausages in a variety of flavours that change regularly. Local producers are given due credit on a blackboard outside the shop: recently featured were John Bishop (beef and lamb from Colwall) and Chris Tindle (Gloucester Old Spot pork from Upton Bishop). The shop also sells a selection of cooked meats, pies, eggs and dairy products.

THE WOODHOUSE FARM COTTAGES

Staplow, Ledbury, Herefordshire HR8 1NP
Tel: 01531 640030
e-mail: sue@thewoodhousefarm.co.uk
website: www.thewoodhousefarm.co.uk

Winners – Self-Catering Holiday of the year 2009 – England.
Located just outside the ancient town of Ledbury sit **The Woodhouse Farm Cottages**, surrounded by apple orchards and in an outstandingly beautiful part of the most unspoilt county in England. Nestled in this Herefordshire haven are three stunning properties available to let that guarantee luxury in rural surroundings. There is a choice between Barn Croft, which sleeps six in a spacious and sunny stone barn conversion opening onto picturesque gardens complete with moat; The Wainhouse, a beautifully converted wagon store with pretty brick arches overlooking a stone-flagged terrace, sleeping two; and The Woodhouse, a Grade 11 Star Listed building, a medieval hall-house, lovingly restored from the 1430s with traditional methods and materials, sleeping six to eight people. There really is little description that can do these properties justice; the elegant combination of fine furniture, original beams, woodburning stoves, rich fabrics with all the luxurious modern comforts you could imagine, such as digital freeview and DVDs, radio, games, CDs, clever underfloor heating and free broadband.

Treats are available to order such as hampers personal chefs and beauty treatments, all to ensure that a stay at The Woodhouse Farm Cottages will be one to remember. They make the perfect retreat to hold a special occasion such as a reunion or wedding, as garden marquees and catering are available, with plenty of information provided for those looking for a stress-free holiday in this scenic area of Herefordshire.

🏛 historic building   🏚 museum   🏛 historic site   🌣 scenic attraction   🌱 flora and fauna

Mary Magdalene washing the feet of Christ.

BROCKHAMPTON

5 miles N of Ross off the B4224

🏛 Church 🚶 Marcle Ridge

Tudor Gatehouse, Brockhampton

The **Church of All Saints** is one of only two thatched churches in the country and dates from 1902, designed by William Lethaby, who had close ties with Westminster Abbey, and built by Alice Foster, a wealthy American, as a memorial to her parents. The Norfolk thatch is not the only unusual aspect here, as the church also boasts stained glass made in the Christopher Whall studios and tapestries from the William Morris workshop from Burne-Jones designs.

This is, like so much of the county, great walking country, with the **Marcle Ridge** and the 500ft Woolhope Dome nearby.

TOM DICKINS FINE ART

Upper Eggleton Court, Stretton Grandison, nr Ledbury, Herefordshire HR8 2TR
Tel: 01531 670080   Fax: 01531 670081
e-mail: sales@tomdickins.co.uk
website: www.tomdickins.co.uk

Tom Dickins Fine Art is the home, workplace and studio of the illustrator, sculptor and fine artist Minter-Kemp and her husband Tom Dickins. Best-known for her humorous greetings cards, which sell all around the world, Minter-Kemp paints portraits, oil paintings and watercolours as well as producing bronze sculpture. She is unusually versatile.

The showroom downstairs offers you the opportunity to buy her cards (including the charity Christmas card range sold in aid of Breast Cancer Haven) as well as prints, bone china mugs, placemats, coasters, books, wrapping paper and her original work. Upstairs the gallery periodically houses her exhibitions. It is a busy working gallery in a beautiful setting and is open weekdays only (9am to 5pm) and at weekends by appointment. Most products can also be viewed and purchased on the website, including retro greeting cards by Martin Wiscombe whose work is also published by Tom Dickins. Do drop in – you never know what you'll find in the middle of nowhere!

WOOLHOPE
7 miles N of Ross off the B4224

> 🏛 Church

A small village enjoying lovely views of the Black Mountains, Woolhope is named after Wuliva, the sister of Lady Godiva who owned the manor in the 11th century. In the 13th-century sandstone **Church of St George** is a modern stained-glass window depicting the siblings. Godiva rides through the streets on her white horse (all in the best possible taste), is seen petting a cat and a dog, while her sister has a dog and some rabbits at her feet.

WILTON
1 mile W of Ross on the A40

> 🏛 Castle

Wilton, just a short walk from Ross, stands at a crossing point of the River Wye. The bridge was built in 1599, some years after a river disaster that claimed 40 lives. Over the bridge are the ruins of **Wilton Castle**, of which some walls and towers still stand. An 18th-century sundial on the bridge bears this numinous inscription:

> *"Esteem thy precious time,*
> *which pass so swiftly away:*
> *Prepare them for eternity*
> *and do not make delay."*

PETERSTOW
2 miles W of Ross on A49

> 🌿 Broome Farm   🌿 Kyrle House

At **Broome Farm**, half a mile off the A49, traditional farmhouse cider has been brewed since the early 1980s, winning many prizes throughout the 1990s and featuring apples with evocative names like Fox Whelp or Yarlington Mill. Also at Peterstow is **Kyrle House**, whose country garden contains herbaceous borders, a small grotto, sunken garden and secret garden. Private visits are welcome.

FOWNHOPE
7 miles NW of Ross on the B4224

A pleasant village set beside the River Wye. Every year on Oak Apple Day, in May or June, the Green Man Inn celebrates the restoration of Charles II with the Heart of Oak Club Walk. The inn's most famous landlord was Tom Spring, a champion bare-knuckle prizefighter who died in 1851. Fownhope's church, known as the 'Little Cathedral', has a special treasure in the form of a Norman tympanum depicting the Virgin and Child with a winged lion and eagle amongst foliage.

HOLME LACY
8 miles NW of Ross on the B4399

> 🏛 St Cuthbert's Church   🏛 Dinedor Court
>
> 🏛 Rotherwas Chapel

Holme Lacy was originally the estate of the de Lacy family in the 14th century, but later passed into the hands of the illustrious Scudamore family. The 1st Viscount Scudamore was the first person to classify the varieties of cider apple, and actually introduced the well-known Red Streak Pippin strain. The fine Palladian mansion dates from 1672 and once sported woodwork by Grinling Gibbons. **St Cuthbert's Church**, standing away from the village on a bend of the Wye, has a remarkable collection of 16th- and 17th-century monuments of the Scudamores, and also some fine furnishings and medieval stalls with misericords.

Near the village of Holme Lacy is **Dinedor Court**, a splendid 16th-century listed farmhouse with an impressive oak-panelled dining hall. English Heritage is responsible for **Rotherwas Chapel** in Dinedor. This is a Roman Catholic chapel dating from the 14th and 16th centuries and featuring an interesting mid-Victorian side chapel and high altar.

SELLACK
3 miles NW of Ross on minor roads or off the A49

A popular waymarked walk takes in three marvellous churches in three delightful villages. The church in Sellack is uniquely dedicated to St Tysilio, son of a king of Powys, and is Norman in origin.

A short drive north of Sellack, in the churchyard at King's Caple, is a plague cross remembering victims of the Black Death of 1348. The church dates mainly from the 13th century and a fascinating little detail is to be found on the benefactors' board on the west wall. The local charities listed include Cake Money, a gift in perpetuity from a former vicar of King's Caple and Sellack. Pax cakes, signifying peace, are still distributed to the congregations on Palm Sunday.

HOARWITHY
6 miles NW of Ross off the A49

🏛 Church 🐎 World Horse Welfare Centre

By far the most extraordinary of the three walk-linked churches lies in the unspoilt village of Hoarwithy on the willow-lined banks of the Wye. **St Catherine's Church** is a splendid piece of architecture that owes its origin to the Reverend William Poole, who arrived in 1854 and didn't like what he saw – the chapel was, he said, "as bare as the palm of the hand". Poole spent the next 30 years supervising the building of a new church round the chapel. The result is an Italianate building complete with a campanile, arcades, beautiful tiled floors

and a white marble altar with lapis lazuli inlay. The **World Horse Welfare Centre** at Glenda Spooner Farm is a recovery and rehabilitation centre for horses and ponies set in glorious countryside. In a quiet lane easily reached from the A49, it's a peaceful haven for around 50 animals at any one time. Open for visits Wednesday and Saturday afternoons (01935 841442). Worth a look in Little Birch, just to the north west, is Higgin's Well, named after a local farmer and restored at the time of Queen Victoria's Diamond Jubilee in 1897.

Hereford

🏛 Cathedral 📖 Chained Library
📖 Mappa Mundi 🏛 Museums 🍎 Cider Mills
🎨 Hatton Gallery 🎵 Three Choirs Festival

The county town-to-be was founded as a settlement near the unstable Welsh Marches after the Saxons had crossed the Severn in the 7th century. A royal demesne in the 11th century, it had a provincial mint, and was an important centre of the wool trade in the Middle Ages. Fragments of Saxon and medieval walls can still be seen, but the city's crowning glory is the magnificent **Cathedral**, known as the 'Cathedral of the Marches'. Largely Norman, it also has examples of Gothic, Early English, Decorated, Perpendicular and Modern architecture. The Cathedral demands an extended visit, as it contains, in the impressive New Library building, two of the country's most important historical treasures. **Mappa Mundi** is the renowned medieval world map, the work of Richard of Haldingham. Drawn on vellum, it has Jerusalem as its centre and East at the top, indicating that direction as the source of all things good and religiously significant. Richard was Treasurer of Lincoln

THE HEREFORD DELICATESSEN

4 The Mews, St Owen Street, Hereford, Herefordshire HR1 2JB
Tel: 01432 341283

Liz Amos has a lifelong interest in all aspects of good food and when the chance came to turn a passion into a business she seized it with both hands and took the opportunity to open the **Hereford Delicatessen**. In her deli just off one of Hereford's main shopping streets she caters for a growing band of regulars as well as the many visitors who come to the city throughout the year. She knows what her customers want, combining an insistence on prime produce – local as far as possible – with great value for money.

The deli counters display a fine selection of cooked and cured meats, cheeses, olives, olive and other oils, vinegars, chutneys, pickles and preserves, pasta and other dry goods, freshly baked bread and scrumptious cakes and pastries. Liz prepares all the fillings for the sandwiches that are an important part of her business, a daily selection that usually includes Wiltshire ham, Herefordshire beef, a variety of cheeses, Albacore tuna and Scottish smoked salmon. And if you've got a special favourite she'll try to make sure she's got it on your next visit.

The deli has an area where customers can take a break from shopping, from work or from the tourist trail to enjoy a snack and a cup of tea or coffee and a glance at the daily papers. The Hereford Delicatessen is open from 8am to 6pm Monday to Saturday.

ARTISAN YARNS

The Small Gallery,
No 1 Capuchin Yard, Church Street,
Hereford HR1 2LR
Tel: 01432 379142
e-mail: thesmallgallery@tiscali.co.uk
website: www.artisanyarns.co.uk

Artisan Yarns is run by Anne Shoring from her exhibition space in the Small Gallery just five minutes from the Cathedral. Textile artist, dyer, knitter and stitcher Anne took over her current work space and turned it into a combined workshop/exhibition area. One day she had dyed some yarn and hung it up to dry in the gallery. She sold the lot almost immediately, thus determining the future course of her career, running Hereford's inspirational resource for contemporary and traditional textiles and yarns designed with today's artists and knitters in mind.

She sells her beautiful, naturally dyed silk and linen yarns from the gallery and from various markets and exhibitions. Some are hand-dyed and source locally, others locally handspun, others included for organic or ethical quality or as simply luxurious. Materials include silk, cashmere, angora, British real wools, Italian superwash merino, linen, hemp, nettle, cotton, bamboo, jelly yarn and recycled sari silk and ribbon. Brands include Cariad, Tilli Thomas, Cornish Organic, Green Mountain Spinning, Frabjious Fibres, Colinette, Artisano, Yarn d'Amour, Orkney Angora, Rockpool Candy, Yarn Undyed from AC Woods and Artists Palette. Artisan yarns is open from 10 to 5 Wednesday to Saturday or you can meet Anne at Hereford's Stitch 'n' Bitch Group at the green Café, St Owen Street on the first Tuesday and third Thursday of the month between 6pm and 9pm.

Hereford Cathedral

Cathedral, which might explain why Lincoln appears rather more prominently on the map than Hereford. The Cathedral has many other treasures, including the shrine of St Thomas of Hereford in stone and marble, the painted and gilded shrine to St Ethelbert, martyred in AD794, the Thomas Traherne stained-glass windows, the Norman font, the Bishop's Throne and the John Piper tapestries. For details of the Cathedral's opening hours and guided tours, call 01432 374202.

The **Chained Library** at All Saints Church, houses more than 1,400 rare books, including over 200 medieval manuscripts, all chained to their original 17th-century book presses. The actor/theatre manager David Garrick was born in Hereford in 1717 and was christened at All Saints. Another notable child of Hereford was Nell Gwyn(ne), favourite of Charles II. Born in 1650, she is

18 BROAD STREET

18 Broad Street, Hereford, Herefordshire HR4 9AP
Tel: 01432 358830

Vintage and antique jewellery is the speciality of **18 Broad Street**, which occupies small, charming premises in a prime position very close to Hereford's magnificent Cathedral.

Behind the blue-and-white frontage with its small-paned window display cabinets in a single room provide a simple but very effective setting for showing the jewellery, which includes rings, necklaces, bracelets, brooches, pendants, watches and dress watches, covering several periods and styles, but with only the very occasional new piece. The owner sources stock from far and wide, with jewellery from the UK, from Europe and North America.

The pieces are in a variety of familiar and some less familiar metals, some of them set with precious and semi-precious stones. The shop is open from 10am to 5pm Monday to Friday.

Also offers a bespoke repair and restoration service.

remembered by a plaque on the wall of the Bishop's Garden.

Hereford is full of fascinating buildings and museums. **Hereford Museum and Art Gallery** has a changing art gallery programme and hands-on exhibitions. The **Old House**, right in the centre of High Town, brings alive the 17th century in a three-storey black-and-white house filled with fascinating exhibits. Churchill House Museum, whose grounds include a fragrant garden, displays furniture, costumes and paintings from the 18th and 19th centuries; among its rooms are a costume exhibition gallery and Victorian nursery, parlour, kitchen and butler's pantry. The **Hatton Gallery** shows the work of local artist Brian Hatton. The **Coningsby Museum & St John Medieval's Museum** at Coningsby is a 13th-century building in an ancient quadrangle of almshouses. Displays include costume models of Nell Gwyn, and the history of the Ancient Order of St John and its wars during the Crusades. Open Wednesday and Saturday (01432 358134). Hereford's restored pumping station is home to the **Waterworks Museum**, where Victorian technology is alive and well in the shape of a collection of pumps (some of which can be operated by visitors), a Lancashire Boiler and Britain's largest triple expansion engine. Children can lift water like Roman slaves and follow trails. Call 01432 357236 for opening times. The **Herefordshire Light Infantry Museum** houses an important collection of uniforms, colours, medals, equipment, documents and photographs connected with the regiment and campaigns such as Gallipoli, Egypt,

---

OFF THE WALL

20 St Owen Street, Hereford, Herefordshire HR1 2PL
Tel: 01432 354892
e-mail: otwgifts@googlemail.com
website: www.offthewallgifts.co.uk

Off the Wall is the brainchild of Derek and Ginny Elsmere, who in 2005 took over a shop called The Best of Brass, specialising in brass fireplaces and artwork to hang above them. They changed the name and exchanged the brass for their own unique and ever-growing array of gifts, collectables and things for the home, expanding the sales area and establishing a gallery. Located in one of Hereford's main shopping streets, Off the Wall is filled with an amazing variety of items to suit all pockets and occasions spread over two floors.

Derek and Ginny add a sense of humour to their friendliness and expertise, and customers can be sure of a welcoming smile from them and a wag of the tail from their dogs Dillon and Nell. The displays cover artwork by locally and nationally known artists, ceramics, mugs, figurines from well-known brands like Willow Tree and Border Fine Arts, jewellery, quirky toast racks, egg cups and lapel pins, educational and play toys, greetings cards, prints and books by Simon Drew, and interesting and amusing pieces with a local or musical theme. The first floor is given over to fine art prints by artists like Mary Ann Rogers and Nigel Hemming, complemented by a complete framing service with a huge choice of frames to choose from.

🏛 historic building   🏛 museum   🏛 historic site   ⚜ scenic attraction   🌱 flora and fauna

ANDREW LAMPUTT
SILVERSMITH & JEWELLER
28 St. Owen Street, Hereford HR1 2PR
Tel: 01432 274961 Fax: 01432 340163
e-mail al@andrewlamputt.co.uk
website: www.AndrewLamputt.co.uk

PROVIDING
CHOICE, QUALITY
& SERVICE

TROLLBEADS

Andrew Lamputt Silversmith & Jeweller, established in 1985 is a family run business near the Town Hall in Hereford City Centre. Often known as "The Silver Shop", where a dazzling array of pieces both antique and modern can be found, especially for those seeking an unusual and often difficult to obtain present. This is one of the best silverware and jewellery shops in the West Midlands. Silverware dominates the showroom interior and creates an amazing visual display, which is unique in the area. A shop for all types of quality gifts for all occasions. The business is highly specialized, (although the public frontage depicts a retail jewellery shop), Andrew Lamputt boasts highly skilled employees who spend most of their working week restoring antique & second hand silverware and Estate Jewellery for both customers and for resale.

Andrew Lamputt specializes equally in **Fine Quality Antique and Modern Jewellery**, together with a wide selection of new items of both jewellery and silver to complement the range. Specialist gem and diamond set rings in gold and platinum. Trollbeads, Hot Diamond, Ortak and Kit Heath Agent. Visit Andrew Lamputt Silversmith & Jeweller in Hereford, where a unique buying experience awaits together with a warm welcome.

TANZANITE &
DIAMOND RING

BADDER FABRICS OF HEREFORD

36 Aubrey Street, Hereford HR4 0BU
Tel: 01432 379137 Fax: 01432 379138
e-mail: badderfabrics@hotmail.co.uk

There really is no better place than Badder Fabrics for all your haberdashery and fabric needs, with a range of stunning fabrics and accessories stocked high to the ceiling all year round.

Lifelong fashion enthusiast and owner Lillian Badder has created high standards in her self-styled shop, taking great pride in not only what she can offer in terms of textiles, but also in what herself and her staff can offer in advice and quality customer care. Her passion for creating things and sumptuous fabrics combine to offer a unique service in Badder Fabrics that contains the option of dressmaking and alterations, perfect for making a once in a lifetime statement with your own meticulously handmade wedding or prom dress. In Lillian's own words she 'can take anything up or down, in or out!'

This quaint shop holds much more than expected, stocking a massive range of both plain and patterned materials over two floors, including a selection of sewing machines for every budget, you are sure to come away with the perfect piece.

Palestine and NW Europe. Visits by appointment only (01432 850328).

Hereford and cider are old friends, and the **Cider Museum** tells the interesting story of cider production down the years. One of the galleries houses the King Offa Distillery, the first cider brandy distillery to be granted a licence for more than 200 years. Among the many attractions are the reconstructed farm ciderhouse, the champagne cider cellars, the vat house, the coopers' workshop and beautiful old books illustrating the varieties of cider apples and perry pears grown from earliest times. The Strongbow Vat, which holds 7.4 million litres and is more than 20 metres high, is the largest in the world. Visitors can sample cider brandy produced at the distillery, which is open for visits Tuesday to Saturday throughout the year (01432 354207). On the outskirts of the city are the **Cider Mills** of HP Bulmer, the world's leading cider producer.

The original Saxon part of the city includes historic Church Street, full of 17th-century listed buildings (most of them modernised in the 19th century). Church Street and Capuchin Yard - the name derives from the hood worn by the Franciscan friars who built a chapel nearby - are renowned for their small specialist shops and craft workshops.

Hereford stages important musical events throughout the year, and every third year hosts the **Three Choirs Festival**, Europe's oldest music festival.

The Golden Valley

KILPECK
8 miles SW of Hereford off the A465

🏛 Church

The parish **Church of St Mary and St David** is one of the most fascinating in the whole county and generally regarded as the most perfect Norman church in England. Built by Hugh de Kilpeck (son of William Fitznorman, who built Kilpeck Castle) round an earlier Saxon church, it has changed little since the 12th century. Much of the church is unique in its rich decoration, but the gem is the portal over the south doorway, with all manner of elaborate carvings. Most of the carvings throughout the church have no apparent religious significance, with some bordering on the bizarre, if not downright bawdy! Very little remains of the castle, it having been largely demolished by Cromwell's men, but on a clear day the castle mound affords very fine views.

Golden Valley

ULIFAS MILLINERY

1 Welbeck Avenue, Tupsley, Hereford HR1 1NG
Tel/Fax: 01432 278086
e-mail: ulifas@aol.com

Emma Lewis studied fashion at the Herefordshire College of Art & Design followed by BA (Hons) Degrees in both Fashion and Marketing at Universities in London and Los Angeles. During this time she worked for Milliners in both cities where she made one-off hats for celebrities, including some of the major Hollywood Stars.

On returning to England in 1995 Emma set up **Ulifas** designing hats and clothing. Her hats being made using traditional millinery techniques have recevied wide acclaim including top awards at the 2008 Chelsea Flower Show and Ladies Day at the Races. She produces a wide range of hats using sinamay, felts, and straws. These are hand-dyed to match outfits, made to each person's head size and decorated with flowers and feathers. Fascinators are also available and made to match outfits.

Visits to her Boutique are by appointment only. Call the number above or Emma's mobile 07906 144389. Tupsley lies on the A438 on the eastern edge of Hereford.

Who or what was 'Ulifas'? He was a Bishop from Alexandria - the first to convert the Goths to Christianity, producing a Bible in their language and inventing Gothic script.

EWYAS HAROLD

12 miles SW of Hereford on the B4347

A village at the foot of the lovely Golden Valley, in an area of fine walks. West of the village lay the ancient Welsh kingdom of Ewias; the motte and bailey castle that was part of the border defences has disappeared, leaving only the distinctive mound. A Cistercian Abbey was founded here in the 12th century and the building, which was substantially restored by John Abel in the 17th century, is still in use as a parish church.

ABBEY DORE

12 miles SW of Hereford on the B4347

🏛 Abbey 🌿 Abbey Dore Court

🌿 Pentwyn Cottage Garden

Occupying a sublimely beautiful setting beside the river are the impressive remains of

a 12th-century **Cistercian Abbey**, part of which is still in use as the parish church. Most of the building dates from around 1180, but the battlemented tower was added in the 1660s by the Scudamore family, lords of the manor. They also commissioned the noted carpenter John Abel to create the impressive wooden chancel roof and the superb, heavily carved screen.

On the other side of the river, the garden at **Abbey Dore Court** is home to many unusual shrubs and perennials along with specialist collections of euphorbias, hellebores and peonies. There's also a small nursery, a gift shop and a restaurant.

In Bacton itself, a mile along the B4347, is **Pentwyn Cottage Garden**, where visitors can walk round the peaceful garden before enjoying a cream tea. From the remote, lonely roads that lead west towards Offa's Dyke and

Llangua and the Monnow Valley Walk

Distance: *4.5 miles (7.2 kilometres)*

Typical time: *120 mins*

Height gain: *180 metres*

Map: *Explorer OL 13*

Walk: *www.walkingworld.com ID:2701*

Contributor: *Pat Roberts*

Parking is in a layby on the minor road to Llangua, just off the A465 from Abergavenny to Hereford, just south of the traffic lights and bridge over the River Monnow south of Pontrilas.

DESCRIPTION:

The Monnow Valley Walk has been produced in book form by Ira and Harry Steggles and traces the River Monnow from Monmouth to Hay-on-Wye. On this walk we follow part of it on the outward route before returning across Cupid's Hill and rejoining the River Monnow and following the river bank back to Llangua.

FEATURES:

Hills or Fells, River, Wildlife, Birds, Flowers, Great Views, Butterflies.

WALK DIRECTIONS:

1 | Walk on the verge of the A465 towards the traffic lights. Cross the bridge on the painted footpath and then cross the road to the west side. We are now following the Monnow Valley Walk.

2 | Immediately after the traffic lights, go through the gate on the left. Ignore the finger post on the side of the road as it is misleading.

Through the gate bear diagonally left to reach a post bearing the Monnow Valley logo and walk under the railway bridge. Through a gate and left to walk with the River Monnow on your left. Over a stile and continue, reaching a wood and a footbridge. Halfway across the next field bear slightly right to reach a stile in the hedge.

3 | Go over the stile onto a lane and right and up. The lane becomes tarmaced and bends left. At the top the lane bends right but we continue on a track ahead, signed 'Vroe'. The track drops down to pass between the two houses and reaches a ford.

4 | Just before the ford take the footbridge over the stream. Through a gate/stile and, keeping about 40 metres from the left hedge, up to another stile. Over the stile and diagonally left up quite a steep field to reach another gate/stile.

5 | Over the stile and immediately left over another stile. We have now left the Monnow Valley Walk. Keep to the left of the next three fields, climbing stiles as nessessary. The fourth field starts to lose height halfway across. Start to bear slightly right to a kissing gate.

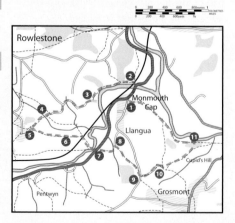

6 | Go through the kissing gate and head across the field to a metal gate onto the railway. CROSS WITH CAUTION and up to another field. Continue across to a metal bridge over the Monnow and on to the A465. Cross with care.

7 | Up the steps, over the stile and up diagonally left to reach a fence. Turn left with the fence on your right. Reach a stile in the corner, over and down to another stile and onto a farm drive.

8 | Cross the drive diagonally and over the stile. Follow the arrow left to another hedge then turn right to walk up with the hedge on your left. Take time to look back and enjoy the views back over the walk and over to the Black Mountains. Go through a gate and up the next field to another gate. Through this gate and slightly left to a stile onto the road then turn right and up for 200 metres.

9 | Just before Little Kingsfield Cottage go left and onto the farm drive. From here the path has been moved and does not match some maps. PLEASE FOLLOW SIGNS.

10 | Before reaching the bend in the drive look out for the gate and footpath sign on the right. Through the gate and down the field, hedge on your right, to a stile. Over and immediately left to the gates before the house. Follow arrows right over stile and small footbridge and immediately left to walk with hedge on your left. Through gate and follow hedge in next field to another stile. Down the next field to reach the river bank where we rejoin the Monnow Valley Walk.

11 | Left with the River Monnow on your right, over stiles and across fields as nessessary to reach a stile onto the road next to the car park.

the boundary with Wales, motorists should leave their cars, stretch their legs and drink in the wonderful scenery.

The villages of Longtown and Clodock lie at the foot of the Olchon Valley, while further north are the Olchon Waterfall, Black Hill, the rocky ridge of the Cat's Back and the ruins of Craswall Priory, which was founded in the 13th century by the rare Grandmontine order and abandoned 200 years later.

PETERCHURCH
10 miles W of Hereford on the B4348

The chief village of the Golden Valley, with a very fine parish church. In AD786, King Offa brought monks to the village to found the original church. It was a sign of Offa's great power and influence that a bishop from Rome was included in the missionary party established here.

DORSTONE
12 miles W of Hereford off the B4348

🏛 Snodhill Castle 🗿 Arthur's Stone

A very attractive village with neat sandstone cottages set around the green. St Faith's Church has a connection with Canterbury, as Richard de Brito, one of the knights who murdered Thomas à Becket, established a church here after serving 15 years penance in the Holy Land for his crime. He returned to build the church and is buried in the churchyard.

South of Dorstone lie the ruins of **Snodhill Castle**, from which the views are spectacular even for this part of the world. To the north, on wild, exposed Merbach Hill, is the much-visited landmark of **Arthur's Stone**, a megalithic tomb of great antiquity that was used for the burial of tribal chieftains. Some say (but few believe) that the body of King Arthur himself was buried here. To the north again, in the village of Brewardine, is the grave of the diarist Francis Kilvert, who was rector of the Church of St Andrew for two years until his death in 1879. His diaries record his life in the remote Welsh borders.

Along the Wye Valley

The A465 out of Hereford soon reaches Belmont Abbey, whose architect, the renowned Pugin, was responsible for part of the House of Commons. One of the stained-glass windows in the church at Clehonger is probably also his work.

SWAINSHILL
3 miles W of Hereford on the A438

🌿 The Weir

The Weir (National Trust) in Swainshill is a charming 10-acre riverside garden, spectacular in early spring, with drifts of flowering bulbs giving way to summer wild flowers and autumn colours. The 1920s walled garden is currently being restored. The Weir enjoys grand views along the River Wye and across the Herefordshire countryside. Limited opening, call 01981 590509.

MADLEY
6 miles W of Hereford on the B4352

🏛 Lulham Pew

There's more fine stained glass from the early 1300s in the Church of the Nativity of the Virgin at Madley, which also claims to have one of the largest stone fonts in the country. A curiosity here is the **Lulham Pew** in the north aisle. Constructed mostly from a medieval screen, it has high sides and curtains, thus

---

THE OLD RECTORY

Byford, Herefordshire HR4 7LD
Tel: 01981 590218 Mobile: 07866 765105
e-mail: info@theoldrectory.uk.com
website: www.theoldrectory.uk.com

The Old Rectory is a handsome white-painted Georgian country house in Byford, a charming little village near the River Wye in beautiful rural Herefordshire. Resident owners Audrey and Charles Mayson welcome Bed & Breakfast guests into an ambience that generates an immediate feeling of being among friends, starting with tea on arrival and extending throughout the stay.

They have three spacious, beautifully appointed and traditionally furnished bedrooms – a double with en suite shower, a double with en suite bath and a twin with en suite bath and shower. Delicious breakfasts with local and home-grown produce are served in the dining room, where three floor-to-ceiling windows overlook the lovely garden with its handsome Cedar of Lebanon.

The Old Rectory is well placed for touring a part of the world that has an almost endless variety of attractions for the visitor, including Black & White villages, charming little market towns, the Black Mountains, Brecon Beacons, the Malvern & Shropshire Hills, Offa's Dyke, Arthur's Stone, the Forest of Dean, castles, churches, historic houses, gardens and galleries. The house has plenty of maps and local guides, and the owners are ready with advice on what to see and do. The accommodation is available from March to October. Sorry no pets, and credit cards not accepted.

🏛 historic building   🖼 museum   🏛 historic site   🍃 scenic attraction   🌿 flora and fauna

THE RED LION

Madley, Herefordshire HR2 9PH
Tel: 01981 250292
e-mail: pat@redlionmadley.co.uk

Visitors come from near and far to the village of Madley to see the Church of the Nativity of the Virgin with its superb 14th century stained glass, decorated tracery, huge stone font and the famous Lulham Pew. And when they've admired the church, those seeking hospitality and refreshment make tracks for the **Red Lion**.

This splendid country inn is run by Alan and Pat, who have many years' experience in running pubs all over the UK. They recently returned from a brief retirement in Portugal to take over the Red Lion and they have already built up a loyal band of regulars from Madley and the surrounding communities. Locals meet in the convivial bar to enjoy a pint – there's always a good selection of draught and bottled beers – and set the world to rights. Families are always made welcome, and children will keep busy and happy on the swings and slides in the play area by the lawned garden. The inn also has a patio area. Food is an important part of the Red Lion's business and Alan seeks out the best local produce for his tasty, wholesome dishes. His meat comes from an excellent local butcher, with steaks and gammon steaks among the favourites on the menu. Other popular orders include homemade curries and chillies.

The Red Lion is open from 12 to 3.30 and 6 to 11.30 Monday to Friday and all day Saturday and Sunday. Food is served between 12 and 3 and 6 and nine except monday. Opening hours every day 12 - 3 and 6- 11.30 saturday and sunday all day. 12 o clock.

In the Granary in the grounds of the inn are eight recently renovated rooms with en suite showers, TV and hot drinks tray. The inn is an

excellent B&B base for a walking, cycling or touring holiday. Golf and horse riding are available nearby; fishing is provided by nearby ponds and lakes, and the River Wye, a world-renowned fishing river, is a ten-minute drive away. Nearby attractions include The Weir (National Trust) at Swainshill, Moccas Court set in Capability Brown parkland and the much-visited landmark of Arthur's Stone.

The Red Lion, which stands on the B3452 six miles east of Hereford, started life as a coaching inn – mail was brought here by mail coach and distributed to the locality from the inn. The inn is built on a well located under the hallway of the cellar and a stream runs under the rear car park.

allowing the Lulham family to pursue their devotions in privacy. They didn't even emerge to take Communion but received it through a small door in the pew. According to legend, St Dyfrig, the man who some say crowned King Arthur, was born at Madley.

MOCCAS
10 miles W of Hereford off the B4352

🏛 Moccas Court

Moccas Court, designed by Robert Adam and built by local architect Anthony Keck, stands in seven acres of Capability Brown parkland on the south bank of the Wye. In the grounds stands the beautiful Church of St Michael, built in Norman times using the local stone known as tufa limestone. Dominating the chancel is the impressive effigy of a 14th-century knight with a dog lying at his feet – contemporaries would understand this signified that the knight had not died on the battlefield but in his own bed.

HAY-ON-WYE
18 miles W of Hereford on the B4348

🎪 Book Festival

And so to the border town of Hay-on-Wye, where bookworms will wriggle with delight as they browse through its dozens of secondhand bookshops. Richard Booth, known as the King of Wye, opened the first bookshop here nearly 50 years ago and was a leading player in establishing the annual **Hay Book Festival**. The famous diarist Francis Kilvert was a local man, and his Diary is just one of millions of books on sale. But books are not the only attraction: Hay also has a large number of antiques, crafts and clothes shops, and is home to a major conkers championship. The River Wye is never far away, with its shifting moods and ever-changing scenery. Just north of Hay stand the ruins of Clifford Castle, where in 1140 Jane Clifford, 'Fair Rosamund', mistress of King Henry II, was born.

North of Hereford

MORDIFORD
4 miles E of Hereford on the B4224

🏛 Mordiford Dragon   🌿 Haugh Wood

Mordiford was once a centre of the mining industry and the home of the baleful man-eating **Mordiford Dragon**. The story goes that the dragon was found by a local girl while it was still small. She nurtured it lovingly, and although it was at first content to feed on milk, and later chickens and the odd duck, it eventually developed a taste for cows and finally people. The beast terrorised the locals, and indeed one of the paths leading from the woods is still known as Serpents Lane. It was here that he would slink along the river to drink, and it is said that no grass ever grows there. No one was brave enough to face the beast until a man called Garson, who happened to be awaiting execution, decided that he had nothing to lose. He hid in a barrel by the river, and when the creature appeared he shot it through the heart. That was the end of the dragon, and also of poor Garson, who was killed in the fiery breath of the dragon's death throes.

Mordiford stands on the River Lugg, just above the point where it joins the Wye, and the River Frome joins the Lugg a little way above the village. Mordiford Bridge, with its elegant span of nine arches, was once the source of regular revenue for the kings of the country: apparently every time the king crossed the bridge the local lords had to provide him with a pair of silver spurs as a levy on the manor.

WHITE HAYWOOD FARM

Craswall, Herefordshire HR2 0PH
Tel: 01981 510324
e-mail: info@blackmountainsfarmrestaurant.co.uk
website: www.blackmountainsfarmrestaurant.co.uk

Pauline and Philip Goodwin offer farmhouse cooking at its very best in a traditional 400-year-old stone barn beneath the Cat's Back Ridge in the Black Mountains. They are the fourth generation at **White Haywood Farm**, a 164-acre mixed livestock farm set amid stunning scenery, but the first to expand the business with a restaurant – and from the start they have been attracting food-lovers from all over the region.

Top items on the menu include dishes based on naturally reared meat from the farm, the animals with great care on the lush green pastures and refreshed by spring water. Among the favourites are steaks, lamb chops, pork in cider sauce and beef & onion pie. Other choices could be baked trout, honey-and-mustard duck breast and cheese-topped vegetable bake.

The excellent food, served by the owners' daughters Abigail and Rebecca, is accompanied by a well-chosen, well-priced wine list. Pauline and Philip participate in the Countryside Stewardship Scheme and are continuously striving to maintain and improve the wildlife habitats on the farm. They have recently added another string to their bow by bringing on stream two family rooms at the end of the barn for B&B guests.

MONKTON FARM SHOP

Ocle Pychard, Herefordshire HR1 3QQ
Tel: 01432 820579
e-mail: bill@griffithsforestry.co.uk

Monkton Farm Shop is part of a thriving business in which all the members of the Griffiths family are closely involved. The meat and poultry on display in the shop comes from local farms, with cuts and joints to cater for all needs – customers can also phone in their orders in advance. Much of the seasonal fruit and vegetables comes from the farm, including strawberries, raspberries, apples, asparagus and beans.

On the deli counter are cooked and cured meats, cheese, olives, oils and vinegars, bread baked fresh daily, cakes and biscuits, pasta, sauces, pickles and preserves. The farm shop is the domain of Odeyne Griffiths, and other members of the family are responsible for other enterprises on the site. The bright, conservatory-style café is open all day, serving snacks and meals prepared each day (often by Odeyne) making excellent use of the farm's and local produce in sandwiches, quiches and other hot and cold dishes, including a popular three-course Sunday lunch.

Odeyne's husband Bill runs a successful forestry business and is ready with help with garden projects at The Monkton Garden Centre, which sells a wide variety of shrubs, trees, flowers and plants, climbers, herbs, vegetables compost and other gardening aids and accessories. The farm is located a short drive northeast of Hereford off the A465 or northwest of Ledbury off the A417.

The Forestry Commission's **Haugh Wood** is best approached from Mordiford.

SUTTON ST NICHOLAS
4 miles NE of Hereford off the A465

🏛 Wergin Stone   🏛 Sutton Walls

Just outside the village is a group of stones known collectively as the **Wergin Stone**. In the hollow base of one of the stones, rents or tithes were laid, to be collected later by the local squire. There is a story that in 1652 the Devil picked up the stone and removed it to a spot a little distance away. It took a team of nine oxen to return the stone to its original place, though why the villagers bothered is not related. South of the village is the Iron Age hill fort of **Sutton Walls**, where King Offa once had a palace. One day in AD794, Offa, the King of Mercia, promised the hand of his daughter Alfreda to Ethelbert, King of East Anglia. Ethelbert journeyed to Sutton Walls, but the trip was full of bad omens: the earth shook, there was an eclipse of the sun, and he had a vision that his mother was weeping bloody tears. In spite of all this he pressed on, but after he had reached the palace, and before the wedding ceremony, Offa had him beheaded. There is little now to see at the camp, as a lot of the land has been worked on. Many skeletons have been unearthed, some showing signs of a violent end.

Just outside Sutton, Overcourt Garden Nursery is situated in the grounds of a Grade II listed 16th-century house with connections to the Crusader Knights of St John. A wide range of unusual plants is for sale. Private visits are welcome.

BROMYARD
13 miles NE of Hereford on the A44

🏛 Time Machine Museum   🍃 The Nostock Festival

Bromyard is an attractive market town on the River Frome with hills and good walking all around. In the town itself the **Time**

The Time Machine Museum and Coffee Shop

12 The Square, Bromyard,
Herefordshire, HR7 4BP
Tel: 01885 488 329
e-mail - info@timemachineuk.com
website: www.timemachineuk.com

A visit to the **Time Machine Museum** transports you to a large and exciting display of TV, Film, Science Fiction and rare and collectable toys of yester year, including Thunderbirds, Stingray, Captain Scarlet, Supercar, Dr. Who, Star Wars, Bears, Dolls, Pedal Cars, Railways, Disney and much more more.

The museum is one of the most informative you will visit, with hundreds of rare and exciting exhibits. Afterwards browse the Collectors Shop and relax and reflect in The Time Machine coffee shop, set in an Elizabethan retro style.

Opening Hours: Apr 1st - Sep 30th - Open everyday 10:30am - 5:00pm.
                   Oct 1st - Mar 31st - Open everyday except Monday and Tuesday 11am - 4pm.

🏛 historic building   🏛 museum   🏛 historic site   🌀 scenic attraction   🌿 flora and fauna

GRENDON MANOR GUEST HOUSE

Bredenbury, Bromyard, Herefordshire HR7 4TH
Tel: 01885 482226
e-mail: jane.piggott@btconnect.com
website: www.grendonmanor.co.uk

Set in the stunning countryside just outside the historic town of Hereford, Grendon Manor offers the ideal retreat for those looking for a rural getaway. Grendon Manor and farm has been in the Piggott family for over 70 years, and is now run by Massie and Jane Piggott who have been providing a quality space to relax in style for over three years now.

Grendon Manor dates back to the 16th century, taking guests back in time, but not without comfort. This beautiful manor house retains its original stripped wooden beams throughout, but is brought to life by the vibrant and stylish shabby chic décor that lines the walls. Hidden inside Grendon Manor's rustic exterior are 5 sumptuous bedrooms to let, each with ultra modern new en suite bathrooms that simply ooze luxury. There is also an oak panelled lounge filled with deep sofas for guests to unwind in. And if you're feeling peckish, Jane's legendary cuisine will satisfy the deepest appetite – catering privately for up to 12 people in an elegant dining room opening onto Grendon Manor's extensive rear garden's offering a beautiful panoramic view of the surrounding countryside. In the grounds there is also a small church, available for wedding bookings, making Grendon Manor the perfect one stop shop for a get together in the country.

LITTLEBRIDGE HOUSE B&B

Tedstone Wafer, Bromyard, Herefordshire HR7 4PN
Tel: 01885 482471
e-mail: littlebridge_1@tiscali.com
website: www.littlebridgehouse.com

Littlebridge House has been the family home of the Williams family for more than 50 years, and since 1989 Gill has been offering good-value Bed & Breakfast accommodation in this lovely rural setting on the B4203 three miles north of Bromyard. The handsome and imposing early-Victorian house has three comfortable guest bedrooms with en suite shower room, co-ordinated soft furnishings, TV, radio-alarm clock, hot drinks tray, shaver point and hairdryer. Cots are available on request and babysitting can be arranged with a little notice. The house has a comfortable lounge with a woodburning stove and a bright, sunny dining room where a full English breakfast and an optional evening meal are served, both making excellent use of local or home-grown produce.

The large gardens surrounding Littlebridge House are perfect for a leisurely stroll or for children to romp, and well-known nearby walks command stunning walks over National Trust land with views to the Black Mountains and Malvern Hills. The National Trust's Lower Brockhampton Estate, the Hop Pocket Craft Centre and churches at Edvin Loach and Edwyn Ralph are all nearby, and there's also plenty to see in Bromyard, including the charming Time Machine Museum, the Heritage Centre and the annual Gala and Folk Festival.

Machine Museum (formerly the Teddy Bear Museum - see panel on page 30), housed in a former bakery, is a magical little world of teddy bears, dolls, pedal cars, prams, puppets, Disney-related toys and props and memorabilia from *Dr Who, Star Wars, Thunderbirds, Stingray* and *Captain Scarlet* (01885 488329). In late June and early July, the Bromyard Gala takes place, which has built up to a major event over the years. Later on, **The Nostock Festival** and Folk Festival bring in the crowds.

EDVIN LOACH
3 miles N of Bromyard off the B4203

The remains of one of Britain's rare Saxon churches can be found here. The church at nearby Edwyn Ralph is noted for its unusual monument and medieval effigies under the tower.

LOWER BROCKHAMPTON
2 miles E of Bromyard off the A44

🏛 Brockhampton Estate

The 1,900 acres of wood and farmland that comprise **Brockhampton Estate** (National Trust) are the essence of Herefordshire. Springtime sees the park at its best when daffodils provide a mass of colour but there are delightful woodland and lakeside nature walks to be enjoyed throughout the year. Within the grounds of the traditionally farmed estate stands a late 14th-century half-timbered moated manor house with a very unusual detached gatehouse and the ruins of a 12th-century chapel (01885 488099).

STANFORD BISHOP
3 miles SE of Bromyard off the B4220

The Church at Stanford Bishop once possessed an old oak chair in which it is believed St Augustine sat when he presided over a synod of bishops here in AD603. The chair was retrieved by an antiquarian visiting the church during a 19th-century restoration, minutes before workmen were about to chop it up for firewood. The chair is now in Canterbury Cathedral.

BISHOP'S FROME
3 miles S of Bromyard on the B4214

🏛 Church   👁 Hop Pocket Craft Centre

St Mary's Church is notable for its massive font more than 700 years old. Entry to the church is by way of a handsome lychgate, a 19th-century porch and a beautiful Norman doorway. Inside, a battered figure of a knight in armour lies sword in hand and with a lion at his feet. Lying close to the Worcestershire border, in hop country, is the **Hop Pocket Craft Centre** (see panel opposite), which has working kilns and machinery, shops, a craft shop and a restaurant. It lies just off the A4103 Hereford-Worcester road.

HOPE UNDER DINMORE
8 miles N of Hereford on the A49

👁 Queenswood Country Park   🌿 Hampton Court

To the south of the village, at Dinmore Hill, stretch the green spaces of **Queenswood Country Park**, a popular place for walking and enjoying the panoramic views. The Park includes 67 acres of arboretum with over 500 rare and exotic trees from all over the world, and 103 acres of SSSI-designated woodland rich in wildlife. It offers waymarked trails, panoramic views, picnic areas, barbecue facilities, a children's adventure play area and a Tourist Information Centre open March to December. Park open all year dawn to dusk. Free entry.

A more recent addition to the county's notable gardens is **Hampton Court** (see panel on page 34), magnificent organic gardens in

HOP POCKET CRAFT CENTRE, RESTAURANT & SHOPPING VILLAGE

Bishop's Frome, Herefordshire WR6 5BT
Tel: 01531 640323 Fax: 01531 640684
e-mail: info@thehoppocket.com
website: www.thehoppocket.com

From small beginnings in 1988 the Pudge family have created an excellent rural shopping village of enormous and varied appeal. The centre is open from 10 to 5.30 Tuesday to Saturday, 11 to 5 Sunday, closed Mondays except Bank Holidays; open Wednesday to Sunday only January and February. Entry is free and there's a large free car park.

The **Craft Shop** is an Aladdin's Cave of handmade crafts and gifts large and small to suit all pockets. Specialities include hop garlands – traditional garlands for the home, to train along a beam or over a kitchen cupboards, and a popular feature of country weddings.

The **Farmhouse Fayre Restaurant** serves freshly cooked snacks and meals, sandwiches, cakes and cream teas.

The **Wine Company** stocks a wide selection (some of it local) of wines, beers, ciders and spirits, with a chance to sample before buying. Tel: 01531 640592

The **Shopping Village** is home to 20 or so unusual independent shops, a world of gifts you won't find on the High Street: gift ideas, home furnishings, jewellery, pine furniture, kitchen accessories and cookware, clothes, shoes, glassware, tiles, scarves, bags, wooden toys, contemporary artwork and lots more.

Hop Pocket is a delightful place to visit, but a big range of products can be browsed and ordered online.

HOP POCKET GARDEN CENTRE

Bishop's Frome, Herefordshire WR6 5BT
Tel: 01531 640121 e-mail: cweston@hop-pocket.co.uk website: www.hop-pocket.co.uk

Clive Weston is based at the Hop Pocket Shopping Village and supplies a huge range of annuals, perennials, plants, trees and shrubs, ornamental grasses, hanging baskets ready made or made to order, pots, troughs, feeds, bird tables, wind chimes, weather vanes, pergolas and arbours. As well as many unusual plants they also supply statues, tools and gifts.

Hampton Court Herefordshire

Hampton Court Estate, Hope-Under-Dinmore,
Leominster, Herefordshire HR6 0PN
The Castle: Tel: 01568 797676 Fax 01568 797472
The Garden: Tel. 01568 797777 Fax 01568 797472
e-mail: gardens@hamptoncourt.org.uk
website: www.hamptoncourt.org.uk

Hampton Court was founded in 1430 as a reward for a knight's bravery at Agincourt. The castle and gardens have been remodelled several times during their long history, each generation adding new features according to the fashions of the day. In the 18th century Lord Coningsby established the gardens and the Victorian Arkwright dynasty added rose gardens and a naturalistic fernery. The estate declined after the second world war until its sale in 1994 to the Van Kampen family, when a massive programme of building restoration was begun.

Attention turned to the gardens in 1996 and designers Simon Dorrell and David Wheeler were chosen to provide an appropriately elaborate setting for the newly restored castle. Original Victorian garden walls enclose stunning new flower gardens divided by canals, island pavilions and pleached avenues. The kitchen garden is an ornamental garden of fruit and vegetables. It is managed organically, supplying produce to the Orangery Restaurant for its seasonal menu.

There is a maze of a thousand yews with a gothic tower at its centre. Climb to the top for a panoramic view of the gardens or descend underground to a tunnel that leads to a waterfall in the sunken garden. Beautiful herbaceous borders stretch out from a one hundred and fifty year old wisteria tunnel that leads to vast lawns and ancient trees beside the castle. Beyond the lawns are riverside and woodland walks.

Adjoining the castle, in a grand conservatory designed by Joseph Paxton, is the Orangery Café. Here delicious lunches and teas can be enjoyed. The garden shop, in the garden bothy, sells plants from the garden, homemade produce from the castle kitchens and local crafts and gifts.

🏛 historic building 🏛 museum 🏛 historic site 🍃 scenic attraction 🌱 flora and fauna

historic castle grounds. Within the 1,000-acre estate surrounding a fortified medieval manor house are walled vegetable and flower gardens, pools, canals, island pavilions, a maze with a secret tunnel and a waterfall in a sunken garden. There are river and woodland walks, a restaurant and shop (01568 797777).

Leominster

🏛 Priory Church   🏛 Grange Court

🏛 Museum

The hub of the farming community and the largest town in this part of the county, Leominster became wealthy in the Middle Ages through the wool trade of its local Ryeland sheep; the fleeces came to be known as 'Leminster Ore' meaning Leominster Gold. The town still prospers today and is well-known as one of the most important antiques centres in the region. Some have linked the unusual name with Richard the Lionheart, but there was in fact an earlier king with a similar nickname. In the 7th century, Merewald, King of Mercia, was renowned for his bravery and ferocity and was known as 'the Lion'. He is said to have had a dream concerning a message from a Christian missionary, while at the same time a religious hermit had a vision of a lion coming to him and eating from his hand. They later met up at what was to be Leominster almost by accident, and when the King heard of the hermit's strangely coincidental dream, he was persuaded to convert to Christianity. Later, Merewald requested that a convent and church be built in the town; a stone lintel on the west door of the church depicts the chance meeting of

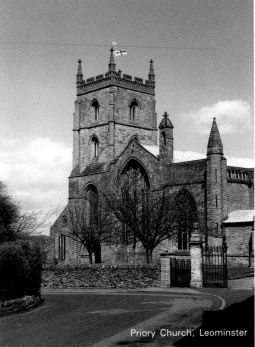

Priory Church, Leominster

King and hermit. Other, more likely explanations of the name revolve around Welsh and medieval Latin words for 'stream' and 'marsh'.

The magnificent ruins of the **Priory Church of St Peter and St Paul**, originally King Merewald's convent, was founded in 1123, and the three naves, built in the 12th, 13th and 14th centuries, attest to its importance. A curio here, standing in the north aisle, is the last ducking stool to be used in England. It's recorded that the miscreant was one Jennie Pipes, the year was 1809, but it's not known which of the two crimes that were punished in this way she had committed – being a 'scold' or selling adulterated goods.

A short walk away, in Priory Park, is

THE QUARRY FARM SHOP
QUALITY MEAT AS IT USED TO BE PRODUCED

Luston, Herefordshire HR6 0AW
Tel: 01568 613156
e-mail: sales@quarryfarmshop.co.uk
website: www.quarryfarmshop.co.uk

Quarry Farm is cared for by the Jones family, and every aspect of running the farm and the shop is in the hands of various members of the family. Lewis and Sarah are responsible for the livestock, which they raise on the farm using traditional methods, mainly grass-fed with no additives, hormones or unnecessary drugs.

They also source meat from a few carefully selected local family farms, always with an overriding concern for the highest standards of animal welfare and for where and how the meat is produced and the distance from producer to plate – their own livestock is slaughtered in an abattoir very close to the farm. The farm shop is a more recent venture set up by Richard, who puts his training as a butcher to excellent use. Beef, lamb, pork, seasonal game and poultry are all of consistently high quality, and the cooked meats, bacon, sausages and sausage rolls are always in great demand.

Mum in the farm's kitchen is kept busy producing a mouth-watering variety of flavour-packed ready meals and scrumptious pies and cakes, while Dad is responsible for deliveries, ensuring that the customer receives his order in the very best condition. The fruit and vegetable section of the farm shop is also top-notch, and the fruit, fresh and frozen, the meringues, the cream and the organic ice cream are just waiting to be turned into luscious desserts. Other items on the shelves include bread, preserves and pickles, eggs, crisps, chocolates and fruit juices. The family guarantee that all who visit this outstanding enterprise enjoy a pleasurable shopping experience, and the reputation for quality, reliability and service has spread far beyond the immediate area.

Holidaymakers, especially those staying at self-catering establishments, are regular buyers of the super breakfast boxes and local households and catering outlets are grateful for the barbecue packs and the 10kg and 20kg freezer packs of the farm's own red Hereford beef. The farm also offers a full catering service that includes barbecues, paella and traditional pig roasts. Quarry Farm is open from 8 to 4 on Monday, from 8 to 6 Tuesday to Friday and from 8 to 5.30 on Saturday. Customers can also visit the farm's website to browse through the lists and order online. The village of Luston is situated on the B4361 between Ludlow and Leominster.

Grange Court, a fine timbered building that for many years stood in the market place. Built in 1633, it is the work of the royal carpenter John Abel, and shows typical Abel flamboyance in its elaborate carvings.

Leominster Museum tells the story of Leominster and its people since pre-Roman times.

Around Leominster

KIMBOLTON
3 miles NE of Leominster off the A49

There are two delightful gardens to visit near Kimbolton. At Stockton Bury (turn right off the A49 on to the A4112) the sheltered four-acre garden has an extensive variety of plants set among medieval buildings, a kitchen garden, pigeon house, tithe barn, cider press and ruined chapel.

ASHTON
3 miles N of Leominster on the A49

🏠 Berrington Hall

Four miles north of Leominster on the road to Ludlow stands the National Trust's **Berrington Hall**, an elegant late 18th-century mansion designed by Henry Holland (later architect to the Prince Regent) in parkland laid out by his father-in-law Capability Brown. Features of the interior include a spectacular staircase hall, gilt tracery, fine furniture and paintings, a display of costumes from the Charles Wade collection of Snowshill Manor, a nursery, Victorian laundry and tiled

HIGHGATE HOUSE B&B

29 Hereford Road, Leominster,
Herefordshire HR6 8JS
Tel: 01568 614562
e-mail: cyrilmerriman@btinternet.com
website: www.highgate-house.co.uk

Highgate House is the home of Margaret and Cyril Merriman, a late-Victorian house a ten-minute stroll from the centre of Leominster. The owners have retained many delightful features, including a beautiful tile hall floor and fireplaces in most of the rooms. The whole place is decorated and furnished in keeping with its age and character, and the owners have imbued their home with a particularly warm and inviting ambience.

The Bed & Breakfast accommodation comprises three quiet, spacious bedrooms, two with en suite facilities, the other a family room with a private bathroom. The rooms are provided with Freeview TV and hospitality tray. Guests can relax in the roomy lounge and plan the day's activities, and Margaret's wonderful multi-choice breakfasts make a perfect start to a day's walking, golf or sightseeing.

The town of Leominster, on the famous Black & White Village Trail, has much to attract the tourist, including the imposing Priory Church of St Peter & St Paul, the Folk Museum, the Lion gallery a 13th century chapel dedicated to Thomas à Becket and a number of antique shops. The National Trust properties of Berrington Hall, Croft Castle are within 7/8 miles.

Georgian dairy. Most notable of all are perhaps the beautifully decorated ceilings: in the drawing room, the central medallion of Jupiter, Cupid and Venus is a composite scene taken from The Council and The Banquet of the Gods by Penni and del Colle in the Villa Farnesina in Rome. In the grounds are a walled garden with a collection of pre-1900 local apple trees, a woodland walk and a living willow tunnel in the children's play area. One of the trails takes in a Site of Special Scientific Interest with a heronry.

YARPOLE
4 miles N of Leominster off the B4361

🏛 Churches   🏛 Croft Castle

In this delightful village with its jumble of cottages and their colourful gardens stands the **Church of St Leonard**, which has a detached bell tower, a wooden structure with a stone outer wall. At neighbouring Eye are Eye Manor and the **Church of St Peter and St Paul**, where Thomas Harley, a Lord Mayor of London, is buried. An unusual feature of this church is the pulpit with carvings of Native Americans.

Near Yarpole, reached from the B4362 between Bircher and Mortimer's Cross, stands **Croft Castle**, an atmospheric property in the care of the National Trust. Behind a defensive exterior that tells of the troubled times of Marcher territory, the state rooms are elegant and comfortable, with rare furniture, fine plasterwork and portraits of the Croft family, who have been associated with the house since 1086. In the park are ancient oaks and an avenue of 350-year-old Spanish chestnut trees. Also looked after by the National Trust, and just a short walk away, is Croft Ambrey, an Iron Age fort that affords stunning views.

ORLETON
6 miles N of Leominster off the B4361

🏛 Richard's Castle

The churchyard at Orleton is thought by some to be the likely setting for the Resurrection at the Day of Judgment, and for that reason people from all over the country used to ask to be buried here in the hope that they would be among the first in the queue when life began again. The road north from Orleton leads to **Richard's Castle** on the Shropshire border. This Norman castle, which lies in ruins on the hillside above the church, was, like so many others, built as a defence against the marauding Welsh. The church played a similar role, and in the 14th century it was refurbished for use as a chapel by the Knights Hospitallers.

MORTIMER'S CROSS
7 miles NW of Leominster on the A4110/B4362

🏛 Battle Site

The site of one of England's greatest and bloodiest battles. Here, on 3 February 1461, a decisive battle in the War of the Roses was fought, with the Yorkists defeating the Lancastrians. Hundreds died that day, but 19-year-old Edward Mortimer, the Duke of York's eldest son, survived and was crowned King Edward IV in the following month. Visit the **Battle Centre** at Watermill.

WIGMORE
11 miles NW of Leominster on the A4110

🏛 Castle   🏛 Abbey

A few miles on from Mortimer's Cross, Wigmore is noted for its ruined **Castle** and **Abbey**. With its impressive vantage point, the hillside at Wigmore was a natural site for

CARADOC HOUSE B&B

49 Watling Street, Leintwardine,
Craven Arms, Herefordshire SY7 0LL
Tel: 01547 540238
e-mail: robinnsue@btinternet.com
website: www.caradoc.org.uk

Caradoc House is a late Georgian house in the peaceful village of Leintwardine on the Shropshire/Herefordshire border just 8 miles southwest of Ludlow set in glorious unspoilt countryside.

Robin and Sue Benson enjoy meeting and looking after their Bed & Breakfast guests, and tea and cakes on arrival and a wag of welcome from Basil the Dalmatian set the scene of relaxed hospitality that makes staying here such a pleasure. The accommodation comprises a double room with en suite facilities and a twin with a private bathroom; both are very comfortable and well-appointed, with crisp cotton bed linen, a hot drinks tray and lovely fresh flowers. The guest drawing room has a real fire, TV, board games and maps and other local information. There's a good choice for breakfast, including home-grown fruit, home-made preserves and delicious local honey as well as a classic cooked plateful. Caradoc House is a great base for a walking or cycling holiday, with miles of quiet lanes, tracks and trails – Offa's Dyke Path, the Mortimer Trail and the Herefordshire way are all nearby. The hosts are happy to take care of wet clothes (the Aga does an excellent job!) and the house has storage space for bicycles – bike hire can be arranged locally.

UPPER BUCKTON FARM

Buckton, Leintwardine, Craven Arms,
Herefordshire SY7 0JU
Tel: 01547 540634
e-mail: ghlloyd@btconnect.com

The location, the fine home cooking and the accommodation bring guests back year after year to **Upper Buckton Farm** set in 450 acres of unspoilt countryside looking south over the River Teme towards the forested Wigmore Rolls. In their handsome Georgian house Hayden and Yvonne have three letting bedrooms – one is a double with en suite shower room, the others doubles/twins with private bathrooms. All rooms come with fluffy towells and bathrobes along with beautiful cotton embroidered bed linen. The whole house is comfortably and traditionally furnished, with antiques and interesting paintings and a wonderfully relaxed, civilised ambience.

Guests can enjoy afternoon tea or after-dinner coffee round the log fire in the sitting room, or on a warm summer's day drinks can be taken on the veranda overlooking the croquet lawn. Yvonne is a superb cook, making excellent use of produce from the farm and garden and local meat, including spring lamb, free-range pork and chicken, super sausages, seasonal game and fresh fish caught of the coasts of Cornwall. A delicious meal is enhanced by a fine wine list chosen by Hayden from a top wine merchant in Shrewsbury. The grounds that surround the house are full of interest, with old-fashioned meadowland, a haha, a marlpit, a heronry, a weir, a millstream and the site of a 12th century motte & bailey castle. They also contain a point-to-point course that hosts two meetings a year, the Teme Valley and the United Hunts. The area attracts walkers, painters, golfers, horse riders and birdwatchers – the red kites over the Elan Valley are a wonderful sight.

building a castle, which is what William FitzOsbern did in the 11th century. This was one of a chain of fortifications built along the Welsh border. By the time of his death in 1071, FitzOsbern had also built Chepstow, Berkeley, Monmouth, Guenta (perhaps Winchester?) and Clifford, and had rebuilt Ewyas Harold. Wigmore passed into the hands of the Clifford family, then the ambitious Mortimers, and it was no doubt here that the future Edward IV prepared himself for the battle at Mortimer's Cross. Enough of the ruins remain to show that Wigmore was once a very important castle, and one which protected the village and its environs for many centuries until the Civil War.

BRAMPTON BRYAN
16 miles NW of Leominster on the A4113

Many of the thatched cottages in the village, as well as its castle, had to be rebuilt after a siege during the Civil War in 1643. The chief relic of the castle is the gatehouse, which now stands in the gardens of a charming 18th-century house near the Church of St Barnabus. Sir Robert Harley, a relation of Thomas Harley of Berrington Hall, owned the castle and it was due to his allegiance to Cromwell that it was besieged not once but twice by the Royalist army. Following the eventual destruction of the castle by the Royalists, Harley fell out with Cromwell. They remained at loggerheads until Cromwell died, and on that day in September 1658, it is said that a violent storm swept through Brampton Bryan Park, destroying a great number of trees. Harley was convinced that the storm was caused by the Devil dragging Cromwell down to Hell.

SHOBDON
8 miles W of Leominster on the B4362

🏛 Church   🏚 Shobdon Arches

🌿 Lingen Nursery   🌿 Bryan's Ground

The **Church of St John the Evangelist**, which stands on the site of a 12th century priory, is the most amazing in the county. In the 1750s, Lord Bateman demolished the medieval priory (relocating selected fragments as a hilltop folly a quarter of a mile away), and built a new church that has been described as "a pastiche of the Countess' boudoir in Mozart's opera *The Marriage of Figaro*". The overall effect is of being inside a giant wedding cake, with white and pale blue icing everywhere, and lovely stained glass adding to the dazzling scene. Such is its flamboyance, the *Shell Guide* declared that this church was "an inconceivable place to hold a funeral". It has to be seen to be believed.

Just north of the village are the **Shobdon Arches**, a collection of Norman sculptures that have sadly been greatly damaged by centuries of exposure to the elements, but which still demonstrate the high skills of the sculptors of the 12th century.

Country roads signposted from the B4362 lead west from Shobdon to Lingen, where the **Nursery and Garden** are a horticultural haven for visitors to this remote area of the Marches. The gardens are home to National Collections of Iris Sibirica and Herbaceous Campanula.

Even nearer the Welsh border, between Kinsham and Stapleton (signs from the B4362 at Combe) is **Bryan's Ground**, a three-acre Edwardian garden with towers and topiary, follies and fragrant flowers, a specialist collection of old roses, formal pools and potager, and paths to a five-acre arboretum beside the river.

THE RADNORSHIRE ARMS HOTEL

High Street, Presteigne, Powys LD8 2BE
Tel: 01544 267406 Fax: 01544 260418
e-mail: info@rahwales.com
website: www.radnorshirearmshotel.com

One of Presteigne's most striking buildings is the **Radnorshire Arms Hotel**, a lovely half-timbered structure that was originally built as a house for Sir Christopher Hatton, one of Elizabeth I's leading courtiers. A Grade II listed building, the hotel, with its wealth of original exposed beams and timber-panelled walls, exudes an atmosphere of luxurious comfort and classic Jacobean elegance.

The hotel today is as rich in amenities as its 17th century structure is in history. There are 10 en suite rooms and one family suite on a bed and breakfast rate and 8 spacious garden rooms, all ensuite and fully equipped to the highest standard with WiFi access. The garden rooms are pet-friendly and have a room only or bed and breakfast rate.

For the ultimate dining experience, the Oak Room and The Hattons both offer a superb range of fresh, home-cooked meals; including vegetarian and special diets which make the most of the exceptional local and seasonal produce. Other amenities include a residents' lounge, drying room, a traditional bar and a large landscaped garden with a children's play area. There is assisted disabled access to the garden rooms, and full access to the bar and restaurants and parking is via 2 car parks, one situated at the front and the other at the rear of the hotel. A garage facility is available by prior booking for cyclists and motorbikes.

EARDISLAND

8 miles W of Leominster on the B4529

🏠 Church 🏠 Dovecote 🏠 Burton Court

"An uncommonly pretty village", said Pevsner of this renowned spot on the banks of the River Arrow. Certainly glorious, Eardisland is one of the most beautiful villages in the county (and the competition is very strong), and with its inns, bowling green, river and charming buildings spanning the centuries, this is essential England. Dominating the scene is the 12th-century **Church of St Mary the Virgin** where, each year, from Easter until late autumn, an exhibition of village and parish life is staged. At Holmlea stands the **Eardisland Dovecote**, a unique Georgian dovecote in a

River Arrow, Eardisland

🏠 stories and anecdotes 🦃 famous people 🎨 art and craft 🏃 entertainment and sport 🚶 walks beautiful riverside setting in the centre of a conservation village. A mile outside Eardisland is **Burton Court**, whose centrepiece is the sumptuous 14th-century Great Hall. Many additions have been made to the building down the years, and the present entrance, dating from 1912, is the work of Sir Clough Williams-Ellis of Portmeirion fame. Highlight of the various attractions is a collection of European and Oriental costumes, but of interest, too, are a model ship collection, a wide range of natural history specimens and a working model fairground. The Court is open only for pre-arranged group visits.

PEMBRIDGE
10 miles W of Leominster on the A44

🏛 Church   🌿 Old Chapel Gallery

The influential Mortimer family were responsible for the medieval prosperity of historic Pembridge, and many handsome buildings bear witness to their patronage and its legacy. The most famous building is the 14th-century **Church**, a three-storey structure in stone and timber with a marvellous timber Belfry. The bell and the clock mechanism can be viewed from inside the church. Two other buildings that the visitor should not miss are the delightful 16th-century Market Hall standing on its eight oak pillars and the **Old Chapel Gallery** (see panel opposite) in a converted Victorian chapel. A little way south of Pembridge is Dunkerton's Cider Mill, where cider and perry are produced from organically grown local fruit. Open Monday to Saturday.

LYONSHALL
14 miles W of Leominster on the A480

🏛 Church   🏛 Castle

The remains of the **Church** and **Castle** are at some distance from the main body of the

village, a fact which is often attributed to the plague causing older settlements to be abandoned. The Church of St Michael and All Angels dates mainly from the 13th century and was restored in 1870 when close to collapse. The ruins of the castle include some walls and part of the moat, making this the most 'complete' of all the castle ruins in the area. Among the fine old buildings in the village itself are the Royal George Inn (see panel opposite), Ivy House, The Wharf and The Woodlands. There are two 12th-century water corn mills in the parish, one of them, Bullock's Mill, being documented continuously from 1580 to 1928.

KINGTON
15 miles W of Leominster on the A44

🏛 Cwmmau Farmhouse   📷 Museum

🏛 Wapley Hill   🏛 Offa's Dyke

🌱 Small Breeds Farm Park & Owl Centre

🌱 Hergest Croft Gardens   🏛 Hergest Court

The road up to Kington passes many places of interest, and for two in particular a short pause will be well worth while. The National Trust's **Cwmmau Farmhouse**, which lies four miles south of Kington between the A4111 and A438 at Brilley, is an imposing timber-framed and stone-tiled farmhouse dating from the early 17th century. Viewing is by guided tour only. Call 01497 831251. **Kington Museum** tells the story of Kington from Roman times to the present day. Open April to September, Tuesday to Saturday.

A splendid place for a family visit is the **Small Breeds Farm Park and Owl Centre**. The Owl Centre houses one of the finest displays of owls in the UK, and in the Pet Animal House can be seen guinea pigs, mice, chinchillas, rabbits and chipmunks. Other

OLD CHAPEL GALLERY

Established in 1989 by Yasmin Strube, **Old Chapel Gallery** has become recognised as a centre of excellence for the arts, where work by both reputable local and nationally known artists and makers can be seen alongside innovative work by talented newcomers. The emphasis is on quality and originality, from glass, ceramics, jewellery, iron-work, sculpture, furniture, to textiles and knitwear and a diverse range of original watercolours, oils, pastels, etchings and aquatints. The gallery hosts regular and ever changing exhibitions and showcases. There is also an annual garden sculpture exhibition.

A range of services are available through the gallery including commissioning and a "take it on appro" service for local and regular customers.

The gallery has developed a website for on-line shopping.

The gallery is selected for quality by the Crafts Council and is a member of the ICGA.

Friendly and knowledgeable staff are always on hand to welcome you and make your visit informative, pleasurable and memorable.

Old Chapel Gallery is OPEN DAILY 11 - 5

East Street, Pembridge Herefordshire HR6 9HB
e-mail: oldchapelgallery@googlemail.com
website: www.oldchapelgallery.co.uk Tel: 01544 388842

THE ROYAL GEORGE INN

Lyonshall, nr Kington, Herefordshire HR5 3JN
Tel: 01544 340084
e-mail: sue.geyton@btinternet.com
website: www.royalgeorgelyonshall.co.uk

In 1840 there were seven pubs in Lyonshall, now there's just one. The **Royal George Inn** is at the heart of the community, and the community is very much in the hearts of Kevin and Sue Geyton and their family. The friendliest of hosts, they have an equally warm welcome for familiar faces and for occasional visitors, including families with children and dogs. Dating from the 17th century and updated in uncluttered contemporary style, the inn has a number of bars and dining areas where a good choice of drinks and super home-cooked food is served. Sue's food ranges from light bites/starters to pub classics such as lasagne, fishcakes, scampi, battered cod, honey-roast ham, burgers, Herefordshire sirloin steaks, curries and pasta. Daily specials like liver & bacon with onion gravy and poached salmon with a caperberry butter sauce extend the choice. Sunday lunchtime brings a choice of traditional roasts and Thursday is steak night – always a popular occasion.

The inn, which is open every session except Monday lunchtime, was just The George until 1782, when it was renamed to commemorate a naval disaster in which the flagship of the fleet The Royal George with the loss of 900 lives.

creatures on the site include ducks, geese and swans in the landscaped waterfowl enclosure, colourful pheasants, doves, bantams, red squirrels and Rhubarb the reindeer in his smart new enclosure with his lady friends Gloria and Cynthia (01544 231109).

Half a mile off the A44 on the Welsh side of Kington are **Hergest Croft Gardens**, four distinct gardens for all seasons from spring bulbs to autumn colour that include a valley of giant rhododendrons, spectacular azaleas, an old-fashioned kitchen garden and a marvellous collection of trees and shrubs. Hergest holds National Collections of maples, birches and zelkovas. Open Easter to 1 November.

Nearby is the impressive Hergest Ridge, rising to around 1,400 feet, and, on its southern edge, **Hergest Court**, once owned by the Vaughan family. Two members of the family who gained particular notoriety were Thomas 'Black' Vaughan and his wife, who was known as Gethen the Terrible. She is said to have taken revenge on a man who killed her brother by taking part in an archery competition disguised as a man. When her turn came, she shot him dead at point-blank range and escaped in the ensuing melee. Thomas died at the Battle of Banbury in 1469, but, being a true Vaughan, that was not the last of him. He is said to have haunted the church in the guise of a bull, and even managed to turn himself into a horsefly to annoy the local horses. He was back in taurine form when he was finally overcome by a band of clerics. One of the band managed to shrink him and cram him into a snuff box, which was quickly consigned to the waters of Hergest Pool. Later owners of the estate found and unwittingly opened the box, letting Black

GLYN SLADE-JONES BUTCHERS

39 High Street, Kington, Herefordshire HR5 3BJ
Tel: 01544 230470

On the High Street of Kington, **Glyn Slade-Jones** is a family butchers of distinction with a reputation for quality and service that stretches back more than 25 years. Glyn and his mother and business partner Marjorie have earned numerous awards for the business, including Flavours of Herefordshire (three times) and Best Local Food Retailer in the West Midlands 2008 (sponsored by the Countryside Alliance). These awards are a spur to maintain the high standards, because, as Glyn says, 'your'e only as good as the last pork chop you sell'.

Most of the meat comes from farmers within a few miles of the shop, and some from their own farm near Lyonshall. Everything they sell here is excellent, but for Glyn and for many of his regular customers pride of place go to his amazing sausages, which are responsible for many of the awards. The choice changes all the time, sometimes with ideas from the local community, but a typical selection could include plain pork, pork & leek, pork & peppers, pork with smoked bacon & tomato and beef with horseradish. When available, Marjorie's pork pies and other pastries and her chutneys and preserves should definitely not be missed. This outstanding butchers business is open from 7.30 to 5 (till 1 Wednesday, till 2.30 Saturday.

🏛 historic building   🏛 museum   🏛 historic site   🍃 scenic attraction   ⚘ flora and fauna

THE OXFORD ARMS

Duke Street, Kington, Herefordshire HR5 3DR
Tel: 01544 230322
e-mail: fredhawkins@btconnect.com
website: www.the-oxford-arms.co.uk

Fred, Sadie and Molly Hawkins came to The **Oxford Arms** in February 2008 with the aim of running an old-fashioned pub with good home-cooked food, real ales and a warm welcome for one and all – all of which they've achieved in some style. The inn started life in the 17th century as a coaching inn called The Salutation – the name was changed at the end of the 19th century in honour of the Earl of Oxford, a big local landowner. Before that it was an important stop on coaching runs to Leominster, Aberystwyth and London; those grand days may be over, but the old lady is getting plenty of love and attention from the Hawkins family and their growing band of regulars. The interior is warm and inviting, with two bars, a cosy dining room, a wood-panelled bar counter...and a classic red telephone box. Herefordshire real ales quench country thirsts, and appetites are satisfied by a selection of classic pub dishes, including steaks, the stew of the week served in a giant Yorkshire pudding, and always a good selection of homemade vegetarian choices.

The inn also offers comfortable guest accommodation in three good-size rooms, one with en suite facilities, the others with private bathrooms across the corridor. This super inn is open Monday and Tuesday from 6pm, Wednesday, Thursday, Friday and Sunday, lunchtimes and evenings and all day Saturday from 12noon to 12 midnight. Food is served at all sessions that we are open, 12noon - 2.30pm and 6pm - 9pm.

HERGEST RIDGE VIEW SELF-CATERING ACCOMMODATION

Kingswood, nr Kington, Herefordshire HR5 3HH
Tel: 01544 230137

Marjorie Jones, mother and business partner of Glyn at the family butchers, has two cottages for self-catering guests on either side of her home at Kingswood, a short drive west of Kington. Standing on a quiet country lane, **Mavis Cottage** enjoys stunning views over Hergest Ridge to the Welsh borders from its elevated position. It has a lounge, a Victorian conservatory-style dining room, kitchen and bathroom on the ground floor and two bedrooms – a double and a twin – upstairs. A few steps away, **Steepholm** is a delightful single-storey stone cottage with living and dining areas, kitchen, bathroom, double and twin bedrooms and the same great views. Both have everything needed for comfortable, go-as-you-please stay, including excellent cooking arrangements, a woodburning stove, washing machine, fridge-freezer TV, books and board games and secluded gardens....and Marjorie is usually close by to give assistance and information about the local

attractions. And what better place to buy supplies for a princely meal than the family butchers in Kington! The cottages are an ideal base for touring, for a walking holiday – Offa's Dyke Path is nearby – or for just relaxing, recharging the batteries and enjoying those glorious views.

Vaughan loose once more. The next band of intrepid clerics confined the spirit under an oak tree, but he is currently at large again - though not sighted for many years. These feisty Vaughans are buried in the Vaughan Chapel in Kington parish church.

Kington itself lies on the England/Wales border and, like other towns in the area known as the Marches, had for many years to look closely to the west, whence the wild Welsh would attack. Kington's castle was destroyed many centuries ago, but outside the town, on **Wapley Hill**, are earthworks of an ancient hill fort that could be the site of King Caractacus' last stand.

Most notable by far of all the defences in the region is **Offa's Dyke**, the imposing ditch that extends for almost 180 miles along the border, from the Severn Estuary at Sedbury Cliffs near Chepstow, across the Black Mountain ridge, through the Wye Valley and north to Prestatyn on the North Wales coast. Offa was a Mercian king of great influence, with strong diplomatic links with the Popes and Charlemagne, who ruled the land south of the Humber from AD757 to AD796. Remnants of wooden stakes unearthed down the years suggest that the Dyke had a definite defensive role, rather than acting merely as a psychological barrier. It was a truly massive construction, in places almost 60 feet wide, and although nowadays it disappears in places, much of it can still be walked, particularly in the Wye Valley. A stretch north of Kington is especially well preserved and provides excellent, invigorating walking for the energetic. The walk crosses, at Bradnor Hill, the highest golf course, over 1,200 feet above sea level. Other major traces of the Dyke remain, notably between Chepstow and Monmouth

and by Oswestry, and at many points Offa's Dyke Path, opened by the Countryside Commission in 1971, diverts from the actual Dyke into magnificent scenery. At Kington, Offa's Dyke links to the Mortimer Trail, a 30-mile route to Ludlow, following the ridges of the hills and woods in the northwest corner of Herefordshire.

DILWYN
7 miles SW of Leominster on the A4112

The village lies in a hollow, so its Old English name of Secret Place is an appropriate one. The main body of the parish church was built around 1200, with additions in the following century and a spire put up in the 1700s. The workmen who built the church were also associated with nearby Wormsley Priory, and one of the figures in Dilwyn's church is thought to be a member of the Talbot family, founders of the priory. The church registers go back over 400 years, providing a valuable trail of local history.

WEOBLEY
9 miles SW of Leominster on the B4230

🏛 Museum

The steeple of the parish church of St Peter and St Paul is the second highest in the county, a reminder that this prettiest of places (pronounced Webbly) was once a thriving market town. One of its more unusual sources of wealth was a successful glove-making industry that flourished in the early 19th century when the Napoleonic Wars cut off the traditional French source of gloves. At certain times in its history Weobley returned two Members of Parliament, but there have been none since 1832. One of the effigies in the church is of Colonel John Birch, who was rewarded for his successes with Cromwell's army with the Governorship of Hereford and who later became a keen Royalist and Weobley's MP. Little but the earthworks remain of Weobley Castle, which was built before the Norman Conquest and was captured by King Stephen in 1138. One of Weobley's many interesting buildings is called The Throne, but it was called The Unicorn when King Charles I took refuge after the Battle of Naseby in 1645. **Weobley Museum**, on the site of an old police station, has exhibitions of local history and regularly changing displays.

KINNERSLEY

5 miles SW of Weobley on the A4112

🏰 Castle

On the main road lie the village and **Kinnersley Castle**, which has the look of a fortified manor house. Famous occupants down the years include the Morgans (the 17th century buccaneer Sir Henry Morgan was one of them) and the Vaughans. Black

Vaughan's huge dog is believed to have been the inspiration for Conan Doyle's *Hound of the Baskervilles*.

EARDISLEY

8 miles W of Weobley on the A4111

🏰 Church   🌳 Great Oak

The greatest treasure of Eardisley's **Church of St Mary Magdalene** is its font, dating from the early 12th century. The figures depicted around the font represent not only familiar religious themes, but also two men in armed struggle. It is thought that these are a 12th-century lord of the manor, Ralph de Baskerville, and his father-in-law, Lord Drogo, whom he killed in a dispute over land. As a penance, Ralph was ordered by the church authorities to commission this extraordinary font.

Outside this pretty village, the most notable feature, standing majestically by an old chapel, is the **Great Oak**, which is believed to be some 800 years old.

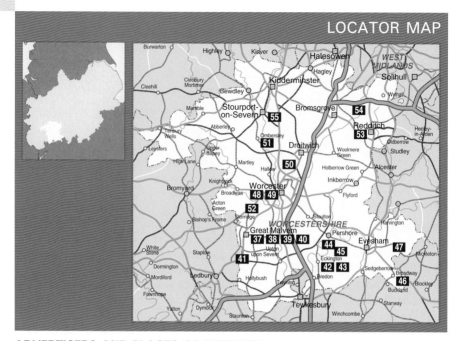

LOCATOR MAP

ADVERTISERS AND PLACES OF INTEREST

🏠 historic building   🏛 museum   🏚 historic site   🍂 scenic attraction   🌿 flora and fauna

2 | Worcestershire

In the southern part of the county lies the spectacular ridge of the Malvern Hills, with marvellous walking and breathtaking views. Moving eastwards we reach the towns of Upton-upon-Severn, Pershore and Evesham, along with many charming villages and ancient sites. The Vale of Evesham is one of the country's most important and prolific horticultural regions, and in springtime the Vale is alive with colour from the blossom of the fruit trees. High-quality fruit and vegetables are distributed from here throughout the country, and motorists will come across numerous roadside stalls selling a wonderful array of produce. At the eastern edge of this part of the county lies Broadway, a quintessential Cotswold village of outstanding beauty, beloved of tourists and not to be missed on any visit to this most delightful part of the world.

Set on either side of the curving River Severn, Worcester is a bustling county capital and cathedral city. Its architecture spans many centuries and there are some marvellous examples from all of them. In the heart of England, this is an area characterised by red earth, apple orchards, hop yards, quiet inns, stone farmhouses and black-and-white timbered dwellings. As a visible legacy of the ancient forest that once surrounded Worcester, the half-timbered buildings lend colour and variety to the villages around this historic city.

Most of Worcestershire's industry was centred in the northern part of the county,

and there are numerous examples of industrial archaeology to interest the historian. Salt and scythes, carpets, porcelain and needles all contributed to the local economy, along with ironworks and corn mills, and many fine old buildings survive as monuments to industries that have dwindled or disappeared.

Canals were once as important a means of transport as the roads, and in this part of the county the Worcester & Birmingham Canal, the Staffordshire & Worcester Canal and the Droitwich Canal were considered to be more reliable than the roads and quicker than the Severn. They lost a good deal of their practical advantages when the railways arrived. Then, as the railway network shrunk over the past 40 years, it's back to the roads for most local communications. However, the Severn Valley Railway, from Kidderminster to Bridgnorth, has survived and flourished, and today people come from far and wide for the chance to ride behind a steam engine through some incredibly beautiful scenery.

Enthusiasts have also ensured that much of the canal system has survived, finding a new role as a major leisure and tourist attraction. The route north from Droitwich towards Bromsgrove takes in much that is of interest to the industrial historian, including the Worcester & Birmingham Canal. Opened in 1815 and 30 miles in length, the canal passes Stoke Works and Stoke Prior, where John Corbett set up his salt works after leaving Droitwich.

Great Malvern

🏛 Priory Church of St Mary & St Michael

🏛 Museum 🏛 St Anne's Well 🎭 Theatres

🎿 Malvern Hills 🎿 The Worcestershire Way

Beneath the northeastern slopes of the **Malvern Hills**, Great Malvern is known for its porcelain, its annual music and drama festivals, Malvern water and Morgan cars. Though invaded by tourists for much of the year, Great Malvern has retained its dignity and elegance, with open spaces, leafy avenues and handsome houses. Close to the start of the Malvern walking trail, on a path leading up from the town, is a Regency cottage housing one source of the famous water – **St Anne's Well** – where one can enjoy a sample and take in the views. Great Malvern was for many centuries a quiet, little-known place with a priory at its heart, and even when the curative properties of its spring waters were discovered, it took a long time for it to become a fashionable spa resort. Hotels, baths and a pump room were built in the early 19th- century, and the arrival of the railway provided easy access from the middle of the century. The station is one of many charming Victorian buildings, and with its cast-iron pillars, stone ornaments and beautifully painted floral designs, is a tourist attraction in its own right.

GREAT MALVERN DELI & COFFEE HOUSE

*11 Abbey Road, Great Malvern,
Worcestershire WR14 3ES
Tel: 01684 899091*

Aruna Buxton's **Great Malvern Deli & Coffee House** stands in a Georgian building just below street level in the heart of town. In the cosy main room or sitting outside visitors can enjoy a fine variety of home-made fare, including soups, sandwiches and panini, hams and other cooked and cured meats, pâtés, cheese, cakes, ice creams, iced yoghurt and fruit juices. Dietary food is available with a little notice. The Deli also sells a selection of olives and olive oils, chutneys, jams, honey and pasta, and home-made English chocolates make an lovely treat or present. This excellent place is open from 9.30 to 5 Monday to Saturday.

THE KNITTING PARLOUR

*12 Graham Road, Great Malvern,
Worcestershire WR14 2HN
Tel: 01684 892079*

Pat Jones and her daughter Vicki own and run the **Knitting Parlour**, a modern knitting shop that attracts customers from as far afield as Birmingham and Bristol. Behind the big window display the shelves and tables of the 2009 winner of the Knitting Retailer of the Year are filled with a wide variety of wools, yarns, threads, cotton fabrics, books, patterns and accessories from leading brands including Rowan and Rowan Classic, Debbie Bliss, Sublime, Sirdar, Noro, Colinette, Gedifra and Amy Butler. The Parlour holds monthly Rowan workshops and courses on a variety of knitting and related topics. Shop hours are 9.30 to 5 Monday to Saturday.

🏛 historic building 🏛 museum 🏛 historic site 🞄 scenic attraction 🌿 flora and fauna

CRIDLAN & WALKER

PURVEYOR OF ORGANIC MEATS

*Abbey Gateway, 23 Abbey Road, Great Malvern,
Worcestershire WR14 3ES
Tel: 01684 573008 Fax: 01684 566017
e-mail: newventure3@aol.com website: www.cridlanandwalker.com*

Quality has always been a byword at **Cridlan & Walker**, a long-established purveyor of organic meats with a reputation that extends far beyond the neighbouring communities. Owners and staff pride themselves on the range of meat, game and poultry, and on their home-produced sausages, bacon and burgers. They also produce South African specialities including Ostrich, Boerewors, Biltong, Droewors & Kassler rib along with a variety of superb home-made pies, pasties, quiches and sausage rolls either freshly baked or to 'take and bake'. And for a quick, tasty snack to go, a country roll filled with roast pork & all the trimmings is hard to beat. Meat is king, but customers in the know also take their pick from the eye-catching displays of prime seasonal fruit and vegetables.

COWLEIGH PARK FARM

*Cowleigh Road, Great Malvern, Worcestershire WR13 5HJ
Tel: 01684 566750
e-mail: info@cowleighparkfarm.co.uk
website: www.cowleighparkfarm.co.uk*

Cowleigh Park Farm is a delightful timber framed, former farmhouse, nestling at the foot of the Malvern Hills. This 400 year old, Grade II listed home is set within it's own grounds and is peacefully located in a tranquil setting ensuring a relaxing stay. It offers 3 comfortable, bed and breakfast rooms each with colour TV, Wi-Fi and ensuite bath/ shower rooms. Owners Ruth and John Lucas offer sumptuous breakfasts featuring prime local produce. Also available on a self catering basis are the adjoining Cider Press (sleeps 2) and the Farmhouse Cottage (sleeps 6). Car parking available within the grounds of the property, and guests are welcome to share the pleasant gardens. Cowleigh Park Farm is on the Worcestershire Way with footpaths leading onto the hills and towards the Teme Valley and Herefordshire.

The **Priory Church of St Mary and St Michael** is a dominant feature in the centre of the town. Its windows, the west a gift from Richard III, the east from Henry VII, contain a wonderful collection of 15th-century stained glass. Another unique feature is a collection of more than 1,200 wall tiles on the chancel screens, which also date from the 15th century. The Victorian bell-frame on which the bells are hung has recently been the subject of much discussion: English heritage insist that the frame is of special historic interest and therefore must be restored and not replaced. Among many interesting graves in the cemetery is that of Jenny Lind, The Swedish Nightingale, who was born in Stockholm in 1820 and died at Wynd's Point, Malvern, which she used as a summer retreat, in 1887. In the churchyard at West Malvern Peter Mark Roget (the Thesaurus man) is buried - "interred, entombed, coffined, laid to rest, consigned to earth". The 14th-century Abbey Gateway, whose huge wooden gateposts can be seen in the archway, houses the **Malvern Museum**. Open Easter to

THE RAILWAY INN

78 Wells Road, Malvern Wells, Worcestershire WR14 4PA
Tel: 01684 572168
e-mail: misstcawley@aol.com

Since arriving here in October 2008 Russell and Theresa have been building a great reputation for hospitality and good food at the **Railway Inn**. It's equally popular with the local community, with visitors to the local showground and theatres and with tourists. Open from 12 to 10 seven days a week for food and drink, the inn enjoys a delightful hilltop setting with fantastic views over open countryside, rivers, forests and villages. The cosy locals bar is a great place to meet for a drink and a chat, and the snugs are quiet retreats to relax with a drink and a newspaper. The inn also has a charming terrace and patio.

Prime meat from local farmers and butchers feature strongly on Russell's menu, with Aberdeen Angus steaks, pork from Woodland Pigs, steak & ale pie, sausages & mash, liver & bacon, home-cooked gammon and the Sunday roasts among the favourites. The fish specials are always popular, there are always several vegetarian main courses, and treacle sponge is a great way to round off an excellent meal. The Railway Inn is also a fine base for touring the region: the three en suite rooms alongside the inn comprise two twins and a family room. Free Wi-Fi is available.

October, its displays include the geology of the Malvern Hills, the history of Malvern spring water and the development of Morgan cars. In Tanhouse Lane stands the factory of Boehm of Malvern, where the remarkable American, Edward Marshall Boehm (call it 'Beam'), founded the centre that has become known worldwide for the quality of its porcelain. Great Malvern has a distinguished tradition of arts and culture, much of it the legacy of Sir Edward Elgar and George Bernard Shaw, and The **Malvern Theatres** are an exciting setting for performances of music and drama including pre-West End runs. Malvern is the home of the excellent English Symphony Orchestra, formed in 1980 by William Boughton. In addition, The Malvern Theatres host many superb performances by notable singers, actors and speakers.

Great Malvern is the largest of six settlements that make up the Malverns: to the south are Malvern Wells and Little Malvern, to the north North Malvern, and to the northeast Malvern Link. The **Worcestershire Way** is a 31-mile walking trail that links Great Malvern with Bewdley, through Abberley, Knightley and Markwick and the valleys of the Teme and Severn.

Around Great Malvern

LITTLE MALVERN
4 miles S of Great Malvern on the A449

🏛 Little Malvern Court 🏛 Little Malvern Priory
🏛 St Peter's Church

At Little Malvern stands the Church of St Wulstan, where a simple headstone marks the grave of Sir Edward Elgar and his wife Caroline. Their daughter is buried next to them.

Little Malvern Court, off the A4104, enjoys a glorious setting on the lower slopes of the Malvern Hills. It stands next to **Little Malvern Priory**, whose hall, the only part that survived the Dissolution, is now incorporated into the Court. Of the priory church, only the chancel tower and south transept remain. The Court was once a Catholic safe house, with a chapel reached by a secret staircase. The Court and gardens are open Wednesday and Thursday afternoons from mid-April to mid-July.

Just to the north at Malvern Wells, where the first medicinal wells were discovered, stands **St Peter's Church**, dating from 1836 and notable for some original stained glass and a William Morris window of 1885.

The showground at Malvern Wells hosts major spring and autumn garden shows as well as antiques and crafts shows.

Around the Malverns

🏛 British Camp

The whole area is glorious walking country, with endless places to discover and explore. **British Camp**, on Herefordshire Beacon, two miles west of Little Malvern, is one of the most important Roman settlements in Britain, and a little way south is Midsummer Hill, site of another ancient settlement.

COLWALL
2 miles SW of Great Malvern off the B4218

🌿 Picton Garden

On the west side of the Malverns, Colwall lies just across the border in Herefordshire. Its chief claim to fame is the enormous lump of limestone thatstands at its centre. How it got there no one knows, but the Devil and a local giant are among the suspects. Less mysterious are the attractions of the **Picton Garden**, which contains a National Collection of Michaelmas daisies that flower

in September/October. The 14th-century poet William Langland, author of *Piers Plowman*, lived at Colwall.

BIRTSMORTON
7 miles S of Great Malvern off the B4208

In the Church of St Peter and St Paul are monuments to the Nanfan family, owners of the nearby Birtsmorton Court. Other notable residents of this magnificent building (not open to the public) include William Huskisson, a former colonial secretary, who in 1830 became the first person to be killed in a railway accident.

HANLEY CASTLE
6 miles SE of Great Malvern on the B4209

The village takes its name from the castle, which was originally a hunting lodge for King John, and which disappeared, except for its moat, many centuries ago. There's still plenty to see in this attractive little spot, including picturesque cottages, a 15th-century inn (The Three Kings), a 16th-century grammar school and the Church of St Mary, built in stone and brick.

UPTON-ON-SEVERN
7 miles SE of Great Malvern on the A4104

🏛 The Pepperpot   🏛 The Tudor House

An unspoilt town that gained prominence as one of the few bridging points on the Severn. The first records indicate that it was a Roman station, and it is mentioned in the Domesday Book. It became an important medieval port, and its strategic position led to its playing a role in the Civil War. In 1651, Charles sent a force to Upton to destroy the bridge, but after a long and bloody struggle the King's troops were routed and Cromwell regained the town. A Dutch gabled building used for stabling

🎦 stories and anecdotes   🦜 famous people   🎨 art and craft   🌿 entertainment and sport   🚶 walks

during the conflict still stands. The medieval church, one of the most distinctive buildings in the whole county, is affectionately known as **The Pepperpot**, because of its handsome tower with its copper-covered cupola, the only surviving part of the church. This former place of worship is now a heritage centre, relating the Civil War battles and the town's history. The Church of St Peter and St Paul, built in 1879, has an interesting talking point in a large metal abstract hanging above the altar. The **Tudor House**, which contains a museum of Upton past and present, is open daily on summer afternoons. The White Lion Hotel, in the High Street, has a history going back to 1510 and was the setting for some scenes in Henry Fielding's *Tom Jones*. The commercial trade has largely left the Severn, replaced by a steady stream of summertime pleasure craft.

RIPPLE
10 miles SE of Great Malvern off the A38

  🌿 Giant's Grave

The village square with its stocks and whipping post is tiny, making the Church of St Mary seem even larger than it is. Note the series of 12 misericords each depicting the seasonal activities of country life. They are full of detail and wondrously carved. In the churchyard is the **Giant's Grave**, the final resting place of Robert Reeve who was said to be 7ft 4in tall when he died in 1626, aged 56. On his well-preserved gravestone the epitaph reads:

> *Ye who pass by behold my length*
> *But never glory in your strength*

EARLS CROOME
6 miles SE of Great Malvern on the A4104

  🏛 Croome Park

There are several attractions in the area of Earls Croome. **Croome Park** was Capability

Brown's first complete landscape. Commissioned by the 6th Earl of Coventry in 1751, the Park made Brown's reputation and set a pattern for parkland design that lasted half a century. At Croome he established the English Landscape Style, a vision of Ideal Nature that was admired and copied throughout the Western world. The restoration of the park, one of the largest landscape restoration projects undertaken, included the replanting of many unusual trees and shrubs, the establishment of a wildflower meadow and pasture, and the creation of pathways to the ice house through the Wild Walk shrubbery. The buildings have equally distinguished pedigrees, with Robert Adam and James Wyatt as architects. The Hill Croome Dovecote is a very rare square building next to the church in Hill Croome. Dunstall Castle folly at Dunstall Common is a folly in the style of a Norman castle, put up in the 18th century and comprising two round towers and one square, connected by arches.

At Croome d'Abitot, a little way north of Earls Croome, the 18th-century Church of St Mary Magdalene is filled with memorials to the Coventry family – it stood on their estate.

ECKINGTON
10 miles SE of Great Malvern on the B4080

  🌿 Bredon Hill

The small village of Eckington can be traced back to AD172; it was originally a Roman settlement on land belonging to the British tribe of Dobuni. The bridge over the Avon, which dates from the 15th century, has an adjacent car park that is a popular picnic site.

The area south of Pershore towards the boundary with Gloucestershire is dominated by **Bredon Hill**, which is surrounded by charming villages such as Great and Little

ECKINGTON MANOR

Manor Farm, Eckington, Pershore
Worcestershire WR10 3BH
Tel: 01386 751600
e-mail: info@eckingtonmanor.co.uk
website: www.eckingtonmanor.co.uk
website: www.lowerendhouse.co.uk

Visitors to **Eckington Manor** can look forward to outstanding hospitality provided by owner Judy Gardner and her staff, whether they're here on a cookery course or enjoying a break in a luxurious 13th century timber-framed hall house (or both!). The cookery school, with our resident head chef and tutor at the helm, is contained within the framework of a Dutch barn on a 260-acre working livestock farm in a quiet country setting, south of Pershore. The school runs a number of hands-on cookery courses lasting one, two or three days and catering for all levels of experience, as well as cookery demonstrations. The aim of the courses is to teach the art of cooking using fresh local seasonal produce wherever possible, and also imparting an appreciation and awareness of the provenance of food ingredients. Raw materials used in the school include the outstanding produce from the farm, including lamb, Aberdeen Angus and Highland beef and Gloucester Old Spot pork and fresh fruit, vegetables, herbs and honey from the orchards and kitchen gardens. Teaching is usually done in small groups, but one-to-one master classes are also available. Challenging and fun, the courses cover a variety of topics, including Great British Classics, Easy Entertaining, Cooking with Fish, Bread Making and Aga Cooking. Teaching is carried out in a spacious, air-conditioned state-of-the-art classroom equipped with ten individual kitchens. The school can also organise team building events and private parties. Students on the courses can buy first-class produce such as preserves, chutneys, pies and home- reared meat from the farm.

Luxurious accommodation is available in Lower End House, a 13th century timber-framed hall house situated in the grounds of the farm. The whole place has been beautifully restored and renovated, providing up-to-date comfort and amenities while retaining period features such as inglenook fireplaces, flagstone floors and exposed wooden beams. Each of the four guest bedrooms has its own charm and character; three are doubles/twins with beautiful Fired Earth en suite bathrooms with the White Company toiletries and sumptuous fluffy towels; the fourth, equally well appointed, is a twin with a separate, dedicated bathroom. All the rooms have the finest Egyptian cotton bed linen, flat-screen TV with Freeview digital channels and free broadband internet access. The whole place can be booked for corporate and private groups. Lower End House provides a supremely comfortable and civilised retreat, a rural sanctuary where guests can relax, unwind and recharge their batteries. It is also an ideal base for a walking or sightseeing holiday – or of course as the perfect place to stay while on an Eckington Manor cookery course.

Great Comberton and Little Comberton

Distance: *3.5 miles (5.6 kilometres)*
Typical time: *120 mins*
Height gain: *25 metres*
Map: *Explorer 190*
Walk: *www.walkingworld.com ID:2627*
Contributor: *Ron and Jenny Glynn*

ACCESS INFORMATION:

On unclassified road off the A44 south of Pershore. Considerate parking on the village streets, please.

DESCRIPTION:

A gentle little walk in Worcestershire farmland from Great Comberton to Little Comberton, and to the edge of Bricklehampton with the splendid backdrop of Bredon Hill for most of the way. The old and lovely thatched and timbered Tudor cottages of Little Comberton are quite breathtaking, and the church with its large tower is another pleasure to behold.

FEATURES:

Pub, Church, Wildlife, Birds, Flowers, Great Views, Butterflies, Mostly Flat.

WALK DIRECTIONS:

1 | From the junction, a few yards from the War Memorial, walk along the road signed to Little Comberton and Elmley Castle, and take the public footpath on the right. Head diagonally left over field where there is a footbridge by a telegraph pole. Go on over it and continue in same direction to a gate, then over a field following a line of telegraph poles. Take footbridge and walk across meadow to far corner, then a stile to walk between houses in Little Comberton.

2 | Turn right past pretty cottages and houses. Turn right into Manor Lane and pass beautiful

Tudor half-timbered houses, following lane round to pass the lovely church. Turn left, then follow the road for few yards.

3 | Turn right into a large lawned area and head for the right of a large lime at far end. Take the gate beneath its branches and turn left, then right, to walk round edge of field with the tree-clad Bredon Hill opposite. Continue over a stile, turning left, then right, beside hedge. Pass two stiles on the right and continue round edge of field and into another, with Nash's Farm on the left. Eventually reach an obscured stile in corner, and climb over it to walk on an overgrown path by Old House Farm, taking another stile into an orchard. Take stile on left and walk over to a gate beside a bungalow on a narrow, overgrown path.

4 | Come out into Little Comberton and turn left to walk along to telephone kiosk, then turn right along main road through village, leaving it to walk on past pretty cottages.

5 | Turn left through a large gate and walk along the field to the corner, through a gate, then over a footbridge into pastures. Go on to climb a stile out onto road.

6 | Turn left along it, the magnificent Bredon Hill ahead, and follow road round, and along to Great Comberton.

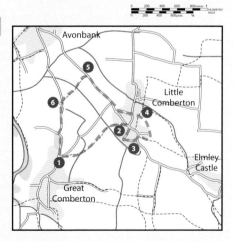

BLUE GECKO PLANTS

Tewkesbury Road, Eckington, Pershore,
Worcestershire WR10 3DE
Tel: 01386 751802
e-mail: cath@bluegeckoplants.com
website: www.bluegeckoplants.com

After studying Plant Sciences and working at large wholesale nurseries for a number of years, Catherine Thorpe revived an old nursery on the B4080 Tewkesbury Road out of Eckington when she established the delightfully named **Blue Gecko Plants**. Since the enterprise opened in 2006 it has built an enviable reputation for an interesting range of high-quality plants presented in a stylish, inviting environment. Set in seven acres in the heart of the Vale of Evesham Blue Gecko Plants sells a wide variety of hardy shrubs, herbaceous perennials, climbers, ornamental trees, camellias, conifers, bamboos, grasses, ferns, herbs and vegetable plants. The majority of plants in stock are grown on site by Catherine with the help of her parents. The nursery also sells compost, ceramic and terracotta pots, garden ornaments, garden-related gifts and greeting cards. National Garden Gift Vouchers are also sold and accepted. Catherine and her team are always ready with help and advice on planting matters at Blue Gecko Plants, which is open from 10am to 5pm every day except Monday.

Comberton and Elmley Castle on the north side, and Bredon, Overbury and Kemerton to the south. Bredon Hill is almost circular, a limestone outcrop of the Cotswolds covering 12 square miles, accessible from many of the villages that ring it, and rising to over 900 feet. On the crest of its northern slope, best accessed from Great Comberton, are the remains – part of the earthworks – of the pre-Roman settlement. Much more visible on the top is a curious brick tower called Parsons Folly, built by a Mr Parsons in the 18th century.

ELMLEY CASTLE
13 miles SE of Great Malvern on a minor road

Just one of the many enchanting villages around Bredon Hill, no longer boasting a castle but with this memorandum of 1540: "The late Castle of Elmley standing on high and adjoining the Park, compassed in with wall and ditch is uncovered and in decay."

The village's main street is very wide and lined with trees, with a little brook flowing to one side. Picturesque cottages with thatched roofs lead up to a well-preserved 15th-century cross, then to St Mary's Church with its handsome tower and battlements. Inside are some of the finest monuments to be found anywhere in England, most notably the 17th-century alabaster tomb of William Savage, his son Giles and Giles' wife and children.

BREDON
14 miles SE of Great Malvern off the B4080

🏠 Bredon Barn

Plenty to see in this sizeable village, notably the Church of St Giles with its 14th-century stained glass and some very elaborate stone monuments; an Elizabethan rectory with stone figures on horseback on the roof; and some fine 18th-century stables. **Bredon Barn**, owned by the National Trust, is a huge 14th-century barn built of local Cotswold stone. 132 feet in length, it has a dramatic aisled interior, marvellous beams and two porches at the wagon entrances. Open April - November.

PERSHORE
9 miles E of Great Malvern on the A4104

🏛 Abbey   🌿 Pershore College

A gem of a market town, with fine Georgian architecture and an attractive setting on the banks of the Avon. Its crowning glory is the **Abbey**, which combines outstanding examples

---

FOUR ACRES NURSERIES

Great Comberton Road, Pensham, Pershore,
Worcestershire WR10 3DY
Tel: 01386 550357

Linda Davies owns and runs **Four Acres Nurseries**, which she established in 2002 in a peaceful, attractive location under Bredon Hills. Gardeners and plant-lovers will find an excellent range of lavenders, salvias, foxgloves, geraniums, phlox and other annuals and perennials, along with patio and bedding plants, garden accessories and hanging baskets, ready made or assembled to individual requirements. Linda and her staff are always ready with help and advice at the nurseries, which can be found off the B4084, east of Pershore on the road to Evesham.

OAKLANDS FARMHOUSE

Oaklands House, Oaklands Farm, Pershore Road,
Bricklehampton, Pershore, Worcestershire WR10 3JT
Tel: 01386 861716

For many years Barbara Stewart has been welcoming guests to her top-quality B&B establishment at **Oaklands Farmhouse**. The house stands in attractive gardens off the B4084, signposted between Pershore (2 miles) and Evesham (3 miles). The River Avon is an easy walk away, the surrounding fields are filled in summer with market gardeners' produce, and the house commands far-reaching views to the Bredon Hills.

The accommodation in the recently refurbished 200-year-old farmhouse comprises two lovely bedrooms, one with en suite shower, the other with a private bathroom with bath and separate shower. Both rooms have TV, radio-alarm clock, tea tray, electric blanket and hairdryer. There's a lovely country feel to the décor and furnishings that's entirely appropriate for the age of the building and its rural setting. Day rooms include a snug with a log-burning stove and a pleasant dining area where a delicious English , Scottish or Continental breakfast is served.

The Malvern and Bredon Hills provide excellent walking amid magnificent scenery, and it's an easy drive to Cheltenham, Worcester and Stratford for a great variety of culture, leisure and shopping. She welcomes children of 12 or over, but not pets.

---

of Norman and Early English architecture. The Abbey was founded by King Oswald in AD689, and in AD972 King Edgar granted a charter to the Benedictine monks. Only the choir remains of the original church, but it is still a considerable architectural treasure. The south transept is the oldest part, while among the most impressive features is some superb vaulting in the chancel roof.

Pershore Bridge, a favourite picnic spot, still bears the marks of damage done during the Civil War. A mile east of town on the B4084 is **Pershore College**. Originally part of the Wyke Estate, the college has been developed round an early 19th-century mansion and is the Royal Horticultural Society's Centre for the Midlands and the Regional Centre of Excellence for the food and drink industry. The grounds contain many unusual trees and shrubs, and in the glasshouses are tropical, temperate and cool decorative plants. The College houses the National Collections of Penstemons and Philadelphus.

Pershore's main horticultural claim to fame are its plums, and a new variety called Pershore Emblem joins the long-established Pershore Purple and Pershore Yellow Egg.

Tewkesbury

🏛 Abbey   🏛 Museums   🏛 Battle of Tewkesbury

Actually just across the border into Gloucestershire, Tewkesbury is a town of historic and strategic importance close to the confluence of the Severn and Avon rivers. At the centre of the town is **Tewkesbury Abbey**, the cathedral-sized parish church of St Mary. Founded in the 8th century and completely rebuilt in the 11th, it was one of the last to be dissolved by Henry VIII, and in 1540 it was saved from destruction by the townspeople,

who raised £453 to buy it from the Crown. Many of its features are on a truly grand scale, and the vast main tower is the tallest surviving Norman main tower in the world. Three museums tell the story of the town and its environs: the **Little Museum**, laid out in a typical old merchant's house, part of Abbey Row Cottages dating from 1450; **Tewkesbury Museum**, with displays on the social history and archaeology of the area; and the **John Moore Countryside Museum**, a natural history collection of preserved mammals and birds, hand tools and wildlife sculptures made from scrap metal, displayed in a 15th-century timber-framed house. The **Battle of Tewkesbury**, one of the fiercest in the Wars of the Roses, took place in 1471 in a field south of the town, which ever since has been known as Bloody Meadow. The 17-year-old son of Henry VI was killed in the conflict, and a plaque marking his final resting place can be seen in the Abbey.

Evesham

🏛 Almonry Heritage Centre   🚶 Spring Blossom Trail
🚶 Country Park

A bustling market town at the centre of the Vale of Evesham, an area long known as the Garden of England, with a prolific harvest of soft fruits, apples, plums and salad vegetables. The **Spring Blossom Trail** is a circular driving trail around the Vale of Evesham, taking in the sights and smells of springtime blossom. The River Avon performs a loop round the town, and the Abbey park is a good place for a riverside stroll; it is also the start point for boat trips. The magnificent 110-foot bell tower is the only major building remaining of the Abbey, which was founded around AD700 by Egwin, Bishop of Worcester, and

Bell Tower, Evesham

The Centre is open Monday to Saturday all year, also Sundays March to October.

There are many other interesting buildings in Evesham, including the neighbouring churches of All Saints and St Lawrence. The former is entered through a porch built by Abbot Lichfield in the 16th century, and the Lichfield Chapel, with a lovely fan-vaulted ceiling, contains his tomb. Much of the building, as well as the stone pulpit, dates from Victorian times, when major restoration work was carried out. The latter, declared redundant in 1978, was also the subject of extensive restoration in the 1830s and again in the 1990s. In the market place is a free-standing grand old timbered building called the Round House – a curious name, because it is actually square. One theory claims that it was so called because "you can walk all round it".

A little way north of Evesham is **Evesham Country Park**, where the attractions include a stretch of the River Avon, a wildlife visitor centre, shops, a garden centre and the charming Evesham Vale Light Railway. Nearby, in the village of Offenham, is a rare sight – a terrace of seven half-timbered medieval cottages from the 1460s, which share one long continuous thatched roof. They stand on Main Street at the end of which is another rarity – a permanent maypole of red, white and blue crowned by a golden cockerel.

was one of the largest and grandest in the whole country. It was knocked down by Henry VIII's men at the time of the Dissolution of the Monasteries. The story of the town is told in vivid detail at the **Almonry Heritage Centre**, which was formerly the home of the Abbey Almoner and was built around 1400. The almoner was responsible for the distribution of alms to poor pilgrims and townspeople during the 850-year lifetime of the Abbey. It now houses a unique collection of artefacts as well as exhibitions showing the history of the Abbey, the defeat of Simon de Montfort at the Battle of Evesham (the Leicester Tower stands on the site of the Battle), the involvement of the town in the Civil War, and stories from more recent campaigns. The Almonry gardens have more exhibits, including agricultural equipment and a cannon from the Crimea campaign of 1854.

Around Evesham

ASHTON UNDER HILL
5 miles SW of Evesham off the A46

Ashton under Hill sits at the foot of Bredon Hill, its main street flanked by stone, half-timbered black and white buildings. At the crossroads stands an unusual survival, an 18th-century cross with a sundial.

🏠 historic building　🏛 museum　🏛 historic site　🌱 scenic attraction　🌿 flora and fauna

BROADWAY
6 miles SE of Evesham on the A44

🏛 Broadway Tower   ⚑ Broadway Beacon

🌿 Snowshill Lavender

One of the most beautiful villages in England and a magnet for tourists throughout the year. The quintessential Cotswold village, its eponymous broad main street is lined with houses and cottages built of golden Cotswold stone. Broadway was settled as far back as 1900BC, and later the Romans came and occupied the hill above the village. Broadway was probably re-established after the Battle of Dyrham in AD557 by conquering Saxons advancing towards Worcester. The parish records tell of hospitality being offered at a Broadway hostelry as early as 1532. This was the time of the advent of the horse-drawn carriage, when Broadway became an important staging post. A journey from London to Worcester took about 17 hours including stops and a change of horse, and at one time Broadway boasted an incredible 33 public houses.

In the centre of Broadway is a wide village green from where the main street continues gently upwards for nearly a mile, with the surrounding hills always in view. The gradient increases at Fish Hill, then rises to more than 1,000 feet above sea level at **Broadway Beacon**. At the top of the Beacon is **Broadway Tower**, standing in a delightful country park with something to interest all ages, from animal enclosures and an adventure playground to nature walks and barbecue sites.

THE GOLDSMITHY

JEWELLERY DESIGNERS, MAKERS & REPAIRERS

High Street, Broadway, Worcestershire WR12 7DT
Tel: 01386 853297
website: www.goldsmithy.co.uk

Jewellery is always a special purchase and having something hand-made makes it especially so. **The Goldsmithy** is the retail outlet for exclusive bespoke jewellery designed and hand-made by the father-and-son team of Terry and Simon Waldron – Terry started the business in the 1970s. Most pieces on display are crafted in their own workshop in a classic Cotswold stone building overlooking the Green in Broadway.

They produce pieces to suit all budgets and tastes, from simple wedding and signet rings to large, dramatic pieces, in a variety of metals and many featuring precious and semi-precious stones including diamonds, sapphires, rubies, emeralds, aquamarines, tanzanites, tourmalines, jade, opals and pearls. Clients are invited to feel very much part of the whole process, from the design stage, choosing the metals and the gems to seeing the completed article. The Goldsmithy also remodels and repairs customers' pieces and will give assistance with insurance and replacement matters.

The owners are members of the National Association of goldsmiths; they are three times winners of the de Beers Diamonds International Award and Academy members – the most prestigious awards for jewellery design in the industry.

📖 stories and anecdotes   🐦 famous people   🎨 art and craft   🎭 entertainment and sport   ⚑ walks

The tower was built as a folly by the 6th Earl of Coventry in 1799 as part of the great movement of the time towards picturesque and romantic landscapes. James Wyatt designed the tower, which now contains various displays and exhibitions including the William Morris Room – Morris used the Tower as a country retreat.

Broadway's St Michael's Church (1839) boasts an intricate Elizabethan pulpit that came from the nearby St Eadburga's Church and was installed in a thanksgiving service marking the end of World War I.

In the late 19th century, Broadway was a haunt of artists, musicians and writers, including JM Barrie, Ralph Vaughan Willams, Henry James, Edward Elgar and John Singer

Sargent. It was later a centre of the Arts and Crafts Movement.

South of Broadway, at Snowshill, **Snowshill Lavender** has 53 acres of rolling lavender fields, with more than 30 varieties.

CHILDSWICKHAM
4 miles SE of Evesham off the A44

🏛 Cider Mill Museum

The Church of St Mary the Virgin, its tall, slender spire a prominent landmark, is a good place to start a walk round the old part of the village. Close by, on the Broadway road, is the Barnfield **Cider Mill Museum**, where visitors can see a display of cider-making down the years before sampling cider, perry or one of the wines produced from local plums and berries.

BRETFORTON
4 miles E of Evesham on the B4035

🏛 Fleece Inn

A pub in the care of the National Trust is a rarity indeed, and it's well worth a trip to Bretforton to visit the **Fleece Inn**, a medieval half-timbered building that was originally a farmhouse. It has changed very little since being first licensed in 1848, and an interesting feature is the Witches' Marks carved in the hearth to prevent witches coming down the chimney. It also has a precious pewter collection. The Thatched Barn is available to hire for functions and has a civil ceremony wedding licence. It hosts the Vale of Evesham Asparagus Festival. The Church of St Leonard boasts a number of interesting and intricate carvings, notably a scene depicting St Margaret emerging (through a hole she made with her cross) from the side of the dragon that had just swallowed her.

Broadway Tower

🏛 historic building   📷 museum   🏛 historic site   🌿 scenic attraction   🌱 flora and fauna

RIDING CENTRE
BRETFORTON EQUESTRIAN

Lower Hind Farm, Station Road, Bretforton, Evesham,
Worcestershire WR11 7HX
Tel: 01386 833369
e-mail: riding@bretfortonequestrian.co.uk
website: www.bretfortonequestrian.co.uk

Bretforton Equestrian Riding Centre offers a wide range of lessons for all levels of rider, from starting out on a new interest to improving riding skills and equestrian knowledge. The aim of the owners is to make the lessons both educational, challenging and enjoyable, and all the lessons are conducted by BHS qualified instructors. The wellbeing of the horses is paramount: they are regularly checked by vets and schooled by the centre's instructors, as well as leaving the centre from time to time to compete in outside events. Lessons are preceded by a half-hour assessment so that riders can be put in the correct group for their level and ability. Most lessons are in small groups, but individual lessons are available at certain times of the week for those who require one-to-one tuition.

Riding lessons are the main offering, but care of horses is also very important and Bretforton Equestrian encourages its clients to attend the stable management courses to acquire a basic understanding of the needs of a horse and the commitment required to own a horse. The centre has indoor and outdoor arenas, a lecture room and a small shop stocked with riding essentials.

HONEYBOURNE

4 miles E of Evesham on minor roads off the B4035

🐦 Domestic Fowl Trust and Honeybourne Rare Breeds

The **Domestic Fowl Trust and Honeybourne Rare Breeds** is a conservation centre for rare breeds of poultry and livestock. Over 100 breeds are on view on the 29-acre farm. Visitors can wander along the grass pathways to see breeding flocks of chickens (including British and American bantams), ducks, geese and turkeys. The farm animals include the rare Irish Moiled cows and some of the rarest breeds of sheep and goats. Books, gifts and animal equipment and feedstuffs are available from the shop, and the centre also has an activity room for children, a poultry museum,

the Speckled Hen tearoom and an information centre.

MIDDLE LITTLETON

3 miles NE of Evesham off the B4085

🏛 Tithe Barn 🐦 Windmill Hill Nature Reserve

The Littletons – North, Middle and South – lie close to each other and close to the River Avon. In Middle Littleton is a huge and wonderful **Tithe Barn**, built in the 13th century and once the property of the Abbots of Evesham. Now owned by the National Trust, it is still in use as a farm building, but can be visited.

Nearby, a bridleway leads off the B4510 to **Windmill Hill Nature Reserve**, an area of fertile limestone that continues up to Cleeve Prior, where the Church of St Andrew is well worth a visit.

🎭 stories and anecdotes 🐦 famous people 🎨 art and craft 🎭 entertainment and sport 🚶 walks

Worcester

- 🏛 Cathedral 🏛 Greyfriars 🏛 City Museum
- 🏛 Royal Worcester Porcelain
- 🏛 Commandery Civil War Centre
- 🏛 Museum of Local Life 🌿 Three Choirs Festival
- 🌳 Worcester Woods Country Park

The **Cathedral**, with its 200-foot tower, stands majestically beside the Severn. The 11th century crypt is a classic example of Norman architecture and was built by St Wulstan, who is remembered in a stone carving. He was the only English bishop not to be replaced by a Norman after the Conquest. To many of the local people the task of building the Cathedral must have seemed endless; the central tower collapsed in 1175 and a fire destroyed much of the building in 1203. The Cathedral had only just been re-dedicated after those disasters when Bishop Blois began pulling it down again, only to rebuild it in the fashionable Gothic style. The nave was rebuilt in the 14th century under the auspices of Bishop Cobham, but the south side was not completed until much later, and in a far less elaborate style. King John requested that he be buried in the choir, and his tomb stands near the high altar. It is a masterpiece of medieval sculpture, showing the King flanked by the Bishops Oswald and Wulstan. Prince Arthur, elder brother of Henry VIII, is also entombed near the high altar. One of the many stories about the Cathedral concerns the 'Grumpy Monk', so grumpy that his brothers decided to get their own back when he died. They buried him under a step in the cloisters so they could have the satisfaction of treading on him whenever they passed by. He lies there to this day, still being trodden on by visitors.

There's a great deal more to see than the

The Greyfriars

Friar Street, Worcester WR1 2LZ
Tel: 01905 23571
e-mail: greyfriars@nationaltrust.org.uk
website: www.nationaltrust.org.uk

Built in 1480, The Greyfriars is a beautiful timber-framed merchant's house located in Worcester city centre. Throughout its history the house has been home to some of the city's most affluent merchant families.

Saved from demolition in the 1940s, it now houses the fascinating, and somewhat unusual collections of the siblings who rescued the house - Matley and Elsie Moore.

Visitors can enjoy the beautiful interior, featuring the oak panelled Great Hall, Library, Bedroom and Parlour. The house contains a rather eclectic collection, including the Copeland and Garrett toilet service in the Dining Room and screens made from antique leather. Throughout the house are delicate tapestries and a variety of 16th and 17th century furniture. In the charming walled garden visitors can relax with light refreshments in the summer and purchase plants cultivated at nearby Hanbury Hall.

🏛 historic building 🏛 museum 🏛 historic site 🌀 scenic attraction 🌿 flora and fauna

GRAYS AT THE NORTHWICK INTERIORS & LIFESTYLE

142 Ombersley Road, Worcester WR3 7HA
Tel: 01905 754040 Fax: 01905 757676
e-mail: Northwick@btconnect.com
website: www.thenorthwick.co.uk

From traditional to contemporary, a complete interiors service awaits visitors to **Grays at the Northwick Interiors and Lifestyle**.

David and Helen Gray deserve an Oscar for creating a new starring role for what had been a sad, derelict cinema. A classic 1938 Art Deco cinema two miles north of the city centre lay neglected for 12 years before they turned it into a vibrant, glamorous setting for displaying a wide variety of furniture, fabrics, lamps, cushions, accessories, gifts and collectables – an eclectic collection well sourced and well priced.

Much of the furniture is in keeping with the spirit of the cinema, including mirrored cabinets and dressers, monochromatic dining sets, pieces in pale wood and glass and striking crystal chandeliers. Supporting the furniture (but definitely not B features) are fabrics by the best-known makers (also a fabric library and a great choice of wallpaper and paint), plants and decorative cast-iron garden seats and tables, gifts and lifestyle items to suit all pockets and a splendid 16-seater café serving all-day breakfasts, sandwiches, snacks and excellent coffee.

Grays also offers a complete design service. Clients come from near and far to this splendid place, which is open from 9 to 5.30 (Sunday 10 to 4.30).

📽 stories and anecdotes   ⚲ famous people   ⚲ art and craft   ⚲ entertainment and sport   ⚲ walks

Greyfriars, Worcestershire

Cathedral, of course, and in the **City Museum and Art Gallery** are contemporary art and archaeological displays, a 19th-century chemist's shop and the military collections of the Worcestershire Regiment and the Worcestershire Yeomanry Cavalry. Friar Street has many lovely old timber houses. **Greyfriars** (see panel on page 64), in the care of the National Trust, is a medieval house that has managed to survive right in the heart of the city, and passing through its archway visitors will come across a pretty walled garden. The imposing Guildhall in the High Street is a marvellous example of Queen Anne architecture, designed by a local man, Thomas White. The **Commandery Civil War Centre** is a stunning complex of buildings behind a small timber-framed entrance. At the Battle of Worcester in 1651, the Commandery was used as the Royalist headquarters, and today is the country's only museum devoted to the story

of the Civil War. The story takes in the trial of Charles I, visits a Royalist encampment on the eve of the battle and enacts the last battle of the war narrated by Charles II and Oliver Cromwell. Period rooms offer a fascinating glimpse of the architecture and style of Tudor and Stuart times.

The **Royal Worcester Porcelain Visitor Centre** is an absolute must on any sightseer's list. Royal Worcester is Britain's oldest continuous producer of porcelain and is world-famous for its exquisite bone china. The factory was founded in 1751 by Dr John Wall with the intention of creating "a ware of a form so precise as to be easily distinguished from other English porcelain". The collection in the museum contains some of the company's finest treasures, and visitors can take a guided tour of the factory to observe the many stages of production. The premises include a shop and a restaurant where the food is, naturally, served on Royal Worcester china. In the 1930s the company was acquired by (Charles William) Dyson Perrins, the grandson of William Perrins, founder of the Worcester Sauce company. Closed Sundays and Bank Holidays.

The **Museum of Local Life** reflects the history of Worcester and its people, with displays covering the past 700 years. There's a Victorian kitchen scene and schoolroom, and a variety of changing exhibitions throughout the year. The site is a 16th-century timber-framed building in wonderful Friar Street. Famous sons of Worcester, where the **Three Choirs Festival** was first held in 1717, include Sir Edward Elgar, born at nearby Broadheath; his statue is a notable landmark opposite the Cathedral.

To the east of the city, and signposted from the M5 (J6) and from the city centre via the A44, **Worcester Woods Country Park**, open daily, has 50 hectares of ancient oak woodland, 10 hectares of traditional wildflower meadow, waymarked trails, a picnic area, children's play area, visitor centre, café and shop.

Around Worcester

POWICK
2 miles S of Worcester on the A449

Powick Bridge was the scene of the first and last battles in the Civil War; the last, in 1651, ending with Charles hiding in the Boscobel Oak before journeying south to a nine year exile in France. Cromwell's power had been overwhelming, and the long years of strife were at an end. Powick Bridge's skyline is today dominated by Worcester's first power station, built in 1894.

SPETCHLEY
3 miles E of Worcester on the A422

🏛 Church

All Saints Church, 14th century with a 16th-century chapel, is home to a fine collection of monuments to the Berkeley family, who owned adjoining Spetchley Park. The park, which extends over 12 hectares, has lovely formal gardens, wooded areas, lawns and a lake with an ornamental bridge.

HUDDINGTON
6 miles E of Worcester on minor roads

🏛 Huddington Court

Two buildings of particular note: the simple little Church of St James, with a timber-framed bell turret; and **Huddington Court**. The Court has been described as the most picturesque house in Worcestershire. An excellent example of a 16th-century timber-framed building, it was once the home of the Wintours, a staunchly Catholic family who were involved in the Gunpowder Plot. When the plot was exposed and the conspirators finally arrested, both Thomas and Robert Wintour, cousins of Robert Catesby, confessed their guilt and were executed. The Court is a private residence, but you can get a good view of it from the churchyard.

A mile or so north of Huddington lies the village of Himbleton, where the Church of St Mary Magdalene has a picturesque bell turret with a memorial clock.

ROUS LENCH
7 miles E of Worcester on a minor road

🏛 Rous Lench Court

The Lenches are attractive little villages in an area known for its particularly rich soil. Rous Lench church has a chapel with monuments to the Rous family and an oil painting of Jesus in the house of Simon the Pharisee. The road to the hilltop village of Church Lench (a mile south), with the church at the very top of the hill, passes by **Rous Lench Court**, the seat of the Rous family for many centuries from 1382. The Court is a splendid half-timbered mansion with a tall Italianate tower in the beautiful gardens.

INKBERROW
8 miles E of Worcester off the A42

🏛 Old Bull Inn

A very pleasant and pretty spot to pause awhile, with the Church of St Peter (note the alabaster of John Savage, a High Sheriff of Worcester who died in 1631), the inn and other buildings round the village green, some in red brick, others black and white half-timbered. The **Old Bull Inn** has two claims to fame - one that William Shakespeare stayed there in 1582, the other that it is the original of The Bull at Ambridge, home of *The Archers*. Photographs of the cast adorn the walls, and the inn has become a place of pilgrimage for fans of the programme.

The Old Vicarage, a handsome 18th-century building in the Tudor style, was host in an earlier guise to King Charles I, who stayed there on his way to Naseby; some maps he left behind are kept in the church.

At nearby Dormston, a timber-framed dovecote stands in front of the Moat farmhouse.

One mile south of Inkberrow is the village of Abbots Morton, whose dwellings are mainly 17th-century yeomen's houses. The village was once the site of the Abbot of Evesham's summer residence, but only some mounds and fishponds now remain.

ODDINGLEY

5 miles NE of Worcester on minor roads

The parish church of Oddingley stands on a hill overlooking the Worcester & Birmingham Canal. Its principal treasure is the mostly 15th-century stained glass in the east window, which is regarded as some of the finest of that period. Behind the communion rail is a memorial to a rector, George Parker, who was murdered in 1806 because of a dispute over tithes.

DROITWICH

6 miles NE of Worcester on the A38

🏛 Church of the Sacred Heart

🏛 Heritage & Information Centre

🌱 Salwarpe Valley Nature Reserve

This was Salinae, the place of salt, in Roman times. Salt deposits, a legacy from the time when this area was on the seabed, were extracted for 2,000 years until the end of the 19th century. The natural Droitwich brine contains about 2.5 pounds of salt per gallon -

10 times as much as sea water - and is often likened to the waters of the Dead Sea. The brine is pumped up from an underground lake that lies 200 feet below the town. Visitors do not drink the waters at Droitwich as they do at most other spas, but enjoy the therapeutic properties floating in the warm brine. The first brine baths were built in the 1830s and were soon renowned for bringing relief to many and effecting seemingly miraculous cures. By 1876, Droitwich had developed as a fashionable spa, mainly through the efforts of John Corbett, known as the Salt King.

This typical Victorian businessman and philanthropist introduced new methods of extracting the brine and moved the main plant to Stoke Prior. The enterprise was beset with various problems in the 1870s and Corbett turned his attention to developing the town as a spa resort. He was clearly a man of some energy as he also served as an MP after the 1874 General Election. Many of the buildings in present-day Droitwich were owned by Corbett, including the Raven Hotel (a raven was part of his coat of arms) in the centre. His most remarkable legacy is undoubtedly Chateau Impney, on the eastern side of town at Dodderhill. It was designed by a Frenchman, Auguste Tronquois, in the style of an ornate French chateau, with soaring turrets, mansard roof and classical French gardens. It was intended as a home for Corbett and his wife Anna, but she apparently didn't like the place; their increasingly stormy marriage ended in 1884, nine years after the completion of the flamboyant chateau, which is now a high-class hotel and conference centre.

The **Heritage and Information Centre** includes a local history exhibition (Salt Town to Spa) and a historic BBC radio room (01905 774312).

In the centre of the town is St Andrew's

Church, part of whose tower was removed because of subsidence, a condition that affected many buildings, some of which stand at fairly alarming angles. One of the chapels, dating from the 13th century, is dedicated to St Richard de Wyche, the town's patron saint, who became Bishop of Chichester. On the southern outskirts of Droitwich is the **Church of the Sacred Heart**, built in Italianate style in the 1930s and remarkable for its profusion of beautiful mosaics made from Venetian glass. Many of these mosaics also commemorate the life of St Richard.

One of Droitwich's most famous sons is Edward Winslow, born the eldest of eight children in 1595. He was one of the pilgrims who set sail for the New World to seek religious freedom and later became Governor of the colony. A bronze memorial to Edward Winslow can be seen in St Peter's Church.

Salwarpe on the southwest fringes of Droitwich, is truly a hidden hamlet, approached by a stone bridge over James Brindley's Droitwich Canal. Opened in 1771, the canal linked the town to the River Severn at Hawford. The Church of St Michael, by the edge of the canal, has several monuments to the Talbot family, who owned nearby Salwarpe Court. **Salwarpe Valley Nature Reserve** is one of very few inland sites with salt water, making it ideal for a variety of saltmarsh plants and very well worth a visit.

HAWFORD
4 miles N of Worcester off the A449

The site of another amazing dovecote, this one half-timbered, dating from the 16th century and owned by the National Trust.

BUTTERMILK BED AND BREAKFAST

Four Gables, Longlands, nr Worcester WR3 7SX
Tel/Fax: 01905 451588
e-mail: enquiries@buttermilk-bandb.co.uk
website: www.buttermilk-bandb.co.uk

Martyn and Caroline Jones welcome Bed & Breakfast guests to **Buttermilk**, their home in a quiet country setting in the village of Ladywood. The well appointed accommodation consists of three generously sized rooms decorated and furnished to a very high standard. On the ground floor are a twin with en suite bath and shower and wheelchair access and a double with en suite shower, its own side entrance, private garden and full wheelchair access; upstairs is a double with en suite shower. Wireless-free access is provided. Disabled aids are available upon request. Excellent breakfast which is sourced locally and seasonally offers cereals, juices, yoghurt and fresh fruit and a choice of Continental platter or full English with home-made preserves and eggs from the owners' free-range hens. For the winter visitor, there is a welcome pot of coffee on the Breakfast Room's wood burning stove. Dinner is available, by prior arrangement, for groups of 4 or more

Though secluded, Buttermilk is certainly not remote: Droitwich is a mile and a half away, it's 4 miles to Worcester and 3 from J6 of the M5. It's an ideal base for touring, walking or just relaxing and enjoying the stunning views over the Salwarpe and Severn Valleys maintaining an air of tranquillity, so welcome after a busy day of sight seeing or business.

OMBERSLEY
6 miles N of Worcester off the A449

🏛 St Andrew's Church

A truly delightful and very English village with some superb black and white timbered dwellings with steeply sloping roofs. **St Andrew's Church**, rebuilt in 1825, contains memorials to the Sandys family and their family pew. Large and square, it stands beside the pulpit and is comfortably furnished with cushioned seats, matching blue embroidered kneelers and an ornate open fireplace. For heating, the congregation had to rely on the impressive Howden Heating Stove, set against the north wall. Installed in 1829, it rises some 12 feet and is in the shape of a miniature church tower complete with buttresses, arcaded top and a fuel opening just like a church doorway.

The Sandys family lived at nearby Ombersley Court (private), a splendid Georgian mansion that can be seen from the churchyard.

WICHENFORD
5 miles NW of Worcester on the B4204

🏛 Dovecote

A famous landmark here is the National Trust's **Wichenford Dovecote**, a 17th-century timber-framed construction with a lantern on top. With its 557 nesting holes, it is the largest surviving dovecote in England. When it was constructed, only the Lord of the Manor had the right to build one and to kill the birds for winter meat – a source of resentment to the villagers whose crops were pillaged by these voracious birds.

CHECKETTS MASTER BUTCHERS & FISHMONGERS

Main Road, Ombersley, Worcestershire WR9 0EW
Tel: 01905 620284
e-mail: enquiries@checketts.co.uk
website: www.checketts.co.uk

For over a century **Checketts** has been selling top-quality meat, most of it sourced from within 30 miles. Throughout that time the name of Checketts has been synonymous with quality, service and hygiene, and that remains true for all the meats on display, from British beef joints, steaks and mince to English lamb, outdoor-reared pork, free-range poultry, seasonal game, home-cured bacon, burgers, flavour-packed pies, brilliant sausages with their unique secret seasoning and a section of deli products.

The same high standards that have earned Checketts Butcher of the Year Awards now extend to Checketts Fresh Fish, opened at the end of 2007 behind the butchers and deli. David Checketts and his colleague Ian Dugmore present what is probably the largest fresh fish display in

Worcestershire. The range includes traditional British favourites like cod, haddock, plaice, sole, salmon, turbot, sea bass, scallops and lobster along with seafood from distant waters such as tuna, swordfish, yellow-tailed snapper and enormous tiger prawns. They also sell a selection of pre-prepared products – seafood soups and pâtés, fishcakes, ready-battered cod and haddock, rollmop herrings and speciality seafood platters. Orders for meat and fish can be placed on the hot line 01905 620750 or through the comprehensive website.

🏛 historic building 📷 museum 🏛 historic site ⚘ scenic attraction 🌱 flora and fauna

CLIFTON

10 miles NW of Worcester on the B4204

🏛 Church of St Kenelm

In lovely countryside near the River Teme, the village boasts a number of charming dwellings around the green and the **Church of St Kenelm**. Parts of the church go back to the 12th and 14th centuries. Collectors of unusual tombstones will find two here. Just inside the porch is the grave of "Elizabeth Taylor, Gent." who "Lived and dyed A Virgin"; on the north wall a marble tablet includes an inscription recording that "William" achieved the intriguing feat of being born on August 22nd 1714 and dying on November 23rd 1713.

There are other interesting churches at nearby Shelsey Beauchamp, in red sandstone, and Shelsey Walsh, which has many treasures, including the tomb of Sir Francis Walsh. The name of Shelsey Walsh will be familiar to fans of motor sport as the location of a very famous hill climb.

LOWER BROADHEATH

3 miles W of Worcester off the A44

🏛 Elgar Birthplace Museum

The **Elgar Birthplace Museum** is a redbrick cottage that is crammed with items from the great composer's life. He was born here in 1857 and, despite long periods spent elsewhere, Broadheath remained his spiritual home. The violin was his first instrument, though he eventually succeeded his father as organist at St George's Church in Worcester. He played at the Three Choirs Festival and began conducting locally. He married in 1889 and was soon devoting almost all his time to composing, making his name with *The Enigma Variations* (1899) and *Dream of Gerontius* (1900). He was knighted in 1904 and, when in 1931 he was made a baronet by King George V, he took the title 1st Baronet of Broadheath. The **Elgar Centre** beside the cottage hosts regular recitals, lectures, exhibitions and other events. In March 2009, the distinguished conductor Sir Mark Elder unveiled a bronze sculpture by Jemma Pearsonat the bottom of the cottage garden showing the composer sitting on a bench looking out towards his beloved Malvern Hills. Jemma also created the sculpture of Elgar that stands in Hereford Cathedral. The 40-mile Elgar Route is a circular driving route passing through West and great Malvern. It takes in 40 places of interest associated with Sir Edward.

LEIGH

5 miles W of Worcester off the A4103

🏛 Church 🚶 Leigh Brook

The **Church of St Eadburga** is very fine indeed, with some imposing monuments and a marvellous 15th-century rood screen. A curious legend attaches to the church. A man called Edmund Colles is said to have robbed one of his colleagues who was returning from Worcester and known to be carrying a full purse. It was a dark, gloomy night, and as Colles reached out to grab the man's horse, holding on to the bridle, the other struck at him with a sword. When he visited Edmund the next day, the appalling wound testified to the man's guilt; although forgiven by his intended victim, Colles died shortly after and his ghost once haunted the area. A phantom coach pulled by four fire-breathing steeds would appear and race down the hill to the church by Leigh Court, where they would leap over the tithe barn and disappear beneath the waters of the River Teme. A midnight service attended by 12 clergymen eventually laid the ghost to rest. Leaping over the tithe barn was

SHARON MCSWINEY

Studio A, The Fold, Bransford,
Worcestershire WR6 5JB
Tel: 01886 830125
e-mail: info@sharonmcswiney.co.uk
website: www.sharonmcswiney.co.uk

Sharon McSwiney & her husband Tim design and make extensive collections of quirky, imaginative, stylish jewellery and metalwork for the home and garden. A visit would be a unique opportunity to see a working jewellery & metalwork studio in Worcestershire.

A selection of distinctive jewellery in various metals & finishes is shown together with a large range of greetings cards. Decorative copper and brass wall panels are displayed alongside one-off metalwork block pictures, these pieces can also be made to commission.

Sharon & Tim's shop also exhibits a range of unusual and affordable gift ideas from UK designer makers including glass, ceramics and textiles. You are welcome to call into the studio Tues – Sat 10am until 5pm where it may be possible to see the artist at work, view designs in progress or even chat about commissioning a unique piece for yourself!

The studio is located half way between Malvern and Worcester on the A4103 within a craft centre including a licensed cafe and large free car park.

It's sure to be a fascinating and inspiring visit.

no mean feat (though easier of course if you're a ghost), as the 14th-century barn is truly massive, with great cruck beams and porched wagon doors. Standing in the grounds of Leigh Court, a long gabled mansion, the barn is open for visits on summer weekends.

Leigh Brook is a tributary of the Teme and wends its way through a spectacular valley cared for by Worcestershire Nature Conservation Trust. The countryside here is lovely, and footpaths make the going easier. Up on Old Storridge Common, birch, ash, oak and bracken have taken a firm hold, and there is a weird, rather unearthly feel about the place. Nearby, the hamlet of Birch Wood is where Elgar composed his *Dream of Gerontius*.

ALFRICK
7 miles W of Worcester off the A44

🌾 Nature Reserves

Charles Dodgson (Lewis Carroll) once preached at the village Church of St Mary Magdalene, which enjoys a delightful setting above the village green. In the vicinity are two major attractions for nature-lovers. A little way to the northwest is **Ravenshill Woodland Nature Reserve** with waymarked trails through woodland that is home to many breeding birds, while a mile south of Alfrick is the **Knapp and Papermill Nature Reserve**, with 25 hectares of woodland and meadows rich in flora and fauna.

Bromsgrove

🏛 Avoncraft Museum of Historic Buildings

🏛 Museum   🏛 AE Housman

🏛 BT National Telephone Kiosk Collection

🏛 Church of St John the Baptist

A visit to the **Avoncraft Museum of Historic Buildings**, just south of Bromsgrove, is a walk through seven centuries of English history, with each building providing a snapshot of life in its particular period. The first building, a timber-framed merchant's house from Bromsgrove, was brought to the site in 1967, since when over 20 more have been installed. In addition to the buildings themselves, the Museum has regular demonstrations of such crafts as wood-turning, windmilling, racksawing, brick-making, chain-making and nail-making. There's also a shop, refreshment area, picnic site, a children's area, horse-drawn wagon rides and farm animals wandering around freely. One of the most treasured exhibits is the original 14th-century beamed roof of

Guesten Hall from Worcester Cathedral, now covering a modern brick building. In an area behind the shop is another unique collection, the **BT National Telephone Kiosk Collection** (01527 831809).

Bromsgrove Museum, near the town centre, has displays of local crafts and industries, including glass, salt and nail, and the Bromsgrove Guild, an organisation of craftsmen founded in 1894. The Guild of highly skilled craftsmen had its finest hour when commissioned to design and make the gates and railings of Buckingham Palace. Another popular exhibit is a street scene of Victorian shops.

Besides the museums, there is plenty to see, including some very handsome timber-framed buildings in the High Street, where stands a statue of **AE Housman**, the town's most famous son. Alfred Edward Housman was born one of seven children at Fockbury, Bromsgrove, in 1859, and spent his schooldays in the town. After a spell at Oxford University, and some time teaching at his old school, he entered the Civil Service in London, where he found time to resume his academic studies. He was appointed Professor of Latin at University College, London, in 1892 and soon afterwards he published his first and best-known collection of poems – *A Shropshire Lad*. His total output was not large, but it includes some of the best-loved poems in the English language. He died in 1936 and is buried in the churchyard of St Lawrence in Ludlow. The forming, in 1972, of a Housman Society brought his name to the forefront of public attention, and in the region of Bromsgrove walking and motoring trails take in the properties and places associated with him.

Bromsgrove has a prestigious annual music festival held during the month of May, when

Bromsgrove Museum

🎞 stories and anecdotes   🍗 famous people   🎨 art and craft   🎭 entertainment and sport   🥾 walks

the town plays host to a wide range of musical entertainment from orchestral concerts to jazz, and featuring many well-known artists. Another annual event is the revival of the Court Leet, an ancient form of local administration. A colourful procession moves through the town and there's a lively Elizabethan street market.

The **Church of St John the Baptist** – see his statue over the south porch entrance – contains some superb 19th-century stained glass and an impressive collection of monuments, notably to members of the Talbot family. Side by side in the churchyard are the tombs of two railwaymen who were killed in 1840 when the boiler of their engine exploded while climbing the notorious Lickey Incline (see Burcot below).

BURCOT

3 miles NE of Bromsgrove on the B4184

Locks at Tardebigge

Burcot was long associated with the Floyd family of blacksmiths, who had been blacksmiths in Ireland for 500 years before coming here to work at the long-established forge. During World War I, three members of the Floyd family and one employee made 25,000 shoes for cavalry horses.

The stretch of railway that includes the Lickey Incline is, at 1 in 37.7, the steepest gradient on the whole of the British rail network. One specially powerful locomotive, 58100 (better known as Big Bertha), spent its days up until the late 1950s helping trains up the bank, a task that was later performed by massive double-boilered locomotives that were the most powerful in the then British Railways fleet. The steepness of the climb is due to the same geographical feature that necessitated the construction of the unique flight of **Locks at Tardebigge**, between Bromsgrove and Redditch. In the space of 2.5 miles the canal is lifted by no fewer than 30 locks. In the actual village of Tardebigge, on the A448, the Church of St Bartholomew enjoys a lovely setting with views across the Severn lowlands. Built in 1777 to the design of Francis Horn of Warwick, it has a slender tower capped by a delicate needle spire.

Around Bromsgrove – South

HANBURY

3 miles S of Bromsgrove off the B4090

Hanbury Hall   Jinney Ring Craft Centre

Hanbury Hall is a fine redbrick mansion in William & Mary style, completed by Thomas Vernon in 1701. Internal features include murals by Sir James Thornhill, known particularly for his Painted Hall in the Royal Naval Hospital, Greenwich, and frescoes in the dome of St Paul's. See also a splendid collection of porcelain, the Long Gallery, the Moorish gazebos at each corner of the forecourt and the formal gardens with orangery and an 18th-century ice house.

In beautiful rural surroundings a mile north of the village of Hanbury stands the award-winning **Jinney Ring Craft Centre**, based on converted old timbered barns. Craftspeople with many diverse skills can be seen at work in their own studios, including ceramicists, two potters, a violin-maker, a wooden pen maker, a jeweller, a picture-framer, a leatherworker, a glass-maker, a sign-maker, a chocolate maker and an antiques restorer. Also on the premises is a craft gallery with changing exhibitions by British craftsmen and artists, a clothes and knitwear department, a plant centre and falconry at the end of the garden. The Centre hosts many events throughout the year, including cookery courses, beer festivals and blues festivals.

FECKENHAM

7 miles SE of Bromsgrove on the B4090

A pretty village with half-timbered, redbrick and Georgian houses and the fine Church of St John the Baptist. Inside the church a board displays the benefaction thatCharles I bestowed upon the village in 1665 - 6 pounds 13 shillings and fourpence, payable out of forest land to the school. The forest in question once surrounded the village, but the trees were all felled for fuelling the saltpans and no trace of the forest now remains.

REDDITCH

6 miles E of Bromsgrove on the A448

🏛 Forge Mill Needle Museum

🚶 Arrow Valley Country Park

A New Town from the 1960s, but there is plenty of history here, as well as some great walking. The **Arrow Valley Country Park**, is a vast expanse of parkland with nature trails, picnic areas and lovely walks. Sailing, canoeing, windsurfing and fishing are popular pastimes on the lake. There is a café, shop and countryside centre. One walk follows the river upstream to the ruins of Bordesley Abbey, a medieval Cistercian Abbey. Nearby is the **Forge Mill Needle Museum**, opened by the Queen in 1983, telling the fascinating story of the Redditch needle-making industry (01527 60806).

HUMPHRIES SHOES

30-32 Evesham Walk, Kingfisher Centre, Redditch, Worcestershire B97 4HH
Tel: 01527 62416
e-mail: sales@humphriesshoes.co.uk
website: www.humphriesshoes.co.uk

Humphries Shoes is a traditional family business established in 1862 at Redditch by Walter Humphries and run today by the fourth and fifth generations of the family. Walter began the business by handcrafting individually measured boots which were fitted for each of his customers. He was able to make three pairs of boots every two days. Over the years the small business became a first-class shoe store, stocking a wide range of styles from all the top British manufacturers together with some overseas brands. The emphasis has always been on fitting, quality and value for money and it was one of the very first shoe stores to offer fitted shoes for children.

Today, being the Main Fitting Centre, Humphries Shoes is the top destination in the region for fitted children's shoes, with an unrivalled range that includes Clarks, Start-Rite, Lelli Kelly, Geox, Timberland and Skechers – all **professionally fitted** with the **friendly service** expected from a family business.

Naturally, there's also an unbeatable selection for adults: Clarks, Rieker, Ecco, Lotus, Hotter, Gabor, Geox, Anatomic Gel, Josef Seibel, Equity, Rihde, Van Dal, Riva, Timberland, Skechers, Pikolinos, Tamaris, Barker, Loake and Grenson. The shop also stocks a selection of handbags from Radley, Tula, Gigi and Bullaggi. Shop hours are 9 to 5.30 (Sunday 10.30 to 4.30). Other Humphries Shoes branches are in Alcester, Warwickshire and Stow-on-the-Wold, Gloucestershire.

🏛 stories and anecdotes   🕊 famous people   🎨 art and craft   🎭 entertainment and sport   🚶 walks

ALCOTT FARM B&B AND SELF-CATERING

Icknield Street, Weatheroak, Alvechurch, Worcestershire B48 7EH
Tel: 01564 824051 Fax: 01564 829799
e-mail: alcottfarm@btinternet.com
website: www.alcottfarm.co.uk

For many years Jane and John Poole have been welcoming guests to **Alcott Farm**. The Bed & Breakfast accommodation comprises four large ensuite bedrooms - two doubles, one being on the ground floor, and two twins. Adjacent to the farmhouse is a self catering cottage which sleeps two people. There are many good pubs and restaurants nearby, as well as easy access to the motorway network, Birmingham city centre and airport. Alcott Farm is an ideal base for business people, tourists & walkers. It is also a perfectly located venue for those who are working or visiting the NEC.

WYTHALL

10 miles NE of Bromsgrove on the A435

🏛 Transport Museum

Right on the other side of Redditch, and well on the way to Birmingham, is the **Transport Museum**. Founded in 1977, the museum's two large halls house a marvellous collection of almost 100 buses and coaches, battery vehicles and fire engines, many having seen service in Birmingham and the West Midlands. It includes the largest collection of buses from the Midland Red fleet and many Bristol vehicles. Open weekends March to end November, also Wednesdays May to August.

WASELEY HILL

5 miles N of Bromsgrove of the B4551

🕺 Lickey Hills

Five miles north of Bromsgrove lies Wasely Hill where open hillside and woodland offers great walking and spectacular views from the top of Windmill Hill. There is also a visitor centre. Just to the east there is more great walking and views in a varied landscape around the **Lickey Hills**, which also has a visitor centre.

BELBROUGHTON

6 miles N of Bromsgrove on the B4188

🕺 Clent Hills

This village was once a centre of the scythe-making industry. Holy Trinity Church occupies a hillside site along with some pleasing Georgian buildings.

A little to the north are the village of Clent and the **Clent Hills**, an immensely popular place for walking and drinking in the views. On the top are four large upright stones that could be statement-making modern art but for the fact that they were put there over 200 years ago by Lord Lyttleton of Hagley Hall. Walton Hill is over 1,000 feet above sea level.

HAGLEY

8 miles N of Bromsgrove off the A491

🏛 Hagley Hall

In 1756, George, 1st Lord Lyttleton, commissioned the creation of what was to be the last great Palladian mansion in Britain, **Hagley Hall**. Imposing without, exotic and rococo within; notable are the Barrell Room with panelling from Holbeach Hall, where two of the Gunpowder Plotters – the Wintour

🏛 historic building   🏛 museum   🏛 historic site   🌀 scenic attraction   🌿 flora and fauna

brothers – were caught and later put to death in the favourite way of hanging, drawing and quartering. Temples, cascading pools and a ruined castle are some of the reasons for lingering in the park, which has a large herd of deer.

Another attraction at Hagley is the Falconry Centre on the A4565, where owls, hawks, falcons and eagles live and fly.

DODFORD
3 miles W of Bromsgrove off the A448

Not far out of Bromsgrove, north of the A448, lies the village of Dodford, whose Church of the Holy Trinity and St Mary is an outstanding example of an Arts and Crafts church, designed in 1908 by the Bromsgrove Guild in their interpretation of the neo-Gothic style.

CHADDESLEY CORBETT
4 miles W of Bromsgrove on the A448

A fairly sizeable village, dominated at its southern end by the 14th-century Church of St Cassian. It is the only church in England to be dedicated to this saint, who was born in Alexandria in the 5th century and became a bishop in Africa. He was also a schoolmaster and was apparently killed by his pupils.

HARVINGTON
5 miles W of Bromsgrove near junction of A448/ A450

🏠 Harvington Hall

Harvington Hall is a moated medieval and Elizabethan manor house with a veritable maze of rooms. Mass was celebrated here during times when it was a very dangerous thing to do, and that is perhaps why the Hall has more priest holes than any other house in the land.

Harvington Hall

Kidderminster

🏠 St Mary's Church   📷 Railway Museum

🌱 Stone House Cottage Garden

Known chiefly as a centre of the carpet-making industry, which began here early in the 18th century as a cottage industry. The introduction of the power loom brought wealth to the area and instigated the building of carpet mills. Standing on the River Stour, the town has a variety of mills, whose enormous chimneys dominate the skyline and serve as architectural monuments to Kidderminster's heritage. **St Mary's Church**, on a hill overlooking the town, is the largest parish church in the county and contains some superb tomb monuments. The Whittall Chapel, designed in 1922 by Sir Charles Gilbert Scott, was paid for by Matthew

Whittall, a native of Kidderminster who went to America and made a fortune in carpets. Three beautiful windows depicting the Virgin Mary, Joan of Arc and Florence Nightingale, were given by his widow in his memory.

Kidderminster's best-known son is Rowland Hill, who founded the modern postal system and introduced the penny post; he was also a teacher, educationalist and inventor. His statue stands outside the Town Hall. By the station on the Severn Valley Railway is the **Kidderminster Railway Museum** with a splendid collection of railway memorabilia. Run by volunteers, it is housed in an old (1878) GWR grain store and is usually open at the same time as the train operating dates on the Severn Valley Railway (see under Bewdley).

Just outside town, at Stone, on the A448, is **Stone House Cottage Garden**, a lovely walled garden with towers. Unusual wall shrubs, climbers and herbaceous plants are featured, most of them for sale in the nursery.

In the Stour Valley just north of Kidderminster is the village of Wolverley, with charming cottages and pretty gardens, the massive Church of St John the Baptist, and the remains – not easy to see – of prehistoric cave dwellings in the red sandstone cliffs.

Around Kidderminster

HARTLEBURY
7 miles W of Bromsgrove off the A449

🏛 Castle   🏛 Museum   🌱 Leapgate Country Park

Hartlebury Castle (see panel opposite), a historic sandstone castle of the Bishops of Worcester and a prison for captured Royalist troops in the Civil War, houses the **Worcester County Museum**. In the former servants'

quarters in the north wing numerous permanent exhibitions show the past lives of the county's inhabitants from Roman times to the 20th century. Visitors can also admire the grandeur of the three Castle State Rooms. The Museum is open from 10am to 5pm Tuesday to Friday, 11am to 5pm weekends and Bank Holiday Mondays.

On Hartlebury Common, **Leapgate Country Park** is a nature reserve in heath and woodland, with the county's only acid bog.

SHATTERFORD
3 miles NW of Kidderminster on the A442

🌱 Wildlife Sanctuary   🌱 Kingsford Country Park

Shatterford **Wildlife Sanctuary** is home to Sika deer, red deer, goats, sheep, wild boar, pot-bellied pigs and koi carp.

Two miles further north, off the A442, **Kingsford Country Park** covers 200 acres of heath and woodland that is home to a wide variety of birdlife. It extends into Kinver Edge, across the border into Staffordshire, and many waymarked walks start at this point.

BEWDLEY
3 miles W of Kidderminster on the A456

🏛 Museum   🏛 Severn Valley Railway

On the western bank of the Severn, linked to its suburb Wribbenhall by a fine Thomas Telford Bridge, Bewdley was once a flourishing port, but lost some of its importance when the Staffordshire & Worcestershire Canal was built. It's a quiet, civilised but much visited little town with some good examples of Georgian architecture, and has won fame with another form of transport, the **Severn Valley Railway**. Guaranteed to excite young and old alike, the Severn Valley Railway operates a full service of timetabled trains hauled by a variety of steam locomotives. Among those listed as operational

Hartlebury Castle

Hartlebury, nr Kidderminster,
Worcestershire DY11 7XZ
Tel: 01299 250416
e-mail: museum@worcestershire.gov.uk
www.worcestershire.gov.uk/museum

Worcestershire County Museum is housed in the servants quarters of Hartlebury Castle, home to the Bishop of Worcester for over 600 years. The museum collection ranges from fascinating toys and domestic items to beautiful costume and ancient archaeological finds. The building also contains room sets such as the Schoolroom as well as original rooms within the Castle including the Scullery, Housekeeper's Room and Nursery. On most days visitors can also view the Bishop's State rooms.

Within the grounds of the Castle you can also visit the Cider Mill and the Transport Gallery housing a fascinating array of horse-drawn vehicles including a fire engine, hansom cab and a large collection of Gypsy caravans.

A café area in the historic Castle Kitchen serves a range of freshly made lunches, afternoon teas and refreshments using both local and fair trade products. The café is also available for private hire and functions. There are also two outdoor picnic areas in Old Moat Coppice and the Orchard. An external glass lift gives all visitors access to the first and second floors of the Museum.

in June 2009 are two ex-Gwr Manors 7802 and 7812; ex-GWR Prairies 5164 and 4566; two Collett-designed ex-GWR 0-6-0 Pannier Tanks, 5764 and 7714; Ivatt 2-6-0 46443; and Stanier 2-6-0 42968. The service runs from Kidderminster to Bridgnorth, home of the railway since 1965, and the route takes in such scenic attractions as the Wyre Forest and the Severn Valley Country Park and Nature Reserve. Each of the stations – Bridgnorth, Hampton Loade, Country Park Halt, Highley, Arley, Bewdley and Kidderminster – is an architectural delight, and there are buffets at Bridgnorth and

Kidderminster, and a tearoom at Bewdley. The Engine House at Highley (in Shropshire) has a large display of steam locomotives, including an ex-LMS 'Jinty', a Stanier 8F and Standard 4-6-0 80079, and a Visitor and Education centre. Visitors can realise a childhood dream by

River Severn, Bewdley

🎬 stories and anecdotes 🐦 famous people 🎨 art and craft ✒ entertainment and sport 🚶 walks

driving and firing a steam locomotive - call 01299 404740 for all information concerning the railway, the timetables and the special events that take place throughout the year.

Bewdley Museum, which also incorporates the Tourist Information Centre, is a great place for all the family, with exhibitions themed around the growth and trades of the town, including basket and besom makers, charcoal burners, pewterers, brass founders and wheelwrights. There are daily demonstrations of rope-making and clay pipe-making, and a fascinating programme of events throughout the year. Bewdley was the birthplace of Stanley Baldwin, three times Prime Minister between the World Wars. On the A456 between Bewdley and Kidderminster, the West Midland Safari & Leisure Park at Spring Grove provides a fantastic day out for the whole family.

CALLOW HILL
5 miles W of Kidderminster on the A456

🛉 Wyre Forest

The **Wyre Forest** Visitor Centre is set among mature oak woodland with forest walks, picnic area, gift shop and restaurant. Wyre Forest covers a vast area starting northwest of Bewdley and extending into Shropshire. The woodland, home to abundant flora and fauna, is quite dense in places. It was once inhabited by nomadic people who made their living from what was around them, weaving baskets and brooms, burning charcoal and making the little wooden whisks that were used in the carpet-making process. Just south of Callow Hill, the village of Rock has an imposing Norman church in a prominent hillside position with some lovely windows and carving.

STOURPORT-ON-SEVERN
3 miles S of Kidderminster on the A451

At the centre of the Worcestershire waterways is the unique Georgian 'canal town' of Stourport, famous for its intricate network of canal basins. There was not much trade, nor even much of a town, before the canals, but prosperity came quickly once the Staffordshire & Worcestershire Canal had been dug. The commercial trade has gone, but the town still prospers, the barges laden with coal, timber, iron and grain having given way to pleasure craft. Many of the old barges have been renovated and adapted to this new role.

ASTLEY
5 miles S of Kidderminster on the A451

Stanley Baldwin (1867-1947), born in Bewdley, died at Astley Hall, opposite which stands a memorial stone inscribed "Thrice Prime Minister". (His ashes are buried in the nave of Worcester Cathedral.) Astley is also home to Astley Vineyards, a working vineyard producing award-winning white wines, with a vineyard trail and a shop. Visitors can arrive by car, by bus or by boat as they have mooring facilities.

Abberley Valley

ABBERLEY
7 miles SW of Kidderminster off the A451

🏛 Church of St Michael

A truly delightful little place, surrounded by hills. The Norman **Church of St Michael** was saved from complete dilapidation in the 1960s, and the part that survives, the chancel, is well worth a visit, not only for its charming ambience, but also for the treasures it holds. On the other side of the hill is Abberley Hall, now a school, with a Big Ben-like bell tower that can be seen for miles around. Old Boys include former Foreign Secretary Geoffrey Howe and the late actor Sir Anthony Quayle.

GREAT WITLEY
8 miles SW of Kidderminster on the A443

🏛 Church 🏛 Witley Court

🎨 Jerwood Sculpture Path

There are two great reasons not to miss this place. **Great Witley Church**, almost ordinary from the outside, has an unbelievable interior of Baroque flamboyance that glows with light in a stunning ambience of gold and white. Masters of their crafts contributed to the interior, which was actually removed from the Chapel of Canons in Edgware: Joshua Price stained glass, 23 ceiling paintings by Antonio Bellucci, plasterwork by Bagutti.

Next to the church are the spectacular and hauntingly beautiful remains of **Witley Court**, a palatial mansion funded by the riches of the Dudley family. Destroyed by fire in 1937, it stood a neglected shell for years, until English Heritage took over these most splendid of ruins and started the enormous task of making them safe and accessible. If you only see one ruin in the whole county, this should be it. Restoration work on the west wing has made several rooms accessible to the public for the

first time. Across from the ruins is a magnificent fountain, said to be the largest in Britain. Inspired by Bernini's fountains in Rome, it rises 26 feet and is crowned by an opulent sculpture that depicts Perseus rescuing Andromeda from a sea monster. Also within the grounds is the **Jerwood Sculpture Park**, which has a permanent collection including work by Elizabeth Frink and Anthony Gormley and also stages temporary exhibitions during the summer months.

TENBURY WELLS
12 miles SW of Kidderminster on the A456

🏛 Museum 🌱 Burford House

The A443 leads from Great Witley towards Shropshire and the border town of Tenbury Wells in a delightfully rural setting on the River Teme. The 'Wells' was added when a source of mineral water was discovered, but its heyday as a spa resort was very brief. **Tenbury Museum** tells the spa story and depicts other aspects of local life, including hop-growing and the railway days. In the market place is a curious oval-shaped building with rather ecclesiastical-looking windows. This is the Market House, which was built in 1811 and used as a corn and butter market.

Set in sweeping lawns on the banks of the River Teme, in the village of Burford a mile west of Tenbury (and just in Shropshire) stands **Burford House**, whose four-acre gardens are filled with well over 2,000 varieties of plants. This is the home of the National Collection of Clematis, and in the nursery attached to the garden almost 400 varieties of clematis are for sale, along with many other plants and gifts. The ground floor of the house is open as a gallery of contemporary art. Teas and light meals are served in the Burford Buttery (01584 810136).

🎭 stories and anecdotes 🕊 famous people 🎨 art and craft 🌿 entertainment and sport 🚶 walks

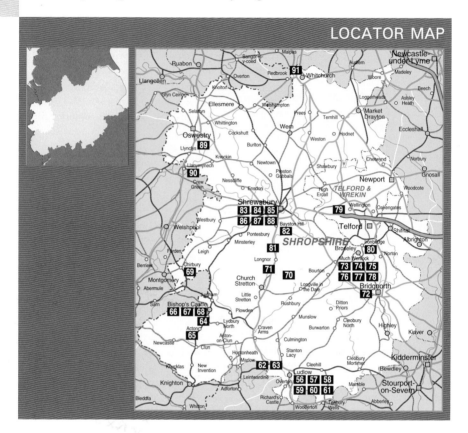

LOCATOR MAP

ADVERTISERS AND PLACES OF INTEREST

🏛 historic building   🏛 museum   🏛 historic site   🌢 scenic attraction   🌱 flora and fauna

3 | Shropshire

The tranquil, romantic face of Shropshire belies an often turbulent past that is revealed at scores of sites by the remains of dykes, ramparts and hill forts, and by the castles of the marcher lords, who seem to have divided their time between fighting the Welsh and fighting each other. The county boasts some of Britain's most important Roman sites, notably at Wroxeter, which at one time was the fourth largest Roman town in the land. Shropshire beckons with a landscape of great variety: the little hills and valleys, the lakes and canals of the northwest, the amazing parallel hill ranges towards the south, the rich farming plains around Oswestry, the forests of Clun and Wyre, Ironbridge Gorge, the birthplace of the Industrial Revolution. This stretch of the Severn Valley is now a World Heritage Centre, ranking it alongside the Pyramids,

the Grand Canyon and the Taj Mahal. Add to this the historic towns of Shrewsbury, Ludlow and Oswestry, several interesting museums, the churches and the stately homes and the glorious gardens, and you have a part of the world just waiting to be explored, whether by car, bike or on foot. South Shropshire affords a trip through history, including the wonderful town of Ludlow and the spectacular scenery of Wenlock Ridge, Long Mynd and Clun.

Ludlow Castle

ADVERTISERS AND PLACES OF INTEREST

🎬 stories and anecdotes   🐦 famous people   🎨 art and craft   🎭 entertainment and sport   🚶 walks

Ludlow

🏠 Castle   🏠 Church of St Laurence

🏛 Museum   🌿 Festival

Often called 'the perfect historic town', Ludlow is an enchanting place with more than 500 listed buildings and a medieval street pattern that has been kept virtually intact. There are some lovely walks along the banks of the River Teme with its plentiful wildlife, markets on Mondays, Wednesdays, Fridays and Saturdays, a livestock market on Mondays, and regular flea markets on Sundays.

Ludlow Castle was built by the Normans in the 11th century, one of a line of castles along the Marches to keep out the Welsh. Under its protection a large town was planned and built - and prospered, due to the collection and sale of wool and the manufacture of cloth. The Castle has been home to many distinguished families and to royalty: Edward V, Prince Arthur and other royal children were brought up in Ludlow, and the Castle became the headquarters of the Council of the Marches, which governed Wales and the border counties until 1689. The parish **Church of St Laurence** is one of the largest in the county, reflecting the town's affluence at the time of its rebuilding in the 15th century. There are fine misericords and stained glass, and the poet AE Housman, author of *A Shropshire Lad*, is commemorated on the outer wall of the church; his ashes lie outside the north door. Other places that should be seen include Castle Lodge, once a prison and later home

---

THE WOOL SHOP

13 Broad Street, Ludlow, Shropshire SY8 1NG
Tel: 01584 872988
website: www.ludlow-woolshop.co.uk

Owner Jean Brindley and her staff bring years of knowledge and experience to the **Wool Shop**, their specialist shop located in one of the oldest streets in Ludlow. The two rooms in the shop cater for all knitting and sewing needs, selling an amazing range of wools, yarns, threads, fabrics, haberdashery, tapestries, needles, patterns, books, sewing equipment and accessories that include all the best-known brands. The long-established business is based on the principles of selling and making quality products and services, growing the product range by following trends, improving standard products and listening to customers. The emphasis on providing help and advice as well as selling goods has earned the Wool Shop a large and loyal group of happy customers; Jean

knows her customers well and is always pleased to see new faces.

Their unique service lets them make distinctive and unusual garments for their customers, and other services include knitting-up and knit'n'natter Wednesday afternoons. Shop hours are 9 to 5 Monday, Tuesday, Wednesday and Friday; 9 to 1 Thursday; 9 to 4 Saturday. Customers can also order by phone or e-mail.

🏠 historic building   🏛 museum   🏚 historic site   🌊 scenic attraction   🌿 flora and fauna

CHOCOLATE GOURMET

16 Castle Street, Ludlow, Shropshire SY8 1AT
Tel: 01584 879332
e-mail: sales@chocolategourmet.co.uk
website: www.chocolategourmet.co.uk

John Betjeman called Ludlow 'the loveliest town in Britain', a
view definitely shared by Janette Rowlatt. She combined her love
of the town with a long-held fascination for chocolate when she
opened **Chocolate Gourmet** in 1999, providing the local area with the
finest chocolate in its various forms from around the world. In an
attractive Georgian brick building close to the Castle, the main museum
and the open-air market she tempts the good people of Ludlow and
visitors to the town with an amazing array of chocolate bars, chocolate
boxes, truffles and fudge.

Bars include the El Ray range (up to 73% cocoa content), Valrhona,
Michel Cluizel from Normandy (some 85% and a tiny bar with an incredible 99%), Amedei from
Tuscany and the Cocoa Tree with organic fruit and nuts. Truffles come with a mouth-watering range
of fillings – fresh cream, praline, marzipan, cherry and raspberry fondant, marc de champagne – and
fudge by Burnt Sugar is made with unrefined Fairtrade sugar from a co-operative in West Kenya.
Boxes can be filled with the customer's own choice for any special occasion and trimmed with
exquisite ribbons. Shop hours are 10.30am to 5.30 pm (Sunday 11 to 4.30)

In 2004 Janette opened a second Chocolate Gourmet at 72 Wyle Cop, one of Shrewsbury's
most prestigious shopping streets. Tel: 01743 343477 or sales@chocolategourmet.co.uk

ANDREW FRANCIS

1 Market Street, Ludlow,
Shropshire SY8 1BD
Tel: 01584 872008 Fax: 01584 711785

Andrew Francis has been a butcher for 25 years,
15 of them in Ludlow and the last two here in the
centre of town a short walk from the Castle.

Quality is the keynote throughout the range on
sale: Hereford and Welsh black beef, Berkshire and
Gloucester Old Spot pork, prime local lamb, wild
venison from Mortimer Forest in steaks, joints,
casserole meat and sausages, wild duck, rabbit,
pigeon, home-cured bacon and ham, free-range
poultry and eggs. Andrew's award-winning
sausages, pork pies and steak pies are all cooked on
the premises.

Outside catering includes hog roasts and
barbecues, and the shop supplies many of the top
local pubs, restaurants and hotels, including the
renowned Feathers Hotel a few streets away. In
spring and summer, hanging baskets make a
colourful sight outside the shop, which is open from
7am to 5pm (6am to 5pm Friday and Saturday;
closed Sunday).

THE SILVER PEAR

68-69 Broad Street, Ludlow,
Shropshire, SY8 1NH
Tel: 01584 879096
Fax: 01584 879124
e-mail: sales@silverpear.co.uk
website: www.silverpear.co.uk

A beautifully restored 13th century building in Ludlow's finest street is home to The Silver Pear, an exciting contemporary emporium of design-led products and home accessories. Janet Tuffley opened her small department store in 1999 to fill a perceived gap in the market for such goods and created one of the best businesses of its kind in the whole region. The ever changing stock on display includes luxury bathroom goods from L'Occitane, Cath Kidston and Geo.F.Trumper. Stunning jewellery by Thomas Sabo, Coeur de Lion, Riley Burnett, Dower & Hall. Handbags by Orla Kiely and Lupo; scarves, watches, clocks, silk ties, wallets and gadgets. Interiors; candles, photo frames, cushions, rugs and lighting. Kitchenware by Alessi, Joseph Joseph, Sophie Conran and Maxwell Williams. Glassware by LSA; bowls, decanters, drinking glasses, vases and jugs. A children's department; toys, clothes, and shoes. Party paraphernalia; gardening accessories, books - the list is almost endless with gifts to suit every occasion and customers can also purchase online.

The Silver Pear also offers a comprehensive and personalised Wedding List Service including 2 free nights in one of the luxury self-catering apartments superbly situated above the store which are also available to let. Please visit www.silverpearapartments.co.uk.

BROMLEY COURT B&B

18-20 Lower Broad Street, Ludlow, Shropshire SY8 1PQ
Tel: 01584 876996
e-mail: bromley.court18@btinternet.com
website: www.ludlowhotels.com

'Luxury suites in the heart of Ludlow'

Bromley Court comprises three individual Tudor cottages clustered around an enclosed courtyard in the heart of Ludlow. Close to Ludlow's shops, square, castle and church, and within yards of the River Teme's stunning Horseshoe Weir and country walks. Each beamed cottage provides self-contained, private luxury, with an en-suite bedroom, a well-equipped sitting room and a breakfast bar. On sunny mornings, consider breakfasting al fresco in the sheltered courtyard. Perfect for a leisurely start at any time of day...

Each cottage is replenished daily with the finest local produce from Ludlow's award-winning **Deli on the Square** (on the town square, reached in minutes through the 13th Century Broadgate). The Deli is at the forefront of forging Ludlow's foodie reputation and specialises in local, British and Continental cheeses – over 140 varieties. Plus local treats, charcouterie, hampers, olive oils, vinegars, mustards and more. A must-visit shop!

🏠 historic building   🏛 museum   🏚 historic site   🦆 scenic attraction   🌿 flora and fauna

THE ARCHWAY - S J ALLSOP

6 New Road, Ludlow, Shropshire SY8 2NX
Tel: 01694 771371
e-mail: sandra-allsop@hotmail.co.uk
website: www.thearchwaycentre.co.uk

The Archway Centre is a lovely place to visit to refresh yourself from tip to toe within the one complex, easily found on the outskirts of historic Ludlow. A snapshot of each business is shown below, we also have a lovely informal courtyard and café to cater for visitors who would like to stay with us for the day.

Tone 'n' Shape offers a relaxing and enjoyable way to loose those inches. The 7 tables are dedicated to each muscle group and designed to improve flexibility, increase circulation and muscle tone. Trained staff help people of all ages to use the beds safely and effectively.
Tel 01584 879692

Amber Holistic & Beauty, Teresa offers liquid and powder nail care, facials, aromatherapy, Swedish and hot stone massage, reflexology, eye enhancements tanning treatments, manicure, pedicure and waxing.
Tel: 07817 561510

Red Hair Studio is a stylish, modern salon run by Lindsey Piper with her experienced team and offers a very friendly, relaxed environment, uses latest techniques in hair design and offers little extras like a complimentary blow dry with colours to keep clients loyal and happy. Tel: 01584879333

Epil Pro Hair removal, Jo Beadman offers a truly non-invasive , pain free treatment for all skin types and all hair colours. Tel: 07779 341586

Skin Solutions, Madelaine offers tattoos, non laser tattoo removal, body piercing, advanced facials, manicure and nail extensions, electrolysis and thread vein removal, eye lash treatment, full exfoliation and Hopi ear candling. Tel: 07869 132752

Additional treatment rooms are available at competitive daily/weekly rates for therapists in similar disciplines. General enquiries call Sandra Allsop 07967 976164, The Archway Centre, 6 New Road, Ludlow, SY8 2NX.

of the officials of the Council of the Marches, and the fascinating houses that line Broad Street.

Ludlow Museum, in Castle Street, has exhibitions of local history centred on, among other things, the Castle, the town's trade and special features on local geology and archaeology. At one time in the last century glove-making was one of the chief occupations in the town. Nine master glovers employed some 700 women and children, each required to produce 10 pairs of gloves a week, mainly for the American market.

The **Ludlow Festival**, held annually since 1960 and lasting a fortnight in June/July, has become one of the major arts festivals in the country. The centrepiece of the festival, an open-air performance of a Shakespeare play in the Castle's inner bailey, is supported by a number of events that have included orchestral concerts, musical recitals, literary and historical lectures, exhibitions, readings, workshops and food and drink celebrations.

Around Ludlow

CLEOBURY MORTIMER
8 miles E of Ludlow on the A4117

🏛 St Mary's Church

A famous landmark in this pleasing small town just west of the Forest of Wyre is the crooked spire of **St Mary's Church**, whose east window commemorates the 14th-century poet, William Langland. His best-known work is Piers Plowman, an indignant tract against rural poverty in a landscape still recognisable as south Shropshire.

It was in Cleobury Mortimer that Maisie Bloomer, a witch, gained notoriety in the 18th century. Curses and love potions were

her speciality, and the villagers were in no doubt that she was in league with the Devil.

Two miles east of Cleobury stands Mawley Hall, an 18th-century stone house with some very fine internal features.

CLEE HILL
4 miles E of Ludlow on the A4117

🏃 Brown Clee

The Clee Hills to the north of the village include the highest peaks in the county. The summit of **Brown Clee** is 1,750 feet above sea level.

STANTON LACY
2 miles NW of Ludlow off the B4365

This charming little village with its black and white cottages sits on the bank of the River Corve and is notable for its Church of St Peter, which has some Saxon features and Victorian stained glass.

BROMFIELD
3 miles NW of Ludlow on the A49

🏛 St Mary's Church   ✒ Racecourse

Although the busy A49 runs through the centre of the village, **St Mary's Church** is beautifully sited close to where the River Teme joins up with the River Onny. Originally a priory, it became a private residence for one George Foxe following the dissolution of the monasteries. What is now the chancel was once the dining room, but the extraordinary painted ceiling was created after the building once again became a church in the mid 1600s. The swirling figures with their ribbons bearing biblical texts have been described as "the best example of the worst style of ecclesiastical art". Another striking feature here is the huge mural coat of arms of Charles II on the south wall.

LUDLOW FOOD CENTRE

Bromfield, Ludlow, Shropshire SY8 2JR
Tel: 01584 856 000
e-mail: greatfood@ludlowfoodcentre.co.uk
website: www.ludlowfoodcentre.co.uk

The **Ludlow Food Centre** offers a unique food shopping experience. The Centre's aim is to provide customers with fresh, local, seasonal and handmade food with exceptional taste and flavour. More than 80% of the produce on sale is sourced from Shropshire and the surrounding counties of Herefordshire, Worcestershire and Powys. Much of the produce is purchased directly from the grower or producer thereby keeping food miles to a minimum and prices at a realistic level. The Food Centre is part of the Earl of Plymouth's Oakly Park Estate from which it sources all its beef, lamb and rare breed pork. The meat is brought back to the Food Centre's butchery to be matured and prepared with skill and attention to detail. The centre likes to buy from small artisan producers where quality and taste count. Daily deliveries ensure that produce arrives on the shelf in absolutely peak condition. By following the seasons, a mouth-watering array of different products are displayed throughout the year, supplemented where necessary by carefully selected produce from abroad. The centre also stocks a wide range of organic and fairtrade products.

Purpose built using sustainable materials and the latest energy management systems the Food Centre has a unique layout that feels spacious and airy. The Food Hall is surrounded by eight kitchens that can be viewed through large picture windows. Among the kitchen units is a bakery making fresh bread 7 days a week, a dairy producing a range of ice-creams and award winning cheeses with milk from the Estate, a production kitchen that supplies the deli, a coffee roasting area and a jam and pickle kitchen that makes with the seasons.

You can sample some of this fare in the Conservatory Barn Café which offers seasonal food at sensible prices. Everything is home-made and includes freshly roasted and ground coffee, cakes and scones, ploughmans featuring the Centre's own cheeses, home-made pies and quiches and an ever-changing selection of freshly prepared hot lunches.

Overlooking the food hall is the Conference Centre which is equipped with all the latest audio-visual equipment and is available to hire to hire with catering being provided by the Centre's kitchen if required.

A rather unexpected amenity within the centre is a Post Office which offers all the usual counter services and also stocks a wide range of convenience goods as well as newspapers, stationery, hand-made cards and a small selection of eco-friendly cleaning products and is open 7 days a week.

The centre is located just off the A49, next to the Clive Hotel in the village of Bromfield, 2 miles northwest of Ludlow.

stories and anecdotes   famous people   art and craft   entertainment and sport   walks

THE CLIVE BAR AND RESTAURANT WITH ROOMS

Bromfield, Ludlow, Shropshire SY8 2JR
Tel: 01584 856565 Fax: 01584 856661
e-mail: info@theclive.co.uk website: www.theclive.co.uk

A handsome three-storey Georgian building attracts visitors with top-class cooking in friendly, relaxed surroundings, with ales and wines to match and excellent overnight accommodation. The former farmhouse has been developed to offer a delightful blend of traditional and contemporary, with original features in the bar and a more modern look in the restaurant. The chefs set great store by fresh local produce, seeking out the best local meat, vegetables and smoked products and fish fresh from Cornwall. Typical dishes on the ever-changing menus could include Wenlock Edge Farm air-dried beef and Ragstone cheese salad with a cassis dressing, rack of Welsh lamb with dauphinoise potatoes, pan-fried scallops with tomato salsa, strudel of lightly spiced summer vegetables on baby fennel and, to finish, summer fruit kebabs with creamed rice and a peach conserve. To accompany the superb food is an extensive list of wines from Old and New Worlds, with many available by the glass. The bar, with its adjoining courtyard, is a great place to meet for a drink and a snack, with local ales, a good choice of wines and organic cider and apple juice.

Fifteen en suite bedrooms in skilfully and tastefully converted outbuildings provide very comfortable up-to-date accommodation; all have TV, radio, hot drinks tray, mini-bar and free Wi-Fi, and some have facilities for disabled guests. A boardroom is available for meetings, with a range of presentation and communication facilities.

About a mile northeast of Bromfield is **Ludlow Racecourse** (National Hunt) where Bronze Age barrows have been brought to light.

ONIBURY

5 miles NW of Ludlow off the A49

🌱 The Wernlas Collection

"I didn't know chickens could be so beautiful," was the comment of one visitor to **The Wernlas Collection**, a living museum of rare poultry. The setting of this 20-acre smallholding is a joy in itself, and the collection is an internationally acclaimed conservation centre and vital gene pool where over 15,000 chicks, both traditional and rare, are hatched each year, all year round. Besides the 220 breeds of chickens there are rare breeds of goats, sheep and pigs, and some

donkeys. The gift shop is themed on chickens - a chickaholic's paradise, in fact - and eggs and vaccinated and salmonella tested chicks are also on sale.

STOKESAY

7 miles NW of Ludlow off the A49

🏛 Castle   🏛 Church of St John the Baptist

The de Say family of nearby Clun began building **Stokesay Castle** in about 1240, and a Ludlow wool merchant, Lawrence de Ludlow, made considerable additions, including the Great Hall and fortified south tower. It is the oldest fortified manor house in England and is substantially complete, making it easy to see how a rich medieval merchant would have lived. Entrance to this magnificent building is through a splendid timber-framed gatehouse and the cottage-

---

🏛 historic building   🏛 museum   🏛 historic site   🏞 scenic attraction   🌱 flora and fauna

Stokesay Castle

style gardens are an extra delight. An audio tour guides visitors round the site.

The adjacent parish **Church of St John the Baptist** is unusual in having been restored during Cromwell's rule after sustaining severe damage in the Civil War. A remarkable feature in the nave is a series of biblical texts written in giant script on the walls. The 17th-century box pews and pulpit are still in use and, outside, the churchyard is managed as semi-wild, allowing some 88 species of wild flowers to flourish.

Centre, visitors can discover the heritage, wildlife and traditions of the area in a striking all-weather building with a grass roof made from 1,000 square metres of turf weighing more than 70 tons. Rocks that have travelled 7,000 miles from the equator over the last 560 million years; a mammoth skeleton from Shropshire's last Ice Age 13,000 years ago, and a simulated balloon flight over the hills are just some of the attractions. Outside, visitors can wander through 25 acres of attractive meadows sloping down to the River Onny. The centre has a gift shop, café and information point, and there's a programme of regular events and craft exhibitions throughout the year. Brought on stream in May 2008, the Secret Hills Exhibition tells some stories of the Shropshire Hills, and there's a superb film panorama shot from a number of balloon flights.

Craven Arms

🏛 Secret Hills

The village takes its name from the hotel and pub built by the Earl of Craven. The coming of the railways brought expansion and development. Once at the centre of several roads that were used by sheep-drovers moving their flocks from Wales to the English markets, in its heyday, Craven Arms held one of the largest sheep auctions in Britain, with as many as 20,000 sheep being sold in a single day.

Shropshire's landscape has inspired the music of Vaughan Williams, the poems of AE Housman and the novels of Mary Webb. At the **Secret Hills**, Shropshire Hills Discovery

Around Craven Arms

ASTON ON CLUN
3 miles W of Craven Arms off the B4368

🌱 Arbor Tree Dressing

Not one of Housman's Cluns, but well worth a mention and a visit. The village's **Arbor Tree Dressing** ceremony was first held in 1786. Following the Battle of Worcester in 1651, King Charles spent some time up a tree (see under Boscobel page 110) and to commemorate his escape he proclaimed Arbor Day, a day in May, as a national holiday when trees were dressed. The custom generally died out but was revived here in 1786 when a local landowner married. As Aston was part of his

📖 stories and anecdotes   🐦 famous people   🎨 art and craft   ✒ entertainment and sport   🚶 walks

Clun Castle

estate he revived the tradition of dressing the Black Poplar in the middle of the village, a custom that still survives.

CLUN
8 miles W of Craven Arms on the A488/B4368

🏛 Castle   🏛 Church of St George   🏛 Museum

🏛 Bury Ditches

A quiet, picturesque little town in the valley of the River Clun, overlooked by the ruins of its **Castle**, which was once the stronghold of the Fitzalan family. The shell of the keep and the earthworks are the main surviving features. The **Church of St George** has a fortress-like tower with small windows and a lovely 17th-century tiered pyramidal top. There are also some splendid Norman arcades with circular pillars and scalloped capitals. The 14th-century north aisle roof and restored nave roof are an impressive sight that will keep necks craning for some time. Some wonderful Jacobean woodwork and a marvellous medieval studded canopy are other sights worth lingering over at this beautiful church, which is a great tribute to GE Street, who was responsible for its restoration in 1876. Agricultural implements and geological finds, and in particular flints,

are the main attractions in the little **Local History Museum** in the Town Hall, in a ground-floor area that was once an open jail. **Bury Ditches**, north of Clun on the way to Bishop's Castle, are an Iron Age fort on a seven-acre tree-covered site.

Down the valley are other Cluns: Clunton, Clunbury and Clungunford. The quartet were idyllically described by AE Housman in *A Shropshire Lad*:

> *In valleys of springs and rivers,*
> *By Onny and Teme and Clun,*
> *The country for easy livers,*
> *The quietest under the sun.*

BISHOP'S CASTLE
9 miles NW of Craven Arms off the A488

🏛 Museums   🏛 Mitchell's Fold   🌿 Stiperstones

This small and ancient town lies in an area of great natural beauty in solitary border country. Little remains of the castle, built in the 12th century for the Bishops of Hereford, which gave the place its name, but there is no shortage of fine old buildings for the visitor to see. The **House on Crutches Museum**, sited in one of the oldest and most picturesque of these buildings, recounts the town's history. Its gable end is supported on wooden posts – hence the name. Also in town is a **Railway Museum** that charts the rise and fall of the Bishop's Castle Railway, which ran between Craven Arms and Lydham from 1865 to 1935. Traces of the railway, including embankments, bridges and station buildings, can be seen along the A489. North of Bishop's Castle lie the **Stiperstones**, a

POTS & DOTS

Penan Heath, Colebatch, Bishop's Castle,
Shropshire SY9 5LW
Tel: Yvonne: 01588 630285 Max: 01588 638961
Mob: 0781 0781 938
Yvonne's e-mail: potsanddots@orange.net Yvonne's website: www.potsanddots.co.uk
Max's e-mail: maxbaccanello@hotmail.com Max's website: www.maxbaccanello.com

Yvonne Baccanello and her son Max practise their manifold artistic talents in studios at their farmhouse home a short drive south of Bishop's Castle. At **Pots & Dots** Yvonne's speciality is ceramic kitchenware and tableware, including pots, jugs, mugs, bowls, salt & pepper sets, plates and butter dishes. They come in a range of colours with a variety of glazes, and all are microwave and dishwasher proof. The 'dotty' items are something of trademark, and with each dot glazed on three times, they are great to hold and feel as well as to look at. Yvonne's pieces make excellent gifts and can be named and dated to commemorate special occasions.

Yvonne's son Max, born in 1988, is rapidly making his mark as an artist in various media. After a scholarship to Shrewsbury School and a spell at Chelsea College of Art and Design he then began studying at the Charles H Cecil Studio in Florence, where tuition is focused on academic portraiture in the lineage of traditional representational art and sight size technique. Max works almost exclusively from life in his oil paintings, pencil and charcoal drawings and sculptures in clay, bronze and marble. He is happy to discuss commissions for portraits and also for landscapes and still lifes, and prints are available on a selection of his charcoal drawings. Many of his works can be seen on his website. Visits to the Yvonne's and Max's studios by appointment.

THE WHITE COTTAGE

Acton, nr Bishop's Castle, Shropshire SY9 5LD
Tel: 01588 630330
e-mail: staying@thewhitecottageacton.co.uk
website: www.thewhitecottageacton.co.uk

The White Cottage, the home of Tim Dicker and Mary Wraith, is situated halfway between Bishop's Castle and Clun in an Area of Outstanding Natural Beauty among the South Shropshire Hills. In the garden of their home stands The Bothy, a charming stone-built barn that provides a cosy retreat for B&B or self-catering guests.

Recently renovated and refurbished, it has a bedroom with a super kingsized bed, a shower room and a fully-fitted little kitchen with table and chairs. TV with DVD player is provided and guests will delight in the collection of interesting paintings, ceramics and sculpture. Ornamental pots with plants and trees, and more sculpture, decorate the private sitting area outside the French windows whilst the main cottage gardens provide additional sitting areas with outstanding views.

The breakfast menu is truly delicious and offers an interesting choice of local produce as well as home made yoghurt, fruit salads and compotes, preserves and main courses. It is served in the kitchen or garden at The White Cottage or can be delivered to the front door of The Bothy.

The setting, up a private track off a country lane, is both beautiful and peaceful, and the area is ideal for a touring, walking or cycling holiday – Offa's Dyke Path, the Shropshire Way and Jack Mytton Way are all nearby. Birdlife abounds, and the sight of wild deer at the gate add to the charm of a stay in this lovely place.

stories and anecdotes   famous people   art and craft   entertainment and sport   walks

theGALLERY

3 Market Square, Bishop's Castle,
Shropshire SY9 5BN
Tel: 01588 630128
website:www.thegallerybc.co.uk

In a prominent position on the attractive market square in Bishop's Castle, **theGALLERY** is a showcase for the very best of designer-made glass, ceramics and jewellery, along with original artwork and prints, woodwork and metalwork, textiles, studio pottery and home furnishings.

theGALLERY, previously known as Bishop's Gallery, was relaunched in March 2008 by Jacs Collins, who came here after a 20-year career in interior design in Surrey. A painter and designer with a degree in textile design, she has dedicated the display space to as many local artists and craftmakers as possible, and each month brings a new exhibition on a wide variety of themes.

The applied art and craft work on display is carefully selected from makers with the skills and experience to be among the best in their field and everything in theGALLERY is handmade in the UK. Many pieces are unique or limited edition and most are signed by the makers as well as being instantly recognisable by the inherent signature of style and quality.

theGALLERY stock also regularly includes-

"Inside Knowledge" which is a small range of modern furnishings and accessories, showcasing a personal selection of contemporary designer style including hand printed fabrics, wallpapers, bags and cushions while "Rural Retro" is an eclectic collection of re-cycled, re-vived and re-loved items of mid century modern studio pottery, welsh blankets, fabrics and original 1960's Ercol or G Plan furniture items.

theGALLERY is usually open from 11.00am on Tuesdays, Thursdays, Fridays and Saturdays-also occasional Sundays and Bank Holiday Mondays.

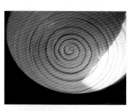

Opening times and days might vary according to seasons, whim and weather- so it's best to call before making a special journey.

www.thegallerybc.co.uk lists current opening times as well as all of the exhibiting Artists and Makers, exhibition news and "one-off" vintage items to buy.

MIDDLE WOODBATCH FARM

Woodbatch Road, Bishop's Castle,
Shropshire SY9 5JT
Tel: 01588 630141 mob: 07989 496875
e-mail: steven.austin5@btinternet.com
website: www.middlewoodbatchfarm.co.uk

The Austin family have lived and worked at **Middle Woodbatch Farm** since 1936. The farm stands in a beautiful tranquil spot on the English /Welsh border, 1.5 miles from the small market town of Bishops Castle, in a Designated Area of Outstanding Natural Beauty. From its elevated rural location the farm commands breath-taking views of the Shropshire hills &The Long Mynd.

Mary & her husband Steve welcome guests to their 4 star 17th centuary farmhouse into an atmosphere of relaxed friendly hospitality.

The three guest rooms Owl, Badger & Fox, named after some of the farms regular inhabitants enjoy superb views of the surrounding countryside and are furnished to a high standard with luxurious bed linen, quality Egyptian cotton towels, hairdryers, TV, clock/radio, tea & coffee facilities and WI-FI internet access plus many other extras. All the rooms have fully tiled en-suite bathrooms with large spacious walk in showers and a complimentary basket of toiletries. The house also has a cosy guest lounge, but guests are welcome to use the family sitting room which has a lovely wood burner to thaw out by during the winter months.

Breakfast served in the dining room includes, fresh fruit, yoghurts, juices, cereals, local bacon & sausage, tomatoes and mushrooms and our own free range chicken and duck eggs, and there is always home baked bread using local organic flour. Full vegetarian options always available! This is a great way to start a days walking, cycling, mountain biking or just relaxing and enjoying the beautiful surroundings, our prime location suits all.

We are fortunate to be surrounded by an extensive network of footpaths & bridleways; The Shropshire Way & the Blue Remembered Hills bridleway that come through the farm yard, we are also a stones throw from the Offas Dyke, Kerry Ridgeway, Jack Mytton Way, BC Ring and The Long Mynd. Our secluded rural location is also perfect for bird & wildlife watching.

Guests arriving from Shrewsbury and the A5, take the A488 bishops Castle road (approx22 miles). On reaching the 2nd town sign, turn right, past the high school, just after the church, keep to the left (do not go up into the town).After about 250 yds just past a high block wall turn left onto Woodbatch road, follow the road round to the right where it turns into a single track road, follow this to the end (approx1.5 miles).

Nipstone Rock

Distance: *2.5 miles (4.0 kilometres)*

Typical time: *90 mins*

Height gain: *80 metres*

Map: *Explorer 216*

Walk: *www.walkingworld.com ID:2541*

Contributor: *Jim Grindle*

ACCESS INFORMATION:

Stiperstones village and the Bog are signposted from the A488 near Minsterly; the A488 joins the A5 Shrewsbury bypass. There is ample free parking by the Bog crossroads. For travel information call 0870 608 2608.

ADDITIONAL INFORMATION:

At the crossroads is an outdoor activity centre in an old school. At summer weekends, and mid-week at times, a volunteer group offers refreshments here; there are also toilets. For details e-mail info@thresholdscentre.co.uk or visit www.shropshire-cc.gov.uk/discover.nsf

Mary Webb, the Shropshire author, set one of her novels, *The Golden Arrow*, in the Stiperstones area and there are many legends concerning the rocks - don't spend the night in the Devil's Chair for instance, or else... A film of her novel, *Gone to Earth*, was made here. The district has been known since Roman times though, as an intensively industrialised mining area, mainly lead and barytes, and many chimneys and spoil heaps can be seen on the western slopes. The main geological feature is the quartz capping of the ridge, some 480 million years old and shattered by frost in the last Ice Age resulting in the huge outcrops we see today.

DESCRIPTION:

The walk starts from The Bog, an area that even 50 years ago had some fading signs of the intense industrial activity of Victorian days. The start is relatively high and gives good views for very little climbing. Some mapped areas of woodland have

been removed to restore the heather habitat, part of the Stiperstones Purple Project by English Nature.

FEATURES:

Hills or Fells, Pub, Toilets, Birds, Flowers, Great Views, Butterflies, Good for Kids, Industrial Archaeology, Tea Shop, Woodland.

WALK DIRECTIONS:

1 | At the higher end of the Bog car park is a signpost for two waymarked walks. Turn right, following The Mucklewick Walk. This takes you past a small pond where you are directed to the left through trees. You reach a flight of steps going up to the right. At the top is a stile next to the telegraph pole. Cross the stile and follow the line of poles uphill to a stile in a fence. After this the footpath goes diagonally left away from the line of poles and ends at a stile on a lane.

2 | Don't cross this stile but turn round and look across the large field. Go first just to the left of the telegraph pole in front and then follow the line of trees making for the extreme left end of the wood in front.

3 | At the end of the wood and to the right of the more obvious gate is a stile with signposts for the Shropshire Way (a buzzard) and the Mucklewick

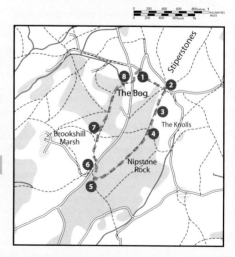

Walk. Cross this and follow a path along the edge of the wood to a stile at its far end. At the moment you can go around the stile. Just in sight is a crossing track with signposts.

4 | Cross the track and go through the gate. The route is now well signposted both for the Mucklewick Walk and the Shropshire Way (the buzzard symbol). It leads past the Nipstone Rock, the last of the Stiperstones over to your right across the fence. After this it goes into another plantation where you must watch for a signpost at the bottom of a drop in the ground.

5 | At this point the two waymarked routes divide - our route goes to the right, following the Mucklewick Walk. 100m away it comes to a stile and a lane. Cross the lane to the far stile and then go to the hedge and fence beyond. At the fence the Mucklewick Walk is signposted to the left, but our route goes to the right, following a farm track for a very short distance almost as far as a gateway with a cattle-grid.

6 | Leave the track and follow the hedge to a stile. Continue by the hedge (really a line of trees with some laburnum) until you see the way into the next field. There is no gate, just a gap. When you have gone through it you will have a fence on your right with a farm behind it. Follow the fence, which bends a few times, to its corner where there is a stile leading into a wood.

7 | The path goes along the edge of the wood but soon ends at a newish forest road. Cross this onto a grassy firebreak and continue when the surface is stony. The route is well signposted at all junctions. There is no change in direction, but several gates. After passing a reedy lake, which you can just about make out on your left, the forest paths end at a metal gate. Keep straight ahead over the crossing track and you will come to a lane.

8 | Turn left and after about 20m you will see the wide open area which is the car park. Turn right and cross to the far side where the walk started.

SOL DELICATESSEN

The Main Shop, The Porch House,
35 High Street, Bishop's Castle,
Shropshire SY9 5BE
Tel: 01588 638190

Bishop's Castle is an ancient little town with a number of fine old buildings, two museums and two breweries. It's well worth a leisurely stroll, and food-lovers will make sure that the stroll includes a stop at **Sol Delicatessen**.

This excellent place has been owned and run by Robin Fox since 2006, in one of the oldest shop premises in town. Robin cooks all the quiches, vegetarian dishes and cakes, whilst meat pies and pâtés are all supplied by a local chef. Fresh bread is baked daily and sandwiches are made to order. Locally sourced chutneys, jams and honey, together with a fine selection of European wines are complemented by an extensive range of classic cookware essentials.

Sol Delicatessen is open from 9 to 5 Monday to Saturday. Bishop's Castle lies off the A488 9 miles northwest of Craven Arms.

THE HERBERT ARMS

Chirbury, Montgomery, Powys SY15 6BG
Tel: 01938 561216
website: www.herbertarmschirbury.co.uk

The Herbert Arms is a pleasant old inn located in the village of Chirbury, at the junction of the A490 and B4386 close to Montgomery on the border with Shropshire. Sisters Kathryn and Sarah acquired the premises in 2008, and with Sarah's partner Stéphane they have expanded its role from country local (a role it still fulfils admirably) to a destination dining pub that attracts lovers of good food from all over the region.

The interior is inviting and unpretentious, with cosy fires and quarry-tiled floor, and in the restaurant at the rear happy diners return time after time to savour a memorable culinary experience. 'The Frenchman and the Farmers' Daughters' wow the customers with classic-inspired cuisine bringing top-notch cooking (Stephane's CV includes 7 years at Michel Roux's Waterside Inn) based on the very best seasonal produce, sourced locally wherever possible. A typical evening menu, with about half a dozen choices for each course, might include homemade black pudding with caramelised apples and Madeira sauce; vintage cheddar cheese souffle with pickled beetroot salad; crisp pork belly, roasted pear & braising jus, roast lemon sole, crushed potato & bouillabaisse, dark chocolate & caramelised walnut delice and iced prune & armagnac parfait. Special dietary requirements can be catered for with a little notice.

The Herbert Arms is open for food lunch and dinner Wednesday to Saturday and lunch on Sundays. The bar is open Tuesday evening, Wednesday and Thursday lunchtime and evening and all day Friday to Sunday.

rock-strewn quartzite outcrop rising to a height of 1,700ft at the Devil's Chair. A bleak place of brooding solitude, the ridge is part of a 1,000-acre National Nature Reserve and on the lower slopes gaunt chimneys, derelict buildings and neglected roads and paths are silent reminders of the lead-mining industry that flourished here from Roman times until the 19th century. To the west, on the other side of the A49 near Chirbury, is **Mitchell's Fold** stone circle, a Bronze Age circle of 15 stones. This is Shropshire's oldest monument, its origins and purpose unknown.

ACTON SCOTT
5 miles NE of Craven Arms off the A49

🌱 Acton Scott Historic Working Farm

Signposted off the A49 just south of Church Stretton, **Acton Scott Historic Working Farm** offers a fascinating insight into daily life on an upland farm as practised in the South Shropshire hills at the close of the 19th century. Owned by Shropshire County Council, it is a living museum with a commitment to preserving both traditional farming techniques and rural craft skills. Every day visitors can see milking by hand and butter-making in the dairy. There are weekly visits from the wheelwright, farrier and blacksmith, while in the fields the farming year unfolds with ploughing, sowing and harvesting. Special attractions include lambing, shearing, cider-making and threshing with steam and flail. The waggoner and his team of heavy horses provide the power to work the land, while the stockman looks after the farm's livestock, among which are many rare breeds of cattle, sheep and pigs. The farm is open to visitors from 10am - 5pm Tuesday

🏛 historic building   🏛 museum   🏛 historic site   🍃 scenic attraction   🌱 flora and fauna

to Sunday and Bank Holidays between April and October.

Church Stretton

🏠 Church of St Laurence   ⚔ Long Mynd

⚔ Carding Mill Valley   ⚔ Rectory Wood

The town has a long history - King John granted a charter in 1214 - and traces of the medieval town are to be seen among the 18th and 19th-century buildings in the High Street.

Elsewhere in the town, many of the black-and-white timbered buildings are not so old as they look, having been built when the town had ideas of becoming a health resort. Just behind the High Street stands the **Church of St Laurence**, with Saxon foundations, a Norman nave and a tower dating from about 1200. Over the aisle is a memorial to a tragic event that happened in 1968 when three boys were killed in a fire. The memorial is in the form of a gridiron, with flakes of copper simulating flames. The gridiron is the symbol of St Laurence, who was burnt to death on one in AD258. The Victorian novelist Sarah Smith, who wrote under the name of Hesba Stretton, was a frequent visitor to nearby All Stretton, and there is a small memorial window to her in the south transept.

A mile from the town centre are **Carding Mill Valley** reservoir and the extensive ridge known as **Long Mynd**. The valley and the moorland into which it runs are National Trust property and very popular for walking and picnicking. This wild area of heath affords marvellous views across Shropshire to the Cheshire Plains and the Black Mountains. Just

🎭 stories and anecdotes   🦜 famous people   🎨 art and craft   🎟 entertainment and sport   ⚔ walks

HEATHER BRAE

Leebotwood, nr Church Stretton, Shropshire SY6 6LU
Tel: 01694 751757
website: www.heatherbraeshropshire.co.uk

Jane Tyler and Mary Mullock renovated an old garage and turned it into a delightful lifestyle shop that has quickly won many loyal friends. **Heather Brae** is filled with a carefully chosen, eclectic selection of items large and small for the house and garden, and a wide variety of gift ideas. On display are chinaware and pottery, tins and jars and other kitchenalia, brooches, vintage and contemporary jewellery, semi-precious stones, home-made soaps, candles and lanterns, embroidery, dolls and toys and mobiles, leather goods, watercolours and cards for all occasions.

For the outside and garden there are sculptures and ornaments, benches, and superb locally made wrought-iron arches. It's a great place for browsing and the stock is constantly changing,

so every visit is guaranteed to reveal new and delightful surprises. Hard to beat when looking for a personal treat or an unusual present, Heather Brae is open from 10 to 5.30 every day except Sundays in the winter.

below Long Mynd is **Rectory Wood**, which once formed part of the rectory church at Church Stretton. Three marked walks in the vicinity of the woods include a sculpture trail, and the woodland itself provides a valuable habitat for birds, bats and other wildlife. The area is a designated a Site of Special Scientific Interest.

Around Church Stretton

LITTLE STRETTON
2 miles S of Church Stretton on the B4370

🏛 All Saints Church

The village of Little Stretton nestles in the Stretton Gap, with the wooded slopes of Ragleth to the east and Long Mynd to the west. It is a peaceful spot, bypassed by the A49, and

is a delightful place for a stroll. The most photographed building is **All Saints Church**, with a black and white timbered frame, a thatched roof and the general look of a cottage rather than a church. When built in 1903 it had an iron roof, but this was soon found to be too noisy and was replaced with thatch (heather initially, then the straw that tops it today). Among many other interesting buildings are Manor House, a cruck hall dating from 1500, and Bircher Cottage, of a similar vintage.

"Switzerland without the wolves and avalanches" is a description sometimes applied to this beautiful, serene part of the world.

ACTON BURNELL
7m NE of Church Stretton off the A49

This charming small village takes its name from Robert Burnell who was Bishop of

🏛 historic building   🏛 museum   🏛 historic site   ♨ scenic attraction   🌿 flora and fauna

Bath and Wells and Lord Chancellor to Edward I. In his latter role he entertained the king here in 1283 and one of the first true Parliaments took place in the castle (more of a fortified residence, really) whose ruins of bright red sandstone stand behind the church. Burnell had built the church of St Mary only a decade before the king's visit. It's an elegantly proportioned early Gothic building with a simple interior that shows off to advantage the impressive late 16th-century alabaster tomb of a later Lord of the Manor, Sir Richard Lee.

Bridgnorth

🏰 Castle 🏰 Bishop Percy's House

🏛 Museums 🏛 Castle Hill Cliff Railway

🏛 Severn Valley Railway

The ancient market town of Bridgnorth, straddling the River Severn, comprises Low Town and, 100 feet up sandstone cliffs, High Town. The year 1101 is a key date in its history – the year in which the **Norman Castle** was built by Robert de Belesme from Quatt. All that remains of the castle is part of the keep tower, which leans at an angle of about 17 degrees (more than that of the Leaning Tower of Pisa) as a result of an attempt to demolish it after the Civil War. The castle grounds offer splendid views of the river, and when King Charles 1 stayed here in 1642 he declared the view from the Castle Walk to be the finest in his dominion. The **Northgate Museum** is a good place to start a tour of this interesting town. It occupies rooms over the arches of the North Gate, which is the only one of the town's original fortifications to survive - though most of it was rebuilt in the 18th century. The **Costume and Childhood Museum** incorporates a

costume gallery, a complete Victorian nursery, toys from Victorian times to the 1960s and a collection of over 700 rare minerals from all over the world. It's a really charming place that appeals to all ages, and its popularity is a great tribute to the four generations of a local family who have assembled the childhood collections. The Civil War caused great damage in Bridgnorth and the lovely Town Hall is one of many timber-framed buildings put up just after the war. The sandstone arched base was completed in 1652 and later covered in brick; Charles II took a great interest in it and, when improvements were needed, he made funds available from his own purse and from a collection he ordered be made in every parish in England.

St Mary's Street is one of the three streets off High Street that formed the planned new town of the 12th century. Many of the

Bishop Percy's House, Bridgnorth

THAT'S NICE!

High Street (Posterngate), Bridgnorth,
Shropshire WV16 4BX
Tel: 01746 768020
e-mail: Michael.southall@btinternet.com

'Timeless Interiors, Stylish Accessories, Inspirational Gifts'
Owners Wendy and Mick pride themselves on seeking out the
very best in home furnishings for their clientele to create the
Country Living look in their homes and gardens. In **That's Nice!**
their attractive premises on Bridgnorth High Street, Mick and
Wendy assemble an ever-changing array of lovely things for the
person and home in a variety of styles ranging from fabulously
elegant to shabby chic! That's Nice! stocks bags and baskets,
jewellery, clocks, frames, mirrors, lamps and gorgeous
chandeliers, garden accessories

and furniture from armoires to lamp tables. That's Nice! stock is
ever changing to keep the shop looking fresh with several
exclusive one-off ranges and if a piece is not in stock- just ask! -
And Mick and Wendy will do their best to find it. They also
specialise in restoring and revamping vintage furniture giving it a
fresh, up-to-date look whilst offfering a quality service.

That's Nice! is open seven days a week.

houses, brick faced over timber frames, have
side passages leading to gardens that
contained workshops and cottages. **Bishop
Percy's House** is the oldest house standing
in the town, a handsome building dating
from 1580 and one of the very few timber-
framed houses to survive the fire of 1646. It
is named after the Reverend Dr Percy, who
was born in the house in 1729 and became
Bishop of Dromore.

For many visitors the most irresistible
attraction in Bridgnorth is the **Castle Hill
Cliff Railway**, a funicular railway built in
1892 to link the two parts of the town. The
track is 200 feet long and rises over 100 feet
up the cliff. Originally it operated on a water
balance system, but it was converted in 1943
to electrically driven colliery-type winding
gear. John Betjeman likened a ride on this
lovely little railway to a journey up to heaven.

For all but the very energetic it might feel like
heaven compared to the alternative ways of
getting from Low to High Town - seven sets
of steps or Cartway, a meandering street that's
steeped in history.

The bridge across the Severn, rebuilt in
1823 to a Thomas Telford design, has a clock
tower with an inscription commemorating the
building, in 1808, of the first steam
locomotive at John Hazeldine's foundry a
short distance upstream.

Talking of steam locomotives, Bridgnorth is
the northern terminus of the wonderful
Severn Valley Railway (see under Bewdley in
Worcestershire).

One of the stations on this marvellous
railway is at Highley, where a popular
attraction is the Visitor and Education centre
in the Engine Shed, with an exhibition and a
large display of steam locomotives.

Dudmaston, Bridgnorth

rhyme wood sculptures (01299 841255). The longest bridleway in Shropshire, and one of the longest in the country, passes close by. This is the **Jack Mytton Way**, named after a 19th-century hard-living squire and sometime MP for Shrewsbury. It runs all the way to Llanfair Waterdine in the Teme Valley, a distance of some 70 miles.

Around Bridgnorth

QUATT
4 miles SE of Bridgnorth on the A442

🏛 Dudmaston Hall

Quatt is the location of the National Trust's **Dudmaston Hall**, a late 17th-century house with fine furniture, Dutch flower paintings, modern pictures and sculptures (Hepworth, Moore), botanical art, watercolours, family and natural history and colourful gardens with lakeside walks, a rockery and a wooded valley. The church at Quatt contains some splendid monuments and memorials to the Wolryche family.

BILLINGSLEY
5 miles S of Bridgnorth on the B4363

🐦 Rays Farm Country Matters 🎋 Jack Mytton Way

In eight acres of ancient woodland in a beautiful valley near the village, **Rays Farm Country Matters** is home to many farm animals including Highland cattle, deer, reindeer, donkeys, goats, llamas, alpacas, pigs, ferrets, red squirrels, and more than 50 owls. Other features include a bird viewing hide, myth and magic woodcarvings and nursery

MUCH WENLOCK
8 miles NW of Bridgnorth on the A458

🏛 Guildhall 🏛 Holy Trinity Church
🏛 Museum 🏛 Priory of St Milburga

The narrow streets of Much Wenlock are a delight to explore, and among the mellow buildings are some absolute gems. The **Guildhall** is one of them, dating from 1540 and added to in 1577 with a chamber over the stone medieval prison. The Guildhall was until recently used as a courtroom, and the Town Council still meets here once a month. The **Museum** is housed in the former market hall, which was built in 1878. There are interesting displays on the geology, flora and fauna of Wenlock Edge (see below), as well as local history items including Dr William Penny Brookes' Olympian Games. A forerunner of, and inspiration for, the modern Olympic Games, they are an annual event in the town every year, having started in 1850. The good doctor lived in Wilmore Street.

Holy Trinity Church, "mother" to ten churches in villages around Much Wenlock, is a dominant presence in the town, though less conspicuous than it was until 1931 when its spire was removed. Its nave and chancel are Norman, the porch 13th century. The Parish

IPPIKIN GALLERY & SHOP

59 High Street, Much Wenlock, Shropshire TF13 6AE
Tel: 01952 728371
e-mail: ippikin@googlemail.com website: www.ippikin.com

Ippikin was a highway man who robbed passing travellers along the Wenlock Edge. It is said that Ippikin hid his stolen treasure under a rock on the Wenlock Edge. On a particularly stormy night Ippikin was standing on his rock marvelling at his riches when an untimely lightning bolt struck him down. The legend of Ippikin and his treasures lives on and Ippikins rock is a popular place to visit along the Wenlock edge just out of the town of Much Wenlock.

Inside the town however a different type of treasure trove exists. **Ippikin Wool Gallery** is a shop that is abundant with bright buttons, hand dyed yarns, contemporary knits, locally handmade jewellery, rag rugs, funky ribbons, fair trade products and embroidery threads. Lesley butler started Ippikin wool shop with help from her sister Belinda Logan in 2006. Now three years on Lesley continues to run Ippikin and it has now become a family affair with help from friends too. The helpers range from Lesley's mother, Janet Jones, who contributes with the knitted garments to local artist with their own style of art including free formed knits and handmade jewellery. Ippikin is a welcoming shop and offers friendly advice. Workshops are available throughout the year classes range from knitting for beginners to freeform knitting and crocheting.

Ippikin is open from 10 to 4 Monday to Saturday.

THE WENLOCK COLLECTION

53 High Street, Much Wenlock, Shropshire TF13 6AE
Tel: 01952 728285
e-mail: margaret@wenlockcollection.co.uk
website: www.wenlockcollection.co.uk

Set in a splendid medieval building in the charming market town of Much Wenlock, the **Wenlock Collection** is a must for both collectors and those who enjoy items of beauty. There is a wealth of wonderful Moorcraft Pottery. Moorcroft pottery has been enriching homes since 1912 and is still a world leader in art pottery. There is a beautiful collection of Elliot Hall enamels in small limited editions each one free hand painted by the artist, alongside Bronte porcelain, Tula handbags and a kitchen room full of useful and decorative items ideal for gift giving. Items from the short-lived but much sought after Cobridge Pottery are featured, along with many pieces from the Spode factory in Stoke. Many of the goods are displayed on handmade furniture by professional craftsmen (these pieces can be customised for individual clients) and also there is an extensive collection of reproduction chairs. The owner Margaret Himsworth will give you a warm welcome and can talk to you about all of the products if you so wish.

twenty twenty

3-4 High Street, Much Wenlock, Shropshire TF13 6AA
Tel: 01952 727952 e-mail: info@twenty-twenty.co.uk
website: www.twenty-twenty.co.uk

Twenty Twenty is a contemporary art and craft gallery with an
excellent reputation. The gallery is based in the delightful and historic
town of Much Wenlock, on Wenlock Edge. Owner Mary Elliott has
selected some of the best artists and makers in all disciplines from all
over the British Isles; many are from Shropshire and the surrounding
counties.

Paintings & Prints:

Original members of the Brotherhood of Ruralists, such as David
Inshaw often exhibit at the gallery and Annie Ovenden is represented
by Twenty Twenty so there is a good selection of her paintings,
drawings and prints available. Sue Campion R.BA., a great colourist
and well known for her Shropshire landscapes is a regular exhibitor.
Artists linked with the South and South West such as Alfred
Stockham R.W.A and Margot Bandola, frequently have original
paintings on show. Local artists with big reputations, include Bob
Bates, Peter Tarrant, Betsy Smith, Norman Lamputt and Frans
Wesselman.

Jewellery and Silverware:

Twenty Twenty has gradually built a fine collection of British jewellers
many of whom are part of the permanent display. Catherine Hills
produces beautiful gold and silver pieces, inspired by natural forms;
silversmiths Louise Chesshire and Victoria Delany make silver bowls
and spoons as well as original hand-made jewellery.

Ceramics and Glass:

From whimsical, hand-modelled work by Helen Kemp and Janet Creed,
to painterly, sculptural forms by Dennis Farrell and decorative but
practical pots by Elspeth Soper. Wonderful stained glass by Tamsin
Abbott and hand-blown glasses by Tim Casey make great gifts.

Furniture:

Hugh Elliott designs beautiful occasional tables which are made in
Shropshire in solid oak, each piece is signed and numbered and
stamped with his Curlew brand.

Twenty Twenty has regular exhibitions featuring new artists and old
favourites, by joining the mailing list you can be invited to private
views and get first choice of new work available. You can also check
out the website to see what is on.

Twenty Twenty is part of the Arts Council –run Own Art scheme to
make art ownership accessible to a wider selection of the public.

The gallery is open Tues-Sat from 10am to 5pm.

TWICKEL HOUSE

23 Barrow Street, Much Wenlock,
Shropshire TF13 6EN
Tel: 01952 727165
e-mail: jemima@twickel-dental.co.uk

Twickel House is one in a million and whatever you choose from here you will come away with a one in a million piece. This unique shop is situated just off the high street in the beautiful Shropshire town of Much Wenlock.

Owner Jemima Willis has much experience in interior design and fashion and left the urban jungle of London for this olde English town where she has created a truly individual shop where everyone can find the perfect item. She stocks a massive range of products from women's designer clothes, jewellery, furniture, beautiful home accessories, mirrors, greeting cards and gift ware. Inside the doors you will find hundreds of trinkets, each individual with many items being handmade and one of a kind. You will find anything from funky felt baby booties for your kids to elegant light fixtures, beautiful carpentry or extraordinary textile tea cosies to make your home as individual as you are. Jemima works tirelessly to ensure that the stock is constantly changing meaning that you won't find anything like the stuff from Twickel House anywhere in Shropshire. The shop spans over two floors full to bursting of gift ideas and trinkets. There is plenty of parking just behind the high street.

A contented potter in Twickel House will surely leave you happy with your purchase and ready for an afternoons happy browsing in Much Wenlock. The small town itself is full of quaint little shops catering for both young and old, collectors of all sorts, readers, gardeners and anyone who just likes to window shop. Much Wenlock is a medieval town that offers a pleasant trip down memory lane with plenty of historic attractions with some areas dating back to 680 AD and a range of medieval, Victorian and Georgian architecture all crafted from locally quarried limestone, timber frames and bricks. It is a fantastic place to sit back and watch the world go by underneath the Jubilee Clock tower on the main high street and Twickel House is a fantastic addition to it, adding a funky and individual twist to what is one of the most character filled towns in Shropshire.

THE RAVEN HOTEL

Barrow Street, Much Wenlock,
Shropshire TF13 6EN
Tel: 01952 727251 Fax: 01952 728416
e-mail: enquiry@ravenhotel.com
website: www.ravenhotel.com

The Raven Hotel is at its heart a 17th century coaching inn, built round a courtyard and incorporating parts of several older buildings. Always the hub of the local community, it has evolved with the town of Much Wenlock – its architecture, its people, its spirit – and has added period charm, genuine warmth and high levels of service, hospitality, comfort and cuisine for today's discerning guests. Its lofty and hard-earned reputation is safe in the hands of the present owners, management and staff, and return bookings and comments in the visitors book are testimony to the quality of the product offered at The Raven.

The guest accommodation comprises 20 superbly appointed bedrooms, each individual in style, décor and furnishings, in harmony with the various architectural features of the building. All the rooms have sparkling en suites with powerful showers, TV with satellite channels, internet connection and tea/coffee tray. All the bedrooms are highly desirable, and among the most sought after are No 2, a romantic four-poster room, and No 15, a galleried suite with its bedroom area overlooking the roomy living space.

Though not quite old enough to have witnessed Henry the Eighth's dissolution of Wenlock Priory, The Raven has seen a number of royal visitors down the years and has also been closely connected with the Much Wenlock Olympics and the birth of the modern Olympic Games. The man responsible for the Much Wenlock Olympics was William Penny Brookes, and news of the venture brought none other than Baron de Coubertin to the town and the hotel. Guests can see artefacts from those years, including original letters from the Baron to Brookes. And in 1994 the connection was again affirmed by a visit from Juan Antonio Samaranch, the then President of the International Committee, who laid a wreath at Brookes' grave.

Food is a vital part of The Raven's success, with a reputation for fine dining based on the talented team in the kitchen who source fresh seasonal ingredients from the top producers/suppliers in the region. Menus combine the best traditional and contemporary elements of British and European cooking, with inspirational menus matched by discreet, attentive service and well-chosen wines.

The restaurant is located in what is thought to be the town's original 15th century almshouses. The Raven is a popular venue for functions, parties and social events and also offers an outside catering service, bringing its culinary and presentation skills to the client's chosen location with anything from a cold buffet to a seven-course banquet.

MEMORIES ANTIQUES & COLLECTABLES

1 Wilmore Street, Much Wenlock,
Shropshire TF13 6HR
Tel: 01952 728368

Mary Nicklin was born in Much Wenlock and ran an antiques business in the Malthouse before setting up **Memories Antiques & Collectables** here in Wilmore Street. Much of the stock comes from the region, and virtually all from the UK. Mary has a keen eye for products to enhance the home – some pieces pretty, some unusual, some nostalgic, some quirky, all interesting – and since Mary is constantly on the look out for interesting pieces you never know what you'll find from one visit to the next: whether it's a napkin ring or a substantial piece of furniture it will always be an item of interest and quality. The majority of what's on display comes from out of production lines. Porcelain is something of a speciality, and Mary always has a variety of Coalport on show. Furniture ranges from occasional tables to bookcases, dining chairs and dressers. In the two cabinets of silver you might find anything from spoons, knives and salvers to lighters, compacts and hair brushes. Other items run from tea sets and display plates to ceramics, glassware, lighting, pictures and prints, along with costume and some silver jewellery. Mary is always interested in buying interesting antiques and she can also arrange house clearances. This browser's delight is open from 10 to 5 Monday to Saturday and from 2 to 4 on Sunday.

Registers date from 1558.

The sight that simply must not be missed on a visit here is the ruined **Priory of St Milburga**, maintained by English Heritage. The Priory was originally a nunnery, founded in the 7th century by a Mercian princess and destroyed some 200 years later. Leofric, Earl of Mercia and husband of Lady Godiva, re-established it as a priory in 1050, and the current spectacular ruins belong to the Cluniac Priory rebuilt in the 12th and 13th centuries. The best remaining features are the wall carvings in the cloisters and the Norman interlacing of arches and doorways in the Chapter House. The Prior's Lodge, dating from about 1500, is particularly impressive with its steeply pitched roof of sandstone tiles above the rows of mullioned windows. Away from the main site is St Milburga's Well, whose waters are reputed to cure eye diseases.

WENLOCK EDGE

7 miles W of Bridgnorth on the B4371

Wenlock Edge is one of the most spectacular and impressive landmarks in the whole county, a limestone escarpment dating back 400 million years and a paradise for naturalists and lovers of the outdoors. It runs for 15 miles all the way down to Craven Arms. For centuries its quarries have produced the stone used in many of the local buildings; it was also a source of lime for agricultural fertiliser and much went into the blast furnaces that fired the Industrial Revolution.

EARDINGTON

2 miles SW of Bridgnorth on the B4555

🏛 Daniel's Mill

Eardington is a southern suburb of Bridgnorth where, a mile out of town on the

🏚 historic building   🏛 museum   🏛 historic site   🏞 scenic attraction   🌿 flora and fauna

B4555, stands **Daniel's Mill**, a picturesque working watermill powered by an enormous (38ft) wheel. Family-owned for 200 years, the mill still produces flour.

MORVILLE
2 miles W of Bridgnorth on the A458

🏠 Morville Hall   🌿 Dower House Garden

Morville Hall, 16th century with 18th-century additions, stands at the junction of the A458 and B4368. Within its grounds, the **Dower House Garden** is a one-and-a-half acre site designed by Dr Katherine Swift and begun in 1989. Its aim is to tell the history of English gardens in a sequence of separate gardens designed in the style of different historical periods. Particular attention is given to the use of authentic plants and construction techniques. Old roses are a speciality of the garden. Parking is available in the churchyard of the fine Norman Church of St Gregory, which is also well worth a visit.

Telford

🏛 Steam Railway Trust

🌿 Hoo Farm Animal Kingdom   🌿 Wonderland

Telford is a sprawling modern development that absorbed several existing towns in the region of the Shropshire coalfield. Wellington, Hadley, Ketley, Oakengates, Madeley and Dawley were among the towns to be incorporated, and the name chosen in the 1960s commemorates Thomas Telford, whose influence can be seen all over the county. Thomas Telford was a Scot, born in Eskdale in 1757, who came to Shrewsbury in 1786. Appointed County Surveyor, he quickly got to work on such enterprises as Shrewsbury jail, Bridgnorth, a host of bridges, an aqueduct, canals and the Holyhead Road. He designed

distinctive milestones for the road, one of which is now at the Blists Hill Museum. Telford's many ambitious developments include the huge (450 acres) Town Park, with nature trails, sports fields, lakes, gardens and play areas. **Wonderland** is an enchanting and enchanted woodland whose fairytale attractions include Snow White's Cottage, the Three Little Pigs and the Wrekin Giant. On the northern outskirts, at Preston-on-the-Weald Moor, is **Hoo Farm Animal Kingdom**, which numbers among its inhabitants ostriches, chipmunks, deer and llamas. Events include lamb feeding, milking and the famous sheep steeplechase.

Telford Steam Railway Trust keeps a number of vintage locomotives, some of them ex-Great Western Railway, in working condition at the old shed and yard at Horsehay. It operates over a section of the old Wellington & Severn Junction Railway.

Around Telford

OAKENGATES
1 mile NE of Telford on the A5

Oakengates, on the eastern edge of the metropolis of Telford, is the birthplace of Sir Gordon Richards, perhaps the greatest jockey this country has ever produced. His father was a miner and the young Gordon first learned to ride on pit ponies. When he retired from the saddle, he had ridden 4,872 winners and was champion jockey for 20 years. Frankie Dettori and Kieren Fallon have a long way to go!

SHIFNAL
3 miles E of Telford on the A464

🏛 RAF Museum

Once a staging post on the Holyhead Road,

Shifnal has an unexpectedly large church with a Norman chancel arch, a 14th-century east window, carved Italian pulpit and an Italian reredos.

Old Church Ruins, Tong

On the A41, at Cosford near Shifnal, the **RAF Museum** is home to an important collection of aircraft, from the little Red Arrows Folland Gnat to Hurricanes, Spitfires, Messerschmitts and the mighty Belfast, along with aero engines and missiles from all over the world. Attractions include a Fun 'n' Flight Centre and the National Cold War Exhibition, reflecting the social, cultural and political history of the Cold War era, c1947 to 1991. The museum also features Britain's three famous V Bombers, the Vulcan, Victor and Valiant, and others suspended as if in flight, including a Dakota, Canberra, Meteor and Lightning.

NEWPORT
6 miles NE of Telford off the A41

A handsome town which lost many of its buildings in a fire in 1665. Most of the buildings on the broad main street are Georgian or early Victorian. There's plenty to keep the visitor active in the area, including the Lilleshall National Sports Centre and the ruins of Lilleshall Abbey, the extensive and evocative remains of an Augustinian abbey.

TONG
5 miles E of Telford on the A41

🏛 Church of St Bartholomew

Tong is an attractive village that once had a castle, founded, according to legend, by the wizard Merlin. Where was he when the castle

was blown up in 1954? The Vernons and the Durants were the Lords of the Manor in Tong for many years and they are commemorated in the 15th-century **Church of St Bartholomew**. The Vernons were a particularly distinguished lot: one was a Speaker of the House of Commons and another was Lord High Constable to Henry V. In the Golden Chapel, which has a superb gilded, fan-vaulted ceiling, there is a bust of Arthur Vernon, who was a don at Cambridge University. Venetia Stanley, descended from the Vernons and the Earls of Derby, was a famed beauty who was lauded by poets and artists. She counted Ben Jonson, Van Dyck and the Earl of Dorset among her lovers, but in 1625 she made the unfortunate move of marrying Sir Kenelm Digby, whose father had been executed for his part in the Gunpowder Plot. She died tragically young, some say at the hands of her jealous husband.

BOSCOBEL
7 miles E of Telford off the A41

🏛 Boscobel House

After Charles II was defeated by the Roundheads at the Battle of Worcester in 1651, he fled for his life and was advised to seek refuge in a remote hunting lodge called **Boscobel House**, already known as a safe house for royals on the run. By day the King hid in the branches of an old oak tree, while at night he would creep into the house and hide in secret rooms with one of his trusty officers. He eventually escaped and nine years later was restored to the throne. The house has changed considerably since Charles's time, but it's still full of atmosphere and interest, with an exhibition giving a vivid account of the King's adventures. Every visitor naturally wants to see the famous oak in which he hid, but it is no longer standing, destroyed by souvenir-hunting loyalists. Today there stands a descendant of the original, itself now more than 300 years old.

BROSELEY
5 miles S of Telford on the B4373

🏠 Benthall Hall 🏠 Pipe Museum

Broseley, which stands on the south side of the River Severn opposite Ironbridge, was the headquarters of John Wilkinson, the great ironmaster and head of a giant empire. He built a coke smelting ironworks here and it was while he was living at The Lawns in Broseley that he commissioned the Shrewsbury architect Thomas Pritchard to design the world's first iron bridge. He also launched the first iron boat, The Trial, on the Severn in 1787 and even designed his own iron coffin. His name lives on in Wilkinson Sword razor blades. Just north of Broseley, off the B4375, on a plateau above a gorge, stands **Benthall Hall**, a 16th-century building in the care of the National Trust, with mullioned windows and a magnificent interior with a carved oak staircase, elaborate plaster ceilings and the Benthall family's collection of furniture, ceramics and paintings. There's a carefully restored plantsman's garden and, in

the grounds, an interesting Restoration church. Broseley was the centre of an ancient local industry in clay products and tobacco pipes, and the **Broseley Pipeworks Clay Tobacco Pipe Museum** in the Hall, untouched for more than 40 years, is a time-capsule factory where the famous Broseley Churchwarden pipes were made for 350 years until 1957. Tools lie on benches where they were left, clay is stacked in the yard ready for use, and saggars lean against each other waiting to be filled.

IRONBRIDGE AND IRONBRIDGE GORGE
4 miles SW of Telford on the B4373

🏠 Museums 🏛 Buildwas Abbey

🏛 Bridge 🏛 Tar Tunnel

This is it, the town at the centre of Ironbridge Gorge, an area that has been designated a World Heritage Centre by UNESCO, ranking alongside the likes of the Pyramids, the Grand Canyon and the Taj Mahal. It was the first British site on the list. The **Bridge** itself is a pedestrian right of way with a museum in the tollgate at one end, and the series of museums that spread along the banks of the Severn in Ironbridge, Coalbrookdale, Coalport and Jackfield pay tribute to the momentous events that took place here 250 years ago. The first iron wheels were made here, and also the first iron rails and the first steam railway locomotive.

The **Museum of the Gorge** offers the ideal introduction to the attractions, filled with stories of how industry changed the Gorge. The **Museum of Iron** in Coalbrookdale in the most historic part of the valley shows the whole story of how the Darby family revolutionised early iron making. The Great Warehouse is full of surprises, including classical statues, garden ornaments, magnificent furniture and curious objects, all made of iron. Next to it is the original furnace used by Abraham Darby when he first smelted iron with coke; a little way north are Rosehill House, one of the homes of the Darby family, and Dale House, where Abraham Darby's grandson made his plans for the iron bridge.

Also in Coalbrookdale is **Enginuity**, where visitors can become apprentice engineers for the day, free to experiment with all the gadgets

The Jackfield Tile Museum

Ironbridge Gorge, Shropshire TF8 7LJ
Tel: 01952 435900
e-mail: marketing@ironbridge.org.uk
website: www.ironbridge.org.uk

The Jackfield Tile Museum in Shropshire's Ironbridge Gorge has re-opened its doors after major restoration with a spectacular new suite of tiled period room settings which capture the extravagance and beauty of Victorian 'tile mania' – a great source of inspiration for room designers today.

Also on offer are galleries filled with thousands of sumptuous tiles, hands-on workshops where families can decorate their own tiles and visits to the Craven Dunnill tile factory alongside. Here skilled crafts people can be seen making intricately designed tiles by hand for private homes, historic houses and public spaces.

For anyone who has broken or damaged a special tile, the Craven Dunnill team offer a custom service to restore or replicate the design to bring the display back to its original splendour – a great bonus for today's interior designers as well as those restoring historic buildings. Alternatively visitors can create their own designs, or order from the extensive selection of British hand-made tiles displayed in the museum shop.

Jackfield Tile Museum is housed in the original Craven Dunnill factory built in the 1870s. Visitors can view five themed galleries starting with the history of tile making in the Severn Valley followed by the restored 19th century, gas-lit Tile Trade Showroom. This large vaulted room would have been used by commercial buyers and architects to select ranges of tiles for retailing and decoration prior to the production of trade catalogues. Other galleries display examples of different decorative styles and art pottery as well as explain the various tile making processes, such as encaustic production, tube lining, embossed and hand painted designs.

The museums are open seven days a week from 10am until 5pm; activities and workshops vary day-to-day, for further information, contact the Ironbridge Tourist Information Centre visit www.ironbridge.org.uk.

🏛 historic building   🏛 museum   🏛 historic site   🌿 scenic attraction   🌱 flora and fauna

and acquire the know-how involved in producing everyday items. You can find out whether you can pull a real locomotive; test your speed and accuracy against a robot; control water to generate electricity or work as a team to make the Crazy Boiler blow its top!

The Iron Bridge

The **Old Police Station**, owned by John and Lynn Youngman, is one of Ironbridge's less well-known museums, but one that is well worth a visit, and for a variety of reasons. The Victorian station and its cells have been painstakingly restored to provide a fascinating insight into the judicial and prison systems at the turn of the century. After it closed for duty in 1964, it was used for various purposes before becoming home to police memorabilia from handcuffs and truncheons to uniforms and documents. The cells are particularly arresting – Cell 4 was the birching centre for Shropshire, and a birching stool still stands in the middle of the room. In the upper-floor theatre, using the unique backdrop of the former station and courthouse, Courthouse Productions puts on a wide variety of corporate and personal events, from plays with a buffet supper to Courtroom trial re-enactments; from Victorian Music Halls to jazz and other musical events. Also on the premises is a tearoom where home baking, traditional afternoon teas and a Victorian buffet are among the offerings. Weddings are catered for at the station, and for an eve-of-wedding

night with a difference, the groom and best man can spend a night in the cells after the evening's celebrations, then wake up to a healthy breakfast before being delivered in style to the church! Also to be found in the Police Station is the Left Centre, which holds a vast stock of knives, scissors, kitchen tools and writing aids for left-handers, plus anti-clockwise clocks and "the best of ambidextrous".

Also at Coalbrookdale is the **Ironbridge Open Air Museum of Steel Sculpture**, a collection of 60 modern steel sculptures of all shapes and sizes set in 10 acres of beautiful countryside.

The **Jackfield Tile Museum** (see panel opposite), on the south bank, stands on the site of a world centre of the tile-making industry. The museum houses a fine collection of wall and floor tiles from Victorian times to the 1950s. Demonstrations of traditional tile-making take place regularly, and visitors can have a go in one of the hands-on workshops. Back across a footbridge, the Coalport China Museum has marvellous displays of two centuries of porcelain. The National Collections of Coalport and Coughley China are displayed in the original riverside buildings in which many of the pieces were made. Coalport was once one of the country's largest manufacturers of porcelain, starting life here but moving its factory to Stoke in the 1920s. Nearby is the extraordinary **Tar Tunnel** with its pools of natural bitumen. It was a popular attraction for tourists in the 18th century, and it remains one of the most interesting geological phenomena in Britain. The tunnel was started in 1786, under the direction of ironmaster William Reynolds, who intended that it should be used for a canal to reach the shafts to the coal seams three quarters of a

mile away on Blists Hill. After they had driven the tunnel about 300 yards the miners struck a spring of natural bitumen. Reynolds immediately recognised the importance of the discovery and sent samples of the bitumen to eminent scientists, who declared that the properties of the bitumen were superior to those of tar made of coal. The tunnel was almost forgotten over the years, but in 1965 the Shropshire Mining Club persuaded the owner of the village shop in Coalport to let them explore the darkness that lay beyond a door opening from his cellar. They rediscovered the Tar Tunnel, but it was another 18 years before visitors were allowed access to a short stretch.

At **Blists Hill Victorian Town** visitors can experience the atmosphere and way of life of a working Victorian community; there's a

THE GOLDEN BALL INN

Newbridge Road, Ironbridge, Shropshire TF8 7BA
Tel: 01952 432179 Fax: 01952 433123
e-mail: goldenballinn@yahoo.co.uk
website: www.goldenballinn.com

The **Golden Ball** is an independently owned hostelry in the unique World Heritage Site of Ironbridge Gorge. These are the oldest licensed premises in the area and started brewing ale some 50 years before the Iron Bridge was built. Many original features survive from brewhouse days, including the water pump, the fireplace where the 'mash' was prepared and beams and floors in the gaggle of little rooms. The inn is equally popular with the local community and with the visitors who flock throughout the year to this extraordinary hub of England's industrial heritage.

The bar is open all day for a fine selection of real ales and other draught and bottle beers and cider, and there's an extensive choice of wines to accompany the excellent food served lunchtime and evening and all day Saturday and Sunday. Prime seasonal produce, much of it local, is prominent on the daily changing blackboard menus of dishes such as rack of Welsh Borders lamb, Wenlock Edge Farm faggots with onion gravy, steaks, beer-battered cod and gammon & leek pie. When the sun shines, food and drink can be enjoyed out in the courtyard and garden. Ironbridge is much more than a quick tourist stop, and the Golden Ball is the perfect base for exploring the numerous museums and other fascinating sites. The inn has four well-equipped en suite bedrooms for B&B guests – a double, a twin, a four-poster room and a twin with a separate sitting area.

🏛 historic building   🏛 museum   🏛 historic site   🍃 scenic attraction   🌿 flora and fauna

shop, domestic animals, a squatter's cottage, a schoolhouse and a bank that distributes its own tender.

Passport tickets are available to admit holders to all the Ironbridge Gorge Museums. Call 01952 884391 for details.

Two miles west of Ironbridge, on a minor road off the B4378, stands **Buildwas Abbey**, one of the finest ruined abbeys in England. After 850 years the church is virtually complete except for the roof, and the setting, in a meadow by the Severn against a backdrop of wooded grounds, is both peaceful and evocative. The place is full of things of interest, like the lead-glazed tiles depicting animals and birds in the Chapter House. Just north of Ironbridge stands the village of Cawley, birthplace in 1848 of Matthew Webb, the first man to swim the English Channel. This feat earned him great fame, but another adventure cost him his life: he died in 1883 attempting to swim through the whirlpools at the foot of Niagara Falls.

WELLINGTON
2 miles NW of Telford on the A442

🏠 Sunnycroft 🏠 Aqueduct 🌱 The Wrekin

Wellington is part of the new town of Telford but still retains much of its Victorian look. The Church of All Saints is the work of George Steuart, better known for St Chad's in Shrewsbury. Among the town's attractions is the National Trust's **Sunnycroft**, a late-Victorian gentleman's suburban villa typical of the kind that were built for wealthy business and professional men. The house and its contents are largely unaltered, and in the grounds are pig sties, stables, a kitchen garden, orchards, a conservatory and a Wellingtonia avenue. Call 01952 242884 for details of opening times and guided tours.

A couple of miles north of Wellington, at Longdon-on-Tern, stands the **Aqueduct** built by Thomas Telford as a pilot for other, better-known constructions.

South of here, on the other side of the M54/A5, is one of the best-known landmarks in the whole country. **The Wrekin**, which reaches up over 1,300 feet, is the site of a prehistoric hill fort, visible for many miles around and accessible by a network of public footpaths. The reward for reaching the top is a beautiful panoramic view stretching to the neighbouring counties. In Roman times it was used as a base by the Cornovii tribe before they were moved to Viroconium. Shropshire folklore tells us that it was put there by a malicious giant who was carrying a huge load of earth to dam the Severn and flood Shrewsbury, simply because he didn't like the people. The giant met a cobbler who persuaded him against this evil act, whereupon the giant dropped the load he was carrying – and that's The Wrekin.

WROXETER
7 miles W of Telford on the B4380

🏠 Viroconium

In the village of Wroxeter, beside the B4380, is one of the most important Roman sites ever brought to light. **Viroconium** was the first town to be established by the Romans in this part of the country and developed into the fourth largest city in Roman Britain with more than 5,000 soldiers and civilians living here. It's an absolutely fascinating place, where the highlights include extensive remains of a 2nd-century bathhouse complex. Some of the major excavated items are on display here, many more at Rowley's House Museum in Shrewsbury. Also in the village is Wroxeter Roman Vineyard where there is not only a vineyard producing both red and white wines, but also additional attractions in the shape of rare-breed animals and a lavender field.

ATCHAM
7 miles W of Telford on the B4380

🏛 Attingham Park   🌱 Attingham Home Farm

The village stands at the point where the Severn is crossed by the Roman road. The splendid old seven-arched bridge is now redundant, having been replaced by a new neighbour some time ago, but is still in situ. The old bridge was designed by John Gwynne, who was a founder member of the Royal Academy and the designer of Magdalen Bridge in Oxford.

Attingham Park, run by the National Trust, is perhaps the finest house in Shropshire, a splendid neo-classical mansion set in 250 delightful acres. Designed by

George Steuart for the 1st Lord Berwick, and altered by Nash, it has the grandest of Regency interiors, ambassadorial silver, Regency furniture and Grand Tour paintings hanging in the John Nash gallery. The tearoom is lined with paintings of the 5th Lord Berwick's Herefordshire cattle. An ongoing restoration project continues in 2010 with the Dining Room and Picture Gallery. Humphry Repton landscaped the park where visitors can enjoy woodland and riverside walks and see the deer.

From the park, visitors can take a trailer ride to **Attingham Home Farm**, the original home farm of the grand house. It comprises buildings dating mainly from about 1800 and the yard retains the atmosphere of a traditional Shropshire farm. Many breeds of farm animals are represented: Oxford, Sandy, Iron Age, Vietnamese pot-bellied pigs; Jacob,

---

WHEAT HALL

Dorrington, nr Shrewsbury, Shropshire SY5 7NF
Tel: 01743 718311
e-mail: lucy@wheathall.co.uk
website: www.wheathall.co.uk

Lucy Hinds and her family welcome self-catering guests to a luxuriously appointed cottage in the grounds of **Wheat Hall**, their home in an Area of Outstanding Natural Beauty in the heart of Shropshire. A lot of time and thought went into the conversion of the Hall's former coach house, which combines a number of original features with a fresh contemporary feel. Two bedrooms with double or twin beds and an optional extra bed provide very comfortable accommodation for up to five guests. The cottage has an entrance hall, a semi-open-plan sitting room with TV and DVD player and a well-equipped kitchen with a modern dining table and six chairs.

There's ample on-site parking, cycle storage space and a small barbecue area, and guests can also use the family garden.

The cottage is an ideal place to relax and unwind, enjoying the views and meeting the owners' Dalmatians, horses and chickens. It's also an excellent base for a walking, cycling or touring holiday, with Shrewsbury and many historic and scenic attractions close by.

🏛 historic building   🏛 museum   🏛 historic site   🔷 scenic attraction   🌱 flora and fauna

Shetland and Ryeland sheep and Jerseys, Longhair, Dexter, Red Poll and British White cattle. The rabbit house is particularly popular with youngsters, and there are usually some orphaned lambs for children to bottle-feed. The farm makes its own ice cream from milk from the Jerseys – milking at 3.30pm.

Shrewsbury

🏠 Castle   🏠 Abbey   🏠 Lord's Hill Column

🏠 St Chad's Church   🏠 St Mary's Church

🚶 Quarry Park   🚶 Brother Cadfael Walk

🏛 Coleham Pumping Station   🏠 Bear Steps

🏛 Battlefield   🏛 Shropshire Regimental Museum

High the vanes of Shrewsbury gleam,
Islanded in Severn stream

So wrote AE Housman in *A Shropshire Lad* and the town is indeed almost an island,

caught in a wandering loop of the River Severn. It was on two hills within this protected site that the Saxon town developed. The Normans under Roger de Montgomery took over after the conquest, building the castle and the great Benedictine abbey. In the 15th and 16th centuries Shrewsbury prospered through the wool trade, and evidence of its affluence shows in the many 'Magpie' black and white timbered buildings that still line the streets. In Victorian times steam made Shrewsbury an important railway centre, while at the same time Charles Darwin, born and educated in the town, was rocking the world with his theories. Everywhere there is a sense of history, and the Museums do a particularly fine job of bringing the past to life, in terms of both human and natural history. Rowley's House is a glorious timber-framed building

---

CHATFORD HOUSE BED & BREAKFAST

Chatford, Bayston Hill, Shrewsbury,
Shropshire SY3 0AY
Tel: 01743 718301 / 07841990179
e-mail: b&b@chatfordhouse.co.uk
website: www.chatfordhouse.co.uk

Chatford House is a Grade II listed 17th century building, a place of charm and character on a small holding in a hamlet in beautiful Shropshire countryside five miles south of Shrewsbury. It's the home of Christine and Rupert Farmer, who have the warmest of welcomes for their guests – the hospitality starts with tea or coffee and home-made cake greeting arrivals in the sitting room or outside in the pretty country garden.

The guest accommodation comprises of three recently refurbished first-floor rooms, all decorated and furnished in a style that respects the origins and pedigree of the house. The Wrekin and The Lyth have super king-size/twin beds and en suite power showers, while the master bedroom, The Lawley, has a luxurious king-size brass bed and an oak-floored bathroom with power shower and corner bath. A delicious Aga cooked breakfast using locally sourced meats, eggs fresh from the hen run and fruit from the orchard, is a fine way to set out on a day's walking, cycling or sightseeing. Though quiet and secluded, Chatford House is an easy drive from Shrewsbury and the A5/A49 junction – take the A49 towards Hereford for two miles and turn right onto a country road leading you to Chatford. All guests must prebook before arrival.

🎬 stories and anecdotes   🐦 famous people   🎨 art and craft   🎭 entertainment and sport   🚶 walks

OCACIA

18 St Mary's Street, Shrewsbury SY1 1ED
Tel: 01743 365003

St Mary's Street is a busy lively shopping street just
north of Shrewsbury's High Street (A5191). It offers a
wide variety of retail outlets, from familiar chains to
interesting independent shops. Prominent among the
latter is **Ocacia**, a small shop filled with gift ideas and
nice things for the home.

Owner Jenny Carson welcomes browsers in the
three rooms of homeware and gifts, and the friendly,
relaxed atmosphere makes it a pleasure to look for
things to enhance the home. The constantly changing
stock covers ceramics that's both decorative and
practical, kitchenware, clocks, lamps, bags and baskets
and storage boxes, cushions and textiles, soaps and
toiletries, gift wrap and a wide selection of cards for all
occasions. There's also plenty to delight the kids,
including puppets, teddies, rag dolls and soft toys. Shop
hours are 9.30 to 5 Monday to Saturday.

Shoppers should find time to visit St Mary's Church
just across the road from Ocacia. This fine building is
noted for its tall spire and some magnificent stained glass and memorials.

of the late 16th century, with an adjoining
brick and stone mansion of 1618, the home
of William Rowley, 17th-century draper,
brewer and leading citizen. The collection of
pieces from Viroconium and spectacular
displays of costumes, natural history and
geology that were until the end of 2006
housed here will be shown in the Music Hall,
which already has the Tourist Information
Centre and is still being developed. Rowley's
house remains a building of some
significance. A short walk away is Clive
House, where Clive of India lived in 1762
while he was Mayor of the city. It is now a
private house.

Noted for its commanding position and
wonderful views, **Shrewsbury Castle** was
founded in 1083. That was when Roger de
Montgomery, a kinsman of William the
Conqueror, was granted Shrewsbury and

much of Shropshire as a reward for loyalty,
and the Castle was part of the Norman
attempt to control the lawless Welsh border.
By the time of Elizabeth I it had become a
virtual ruin, and of the original structure
only the gateway survives, along with one
side and two towers dating from the 13th
century. It last saw action in the Civil War
and was converted by Thomas Telford into a
private residence. It now houses the
Shropshire Regimental Museum, which
tells the story of the four Shropshire
regiments – the King's Shropshire Light
Infantry, the Shropshire Yeomanry Cavalry,
the Shropshire Royal Horse Artillery and the
4th Battalion King's Shropshire Light
Infantry TA. Among the many treasures on
display are colours bearing battle honours,
regimental silver and china, weapons and
medals, including three Victoria Crosses.

POPPY'S TEA ROOM & RESTAURANT AND POPPY'S SWEET SHOP

With its narrow streets and alleyways, historic buildings, churches and museums, Shrewsbury is a marvellous place to visit. Just of the High Street and close to Wyle Cop shopping street, Geoff and Anne Meredith run two real gems in this gem of a town – a traditional tea room offering exceptional value for money and a sweet shop like sweet shops used to be.

POPPY'S TEA ROOM & RESTAURANT

8 Milk Street, Shrewsbury SY1 1SZ
Tel: 01743 272709
e-mail: celticfoodbar@btopenworld.com

In an attractive Grade II listed building, **Poppy's Tea Room & Restaurant** is open from 8am to 5pm Monday to Saturday for a wide variety of freshly prepared, wholesome hot and cold snacks and meals. The menu includes all-day breakfasts, soups, salads, baguettes, panini, jacket potatoes, mid-morning specials, kids' dishes, cakes and cream teas. Drinks include Poppy's own brand teas and coffees, which can also be bought to take away in packets. Waiters and waitresses provide friendly, efficient service. Poppy's is a great place to take a break from work, shopping or sightseeing, but it's well worth a special visit in its own right, and for those who don't have time to spare many items on the menu can be ordered to take away. There are seats for 90 on two levels inside and 30 more in the pleasant courtyard that links the tea room to the sweet shop.

POPPY'S SWEET SHOP

18 Princess Street, Shrewsbury SY1 1LP
Tel: 01743 272709
e-mail: poppyssweet@btinternet.com

'The Way Things Used To Be'
Children will be in seventh heaven and grown-ups are certain to get a nostalgic kick from a visit to **Poppy's Sweet Shop**. The shelves are stacked with 100 or more different goodies, many of them in old-fashioned jars. There are sherbet lemons, acid drops, pear drops, jellies, Everton mints, fudge, aniseed balls and aniseed twist, licorice, flying saucers and dozens more, all guaranteed to bring back childhood memories to grown-ups and win over new generations of young sweet-lovers. The shop also stocks Penny sweets, sugar-free sweets and Shugbury's super ice cream made on a farm at Hurleston in Cheshire. Poppy's can supply wedding favours and party bags for boys and girls. The shop is open from 10am to 4.30pm Monday to Saturday.

THE GOLDEN CROSS HOTEL

14 Princess Street, Shrewsbury SY1 1LP
Tel: 01743 362507 Fax: 01743 362577
e-mail: info@goldencrosshotel.co.uk
website: www.goldencrosshotel.co.uk

The **Golden Cross Hotel** is the oldest licensed premises in Shrewsbury, with an unbroken history of hospitality that dates back to 1428. First recorded as the Golden Cross in 1780, it had been previously called the Sextry – it was the sacristy for St Chad's Church, where the church plate and vestments were kept. (The ruins of the old church stand across the road from the hotel; it collapsed in 1788 and was replaced by the present St Chad's, which stands nearby on a hilltop above the River Severn.) The hotel's fascinating history has seen it as an alehouse and tavern and, for a while in the 18th century, as a takeaway sausage shop. During the Civil War it was a regular meeting place for a group of Royalists from the town, and in 1796 a corrupt Tory politician used the place to ply the locals with food and drink in an attempt to buy their votes. For some years at the beginning of the 20th century it was owned by the Worthington Brewery and in 1962 it welcomed the former jump jockey Michael O'Dwyer as one of its most popular landlords. The tradition of hospitality is being maintained in fine style by Gareth and Theresa Reece, who have enhanced its standing as a hotel, a restaurant and a favourite place for locals and visitors to meet for a drink.

The guest accommodation under the eaves of this splendid old building comprises five very comfortable en suite rooms, each with its individual charm and character. Top of the range is a luxurious four-poster room. The convivial bar offers a full range of real ales, beers, ciders, wines, spirits, liqueurs and soft drinks, and eighty covers in the two dining areas provide a stylish setting for enjoying the excellent food prepared from local produce by a talented kitchen brigade. Typical dishes range from Cornish crab, smoked salmon & avocado torte with sesame tuille to British stalwarts like beer-battered haddock and slow-cooked belly of pork. Desserts such as orange crème brûlée with iced rhubarb parfait round things off in style, and the food is complemented by an eclectic wine list.

The restaurant is open lunchtime and evening seven days a a week. The hotel is also a popular venue for functions, parties and other celebrations. Shrewsbury is a wonderful place to visit, and with its sense of history, comfort, service and fine food the Golden Cross is the perfect base from which to explore the wealth of the town's historic buildings, churches and museums.

🏛 historic building   🏛 museum   🏛 historic site   🌣 scenic attraction   � flora and fauna

Begun in the same year as the castle, **Shrewsbury Abbey** survived the dissolution of the monasteries in 1540 and still serves as the parish church. The Abbey was founded, like the Castle, by Roger de Montgomery, on the site of a Saxon wooden church. In 1283 a parliament met in the Chapter House, the first national assembly in which the Commons were involved. The Abbey Church remains a place of worship, and in 1997 a stained glass window depicting St Benedict was dedicated to the memory of Edith Pargeter. Writing under the name of Ellis Peters, she created the character of Brother Cadfael, who lived at the Abbey and became one of the country's best-loved fictional characters when portrayed by Derek Jacobi in the television series.

To the east of the abbey, in front of the Shire Hall, rises the lofty **Lord Hill's Column**. Four magnificent sculpted lions guard the base of this, the largest Grecian Doric column in the world, which reaches a total height of 133 feet 6 inches. Inside, there's a spiral staircase that unfortunately is not open to the public for safety reasons. Completed in 1816, the column celebrates Rowland Hill who was born in Shropshire and achieved distinction as a soldier in the Napoleonic wars, notably at Waterloo. He was created a viscount and later succeeded the Duke of Wellington as commander-in-chief.

Shrewsbury has more than 30 churches and among the finest are **St Mary's** and **St Chad's**. St Mary's, the town's only complete medieval church, originated in the late Saxon period, but the earliest features of the present building are of the 12th century. The stained glass, monuments and fittings are quite out of the ordinary, and the spire has claims to being

OBERON

25 Wyle Cop, Shrewsbury SY1 1XB
Tel: 01743 246534
e-mail: oberon.shrewsbury@hotmail.co.uk

In the historic shopping street of Wyle Cop is one of Shrewsbury's best known fashion shops Oberon, which has been a firm fixture on the street for more than 25 years. Established by Stacey Hill the shop has become a destination of choice for hundreds of loyal customers drawn to it from throughout the country. It sells an eclectic mix of contemporary clothes which are individual and inspiring. There range includes the very popular Great Plains, Noa Noa, Nougat, and Sandwich and also lesser known but very individual brands such as Out of Xile and Masai. Oberon was one of the first shops in the country to discover the Spanish brand Desigual. As well as the beautiful clothing Oberon also stocks an impressive range of bags shoes and other accessories including the famous Radley bags and the Spanish shoe brand Unisa.

Oberon staff are always happy to help ladies choose something and are great with coming up with ideas for those who are a little unsure. Stacey is also passionate about jewellery and in the offshoot of Oberon immediately opposite she sells a selection of sterling silver and stone set jewellery from all corners of the globe including a superb range of amber. With beautiful pendants necklaces rings earrings you would be very hard pressed not to find a perfect gift or be tempted for yourself!

Oberon is open 6 days a week 9.30-5.30 also Sundays and late night Wednesdays during December.

📖 stories and anecdotes   🐦 famous people   ✐ art and craft   ♪ entertainment and sport   🚶 walks

HERITAGE HOUSE

18-19 Castle Street, Shrewsbury SY1 2AZ
Tel: 01743 231300
e-mail: info@heritagehouse.uk.com
website: www.heritagehouse.uk.com

'Welcome to the Home of 100% Solid Oak Furniture'

Only 100 yards from the Train Station, on the main thoroughfare into the centre of Shrewsbury, Heritage House is one the towns largest independent furniture retailers, specialising in 100% solid oak furniture, the vast majority of which is designed within the company.

Their extensive showroom covers 2 floors of one of the towns many period properties and showcases furniture designed for both contemporary and traditional environments.

Complimenting their wonderful furniture is a wealth of accessories, including, lighting, gifts and soft furnishings all inspired to transform a room into a space for living.

On hand are well informed, helpful staff, whose knowledge and enthusiasm will ensure a visit to Heritage House is as enjoyable as it possibly can be.

How to order:

Orders can be placed online, by phone or by visiting their showroom. Out of County delivery is available from as little as £25, ensuring almost everyone in the UK can benefit from the outstanding quality and value Heritage House offers.

the third highest in the land. One of the memorials is to Admiral Benbow, a national hero who died in 1702 and who is also remembered in innumerable pub signs.

St Chad's is the work of Attingham Hall's designer George Steuart, who was commissioned to design a replacement for the original church, which fell down in 1788. His church is very unusual in having a circular nave.

The best examples of Shrewsbury's Tudor buildings are to be found in **Bear Steps**, close to the main square. This charming group of Tudor cottages and a timbered hall now houses two floors of paintings and craft exhibits, usually featuring local artists and images.

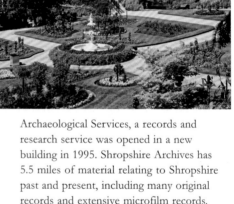
Quarry Gardens, Shrewsbury

Guided tours and suggested walks cover all aspects of this marvellous town, including a **Brother Cadfael Trail** and walks in the surrounding beautiful countryside. One walk takes in the spot to the north of town now known as **Battlefield**, where in 1403 the armies of Henry IV and the insurgent Harry Percy (Harry Hotspur) met. Fifty thousand men were deployed in all, and in the brief but bloody battle Hotspur was among the many casualties. A church was built near the mass grave, where 1,600 bodies are buried, a monument to the fallen and also an oasis of wildlife in the town environment. Battlefield Church is open at weekends during the summer.

Complementing the town's Museum and Archaeological Services, a records and research service was opened in a new building in 1995. Shropshire Archives has 5.5 miles of material relating to Shropshire past and present, including many original records and extensive microfilm records.

A museum with a difference is **Coleham Pumping Station** at Longden Coleham. The station, which looks like a Victorian chapel, was built in 1900 to house the two massive steam-driven beam engines to pump sewage. The engines, which were built by Renshaws of Stoke, powered Shrewsbury's sewage system until 1970.

Shrewsbury Flower Show is a wonderful two-day summer show. Each August for more than a century the show has been held in the picturesque grounds of **Quarry Park**, which slope down to the Severn. At the centre of the 29-acre site is The Dingle, a colourful sunken flower garden.

stories and anecdotes　　famous people　　art and craft　　entertainment and sport　　walks

Around Shrewsbury

WOLLASTON
8 miles W of Shrewsbury on the A458

The church here has a memorial to Thomas Parr, widely claimed to be the longest-lived Englishman, dying at the ripe old age of 152. He lived through 10 reigns, married for the first time at 88, raised a family and married again at 122. He is buried in Westminster Abbey, so someone must have believed his story.

MONTFORD
4 miles W of Shrewsbury off the A5

It's worth pausing at Montford to look at the church where Charles Darwin was buried for a time. His body was subsequently moved to Westminster Abbey, showing that the furore caused by his theories had largely died down soon after his death – but not entirely, as *The Origin of Species* and *The Descent of Man* can still arouse fierce debate. Just beyond Montford are the ruins of Shrawardine Castle.

MELVERLEY
10 miles W of Shrewsbury off the B4393

🏛 Church of St Peter

Country lanes lead to the remarkable **Church of St Peter**, which stands serenely, if somewhat precariously, on the banks of the River Vyrnwy. From the outside, flanked by two massive yew trees, the church looks rather like a black and white manor house; the interior reveals one of England's few timber-framed churches. It was built in 1406 after its predecessor was destroyed by Owen Glendower. Great open screens of oak divide the interior into three areas and most of the furnishings - pulpit, altar table and chairs - are Jacobean.

NESSCLIFFE
9 miles NW of Shrewsbury on the A5

🦌 Country Park

Near the village of Nesscliffe, which lies halfway between Shrewsbury and Oswestry, is **Nesscliffe Hill Country Park**, where paths lead up through woodland to the summit and fine views over Shropshire. The hill is a sandstone escarpment, popular for walking and rock climbing; cut into the face of an abandoned quarry are caves, one of them reputedly the lair of the 16th-century worthy-turned-highwayman Humphrey Kynaston.

A short distance north of Nesscliffe, on the B4397, is the village of Ruyton-Xl-Towns, which acquired its unusual name in medieval times when 11 communities were united into the borough of Ruyton.

HADNALL
5 miles NE of Shrewsbury on the A49

Hadnall is the burial place of Rowland Hill – not the man who conceived the idea of the Penny Post in Victorian times, but the distinguished soldier who was Wellington's right-hand man during the Peninsula War and covered himself with glory by routing Napoleon's Imperial Guard at the Battle of Waterloo. Hill was created a viscount and after succeeding Wellington as Commander-in-Chief retired to Hardwicke Grange near Hadnall. That house no longer stands and the viscount himself is buried beneath the church tower.

Oswestry

🏛 Church of St Oswald   🏛 Croeswylan Stone

🏛 Heritage Centre   🏚 Wat's Dyke

🏛 Cambrian Museum of Transport

🏚 Old Oswestry   🏚 St Oswald's Well

Close to the Welsh border, Oswestry is an

🏛 historic building   🏛 museum   🏚 historic site   🦌 scenic attraction   🌿 flora and fauna important market town whose look is mainly Georgian and Victorian, due in part to the fires that regularly ravaged timber-framed buildings. The town grew up around St Oswald's Well. Oswald was a Saxon king who was killed in a battle in AD642 against a rival Saxon king, Penda of Mercia. Oswald's body was dismembered and hung on the branches of a tree. An eagle swooped and carried off one of his arms and where the limb fell to the ground a spring bubbled up to mark the spot. **St Oswald's Well** soon became a place of pilgrimage renowned for its healing powers.

There are many fine old buildings in Oswestry, none finer than the **Church of St Oswald**. It played an important part in the Civil War, when it was used as an observation point during the siege of the town by the Parliamentarians. The oldest section is the tower, which dates back to around 1200. The interior is beautiful, and among the treasures are a font presented by Colonel Lloyd of Llanforda as a thanksgiving for the restoration of the monarchy, a Gilbert Scott war memorial and a memorial to Hugh Yale, a member of the family that founded Yale University.

Standing in the grounds of the church is the 15th-century Holbache House. Once a grammar school, this handsome building now houses the Tourist Information Centre and the **Heritage Centre** showing displays of local interest and exhibitions of arts and crafts. Ferrequinologists (railway buffs) will make tracks for the **Cambrian Museum of Transport** on Oswald Road. Oswestry was the headquarters of the Cambrian Railway Company until it amalgamated with the Great Western Railway in 1922, and as late as the 1960s there were over 1,000 railwaymen in the area. Locomotives, carriages and wagons have been built and repaired in Oswestry for over 100 years, and the maintenance of 300 miles of track was directed from offices in the station building. One of the old engine sheds now houses a small museum with a collection of railway memorabilia as well as some old bicycles and motorbikes. One of the locomotives is regularly steamed up by the volunteers of the Cambrian Railway Society. At Llynclys South Station a short section of track has been restored.

In 1559 a plague killed almost a third of the town's population and the **Croeswylan Stone** commemorates this disaster, marking the spot to which the market was moved during the plague. It is sometimes referred to as the Cross of Weeping.

On the northern edge of town, **Old Oswestry** is an impressive example of an Iron Age fortress,

Old Oswestry

first occupied in about 300BC. It was on the border of the territory held by the Cornovii and is one of several in the region. At the southwest corner of the fort can be seen **Wat's Dyke**, built at the same time and for the same purpose – delineating the border between Saxon Mercia and the Welsh – as the better-known Offa's Dyke. Who was Wat? We don't know, but he could have been one of Offa's officers. The World War I poet Wilfred Owen was born in Oswestry in 1893.

Around Oswestry

MAESBURY

2 miles S of Oswestry off the A5 or A483

The village was one of the main transit points on the Montgomery Canal, and many of the canal buildings at Maesbury Marsh are still standing, along with some boatmen's cottages.

Immediately south of Maesbury Marsh is the village of Woolston, where St Winifred's Well is said to have been a resting place for saints' bones being carried to their final destinations.

LLANYMYNECH

7 miles S of Oswestry on the A483

  🔥 Llanymynech Hills   🔥 Offa's Dyke

  🔥 Montgomery Canal

A small diversion is well worthwhile to visit Llanymynech, once a town of some standing, with a major canal and a thriving industry based on limestone. It was also a railway junction. The Llanymynech Hills, which include a section of Offa's Dyke, make for

---

WHITE HOUSE

Maesbury Marsh, nr Oswestry,
Shropshire SY10 8JA
Tel: 01691 658524
e-mail: whitehouse@maesburymarsh.co.uk
website: www.maesburymarsh.co.uk

Standing in 7 acres alongside the historic Montgomery Canal, **White House** sit off a country road off the A483, just south of the Oswestry. A delightful stone cottage, over the years extended to now offer quite, comfortable Bed & Breakfast accommodation in three en-suite guest bedrooms. The large Master Suite, on the ground floor, has a four poster bed, a sofa bed, to create a family room, a whirlpool bath and a "wet room" shower. The other rooms are on the first floor and have pleasant views over the courtyard or garden.

All rooms have state-of-the-art TV (Freeview + DVD/CD + iPod connections), the Master Suite has full Sky. All rooms have a fridge; hot drinks tray and free Broadband Internet, phone calls to UK landline phones are free. Resident owners Ross and Isabel Southwell, who bought the house in April 2009, provide evening meals. Vegetarian cooking is a speciality but meat eaters and vegans are also catered for and the menu always offers two starters, three mains and two desserts (bring your own wine). Breakfast, a tour-de-force, is a perfect way to prepare for a day's touring, cycling, walking (Offers Dyke runs nearby), canoeing or just relaxing with a stroll in the garden or the canal towpath. Complementary afternoon tea can be taken in the sun-trap courtyard, the only place where smoking is permitted. Drying and ironing facilities are available and there is good selection of books, magazines, maps and local information. **White House** does not accept credit card, just cash or personal cheques.

🏛 historic building   🏛 museum   🏛 historic site   🍃 scenic attraction   🌿 flora and fauna

THE MANSE B&B

North Road, Llanymynech, North Powys SY22 6EN
Tel: 01691 831075
e-mail: info@stayatthemanse.co.uk
website: www.stayatthemanse.co.uk

The Manse B&B offers comfortable, reasonably priced
accommodation in a handsome Edwardian house dating from 1906.
It stands just 200 yards from the Offa's Dyke path so is particularly popular with walkers for
whom a drying area is available for wet clothes and equipment. They also appreciate the hearty
breakfasts provided by owners Jenny and Peter Wright. The Manse has a choice of double, twin or
single room with en suite facilities. All rooms have colour TV, tea/coffee making facilities,
hairdryer, internet wi fi and thermostatically controlled radiators.

good walking, with the old limestone workings to add interest – you can still see the old bottle lime kilns and an unusual Hoffman rotary kiln. The quarried limestone was taken to the kilns on a tramway and, after processing, to the nearby canalside wharf. Part of the quarry is now a designated nature reserve and supports abundant bird life. On top of the hill are traces of an ancient hill fort. The Montgomery Canal was built at the end of the 18th century mainly for the transportation of limestone from the Llanymynech quarries. Large sections of it are now unnavigable, indeed dry, but a restoration project aims to open 35 miles of waterway from Oswestry through Welshpool to Newtown. Until the boats return there are some delightful walks along the towpath, as well as fishing where it is possible.

ELLESMERE
8 miles NE of Oswestry on the A495

🏛 Old Town Hall 　🏛 Old Railway Station

🏛 Welshampton Church 　⚓ Llangollen Canal

🚶 The Mere

The centre of Shropshire's Lakeland, Ellesmere is a pretty market town where the market is held every Tuesday, just as it has been since 1221. The town has been regional

winner of the Britain in Bloom competition in both 2000 and 2001 and along its medieval streets rise Georgian and half-timbered buildings. The **Old Town Hall** and the **Old Railway Station** are two of the most striking buildings, but nothing except the mound remains of the castle. The most impressive of all is the parish church of St Mary the Virgin, built by the Knights of St John. It is particularly beautiful inside, with an exceptional 15th-century carved roof in the chapel.

The church overlooks **The Mere**, largest of several lakes that are an equal delight to boating enthusiasts, anglers and birdwatchers. Herons, Canada geese and swans are among the inhabitants of The Mere. For an insight into the creation some 15,000 years ago of the Shropshire meres, a browse around the Meres Visitor Centre is recommended. From the centre, there's a pleasant half-mile promenade along the lakeside and through Cremorne Gardens.

Ellesmere forms the hub of a regional canal network with the **Llangollen Canal** linking the Shropshire Union Canal to the Mersey. It was from his offices in Ellesmere that Thomas Telford designed and supervised the building of the entire canal whose most spectacular

🗿 stories and anecdotes 　🐦 famous people 　🎨 art and craft 　✒ entertainment and sport 　🚶 walks

feature is the aqueduct, 125 feet high and 1,000 feet long, which spans the Vale of Llangollen. The project was initiated by the Duke of Bridgewater who in just one day raised over a million (18th-century) pounds at a hotel in the town to fund the scheme.

A mile or so east of Ellesmere, on the A495, is Welshampton, whose **Church** was built by Sir George Gilbert Scott in 1863. One of its memorial windows is dedicated to a Basuto chieftain; he had been a student of theology at Canterbury and part of his studies brought him to Welshampton, where he lodged with the vicar. Unfortunately he fell ill and died in the same year that saw the completion of the church.

Market Drayton

🏛 Butter Cross   🚶 Shropshire Union Canal

🚶 Newcastle Way   🚶 Discovery Trail

Market Drayton was mentioned in the Domesday Book as Magna Draitune. It changed its name when Abbot Simon Combermere obtained a Royal Market Charter in 1245:

Know that we have granted and by this our present charter confirmed to Brother Simon Abbot of Combermere and the monks serving God there that they and their successors forever shall have a weekly market in their manor of Drayton on Wednesday.

And so they have, every Wednesday since.

The fire of 1651 razed most of the town, so there is now quite a diversity of styles among the buildings, including black and white half-timbered residences and former coaching inns. One of the most interesting structures is the **Butter Cross**, built in 1842 to enable farmers' wives to display their wares protected from the weather. The crest it carries is of the Corbet family, Lords of the Manor since 1650.

Market Drayton is often referred to as The Home of the Gingerbread. Gingerbread was baked here for more than 200 years. The bakery no longer exists but traditional Billington's Gingerbread can still be bought in local shops in the town. Traditionally it was dunked in port. Also available is a selection of Gingerbread figures made in all shapes and sizes by a local business called Image on Food. Gingerbread is very good to nibble on the **Discovery Trail** that takes in the sights of the town. Gingerbread dates back far more than 200 years, of course, and Shakespeare had a good word for it:

An' I had but one penny in the world thou shouldst have it to buy gingerbread.

Just a few hundred yards from the town centre, the **Shropshire Union Canal** gives

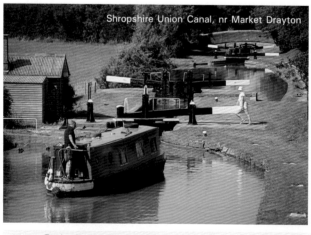

Shropshire Union Canal, nr Market Drayton

🏛 historic building   🏛 museum   🏛 historic site   🕊 scenic attraction   🌿 flora and fauna

boaters the chance to moor up and explore the town, while the towpath walk takes in flights of locks, wharfside cottages and the breathtaking 40-steps Aqueduct.

Market Drayton's most famous son (actually born just outside) was Clive of India, whose childhood escapades in the town included climbing the church tower and sitting on one of the gargoyles, and building a dam to flood a shop whose owner was unwilling to pay protection money. Baron Clive of India, Governor of Bengal, was MP for Shrewsbury from 1760 until his death. He is buried in St Margaret's Church, Moreton Say, 12 miles northwest of Shrewsbury. The **Newcastle Way** is a long-distance walking route that runs for 25 miles between Market Drayton and Mow Cop in Staffordshire. It links the Staffordshire Way at Mow Cop with the Shropshire Union Canal towpath at Market Drayton.

Around Market Drayton

HODNET
4 miles SW of Market Drayton on the A53

🏠 Hodnet Hall

The sizeable village of Hodnet is overlooked by the church of St Luke from its hilltop position. The church is Norman, with some unusual features including a christening gate and wedding steps, and it has a very distinctive octagonal tower. There are some ornate carvings around the 17th-century font, and a chapel is dedicated to the Heber-Percy family, owners of **Hodnet Hall**. The most illustrious member of the family was Bishop Heber, who wrote, among many other hymns, From Greenland's Icy Mountains. Hodnet Hall is an Elizabethan-style mansion built in the 1870s, but the real reason for a visit here is the

wonderful gardens, which extend over 60 acres and were carefully planted (Brigadier Heber-Percy masterminded the transformation) to provide a show of colour throughout the seasons. The gardens are only open to the public on certain weekends during the summer. Call 01630 685786 for dates.

MARCHAMLEY
4 miles SW of Market Drayton on the A442

🏠 Hawkestone Hall

The beautiful Georgian mansion **Hawkestone Hall** was the ancestral home of the Hill family from 1556 until 1906. The Hall is now the seat of a religious order, but the principal rooms, including the splendid Venetian Saloon, are open for a short time in the summer (01630 685242). The Pleasure Gardens comprise terraces, lily pond, herbaceous borders and extensive woodland.

MORETON CORBET
6 miles N of Shrewsbury on the B5063

🏠 Castle

Take the A53 to Shawbury and turn left on to the B5063 and you'll soon come across the splendid ruins of **Moreton Corbet Castle**, seat of the local bigwig family. Its stark greystone walls are an entrancing and moving sight, and not at all like a castle. In fact, what remains is the shell of a grand Italian-influenced mansion that was never completed (Corbet's funds ran out) and was severely damaged in the Civil War.

WEM
11 miles N of Shrewsbury on the B5476

🏠 Astley House

A peaceful enough place now, but Wem has seen its share of strife, being virtually

🏠 stories and anecdotes   🐦 famous people   🎨 art and craft   🚲 entertainment and sport   🚶 walks

destroyed in the Wars of the Roses and attacked in the Civil War. On the latter occasion, in 1643, Lord Capel at the head of 5,000 Royalist troops got a pretty hostile reception, and his defeat by a much smaller band, including some townswomen, gave rise to this mocking couplet:

> *The women of Wem and a few volunteers*
> *Beat the Lord Capel and all his Cavaliers.*

It was another woman – actually a 14-year-old girl called Jane Churm – who nearly did what Capel proved incapable of doing. In setting alight the thatch on the roof of her home she started a fire that destroyed 140 properties in one hour. Some notable buildings survived, including **Astley House**, home of the painter John Astley. This and

many of the town's most impressive houses are in Noble Street. Famous people associated with Wem include Judge Jeffreys of Bloody Assize fame, who became Baron Wem in 1685, with his official residence at Lowe Hall. Wem is the home of the modern sweet pea, developed by the 19th-century nurseryman Henry Eckford. The Sweet Pea Show and the carnival are great occasions in the Wem calendar.

WHITCHURCH
17 miles N of Shrewsbury on the A49

St Alkmund's Church

First developed by the Romans as Mediolanum, Whitchurch is the most important town in the northern part of the

---

LOCKSIDE CAFÉ

Bridge 29, Llangollen Canal, Grindley Brook,
Whitchurch, Shropshire, SY13 4QH
Tel: 01948 663385
e-mail: jane@lockside.biz website: www.lockside.biz

The Llangollen Canal is a 47-mile picturesque stretch of the Shropshire Union and **Lockside Café** enjoys a wonderful setting at Grindley Brook where the canal descends to meet the Cheshire plain. Grindley Brook, the most northerly settlement in Shropshire, stands on the main A41 trunk road a mile and a half north of Whitchurch. It is best known for its staircase of 6 locks. The Café serves the local community as well as boaters on this, one of the most popular and busiest stretches of canal on the whole of the British Waterways network.

It is also a great part of the world for walkers, with the Sandstone Trail running alongside the canal at this point. The Bishop Bennett Way, the Marches Way and the Shropshire and Cheshire Ways, also start or meet close to here. Lockside is, as the name suggests, set right alongside the locks and sells snacks, light meals and a selection of home baking. As well as seating inside there is plenty of seating outside in the Café garden where you can relax the time away with a cappuccino or even a glass of beer or wine watching the comings and goings on the locks only a few feet away. The café compliments this by stocking a range of local produce and specially made jams and pickles, plus a selection of canal gifts and mementoes. Lockside is open 7 days a week from 9am – 5pm – Easter through to November. *Images courtesy of Sheila Halsall of Vision Cards.*

---

historic building   museum   historic site   scenic attraction   flora and fauna

county. Its main street is dominated by the tall sandstone tower of **St Alkmund's Church**, in whose chapel lies the body of Sir John Talbot, 1st Earl of Shrewsbury, who was killed at the Battle of Castillon, near Bordeaux, in 1453.

The Shropshire Way passes nearby, so too the Llangollen Canal, and nature-lovers can explore the local wetland habitats – Brown Moss is two miles to the south off the A41. Whitchurch is the home of Joyce Clocks, the oldest tower clockmakers in the world, and is also, somewhat oddly, where Cheshire cheese was created.

Hidden away in the heart of the town are the Old Town Hall Vaults, where the composer Edward German (*Merrie England*, *Tom Jones*) was born in 1862.

LOCATOR MAP

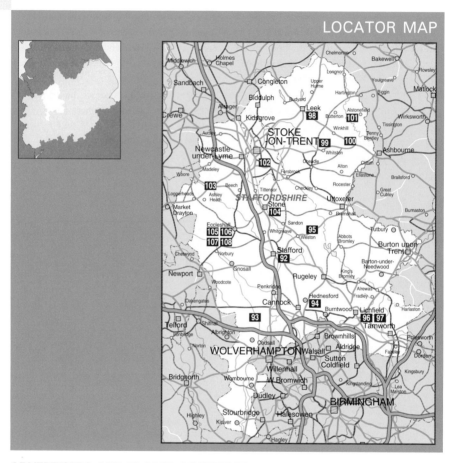

ADVERTISERS AND PLACES OF INTEREST

🏛 historic building   📷 museum   🏛 historic site   🌳 scenic attraction   🌿 flora and fauna

4 Staffordshire

The southwest of Staffordshire encompasses many changing landscapes, from the busy industrial towns of Stafford and Burton-on-Trent to the peace and quiet of Cannock Chase. Along with the Hednesford Hills, the Chase provides a wonderful open area of woodland and moorland that is one of the county's great recreational centres. Well-supported by an interesting and informative visitors' centre, the Chase is a must for anyone visiting this part of Staffordshire. The southeast of the county, although lying close to the Black Country – the depressing product of the heavy industrialisation of the 18th and 19th centuries – has managed to escape in the main. One legacy of the era and a feature throughout the whole of Staffordshire, however, is the canal network. Built to link Birmingham with the Trent & Mersey Canal, the less well-known Coventry Canal and the Birmingham & Fazeley Canal pass through tiny villages and hamlets and the towpaths provide the opportunity to walk in some unexpectedly scenic countryside.

Extending along the southern edge of the Peak District, the Staffordshire moorlands certainly rival their neighbour in terms of scenic attraction. The undulating pastures of the moorlands, along with the fresh air and ancient weather-worn crags, make this the ideal place to walk, cycle or trek. It is also an area full of character, with charming scattered villages, historic market towns and a wealth of history. The Industrial Revolution also left its mark on the landscape, though the two great reservoirs of Rudyard and Tittesworth, built to provide a water supply to the growing industry and population of the Midlands, now offer peaceful havens for a wide variety of plants, animals and birds, as well as recreational facilities such as fishing and boating.

The area around Stoke-on-Trent is famous the world over for its pottery industry. Originally centred on the five towns of Stoke, Tunstall, Burslem, Hanley and Longton, the Potteries were at the heart of the Industrial Revolution. Both coal and clay were found locally, which gave rise to the start of the industry, though imported clay from Cornwall was later used - but it was the foresight and ingenuity of men such as Wedgwood and Minton that really turned the cottage industry into production on a much larger scale. To support the industry in and around the centre, a network of canals and, later, railways was begun. The Trent & Mersey Canal, built by James Brindley with the support of Wedgwood and his friend the Duke of Bridgewater, was finally completed in 1777 and made possible navigation from coast to coast, between the busy ports of Liverpool and Hull. Together, the Trent & Mersey Canal, the Staffordshire & Worcester Canal, begun in the same year, the Shropshire Union Canal to the west and the Middlewich branch of the Llangollen Canal, form a wonderful four counties ring that can be undertaken wholly or partly by boat.

Stafford

🏛 Castle   🏛 The Ancient High House

🦢 Izaak Walton   🎿 Victoria Park

🏛 Church of St Mary   🏛 St Mary's Mews

The county town of Staffordshire has its origins in Saxon times, but the most impressive site is Norman. At **Stafford Castle** visitors can follow the castle trail, wander around the medieval herb garden and explore the visitor centre built in the style of a Norman Guardhouse. The Castle grounds are often used for historical re-enactments by such groups as the Napoleonic Society, and are the site for Sealed Knot battles as well as other outdoor entertainment. Stafford originally had a medieval town wall, which evidence of can still be seen today in the

names of the town's main streets. However, only the East Gate remains of the structure. Stafford lies on the banks of the River Sow, and Green Bridge marks the site of the ancient ford across the river. There has been a bridge on this spot since the late 1200s, but the gate in the town's medieval walls that was also at this point was demolished in 1777. Just to the east of the Bridge is **Victoria Park**, opened in 1908 and later extended to incorporate land reclaimed from the River Sow. There are many pleasant walks through the Park, which includes a mill pond and a weir, in particular to the Windmill at Broad Eye. Built in 1796 by John Wright, the mill moved over to steam power in 1847 and continued to be used until 1880. Like many towns today, Stafford has its busy shopping streets and also an impressive shopping centre. However, many picturesque cobbled lanes still remain and provide the visitor with a quiet and relaxing contrast to the hurly-burly of the 21st century. Of particular note are Church Lane, with its timbered buildings, and Mill Street, with a varied array of shops, restaurants and pubs.

A place well worth visiting during any stay in Stafford is **The Ancient High House**, a beautiful Elizabethan house built in 1595 and now the largest surviving timber-framed town house in England. Through painstaking efforts over several years, Stafford Borough Council has restored this breathtaking piece of architecture to its former glory. Today the building houses the Museum of the Staffordshire Yeomanry. The Ancient High House's varied history can be followed through the permanent displays in the period room settings taking the visitor through the 17th, 18th and 19th centuries and telling the stories of people who came to know this

Ancient High House, Stafford

🏛 historic building   📷 museum   🏛 historic site   🍃 scenic attraction   🌱 flora and fauna

STAFFORDSHIRE

Shire Hall Gallery

Market Square, Stafford ST16 2LD
Tel: 01785 278345 Fax: 01785 27832
e-mail: shirehallgallery@staffordshire.gov.uk
website:www.staffordshire.go.uk/sams

The **Shire Hall Gallery** is a Grade II listed building situated in
the town centre of Stafford. Exhibitions of contemporary
work include fine art, sculpture and photography
throughout the year. The Craft Shop is listed on the Craft Counsel of selected
Galleries, showing work by nationally renowned artists. There is also a coffee bar
selling specialist tea, coffee & home made cakes. Open Monday to Saturday 9.30am-
5pm. Closed for Bank Holidays and exhibition changes.

House so intimately. Not surprisingly, the house has royal connections: both King Charles I and Prince Rupert stayed here in 1642. The House also has a small heritage shop selling a variety of interesting and locally crafted gifts. The Shire Hall Gallery (1798) on the market square was the assize court and still retains the original panelled courtrooms. It is now a venue for contemporary exhibitions and children's workshops, and has a teashop and a workshop.

Close to the High House is the **Collegiate Church of St Mary**, an unusual building that dates in part from the late 1100s, but has received additions in the early English, Gothic and Victorian styles. The huge tower arches in the nave seem to divide the building into two, which is, in fact, exactly what they were intended to do, as St Mary's is two churches under one roof. The nave was the parish church of Stafford with its own altar while the chancel beyond was used by the Deans of the College of St Mary whose duty it was to pray for deceased members of the royal family. Although the College was abolished in 1548, the screens that divided the Church remained until 1841 and today the Church is still referred to as the

Collegiate. Izaak Walton was baptised here on 21 September 1593, and his bust can be seen on the north wall of the nave. Each year, at a civic service, a wreath is placed around the bust to commemorate his probable birthday (9 August). Those interested in ecclesiastical architecture should also find time to visit the little Norman and medieval Church of St Chad.

Best-known today for his work *The Compleat Angler*, **Izaak Walton** was famous throughout his lifetime as a writer of biographies. However, the story of his own life is somewhat obscure, though it is certain that he was born in Stafford in 1593. From humble origins, Walton became accepted into the intellectual and ecclesiastical circles of the day and, during the Civil War, he

Stafford Castle

⟨fi⟩ stories and anecdotes ⟨⟩ famous people ⟨⟩ art and craft ⟨⟩ entertainment and sport ⟨⟩ walks

remained a staunch Royalist and stayed in the Stafford area.

St Mary's Mews dates back to the mid 19th century and is a Grade II listed building. The architect was the renowned Gilbert Scott, the famous church restorer of the 1850s. Other notable buildings include The Infirmary, designed by Benjamin Wyatt and completed in 1772, the Noell Almshouses dating back to 1680, and Chetwynd House, the 17th-century town house of the Chetwynd family and now used as the town's main Post Office.

Around Stafford

GNOSALL

6 miles W of Stafford on A518

🏠 Canal

Some beautiful ash and sycamore trees form a delightful shaded arch over the road through this village (the name is pronounced No Sull) and it also has its very own ghost! On the night of 21 January 1879, a man was attacked at Gnosall canal bridge by an alarming black monster with enormous white eyes. The police were quite sure it was the ghost of a man–monkey who had haunted the bridge for years after a man was drowned in the canal. It is worth staying a while in the village, ghost permitting, to have a look around the fine collegiate Church of St Lawrence. As well as containing some of the best Norman work to be seen in the county, the church, most of which dates from the 13th and 15th centuries, has a particularly ornate west crossing arch.

Despite its name, a large portion of the **Shropshire Union Canal**, some 23 miles, lies within the county of Staffordshire. Indeed, much of this southern section passes through

wonderful countryside. Extending from Ellesmere Port, Cheshire, on the Manchester Ship Canal to Autherley junction near Wolverhampton, the Shroppie, as it is affectionately known, has a long history.

Built by three separate companies, at three different times, the canal was begun as early as 1772 but not finished until 1835, a few months after the death of Thomas Telford, who had worked on its construction. In order to compete with the new railways, the canal had to be built as simply and economically as possible and so, unlike many canals before it, the Shropshire Union's route was short and straight, cutting deeply through hills and crossing lower ground on embankments rather than talking the longer route on level ground.

The canal's Cowley Tunnel, near the village, was originally intended to be longer than its actual 81 yards but, as it was being constructed, the rock towards the southern end, being softer, gave way. The dramatic fault, where the more solid sandstone of the northern end meets the soft marlstones, can still be seen by taking the towpath through the tunnel and cutting.

WESTON-UNDER-LIZARD

11 miles SW of Stafford on the A5

🏛 Weston Park

Situated on the site of a medieval manor house, **Weston Park** has been the home of the Earls of Bradford for 300 years. Disraeli was a frequent visitor here and, on one visit, presented the house with a grotesque stuffed parrot. The parrot became famous when the present Earl, after leaving Cambridge, published a book entitled *My Private Parts and the Stuffed Parrot*. The stuffed parrot still enjoys the hospitality of Weston Park. The parkland at Weston has matured over several hundred

🏛 historic building   🏠 museum   🏚 historic site   🔱 scenic attraction   🌿 flora and fauna

W MAIDEN & SON

30 Stafford Street, Brewood,
Staffordshire ST19 9DX
Tel: 01902 850346

W Maiden & Son has been a successful family business since being established by Bill and Mary Maiden in 1946.

The family has been in the meat trade for generations, and the business is now run by their son, also Bill Maiden.

The shop sells as much locally produced meat as possible, including Longhorn Beef & Lamb from the nearby Chillington Estate.

Special orders and cuts are always available, along with a large selection of game, cooked meats, award winning home cured dry bacon, pies and sausages.

The shop is renowned for home made pies which customers can watch being made most days. There is also a large selection of cheeses, fruit, veg, jams and preserves.

Brewood is an historic village north of Wolverhampton, on the Shropshire Union Canal. The detour from the A5, A449 or M54, to visit this outstanding Butcher, is well worth while.

---

years into a masterpiece of unspoilt landscape. Many have left their mark, yet each successive generation has taken note of its predecessors. Disraeli loved the Park. In one of his letters to Selina, 3rd Countess of Bradford, he refers to the "stately woods of Weston". There are some wonderful architectural features in the Park, including the Roman Bridge and the Temple of Diana, both designed and built by James Paine for Sir Henry Bridgeman in about 1760. Fallow deer and rare breeds of sheep roam the vast parklands and there are plenty of other interesting attractions for visitors of all ages including nature trails, a miniature railway and a Museum of Country Bygones.

FEATHERSTONE
12 miles S of Stafford off the A449

🏛 Moseley Old Hall

Just to the south of the village is **Moseley Old Hall**, which visitors can be forgiven for

thinking belongs to the 19th century. In fact, it dates from the first Elizabethan Age and, inside, much of the original panelling and timber framing is still visible. The Hall once sheltered King Charles II for a short time following his defeat at the Battle of Worcester in 1651, and it is for this that the house is best remembered. Under cover of darkness the defeated King, disguised as a woodcutter, was escorted into the house by Thomas Whitgreave, the owner, and his chaplain, John Huddlestone. He rested here for two days - even evaded capture when Parliamentarians visited the house in search of the monarch - before leaving, again in disguise, and fleeing to France. In 1940, the house was acquired by the Wiggin family and in 1962 it became the property of the National Trust. At that time it had no garden to speak of, but fairly soon two experts re-created the garden in the style of the century.

🎭 stories and anecdotes   🍴 famous people   🎨 art and craft   🎵 entertainment and sport   🚶 walks

The outstanding feature is the knot garden with its box hedges and gravel beds. There is interest everywhere in this wonderful garden, which is full of rare 17th-century plants and herbs. In the barn is an exhibition showing the escape of King Charles.

CANNOCK
9 miles S of Stafford on the A34

Lying on the southern edge of Cannock Chase, this colliery town goes back to the time of the Norman Conquest and appears as Chenet in the Domesday Book. It was an important market town for centuries (Henry III granted the charter in 1259), and the attractive market place still holds busy market days on Tuesdays, Fridays and Saturdays.

On the far side of the market place is the Parish Church of St Luke, which, according to the records, had a chantry and a grammar school linked to it as early as 1143. The battlemented church tower dates from the 1300s and, together with the west end of the nave, is the oldest surviving part of the building. The arms of Humphrey de Stafford, who was killed at the Battle of Northampton in 1460, are on display.

The ancient bowling green has been there for many years and, overlooking the green, is an imposing Georgian house that was once home to the Council. Nearby is the former conduit head building of Cannock Conduit Trust. Founded in 1736 to bring a water supply to the town, the Trust building, known as the Tank House, supplied water to the area until 1942.

HEDNESFORD
8 miles SE of Stafford on the A460

🐾 Hazel Slade Reserve   🏃 Cockpit Hill
🏃 Hednesford Hills

This former mining town lies on the edge of Cannock Chase and its oldest building, The Cross Keys Inn, dates from about 1746. The Anglesey Hotel, built in 1831 by Edmund Peel of Fazeley, was originally designed as a form of summerhouse in a Tudor style with stepped gables and this, too, lies at the heart of Hednesford.

Nearby, the **Hazel Slade Reserve** shows the adaptability of nature with an old-fashioned countryside of small fields, hedges, streams, marshes and woodland. In the 1960s the old broadleaf wood was felled for timber; hedges

The Museum of Cannock Chase

Valley Road, Hednesford, Staffordshire WS12 5TD
Tel: 01543 877666 Fax: 01543 428272
website: www.museumcannockchasedc.gov.uk

This museum illustrates the rich social and industrial heritage of the area, from medieval hunting forest to coal field community, reflecting the social and domestic life of times past. The new Toys Gallery has a collection of toys from the Victorian era right up to present day, including lots to do for 'kids' of 'all ages'. Enter our Coal Face gallery to discover the harsh working conditions of a coal miner. Temporary exhibitions and a full events diary ensure that there is always something new to see or do. Admission free. Open Easter to end September - daily 11am-5pm; October to Easter - Monday to Friday 11am-4pm.

🏛 historic building   🏛 museum   🏛 historic site   🍃 scenic attraction   🐾 flora and fauna

were planted and cattle grazed the cleared fields. However, a small area of the wood managed to recover and grew from the stumps and seeds that remained in the ground. Then, five years later, a pool and marsh started to form as the land began to subside as a result of the local mining activity. The Reserve is a popular place for fishermen as well as those interested in natural history.

Rising over 700 feet above sea level, the **Hednesford Hills** are a prominent local landmark, which bring the countryside of Cannock Chase into the heart of Hednesford. Originally covered in oak and birch, these 300 acres of heathland have been the scene of varied activities over the years. They have been quarried for sand and gravel, mined for coal and used for military training. The land is now a registered common and the hills are a tract of wild landscape with a plethora of heathland plants, abundant wildlife and the opportunity for recreation for the people who live nearby.

The hills have other sporting connections, too. Cockfighting once took place at **Cockpit Hill** though the exact location of the old cockpit is unknown. In the 1900s, prize fighters prepared themselves at the nearby Cross Keys Inn for boxing bouts on the hills, and racehorses were trained on the land. Race meetings were held here regularly until 1840 when the racetrack at Etchinghill, near Rugeley, became more popular. In particular, three Grand National winners were stabled and trained on the Hednesford Hills: Jealousy won the race in 1861, Eremon in 1907 and Jenkinstown in 1910.

CANNOCK CHASE
5 miles SE of Stafford on the A34

🏛 Museum   🏰 Castle Ring   🏰 Broadhurst Green
⛰ Coppice Hill   ⛰ Brereton Spurs

Though close to areas of dense population,

Cannock Chase is a surprisingly wild place of heath and woodland that has been designated an Area of Outstanding Natural Beauty. Covering some 20,000 acres, the Chase was once the hunting ground of Norman kings and, later, the Bishops of Lichfield. Deer are still plentiful. Conifers now dominate, but it is still possible to find the remains of the ancient oak forest and, in the less well-walked marshy grounds, many rare species survive. A popular place for leisurely strolls, the Chase is also ideal for more strenuous walking and other outdoor recreational activities. Excellent view points can be found at **Coppice Hill** and **Brereton Spurs**, while **Castle Ring**, an impressive Iron Age hill fort, is well worth the effort to find.

Amid all this natural beauty, there are also reminders of the 20th century and, in particular, the unique military cemeteries near **Broadhurst Green**, where some 5,000 German soldiers from World War I lie buried. Cannock Chase was used as a training ground during that war and was the last billet for many thousands of soldiers before they left for France. The remnants of the training area can still be seen, as can the prisoner of war camp. The use of the Chase as a training ground was not a new idea: in 1873, there were extensive manoeuvres here with one army base at Etching Hill and the other at Hednesford Hills.

The **Museum of Cannock Chase** (see panel opposite) illustrates the rich social and industrial heritage of the area, from medieval hunting forest to coal field community, reflecting the social and domestic life of times past. The site was once the Valley Colliery; the pit has long since gone, leaving 30 acres of green open space at the Gateway to the Hednesford Hills Nature Reserve. The Toys and Games gallery has a collection of toys from the Victorian era right up to the

🎦 stories and anecdotes   🦅 famous people   🎨 art and craft   ✏ entertainment and sport   🚶 walks

present day, including loads of things to do for kids of all ages. Temporary exhibitions and a full events diary ensure that there is always something new to see or do at the Museum. Visitors can take a self-guided walk round the Museum – admission is free – and then enjoy a walk over the adjacent Nature Reserve following the Colliery Trail or using one of the many other walk leaflets available in the Museum.

RUGELEY
7 miles SE of Stafford on the A51

🏛 Old Chancel   ✸ Ridware Arts Centre

🌿 Wolseley Centre

On first arriving in the town, visitors can be mistaken for thinking that Rugeley is all modern but, at its heart, there are some fine 17th and 18th-century buildings that have survived the years of industrialisation. Between 1860 and 1967, the cattle market was held behind the inn and a market bell was rung from the steps of the hostelry to summon the farmers back from their lunch.

Rugeley's original parish church, the **Old Chancel**, was founded in the 1100s though it is only the tower, chancel and north chapel that remain from those early days; the rest of the building dates back to the 13th and 14th centuries. The nave was demolished in 1823 to help pay for the building of the imposing new church, which, too, is well worth a visit.

Next to the Old Chancel is Church Croft, a fine Georgian house and the birthplace of William Palmer. Later in life, as Dr William Palmer, he brought unhappy notoriety to the town in Victorian times as he poisoned his hapless victims after insuring them. Eventually he was caught, put on trial, found guilty of murder and publicly hanged in Stafford in 1856. The Tudor house rented by the evil Dr Palmer still stands.

Ridware Arts Centre, just outside the town, is within the Tudor walls of the ancient manorial site of Hamstall Hall. Opened in 2002, it houses vibrant studios and workshops and hosts a continuous programme of recreational arts classes (01889 504102). Also nearby is the **Wolseley Centre**, a haven of wildlife and plant life and the headquarters of the Staffordshire Wildlife Trust.

GREAT HAYWOOD
5 miles E of Stafford on the A51

🏛 Shugborough Hall

This ancient village is famous for having the longest packhorse bridge in England. Built in the 16th century, the Essex Bridge (named after the Elizabethan Earl who lived nearby at Shugborough Hall when hunting in the area) still has 14 of its original 40 arches spanning the River Trent. Here, too, is the interesting Roman Catholic Church of St John the Baptist. Built in 1828, the whole church was moved in 1845 from its original site at Tixall to Great Haywood by the local Roman Catholic community. With an ornate west front and Perpendicular windows, it is the richness of the west gallery that is the highlight of the building.

Most visitors to the village however, pass swiftly through it on their way to one of the most impressive attractions in the county, **Shugborough Hall**, the 17th-century seat of the Earls of Lichfield. This magnificent 900-acre estate includes Shugborough Park Farm, a Georgian farmstead built in 1805 for Thomas, Viscount Anson, and now home to rare breed animals and to demonstrations of traditional farming methods such as hand milking, butter and cheese making and shire horses at work. The former servants'

🏛 historic building   📷 museum   🏛 historic site   🏞 scenic attraction   🌿 flora and fauna

quarters have been restored to the days of the 19th century and offer an insight into life below stairs. The mansion itself is a splendid piece of architecture, altered several times over its 300 years, but always retaining its distinct grandeur. Exhibitions of the Staffordshire Arts & Museum Service are held at the Hall. Outside, in the beautiful parkland, can be found an outstanding collection of neoclassical monuments dotted around, and the Lady Walk leads along the banks of the River Sow to the delightful terraced lawns and rose garden.

INGESTRE

4 miles E of Stafford off the A51

🏛 Church of St Mary the Virgin

The beautiful **Church of St Mary the Virgin**, in this small estate village, is something of a surprise. Standing close to the Jacobean Ingestre Hall, the sophisticated church was built in 1676 and has been attributed to Sir Christopher Wren. One of the few churches that Wren designed outside London, it has an elegant interior with a rich stucco nave ceiling and some of the earliest electrical installations in any church. The chancel, which is barrel vaulted, is home to a delightful garlanded reredos and there are many monuments to the Chetwynds and Talbots, who were Earls of Shrewsbury from 1856 and had their seat in the village.

STOWE-BY-CHARTLEY

5 miles E of Stafford on the A518

On the A518 Stafford-Uttoxeter road, a mile east of Weston, Amerton Farm and Craft Centre (see below) has something for everyone.

AMERTON POTTERY

Amerton Farm and Craft Centre,
nr Weston, Staffordshire ST18 0LA
Tel: 01889 270821
website: www.amertonpottery.co.uk

Established in 1994, **Amerton Pottery** is the creation of James Gauge, who produces hand-thrown pottery on the potter's wheel in his studio in the Craft Centre at Amerton Farm. He works in both stoneware and red earthenware to produce a range of work, from simple terracotta pots to beautiful vases, bowls, candle holders and indoor water features, all of which can be seen and bought at the studio.

The pottery also offers a popular paint-a-pot service, enabling visitors to choose from a wide range of plain pottery – little animal figures, mugs, plates, money boxes – to personalise with their own designs with acrylic or ceramic paint. Babies' hand and foot prints make lovely gifts for parents and grandparents, and pieces can be tailored to birthdays, weddings and other big occasions. Special one-off commissions can also be accepted. The studio can accommodate up to 20 customers round five tables, or takeaway packs can be bought with instructions on how to paint a pot at home.

The Farm and Craft Centre complex stands on the A518 midway between Stafford and Uttoxeter.

Burton-on-Trent

🌱 Washlands

The "capital" of East Staffordshire, Burton-on-Trent is famous for its brewing industry. Started many centuries ago, even the monks of the Benedictine Abbey, founded here in 1100, were not the first to realise that the Burton well water was specially suited to brewing. William Bass began brewing in Burton in 1777, and by 1863 the brewery had grown to produce half a million barrels of beer each year on a 150-acre site. In 1998 Bass acquired the Burton premises of Carlsberg-Tetley, creating the biggest brewery site in the UK.

A Benedictine Abbey, founded by a Saxon earl called Wulfric Spot, was established on the banks of the River Trent, where the Market Place now stands. The focus of Burton, it was from here that the town grew. In the 12th century, the monks constructed a large stone bridge of some 36 arches across the River Trent – today's bridge replaced the medieval structure in 1864. The area along the banks of the Trent, between Burton Bridge and the later structure of Ferry Bridge, which opened in 1889, is known as the **Washlands**. Rich in native wildlife, the Washlands is a haven for all manner of birds, small mammals, trees and plants. This ancient area, now a wonderful, traditionally managed recreational centre for the town, has a history dating back beyond that of Burton itself. It was at Washlands, in the 7th century, that St Modwen is said to have built her chapel and settlement on Andresey Island. No evidence of the constructions remain and they are thought to have been destroyed in a Danish raid in AD874. The site of the chapel is marked by a cherry orchard and some yew trees.

Around Burton-on-Trent

TUTBURY
4 miles N of Burton on the A50

🏛 Castle

The historic village of Tutbury is dominated by the imposing remains of the **Castle**, which has stood on a naturally defensive outcrop of rock for many centuries. From 1086 to 1265, Tutbury Castle belonged to the Ferrers family, who had connections here and in Derbyshire, and for a time it belonged to the Duchy of Lancaster. Today, the Castle is in ruins but it remains an attraction particularly for those interested in Mary, Queen of Scots, who was imprisoned here for a while. During the Civil War, Tutbury Castle remained loyal to the Crown while the town was under the control of Parliament. After a three-week siege, the Castle surrendered and in the following year, 1647, Parliament ordered its destruction. In the shadow of the castle stands the Priory Church of St Mary the Virgin, one of the finest of all Norman churches. The town

Tutbury Castle

🏛 historic building   🏛 museum   🏚 historic site   💧 scenic attraction   🌱 flora and fauna

itself is both charming and full of character with many Georgian-fronted shops and a wide variety of antiques showrooms in the Tutbury Mill Mews, which was originally an ironmongery and wheelwright.

HOAR CROSS
7 miles W of Burton off the B5234

🏠 Church of the Holy Angels

The magnificent Roman Catholic **Church of the Holy Angels** is by the Victorian architect GF Bodley and it so impressed Sir John Betjeman that he called it Bodley's masterpiece. It was commissioned by the widow of Hugo Francis Meynell Ingram, in his memory, and much of its beauty it due to this remarkable lady.

ABBOTS BROMLEY
10 miles W of Burton on the B5234

🏠 Hurst Chapel

This delightful 13th-century village in the Vale of Trent has some notable timber-framed buildings, among which are the Goat's Head Inn and the village school. The butter cross in the centre of the village is where the local farmers used to sell their produce. Abbots Bromley is known chiefly for its annual Horn Dance, and the ancient reindeer horns used in the ceremony are kept in the **Hurst Chapel** of the Church of St Nicholas. The origins of this dance are lost in the mists of time, but it is thought that it was first performed at the three-day Bartelmy Fair, granted to the Abbots of Burton by Henry III in 1226 to celebrate St Bartholomew's Day. In early September each year, six male dancers carry the horns around the village with six others and a fool, a hobby horse, a bowman and Maid Marian, the last being a man dressed up as a woman. There's dancing and even mock battles with deer heads and reindeer antlers. The procession starts at about 8am and passes by some local farms before arriving at Blithfield Hall around midday. After lunch, the procession wends its way back to the village, where the horns are returned to the church.

Lichfield

🏠 St John's Hospital & Chapel   🏠 Cathedral
🚶 Stone and Minster Pools   🏛 Heritage Centre
🏛 Wall Roman Site   🎨 The Curborough Collection
🦜 Samuel Johnson Birthplace Museum
🦜 Erasmus Darwin Centre

Despite its 18th century prominence, Lichfield lagged behind other towns in extensive rebuilding programmes and consequently it still retains its medieval grid pattern streets

Lichfield Cathedral

with elegant Georgian houses and, mixed in among them, black and white Tudor cottages. First settled by the Celts, and close to the crossroads of the two great Roman roadways, Rykneld Street (now the A38) and Watling Street (now the A5), Lichfield was one of the most important towns of ancient days; the King of Mercia offered St Chad the seat of Lichfield and, on his death, the town became a place of pilgrimage and an important ecclesiastical centre.

The first cathedral was built here in AD669, but no traces of this building, or the later Norman structure, remain. The **Lichfield Cathedral** seen today dates from the 12th century and is particularly famous for the three magnificent spires that dominate the City skyline. Inside there are many treasures, including the beautiful 8th-century illuminated manuscript *The Lichfield Gospels* and Sir Francis Chantrey's famous sculpture *The Sleeping Children*.

The surrounding Cathedral Close is regarded by many as the most original and unspoilt in the country. Since it is separated from the rest of the city by Stowe and Minster Pools, it is also a peaceful haven of calm. These two wonderful pools, **Stowe and Minster**, are used for fishing, while Beacon Park is the venue for the Festival fireworks

display each July. The Minster Pool is particularly beautiful – it was landscaped in the late 1700s by Anna Seward and is now a haven for wildfowl.

At the very heart of Lichfield is the **Lichfield Heritage Centre**, part of St Mary's Centre in the Market Place. The Staffordshire Millennium Embroideries are on display here. A church has stood on this site since the 12th century and the present building, the third, dates from 1868. As with many ecclesiastical buildings, the decline in the church-going population made St Mary's redundant and, to save it from being demolished altogether, the Centre was formed. A stroll round here is a fascinating experience and, for the energetic, there are spectacular views across the city from the viewing platform on the spire. There are exhibitions on the history and everyday life of the city as seen through the eyes of its inhabitants over the centuries, including the story of the siege of Lichfield Cathedral during the Civil War and displays of the city's silver, ancient charter and archives.

The City has been a place of pilgrims and travellers for centuries and, in 1135, **St John's Hospital** was founded to offer shelter to those passing through Lichfield. One of the finest Tudor brick buildings in the country, the Hospital is now a home for the elderly. **The Hospital Chapel**, with its magnificent stained-glass window by the designer of the celebrated east window at Coventry Cathedral, John Piper, is open daily. A statue of Noah and the Dove by Simon Manby was installed here in 2006.

The **Guildhall**, the meeting place of the city governors for over 600 years, has, at various times been a courthouse, police station

Watling Street Wall Roman Site, Lichfield

🏛 historic building   🏛 museum   🏛 historic site   ᙈ scenic attraction   🌱 flora and fauna

and prison. Behind its Victorian façade, lie the remains of the city jail, complete with stocks and cells - the City Dungeons can be visited on Saturdays throughout the summer.

Lichfield's most famous son is Dr Samuel Johnson, the poet, novelist and author of the first comprehensive English dictionary. The son of a bookseller, Johnson was born in 1709 in Breadmarket Street, and the house is now home to the **Samuel Johnson Birthplace Museum**. Open every day, with free entry, the Museum, as well as exhibiting artefacts relating to his life and works, also has a series of tableaux showing how the house looked in the early 1700s. Dr Johnson was justly proud of his city:

'I lately took my friend Boswell (a Londoner) and showed him genuine civilised life in an English provincial town. I turned him loose in Lichfield, that he might see for once real civility.'

Here are a few more Johnson gems:

'A tavern chair is the throne of human felicity.'

'Depend on it sir, when a man knows he is to be hanged in a fortnight, it concentrates the mind wonderfully.'

'When two Englishman meet their first talk is of the weather.'

2009 sees the 300th anniversary of the birth of Dr Johnson, and the event is being celebrated with a number of special events, culminating in a light and sound show in the Market Square. Memorials to Dr Johnson's stepdaughter, Lucy Porter, can be seen in the medieval St Chad's Church, which has a Norman tower. In the churchyard is a well in the place where St Chad used to baptise people in the 7th century. The ancient practice of well-dressing was revived at St Chad's in 1995 to celebrate the 50th anniversary of

---

THE SPELLBOUND BEAD COMPANY

47 Tamworth Street, Lichfield, Staffordshire WS13 6JW
Tel: 01543 417650
e-mail: info@spellboundbead.co.uk
website: www.spellboundbead.co.uk

Founded in 1984, the **Spellbound Bead Company** has been based in Lichfield since 1996, moving to its present premises a short walk from the centre in 2006. One of the largest specialist bead outlets in the UK, the shop is filled with a range of over 8,000 items, from loose beads in all shapes and sizes in glass, metal, wood and semi-precious stones to mixed packs, books, tools, wires, threads and bead storage boxes. The shop also stocks a unique range of bead kits, and with more than 200 designs there's something for everyone. They contain all the beads and threads required, along with full instructions for making the pictured design; with the starter packs all the kit is included but with no set picture the final look is left to the purchaser. All the staff here make jewellery in some form, and with three experienced tutors on the staff as well as there is always someone on hand to set you in the right direction. Workshops are held throughout the year – pre-booking is essential and dates can be found on the excellent website. Spellbound Beads has a thriving mail order business, and most of the lines available in the shop can be ordered online. The company also displays at a number of shows around the UK. The shop is open Monday to Saturday (half-day Wednesday).

Christian Aid and is now an annual event.

Apart from the historic pleasure that Lichfield gives, there is also plenty of parkland to enjoy and, in particular, the Beacon Park and Museum Gardens. The 75-acre park encloses playing fields and a small boating lake and, in the Museum Gardens, there is a statue of Commander John Smith, captain of the ill-fated *Titanic*, sculpted by Lady Katherine Scott, widow of Scott of the Antarctic.

Anna Seward, the landscaper of Minster Pool, is another of Lichfield's famous sons and daughters. She lived in the Bishop's Palace and was a poet and letter writer as well as being at the centre of a Lichfield-based literary circle in the late 1700s. Erasmus Darwin, the doctor, philosopher, inventor, botanist and poet, and the closest friend of Josiah Wedgwood, lived in a house in Beacon Street on the corner of The Close. **The Erasmus Darwin Centre** (see panel opposite), just three minutes from the Cathedral, is a fascinating place to visit, with touch-screen computers to access Darwin's writings and inventions, and a garden where herbs and shrubs that would have been familiar to the doctor are grown. Erasmus was the grandfather of Charles Darwin, and had his own theories about evolution. David Garrick, probably the greatest actor-manager of the 18th century, had a home here opposite the west gate of the Cathedral. The new Lichfield Garrick Theatre opened in 2003. Lichfield is a festival city, the premier event being the Lichfield International Arts Festival held in July.

Just north of Lichfield, **The Curborough Collection** is a traditional craft centre with an amazing array of crafts and antiques, found in 24 separate units. To the south of the town can be found the impressive **Wall Roman Site**. Known to the Romans as Letocetum, is has the remains of a bath house and mansion, the most substantial to be found in the country.

Around Lichfield

BURNTWOOD
4 miles W of Lichfield on the A5190

🌱 Chasewater Heaths   🏠 Chasewater Railway

The 700 acres of land and water known as **Chasewater Heaths** are an unexpected find in this otherwise urban setting. On the fringes of the village, Chasewater offers a true wilderness experience with a combination of heath and woodland environments. Criss-crossed by paths and bridleways, the collection of plants and animals found here is so rare that a large area has been designated a Site of Special Scientific Interest. The volunteer-run **Chasewater Railway**, a former colliery railway in what is now Chasewater Country Park, operates passenger services behind tank engines between Brownhills West and Norton Lakeside stations. The two-mile trip takes about 25 minutes and trains run every 45 minutes on Sundays and Bank Holiday Mondays from March to October. Old buildings from the industrial days of coal mining can still be seen, as can reminders of the time when this was an inland waterside resort (01534 412121).

ARMITAGE
5 miles NW of Lichfield on the A513

Situated on the banks of the Trent and Mersey Canal, the village is synonymous with sanitary ware – the manufacturer Armitage Shanks is still located on the canalside. Less

---

🏛 historic building   🏛 museum   🏛 historic site   🍃 scenic attraction   🌱 flora and fauna

Erasmus Darwin Centre

Beacon Street, Lichfield, Staffordshire WS13 7AD
Tel: 01543 306260
e-mail: erasmus.d@virgin.net
website: www.erasmus-darwin.org

Visitors to Lichfield can find a covered alley way in-between the houses and bookshop opposite the majestic, three spired Cathedral.

Walking up the alley, they are led to the right, discovering a secluded courtyard of ancient houses, surrounding the herb garden of Erasmus Darwin's House. Through an iron gateway, the visitor then reaches the entrance door to the Doctor's former home. Indoors, an introductory video gives a short biography and audio-guides take the visitor back in time as they journey through the rooms. Touch screen computers, working models, and a silhouette booth are some of the interactives that compliment the historical artefacts on display.

well-known is the splendid Norman font in the church. Close to the village is the only tunnel along the Trent & Mersey Canal with a towpath. Cut through red sandstone rock, it withstood the test of time and the vibrations of the traffic crossing over it, until, finally, the heavy lorries of the late-20th century took their toll. The tunnel was opened out completely, but the tunnel effect remains as the widened road still crosses the cutting.

ALREWAS

5 miles NE of Lichfield on the A38

🌿 National Memorial Arboretum

🌿 Armed Forces Memorial

The main street of this enchanting village is lined with delightful black and white thatched cottages, some of which date back to the 1400s. The village Church of All Saints is equally beautiful. Its doorways are all that remain of the original Norman church; the chancel was built in the 13th century.

The **National Memorial Arboretum**, on the A513 Alrewas-Tamworth road, is the first large arboretum and wildlife reserve to be

created in Britain for 200 years. A substantial grant from the Millennium Commission has transformed a 150-acre former gravel quarry into a sylvan temple whose theme is remembrance, essentially for those who have lost their lives or suffered in the service of their country. The central feature of the Arboretum, which is run by the British Legion, is the Millennium Avenue, created from cuttings from a 2,000-year-old lime tree. In the unique Millennium Chapel, the Last Post, two minutes' silence and Reveille are observed at 11am daily. In October 2007, in the presence of the Queen and the Duke of Edinburgh, the Prince of Wales and the Duchess of Cornwall, the Archbishop of Canterbury conducted a ceremony to dedicate the **Armed Forces Memorial** – a national monument that commemorates members of the UK armed forces (Regular and Reserve) killed on duty or as a result of terrorist action since World War II. The Memorial is a striking and emotive structure designed by Liam O'Connor and inspired by the ancient landscapes of pre-historic Britain and the classical forms of ancient Rome. At the top of

🎬 stories and anecdotes 🐦 famous people 🎨 art and craft ✐ entertainment and sport 🚶 walks

a six-metre mound is a 43-metre diameter stone structure with two curved walls and two straight walls. 200,000 bricks faced with Portland stone panels contain the names of those honoured by the Memorial, which will be maintained by The Armed Forces Memorial Trust, a separate charitable trust whose patron is The Prince of Wales.

FRADLEY
4 miles NE of Lichfield off the A38

🌱 Fradley Pool Nature Reserve

Another dimension in the history of the canal age is revealed in the opening of **Fradley Pool Nature Reserve** at Fradley Junction, where the Coventry Canal joins the Trent & Mersey Canal. The reservoir site includes a variety of habitats, a bird hide, tree sculptures, pools, and gateways and a willow tunnel designed and made by local school groups. On the other side of the canal are a café and a British Waterways Information Centre and shop.

EDINGALE
5 miles E of Lichfield off the A513

🚶 National Forest

A regional forest, **National Forest**, has reshaped the landscape between this village and Alrewas to the west. The project, which stretches over the three counties, blends the new plantations with ancient woodland and includes farmland, villages and open country.

WHITTINGTON
3 miles SE of Lichfield off the A51

🏛 Museum of the Staffordshire Regiment

Whittington is home to the **Museum of the Staffordshire Regiment** (The Prince of Wales'),

housed in the Victorian Whittington Barracks. The regiment incorporates the former South and North Staffordshire Regiments, which were amalgamated in 1959. The Regiment's origins go back to 1705 when the 38th Foot (later the 1st Battalion of the South Staffordshire Regiment) was raised at Lichfield. The Museum exhibits over 9,000 items including uniforms, shako and helmet plates, belt plates and clasps, badges and buttons, and weapons from pistols to machine guns. There's a full-scale World War I trench system, Anderson shelters and relics from the Sikh Wars, the Crimean, Indian Mutiny, Zulu War, Egypt, Sudan, South Africa and both World Wars. Among the medals on display there are no fewer than 13 Victoria Crosses. The Museum also includes archives of other Regiments (01538 483741).

TAMWORTH
8 miles SE of Lichfield off the A5

🏛 Castle   🏛 Town Hall

A modern, busy town, Tamworth is actually much older than it first appears. Straddling the famous Roman Watling Street (now the A5), it has a fascinating and turbulent past. The first reference to the town dates back to

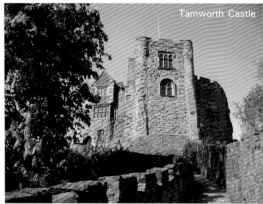
Tamworth Castle

🏛 historic building   🏛 museum   🏛 historic site   🌿 scenic attraction   🌱 flora and fauna

the 8th century when it was the capital of the Kingdom of Mercia. King Offa built a palace here. Raiding Danes managed to destroy the town twice, and it was later invaded by other Scandinavians who left evidence of their visit in some of the street names such as Gungate.

Alfred's daughter, Ethelfleda, was busy here, too, and excavations in the town centre have revealed Saxon fortifications. Dominating Tamworth today is the fine Norman motte and bailey **Castle** set in the Pleasure Grounds, which have truly magnificent floral terraces. The sandstone castle, with its superb herringbone wall, dates originally from the 1180s, having replaced a wooden tower on the present artificial mound constructed shortly after the Norman Conquest. Behind the ancient fortress walls, Tudor and Jacobean buildings tower over the medieval timer-framed Great Hall. Restored period rooms give a fascinating glimpse into life above and below stairs down the centuries. A Saxon nun, Editha, is said to haunt Tamworth Castle, her ghost appearing first in 1139. The story goes that when de Marmion took possession of his lands he expelled the nuns from a nearby convent. The order had been founded by Editha in the 9th century, so the expelled nuns summoned her from her grave. Editha attacked de Marmion in his bedroom and, as a result of the severe beating she gave him, he restored the nuns to their home. The Parish Church of St Editha, founded in AD963, is vast and was rebuilt after the Norman Conquest; then, again, after the Great Fire of Tamworth in 1345. The splendid 15th-century tower at the west end contains a most remarkable double staircase. The mixture of Victorian and modern stained glass found inside is surprisingly harmonious.

The **Town Hall**, built in 1701, is charming with open arches and Tuscan columns below. The building was paid for by Thomas Guy, the local Member of Parliament, who is probably more famous as the founder of the London hospital that bears his name. Thomas Guy also gave the town its 14 almshouses in Lower Gungate, which were rebuilt in 1913.

FAZELEY
9 miles SE of Lichfield on the A4091

Canal

Drayton Manor Family Theme Park has over a million visitors a year. Besides the scary rides and a G-Force rollercoaster, it has a zoo, farm and garden centre and two museums, one of which is particularly interesting as it charts the history of the Peel family, former owners of Drayton Manor.

The **Birmingham & Fazeley Canal**, which joins up with the Trent & Mersey Canal to the west of Alrewas, made this small town one of the key centres of the English canal system for over 200 years, and in the 18th century it had one of the most complete cotton mill complexes in the country. Not only did the Peel family set up their cotton factory here to take full advantage of the canal network, but also other cotton manufacturers also saw the potential for business at Fazeley. The old factory buildings and mills are being restored to their former glory and a wander along the towpath provides interesting glimpses into the industrial history of the area.

SWINFEN
3 miles S of Lichfield on the A38

Heart of the Country Village

On the A38 between Swinfen Island and Weeford Island stands the **Heart of the Country Village**, a country centre set around attractive courtyards in converted farm buildings with a range of shopping outlets and two restaurants.

Leek

🏛 Butter Cross 🏛 Nicholson Institute

📷 Brindley Water Museum 🏃 River Churnet

🏃 Tittesworth Reservoir 🏛 War Memorial

Leek is an attractive textile centre on the banks of the River Churnet, noted for its range and variety of antiques shops. It was here that French Huguenots settled, after fleeing from religious oppression, and established the silk industry that thrived due to the abundance of soft water coming off the nearby moorland. Until the 19th century, this was a domestic industry with the workshops on the top storey of the houses; many examples of these 'top shops' have survived to this day. Leek also became an important dyeing town, particularly after the death of Prince Albert, when Raven Black was popularised by Queen Victoria, who remained in mourning for her beloved husband for many years.

William Morris, founder of the Arts & Crafts movement, lived and worked in Leek for long periods between 1875 and 1878. Much of his time here was spent investigating new techniques of dyeing with Thomas Wardle, but he also revived the use of traditional dyes. Thomas Wardle's wife, Elizabeth, founded the Leek School of Embroidery, with much encouragement from William Morris.

Leek is by no means a recent town that grew up in the shadow of the Industrial Revolution. An ancient borough, granted its charter in 1207, Leek was a thriving market centre rivalling Macclesfield and Congleton.

The **Butter Cross**, which now stands in the Market Place, was originally erected near the junction of Sheep Market and Stanley Street by the Joliffe family in 1671.

Every road coming into the town seems to converge on the old cobbled Market Place and the road to the west leads down to the Parish Church. Dedicated to Edward the Confessor, the original Church was burnt down in 1297 and rebuilt some 20 years later, though the building is now largely 17th century. The timber roof of the nave is well worth a second look and is the church's pride and joy – it is said that each of the cross beams was hewn from a separate oak tree. In the west part of the nave, an enormous 18th-century gallery rises up, tier on tier, giving the impression of a theatre's dress circle.

Although much has been altered inside the church, most notably in 1865 when GE Street rebuilt the chancel, reredos, sanctuary, pulpit and stalls, the rose window designed by William Morris remains. The church also contains work by the Leek School of Embroidery. Outside, in the churchyard, can be found a rather curious inscription on a gravestone: "James Robinson interred February the 28th 1788 Aged 438". To the north side of the Church is an area still known locally as 'Petty France', it holds the graves of many Napoleonic prisoners of war who lived nearby. An oft-told local story relates that one day Bonnie Prince Charlie was passing through the town and knocked on the door of the vicarage asking for accommodation. The vicar's wife was so surprised that she expired from shock on the spot.

Another building worthy of a second glance is the imposing **Nicholson Institute**, with its copper dome. Completed in 1884 and funded by the local industrialist Joshua Nicholson, the

CHRISTOPHER MUDD
DESIGN

Compton Mill, Compton, Leek,
Staffordshire ST13 5NJ
Tel: 01538 37284 Fax: 07768 845942
website: www.christophermudd.com

Furniture in the Tradition of
Fine Craftsmanship

Down the years, the market town of leek has played a prominent role in the worlds of industry, design and craftsmanship. William Morris, the founder of the Arts & Crafts movement, worked in Leek, mainly on new dyeing processes, during the 1870s, and his wife founded the Leek School of Embroidery. The silk industry was also important here, and the in the 17th century local workers in wood put their skills to fine use in creating the superb oak cross beams to be seen in Leek's parish church, each one said to have been hewn from a single tree. The legacy lives on in the workmanship of individuals and the number of antiques shops, and Compton Mill, by the A520 in the Compton district of town, is one of the best centres for antiques and bespoke furniture in the whole of Staffordshire.

The Mill is the home of **Christopher Mudd Designs**, a successor to Roberts & Mudd Antiques founded by Christopher and his father. Christopher has earned an enviable reputation as one of the finest furniture designers and makers in the region, and he also puts his long experience in the antiques industry to excellent use, drawing on classical designs and adapting them for the needs of modern functionality. His furniture includes reproduction and decorative pine, 'shabby chic' and plain (but by no means simple) country pieces. Everything is made here by Christopher and his team of ten or so men and women, all vastly experienced in furniture making and antiques restoration. Each piece is truly bespoke, made to order to fit the customers' needs, no matter how big or small, with many variations in wood, style, colour, finish and details such as hinges and handles. The portfolio covers the whole spectrum of household furniture and the firm also specialises in bespoke kitchens, each commission specific to customer space and undertaken from initial consultation to measurements, design, manufacture, delivery and installation. Every piece of restored antique wood, every home furnishing and every kitchen that leaves the workshop is something the craftspeople feel proud to have created and which the customers feel equally proud to possess. Making furniture to order is the main activity of Christopher Mudd Design, but they still deal in buying and selling antiques, with an ever-changing stock on display.

The showrooms are open from 10 to 5.30 Tuesday to Saturday and from 1 to 5 on Sunday.
Customers who can't get to Leek can view a wide variety of the firm's furniture
on the very comprehensive website.

Institute offered the people of Leek an opportunity to learn and to expand their cultural horizons. Many of the great Victorian literary giants, including George Bernard Shaw and Mark Twain, came here to admire the building. The town's **War Memorial**, built in Portland stone and with a clock tower, has a dedication to the youngest Nicholson son, who was killed in World War I. Leek was the home of James Brindley, the 18th-century engineer who built much of the early canal network. A water-powered corn mill built by him in 1752 in Mill Street has been restored and now houses the **Brindley Water Museum**, which is devoted to his life and work. Visitors can see corn being ground and displays of millwrighting skills. Open Saturday, Sunday and Bank Holiday afternoons from Easter to the end of September, also Monday, Tuesday and Wednesday afternoons from mid-July to the end of August. Leek has a traditional outdoor market every Wednesday, a craft and antiques market on Saturday and an indoor 'butter market' on Wednesday, Friday and Saturday.

The **River Churnet**, though little known outside Staffordshire, has a wealth of scenery and industrial archaeology and, being easily accessible to the walker, its valley deserves better recognition. The river rises to the west of Leek in rugged gritstone country, but for most of its length it flows through softer red sandstone countryside in a valley that was carved out during the Ice Age. Though there are few footpaths directly adjacent to the riverbank, most of the valley can be walked close to the river using a combination of canal towpaths and former railway tracks.

Four miles to the north of Leek on the A53 rise the dark, jagged gritstone outcrops of The Roaches, Ramshaw Rocks and Hen Cloud. Roaches is a corruption of the French word "roches" or rocks and was reputedly given by Napoleonic prisoners: "cloud" is a local word used for high hills. Just below The Roaches there is another delightful stretch of water, **Tittesworth Reservoir**, which is extremely popular with trout fishermen. It has some super trails, a visitor centre with an interactive exhibition, a restaurant and a gift shop.

Around Leek

LONGNOR

9.5 miles NE of Leek off the B5053

🏛 Market Hall   ✏ Craft Centre

🏛 Church of St Bartholomew

Over the county line into Staffordshire yet in the heart of the Peak District, on a gentle slope between the River Manifold and the River Dove, Longnor was once the meeting-point of several packhorse routes. Its **Market Hall** was built in 1873 – outside the hall there is a posting of the market charges of the time. The town's prosperity declined with the onset of the agricultural depression, and there was an accompanying fall in the population. However, this decline has in recent years been reversed. Longnor is now a conservation area and has attracted a good many craftspeople.

Main showroom for the work of local craftspeople and artisans, **Longnor Craft Centre** occupies the beautifully restored Market Hall in the centre of Longnor village. The village also has some fascinating narrow flagged passages that seem to go nowhere, but suddenly emerge into the most beautiful scenery.

Though the late 18th-century **Church of St Bartholomew** is rather plain, the churchyard has a most interesting gravestone. The epitaph tells the tale of the life of William Billinge, born in 1679, died in 1791 – which made him 112 years old at the time of his death. As a soldier Billinge served under Rooke at Gibraltar and Marlborough at Ramillies; after being sent home wounded, he recovered to take part in defending the King in the Jacobite rebellions of 1715 and 1745.

RUDYARD
2 miles NW of Leek off the A523

 Kinver Edge

In fond memory of the place where they first met in 1863, Mr and Mrs Kipling named their famous son, born in 1865, after this village. The nearby two-mile long Rudyard Lake was built in 1831 by John Rennie to feed the Caldon Canal. With steeply wooded banks, the lake is now a leisure centre where there are facilities for picnicking, walking, fishing and sailing. On summer weekends and Bank Holidays, visitors can enjoy a magical three-mile return trip alongside the lake behind the vintage locomotives of the Rudyard Lake Steam Railway. The west shore of the Reservoir is also a section of the Staffordshire Way, the long distance footpath that runs from Mow Cop to **Kinver Edge**, near Stourbridge. This is a sandstone ridge covered in woodland and heath, and with several famous rock houses that were inhabited until the 1950s.

In Victorian times, Rudyard was a popular lakeside resort – in 1877 more than 20,000 people came here to see Captain Matthew Webb, the first man to swim the English Channel, swim in the Reservoir.

RUSHTON SPENCER
5 miles NW of Leek on the A523

 Chapel in the Wilderness

Well known for its lonely church, the '**Chapel in the Wilderness**, this is a pleasant, moorland village nestling under the Cloud. Originally built of wood in the 14th century, the church, which served both Rushton Spencer and neighbouring Rushton James, has been almost rebuilt in stone. One of the graves is that of Thomas Meakin, who died in 1781 but whose grave faces the wrong way. He was originally buried in Stone, but there was a suspicion that he was buried alive. When the grave was opened scratches were found in the coffin and the body was lying face down. When he was laid to rest in Rushton Spencer the grave was positioned the wrong way round in order to keep the ghost in.

BIDDULPH
10 miles W of Leek on the A527

 Biddulph Grange

John Wesley was a frequent visitor to this

Rudyard Lake

 stories and anecdotes    famous people    art and craft    entertainment and sport    walks

isolated moorland town but the history of Biddulph goes back to long before the days of Methodism. After the Norman Conquest, the manor of Biddulph was granted by William the Conqueror to Robert the Forester, an overlord of what was then the extensively forested area of Lyme. The Biddulphs, a staunchly Catholic family, took control of the area. John Biddulph fought under the Royal flag during the Civil War and was killed at the Battle of Hopton Heath. His son entrusted the defence of Biddulph Hall to Lord Brereton who withstood a determined siege until 1644, when he was finally subjected to heavy artillery. The Hall was then demolished to prevent its being re-garrisoned.

Biddulph Grange belonged to the Cistercian monks of the Abbey at Hulton until the Dissolution and its garden is one of the most unusual and remarkable in the whole country. It was created by James Bateman in the mid 1800s as a series of connected parts to show specimens from his extensive collection, which he had harvested from all parts of the globe. Highlights include an Egyptian garden with a pyramid and yew obelisks, a Chinese garden with a joss house, temple and watch tower, a splendid Scottish glen, a dahlia walk and a Wellingtonia avenue.

HARRISEAHEAD
6 miles W of Leek off the A527

🏛 Mow Cop Castle 🏛 Englesea Brook Chapel

Close to the village and perched on top of a hill is **Mow Cop Castle**, which lies exactly on the boundary of Staffordshire and Cheshire. However, the Castle is not all that it appears. The ruined medieval fortress and remains of the round tower are, in fact, what is left of an elaborate summerhouse built by Randle Wilbraham, of nearby Rode Hall, in

Mow Cop Castle, Harriseahead

1754. The history of the site goes back much further and the remains of a prehistoric camp have been found here. In 1807, this ancient site gave birth to Primitive Methodism when Hugh Bourne, a Stoke-on-Trent man, and William Clowes, a champion dancer from Burslem, called a meeting on the hill that lasted almost 14 hours. When Mow Cop Castle was given to the National Trust in 1937, 10,000 Methodists marked the occasion with a meeting at the summit.

A small museum of Primitive Methodism can be visited in the school room of **Englesea Brook Chapel** just north of Balterley. The chapel is one of the oldest Primitive Methodist chapels to survive. Mow Cop is at one end of the Newcastle Way that runs to Market Drayton.

ENDON
4 miles SW of Leek on the A53

This small village is unusual in that it is one of

the few places in Staffordshire that continues the ancient custom of well-dressing that is so common in neighbouring Derbyshire. Probably based on an ancient pagan ritual, the present ceremony, which was revived in 1845, takes place during the Spring Bank Holiday and includes the coronation of a Well-Dressing Queen.

On the Bank Holiday Monday, a village fete and fair is held, where there are traditional Morris dancers and the rural competition of Tossing the Sheaf takes place. In the days before combine harvesters, a heavy sheaf of corn was heaved by pitchfork over a bar that was gradually raised. Today, the game is similar, except that a 15lb sack of straw is used.

CHEDDLETON
3 miles S of Leek on the A520

🏛 Flint Mill   🏛 Churnet Valley Railway

🌿 Deep Hayes Country Park

The restored **Cheddleton Flint Mill**, in the rural surroundings of the Churnet Valley, makes an interesting visit. The water-powered machinery was used to crush flint that had been brought in by canal and then transported, again by water, to Stoke where it was used in the hardening of pottery. The small museum includes a rare 18th-century haystack boiler and a Robey steam engine. There are also collections of exhibits relating to the preparation of raw materials for the pottery industry. Trips by narrow boats along the Caldon Canal can be taken from the mill.

The village station is home to the **Churnet Valley Railway**, which will give great delight to all railway enthusiasts. The Railway has a nostalgic collection of beautifully preserved steam locomotives, diesel multiple units and other railway memorabilia, and operates an 11km journey through the valley. Leekbrook

Junction (no boarding or alighting) is at the northern end, which runs through Cheddleton, Consall and the impressive North Staffordshire Railway-style station at Kingsley & Froghall to Oakamoor. The railway is accessible from Cheddleton or Kingsley & Froghall (01538 360522).

To the west of Cheddleton is **Deep Hayes Country Park**, which lies in a secluded valley by the Caldon Canal and Staffordshire Way. From the ridge there are breathtaking views but, for the less energetic, there is a very pleasant walk around two pools, which has many offshoots into lovely countryside.

CONSALL
4 miles S of Leek off the A520

🌿 Nature Park

This is a beautiful spot hidden in a particularly deep section of the Churnet Valley downstream from Cheddleton. The little cottages keep close company with the small bridges over the Caldon Canal. Originally known as Consall Forge, the hamlet took its name from an old iron forge that existed here

Caldon Canal

in the first Elizabethan Age. As iron making became uneconomic, the forge altered its operation and became one of the major lime making centres after the completion of the Caldon Canal.

Reached through Consall village is **Consall Nature Park**, an RSPB reserve that is a quiet and peaceful haven with much to delight the avid birdwatcher. It is accessible only on foot or by canal. The village itself is very popular with walkers and boaters and has a pub to provide the necessary refreshment. Consall Forge Pottery produces hand-thrown stoneware ceramics – teapots are a speciality.

The splendid Consall Hall Landscape Gardens cover 70 acres and are a true delight to visit. An assortment of lakes, follies, packhorse bridges and summer houses amidst the spectacular planting, provide a surprise at every turn. Light lunches and afternoon teas are also available in the Halcyon Room.

FROGHALL
7 miles S of Leek on the A52

🏛 Froghall Wharf   📷 Caldon Canal

📷 Manifold Valley Light Railway

Froghall Wharf was built along the banks of the **Caldon Canal** to act as a trans-shipment area for limestone as it came down a railway incline from the quarries to the south of Waterhouses. Here the limestone was tipped into narrow boats and, from the mid-1800s, into railway wagons, to be carried to Stoke-on-Trent. The once-busy Wharf declined after 1920 following the construction of the **Manifold Valley Light Railway**, which directly linked the quarries with Leek and the national railway network. From then on the Canal and Wharf fell into a state of disrepair and it was only due to the efforts of the Caldon Canal Society that the navigation has survived. The Canal, once again open to

traffic, is now the sole preserve of pleasure craft and, at the leisurely pace of literally one horse power, narrowboats take visitors along to Consall Forge and back.

CAULDON
8 miles SE of Leek off the A52

This was the site of the quarry from which wagons travelled, down a railway track, to Froghall Wharf.

WATERHOUSES
8 miles SE of Leek off the A523

🚶 Hamps-Manifold Track

Between here and Hulme End, the Leek and Manifold Valley Light Railway, a picturesque narrow-gauge line, used to follow the valleys of the Manifold and the Hamps, criss-crossing the latter on little bridges. Sadly trains no longer run, but its track bed has been made into the **Hamps-Manifold Track**, a marvellous walk that is ideal for small children and people in wheelchairs, since its surface is level and tarred throughout its eight miles. The Track can be reached from car parks at Hulme End, Waterhouses, Weags Bridge near Grindon, and Wetton.

OAKAMOOR
9 miles SE of Leek on the B5417

🦅 Hawksmoor Nature Reserve

This village was once the home of the Thomas Bolton & Sons copper works that produced some 20,000 miles of copper wire for the first transatlantic cable in 1856. Little now remains of the works, which were demolished in the 1960s, but the site of the mill has been turned into an attractive picnic site complete with the very large mill pond. Nearby **Hawksmoor Nature Reserve** and bird sanctuary covers some 300 acres of the Churnet Valley and is managed by a local committee. The trail through the Reserve includes glorious landscapes, abundant natural history and industrial architecture.

ALTON
11 miles SE of Leek off the B5032

🎡 Alton Towers   🏰 Castle

⛰ Toot Hill Rock

The world-famous **Alton Towers** leisure park is the main attraction here, but even this spot has its quieter, lesser known corners. Originally the home of the Earls of Shrewsbury, who also

---

LEE HOUSE FARM B&B

Leek Road, Waterhouses, Stoke-on-Trent, Staffordshire ST10 3HW
Tel: 01538 308439
e-mail: josaphine.little@homecall.co.uk
website: www.leehousefarmbandb.co.uk

Lee House Farm offers homely, comfortable Bed & Breakfast accommodation on the edge of the Peak District National Park, near the Manifold Valley with its renowned scenic trail. Built in 1751, the Grade II listed farmhouse is full of character, with period features including oak beams, fireplaces and window shutters. The three spacious en suite bedrooms all have central heating, television and hot drinks tray. There is ample private parking and secure storage for bicycles. The owners also have a well-equipped self-catering two-bedroom cottage in a converted barn at nearby Cauldon Lowe on the A52.

🎭 stories and anecdotes   🦜 famous people   🎨 art and craft   🎡 entertainment and sport   🚶 walks

owned much of the surrounding area, the 19th-century mansion by Pugin is now just a gutted shell. The surrounding gardens and parkland (which contain most of the attractions) are older and were laid out by Capability Brown. Hundreds of workmen were employed to convert a whole valley into what is still a magnificent mix of formal gardens and parkland. As well as many fountains and pools, there are also numerous paths that lead to charming features such as a cast-iron Chinese pagoda, a Dutch garden, an Italian garden, a Swiss Chalet, a Gothic temple and a vast rock garden. The village of Alton has plenty to offer the visitor. The view up from the valley bottom to the **Castle**, perched on a sandstone rock above the River Churnet, has given this area of Staffordshire the nickname of Rhineland, and the steep climb up to **Toot Hill Rock** is rewarded by magnificent views. The Castle, in its present form, was built mainly by Pugin, who also built the now restored Italianate railway station. Note, too, the old lock-up and water mill.

UTTOXETER
16 miles SE of Leek on the A518

St Mary's Church   Racecourse

Today, the town is perhaps best known for its **Racecourse**, a popular National Hunt track that lies to the southeast of town. Highlight of the course's calendar is the stamina-sapping Midlands Grand National run in the spring. Uttoxeter is a traditional, rural market town, with a busy livestock and street market on Wednesdays. There are several pleasant, old timbered buildings in Uttoxeter, but fires in 1596 and 1672 destroyed most of the town's architectural heritage. As well as a visit to the Heritage Centre, housed in some old timber-framed cottages in Carter Street, **St Mary's Church** should also appear on a sightseer's

itinerary; it has a typical 'preaching box' dating from 1828.

ALSTONEFIELD
8 miles E of Leek off the A515

Tithe Barn

This ancient village, situated between the Manifold and Dove valleys, lies at the crossroads of several old packhorse routes and had its own market charter granted in 1308. The market ceased in 1500, but the annual cattle sales continued right up until the beginning of the 20th century.

Its geographical location has helped to maintain the charm of this unspoilt village. There has been no invasion by the canal or railway builders (it lies at 900 feet above sea level) and it is still two miles from the nearest classified road. Around 150 years ago Alstonefield was at the centre of a huge parish, which covered all the land between the two rivers. There has been a church here since at least AD892, but the earliest known parts of the present Church are the Norman doorway and chancel arch of 1100. There is also plenty of 17th-century woodwork and a double-decker pulpit dated 1637. Izaak Walton's friend, Charles Cotton, and his family lived at nearby Beresford Hall, now unfortunately no more, but the family's elaborate greenish pew is still in the church, and the fishing temple built by Cotton survives in Beresford Dale.

The village also retains its ancient **Tithe Barn**, found behind the late 16th-century rectory. The internal exposed wattle-and-daub wall and the spiral stone staircase may, however, have been part of an earlier building.

ILAM
9 miles E of Leek off the A52

Ilam Hall   Ilam Park

Now a model village of great charm, Ilam

THE OLD SHIPPON

Dales Cottage, The Rakes, Alstonefield, Ashbourne,
Staffordshire DE6 2FS
Tel: 07854821180 Fax: 01335 350103
e-mail: bluebell350103@aol.com

The Old Shippon is a beautifully converted stone barn
bungalow sleeping 2-4 people located in the heart of the
Peak District in the very popular village of Alstonefield,
between Bakewell and Ashbourne.

This self contained accommodation has been refurbished to
modern standards whilst retaining a traditional country feel, making
any stay here a homely one. It comprises a quaint lounge with log
fire, digital TV, DVD and sofa bed for extra guests, a newly fitted
kitchen/diner with all essential appliances, and a tastefully decorated
double bedroom, complete with its own cloakroom and en suite
bathroom. Towels and linen are provided with a hamper service
available containing some of the Peak Districts finest produce
including homemade jam and chutney and locally sourced bacon.
Outdoor furniture is also available in the summer months so that the
well kept gardens of this beautiful property can be fully appreciated.

There are plenty of local attractions nearby easily accessible via
the bus route operating 7days a week with a charming country pub
and farm shop nearby. Tescos and Sainsburys also deliver for all the
home comforts you need. Pets are welcome.

---

was originally an important settlement belonging to Burton Abbey. Following the Reformation in the 16th century, the estate was broken up and Ilam came into the hands of the Port family. In the early 1800s, the family sold the property to Jesse Watts Russell, a wealthy industrialist. As well as building a fine mansion, **Ilam Hall**, for himself, Russell also spent a great deal of money refurbishing the attractive cottages. Obviously devoted to his wife, he had the Hall built in a romantic Gothic style and, in the centre of the village, he had the Eleanor Cross erected in her memory. Ilam Hall is now a Youth Hostel. In a spectacular setting by the River Manifold, the National Trust's **Ilam Park** offers the perfect chance to explore the limestone area of the Peak District. There are glorious views towards Dovedale National Nature Reserve, part of the South Peak Estate. The Visitor centre contains exhibitions and an interactive display about the geology of the area. The tearoom serves dishes using meat from the estate's tenant farmers, who have been awarded the National Trust Fine Farm Produce Award.

Many places in the Peak District have provided the inspiration for writers over the years and Ilam is no exception. The peace and quiet found here helped William Congreve create his bawdy play *The Old Bachelor*, while Dr Johnson wrote *Rasselas* while staying at the Hall. Ilam lies in the valley of the River Manifold and is a popular starting point for walks along this beautiful stretch of river. In summer the Manifold disappears underground north of the village to reappear below Ilam Hall. The village is also the place where the Rivers Manifold and Dove merge. The two rivers rise close

---

📖 stories and anecdotes   🦜 famous people   🎨 art and craft   🏃 entertainment and sport   🚶 walks

Ilam, Dove Dale and Thorpe

Distance: *4.0 miles (6.4 kilometres)*

Typical time: *90 mins*

Height gain: *100 metres*

Map: *Explorer Outdoor Leisure 24*

Walk: *www.walkingworld.com ID:2183*

Contributor: *Phil and Sue Eptlett*

ACCESS INFORMATION:

By car from Ashbourne, take the A515 Buxton road north and after about a mile turn left at the sign for Ilam and Dove Dale. Follow this road through Thorpe to Ilam village. There is limited roadside parking in the village, or use the National Trust car park at Ilam Hall (charge). There is a bus service from Ashbourne three times per day each way, excluding Sunday. Ring 0870 608 2608 for details.

ADDITIONAL INFORMATION:

The National Trust property at Ilam Hall, part of which is a youth hostel, is surrounded by gardens and woodland and is worth a visit. Dove Dale, which stretches for about three miles to Milldale, is

a steep-sided gorge created by the River Dove and was the favourite haunt of Izaak Walton, author of *The Complete Angler.*

DESCRIPTION:

This walk starts in the quaint village of Ilam with its curious tile-clad houses and no intrusion by late 20th-century architecture.

A stroll alongside the River Manifold brings you to the grand stone Coldwell Bridge, which was part of the old packhorse route to Cheadle. A track then ascends to the second of our unspoilt villages at Thorpe. Here the village green and old church take you back to a more tranquil age.

After crossing a meadow and the short walk down Lin Dale, you will arrive at Dove Dale and the well-known stepping-stones that cross the River Dove.

From this point the more energetic can take a short diversion up the conically shaped Thorpe Cloud for fine views of the surroundings.

Continuing down the lower part of Dove Dale brings you to a car park where refreshments can be purchased. It is then a short walk back to the start point at Ilam.

FEATURES:

Hills or Fells, River, Toilets, Stately Home, National Trust/NTS, Wildlife, Birds, Flowers, Great Views, Butterflies, Cafe.

WALK DIRECTIONS:

1 | From the village, take the road to the right of the memorial cross and proceed over the river bridge.

2 | Take the stile and steps on the left immediately after crossing the bridge, which lead down into a meadow. Follow a well-defined, curving path adjacent to the River Manifold, crossing three stiles.

3 | Where the path bends away from the river, cross the stile, turn half-left and take the rising path away from the river and through some trees, following the footpath markers. On emerging from the trees to a

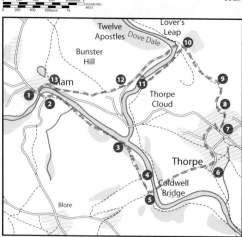

crest, follow the green path across open meadow in the direction of a wooded hillside.

4 | When a stony track is reached, go through the gate and bear slightly left, heading towards a large stone bridge over the river.

5 | This is Coldwell Bridge, which is accessed via a stile adjacent to the gate at the end. After pausing to admire the view of the river from the bridge, continue along the rising old packhorse route to the village of Thorpe.

6 | Enter Thorpe via a gate and take the tarmac road through the village, passing the ancient church and the community centre and pausing at the village green where there is a convenient seat to rest. Continue past the postbox, following the road as it bears right to join the road to Ilam.

7 | Go across the road and carry on through the car park, passing the toilets and exiting on to a stone track going up the meadow beyond.

8 | On reaching a rocky outcrop, turn left on an indistinct path and head for a cluster of trees.

9 | At the trees, follow the path down Lin Dale, keeping the wall to your left. Lin Dale is a short grassy dale under the shadow of conically-shaped Thorpe Cloud.

10 | This brings us to Dove Dale with its popular stepping-stones. Here the more energetic can take a diversion up to the summit of Thorpe Cloud for fine views of the surrounding area. From here take the left path along the bank of the River Dove, or alternatively cross stepping-stones and take the tarmac road on the opposite bank.

11 | Upon reaching a footbridge across the river, cross it and turn left, walking along the opposite bank to a car park where there are toilets and refreshments. Opposite the car park entrance, cross the stile signed to Ilam.

12 | After approximately 100 metres, mount the steps on the right, pass through some trees and go over a stile into a meadow. It is now a straight path across several fields, passing the rear of the Izaak Walton Hotel and a farmyard, heading towards Ilam.

13 | As you reach the outskirts of the village, the path descends to the road via a small gate, from which it is a short walk along the road back to the start point.

together, on Axe Edge, and for much of their course follow a parallel path, so it is fitting that they should also come together. Though Dovedale is regarded, and probably deservedly so, as the most scenic of the Peak District valleys, the Manifold Valley is very similar and, while being marginally less beautiful, it is often much less crowded.

WETTON
7 miles E of Leek off the B5053

🏛 Thor's Cave   🚶 Manifold Valley Trail

Wetton Mill has been sympathetically converted by the National Trust into a café, a very welcome sight for those walking the **Manifold Valley Trail**. There is also a car park here for the less energetic and a picnic area for those who would rather cater for themselves. Much of the hillside either side of the track also belongs to the National Trust and is a splendid place for walks.

Below the Mill can be found the ominous-sounding **Thor's Cave**, situated some 250 feet above the River Manifold. Though the cave is not deep, the entrance is huge, some 60 feet high, and the stiff climb up is well worth the effort for the spectacular views, all framed by the great natural stone arch. The acoustics too are interesting – conversations can easily be carried out with people far below. The openings at the bottom of the crag on which the cave sits are known as Radcliffe Stables and are said to have been used by a Jacobite as a hiding place after Bonnie Prince Charlie had retreated from Derby.

Stoke-on-Trent

🏛 Museums in Stoke, Burslem and Etruria

The city was established as late as 1910 when Fenton joined the five towns (Tunstall,

Burslem, Hanley, Longton and Stoke) immortalised by the novels of Arnold Bennett. Once fiercely independent, the towns became progressively involved with each other as improvements in roads, water supplies and other amenities forced them towards amalgamation. The new city's crest, of an ancient Egyptian potter at his wheel in one quarter, sums up the fortune on which the wealth of the area was created. Each of the old towns is also represented in the crest, and the joint motto translates as "Strength is stronger for unity".

It was the presence of the essential raw materials for the manufacture and decoration of ceramics, in particular marl clay, coal and water, that led to the concentration of pottery manufacture in this area. Though production started in the 1600s, it was the entrepreneurial skills of Josiah Wedgwood and Thomas Minton, who brought the individual potters together in factory-style workplaces, which caused the massive leap forward in production that took place in the 18th century. Their factories were large, but there were also hundreds of small establishments producing a whole range of more utilitarian chinaware; production in the Potteries reached its height towards the end of the 19th century. For those interested in pottery and industrial architecture, Stoke-on-Trent is a wonderful place to visit, with many museums and factories open to the public to tell the story of the city, such as the **Spode Museum & Visitor Centre** in Church Street.

Hanley, one of the five towns of The Potteries, and part of the Stoke-on-Trent conurbation, was the birthplace of Arnold Bennett, Sir Stanley Matthews and John Smith (the captain of the ill-fated *Titanic*). The **Potteries Museum & Art Gallery** houses the world's finest collection of Staffordshire ceramics and offers many more attractions, including a natural history gallery and a lively programme of exhibitions, talks, tours and workshops. The Potteries shopping centre, situated in the heart of Hanley, is every shopper's dream with a fantastic range of famous shops all brought together in a beautiful environment. Natural daylight cascades through the centre's many glazed roofs and plants, trees and water features create an outdoor feel.

Burslem, in the northern suburbs, is the home of **Burleigh Earthenware Pottery**, founded in 1851 by William Leigh and famous for its elegant blue and white patterns. The pottery's products are still made by hand using traditional methods such as underglaze transfer printing. Also in Burslem is the **Royal Doulton Visitor Centre**, which contains the world's largest display of Royal Doulton figures and many other treasures from the company's rich heritage. There are factory tours, demonstrations, a video-theatre, gallery, restaurant and shop. Another Burslem attraction is Ceramica, located in the Old Town Hall, with a huge kiln and an Arnold Bennett study area. Bennett was educated in Burslem and his first novel, *Anna of the Five Towns*, is set in the Potteries. His ashes are buried at Burslem cemetery.

Etruria, to the west of the city centre, was created by Josiah Wedgwood in 1769 as a village for the workers at the pottery factory he built in this once rural valley. Though the factory has gone (it moved to Barlaston in the 1940s), Etruria Hall, Wedgwood's home, is still standing in what is now the National Garden Festival site. The pottery industry dominated the village and the **Etruria Industrial Museum**, next to the Trent & Mersey and Caldon Canals, displays a steam-powered potters' mill as well as other exhibits

---

🏛 historic building　📷 museum　🏛 historic site　⚜ scenic attraction　🌱 flora and fauna

connected with the industry. Wedgwood died at Etruria Hall and is buried in the churchyard of St Peter Vincula, Stoke-on-Trent.

Around Stoke-on-Trent

CHEADLE
5 miles E of Stoke-on-Trent on the A521

🏛 Church of St Giles

The glory of this busy market town is the Roman Catholic **Church of St Giles**, commissioned in 1841 and designed by AWN Pugin. The church has a 200ft spire, and the interior is an exuberant display of bright painting, brass, carving, gilding and Wedgwood and Minton tiles.

KIDSGROVE
5 miles N of Stoke-on-Trent on the A50

🏛 Harecastle Tunnels

Now chiefly a residential town, Kidsgrove is well worth a visit for anyone interested in canals. The two **Harecastle Tunnels** were major engineering feats of their time and they carry the Trent & Mersey Canal from Cheshire into The Potteries. It was Josiah Wedgwood who first dreamt of building a canal to link the area with the major Trent &

Mersey navigation and thus create a waterway link right across the country from Liverpool to Hull. He fought long and hard to get the necessary Bill passed through Parliament, undaunted by the fact that a 3,000-yard-long tunnel would be needed to go through Harecastle Hill. The Bill was passed and, though many scoffed at his plans, Wedgwood's canal and required tunnel, both built by James Brindley, were constructed over an 11-year period.

Those who had their doubts about Wedgwood's grand plan nearly had the last laugh when, some years later, there was almost a catastrophe as Harecastle started to subside. Fortunately, Thomas Telford came to the rescue and another tunnel was built alongside the first, thus averting disaster. The two tunnels can still be seen today and make a very impressive sight: although Josiah's original tunnel is not in use, the Telford tunnel has been restored.

LONGTON
2 miles SE of Stoke-on-Trent on the A50

🏛 Gladstone Working Pottery Museum

The **Gladstone Working Pottery Museum** (see panel below) on Uttoxeter Road is a fascinating museum of the British pottery

Gladstone Working Pottery Museum

Uttoxeter Road, Longton, Stoke-on-Trent ST3 1PQ
Tel: 01782 237777
e-mail: gladstone@stoke.gov.uk   website: www.stoke.gov.uk/museums

Gladstone is the only complete Victorian pottery factory from the days when coal burning ovens made the world's finest bone china. Traditional skills, original workshops, the cobbled yard and huge bottle kilns create an atmospheric time-warp that has no equal. Also visit the gift shop and Gladstone Parlour Tea Room serving morning coffee, delicious hot and cold lunches and afternoon tea. Please allow 2-3 hours for your visit.

🎞 stories and anecdotes   🐦 famous people   💮 art and craft   ✒ entertainment and sport   🚶 walks

industry housed in a Victorian building. It tells visitors the story of how 19th-century potters worked, with the display of traditional skills, the original workshops, the cobbled yard and the huge bottle kilns creating a unique atmospheric time-warp. As the brochure proclaims: "throwing, jiggering, fettling, saggar making, glazing, dipping, firing, painting, sponging, moulding, casting – it's all at Gladstone". Aynsley China, John Tams and Staffordshire Enamels have their factory shops in Longton. Open daily from 10am to 5pm.

BARLASTON
5 miles S of Stoke-on-Trent off the A34

🏛 Wedgwood Visitor Centre & Museum

A visit to The Potteries would not be complete without a visit to the **Wedgwood Visitor Centre & Museum**, set in a beautiful 500-acre country estate just outside Barlaston. The stunning modern museum traces the history of Wedgwood from the founding of the factory in 1759 to the present day through the displays of Queen's Ware, Jasper, Black Basalt and fine bone china. In rooms designed to recapture the style of specific periods, there are hundreds of Wedgwood pieces from those eras. George Stubbs and Joshua Reynolds both painted portraits of the Wedgwood family, which hang in the centre's art gallery. In the craft centre, potters and decorators can be watched as they use traditional skills to create today's Wedgwood products. The centre is open every day.

HANCHURCH
5 miles S of Stoke-on-Trent on the A5182

🌱 Trentham Gardens

This tiny hamlet itself is unlikely to ring any bells with visitors as they pass by, but the nearby gardens are world famous. **Trentham Gardens** were landscaped by Capability Brown and given a more formal style by Sir Charles Barry, whose work can be observed in the lovely Italian gardens. Although the Hall was demolished in 1911, this style can still be recognised in such buildings as the orangery and sculpture gallery, which remain today and form a framework for the outstanding conference, exhibition and banqueting centre that is Trentham.

NEWCASTLE-UNDER-LYME
2 miles W of Stoke-on-Trent on the A53

🏛 Guildhall   🏛 Museum and Art Gallery

This ancient borough, which received its first charter from Henry II in 1173, was, for several centuries, the largest town in north Staffordshire. Today, the town maintains its individuality from its close neighbour, Stoke-on-Trent, and its centre is designated a conservation area. One of the best ways of exploring the delights of Newcastle-under-Lyme is to follow either, or both, of the town trails that take in many of the town's most notable buildings. Both begin in Nelson Place and the first takes in not only the early 19th-century Church of St George and Mayer House, the former home of a famous veterinary family, but also some fine Georgian houses and, in Marsh Parade, the vast 19th-century building that once housed the town's first silk mill.

The second of the two trails takes in the particularly eye-catching Merrial Street before moving on to St Giles's Church, where the base of the tower dates from the 13th century. The original medieval church was replaced by a brick building in 1720, and in 1870 it was again rebuilt, this time by George Gilbert Scott, who managed to capture much of the beauty of medieval times.

🏛 historic building   🏛 museum   🏛 historic site   🌀 scenic attraction   🌱 flora and fauna

BROOKFIELDS FARM SHOP

Stone Road, Blackbrook,
nr Newcastle-under-Lyme,
Staffordshire ST5 5EG
Tel: 01782 680833

For a pleasant, relaxed way to shop for food, a visit to **Brookfields Farm Shop** is takes a lot of beating. Beryl Lockett, Alan, Adam and Gill make this very much a family affair, and lots of the produce on sale is home-grown on the farm. Potatoes, beans, carrots, onions, leeks, courgettes and pumpkins are gathered for sale in their seasonal prime, and other lines include locally produced bacon, sausages and gammon, eggs, cheese, jams and honey, chutneys and pickles, fresh bread, cakes and pastries, ice cream and cut flowers.

The choice is impressive, and success has seen the shop expanding in size and range. It stands near the junction of the A51 and A53, 200 yards from the well-known Swan with Two Necks pub and 5 miles west of Newcastle-under-Lyme. Opening hours are 10 to 5 on Monday, 9 to 6 Tuesday to Saturday and 10 to 4 on Sunday.

One of Newcastle-under-Lyme's oldest buildings also features on the route; the **Guildhall**, built in 1713 to replace an earlier timber building, stands beside the base of a medieval cross. The **Borough Museum and Art Gallery**, set in eight acres of parkland, houses a wonderful collection of assorted items from clocks to teapots, paintings to clay pipes, a reconstruction of a Victorian street and exhibitions of local and national artists (01782 297313). A mile from the town centre, the New Victoria Theatre was Europe's first purpose-built theatre-in-the-round.

MADELEY
7 miles W of Stoke-on-Trent on the A525

🦆 The Pool

Situated on an ancient packhorse route from Newcastle-under-Lyme, this village's name comes from the Anglo-Saxon 'maden lieg',

Madeley Old Hall

🎭 stories and anecdotes   🦅 famous people   🎨 art and craft   🎵 entertainment and sport   🚶 walks

which means 'clearing in the woods'. The focal point of this enchanting place, which has been designated a conservation area, is **The Pool**, formed by damming the River Lea to provide water power for the corn mill that still stands at its northern end. The pool is a haven for a variety of bird life. Madeley's grandest building is the Old Hall, an excellent example of a 15th-century squire's timber-framed residence. The village's large sandstone church can be seen through the trees from the mill pond. Standing in a raised churchyard, with ancient yew trees, All Saints Parish Church was originally Norman, but was extensively enlarged in the 1400s; the chapel was rebuilt in 1872.

Stone

Augustinian monks founded a priory here in the 12th century, of which only one arch and some cloisters now remain, and in 1251 Henry II granted the monks a charter to hold a market. In its heyday as a trading town, some 38 coaches pulled up daily at the bow-windowed Crown Hotel, still one of the most attractive buildings along the High Street. Built during this period of prosperity, the early Gothic Revival Parish Church of St

Michael contains several interesting monuments, including a bust of Admiral John Jervis, Earl St Vincent, the hero of the great naval victory off Cape St Vincent in 1797. The Trent & Mersey Canal played a large part in Stone's early economic development and today it still brings work to the town through the building of holiday canal cruisers and a growing tourist trade. The canal was begun in 1766 and, by 1771, it had reached Stone. The celebrations that accompanied its opening here were so boisterous that one of the four locks in the town and a bridge collapsed under the weight of people. Stone is a true canal town, the dry docks and workshops are still busy today, as they have been for well over 200 years.

Around Stone

ECCLESHALL
5 miles SW of Stone on the A519

🏰 Castle   🏛 Pumping Station

For over 1,000 years **Eccleshall Castle** was the palace of the bishops of Lichfield but, at the beginning of the 19th century, it became a family home when the Carter family moved

STONE ANTIQUES
*12 Radford Street, Stone,
Staffordshire ST15 8DA
Tel: 01785 818291*

Stone Antiques is housed in a delightful little shop in the centre of Stone, a historic town on the Trent & Mersey Canal. Owner Tracy Harris personally chooses the items in stock, taking great pride in sourcing unusual and interesting antiques to give as special gifts or to enhance any room in a home. The ever-changing array includes vintage clocks and watches, antique toys, lights for ceiling, wall or table, paintings, some smaller items of furniture and select pieces from Royal Doulton, Coalport, Beswick and Moorcroft. Tracy also buys scrap gold and buys and sells jewellery. Friendly service and value for money are hallmarks of this lovely little enterprise, which is open from 10 to 4.30.

🏛 historic building   🏛 museum   🏛 historic site   🏵 scenic attraction   🌿 flora and fauna

GOODY 2 SHOES

31 High Street, Eccleshall,
Staffordshire ST21 6BW
Tel: 01785 751697
e-mail: nicole@shoesatgoody2shoes.co.uk
website: www.shoesatgoody2shoes.co.uk

Ladies Footwear for Every Occasion

On the busy High Street of Eccleshall, **Goody 2 Shoes** sells an up-to-the-minute range of ladies' footwear for all occasions, from casual and sporty to day wear and evening wear with definite WOW factor.

The business was founded by Nicole Heath, who saw a shortage of good, fashionable ladies' shoes outlet in the region. She started off in a small terraced house originally called Number 55, but success came quickly and the business soon outgrew these premises, moving to this current Aladdin's Cave of footwear and accessories. Nicole has many years' experience in footwear retail and among the accolades that have come her way is runner-up in 2002 in the UK Footwear Awards, Best Womens Retailer.

Upwards of 300 styles are in stock at any one time, some from names with worldwide recognition, others exclusive in the UK to Goody 2 Shoes and made to the shop's own design and colour range. New arrivals come into stock all the time, and Nicole changes the stock completely every six months. Familiar brands include the long-establsihed German firm Birkenstock (shoes, sandals and clogs); Fitflop (sandals and trainers); Redfoot, specialising in folding shoes and pumps; Melissa from Brazil; and Geox – "shoes that breathe" from Italy. Brands exclusive to Goody 2 Shoes include Pedro Miralles shoes and bags made in Alicante, Bourne, Sachelle, Lisa Kay, Kanna, Pare Gabia and Bou Bou des Colonies – a Parisian boutique label specialising in delicate footwear often adorned with beads or sequins. The impressive range of shoes is complemented by carefully selected accessories including handbags, scarves, watches and fun brooches and necklaces. For a complete ensemble ladies with an eye for fashion can combine a visit here with a trip along the road to the clothes shop Sassy (qv).

About that name Goody 2 Shoes. It comes from an 18th century nursery tale about a poor little girl who had only one shoe. One day someone gave her a pair and she ran around delightedly showing them off and shouting 'Two Shoes!'.

SASSY

7/9 High Street, Eccleshall, Staffordshire ST21 6BW
Tel: 01785 850067
e-mail: jillsilvester@surfree.co.uk

Jill Silvester turned a passion for fashion and design into a popular and successful business when she opened **Sassy** among the many retail outlets on the main street of Eccleshall. She takes great pride in sourcing and stocking the very best in high-quality ready-to-wear ladies' fashion wear, with a select range of accessories to complement the clothes. Aimed mainly at the mid-20s upwards and catering for all sizes and styles, the brands always in stock include Oui, Passport and Adini from Germany, All is Beautiful from France and NYDJ Tummy Tuck jeans from the USA. Among the well-chosen accessories are beautiful Italian scarves, distinctive costume jewellery from Dante, Ticktech and Squadra Blu, and fun, funky and fashionable reading and sun glasses from Clere Vision. The stock in the two sales areas is always changing, so there's always something new and fashionable for the well-dressed ladies of Eccleshall and the surrounding area. And if Tracy hasn't got a specific garment in stock, she can usually order it. If it's smart shoes her customers are looking for, then Goody 2 Shoes (qv) along the road is the place to head for.

Sassy is open from 9.30 to 5.30
(Monday and Saturday from 10, closed Sunday).

MADE OF LEATHER

30 High Street, Eccleshall, Staffordshire ST21 6BZ
Tel: 01785 851722
e-mail: madeofleather@hotmail.co.uk

'Quality Leather Products'

Since opening **Made of Leather** among the shops and inns on Eccleshall's bustling main street, Nicola (Niki) Batllé-Jacques has been sharing her long-held passion for natural fabrics and materials with her many loyal customers. Behind the little bay-windowed frontage of her attractive boutique shop she has assembled an eclectic range of high-quality products, with the main emphasis on leather, ranging from upmarket luggage and bags of all sizes to purses, wallets, briefcases, belts, gloves, travel clocks, manicure sets and passport holders. Among the featured brands are Yoshi, Visconti, Smith & Canova, Pell-Mell bags from Scotland, Kinsey designer bags made not far away in Nantwich, Chatterbox notepads, pill boxes and torches, purses by Rowallen, Saddler and Golunski and gloves and

accessories made by the long-established and world-famous firm of Dents. Other items in stock include Autograph pens and beautiful scarves in wool, silk and linen. Made of Leather is open from 9.30 to 5.30 Tuesday to Friday and 10 to 5 Saturday. Two hours parking is available outside the shop and Eccleshall's main car park is a short walk away.

🏛 historic building 🏛 museum 🏚 historic site ⚘ scenic attraction 🌿 flora and fauna

WILLIAM PERRY THE BUTCHERS

19 Stafford Street, Eccleshall, Staffordshire ST21 6BL
Tel: 01785 850288

2007 sees the 80th anniversary of **William Perry the Butchers**, where the owner and excellent staff take justifiable pride in the quality and consistency of what they sell. The meat comes almost exclusively from local farms, ensuring traceability and minimising 'food miles'. The shop has its own abattoir, and the beef is hung for 3 weeks to allow the full flavours to develop. They make their own sausages, with at least six varieties available at any one time, and their own steak & kidney and chicken & mushroom pies are also among the best-sellers. Bread is delivered fresh daily, and there's always a good choice of cheese, much of it local.

here from Yorkshire. The present simple sandstone house is typical of the best architecture of the William and Mary period and incorporates part of the earlier 14th-century castle. The interior of the house has been augmented by successive members of the family, one of whom added a magnificent Victorian staircase and dome. Perhaps to remind them of the county from which they came, the Carters have collected a very interesting number of 19th-century paintings by Yorkshire artists. The gardens have been created around the ruins of the old castle and have a great deal of romantic appeal.

A little way north of Eccleshall, on the A519 at Cotes Heath, is **Mill Meece Pumping Station**, where two magnificent steam engines that once pumped more than three million gallons of water each day, are kept in pristine condition (01785 617171).

SHALLOWFORD
4 miles SW of Stone off the B5026

🦢 Izaak Walton's Cottage

Set in beautiful grounds in this tiny hamlet in the heart of the Sow Valley, **Izaak Walton's Cottage** is a pretty 17th-century half-timbered cottage once owned by the renowned biographer and author of *The Compleat Angler*. Fishing collections are on show, and there's a small souvenir shop. Within the grounds are an authentic 17th-century herb garden, a lovely picnic area and an orchard.

SANDON
4 miles SE of Stone on the B5066

🏛 Sandon Hall

Near the village stands the ancestral home of the Earl of Harrowby, **Sandon Hall**. Rebuilt in 1850 after the earlier house had been damaged by fire, the Hall is surrounded by 400 acres of parkland, which include a notable arboretum. The Hall is steeped in history and, along with the impressive interior, makes for an interesting and informative visit. The family, too, has led a fascinating life with no less than seven generations in parliament and three successive members of the family holding office in the Cabinet. The museum tells of their lives and includes costumes, toys and the duelling pistols of William Pitt the Younger.

🎭 stories and anecdotes   🦢 famous people   🎨 art and craft   ✒ entertainment and sport   🚶 walks

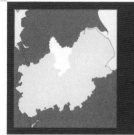

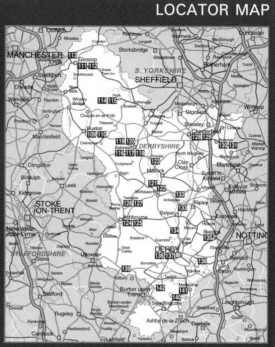

LOCATOR MAP

ADVERTISERS AND PLACES OF INTEREST

🏚 historic building   🏛 museum   🏚 historic site   🌲 scenic attraction   🌿 flora and fauna

5 Derbyshire

Traditionally, Derbyshire marks the start of the north of England, and the county was also at the forefront of modern thinking at the beginning of the Industrial Revolution. The chief inheritor of this legacy is Derby, the home of Rolls-Royce and Royal Crown Derby porcelain, and it remains a busy industrial centre today. An early landmark of this new age is Richard Arkwright's mill and associated village at Cromford. In the south of the county are Calke Abbey and the charming ancient town of Repton.

However, the county is dominated by the Peak District National Park that covers much of its area. The first of the 10 National Parks, it is often divided into White and Dark peak as the landscape changes from deep limestone valleys to bleak, isolated moorland.

Along with numerous attractive villages and small towns, ancient monuments and caves and caverns, the park is home to two of the finest stately homes not just in Derbyshire but in the whole country – Haddon Hall and Chatsworth.

The southern section of the Peak District is probably best-known for beautiful Dovedale. The large car park near Thorpe that gives general access to the Dale is often crowded, but there is plenty of room for everyone and the wonderful valley, just a few hundred yards from the car park, is well worth exploring. It is also the place to have a go at crossing a river on stepping stones, something that has delighted children for many, many years. The River Dove is also a Mecca for keen fishermen. It was a favourite spot for Izaak Walton, who wrote his book *The Compleat Angler* in the area. Lord Byron praised the beauty of the county, writing that "there are prospects in Derbyshire as noble as any in Greece or Switzerland".

The ancient custom of well-dressing is almost exclusively confined to the limestone areas of the county. The porous rock, through which rainfall seeped leaving the surface completely dry just a few hours after heavy rainfall, meant that, for the people of these close-knit communities, the well or spring was of the utmost importance. If this dried up, the lives of the whole community were at risk.

The area of northeast Derbyshire with the District of Bolsover centres around Chesterfield. This was the heart of the county's coal-mining area and many of the towns and villages reflect the prosperity the mines brought in Victorian times. Sadly, the vast majority of the collieries are now closed. For a while the country suffered a period of decline, but visitors today will be surprised at the wealth of history and fine architecture to be seen throughout the region.

Owler Tor, nr Hathersage

The Peak District

In 1951, the Peak District National Park became the first of Britain's National Parks to be established, and ever since then its 555 square miles of glorious scenery have been protected from 'inappropriate development'. Of all the world's national parks, it is the second most popular – only Mount Fuji in Japan attracts more visitors each year.

Referred to as the Dark Peak as well as the High Peak, the northern area of the National Park is not as foreboding as its name might suggest. These high moors are ripe for exploring on foot, and a walk from the Kinder Reservoir will lead to the western edge of Kinder Scout. This whole area is really a series of plateaux, rather than mountains and valleys, with the highest point on Kinder Scout some 2,088 feet above sea level. In this remote and wild area the walker can feel a real sense of freedom - however, it is worth remembering that the moors, with their treacherous peat bogs and unpredictable mists, which can rise quickly even in summer, should not be dismissed as places for a casual ramble.

To the eastern side of this region are the three reservoirs created by flooding of the upper valley of the River Derwent. Howden, Derwent and Ladybower provide water for Sheffield and the East Midlands but their remote location, along with the many recreational activities found there, make them popular places to visit. The Derwent Dam is particularly famous as the site of practice exercises with Barnes Wallis' bouncing bombs for the Dambusters of World War II. The topography of the area was very similar to the Ruhr Valley and it was here that preparations were made for the attack on the Ruhr reservoirs

---

BON APPETIT (BUXTON) LTD

15 Terrace Road, Buxton, Derbyshire SK17 6DU
Tel/Fax: 01298 212414
e-mail: bon-appetit@hotmail.co.uk

Long famous for its spa water, the largest community in the Peak District National Park is now on the map as a centre of good food. **Bon Appetit** has been attracting lovers of good food from Buxton and the surrounding area for several years. Behind the big window in the cheerful green-painted frontage the chill counters, shelves and tables are filled with good things to eat.

Locally sourced meat is to the fore in home-cooked hams, organic pork pies, home-made pies and pâtés, and Bon Appetit also stocks a selection of other English and Continental cooked and cured meats. Excellent pastry features in quiches, tarts and a wide array of home-baked cakes, and sandwiches, baguettes and panini are made to order with a variety of hot and cold fillings. There are salad boxes, soups, jams and chutneys, Derbyshire oatcakes, biscuits, pasta, sauces and condiments, fruit juices and hampers and picnic baskets made up to individual requirements. Bon Appetit is open from 9 to 5.30 Monday to Friday, 9 to 5 Saturday.

---

by Lancasters of 617 Squadron in 1943. The Derwent Dam was also used in the making of the 1954 film *The Dambusters*.

Buxton

🏛 The Crescent 🏛 Opera House
🏛 St Anne's Church 🏛 Devonshire Royal Hospital
🏛 Museum 🎋 Pavilion Gardens
🏛 Church of St John the Baptist

With a population of barely 20,000, the elegant and lofty Georgian town of Buxton is nevertheless the largest settlement within the boundaries of the Peak District National Park. (The second largest town, Bakewell, has fewer than 5,000 inhabitants.) Buxton's gracious architecture can be attributed mainly to the efforts of the 5th Duke of Devonshire who hoped to establish a northern spa town that would rival, possibly surpass, the attractions of Bath in the southwest. In both locations it was the Romans who first exploited the healing waters of apparently inexhaustible hot springs as a commercial enterprise. The Roman name for Buxton was Aquae Arnemetiae – the Spa of the Goddess of the Grove. The waters still bubble up at Buxton, always maintaining an incredibly constant temperature of 28 degrees centigrade. Buxton water is reputed to be particularly pure and especially effective in mitigating the symptoms of rheumatism. Countless sufferers from rheumatism are on record attesting that the balmy Buxton water helped to soothe their painful symptoms: Mary, Queen of Scots, a political prisoner detained at nearby Chatsworth but allowed out on day release to Buxton, was one of them.

In the 18th century, the 5th Duke of Devonshire commissioned the building of

The Crescent to ensure that visitors would flock here. Designed by John Carr of York, the building is similar to the architecture found in Bath and, after suffering from neglect, is about to undergo a huge restoration programme. As with many places, the coming of the railway to Buxton in 1863 marked the height of popularity of the town. Nothing, however, could be done to alter the harsh climate, and the incessant rainfall meant that the Duke's dream of making Buxton the 'Bath of the North', was never truly realised.

Among the other notable architectural features of the town is the Devonshire Royal Hospital. This was originally built as stables for hotel patrons of The Crescent and, after their conversion by the 6th Duke in 1858, the largest unsupported dome in the world (50 metres in diameter) was built to enclose the courtyard in 1880.

Originally built in 1905, the attractive Opera House was restored in 1979 to its grand Edwardian style. After being used as a cinema for many years, it once again hosts live performances on one of the largest stages in England, offering a comprehensive and popular programme throughout the year.

The Pavilion Gardens have a conservatory and octagon within the grounds – antique markets and arts shows are often held here - and it is a very pleasant place to walk around at any time of the year. Laid out in 1871 by Edward Milner, with money donated by the Dukes of Devonshire, the 23 acres include formal gardens, serpentine walks and decorative iron bridges across the River Wye. The conservatory was reopened in 1982 following extensive renovation; there is also a swimming pool filled with warm spa water.

The Church of St John the Baptist was built in Italian style in 1811 by Sir Jeffrey

Wyatville. That same year Wyatville laid out The Slopes, the area below the Market Place in Upper Buxton. The grand Town Hall was built between 1887 and 1889 and dominates the Market Place. Further down Terrace Road is the **Buxton Museum** (see panel below), which explores the Wonders of the Peak through seven time zones. As well as housing an important local archaeology collection, the Museum also has a fine collection of Ashford Marble, Blue John ornaments, paintings, prints, pottery and glassware. It also contains some of the collection from the Derbyshire Constabulary Memorabilia Museum previously housed in Derby.

St Anne's Church, built in 1625, reflects the building work performed here before Buxton's 18th-century heyday when limestone was the most common construction material rather than the mellow sandstone that dominates today.

Buxton, which rivals Ambleside for the title of the highest town in England, is surrounded by some of the most glorious of the Peak District countryside. These moorlands also provide one of the town's specialities – heather honey. Several varieties of heather grow on the moors: there is ling, or common heather, which turns the land purple in late summer; there is bell-heather, which grows on dry rocky slopes; and there is cross-leaved heather, which can be found on wet, boggy ground.

Around Buxton

🏛 Poole's Cavern   ⚜ Axe Edge

To the west of the town lies **Axe Edge**, the highest point of which rises to 1,807 feet above sea level. From this spot on a clear day (and the weather here is notoriously changeable) the panoramic views of Derbyshire are overwhelming. Just beyond, at 1,690 feet above sea level, the Cat and Fiddle Inn is the second highest pub in England. Axe Edge Moor, which receives an average annual rainfall of over four feet, is strictly for hardened walkers. It should come as no surprise that this Moor is the source of several rivers that play an important role in the life of the Peak District. The River Dove and the River Manifold, which join at Ilam, rise not far from one another; the River Wye rises above Buxton to join the Derwent further south; the River Goyt, a major source

Buxton Museum & Art Gallery

Terrace Road, Buxton, Derbyshire SK17 6DA
Tel: 01298 24658 Fax: 01298 79394
e-mail: buxton.museum@derbyshire.gov.uk
website: www.derbyshire.gov.uk

Explore the Wonders of the Peak through seven time zones. Discover when sharks swam in warm 'Derbyshire' seas; when lions and sabre tooth cats terrorised mastodons. Meet the Roman Legionaries, and the scientists unravelling the history of Earth. An audio tour, 'Time Moves On', helps to enhance your visit. For art lovers, enjoy intricate Ashford Black Marble inlay and Blue John ornaments, and a regular programme of exhibitions, featuring work by national and local artists, photographers and craftworkers. Activities for all the family accompany the exhibitions.

🏛 historic building   🖼 museum   🏛 historic site   ⚜ scenic attraction   🌿 flora and fauna

of the Mersey, rises to the west of Axe Edge. The entire length of the River Goyt can be walked, from its source to its confluence with the River Etherow to the north and just outside the boundaries of the National Park.

Those who venture to Errwood Reservoir will be surprised to see rhododendrons growing near the banks of a man-made lake. They once stood in the grounds of Errwood Hall, which was built in the 1830s for the Grimshawe family. The house was demolished before the Reservoir was flooded, but the gardens were left to grow wild. Not far away can be seen the strange-looking Spanish Shrine. Built by the Grimshawes in memory of their Spanish governess, it is a small stone building with an unusual beehive roof.

Also to the west of town, **Poole's Cavern** on Green Lane is a natural limestone cave that was used by tribes from the Neolithic period onwards. It was visited by Mary, Queen of Scots and the 'chair' she used is pointed out during the regular tours of the cavern that are available. Above the cavern and about 20 minutes walk away is Grin Low Country Park and the prominent folly and scenic viewpoint, built in 1896, known as Solomon's Temple.

COMBS
3 miles N of Buxton off the A6

🐾 Chestnut Centre

Combs Reservoir, southwest of Chapel-en-le-Frith, is crossed at one end by Dickie's Bridge. 'Dickie' is said to have lived at a farm in Tunstead where he was known as Ned Dixon. Apparently murdered by his cousin, he nevertheless continued his 'working life' as a sort of guard-skull, alerting the household whenever strangers drew near. Various strange occurrences are said to have ensued when attempts were made to move the skull.

On Castleton Road just a few miles northeast

of the town, the **Chestnut Centre** is a fascinating wildlife conservation centre, popular with children and adults alike. It is famed for its otters, with award-winning otter and owl enclosures set along an extensive circular nature trail that meanders through some historic wooded parkland. The Centre is open all year round from 10.30am to 5.30pm.

CHAPEL-EN-LE-FRITH
4 miles N of Buxton off the A6

🏛 Chapel of St Thomas

This charming town is often missed by travellers on the bypass between Buxton and Stockport, but it repays a closer look. In 1225, the guardians of the High Peak's Royal Forest purchased land from the Crown and built a **Chapel** here, dedicating it to St Thomas à Becket of Canterbury. A century later the chapel was replaced with a more substantial building; further modernisation took place in the early 1700s. The building of the original chapel led to the foundation of the town and also its name, which is Norman French for chapel in the forest. A curious legacy has been passed down allowing owners of freehold land in the district the right to choose their vicar. The interior of the church boasts 19th-century box pews and a monument to 'the Apostle of the Peak', William Bagshawe of nearby Ford Hall, a Nonconformist minister of the late 17th century. In 1648, the church was used as a gaol for 1,500 Scottish prisoners and the dreadful conditions arising from such close confinement caused unimaginable suffering. Their ordeal lasted for 16 days; a total of 44 men died.

WHALEY BRIDGE
6 miles N of Buxton off the A5004

This small industrial town at the gateway to the Goyt Valley grew up around the coal-mining and textile industries. Both have now gone, but the Peak Forest Canal flowing through the town remains very much the centre of activity. The 'bridge' of the village's name crosses the River Goyt, on the site of what may once have been a Roman crossing.

Many of the old warehouses in Whaley Bridge have been restored and converted to meet the needs of the 21st century and, where once narrow boats transported goods and raw materials to and from the town, boats can now be hired for recreational use. The Toddbrook Reservoir was built in 1831 to be a feeder for the Peak Forest Canal. The wharf here is dotted with picturesque narrowboats.

LYME PARK
8 miles NW of Buxton off the A6

Lyme Park (National Trust) is an ancient estate originally granted to Sir Thomas Danyers in 1346 by a grateful King Edward III after a battle at Caen. Danyers then passed the estate to his son-in-law, Sir Piers Legh, in 1388. It remained in the family until 1946, when it was given to the Trust. Not much remains of the original Elizabethan manor house; todays visitors are instead treated to the sight of a fantastic Palladian mansion, the work of Venetian architect Giacomo Leoni. Not daunted by the bleak landscape and climate of the surrounding Peak District, Leoni built a corner of Italy here in this much harsher countryside. Inside the mansion there is a mixture of styles: the elegant Leoni-designed rooms with rich Rococo ceilings; the panelled Tudor drawing room; and two surviving Elizabethan rooms. Much of the three-dimensional internal carving is attributed to Grinling Gibbons, though a lot of the work was also undertaken by local craftsmen. As well as the fantastic splendour of the mansion, the estate includes a late 19th-century formal garden and a medieval deer park.

HAYFIELD
9 miles N of Buxton off the A624

🌄 Kinder Downfall   🐾 Kinder Scout

This small town below the exposed moorland of **Kinder Scout** is a popular centre for exploring the area and offers many amenities for hillwalkers (see walk on page 178). Like its neighbour New Mills, Hayfield grew up around the textile industry, in this case wool weaving and calico printing. Many of the houses seen today were originally weavers' cottages. One of Hayfield's best-known sons was the much-loved actor Arthur Lowe (1914-1982).

Three miles northeast of the town is **Kinder Downfall**, the highest waterfall in the county, found where the River Kinder flows off the edge of Kinder Scout. In low temperatures the fall freezes solid – a sight to be seen. It is also renowned for its blow-back effect: when the wind blows, the fall's water is forced back against the rock and the water appears to run uphill. There are not many natural waterfalls in Derbyshire, so Kinder Downfall appears on most visitors itineraries.

GLOSSOP
13 miles N of Buxton off the A624

🌄 Snake Pass

Glossop is an interesting mix of styles - the industrial town of the 19th century with its towering Victorian mills, and the 17th-century village with its charming old cottages and cobbled streets.

From Glossop, the A57 east is an exhilarating stretch of road with hair-pin bends, known as the **Snake Pass**. The road is frequently made impassable by landslides, heavy mist and massive snowfalls in winter but, weather permitting, it is an experience not to be missed. For much of the length of

Praze FINE FOODS LTD

53 High Street West, Glossop,
Derbyshire, SK13 8AZ
Tel: 01457 860916
e-mail: info@praze.co.uk website: www.praze.co.uk

Opening hours: Tues to Sat 9.30am to 5pm

Share Our Passion For Food.........

......That's the invitation extended by owners Sarah and Tracey at Praze Fine Foods Ltd. Based in the heart of Glossop, their authentic High Street delicatessen, is stocked with a wide range of gourmet foods, including many award-winning products from regional and international producers. They are also members of the Guild of Fine Foods.

Customers are invited to enjoy a stylish, relaxed shopping experience that will delight all lovers of fine food. The range of products includes cheese, pâtés, oils, vinegars, salamis, olives, wines, local ales, chutneys, preserves, antipasti and much more!

Bespoke hampers and gift vouchers are also available.

DERBYSHIRE CLOCKS

104 High Street West, Glossop, Derbyshire SK13 8BB
Tel: 01457 862677

Serving the people of Derbyshire for more than 30 years, Derbyshire Clocks is highly recommended if it is a high quality of service you are after. Restoring and trading in antique clocks and barometers is what owner Terry Lees does best and his passion for his job is evident in his careful restoration of the clocks, which come through his door. He carries out a

full restoration service to all types of clocks and has had a showroom in the area for three decades. His restoration work includes long case clocks (Grandfather clocks), wall clocks (Vienna, Tavern, Drop Dial etc) bracket clocks among many more.

Located in the small market town of Glossop, the shop has an extremely good reputation in the area for its restoration work which consists of casework (the cabinet of the clock), movements and dials (brass and painted). Terry is well known for his friendly manner and high standard of work and many also visit him to buy antique clocks and traditional style lamps. If required, there is a collection and delivery service available. Customers include locals as well as those from further a field, with the shop about 14 miles from Manchester.

Hayfield and Lantern Pike

Distance: *5.6 miles (9.0 kilometres)*

Typical time: *180 mins*

Height gain: *300 metres*

Map: *Explorer Outdoor Leisure 1*

Walk: *www.walkingworld.com ID:2905*

Contributor: *Jim Grindle*

ACCESS INFORMATION:

The start of the walk is at the junction of the A624 and the A6015 and is not far from New Mills on the A6. There is a bus connection with Manchester and a well signposted car park at the start.

ADDITIONAL INFORMATION:

The Sett Valley Trail is traffic-free and was bought from British Rail in 1973 to provide a walking, cycling and horse riding route. Previously it was a popular holiday line for Manchester as well as an essential part of the industrial scene of the valley with its many cotton mills, calico printing works and paper mills. The route has been developed for wildlife, too, with numbers of reed-beds and copses. Lantern Pike is owned by the National Trust to whom it was presented by the Ramblers Association as a memorial to a past president, Edwin Royce. There is a viewfinder/memorial on the summit. The Pennine Bridleway now runs as far north as Burnley and is suitable for mountain bikes and walkers as well as for horse riders.

DESCRIPTION:

This short circular walk has a reasonable height gain, but the summit of Lantern Pike is easily attained by a very gradual climb. Much of the walk follows the Sett Valley Way and the Pennine Bridleway, which means fewer stiles than usual. There are outstanding views, of the Kinder Scout plateau in particular.

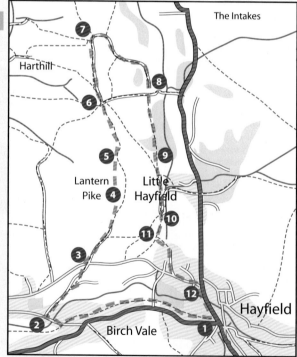

Pub, Toilets, Church, National Trust/NTS, Wildlife, Birds, Flowers, Great Views, Butterflies, Cafe, Gift Shop, Food Shop, Good for Kids, Industrial Archaeology, Moor, Public Transport, Restaurant, Tea Shop, Woodland

WALK DIRECTIONS:

1 | Walk past the Information Centre/Toilet block to join the Sett Valley Trail. Continue along until it is interrupted by a road. Leave the Trail and turn right following the road. Drop to a bridge over the Sett and then look for a Pennine Bridleway sign by a cobbled track going uphill on the right.

2 | The Trail climbs to another road by a group of houses.

3 | Cross the road, turn right and, almost at once, left to continue on the Trail. This climbs slowly again and brings you to a gate with a National Trust sign behind it. Go through the gate and up to the left to reach the summit of Lantern Pike.

4 | The well-worn path leads over the hill and down to the exit from the National Trust land.

5 | Follow the direction of the signpost across the open moorland to a wall on the far side. There you will find a signpost with five arms.

6 | Just to the right of the signpost (and out of shot) is a bridleway gate with a Pennine Bridleway sign. Go through on to an enclosed track and follow it until it divides at Matleymoor Farm.

7 | Turn right and pass the farm. After 100m there is another division in the track. Ignore the turning on the left. Carry on downhill for

1km on the tarred track and look for another tarred track coming from the right.

8 | Here you turn right, doubling back on your route and climbing steeply. Just before a green metal footpath sign about 200m away is a turning on the left leading to a farm. Follow this to a stile and gate at its end. Go through and ahead at first before turning left and following a path across the slope. Cross a stream and avoid taking paths leading downhill on the left. The path leads through a wood and to a high stone wall with a ladder stile by two Scots pines. If you can't see the stile it will be because you have not kept high enough - just go uphill almost to the corner of the field.

9 | Once over the stile keep by the wall on your right to another stile. Cross it and maintain direction with the wall now on your left. The path ends at a stile by a tarred drive with some houses. Cross this stile but not the one immediately opposite across the track. Continue on the drive until it bends sharply to the left. On the right you will find an enclosed track.

10 | Turn down this track until you see a stile on the left just before a bend to the right.

11 | Cross this stile and go down a steepish enclosed path. This leads you down to the outskirts of Hayfield. Turn left on joining a road and watch for a footpath sign by a gate on the right just before you reach a flyover.

12 | The sign directs you across a playing field to the riverbank. Follow the river on your right to a footbridge. Cross the bridge and follow the path to a road. Just over a wall is the car park.

the turnpike road that Thomas Telford built across Snake Pass in 1821, the route follows the line of an ancient Roman road, known as Doctor's Gate, which ran between Glossop and a fort at Brough. The route was so named after it was rediscovered, in the 16th century, by Dr Talbot, a vicar from Glossop.

HADFIELD

14 miles N of Buxton off the A624

🏛 Woodhead Chapel   ⚲ Longendale Trail

The small village of Hadfield is the terminus of the **Longdendale Trail**, a route following the line of a former railway line and part of the Trans-Pennine Trail. Old Hall in The Square is the oldest building in the village,

built in 1646. The Roman Catholic Church of St Charles was built in 1868 by Baron Howard of Glossop; members of the Howard family are buried here.

The Longdendale Trail continues eastward from here. Longdendale itself is the valley of the River Etherow, and is a favourite place for day-trippers. Along the footpath through this wild and desolate valley there are many reminders of the past, including **Woodhead Chapel**, the graveyard of which has numerous memorials to the navvies, and their families, who died in an outbreak of cholera in 1849 while working on the Sheffield to Manchester railway line. Hadfield is the setting for Royston Vasey in the TV series *The League of Gentlemen*.

HALCYON

Station Road, Hadfield, Derbyshire, SK13 1AR
Tel: 01457 853713
e-mail: pamela.hadcross@virgin.net
website: www.halcyonofhadfield.co.uk

The little village of Hadfield lies in the Longdendale valley at the beginning of the Longdendale Trail, a popular walking, cycling, and horse-riding route – part of the Trans-Pennine Way. On arrival in Hadfield - head for Halcyon – less than 2 minutes from the Station. Halcyon offers a self-catering apartment, pot painting studio, and soon, Victorian tea rooms and restaurant.

The top floor of the Victorian shop has been transformed into a luxurious 'city apartment in the country' with hi-tech facilities and magnificent moorland views. The bathroom boasts a spa-bath and double shower wet area. The kitchen is equipped with all appliances. The dining area leads to the 2 bedrooms - Stay in the stylish master bedroom with king size and sofa bed or step back in time in our 'Thirties' themed double room. The spacious living room offers a comfortable corner suite and king size bed settee sleeping an extra 4 persons if required . Visit our website www.halcyonofhadfield.co.uk to see for yourselves.

The studio is set within the elegant stone courtyard behind 101. Choose from our range of over 40 items and paint at your leisure. Your pot is then glazed and fired for you to collect, or can be posted.

The street and courtyard levels, will be traditional tea rooms and superb English restaurant with 50 covers, opening in summer 2010. Produce will be local – Moorland game, Glossop wild boar and Kinder lamb. The arrival of our classically trained head chef is eagerly awaited . He is well respected by Mark Gregory and comes highly praised by Phil Hobbs of Pinewood Studios - 'I would recommend Yuseph to anybody who enjoys the best that food can give. He is a master of his trade and second to none.

🏛 historic building   🏛 museum   🏛 historic site   ⚲ scenic attraction   🌿 flora and fauna

EDALE
8 miles NE of Buxton off the A625

🏃 Pennine Way

In the valley of the River Noe, Edale marks the start of the **Pennine Way**. Opened in 1965, this long-distance footpath follows the line of the backbone of Britain for some 270 miles from here to Kirk Yetholm, just over the Scottish border. Though the footpath begins in the lush meadows of this secluded valley, it is not long before walkers find themselves crossing wild and bleak moorland before heading further north to Bleaklow. Many travellers have spoken of Derbyshire as a county of contrasts, and nowhere is this more apparent than at Edale. Not only does the landscape change dramatically within a short distance from the heart of the village, but the weather can alter from brilliant sunshine to snowstorms in the space of a couple of hours.

Tourism first came to Edale with the completion of the Manchester to Sheffield railway in 1894, though at that time there was little in the way of hospitality for visitors. Today there are several hotels, camping sites, a large Youth Hostel and adventure and walking centres.

CASTLETON
8 miles NE of Buxton off the A625

🏰 Peveril Castle   ⛰ Winnats Pass

🏚 Blue John Mine & Caverns   ⛰ Mam Tor

Situated at the head of the Hope Valley, Castleton is sheltered by the Norman ruin of **Peveril Castle** with its spectacular views over Castleton and the surrounding countryside. The Castle, originally called Castle of the Peak, was built as a wooden stockade in 1080 by William Peveril, illegitimate son of William the Conqueror. Later rebuilt in stone, the keep was added by Henry II. It remains the only surviving example of a Norman castle in Derbyshire, and is among the best preserved and most complete ruins in Britain.

CAUSEWAY HOUSE CRAFTS

Castleton, Hope Valley S33 8WE
Tel: 01433 620343
Fax: 01455 620258
e-mail: enquiries@cinnamon-bear.co.uk
website: www.cinnamon-bear.co.uk

Causeway House Crafts was established by Roger Vincent in 1979 as a small craft shop selling hand-thrown pottery. It has gradually developed to become the largest gift shop in the Peak District village of Castleton, one of the most popular tourist and holiday centres in the area. The shop stocks the world-famous Steiff Teddy Bears; a range of jewellery in modern, vibrant designs by Carrie Elspeth, a young designer based in South Wales; and a wide range of toys, specialising in those by Orchard Toys and Fiesta Crafts - both of which are well-known British brands. The shop also stocks a selection of pictures and prints by well-known artists, including a number of local Peak District artists. Other items on sale include books and maps, greetings cards, studio pottery, handbags and other fashion accessories, candles, garden ware and much more. A limited selection of the stock is available via the shop's website.

To the rear of the craft shop is the Cinnamon Bear Coffee Shop serving lunches, cream teas and some wonderful locally made cakes.

Peveril Castle, Castleton

Approaching Castleton from the west along the A625, the road runs through the **Winnats Pass**, a narrow limestone gorge. Thought to have been formed under the sea, from currents eroding the seabed, the gorge has been used as a road for centuries and is still the only direct route to the village from the west.

Originally laid out as a planned town below its castle, the shape of the village has changed little over the years and it has become a popular tourist centre. The mainly 17th-century Church of St Edmund was heavily restored in 1837, but retains its box pews and a fine Norman arch, as well as a Breeches Bible dated 1611.

The hills to the west of Castleton are famous for their caves. The **Blue John Mine and Caverns** (see Treak Cliff Cavern opposite), which have been in the hands of

the Ollerenshaw family for many years, are probably one of Derbyshire's most popular attractions. Amazing trips down into the caves themselves can be taken. Above ground, in the gift shops, various items can be bought made with the distinctive Blue fluorspar with its attractive purplish veining. It was once prized by the Romans, and it is said that Petronius paid the equivalent of around £40,000 for a wonderfully ornate vase carved from the stone. It is said that in a fit of petty-mindedness he preferred to smash the vase rather than relinquish it to the Emperor Nero.

At the bottom of Winnats Pass lies Speedwell Cavern, a former lead mine that used boats on an underground canal to ferry the miners and lead ore to and from the rock face. Visitors can follow the same boat journey underground in the company of a guide. The mine had a short life: it started up in 1771 and, despite an investment of £14,000, closed in 1790 after only £3,000 worth of lead ore had been extracted.

Peak Cavern, reached by a delightful riverside walk, has the widest opening of any cave in Europe. Up until the 17th century, little cottages used to stand within the entrance. The rope-makers who lived in these tiny dwellings used the cave entrance, dry in all weathers, for making rope. The ropewalk, which dates back some 400 years, can still be seen. Guides re-enact the process of making rope, and one rope-maker's cottage is still extant. The cave was used by the BBC to film an episode of *The Chronicles of Narnia* series. Over the years successive Kings and Queens would entertain deep within the belly of the cave, which would be festooned with candles and other open flames – visitors can see the ledge on which the royal musicians would perch. Peak Cavern was originally known as

TREAK CLIFF CAVERN

Castleton, Hope Valley, Derbyshire S33 8WP
Tel: 01433 620571
website: www.bluejohnstone.com

An exciting and educational few hours is guaranteed on a visit to **Treak Cliff Cavern**, an ancient underground wonderland in the heart of the Peak District National Park.

Treak Cliff Hill is the only place in the world where Blue John stone occurs naturally, and visitors will learn all about this mineral, a unique colour-banded form of fluorspar. (The generally accepted explanation of the name is that it derives from the French bleu et jaune – blue and yellow – which the Derbyshire folk adapted to Blue John.) Tour guides explain how miners in the 1750s constructed a tunnel with hand tools to reach the prized deposits inside the hill. Visitors will see veins of the stone across the cave roof and marvel at The Pillar, the largest piece ever found, and the fossils in the rocks. In the Witch's Cave richer deposits are revealed, before the tour goes deeper to other caves to show the wonders of underground limestone cave formations. The guide will explain where Blue John came from, how the caves were shaped by rushing water and how stalactites and stalagmites are formed – the most extraordinary of the former looks like a stork standing on one leg!

Back on the surface visitors can enjoy a cup of tea or coffee made with water collected from inside the cavern, or take in the marvellous views with a picnic they have brought along. The cavern is of international fame and geological importance and has been designated a Site of Special Scientific Interest. By agreement with English Nature all the deposits on the visitor route are preserved, but Blue John is regularly mined here in parts not seen by visitors. This is cut, polished and made into beautiful ornaments and jewellery which can be bought in the little shop at the cave entrance.

The Castleton Gift Shop, half a mile away in the centre of the village, displays a fine collection of antique and modern ornamental Blue John pieces, along with Blue John mineral specimens, as well as rocks, minerals and fossils from around the world.

The entrance to the Cavern lies on the east-facing slope of an ancient carboniferous reef laid down about 310 million years ago. The Cavern is open throughout the year, weather permitting, but times may vary, so it's best to call before setting out on a visit. All admissions are by guided tour. Children under 16 must be accompanied, dogs are allowed if on a lead. There is no wheelchair access. Polish Your Own Blue John Stone is an activity usually available in school holidays, when visitors can choose, prepare and polish a slice of Blue John to take home. Other activities include Carols by Candlelight at Christmas time.

The Devil's Arse, but the fastidious Victorians felt this was 'inappropriate' and changed it to the name it carries today.

No description of Castleton would be complete without a mention of **Mam Tor**. The name means Mother Hill, and locally the tor is referred to as Shivering Mountain, because the immense cliff face near the summit is constantly on the move with landslips of grit and shale owing to water seepage. A climb to the top of the ridge is worthwhile, as the views are splendid – in particular of the two diverse rock formations which separate the White (limestone) Peak from the northern Dark (gritstone) Peak.

HOPE
9 miles NE of Buxton off the A625

🏛 Church of St Peter

Hope gets its first mention in AD926 as the site of a battle won by King Athelstan. By the time of the Domesday survey of 1086, the parish of Hope had extended to embrace much of the High Peak area and included places such as Buxton, Chapel-en-le-Frith and Tideswell. It remained one of the largest parishes in the country until the 19th century, though a market charter was not granted until 1715. Hope lies at the point where the River Noe meets Peakshole Water; the stream rises in Peak's Hole (better known as Peak Cavern), hence its name.

The parish **Church of St Peter** was built at the beginning of the 1200s; the only part remaining from the original church is the Norman font. The Latin inscription on a chair in the north aisle reads (in translation) 'You cannot make a scholar out of a block of wood' and is said to have been carved for Thomas Bocking, the vicar and schoolmaster here during the 17th century. His name also

Saxon & Steeple Cross, Hope

appears on the fine pulpit; his Breeches Bible is displayed nearby. The Hope Agricultural Show is held every year on August Bank Holiday Monday.

BAMFORD
11 miles NE of Buxton off the A6013

🏛 Church of St John the Baptist   🏛 Bamford Mill

🌿 Ladybower

This charming village situated between the Hope Valley and Ladybower Reservoir, stands at the heart of the Dark Peak below Bamford Edge and close to the Upper Derwent Valley Dams. When the Derwent and Howden Dams were built in the early years of the 20th century, the valley of the Upper Derwent was flooded, submerging many farms under the rising waters. The 1,000 or so labourers and their families were housed at Birchinlee, a temporary village thatcame to be known locally as Tin Town because of its plethora of corrugated iron shacks. During World War II the third and largest reservoir, the **Ladybower**, was built. This involved the flooding of two more villages - Derwent and Ashopton. The dead from Derwent's church were re-interred in the churchyard of St John the Baptist in Bamford. The living were rehoused in Yorkshire Bridge, a purpose-built hamlet located below the embankment of the Ladybower Dam. There is a Visitor Centre at Fairholmes (in the Upper Derwent Valley) that tells the story of these drowned villages.

The topography hereabouts was similar to that of the Ruhr Valley and the Lancaster bombers of 617 Squadron, the Dambusters, used the reservoir to practise dropping Barnes Wallis' bouncing bombs prior to their attack on the Ruhr Dam in 1943. Parts of the film The Dambusters were filmed here in 1954.

Bamford's **Church of St John the Baptist** is unlike any other in Derbyshire. Designed in 1861 by the famous church architect William Butterfield, it has a slender tower and an extra-sharp spire. Also worthy of note, particularly to lovers of industrial architecture, is **Bamford Mill**, just across the road by the river. This cotton mill was built in 1820; it retains its huge waterwheel and also has a 1907 tandem-compound steam engine.

The village lies in the heart of hill-farming country, and each Spring Bank Holiday Bamford plays host to one of the most famous of the Peak District Sheepdog Trials.

Along the A57 towards Sheffield, the road dips and crosses the gory-sounding Cutthroat Bridge. The present bridge dates back to 1830, but its name comes from the late 1500s, when the body of a man with his throat cut was discovered under the bridge that then stood here.

HATHERSAGE
12 miles NE of Buxton off the A625

Moorseats   Churchyard

Once a centre for needle-making, it is difficult to know whether to classify Hathersage as a large village or a small town. In either event, it is a pleasant place with interesting literary connections. Charlotte Brontë stayed at Hathersage vicarage, and the village itself appears as 'Morton' in her novel *Jane Eyre*. The name Eyre was probably gleaned from the monuments to the prominent local landowners with this surname, as can be seen in the village Church of St Michael and its churchyard. The 15th-century head of the family, Robert Eyre, lived at Highlow Hall. Within sight of this Hall he built seven houses, one for each of his seven sons. North Lees was one, and another was **Moorseats**,

River Derwent, nr Hathersage

where Charlotte Brontë stayed on holiday and used as the inspiration for Moor House in *Jane Eyre*.

In Hathersage **Churchyard** lie the reputed remains of Little John, Robin Hood's renowned companion. Whether or not the legend is to be believed, it is worth mentioning that when the grave was opened in the 1780s, a 32-inch thighbone was discovered. This would certainly indicate that the owner was well over seven feet tall.

Bakewell and the White Peak

This region of the Derbyshire Dales, sometimes also known as the Central Peaks and occupying the central area of the Peak District National Park, is less wild and isolated than the remote High Peak area. The two main rivers, the Wye and the Derwent, which both have their source further north, are, in this region, at a more gentle stage of their course. Over the centuries, the fast-flowing waters were harnessed to provide power to drive the mills situated on the riverbanks; any

walk taken along these riverbanks will not only give the opportunity to discover a wide range of plant and animal life, but also provide the opportunity to see the remains of buildings that once played an important part in the economy of north Derbyshire.

Bakewell

🏛 Haddon Hall   🏛 Church   🏛 Museum

The only true town in the Peak District National Park, Bakewell attracts many day-trippers, walkers and campers as well as locals who come to take advantage of its many amenities. The beautiful medieval five-arched bridge spanning the River Wye is still in use today as the main crossing point for traffic. A stone-built town set along the banks of the River Wye, Bakewell enjoys a picturesque setting among well-wooded hills. With only 4,000 inhabitants it is nevertheless generally acknowledged as the capital of the Peak District National Park.

However, for most people it is a dessert that has made the name of Bakewell so famous, but please remember it is referred to locally as a pudding and most definitely not as a tart. Its invention is said to have been an accident when what was supposed to have been a strawberry tart turned into something altogether different. The cooking mishap took place in the kitchens of the White Horse Inn (now the Rutland Arms Hotel), which was built in 1804 on the site of a coaching inn.

Bakewell is the market

Medieval Wye Bridge, Bakewell

town for this whole central area of the Peak District – markets were held here well before the granting of a charter in 1330. Monday is now Bakewell's market day and the cattle market, one of the largest in Derbyshire, is an important part of the area's farming life. The annual Bakewell Show started in 1819 and has gone on to become one of the foremost agricultural shows in the country. Across the River Wye stands the enormous, new Agricultural and Business Centre, where the livestock market takes place.

The large parish **Church of All Saints** was founded in Saxon times, as revealed by the ancient preaching crosses and stonework. Its graceful spire, with an octagonal tower, can be seen for miles around. Bakewell is one of the few places in Derbyshire in the Domesday Book to record two priests and a church, and the churchyard and church itself contain a wonderful variety of headstones and coffin slabs and, near the porch, a most unusual cross. Over 1,200 years old, it stands an impressive eight feet high. On one side it depicts the Crucifixion, on the other are the Norse gods Odin and Loki. The Vernon Chapel in the south aisle contains impressive monuments to The King of the Peak, Sir George Vernon of Haddon Hall, who died in 1567, and also to Sir John Manners, who died in 1584, and his wife Dorothy Vernon – these latter two feature in one of the great romantic legends of the Peak District.

Behind the church is the lovely **Old House Museum,** housed in a building on Cunningham Place that dates back to 1534. It

ID INTERIOR DESIGN

Matlock Street, Bakewell, Derbyshire DE45 1EE
Tel: 01629 813263 Fax: 01629 814361
e-mail: interior.design@btconnect.com

On one of the main shopping streets in the centre of Bakewell, **ID Interior Design** has gained a reputation starting in Sheffield over 60 years for providing a high-quality, personal design service. The studio provides a bespoke interior design consultancy service, and the team of professionally trained designers led by Sarah Cooper are able to undertake a wide range of projects, from individual rooms to complete houses, offices or hotels. The specialists include craftsmen for paint effect, carpet fitting and upholstery, and the workrooms are undoubted leaders in making up of curtains, pelmets, bedspreads and loose covers. Quality and attention to detail are to the fore in everything they do, and no job is too big or too small.

The showrooms on two floors are home to an exciting and inspirational mix of fabrics and upholstery, carpets and rugs, wallpapers and paints, furniture and mirrors, curtain poles, lighting and unusual gifts to suit all budgets. Every item is chosen for good design, quality and individuality.

Owner Sarah Cooper came here in 1982 with a Degree in Interior Design and her customers will testify that she is as keen as ever: her reward is the satisfaction of successfully transforming a room or a whole house for her clients.

Saxon Cross in Churchyard, Bakewell

is thought to be the oldest house in Bakewell. This beautiful building narrowly escaped demolition, and has been lovingly restored by the Bakewell Historical Society and now displays its original wattle-and-daub interior walls. Established as a folk museum, it houses a fascinating collection of rural bygones.

The town is full of delightful, mellow stone buildings, many of which date from the early 1600s and are still in use today. The Old Market Hall is now the Peak District National Park Visitor Centre. Few buildings remain from the days when Bakewell was a minor spa town, but the Bath House, on Bath Street, is one such building. Built in 1697 for the Duke of Rutland, it contained a large bath that was filled with the spa water and kept at a constant temperature of 59 degrees Fahrenheit.

South of Bakewell down the Matlock Road,

on a bluff overlooking the Wye, the romantic **Haddon Hall** (see panel below) stands hidden from the road by a beech hedge. The home of the Dukes of Rutland for over 800 years, the Hall has enjoyed a fairly peaceful existence, in part no doubt because it stood empty and neglected for nearly 300 years after 1640, when the family chose Belvoir Castle in Leicestershire as their main home. Examples of work from every century from the 12th to the 17th are evident in this architectural treasure trove.

Little construction work has been carried out on the Hall since the days of Henry VIII and it remains one of the best examples of a medieval and Tudor manor house. The 16th-century terraced gardens are one of the chief delights of the Hall and are thought by many to be the most romantic in England. The Hall's splendour and charm have led it to be used as a backdrop to television and film productions including *Jane Eyre*, *Moll Flanders* and *The Prince and the Pauper*. Nikolaus Pevsner described the Hall as, "the English castle par excellence, not the forbidding fortress on an unassailable crag, but the large, rambling, safe, grey, loveable house of knights and their ladies, the unreasonable dream-castle of those who think of the Middle Ages as a time of chivalry and valour and noble feelings. None

Haddon Hall

nr Bakewell, Derbyshire DE45 1LA
Tel: 01629 812855 Fax: 01629 814379
e-mail: info@haddonhall.co.uk
website: www.haddonhall.co.uk

Only a mile to the south of Bakewell down the Matlock Road, on a bluff overlooking the Wye, the romantic **Haddon Hall** stands hidden from the road by a beech hedge. The Hall is thought by many to have been the first fortified house in the country, although the turrets and battlements were actually put on purely for show. The home of the Dukes of Rutland for over 800 years, the Hall has enjoyed a fairly peaceful existence, in part no doubt because it stood empty and neglected for nearly 300 years after 1640, when the family chose Belvoir Castle in Leicestershire as their main home. Examples of work from every century from the 12th to the 17th are here in this treasure trove.

Little construction work has been carried out on the Hall since the days of Henry VIII and it remains one of the best examples of a medieval and Tudor manor house. The 16th century terraced gardens are thought by many to be the most romantic in England. The Hall's splendour and charm have led it to be used as a backdrop to television and film productions including *Jane Eyre*, *Moll Flanders* and *The Prince and the Pauper*. Nikolaus Pevsner described the Hall as "The English castle par excellence, not the forbidding fortress on an unassailable crag, but the large, rambling, safe, grey, loveable house of knights and their ladies, the unreasonable dream-castle of those who think of the Middle Ages as a time of chivalry and valour and noble feelings. None other in England is so complete and convincing."

Calton Lees and Edensor

Distance: *4.2 miles (6.7 kilometres)*
Typical time: *120 mins*
Height gain: *140 metres*
Map: *Explorer Outdoor Leisure 24*
Walk: *www.walkingworld.com ID:2434*
Contributor: *Phil and Sue Eptlett*

The start point is from the Calton Lees car park (chargeable) adjacent to the Chatsworth Garden Centre just off the B6012. From whichever direction you approach, just follow the signs for Chatsworth House

ADDITIONAL INFORMATION:

There is an abundance of wildlife to be seen including fish and birds of all types and deer that are free to roam on the estate. In about 1760, the 4th Duke of Devonshire asked Capability Brown, a noted landscape designer, to improve the park the results of which can be seen today. Most notably the creation of Stand Wood, which provides an impressive backdrop to the house and the wide open pastures to the front. He also altered the course of the river.

Fine views of the surrounding area can be seen from Waypoint 6, including Froggatt Edge, Curber Edge and the house surrounded by Stand Wood.

DESCRIPTION:

Starting from the car park at Calton Lees the walk soon follows the bank of the River Derwent across rolling meadow towards Chatsworth House, which is open to the public from Easter to Christmas. Upon reaching the river bridge leading to the house cross the road and take the path to the village of Edensor, which up until the 1830s was sited across the river from the house but was moved to improve the view for His Lordship. After passing through the village

you take a path rising up a large landscaped meadow towards woodland with panoramic views all across the estate and surrounding countryside. Proceeding through the wood and a field, a farm track is soon reached that leads back to the car park. Refreshments are available at the Garden Centre.

FEATURES:

Toilets, Church, Stately Home, Wildlife, Birds, Flowers, Great Views, Butterflies, Food Shop.

WALK DIRECTIONS:

1 | Leave the car park by a path adjacent to the access road and go through the white gate. Immediately cross the road and go directly across the grassland to a weir on the River Derwent.

2 | From the weir walk upstream, keeping the river on your right. As you proceed, the house comes into view with its impressive west face and the Emperor Fountain can be seen in the gardens if it is working. Follow the river until you reach the bridge carrying the access road to the house. If you wish, this is the point to visit the house and gardens

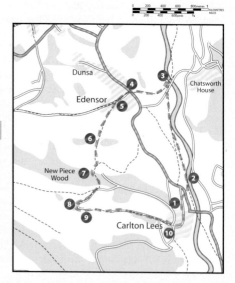

3 | Cross the road and take the path opposite going diagonally across the open parkland to the B6012 road and the village of Edensor.

4 | Cross the road, go through the white gates at the village entrance and proceed taking the road to the right of the church. As you pass through the village, which has not changed since it was moved in the 1830s note the mix of architectural styles, particularly Hollybush Cottage with its unusual spiral chimneys.

5 | Shortly after Hollybush Cottage take the footpath on the left signed to Rowsley. Go up the steps and turn left up further steps immediately before a cottage, then go through a small gate on to open countryside. Here the path is non-existent so starting with your back to the church spire walk across the rising open ground following the very infrequent footpath markers. Upon reaching the first crest head to the right side of a fenced-off copse of trees.

6 | From the copse keep going upward in a straight line towards woodland on the horizon. As the woodland is approached head for the gate in the wall adjacent to some benches. This is the perfect spot to sit and rest and take in the fine view of the house, parkland and surrounding countryside.

7 | When suitably rested go through the gate and follow the track through woodland to a further gate. Go through this gate and proceed across the meadow to a wall, then follow this wall keeping it on your left, until another gate is reached.

8 | Go through the gate and follow the stone track between two cottages and yet another gate.

9 | Keep on the track as it winds down a meadow to the bottom where it turns sharp left. Now follow this track keeping the wall and a stream on your right.

10 | Eventually you come to the final gate, go through and proceed straight ahead where the track becomes a tarmaced estate road. Follow this back to the car park.

other in England is so complete and convincing".

The Hall's chapel is adorned with medieval wall paintings; the kitchens are the oldest extant part of the house, and feature time-worn oak tables and dole cupboards. The oak-panelled Long Gallery features boars' heads and peacocks in the panelling.

Around Bakewell

EDENSOR
2 miles NE of Bakewell off the B6012

🏛 Chatsworth House

This model village (the name is pronounced Ensor) was designed by Sir Joseph Paxton and built by the 6th Duke of Devonshire between 1838 and 1842 after the original village had been demolished because it spoilt the view from Chatsworth House. The village church was built by Sir George Gilbert Scott; in the churchyard is buried the late President Kennedy's sister Kathleen, who had married into the Cavendish family. Both she and her husband, the eldest son of the 10th Duke, were killed during World War II.

The home of the Dukes of Devonshire, **Chatsworth House**, known as the Palace of the Peak, is without doubt one of the finest of the great houses in Britain. The origins of the House as a great showpiece must be attributable to the redoubtable Bess of Hardwick, whose marriage into the Cavendish family helped to secure the future of the palace.

Bess' husband, Sir William Cavendish, bought the estate for £600 in 1549. It was Bess who completed the new house after his death. Over the years, the Cavendish fortune continued to pour into Chatsworth, making it an almost unparalleled showcase for art treasures. Every aspect of the fine arts is here, old masterpieces, furniture, tapestries, porcelain and some magnificent alabaster carvings.

The gardens of this stately home also have some marvellous features, including the Emperor Fountain, which dominates the Canal Pond and reaches a height of 290 feet. It was built by Sir Joseph Paxton to celebrate a visit by the Tsar of Russia in 1844. Paxton also built the world's largest greenhouse here as a prototype for the Crystal Palace, built for the Great Exhibition of 1851. The glasshouse was demolished in 1920. There is a maze and a Laburnum Tunnel and, behind the house, the famous Cascades. The overall appearance of the park as it is seen today is chiefly due to the talents of Capability Brown, who was first consulted in 1761. Sir Joseph is buried in the churchyard of St Peter's Church.

Longshaw Country Park, nr Grindleford

GRINDLEFORD

6 miles N of Bakewell off the B6521/B6001

🎎 Padley Chapel   🌲 Longshaw Country Park

This is one of the smallest Peak District villages, and from here each year in July there is a pilgrimage to **Padley Chapel** to commemorate two Catholic martyrs of 1588. The ruins of ancient Padley Manor House, found alongside the track bed of the old railway line, are all that remain of the home of two devout Roman Catholic families. It was from the manor house that two priests, Robert Ludlam and Nicholas Garlick, were taken to Derby and sentenced to death by hanging,

drawing and quartering. The then owner of the house, Thomas Fitzherbert, died in the Tower of London three years later, while his brother died at Fleet Prison in 1598. In 1933, the charming chapel seen today was converted from the still standing farm buildings.

To the northwest of the village is the **Longshaw Country Park**, some 1,500 acres of open moorland, woodland, and the impressive Padley Gorge. Originally the Longshaw estate of the Dukes of Rutland, the land was acquired by the National Trust in the 1970s.

STONEY MIDDLETON

4 miles N of Bakewell off the A623

🌀 Lover's Leap   🌲 Middleton Dale

This village, known locally simply as Stoney, is certainly well named as, particularly in this part of **Middleton Dale**, great walls of limestone rise up from the valley floor. Further up the Dale there are also many disused limestone quarries as well as the remains of some lead mines. Not all industry has vanished from the area, as this is the home of nearly three-quarters of the country's fluorspar industry. Another relic from the past also survives - a shoe and boot-making company operates from the village and is housed in a former corn mill.

The unusual octagonal village church was built by Joan Padley in thanksgiving for the safe return of her husband from the Battle of Agincourt in the 15th century. The lantern storey was added to the perpendicular tower in 1759.

Higher up the dale from the village is the dramatically named **Lover's Leap**. In 1762, a jilted girl, Hannah Badderley, tried to jump to her death by leaping from a high rock. Her voluminous skirts, however, were caught on some brambles and she hung from the ledge before gently rolling down into a pit and escaping serious injury.

EYAM

5 miles N of Bakewell off the B6521

🎦 Eyam Hall   🎦 Plague Village

Pronounced 'Eem', this village will forever be known as the **Plague Village**. In 1666, a local tailor received a bundle of plague-infected clothing from London. Within a short time the infection had spread and the terrified inhabitants prepared to flee the village. However, the local rector, William

Mompesson, persuaded the villagers to stay put and, thanks to his intervention, most neighbouring villages escaped the disease. Eyam was quarantined for over a year, relying on outside help for supplies of food. To minimize cross infection, food and other supplies were left outside the village, at either the Boundary Stones, or at Mompesson's Well, high above the village. Out of a total of 350 inhabitants, only 83 survived.

The home of the Wright family for over 300 years, **Eyam Hall** is a wonderful, unspoilt 17th-century manor house. The Eyam Hall Crafts Centre, housed in the farm building, contains several individual units specialising in a variety of unusual and skilfully-fashioned crafts.

BRADWELL

9 miles N of Buxton off the B6049

🎦 Bagshawe Cavern

Usually abbreviated in the unique Peak District way to Bradder, Bradwell is a charming little limestone village sheltered by Bradwell Edge. At one time this former lead-mining community was famous as the place where miners' hard hats – hard, black, brimmed hats in which candles were stuck to light the way underground – were made; thus these hard hats came to be known as Bradder Beavers.

A key attraction here is the massive **Bagshawe Cavern**, a cave reached by a descending flight of 98 steps through an old lead mine. Along the half-mile walk to the main show cave there are wonderful rock formations and other interesting sights. For the more adventurous, caving trips are available.

Mompessons Well, Eyam

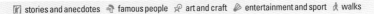

🎦 stories and anecdotes   🐦 famous people   🎨 art and craft   🎭 entertainment and sport   🥾 walks

CHY-AN-DOUR

Vicarage Lane, Ashford-in-the-Water, nr Bakewell,
Derbyshire DE45 1QN
Tel: 01629 813162

Ann and Stuart Rowland have a warm welcome for guests at **Chy-an-Dour**, their home in a quiet setting overlooking the picturesque Peak District village of Ashford in the Water. The happiness of their guests is the owners' aim, and the number of repeat visits is testimony to their success. The three guest bedrooms, a twin and two doubles, are prettily decorated and furnished, with TV and tea/coffee tray among the facilities. Central heating ensures that the house is cosy even in the cooler months, and guests will find plenty of parking for their cars. A full English breakfast provides the prefect start to a day spent exploring the village and the surrounding area.

Ashford developed around a crossing point on the River Wye. The medieval Sheepwash Bridge, one of three bridges in the village, is a favourite subject for artists and photographers, and visitors should find time to look round the great limestone parish Church of the Holy Trinity. The village offers a choice of shops, pubs and eating places; it is also famous for its beautiful well dressings, an ancient tradition that is renewed each year in early June. This is excellent walking and rambling country, and among the attractions within an easy drive are Chatsworth, Haddon Hall, the town of Bakewell (just 2 miles down the Wye), the Kinder Downfall waterfall and the Blue John caverns at Castleton.

ASHFORD IN THE WATER
1 mile NW of Bakewell off the A6

🏠 Church   🏠 Sheepwash Bridge

Not exactly in the water, but certainly on the River Wye, Ashford is another candidate for Derbyshire's prettiest village. It developed around a ford across the river and was once an important crossing place on the ancient Portway. The medieval **Sheepwash Bridge** crosses the Wye, with overhanging willows framing its low arches. It is one of three bridges in the village, and a favourite with artists. There is a small enclosure to one side that provides a clue to its name, as this is still occasionally used for its original purpose – crowds gather to witness sheep being washed in the river to clean their fleece before they are shorn. Mill Bridge dates back to 1664.

Sheepwash Bridge, Ashford in the Water

The great limestone parish **Church of the Holy Trinity**, largely rebuilt in 1871 but retaining the base of a 13th-century tower, has a fine Ashford marble table on show, as well as a tablet to the memory of Henry Watson, the founder of the marble works who was also an authority on the geology of the area. Several of the pillars within the church are made of the rare Duke's Red marble, which is only found in the mine at Lathkill Dale owned by the Duke of Devonshire. Hanging from the roof of Ashford's church are the remains of four 'virgin's crants' – paper garlands carried at the funerals of unmarried village girls.

Ashford is perhaps most famous for its six beautifully executed well-dressings, which are held annually in early June. The village also has a pleasant range of mainly 18th-century cottages, and a former tithe barn that now serves as an art gallery.

MONSAL HEAD
3 miles NW of Bakewell off the B6465

Monsal Dale

Monsal Head is a deservedly renowned beauty spot from which there are tremendous views, particularly over **Monsal Dale** through which the River Wye flows.

WARDLOW
6 miles NW of Bakewell off the B6465

At a crossroads near Wardlow the highwayman Anthony Lingard was hanged in 1812 for the murder of a local widow. He was the last felon to hang in the county, and his execution drew an enormous crowd – so

---

IBBOTSON'S OF ASHFORD

Ashford-in-the-Water, Derbyshire DE45 1QB
Tel: 01629 812528 Fax: 01629 815023

In a handsome old greystone building on a corner site in a pretty village on the River Wye, **Ibbotson's of Ashford** is one of the most delightful and individual food shops in the whole region. It is owned and run by Ken and Kathryn Ibbotson, who have built up a loyal clientele since opening in 2000.

Ken's pickled onions have become a business in themselves, selling to retail outlets and to the trade, and the shop also sells a good range of made-to-order sandwiches, cooked meats, Italian and other products, chutneys, preserves, coffees, ice creams, fresh fruit and vegetables and a range of home-made cakes.

much so that the local lay preacher at Tideswell found himself preaching to virtually empty pews. Determined not to waste this opportunity to speak to so large a congregation, he relocated to the gallows in order to deliver his sermon.

TIDESWELL

8 miles NW of Bakewell off the B6049

Church of St John the Baptist

One of the largest villages in the area, Tideswell takes its name from a nearby ebbing and flowing well. Over 900 feet above sea level, the surrounding countryside offers many opportunities to wander, stroll, or take a leisurely (or energetic) hike through some varied and impressive scenery.

Known as the Cathedral of the Peak, the magnificent 14th-century **Church of St John**

Church of St John the Baptist, Tideswell

the Baptist has a wealth of splendid features. The tower is impressive, the windows are beautiful, there is a fine collection of brasses inside and the 'Minstrel of the Peak', William Newton, is buried in the churchyard.

Today the village is home to a number of craftspeople working in buildings converted from other uses. The excellence of their work is apparent not only in the items they display, but also in the splendid well-dressing they help to enact annually on the Saturday nearest St John the Baptist's Day (24 June).

PEAK FOREST

11 miles NW of Bakewell off the A623

Church of King Charles the Martyr   Eldon Hole

High on the White Peak plateau, Peak Forest takes its name from the fact that it once stood at the centre of the Royal Forest of the Peak. The parish **Church of King Charles the Martyr** speaks of the fierce independence of the village inhabitants. It was built in 1657 by the wife of the 2nd Earl of Devonshire, during a time when there was a ban on building churches. The church that stands today on the site of the former chapel was built in 1878.

A quirk of ecclesiastical law ensured – up until early in the 19th century – that the village was outside the jurisdiction of the bishop. Thus it was not subject to the laws regarding posting the banns before marriage; hence it became known as the Gretna Green of the Peak. To this day if one or other of the couple has lived in the village for 15 days prior to the ceremony they can still be married in the church without banns being read.

Within walking distance of Peak Forest is the 'bottomless' pit of **Eldon Hole**. Once thought to be the Devil's own entrance to

Hell, stories abound in which various people were lowered down on increasingly longer pieces of rope. They all returned, in differing states of mental anguish, but none ever reached the bottom. However, seasoned potholers, who view the hole as no more than a practice run, maintain that it is, in fact, 'only' 180 feet deep.

SHELDON
3 miles W of Bakewell off the A6

🏚 Magpie Mine

Magpie Mine, to the south of the village, produced lead for over 300 years. This important site of industrial archaeology has been preserved, from the Cornish-style chimney stack, engine house and dynamite cabin, right down to the more recent corrugated-iron-roofed buildings.

MONYASH
5 miles W of Bakewell off the B5055

🚶 Lathkill Dale

Monyash was once at the centre of the Peak District's lead mining industry and had its own weekly market (the charter being granted in 1340); the old market cross still stands on the village green.

Today, Monyash, which is situated at the head of **Lathkill Dale**, is busy during the season with walkers keen to explore the valley of the River Lathkill, a road-free beauty spot with ash and elm woods that was designated a National Nature Reserve in 1972. The River Lathkill, like others in the limestone area of the Peak District, disappears underground for parts of its course. In this case, the river rises in winter from a large cave above Monyash, known as Lathkill Head Cave. In summer, the river emerges further downstream at Over Haddon.

ROWSLEY
4 miles SE of Bakewell off the A6

🏚 Caudwell's Mill

This small village, at the confluence of the Rivers Wye and Derwent, is home to the impressive Peacock Hotel. Built originally as a private house, it is aptly named since the carved peacock over the porch is actually part of the family crest of the Manners family, whose descendants still live at nearby Haddon Hall.

On the banks of the River Wye lies **Caudwell's Mill**, a unique Grade II listed historic flour mill. A mill has stood on this site for at least 400 years; the present mill was built in 1874, powered by water from the River Wye, and was run as a family business for over a century up until 1978. Since then the mill has undergone extensive restoration by a group of dedicated volunteers and, using machinery that was installed at the beginning of this century, the mill is once again producing wholemeal flour. Other mill buildings on the site have been converted to house a variety of craft workshops, shops and a restaurant.

On Chatsworth Road near the terminus of the Peak Rail line, Peak Village is an extensive factory outlet shopping centre offering a range of ladies' and men's fashion, sports and outdoor wear, home furnishings, jewellery, toys and books, and eateries. Also at the centre is the charming Wind in the Willows attraction, created by an award-winning team of craftsmen and designers to bring the adventures of Ratty, Mole, Badger and Mr Toad to life.

Matlock

🏚 Church of St Giles   🏚 Riber Castle

🏚 Peak Rail

As the northern, gritstone landscape of the

Peak District is often referred to as the Dark Peak, the southern, limestone plateaux have gained the equally obvious name of White Peak. Though the hilltops are often windswept and bleak, the numerous dales, cut deep into the limestone, provide a lush and green haven for all manner of wild and plant life. Several of the rivers are famous for their trout, particularly the Lathkill, which was greatly favoured by the keen angler and writer Izaak Walton.

Matlock is a bustling town nestling in the lower valley of the River Derwent, and is the administrative centre of Derbyshire, as well as being a busy tourist centre bordering the Peak District National Park. There are actually eight Matlocks making up the town, along with several other hamlets. Most have simply been engulfed and have lost their identity as the town grew, but Matlock Bath, the site of the spa, still maintains its individuality.

Matlock itself, at one time, had the steepest-gradient (a 1-in-5½) tramway in the world; it was also the only tram system in the Peak District. Opened in 1893, the tramcars ran until 1927 and the Depot can still be seen at the top of Bank Street. The old Ticket Office and Waiting Room at Matlock station have been taken over by the Peak Rail Society and here can be found not only their shop, but also exhibitions explaining the history and aims of the society. **Peak Rail** has its southernmost terminus just a few minutes' walk from the mainline station; from here the railway runs through the charming rural station of Darley Dale to the terminus at Rowsley South. Manned entirely by volunteers, this lovely old steam train operates on different days throughout the year. A restaurant car is fitted for every journey. The full journey (one way) takes just 20 minutes, and passengers can alight to enjoy the picnic area at the entrance to Rowsley South Station, or the exhibition coach at Darley Dale platform to learn about the history of the re-opening of the line. Special events are held throughout the year, and engine-driving courses can be taken – the perfect gift for the steam enthusiast!

Inside Matlock's **Church of St Giles** can be seen the faded and preserved funeral garlands or 'virgin crants' that were once common all over Derbyshire. Bell-shaped, decorated with rosettes and ribbons and usually containing a personal item, the garlands were made in memory of a deceased young unmarried girl of the parish. At her funeral the garlands were carried by

---

HOLLIES FARM PLANT CENTRE

Uppertown, Bonsall, Matlock, Derbyshire DE4 2AW
Tel: 01629 822734
Website: www.holliesfarmplantcentre.co.uk

Linda Wells and her son Robert own and run **Hollies Farm Plant Centre**, which lies in glorious Derbyshire countryside at Uppertown, Bonsall, off the A5012 on the edge of the Peak District National Park. The friendly, helpful owners raise most of the plants on site, from all-time garden favourites to more unusual annuals and perennials; their award-winning hanging baskets – buy them straight from the polytunnel or have your own filled – can be seen all over the neighbouring villages. Also is stock are planted containers, basket plants, rockery alpines and shrubs, along with composts and other garden essentials, and the Centre also operates as the village general store.

🏛 historic building   🏛 museum   🏛 historic site   🌀 scenic attraction   🌿 flora and fauna

the dead girl's friends and, after the service, would be suspended from the church rafters above the pew she had normally occupied.

High up on the hill behind the town is the brooding ruin of **Riber Castle**. The castle was built between 1862 and 1868 by John Smedley, a local hosiery manufacturer who became interested in the hydropathic qualities of Matlock. He drew up the designs for the building himself and spent lavishly on its interior décor. Smedley constructed his own gas-producing plant to provide lighting for the Castle and it even had its own well.

Following the death of first Smedley and then his wife, the castle was sold and for a number of years it was a boys' school. During World War II the castle was used as a food store before it was left to become a ruined shell.

Around Matlock

MATLOCK BATH
1 mile S of Matlock off the A6

- 🏠 Peak District Mining Museum
- 🏛 Caverns
- 🏛 The Aquarium
- 🌱 Countryside Centre
- 🦆 Heights of Abraham
- 🌿 Gulliver's Kingdom
- 🚶 High Tor Grounds

As with many other spa towns up and down the country, it was not until the Regency period that Matlock Bath reached its peak. As well as offering cures for many of the ills of the day, Matlock Bath and the surrounding area had much to offer the visitor. The spa town was compared to Switzerland by Byron, and it was much admired by Ruskin, who stayed at the New Bath Hotel in 1829. Many famous people have visited the town, including the young Victoria before she succeeded to the throne.

One of the great attractions of the town is **The Aquarium**, which occupies what was once the old Matlock Bath Hydro that was established in 1833. The original splendour of the Bath Hydro can still be seen in the fine stone staircase and also in the thermal large pool, which is now without its roof. The pool, maintained at a constant temperature of 68 degrees fahrenheit, was where the rheumatic patients came to immerse themselves in the waters and relieve their symptoms. Today, the pool is home to a large collection of Large Mirror, Common and Koi carp while the upstairs consulting rooms now house tanks full of native, tropical and marine fish. Down by the riverbank and housed in the old Pavilion can be found the **Peak District Mining Museum** and Temple, the only one of its kind in the world. Opened in 1978 and run by the Peak District Mines Historical Society, the Museum tells the story of lead mining in the surrounding area from as far back as Roman times to the 20th century. The Museum, which is open daily from 10am to 5pm, also houses a huge engine, dating from 1819, which was recovered from a mine near Winster.

Located in the Victorian Railway Station buildings is the **Whistlestop Countryside Centre**, which aims to inform and educate the public on the wildlife of the county as well as manage wildlife conservation. Set up by the Derbyshire Wildlife Trust and run by volunteers, the Centre has an interesting and informative exhibition and a gift shop, and the staff are qualified to lead a range of environmental activities.

For spectacular views of Matlock Bath, nothing beats a walk on **High Tor Grounds**. There are 60 acres of nature trails to wander around, while some 400 feet below the River Derwent appears like a silver thread through the gorge. A popular viewing point for Victorian visitors to the town, today rock climbers practise their skills climbing the precipitous crags of the Tor.

On the opposite side of the valley are the beautiful wooded slopes of Masson Hill, the southern face of which has become known as the Heights of Abraham. The name was chosen after General Wolfe's victory in Quebec – this part of the Derwent valley being seen to resemble the gorge of the St Lawrence River and the original **Heights of Abraham** lying a mile north of Quebec. It features steep rocky gorges, vast caverns, fast-running rivers, panoramic views and a cable car. The cable car ticket includes access to all the site's attractions, which include two spectacular underground caverns. The 60-acre country park also features woodland walks, the Owl Maze, the Explorers Challenge, a rocks

and fossil shop, coffee shop, restaurant and play and picnic areas.

In 1812, the **Great Rutland Show Cavern**, on the slope, was opened to the public, a new experience for tourists of the time, and it was visited by many including the Grand Duke Michael of Russia and Princess Victoria. Following this success, in 1844, the **Great Masson Cavern** was opened and construction of the Victoria Prospect Tower was begun. Built by redundant lead miners, the Tower became a new landmark for the area and today still provides a bird's-eye view over Derbyshire.

Matlock Bath's Illuminations & Venetian Nights started in 1897 to celebrate Queen Victoria's Diamond Jubilee and is still a popular family-orientated annual event. For several weeks in September and October the event, organised by Darley Dales District

LOOKING GLASS

30 North Parade, Matlock Bath, Derbyshire, DE4 3NS
Tel: 01629 57773
e-mail linlookingglass@aol.com

Opening Hours: 11am to 5pm every day, closed Weds.
Looking Glass is owned & run by Lin Fletcher, a self-taught stained glass artist. Using both lead and copper foil techniques, she works in her studio at the shop and can be seen creating her unique works of art on site. Lin is always happy to discuss commissions for special pieces.

Looking Glass is a small, friendly, independent shop, which began trading in 2006. Since opening it has gone from strength to strength, building up an excellent reputation for quality and choice, both locally and with visitors, many of whom return time and again to find that special gift. You will be offered a warm welcome and excellent customer service, and will enjoy a browse around the interesting and unusual gift ideas on offer.

The shop stocks an eclectic mix of goods from around the world, as well as those from closer to home. With a range of handmade crafts by local artists, a wide selection of Fair Trade & recycled goods, Tiffany style lamps, jewellery and glass, including Murano and Mdina (Malta), there is something for every taste and pocket. As a whole, the shop provides an eye-catching array of bespoke, one-off gifts to treasure for a lifetime.

Council and well supported by local traders, includes lively entertainment in the bandstand, clifftop fireworks and unique parades of illuminated and decorated boats.

To the south of the town centre is a model village with a difference: **Gulliver's Kingdom** theme park, which makes a great day out for all the family. Set on the side of a wooded hill, each terrace is individually themed and includes Fantasy Land, the Old Wild West and the Royal Mine ride. There are plenty of fun rides, a monorail, water slides and other diversions, as well as a cafe and restaurant.

CROMFORD
2 miles S of Matlock off the A5012

Mill   Pumping Station   Cromford Canal

High Peak Trail

Cromford is a model village known the world over. It was developed by Richard Arkwright into one of the first industrial towns. In addition to housing, he also provided his workers with a market place and a village lock-up. Born in Lancashire in 1732, Arkwright was the inventor of the waterframe, a machine for spinning cotton that was powered by water. He built his first mill at Cromford in 1771, the project taking a

further 20 years to complete. It was the world's first successful water-powered cotton spinning mill. The area he had chosen proved to be perfect: the River Derwent, described by Daniel Defoe as "a fury of a river", provided an ample power supply; there was an unorganised but very willing workforce, as the lead-mining industry was experiencing a decline and, probably most importantly, Cromford was away from the prying eyes of Arkwright's competitors. In 1792, Arkwright commissioned the building of the village church, where he now lies. The Mill proved to be a great success and became the model for others both in Britain and abroad, earning Arkwright the accolade Father of the Factory System. His pioneering work and contributions to the great Industrial Age resulted in a knighthood in 1786, and one year later he became High Sheriff of Derbyshire. **Cromford Mill** and the associated buildings are now an International World Heritage site. Tours of the mill, its neighbour Masson Mill and Cromford village are available throughout the year.

Cromford has a rather odd 15th-century bridge, which has rounded arches on one side and pointed arches on the other. It was from this bridge, in 1697, so local folklore has it, that a horse and rider took a flying leap from the parapet, plunged into the river 20 feet below and lived to tell the tale.

For lovers of waterways, there is an opportunity at Cromford Canal to potter along the five-mile stretch of towpath to Ambergate. The old **Leawood Pumping Station**, which transferred water from the River Derwent to the **Cromford Canal**, has been fully

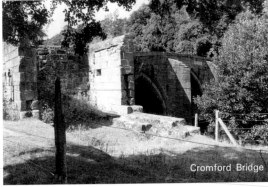
Cromford Bridge

restored. Inside the engine house is a preserved Cornish-type beam engine, which is occasionally steamed up. Close by the Pump House is the Wigwell Aqueduct, which carries the Canal high over the River Derwent.

The **High Peak Trail**, which stretches some 17 miles up to Dowlow near Buxton, starts at Cromford and follows the track bed of the Cromford and High Peak Railway. First opened in 1880, the railway was built to connect the Cromford Canal with the Peak Forest Canal and is somewhat reminiscent of a canal as it has long level sections interspersed with sharp inclines (instead of locks) and many of the stations are known as wharfs. After walking the trail it is not surprising to learn that its chief engineer was really a canal builder. The railway was finally closed in 1967; the old stations are now car parks and picnic areas; there is an information office in the former Hartington station signal box. Surfaced with clinker rather than limestone, the trail is suitable for walkers, cyclists and horses.

Wirksworth Close

WIRKSWORTH

4 miles S of Matlock off the B5023

- 🏛 Church of St Mary
- 🏛 Heritage Centre
- 🏛 National Stone Centre
- 🏛 Steeple Grange Light Railway Society

Nestling in the lush green foothills of the Peak District where north meets south, Wirksworth is home to a distinctive **Heritage Centre** housed in a former silk mill. Visitors can travel through time from the Roman occupation to the present day. Quarrying, lead-mining and local customs such as clypping the church (a ceremony in which the parish church is encircled by the congregation holding hands around it) and well-dressing are explored with interactive and fascinating exhibits. The Centre is open Wednesday to Saturday. One of the town's most interesting sights is the jumble of cottages linked by a maze of jitties on the hillside between The Dale and Greenhill, in particular the area known locally as The Puzzle Gardens. Babington House dates back to Jacobean times. Another former lead-merchant's house, Hopkinsons House, was restored in 1980 as part of a number of restoration schemes initiated by the Civic Trust's Wirksworth Project. The ancient parish **Church of St Mary** is a fine building standing in a tranquil close and bounded by Elizabethan Gell Almshouses and the former (Georgian) grammar school. The church holds one of the oldest stone carvings in the country. Known as the Wirksworth Stone, it is a coffin lid dating from the 8th century.

The **National Stone Centre**, open every

🏛 historic building 🏛 museum 🏛 historic site 🔱 scenic attraction 🌱 flora and fauna day, tells the story of stone, with a wealth of exhibits, activities such as gem-panning and fossil-casting, and outdoor trails tailored to introduce topics such as the geology, ecology and history of the dramatic Peak District landscape. Nearby, the **Steeple Grange Light Railway** runs along a short line over the High Peak Trail between Steeplehouse Station and Dark Lane Quarry. Power is provided by a battery-electric locomotive; passengers are carried in a manrider salvaged from Bevercotes Colliery in Nottinghamshire.

DARLEY DALE
2 miles NW of Matlock off the A6

🏛 Red House Stables 🌳 Darley Yew

The charming name for this straggling village along the main road north from Matlock dates only from the 19th century, and was either devised by the commercially-minded railway company at work in the area, or by the romantically-inclined vicar of the parish. Darley Dale makes up one of three stops on the Matlock-to-Rowsley South Peak Rail line.

One of the most unassuming heroines of this part of Derbyshire must be Lady Mary Louisa Whitworth, the second wife of Sir Joseph Whitworth, the famous Victorian engineer. Following his death in 1887, Lady Mary undertook sweeping changes to the lifestyle of the local poor and needy. The Whitworth Institute was opened in 1890, bringing to the community a wide range of facilities including a swimming pool, an assembly hall, a natural history museum and a library. Lady Whitworth died in France in 1896, and is buried next to her husband at the parish Church of St Helen, in the hamlet of Churchtown. The churchyard is also home to the **Darley Yew**, one of the oldest living trees in Britain, which has a girth of some 33 feet.

The yew pre-dates the Norman origins of the Church and may even be older than the Saxon fragments found here in the mid 1900s.

Darley Dale has an extensive park, which is very pretty in all seasons. Another of this small village's attractions is **Red House Stables**, a working carriage museum featuring some fine examples of traditional horse-drawn vehicles and equipment. One of the finest collections in the country, it consists of nearly 40 carriages, including one of the very few surviving Hansom cabs, a stage coach, Royal Mail coach, Park Drag and many other private and commercial vehicles. Carriage rides are available, making regular trips through the countryside to places such as Chatsworth and Haddon Hall. The carriages and horses can be hired for special occasions.

Darley Dale Church and Yew

STANTON IN PEAK

5 miles NW of Matlock off the B5056

🏛 Nine Ladies 🏛 Rowtor Rocks 🌿 Stanton Moor

Nine Ladies Stone Circle, Stanton In Peak

The gritstone landscape of **Stanton Moor**, which rises to some 1,096 feet and overlooks the village, is encircled by footpaths and is a popular walking area. There are also several interesting features on the moorland. The folly, Earl Grey's Tower, was built in 1832 to commemorate the reform of Parliament. There is also an ancient stone circle, dating from the Bronze Age, with over 70 burial mounds. Known as the **Nine Ladies**, the stone circle has a solitary boulder nearby called the King's Stone. Legend has it that one Sunday nine women and a fiddler came up on to the moor to dance and, for their act of sacrilege, they were turned to stone.

The nearby **Rowtor Rocks** contain caves that were carved out at some stage in the 1600s. Not only was the living space made from the rock, but tables, chairs and alcoves as well, to create a cosy retreat for the local vicar, Reverend Thomas Eyre. Prior to these home improvements, the caves were reputedly used by the Druids, who did not believe in such creature comforts.

CAUDWELL'S MILL TRUST LTD

Caudwell's Mill, Bakewell Road, Rowsley, nr Matlock,
Derbyshire DE4 2EB
Tel/Fax: 01629 734374
e-mail: graemethemiller@yahoo.co.uk

Caudwell's Mill is a unique Grade II* listed roller flour mill, the only complete Victorian water turbine-powered example in the country. It stands on the A6 between Bakewell and Matlock in the lovely Wye Valley. A mill has been on this site for at least 400 years and the current occupant was built in 1874 by John Caudwell. Run as a family business for more than a century, it is now managed by a charitable trust.

The four-storey mill is worked by turbines powered by water from the Wye. The main turbine, dating from 1914, drives the flour mill, while the second turbine, built in 1898 to provide provender (animal feed), now generates electricity for the site. Most of the machinery pre-dates 1914 and is still driven by belts (often made of leather) and pulleys from line shafts.

The many displays, descriptions and hands-on models provide a fascinating and educational insight into how the mill turns wheat into flour, and in the mill shop visitors can buy from a selection of more than 20 flours, along with recipe books, souvenirs and a range of tasty biscuits. A visit to the mill can be rounded off with a stroll along the head race or nature trail or around Rowsley village.

🏛 historic building 🏛 museum 🏛 historic site 🌊 scenic attraction 🌿 flora and fauna

YOULGREAVE
6 miles NW of Matlock off the B5056

🏛 Church of All Saints   🏃 Lathkill Dale

This straggling village, known locally as Pommey, lies in Bradford Dale. The village **Church of All Saints** contains some parts of the original Saxon building though its ancient font is, unfortunately, upturned and used as a sundial. Inside, the working font is Norman and still retains its stoop for holding the Holy Water. It is well worth taking the time to have a look at, since it is the only such font in England. The Church also contains a small tomb with an equally small alabaster effigy; dated 1488, it is a memorial to Thomas Cockayne, who was killed in a brawl when in his teens.

Further up the village's main street is Thimble Hall, the smallest market hall in the Peak District and still used today for selling goods. Typical of the White Peak area of Derbyshire, the Hall dates from 1656; there are also some rather grand Georgian houses to be found in the village.

Lathkill Dale, which can really only be experienced by walking along the path by the banks of the quiet river, is noted for its solitude and, consequently, there is an abundance of wildlife in and around the riverbank meadows. The upper valley is a National Nature Reserve; those who are lucky enough may even spot a kingfisher or two. One of the country's purest rivers, the Lathkill is famed for the range of aquatic life that it supports, as well as being a popular trout river. Renowned for many centuries, it was Izaak Walton who said of the Lathkill, back in 1676;

*the purest and most transparent stream
that I ever yet saw, either at home or abroad;
and breeds, 'tis said, the reddest
and best Trouts in England.*

MIDDLETON BY YOULGREAVE
7 miles NW of Matlock off the A5012

🏛 Lomberdale Hall

Just outside this leafy village is **Lomberdale Hall**, once the home of Thomas Bateman, the 19th-century archeologist who was responsible for the excavation of some 500 barrows in the Peak District over a 20-year period - it is said that he managed to reveal four in one single day. Many of the artefacts he unearthed can be seen in Sheffield Museum. The village lies in the valley of the River Bradford, at the point where it becomes Middleton Dale, and is unusual among villages in this area of the Peak District in that it has a large number of trees.

BIRCHOVER
4 miles W of Matlock off the B5056

🏛 Rowtor Rocks

The strange **Rowtor Rocks**, behind The Druid Inn, are said to have been used for Druidical rites. The Reverend Thomas Eyre, who died in 1717, was fascinated by these rocks and built the strange collection of steps, rooms and seats that have been carved out of the gritstone rocks on the summit of the outcrop. It is said that the Reverend would take his friends there to admire the view across the valley below – a view that nowadays is obscured by trees.

Hermits Cave, Birchover

The equally strange outcrops of Robin Hood's Stride and Cratcliff Tor can be found nearby. A medieval hermit's cave, complete with crucifix, can be seen at the foot of Cratcliff Tor hidden behind an ancient yew tree.

WINSTER
4 miles W of Matlock off the B5056

🏛 Market House

This attractive gritstone village was once a lead-mining centre and market town. Today, it is a pleasant place with antique shops in the high street and some fine late 18th-century houses. Less splendid than the surrounding houses, but no less interesting, are the ginnels – little alleyways – that run off the main street. The most impressive building here, however, must be the **Market House**, owned by the National Trust and found at the top of the main street. The Trust's first purchase in Derbyshire, the rugged, two-storey Market House dates from the late 17th and early 18th centuries and is a reminder of Winster's past importance as a market town. Built from an attractive combination of brickwork and stone, the House is open to the public and acts as an information centre and shop for the Trust.

Although Morris dancing is traditionally associated with the Cotswold area, two of the best known and most often played tunes, *The Winster Gallop* and *The Blue-Eyed Stranger*, originate from the village. Collected many years ago by Cecil Sharpe, a legend in the world of Morris dancing, they were rediscovered in the 1960s. The Winster Morris men traditionally dance through the village at the beginning of Wakes Week in June, finishing, as all good Morris dances do, at one of the local pubs.

Ashbourne

🏛 Market Square   🏛 The Mansion

🏛 St Oswald's Parish Church

🏛 Green Man & Black's Head Royal Hotel

Ashbourne is one of Derbyshire's finest old towns, with a wealth of wonderful Georgian architecture as well as some older buildings, notably the Gingerbread Shop, which is timber framed and probably dates from the 1400s. The triangular cobbled **Market Square** was part of the new development begun in the 1200s that shifted the town to the east, away from the church. Weekly markets have been held in the square since 1296, and still take place every Thursday and Saturday. It was in this market place, once lined with ale houses, that Bonnie Prince Charlie proclaimed his father as King James III, and so started the Jacobite Rebellion. Traditional Ashbourne gingerbread is

Market House, Winster

said to be made from a recipe that was acquired from French prisoners of war who were kept in the town during the Napoleonic Wars.

Also worthy of a second glance is the **Green Man and Black's Head Royal Hotel**. The inn sign stretches over St John's Street and was put up when the Blackamoor Inn joined with the Green Man in 1825. Though the Blackamoor is no more, the sign remains and it claims to be the longest hotel name in the country. Of Georgian origin, the amalgamated hotel has played host to James Boswell, Dr Johnson and the young Princess Victoria. Ashbourne was, in fact, one of Dr Johnson's favourite places; he came to the town on several occasions between 1737 and 1784. He also visited the hotel so often that he had his own chair with his name on it. The chair can still be seen at the Green Man.

A stroll down Church Street, described by Pevsner as one of the finest streets in Derbyshire, takes the walker past many interesting Georgian houses – including the Grey House which stands next to the Grammar School. Founded by Sir Thomas Cockayne on behalf of Elizabeth I in 1585, the school was visited on its 400th anniversary by the present Queen. Almost opposite the Grey House is **The Mansion**, the late 17th-century home of the Reverend Dr John Taylor, oldest friend of Dr Johnson. In 1764, a domed, octagonal drawing room was added to the house, and a new brick façade built facing the street. Next to The Mansion are two of the many almshouses established in Ashbourne during the 17th and 18th centuries. Ashbourne also retains many of its narrow alleyways, opening into yards, in particular The Gallery.

In **St Oswald's Parish Church**, Ashbourne has one of the most impressive and elegant churches in the country, described by George Eliot as "the finest mere parish church in England". James Boswell said that the church

GRAVES OF ASHBOURNE

12 St John Street, Ashbourne,
Derbyshire DE6 1GH
Tel: 01335 342248

Visit **Graves of Ashbourne** for quality top brand names
in men's traditional clothing. Paul Kaufman owner of
this long established gents outfitters, takes pride in
keeping this old fashioned style shop unchanged for the
last 130 years. Over two floors, the shop has the
largest selection of top brands in Derbyshire.

Top brands include: **Aigle, Bladen, Dents, Double Two,
H J Socks, Gabicci, Gurteen, Jockey, Olney, Peter
England, Van Heusen, Viyella and Wolsey.**

was "one of the largest and most luminous that
I have seen in any town of the same size".
St Oswald's stands on the site of a minster
church mentioned in the Domesday Book,
though most of what exists today dates from
rebuilding work in the 13th century.

The alabaster tombs and monuments to the
Bradbourne and Cockayne families in the
north transept chapel are justly famous.
Perhaps the best-known monument is that to
Penelope Boothby, who died in 1791 at the
tender age of five. Thomas Banks' white
Carrara marble figure of the sleeping child is
so lifelike that she still appears to be only
sleeping. The moving epitaph reads: "She was
in form and intellect most exquisite; the
unfortunate parents ventured their all on this
frail bark, and the wreck was total". It is said
that Penelope's parents separated at the child's
grave and never spoke to each other again.

Ashbourne is home to the famous
Shrovetide football game played on Shrove
Tuesday and Ash Wednesday. The two teams,
the 'Up'ards' (those born north of the
Henmore Brook) and the 'Down'ards' (those
born south of it) begin their match at 2pm
behind the Green Man Hotel. The game
continues until well into the evening. The two

goals are situated three miles apart, along the
Brook, on the site of the old mills at Clifton
and Sturston. It is rare for more than one goal
to be scored, the ball moves through the town
in a series of 'hugs', a rugby-like scrum made
up of an unlimited number of people.

Around Ashbourne

HOGNASTON
4 miles NE of Ashbourne off the B5035

🖉 Carsington Water

This hillside village, with its extraordinary
Norman carvings over the church doorway,
lies close to **Carsington Water**, Britain's
newest reservoir, owned by Severn Trent
Water. There is plenty to do here besides the
more usual water sports such as canoeing,
sailing and fishing. An eight-mile track,
mostly off road can be walked or cycled
around the reservior. Opened by the Queen
in 1992, the reservoir has already blended
well with the local countryside. Unlike many
of the Peak District reservoirs, which draw
their water from the acid moorland,
Carsington is able to support a whole host of
wildlife. One controversial resident is the

American ruddy duck. Once unknown outside wildlife reserves, the duck escaped and in little over 50 years the breed has become widespread throughout Europe.

HOPTON

8 miles NE of Ashbourne off the B5035

This village, now by-passed by the main road, is dominated by the Carsington Water Reservoir. The land rises to the north of Hopton and here can be found the Hopton Incline, once the steepest railway incline in the British Isles. Lying on the High Peak Railway line, carriages on their journey from Cromford to Whaley Bridge were hauled up using fixed engines. It is now part of the High Peak Trail.

BRASSINGTON

7 miles NE of Ashbourne off the B5056

🏛 Rainster Rocks   🏛 Harborough Rocks

Protected from the wind by the limestone plateau that soars some 1,000 feet above sea level, the village sits by strange shaped rocks, the result of weather erosion, with names like **Rainster Rocks** and **Harborough Rocks**. Stone Age man found snugs among these formations and there is evidence that animals

like the sabre-toothed tiger, brown bear, wolf and hyena also found comfort here in the caves. As late as the 18th, century families were still living in the caves.

FENNY BENTLEY

2 miles N of Ashbourne off the A515

🏛 St Edmund's Church

Inside **St Edmund's Church** can be found the tomb of Thomas Beresford, the local lord of the manor who fought alongside eight of his 16 sons at Agincourt. The effigies of Beresford and his wife are surrounded by those of their 21 children – each covered by a shroud because by the time the tombs were built nobody could remember what they had looked like. During the Civil War, much of the church and its rectory were destroyed. On returning to his parish after the restoration of Charles II in 1661, the rector resolved to rebuild the rectory, which was all but rubble, and restore the church to its former glory. Both of these he managed. The 15th-century square tower of the fortified manor house, now incorporated into Cherry Orchard Farm - which belonged to the Beresford family and was once the home of Charles Cotton - is a local landmark that can be seen from the main road.

Fortified Manor, Fenny Bentley

TISSINGTON

4 miles N of Ashbourne off the A515

🏛 Tissington Hall   🎋 Tissington Trail

Sitting at the foothills of the Pennines, Tissington is, perhaps, most famous for its ancient festival of well-dressing, a ceremony that dates back to at least 1350. Today this starts on

WHITE PEAK FARM BUTCHERY

The Old Slaughterhouse, Chapel Lane,
Tissington, nr Ashbourne, Derbyshire DE6 1RA
Tel: 01335 390300/07973 120985
e-mail: liz.power@btinternet.com
website: www.whitepeakfarm.co.uk

'Meat at its Peak'

White Peak Farm Butchery is set in the foothills of the Pennines in the stunning village of Tissington. This unique estate village on the A515 3 miles north of Ashbourne, which was built round Tissington Hall, the Jacobean home of the FitzHerbert family, is perhaps best known for its well dressing. But within the local community and for many miles around it is also known for being the home of one the very best butchers in the land. Owner Richard Hobday sources the best local produce and is renowned in Tissington, Ashbourne and the surrounding area for supplying some of the best meat to be found anywhere in the UK, all from animals leading a happy, relaxed life in and around the Peak District national Park.

For his retail trade he sells meat either home-reared or personally selected from farmers he knows and from local livestock markets. He never compromises on quality, so if he has to source his meat from other areas he will, but always with quality in mind. He is a leading expert in his field and is often asked to use his expertise in judging fatstock shows throughout the Midlands and the North West.

The butchery and shop are situated in a little road off the village square in the Old Slaughterhouse, which was purpose-built in Victorian times and served local butchers in villages and towns for over a century before becoming a butchery in 1984. Richard has been in the trade for more than 30 years and has been running White Peak with his cheerful, welcoming and expert staff since 1999.

The beef, the lamb and the pork are cut to the customers' needs, and the shop also sells poultry and seasonal game from the estate. And the White Peak bacon, sausages and black pudding are essential ingredients for a truly memorable breakfast. The shop also sells a selection of outstanding pies, cheeses, pickles and preserves.

Meat-lovers who can't get to the shop can order anything from the range online: topside, sirloin, mince, brisket, rumpsteak, ribs fillet of beef; legs, chops and racks of lamb; pork chops, legs, gammon, bacon; black pudding, sausages with varieties including Czech with red onion and sage, plain pork, pork & leek, pork & apple, venison. Orders are sent out on Tuesdays and Thursdays for guaranteed next day delivery.

Ascension Day and draws many crowds who come to see the spectacular folk art created by the local people.

There are plenty of theories as to why well-dressing began or was revived at Tissington. One centres on the purity of the Tissington wells during the Black Death, which swept through the country in the mid 1300s. During this time some 77 of the 100 clergy in Derbyshire died and the surviving villagers simply returned to the pagan custom of well-dressing. Another plausible theory dates back only as far as the great drought of 1615, when the Tissington wells kept flowing though water everywhere was in very short supply. Whichever theory is true, one thing is certain, that in the past 50 years or so many villages who had not dressed a well for centuries, if ever, are now joining in the colourful tradition.

A total of six wells are dressed at Tissington: the Hall, the Town, the Yew Tree, the Hands, the Coffin and the Children's Wells. Each depicts a separate scene, usually one from the Bible. Visitors should follow the signs in the village or ask at the Old Coach House.

Home of the FitzHerbert family for 500 years, **Tissington Hall** is a distinguished and impressive stately home which was built by Francis FitzHerbert in 1609. The estate consists of 2,400 acres comprising 13 farms, 40 cottages and assorted lettings. The Hall boasts a wealth of original pieces, artwork, furnishings and architectural features tracing the times and tastes of the FitzHerbert family (now headed by Sir Richard FitzHerbert) over the centuries. Tissington Hall and Gardens are open to the public on 28 afternoons throughout the summer.

Following the old Ashbourne to Buxton Hay railway line, the **Tissington Trail** is a popular walk which can be combined with other old railway trails or country lanes in the area to make an enjoyable circular country walk. The Tissington Trail passes through some lovely countryside and, with a reasonable surface, is also popular with cyclists. Along the route can be found many of the old railway line buildings and junction boxes and, in particular, the old Hartington station, which is now a picnic site with an information centre in the old signal box.

THE BLUEBELL INN

Tissington, Ashbourne, Derbyshire DE6 1NH
Tel: 013335 350317 Fax: 01335 350103
e-mail: bluebell350317@aol.com
website: www.bluebelltissington.co.uk

The Bluebell Inn is situated just outside the lovely village of Tissington on the A515 on the Ashbourne/Buxton Road 3 miles north of Ashbourne. It is a traditional pub with a special reputation of delicious cuisine, catering for breakfasts, bar meals, Sunday lunches, banquets, buffets, conferences, weddings, private or children's parties and all special diets are catered for using locally sourced products. The function room is separate to the bar and dining area has seating for up to 100 people, complete with its own bar, disabled activities and dance floor. Food is served between 10:30am-9pm and opening hours are from 10:30am-11:00pm.

ALSOP-EN-LE-DALE

5 miles N of Ashbourne off the A515

🏠 Viator's Bridge

The old station on the Ashbourne-Buxton line that once served this tiny hamlet is today a car park on the Tissington Trail. The tranquil hamlet itself is on a narrow lane east of the main road towards Parwich, just a mile from Dovedale. Alsop-en-le-Dale's parish church of St Michael is Norman, though it was rebuilt substantially during Victorian times. The nave retains Norman features, with impressive double zigzag mouldings in the arches, but the west tower is only imitation Norman, and dates from 1883. One unusual feature that dominates this small church is its extraordinary 19th-century, square mock-Gothic pulpit.

The renowned **Viator's Bridge** at Milldale is only a mile away to the west. It was immortalised in Izaak Walton's *The Compleat Angler* by a character who complains to another about the size of the tiny, two-arched packhorse bridge, deeming it "not two fingers broad".

ARBOR LOW

13 miles N of Ashbourne off the A515

🏛 Stone Circle

This remote **Stone Circle** is often referred to as the Stonehenge of the Peaks, and although many of the stones now lie on the ground, it is still an impressive sight. There are several stone circles in the Peak District but none offer the same atmosphere as Arbor Low, nor the same splendid views. Built around 4,000 years ago by the early Bronze Age people, there are a total of 40 stones each weighing no less than eight tonnes. Probably used as an observatory and also a festival site, it is likely that the stones, which have been placed in pairs, never actually stood up.

MAPPLETON

2 miles NW of Ashbourne off the A515

Mappleton is a secluded and charming village of the Dove Valley, with attractive views and a wealth of exciting natural beauty. The 18th-century Church of St Mary's is unusual in that it has a dome rather than a tower or steeple.

The village's main claim to fame is its annual New Year's Day charity bridge jump when 10 teams of three people each paddle down half a mile of the River Dove and then jump off a bridge. The Dove is not easily navigable, the bridge is 30 feet high and after the jump there is a 500-yard sprint to the pub. It is a grand spectator sport and hundreds of people come to watch.

Arbor Low Stone Circle

🏠 historic building　🏛 museum　🏛 historic site　♨ scenic attraction　🌿 flora and fauna

THORPE

3 miles NW of Ashbourne off the A515

🌄 Thorpe Cloud 🏞 Dovedale and River Dove

Thorpe lies at the confluence of the Rivers Manifold and Dove, and is dominated by the conical hill of **Thorpe Cloud**, which guards the entrance to **Dovedale** (see walk in Staffordshire Chapter). Although the Dale becomes over-crowded at times, there is always plenty of open space to explore on the hill as well as excellent walking. For much of its 45-mile course from Axe Edge to its confluence with the River Trent, the **River Dove** is a walker's river as it is mostly inaccessible by car. The steep sides to its valley, the fast-flowing water and the magnificent white rock formations all give Dovedale a special charm. Dovedale, however, is only a short section of the valley. Above Viator's Bridge it becomes Mill Dale, and further upstream again are Wolfscote Dale and Beresford Dale.

Chesterfield

🏛 Crooked Spire 🐦 George Stephenson

This friendly, bustling town on the edge of the Peak District National Park grew up around its open-air market, which was established over 800 years ago and claims to be England's largest. As the town lies at the crossroads of England, the hub of trade routes from all points of the compass, the town's claim seems easily justified. It was earning royal revenue in 1165, as the Sheriff of Derbyshire recorded in the Pipe Rolls and, in that year, the market earned the princely sum of £1 2s 7d for the Crown. The Pipe Roll of 1182 also mentions a fair in Chesterfield. Such fairs were large markets, usually lasting for several days and drawing traders and buyers from a much wider area. Chesterfield's formal charter, however, was not granted until 1204, but this charter made the town one of the first eight free boroughs in the country. Escaping the prospect of redevelopment in the 1970s, the markets are as popular as ever and are held every Monday, Friday and Saturday, with a flea market each Thursday and a farmers' market on the second Thursday of every month.

The town centre has been conserved for future generations by a far-sighted council, and many buildings have been saved, including the Victorian Market Hall built in 1857. The traditional cobbled paving was restored in the Market Place, and New Square was given a complete facelift. There are several Tudor buildings in the heart of Chesterfield, most notably the former Peacock Inn, which is now home to a café. The Tourist Information Centre that was here is now in a new purpose-built centre in Rykneld Square, near the

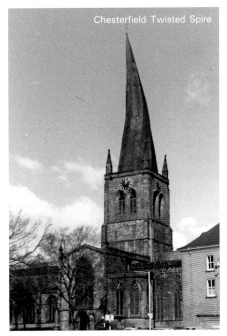
Chesterfield Twisted Spire

FRANK HILL JEWELLER

5 West Bars, Chesterfield S40 1AQ
Tel: 01246 232155 Fax: 01246 278221
e-mail: Andrew@24ctjewellery.co.uk
website: www.24ctjewellery.co.uk

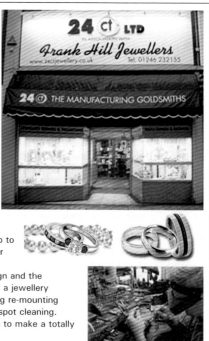

Thirty-five years of experience and expertise go into the design and manufacture of the highest quality jewellery at 24CT Ltd in association with **Frank Hill Jeweller**, with a level of service to match. The main specialities are wedding and engagement rings made in gold, white gold, platinum and titanium. All are made in the workshop on the premises from the highest quality metals hallmarked to British standards. Stones used include diamonds, emeralds, rubies, topaz, sapphire, aquamarine, amethyst and the increasingly popular modern tanzanite.

Clients can browse the website or visit the shop to see examples of what is offered, and can have their own pieces made to their specification. Andrew Thomson and his staff are happy to advise on design and the selection of metals and gemstones. They also offer a jewellery valuation service and a total repair service, including re-mounting stones, re-sizing rings, repairing chains and on-the-spot cleaning. They can also remodel an old piece or melt it down to make a totally new item.

Crooked Spire church. Visitors to the town are drawn to this peculiarly graceful spire reaching high into the skyline; twisting and leaning, it is totally confusing to the eye. The Crooked Spire of St Mary and All Saints Church has dominated the skyline for so long that local folk have ceased to notice its unusual shape. Superstition surrounds it, and sadly the real story to its unusual appearance has been lost over the years. The truth – or at least the best guess – could be the amount of green timber used to build the spire. Green timber is more easily shaped and becomes much stronger as it dries, finally setting like concrete. The builders would have expected the wood to move as it dried and allowed for it, but it's impossible to predict exactly how green timber will dry. It can split, defects can appear and develop – anything can happen. And, clearly, anything did! As well as this, there's no cross bracing in the eight sides of the spire, and the bottom timbers decayed, which is why it leans. Add to that 32 tons of lead that cover the wooden structure, 600 years of weather and, according to one 'expert', bell-ringing, and you get a crooked spire. However, some stories say it was the Devil who, pausing for a rest during one of his flights, clung to the spire for a moment or two. Incense from the Church drifted upwards and the Devil sneezed, causing the spire to twist out of shape.

This magnificent spire rises to 228 feet and leans 9 feet 4 inches from its true centre point. It is eight-sided, but the herringbone pattern of the lead slates trick the eye into seeing 16 sides from the ground. The Crooked Spire is

MAKING IT4U

414 Chatsworth Road, Chesterfield,
Derbyshire S40 3BQ
Tel: 01246 297615
e-mail: yvonneclarkelimited@live.co.uk

"It's an Aladdins cave, there is so much to look at and the staff are very friendly and always willing to help"

In her shop by the junction of the A619 Chatsworth Road and Walton Road, Yvonne Clarke shares her passion for fashion with her growing band of regular customers. **Making It4U** specialises in all aspects of soft furnishings, and Yvonne and her staff are always ready to assist their clients with design solutions, enabling them to get the very best from their purchases and to enhance their homes. Curtains are a speciality, sold customised from stock or made to individual requirements from a small selection of fabrics kept in house or from customers' own fabric. Also made instore are table cloths, runners and napkins, they can also re-cover caravan cushions and some seating stools and headboards. The shop sells a range of designer clothes from Yvonne herself including prom evening wear, mother of the bride outfits, bespoke wedding dresses as well as hat fascinators, scarves, handbags and jewellery. Making It4U is a stockist of Lunar Shoes, with a selection of Lunar bridal shoes and handbags and the shop also offers an alteration and repair service for customers' garments, wherever they were purchased.

This is one of two shops owned by Yvonne. The other is Silhouettes in Bolsover (qv), which carries a wide range of ladies fashion garments and has an upstairs room where clothes are made to her designs. Silhouettes is at Unit 4, Cavendish Walk, Bolsover. Tel: 01246 827005.

open most Bank Holidays and at advertised times; the church is open all year, Monday to Saturday 9am - 5pm (9am - 3pm, January and February), and Sundays at service times only. **George Stephenson** (1781-1848) lived in Tapton House on the edge of town while working on railway construction in the area. He died in Chesterfield and is buried in Trinity Church in Newbold Road.

Around Chesterfield

WHITTINGTON

3 miles NE of Chesterfield off the B6052/A61

🏠 Revolution House

During the 17th century, **Revolution House** was part of an alehouse called the Cock and Pynot (pynot being the local dialect word for magpie). It was here that three local noblemen – the Earl of Devonshire, the Earl of Danby and John D'Arcy – met to begin planning their part in the events that eventually led to the overthrow of James II in favour of his daughter Mary and her husband, William of Orange. The Glorious Revolution took place later in the same year, November 1688, and it was in the year of its 250th anniversary that this modest house was turned into a museum.

Revolution House, a tiny cottage with thatched roof, flower border and charming garden gate, which belies its rather incendiary name, is now open to the public from Easter to the end of September and features period furnishings and a changing programme of exhibitions on local themes. A video relates the story of the Revolution and the role that the house played in those fraught and dangerous days.

BARLBOROUGH

7 miles NE of Chesterfield off the A619

Lying close to the county borders with both Nottinghamshire and Yorkshire, this village still retains its manor house. Lying just north of the village centre, Barlborough Hall (private) was built in 1584 by Lord Justice Francis Rodes to plans drawn up by the designer of Hardwick Hall, Robert Smythson. Those who visit both houses will notice the strong resemblance. As well as building houses, Rodes was also one of the judges at the trial of Mary, Queen of Scots. The Hall is supposed to be haunted by a grey lady, said to be the ghost of a bride who received the news of her groom's death as she was on her way to the 12th-century village church. Barlborough Hall should not be confused with Barlborough Old Hall: this is an easy mistake to make as Barlborough Old Hall is actually the younger of the two! Built in 1618, as the date stone over the front door states, the Old Hall is of a large H-plan design and has mullioned windows.

CRESWELL

9 miles E of Chesterfield off the A616

🏛 Creswell Crags

Lying close to the Derbyshire-Nottinghamshire border, the limestone gorge known as **Creswell Crags** is well worth seeing. Formed thousands of years ago by the erosion of a river that cut through the limestone, this rock, which is porous and subject to erosion underground as well as on the surface, contributes by its very nature to the forming of natural chambers. The subterranean movement of water created a vast network of caves, which were subsequently exposed and used by Neanderthal man as shelters while out

Streetly Chapel, Creswell

hunting. Tours can be taken from the visitor centre where there is also a display of artefacts found in the area. Testimony to the artistry of the later inhabitants of these caves was the discovery of a bone carved with the head of a horse. The carving is about 13,000 years old and can now be seen in the British Museum. The largest cavern, Church Hole Cave, extends some 170 feet into the side of the gorge; it was here that hand tools and the only known Ice Age rock art in Britain were found.

BOLSOVER

7 miles E of Chesterfield off the A632

🏛 Castle

The approach to Bolsover from the north and east is dominated by the splendid, sandstone structure of **Bolsover Castle** (English Heritage - see panel opposite), which sits high on a limestone ridge. A castle has stood here since the 12th century, though the present building is a fairytale folly built for Sir Charles Cavendish during the early 1600s on the site of a ruined castle. By the mid 1700s, much of the building had been reduced to the ruins seen today, though thankfully the splendid keep has withstood the test of time.

Pevsner remarked that not many large houses in England occupy such an impressive position as Bolsover Castle, as it stands on the brow of a hill overlooking the valley of the

Bolsover Castle

Bolsover, Derbyshire S44 6PR
Tel: 01246 822844
website: www.english-heritage.org.uk

'By an unlikely miracle,' wrote the architectural historian Mark Girouard, 'the keep at Bolsover has survived into this century as an almost untouched expression in stone of the lost world of Elizabethan chivalry and romance.'

Dominating the countryside from its hilltop, Bolsover occupies the site of a medieval castle built by the Peverel family shortly after the Norman Conquest. Sir Charles Cavendish bought the old castle in 1612 and began work on his 'Little Castle' project. Despite its embattled appearance, his creation was not designed for defence, but for elegant living.

Sir Charles intended the house as a retreat from the world to an imaginary golden age of chivalry and pleasure. His son William, later Duke of Newcastle, inherited the Little Castle in 1616 and set about its completion, assisted by the architect John Smythson. An extraordinary survival, the exquisitely carved fireplaces and recently conserved murals and painted panelling of its interiors take the visitor on an allegorical journey from earthly concerns to heavenly (and erotic) delights.

William also added the vast and stately rooms of the Terrace Range, now a dramatic roofless shell. To show off his achievement, in 1634 he invited the Stuart court to 'Love's Welcome to Bolsover', a masque specially written by Ben Jonson for performance in the Fountain Garden. Finally he constructed the cavernous Riding House with its magnificent roof, perhaps the finest surviving indoor riding school in Britain: here he indulged his passion for training 'great horses'. There is also a Discovery Centre in the Stables, with audio-visual displays.

The castle battlements and the Venus Garden are in the process of being restored, and the fountain, with 23 new statues, plays again for the first time in centuries. A series of 'Caesar paintings' depicting Roman emperors and empresses has also recently returned to Bolsover. These were commissioned by William Cavendish and copied from originals by the great Venetian artist Titian - which have since been destroyed - making the Bolsover versions uniquely important.

River Rother and Doe Lea. The first castle at Bolsover was built by William Peverel, illegitimate son of William the Conqueror, as part of his vast Derbyshire estates. Nothing remains of that Norman building. Visitors can explore the Little Castle, or Keep, which is decorated in an elaborate Jacobean style with wonderful fireplaces, panelling and wall paintings. The whole building later descended to the Dukes of Portland, and it remains a

SILHOUETTES

Unit 4, Cavendish Walk, Bolsover, Derbyshire S44 6DB
Tel: 01246 827005

The expertise and experience that have made her Making It 4U in Chesterfield such a success are watchwords at Yvonne Clarke's Bolsover outlet **Silhouettes**. This is a ladies boutique of quality and prestige, with a wide, seasonally changing display of garments aimed primarily at the over-40s, catering mainly for sizes 10 to 22. Popular, respected brands regularly in stock include Emreco – making waves with its bright colours, exuberance and vivacity since Emreco Coveri hit the headlines on the Milan catwalks in 1973; Oscar B – clear, contemporary style meets the highest standards of quality and fitting, feminine fashion with casual influences and important little details that surprise; and Adini, Marble and Viz a Viz – created in 1992 to fill the perceived gap in the ladies wear market for discerning women who want to wear fashion that is individual and feminine yet affordable. Silhouettes also stocks a selection of shoes, including the Lunar range (comfort, glitz and glamour) hats, jewellery and other accessories.

Part of the upstairs section of the boutique is given over to designing and making Yvonne's exclusive clothes, some produced for stock to display in the sales area, others made to individual orders from customers. Silhouette is open five days a week, closed Wednesday and Sunday.

Curtains and other soft furnishings, ladies' clothes and garment repair and alterations are the main offerings of Yvonne's other enterprise Making It4U (qv) at 414 Chatsworth Road, Chesterfield. Tel: 01246 297615.

strangely impressive place, though even now it is threatened by its industrial surroundings and the legacy of centuries of coal-mining beneath its walls: subsidence.

AULT HUCKNALL

6 miles SE of Chesterfield off the A617

🐦 Hardwick Hall

The strange name of this village probably means Hucca's high nook of land, and this pleasant place, standing on a ridge close to the Nottinghamshire border, is home to the magnificent Tudor house, **Hardwick Hall** (National Trust). "More glass than wall", it is one of Derbyshire's Big Three stately homes alongside Chatsworth and Haddon, all three glorious monuments to the great landowning families who played so great a role in shaping

the history of the county. The letters E S can be seen carved in stone on the outside of the house: E S, or Elizabeth of Shrewsbury, was perhaps better known as Bess of Hardwick. This larger-than-life figure had attachments with many places in Derbyshire, and the story of her life makes for fascinating reading.

She was born in the manor house at Hardwick in 1520. The house stood only a little distance from the present-day Hall and was then not much more than a farmhouse. The young Bess married her neighbour's son, Robert Barlow, when she was only 12. When her young husband, himself only 14, died a few months later, she naturally inherited a great deal of property. Some 15 years later she married Sir William Cavendish and, when he died in 1557, she was bequeathed his entire fortune. By this time she was the richest woman in England, save for one, Elizabeth, the Queen.

Bess began the building of Hardwick House in 1590, towards the end of her life and after her fourth lucrative marriage to George Talbot, 6th Earl of Shrewsbury. It stands as a monument to her wealth and good taste, and is justly famous for its magnificent needlework and tapestries, carved fireplaces and friezes, which are considered to be among the finest in Britain. One of the highlights is the Threads of Time exhibition, and conservation tours take place between Wednesday and Saturday.

Though Bess is the first person who springs to mind with regard to Hardwick Hall, it was the 6th Duke of Devonshire who was responsible for the Hall's antiquarian atmosphere. He inherited the property in 1811

and, as well as promoting the legend that Mary, Queen of Scots stayed here, he filled the house with furniture, paintings and tapestries from his other houses and from Chatsworth in particular. The philosopher Thomas Hobbes, author of *The Leviathan*, who was tutor to two Dukes of Devonshire, died at Hardwick Hall in 1679 and is buried in the Church of St John the Baptist.

PILSLEY
5 miles S of Chesterfield off the B6039

🌿 Herb Garden

The **Herb Garden** in Pilsley is one of the foremost gardens in the country. It consists of four display gardens, the largest of which is the Mixed Herb Garden, boasting an impressive established parterre. The remaining three gardens each with its own special theme and housing many rare and unusual species are the Physic, the Lavender and the Pot Pourri. Areas of native flowers and wild spring bulbs can be enjoyed from March to September.

HOLYMOORSIDE
3 miles W of Chesterfield off the A632

Surrounded by attractive moorland and lying in the picturesque valley of the River Hipper, this scattered village has grown into a popular residential area for the nearby towns. The custom of well-dressing in the village was revived in 1979 after a gap of about 80 years. Two wells are dressed, a large one and a smaller one for children, on the Wednesday before the late summer Bank Holiday in August.

The dressers follow the tradition of Barlow, where only flowers and leaves are used and not wool, seed and shells, though they do not stick to biblical themes. In 1990 the well-dressing depicted a scene commemorating the 50th anniversary of the

Norman Church, Ault Hucknall

Battle of Britain, one of their most spectacular dressings to date, and won the dressers pictures in the national press.

CUTTHORPE
4 miles W of Chesterfield off the B6050

🏛 Linacre Reservoirs

Before World War II the well-dressings in this village, which take place on the third Friday in July, had no religious links. After the war the custom died out, but was revived again by three people from nearby Barlow in 1978. The three dressed wells are blessed during a service of thanksgiving for the pure water.

Near the village are the three **Linacre Reservoirs**, set in the attractive wooded Linacre Valley. Built between 1855 and 1904, they supplied water to Chesterfield until recently. Today the area is home to many species of fish, waterfowl, mammals and plant life, and is considered one of the most important ecological sites in the area. There are very pleasant walks, nature trails and fishing and a scenic picnic area.

BARLOW
3 miles NW of Chesterfield off the B6051

Barlow is mentioned in the Domesday Book, and was the home of Robert Barlow, the first of Bess of Hardwick's four husbands. Although situated outside the limestone area, Barlow has been dressing its main well for longer than most. It is not known for certain when the custom began in the village, though it is known that, like Tissington, the well here provided water throughout the drought of 1615; this may have marked the start of this colourful practice. The wells are dressed during the second week of August every year. West of the village, Barlow Woodseats are not as uncomfortable as they sound for

this is the name of an irregular gabled 16th-century house, also called Woodseats Hall (private), which has a cruck barn in its grounds. It was home to the Mower family, one of whom, Arthur Mower, was the agent to the Barlow family in the 16th century, and kept a truly remarkable diary from 1555 to 1610. All 52 volumes are now in the British Museum. He records the death of Bess of Hardwick in 1608, recalling her as "a great purchaser and getter together of much goods" and notes that she "builded Chattesworth, Hardwick and Owlcotes".

Alfreton

🏛 Alfreton Hall

This historic town dates back to Saxon times and, despite local legends to the contrary, Alfred the Great was not immortalised in the naming of the place. This attractive former coal-mining town stands on a hill close to the Nottinghamshire border. Along the charming High Street can be found the George Hotel, a fine Georgian building that looks down the length of the High Street. There are also a number of other 18th-century stone-built houses, the most impressive of which is **Alfreton Hall**, the centrepiece of an attractive public park. In soft mellow stone, the Hall was built around 1730, with 19th-century additions. The home until fairly recently of the Palmer Morewood family, owners of the local coal mines, it is now used as an Arts and Adult Education Centre. The park is quite extensive, boasting its own cricket ground and a horse-riding track around its perimeter. In King Street there is a house of confinement, or lock-up, which was built to house lawbreakers and catered mainly for the local drunkards. The close confines of the prison with its two cells, minute windows and thick outer walls must have been a very effective deterrent.

Around Alfreton

SOUTH WINGFIELD
2 miles NW of Alfreton off the A6

🏛 Wingfield Manor

Above the village, on the rise of a hill, stand the graceful ruins of the 15th-century **Wingfield Manor**. Built by Ralph Lord Cromwell, the manor house was used as Mary, Queen of Scots' prison on two separate occasions, in 1569 and 1584, when she was held under the care of the Earl of Shrewsbury. The local squire, Anthony Babington, attempted to rescue the Queen and lead her to safety but the plot failed and, instead, lead to them both being beheaded. One of the less well-known of Derbyshire's many manor houses and mansions, the history and architectural interest provided by the ruins

make it one of the more fascinating homes in the area. A wander around the remains reveals the large banqueting hall with its unusual oriel window and a crypt that was probably used to store food and wine. Whatever its use, it is a particularly fine example and rivals a similar structure at Fountains Abbey.

CRICH
4 miles SW of Alfreton off the A6

🏛 Crich Stand   🚋 National Tramway Museum

High up overlooking the Derwent valley, this lovingly restored village, with its hilltop church and market cross, is probably most famous as the home of the **National Tramway Museum**. Referring to itself intriguingly as 'the museum that's a mile long', it offers a wonderful opportunity to enjoy a tram ride along a Victorian Street scene. The beautifully preserved trams are of course the main centre of interest and include one of the ex-London Transport Feltham trams, considered by many to be the most elegant

National Tramway Village

Crich Tramway Village, Derbyshire DE4 5DP
Tel: 01773 854321
e-mail: enquiries@tramway.co.uk
website: www.tramway.co.uk

National Tramway Museum offers a family day out in the relaxing atmosphere of a bygone era. Explore the re-created period street with its genuine buildings and features, fascinating exhibitions and most importantly, its trams. Unlimited tram rides are free with your entry fee, giving you the opportunity to fully appreciate the Village and surrounding countryside.

Journey on one of the many beautifully restored vintage trams, as they rumble through the cobbled street past a traditional police telephone known as the 'TARDIS', the Red Lion Pub & Restaurant, exhibition hall, workshops, children's play and picnic area, before passing beneath the magnificent Bowes Lyon Bridge. Next it's past the bandstand, through the woods, and then on to Glory Mine taking in spectacular views of the Derwent Valley.

🎬 stories and anecdotes   🦜 famous people   🎨 art and craft   🎭 entertainment and sport   🚶 walks

ever built. Trams run to and fro every few minutes along the cobbled streets, and the site also has a woodland walk and sculpture trail. The museum is open daily from April to the end of October.

Back in the centre of the village is the tower of **Crich Stand**, a local landmark that looks rather like a lighthouse. In fact, this is the Regimental Memorial for the Sherwood Foresters and, erected in 1923, stands almost 1,000 feet above sea level. From its viewing gallery on a clear day, it is said that seven counties can be seen: a climb to the top certainly offers some fantastic views. This large, straggling village, which retains its medieval market cross, was also a flourishing knitting centre at one time; the telltale 18th-century cottages with their long upper windows can still be seen. The part-Norman parish Church of St Michael has a built-in stone lectern, which, though common in Derbyshire, is rare elsewhere in the country.

AMBERGATE
6 miles SW of Alfreton off the A6

🌱 Shining Cliff Woods

Where the River Amber joins the mighty Derwent, Ambergate is one of the main gateways to the Peak District for travellers going north on the A6. A marvellous bridge crosses the Derwent. The village itself is surrounded by deciduous woodland, including the fine **Shining Cliff Woods**, an important refuge for wildlife. The railway, road and canal here are all squeezed into the tight river valley, and the railway station, standing 100 feet above the road, was one of the few triangular stations in Britain. Built in the late 19th century, the church of St Anne was a gift to the village from the Johnson family of the Ambergate Wire Works, now

known as the business concern Richard Johnson and Nephew.

RIDDINGS
2 miles S of Alfreton off the A38/A610

Riddings, now a tranquil village, has twice been the scene of important discoveries. In the mid 1700s, 800 precious Roman coins were uncovered here. A century later, James Oakes, a colliery proprietor and ironmaster, discovered a mysterious liquid flowing on his property. He called in the assistance of his brother-in-law, Lyon Playfair, one of the most brilliant practical scientists of his day. Playfair found the liquid to be petroleum – then an unknown product commercially, although it had been known as naphtha, 'salt of the earth', from Biblical times.

Playfair summoned the help of his friend James Young, who soon after he came to Riddings approached Playfair in dismay to show him that the oil was in a turbid condition. Playfair recognised at once the presence of paraffin, and instructed Young to extract enough paraffin to make two candles – the first paraffin-wax candles ever produced. With one candle in his left hand and the other in his right, Playfair illuminated a lecture he gave at the Royal Institution. From these small beginnings date the enormous petroleum industry and the rich trade in paraffin and its wide range of by-products.

Ripley

Once a typical small market town, Ripley expanded dramatically during the Industrial Revolution when great use was made of the iron, clay and coal deposits found nearby. The town's Butterley ironworks, founded in 1792 by a group of men that included renowned engineer Benjamin Outram, created the roof for London's St Pancras station. Outram's even more famous son, Sir James, enjoyed an illustrious career that saw him appointed Bayard of India, and earned him a resting place in Westminster Abbey.

Around Ripley

HEAGE
1 mile W of Ripley off the B6013

🏛 Windmill

This village is home to a famous tower **Windmill** (see panel below), the only one in Derbyshire to retain all its six sails, fan tail and machinery. The Grade II listed building, situated to the west of the village, is built of local sandstone. Now more than 200 years old, the mill has been restored to full working order and is open to the public at weekends and Bank Holidays. The mill can be visited between 11am and 4pm, April to October.

DENBY
2 miles S of Ripley off the A38/B6179

🏛 Visitor Centre

Denby Visitor Centre is one of the biggest visitor attractions in Derbyshire. The centerpiece is the famous pottery; it was established in 1809 and, 200 years later, classic ranges such as Imperial Blue and Regency Green are still bestsellers. Other on-site attractions include a Factory Shop, a Cookery Emporium offering cookery demonstrations, and a stock of more than 3,000 kitchen gadgets, supplies and equipment.

Heage Windmill

Chesterfield Road, Heage, Belper,
Derbyshire DE56 2BH
Telephone: 01773 853579
website: www.heagewindmill.co.uk

Heage Windmill stands in a very striking position overlooking the village of Nether Heage. A Grade II* listed building, it is the only working, stone-towered windmill with six sails in England and the only working windmill in Derbyshire. The mill started grinding corn in 1797 and, prior to her restoration, was last worked by miller, Thomas Shore in 1919.

The mill has much of her old wooden mechanism in place which drives one of her two pairs of millstones. In the basement, the interpretation centre tells a story of Heage Windmill. The adjacent kiln has been restored as a reception centre with toilets and a shop selling flour, souvenirs and refreshments. There is wheelchair access to the ground floor of the windmill, the interpretation centre and the reception centre. There is a large car park on site.

HEANOR

3 miles SE of Ripley off the A608

🌱 Memorial Gardens   🦌 Shipley Country Park

The hub of this busy town centres on the market place, where the annual fair is held, as well as the twice-weekly market (Fridays and Saturdays). Away from the bustle of the market are the **Memorial Gardens**. This peaceful setting always promises a magnificent spread of floral arrangements, herbaceous borders and shrubberies.

To the south of Heanor is the **Shipley Country Park**, on the estate of the now demolished Shipley Hall. In addition to its magnificent lake, the Country Park boasts over 600 acres of beautiful countryside, which should keep even the most enthusiastic walker busy. Well known as both an educational and holiday centre, there are facilities for horse riding, cycling and fishing. Restoration over the years has transformed former railways into wooded paths, reservoirs into peaceful lakes, and has re-established the once-flowering meadows and rolling hills that had been destroyed by colliery pits.

Belper

🏛 Mills   🏛 Visitor Centre   🦌 River Gardens

Famous for its cotton mills, the town is situated alongside the River Derwent on the floor of the valley. In 1776, Jedediah Strutt, the wheelwright son of a South Normanton farmer, looking to harness the natural powers of the river to run his mills, set up one of the earliest water-powered cotton mills here. With the river providing the power, and fuel coming from the nearby South Derbyshire coalfield, the valley has a good claim to be one of the cradles of the Industrial Revolution. Earlier, in 1771,

Strutt had gone into profitable partnership with Richard Arkwright to establish the world's first water-powered cotton mill at Cromford. Great benefactors to Belper for 150 years, the Strutt family provided housing, work, education and even food from the model farms they established in the surrounding countryside.

The **Mills** are still standing and, along with them, are some unique mill-workers cottages. To discover more about the cotton industry, a visit to the **Derwent Valley Visitor Centre** is a must. It records the influence of the Strutt family on the town and of Samuel Slater, Strutt's apprentice who emigrated to America in 1789, built a mill there and went on to become "the Father of American manufacturers".

The oldest mill still surviving is the two-storey North Mill at Bridgefoot, near the magnificent crescent-shaped weir in the Derwent and the town's main bridge. Built in 1876, the mill has cast-iron columns and beams, and hollow tile floors that provided a warm-air central heating system. It is now the visitor centre. The massive neighbouring redbrick East Mill was constructed in 1912, but now is largely empty. A Jubilee Tower in terracotta was erected on the mill site in 1897 to mark Queen Victoria's 60 years on the throne.

Train travellers through Belper are among those treated to a glimpse of George Stephenson's mile-long cutting, walled in gritstone throughout and spanned by no fewer than 10 bridges. When completed in 1840, it was considered the engineering wonder of its day. In addition to all its industrial history the town goes back to well before the Industrial Revolution. Not only was it mentioned in the Domesday Book (as Beau Repaire - the beautiful retreat), but in 1964 the remains of a Roman kiln were found here.

CROOTS FARM SHOP & KITCHEN

Farnah House Farm, Wirksworth Road,
Duffield, Derbyshire DE56 4AQ
Tel: 01332 843032 Fax: 01332 842175
e-mail: info@croots.co.uk
website: www.croots.co.uk

The Croots family, with Steve and Kay at the helm, are passionate about the quality and freshness of what they sell, and everything on the shelves of **Croots Farm Shop** is testament to that passion. All their efforts are directed towards providing only the very best food and drink for their discerning customers, and the reward for those efforts is a large and ever-growing band of loyal shoppers who come from many miles around to this idyllic farmyard setting signposted on the B5023, a mile off the main A6 running through Duffield. Steve believes that farm shops should be all about food and drink, so there's no place here for the themed giftware that clutters so many inferior establishments.

Steve has been a keen grower of vegetables, herbs and salads all his life, and the farm shop, adapted from the family farm, is stocked with his produce and daily deliveries of fresh seasonal produce, as local as possible to reduce food miles to a minimum. Prominent on display are fruit and vegetables, home-produced lamb, free-range eggs, local ice cream and other dairy products, freshly baked bread, home-made cakes and tarts, pickles and preserves, local beer and fruit juices, flour and other dry goods. The meat counter has its own butcher, which means that everything can be cut to customers' individual needs. The butcher works with local farmers to ensure the highest standards in raising the livestock, and the butchery and preparation for putting the meat on sale. As well as the traditional cuts and joints, the butchery sells tasty home made Award Winning sausages, hams, bacon and pies. From the delicatessen counter come pâtés and pies, quiches, cooked meats, wines, oils and vinegars and hand-crafted cheese, including local Stilton, traditional farmhouse Cheddar, richly flavoured goat's cheese and some from France, Italy and elsewhere on the Continent.

The Kitchen at the farm prepares a wide and mouthwatering selection of food which can be sampled on the premises (accompanied by great views) or bought to take home. Breakfast is served from 9 to 11, lunch from 12 to 2.30, and teas, coffees, cakes and hot and cold snacks are served throughout the day.

Croots Farm Shop is open from 9 to 5 Tuesday to Saturday,
10 to 4 Sunday; closed Monday and Bank Holidays

The **River Gardens** were established in 1905, and today the beautifully tended gardens are a pleasant place for a stroll. Rowing boats can be hired for a trip along the Derwent. The Gardens are a favourite with the film industry, having been used in Ken Russell's *Women in Love*, as well as television's *Sounding Brass* and *In the Shadow of the Noose*.

Around Belper

DUFFIELD
2 miles S of Belper off the A6

🏰 Castle

This ancient parish is a charming place, with Georgian houses and cottages lining the banks of the River Ecclesbourne. For such a cosy place, it seems odd that the Parish Church is situated in isolation down by the river. Inside the Church there is an impressive monument dedicated to Anthony Bradshaw whose great-nephew went on to officiate over the court that called for the execution of Charles I. Also in the village is a large mound, all that remains of **Duffield Castle** (National Trust), which was ransacked and burnt to the ground in 1266.

Ilkeston

🏛 Erewash Museum

The third largest town in Derbyshire, Ilkeston received its royal charter for a market and fair in 1252; both have continued to the present day. The history of the town, however, goes back to the days when it was an Anglo-Saxon hilltop settlement known as Tilchestune. Once

---

ANDREA WELSHER DESIGNS
Dragonflies, 2A Station Road, Ilkeston,
Derbyshire DE7 5LD
Tel: 0115 9326000
e-mail: info@dragonfliesofilkeston.co.uk
website: www.dragonfliesofilkeston.co.uk

The mother-and-daughter team of Christine and Andrea Welsher own and run Andrea Welsher Design, which trades as Dragonflies in the historic town of Ilkeston. What started as a modest cottage business run from Andrea's home has developed into an Aladdin's Cave of crafts, a one-stop shop for craft supplies, bespoke gifts and wedding stationery, all at very realistic prices. Along with their assistant Jane, the owners offer a smile, a cuppa and an amazing array of crafting materials and supplies.

Card making, cross stitch kits and accessories, DMC threads, Dovecraft materials and tools, scrap booking supplies, quilling accessories, glitters, rubber stamps, punches, glues, Gel Gems, Rainbow Toys, jewellery, photo frames, Ashleigh & Burwood candles and incense for home and garden, Aspen Mulling spices, cards and gifts for all ages and all occasions, personalised handmade wedding stationery and cards.......All this and more under one roof, in a warm, friendly ambience that makes browsing and shopping a real pleasure. Shop hours are 9 to 5; closed Wednesday and Sunday.

🏛 historic building 🏛 museum 🏰 historic site 🐟 scenic attraction 🌿 flora and fauna

a mining and lace-making centre, its history is told in the **Erewash Museum**, housed in a fine Georgian house on the High Street. Other fine examples of elegant 18th-century houses can be found in East Street while in Wharncliffe Road there are period houses with art nouveau features.

Ilkeston commands fine wide views from the hillside above the valley of the Erewash, which here bounds the county. The town's church-crowned hilltop provides a landmark that can be seen from far afield.

Around Ilkeston

WEST HALLAM
2 miles W of Ilkeston off the A609

🏠 West Hallam Hall   🎨 The Bottle Kiln

West Hallam stands on a hilltop; its church, set between the great expanse of **West Hallam Hall** and the rectory, is approached via a lovely avenue of limes. The rector's garden has a glorious lime tree, and looks out over the valley to a great windmill with its arms still working as they have done since Georgian times.

One of the premier attractions in the area, **The Bottle Kiln** is a handsome and impressive brick-built former working pottery, now home to contemporary art and craft. Visitors can take a leisurely look at exhibitions (changing throughout the year) of both British studio ceramics and contemporary painting in the European tradition. From figurative and descriptive to abstract, many styles and media are displayed here. In addition, there is a selection of imaginative contemporary British jewellery and craftware on display in and around the old kiln. Two shops filled with jewellery, cards, gifts, objets d'art, soft

furnishings and housewares with an accent on style, design and originality can also be found at this superb site.

DALE ABBEY
3 miles SW of Ilkeston off the A6096

🏠 Windmill   🚶 Hermit's Wood

The village takes its name from the now ruined abbey that was founded here by Augustinian monks in the 13th century. Beginning life in a very humble manner, local legend has it that a Derbyshire baker came to the area in 1130, carved himself a niche in the sandstone and devoted himself to the way of the hermit. The owner of the land, Ralph FitzGeremunde, discovered the baker and was so impressed by the man's devotion that he

Dale Abbey Ruins

bestowed on him the land and tithe rights to his mill in Borrowash. The sandstone cave and the romantic ruined 40-feet-high window archway are popular attractions locally, and a walk around the village is both an interesting and pleasurable experience. Nearby **Hermit's Wood** is an ancient area of woodland with beech, ash, oak and lime trees. It is wonderful at any time of year, but particularly in the spring when the woodland floor is covered with a mist of bluebells.

To the north of the village stands the **Cat and Fiddle Windmill**, built in the 1700s and a fine example of the oldest type of mill. The stone roundhouse is capped with a box-like wooden structure that houses the machinery and is fitted onto an upright post around which it can rotate to catch the wind.

RISLEY
4 miles S of Ilkeston off the B5010

This small village has once again become a quiet backwater now that the main Derby to Nottingham road bypasses it to the south. Apart from ribbon building along the former main road, Risley consists of no more than a small group of old buildings, but they are unique and well worth a visit. In 1593, Michael Willoughby started to rebuild the village church. Although small, even by the standards of the day, it is charming and essentially Gothic in style. In the same year his wife founded a school and, although none of the original schoolhouses exist, those seen today date from the early 1700s and were constructed by a trust founded by the family. The central school building is a perfect example of the Queen Anne style and acted as both the school and schoolhouse, with the boarders sleeping in the garrets. The trustees still maintain this wonderful building, along with the Latin School of 1724, the English School of 1753, and another School House built in 1771.

BREASTON
5 miles S of Ilkeston off the A6005

🏛 Church of St Michael

On the southern borders of the county, close to Nottinghamshire and Leicestershire, Breaston occupies the flat countryside near the point where the River Derwent joins the River Trent before continuing on its long journey to the North Sea. The mainly 13th-century **Church of St Michael** boasts the Boy of Breaston – a small, chubby-faced child immortalised in the 13th century by the mason of the nave arches. He has smiled down on worshippers and visitors for the past seven centuries. The story has it that this boy would come in and watch the masons at work while the church was being built. The master mason decided to make the child part of the church, so that he could always have a good view of it.

Coffins had to be carried to neighbouring Church Wilne for burial up until the early 1800s, as there was no burial ground at Breaston until then. For this reason the footpath over the fields of Wilne continues to be known by villagers as the Coffin Walk.

ELVASTON
8 miles SW of Ilkeston off the B5010

🏛 Castle

Elvaston is gathered around the edge of the Elvaston Castle estate, home of the Earls of Harrington. The magnificent Gothic castle seen today replaced a 17th-century brick and gabled manor house; part of the original structure can be seen on the end of the south front. Designed by James Wyatt, the castle was finished in the early 1800s but, unfortunately, the 3rd Earl died in 1829 and had little time to enjoy his new home.

The grounds of **Elvaston Castle** were originally laid out and designed for the 4th Earl by William Barron. Barron, who was born in Berwickshire in 1805, started work in 1830 on what at first appeared to be an impossible task. The 4th Earl wanted a garden "second to none", but the land available, which had never been landscaped, was flat, water-logged and uninspiring with just two avenues of trees and a walled kitchen garden (but no greenhouses or hot houses). First draining the land, Barron then planted trees to offer shelter to more tender plants. From there the project grew. In order to stock the gardens, Barron began a programme of propagation of rarer tree species and, along with the tree-planting methods he developed specially to deal with Elvaston's problems, his fame spread. The gardens became a showcase of rare and interesting trees, many found nowhere else in Britain. Now owned by Derby County Council, the gardens, after years of neglect, have been completely restored and the delights of the formal gardens, with their fine topiary, the avenues and the kitchen garden can be enjoyed by all visitors to the grounds, which are now a Country Park.

No visit to Elvaston would be complete without a walk down to the Golden Gates. Erected in 1819 at the southern end of the formal gardens, the gates were brought from the Palace of Versailles by the 3rd Earl of Harrington. Little is known of the gates history, but they remain a fine monument and are the symbol of Elvaston.

Derby

🏛 Cathedral 🏠 Pickford House 🏠 Museums

Essentially a commercial and industrial city, Derby's position, historically and geographically, has ensured that is has remained one of the most important and interesting cities in the area. Consequently there is much for the visitor to see, whether from an architectural or historical point of

Derby Cathedral

Pickford's House Museum

41 Friargate, Derby DE1 1DA
Tel: 01332 255363
website: www.derby.gov.uk

Pickford's House Museum, in the historic Friar Gate area, is a beautifully restored Georgian house, and was the home of Derby industrialist Joseph Pickford. The dining room, drawing room and morning room are as they might have been in Pickford's time. A Georgian bedroom and dressing room have been recreated on the first floor, while on the top floor there is a servant's bedroom. The kitchen and laundry have been reconstructed, together with a cellar, pantry and housekeeper's cupboard, so that visitors can get an idea of what life was like for the servants working below stairs in Georgian times. One of the cellars is equipped as an air-raid shelter of the 1940s. The upper floors feature displays of toys and toy theatres, and several rooms showing some of the Museum's excellent collection of historic costumes and textiles.

view. There are, however, two things almost everyone, whether they have been to the city before or not, associate with Derby: Rolls-Royce engines and Royal Crown Derby porcelain. When in 1906 Sir Henry Royce and the Hon C S Rolls joined forces and built the first Rolls-Royce (a Silver Ghost) at Derby, they built much more than just a motor car. Considered by many to be the best cars in the world, it is often said that the noisiest moving part in any Rolls-Royce is the dashboard clock! The home of Royal Crown Derby, any visit to the city would not be complete without a trip to the factory and its museum and shop. The guided tours offer an intriguing insight into the high level of skill required to create the delicate flower petals, hand-gild the plates and to hand-paint the Derby Dwarves.

The city's **Cathedral of All Saints** possesses a fine 16th-century tower, the second highest perpendicular tower in England. The airy building was actually built in the 1720s by James Gibbs. Inside is a beautiful wrought-iron screen by Robert Bakewell and, among the splendid monuments, lies the tomb of Bess of Hardwick. Originally Derby's Parish Church, it was given cathedral status in 1927.

One of Derby's most interesting museums is **Pickford House** (see panel above), situated on the city's finest Georgian street at number 41. It is a Grade I listed building, erected in 1770 by the architect Joseph Pickford as a combined family home and place of work. Pickford House differs from the majority of grand stately homes. Unlike

The Silk Mill

Derby's Museum of Industry and History
Silk Mill Lane, off Full Street, Derby DE1 3AF
Tel: 01332 255308
e-mail: museums@derby.gov.uk
website: www.derby.gov.uk

The Silk Mill, Derby's Museum of Industry and History, is on the site of the world's oldest factories, the Silk Mills, built by George Sorocold in 1702 and 1717. The foundations and parts of the tower from the 1717 mill are still visible. The displays in the Mill tell the story of Derby's industrial heritage and achievements, and of its people. There is a special emphasis on the development of Rolls-Royce aero engines and the railway industry.

most, it does not have a wealth of priceless furniture and works or art. Instead, visitors are able to gain an insight into everyday middle-class life during the 1830s.

Just a short walk from Pickford House is the **Industrial Museum** (see panel above). What better place to house a museum devoted to the preservation of Derby's industrial heritage than the beautiful old Silk Mill? The building stands on one of the most interesting sites in the country and preceded Richard Arkwright's first cotton mill by over 50 years. The tower of the mill is incorporated into the museum.

The **City Museum and Art Gallery** is also well worth visiting. Opened in 1879, it is the oldest of Derby's museums and the displays include natural history, archaeology and social history exhibits. One section of the museum is devoted to a Military Gallery and relates to Derby's local historical regiments. The walk-in World War I trench scene attempts to capture the experience of a night at the front. A ground floor gallery houses the city's superb collection of fine porcelain, manufactured in Derby from the mid 18th century.

Around Derby

DRAYCOTT
5 miles E of Derby on the A6005
(just off the A52)

🌿 St Chad's Water

Draycott is a narrow, elongated village situated in the countryside between Derby and long Eaton, a very short walk from the midshires Way and Route 6 of the National Cycle Route, along the route of the old Derby Canal. The best-known landmark in Draycott is a four-storey mill with a green copper-capped ornamental clock tower. When it was completed in 1907 as part of Nottingham's thriving lace industry, it was the largest manufacturing mill in Europe. Near Draycott is the beautiful **St Chad's Water**, a 12-acre Nature Reserve sitting peacefully beside St Chad's Church. This compact reserve is a haven for birds and other wildlife in the area. Among the migrant birds spotted here are whitethroats, willow warblers, swallows, kingfishers and

THE BEETROOT TREE GALLERY FOR CONTEMPORARY ART

South Street, Draycott, Derbyshire, DE72 3PP
Tel: 01332 873929
e-mail: info@thebeetroottree.com website: www.thebeetroottree.com

Open every day between 10.00am and 5.00pm.
FREE entry to exhibitions.
ART to covet: **FOOD** to enjoy: **SPACE** to relax.
Our visitors say: ...

> *oh it's heaven in here.* (Josie)
> *Truly enjoyable, the hairs on the back of my neck*
> *are standing up.* (Travis)
> *As ever, beautiful – inspirational and thought provoking.*
> *Thank you, I will be back soon.* (Jenny)
> *Amazing work –really lovely. Will come back. Xxx* (Ann)
> *Wonderful ambience.* (Carol)

On South Street in the old village centre of Draycott you will find a renovated late 17th Century Jacobean barn housing an established and internationally renowned contemporary art gallery. The main exhibition space plays host to a full programme of exciting and eclectic shows running throughout the year showing a range of media including painting, textiles, ceramics, glass, photography, metal, jewellery and more. The gallery also displays continuing exhibitions of work by acclaimed designer-makers and a permanent collection of work by resident artist Alysn Midgelow-Marsden. The art materials section offers you the means to develop your own creativity, while the workshop space set in the restored stable runs courses throughout the year for skill development, enjoyment and exploration.

The café and landscaped garden allow for peaceful contemplation, relaxation and restoration of body and mind. A knowledgeable and friendly team will be happy to help when you visit and for information, news and updates please see the website.

chiffchaffs as well as the usual water birds. The swans and their cygnets are a popular annual attraction. A second reserve, Orchid Wood Nature Walk, boasts several species of naturally occurring orchids in the grass and woodland around the walk.

KEDLESTON

4 miles NW of Derby off the A52

🏛 Kedleston Hall

Kedleston Hall has been the family seat of the Curzon family since the 12th century and, until it was taken over by the National Trust, it had the longest continuous male line in Derbyshire and one of the longest in the country. The present elegant mansion was built between 1759 and 1765 by Robert Adam and it remains one of the finest examples of his work. The house has a fine collection of paintings and sculpture, and the Eastern Room is filled with fascinating objects collected by Lord Curzon when he was Viceroy of India between 1899 and 1905. He died in 1925 and is buried in All Saints Church, which is all that remains of the medieval village of Kedleston. Since taking over the property in 1987, the National Trust have embarked on a major restoration programme. The garden has been restored to an 18th-century pleasure ground, and three different walks allow visitors to explore the historic parkland, which includes beautiful lakes and cascades. An exhibition shows how

THE ROUNDHOUSE GALLERY

The Firs, Foston, Derbyshire DE65 5DL
Tel: 01283 585348
e-mail: pj.evans@btconnect.com
website: www.roundhousegallery.co.uk

Philip Evans, a potter for 25 years, owns and runs the **Roundhouse Gallery** with his wife Leah. The family business was established in 1989 in Tutbury, Staffordshire, and in 1991 it was selected by the Crafts Council for the quality and variety of the pottery and ceramics on display. In 1999 the business moved to Foston, where it stands just west of the junction with Coplow Lane. It's a short drive from the A50, east of Uttoxeter and north of Tutbury.

In what started life in the 18th century as a coaching inn, loyal regular clients have seen it grow from those small beginnings in Tutbury to become one of the foremost collections of British pottery, a showcase for the pick of Britain's leading contemporary studio potters. Collectors will find an impressive array of work at prices to suit all pockets, from as little as £5. As well as the constantly changing display the Roundhouse holds a much-acclaimed annual Bakers Dozen featuring the work of 13 potters. The whole place has a very friendly, relaxed feel, and visitors can enjoy a cup of coffee while browsing the unique collections.

the interior of the Hall was transformed during the filming of the film *The Duchess*, starring Keira Knightley.

SUDBURY

12 miles W of Derby off the A50

🏠 Sudbury Hall   🏛 Museum of Childhood

Sudbury is the estate village to **Sudbury Hall**, the late 17th-century mansion and home of a branch of the Vernon family who lived at Haddon Hall. The house is intriguing, the garden restful. Gifted to the National Trust in 1967, the Hall is an unexpected mixture of architectural styles. A splendid example of a house of Charles II's time, the interior of Sudbury Hall contains elaborate plasterwork and murals throughout, wood carvings by Grinling Gibbons, and some fine examples of mythological paintings by Laguerre. Of

particular interest is the **Museum of Childhood**, which is situated in the servants' wing and provides a fascinating insight into the lives of children down the ages. Fascinating displays range from a wealthy family's nursery and an Edwardian schoolroom, to a 'chimney climb' and coal tunnel for the adventurous. The Hall featured in the BBC's *Pride and Prejudice* and *Jane Eyre*. The formal gardens and meadows lead to the tree-fringed lake. Wildlife abounds, including kestrels, grey herons, grass snakes, dragonflies, newts, frogs, toads, little and tawny owls and woodpeckers. Special events are held throughout the year (01283 585305).

Swadlincote

Here at the extreme edge of Derbyshire, well south of the River Trent, Swadlincote shares many characteristics with Staffordshire. Among the town's thriving industries, based on the clay and coal on which it stands, are large potteries founded in 1795 as well as brickworks.

Around Swadlincote

NETHERSEAL
6 miles S of Swadlincote off the A444

Netherseal is a picturesque village on the banks of the River Mease. Seal means forested, and Netherseal was recorded in the Domesday Book as a wooded area on the edge of Ashby Woulds. It was once a mining community with a two-shaft colliery and several related industries. The mining activity has long ceased and the centre of the village is now a conservation area with many listed buildings - including some charming 17th-century almshouses.

TICKNALL
5 miles NE of Swadlincote off the B587

🏛 Calke Abbey

In 1985 the National Trust bought **Calke Abbey**, a large Baroque-style mansion built in 1701 on the site of an Augustinian priory founded in 1133. However, it was not until 1989 that the Trust was able to open the house to the public, for this was no ordinary house. Dubbed 'the house that time forgot' since the death of the owner, Sir Vauncy Harpur-Crewe in 1924, nothing had been altered in the mansion. In fact, the seclusion of the house, and also the rather bizarre lifestyle of its inhabitants, had left many rooms and objects untouched for over 100 years. There was even a spectacular 18th-century Chinese silk state bed that had never been unpacked.

Today, the Trust has repaired the house and returned all 13,000 items to their original

---

SCADDOWS FARM SHOP & CAFÉ
Scaddows Lane, Ticknall, South Derbyshire DE73 7JP
Tel: 01332 865709
e-mail: scaddowsfarmshop@hotmail.com

A friendly welcome and personal, attentive service awaits visitors to Scaddows Farm Shop & Café set in beautiful South Derbyshire countryside on the A514 between Ticknall & Hartshorne. The farm is run by the Webster family who are passionate about traditional home-raised and home-grown produce, growing a wide variety of soft fruit and vegetables. They are rightly renowned throughout the region for the Pick Your Own side of the business, with strawberries, raspberries, gooseberries and blackcurrants in great demand in June and July.

The shop and café are open every day where home grown and local produce are available all year round, along with meat from their award-winning butcher, cheese from Leicestershire, local jams, chutneys, bread, cakes and other delicious treats. This top quality produce is the basis for the menu in the café which offers a selection of mouth-watering snacks including homemade soups, quiches, and their popular cream teas.

Also on site is a quiet, secluded 10-van caravan site with extensive views looking out across the heart of the National Forest and surrounded by places of interest.

🏛 historic building 🏛 museum 🏛 historic site 🝔 scenic attraction 🌿 flora and fauna

positions so that the Abbey now looks just as it did when it was bought in 1981. The attention to detail has been so great that none of the rooms have been redecorated. Visitors can enjoy the silver display and trace the route of 18th-century servants along the brewhouse tunnel to the house cellars. Calke Abbey stands in its own large park with gardens, a chapel and stables that are also open to the public. There are three walled gardens with their glasshouses, a restored orangery, vegetable garden, pheasant aviaries and the summer flower display within the unusual Auricula Theatre. Also, house conservation tours and a children's play area (01332 863822).

MELBOURNE
6 miles NE of Swadlincote off the B587

🏛 Church of St Michael and St Mary

🌿 Melbourne Hall

This small town, which lent its name to the rather better-known city in Australia, is a successful market garden centre. A famous son of Melbourne, who started his working life in one of the market gardens, was Thomas Cook, who was born here in 1808. A strict Baptist, in 1841 he organised an excursion from Leicester to Loughborough to a temperance meeting. He went on to pioneer personally conducted tours and established the famous worldwide travel company.

Full of Georgian charm, Melbourne has many fine buildings that include one of the noblest Norman churches in the country, the **Church of St Michael and St Mary**. This seems rather a grand church for this modest place and, indeed, it is no ordinary parish church. In the 12th century, when the Bishopric of Carlisle was formed, there was a need for a place of safety for the clergy when Carlisle was being raided by the Scots. So this church was built at Melbourne and, while

---

THE FAIR TRADING PLACE

28 Market Place, Melbourne,
Derbyshire DE73 8DS
Tel: 01332 863619
www.fairtrade-melbourne.co.uk

The Fair Trading Place is situated on the Market Place in Melbourne, a pleasant Derbyshire town with a grand church and many other fine buildings.

The business was started by three friends, Alison, Anne and Christine, to promote fair trade, true to their shared passion for trade justice. The shop was officially opened in 2004 by the well known broadcaster George Alagiah, patron of The Fair Trade Foundation. The shop is a member of BAFTS (the British Association for Fair Trade Shops), an umbrella organisation of fair trade shops across the UK. All the goods in the shop are sourced from recognised fair trade suppliers, predominantly from the third world and developing countries, providing browsers with a guarantee of finding a personal treat or gift that's just a little bit different. Among the goods are a wide range of jewellery, stylish bags and scarves, greetings cards, gifts, crafts, toys and foods.

This friendly place is open from 10am to 4pm Tuesday to Friday and 9am to 12.30pm on Saturday.

🎭 stories and anecdotes 🦜 famous people 🎨 art and craft 🎭 entertainment and sport 🥾 walks

Carlisle was subjected to raids and violence, the Bishop retired to Melbourne and continued to carry out his duties. The church was built between 1133 and 1229 and, in 1299, the then Bishop built a palace on land that is now home to Melbourne Hall.

Swarkestone Causeway

The birthplace of the 19th-century statesman Lord Melbourne, and also the home of Lady Caroline Lamb, **Melbourne Hall** is another fine building in this area of Derbyshire. A modest building, the Hall is surrounded by beautiful gardens, the most notable feature of which is a beautiful wrought-iron birdcage pergola built in the early 1700s by Robert Bakewell, a local blacksmith from Derby. The house is only open to the public on afternoons in August, but the formal gardens are open on Wednesdays, Saturdays, Sundays and Bank Holidays throughout the summer season.

SWARKESTONE

9 miles NE of Swadlincote off the A5132

🏠 Bridge

It was at **Swarkestone Bridge** in 1745 that Bonnie Prince Charlie's hopes of seizing the English crown were finally dashed. To everyone's surprise, his advance guard had successfully penetrated so far south and victory seemed within his grasp. But when the Jacobite soldiers reached the bridge with its seven arches and three-quarter-mile long causeway crossing the River Trent, they were confronted by a strong force of King George's troops. If Prince Charlie's soldiers had managed to force their way across the river at this point, they would have faced no other natural barriers along the 120-mile march to London. As it transpired, the Scottish army retreated and fled north. Bonnie Prince Charlie himself managed to escape, but the Jacobite Rebellion was all over bar the shouting.

Legend has it that the original bridge at Swarkestone was built by two daughters of the Harpur family in the early 13th century. The girls were celebrating their joint betrothals when their fiancés were summoned to a barons' meeting across the river. While they were away torrential rain fell, flooding the river, and the two young men drowned as they attempted to ford the raging torrent on their return. The girls built the bridge as a memorial to their lovers. Both girls later died impoverished and unmarried.

REPTON

5 miles N of Swadlincote off the B5008

🏠 Church of St Wystan   🏠 College

This village, by the tranquil waters of the River Trent, is steeped in history. The first

REDSHAWS FAMILY BUTCHERS

5/7 Burton Road, Repton, Derbyshire DE65 6FL
Tel: 01283 703256

Jo and Neil Redshaw welcome one and all to **Redshaws Family Butchers**, which stands near Toyota Island off the A38 south of Derby. It's a very popular place to shop within the village and in the surrounding district, its success based on quality and reliability backed up by good old-fashioned service. There's always a good selection of cuts and joints of locally sourced beef, lamb and pork, along with poultry, seasonal game, superb gammon and bacon, home-made sausages, and pies, cooked meats and Scotch eggs prepared to tried and tested traditional recipes. The Christmas season brings turkeys, ducks and geese, and Christmas cakes and mince pies – everything needed for a great Christmas. Redshaws also sells a selection of preserves and chutneys, and basic essentials such as fresh baked bread available daily. Shop hours are 8.30 to 5.30 (Saturday to 3, closed Wednesday and Sunday).

recorded mention of Repton was in the 7th century when it was established as the capital of the Saxon kingdom of Mercia. A monastery housing both monks and nuns was founded here sometime after AD653 but the building was sacked by the Danes in AD874. A battleaxe, now on display in the school museum, was excavated a little distance from the church. It had apparently lain undisturbed for well over 1,000 years.

The parish **Church of St Wystan** is famous for its Anglo-Saxon chancel and crypt, but it also contains many of the major styles of medieval architecture. When the chancel and part of the nave were enlarged in 1854, the original Anglo-Saxon columns were moved to the 14th-century porch. The crypt is believed to be one of the oldest intact Anglo-Saxon buildings in England. The burial place of the Kings of Mercia, including St Wystan in AD850, the crypt was rediscovered by chance in 1779 by a workman who was digging a hole for a grave in the chancel floor.

The ancient Cross, still at the central crossroads in the village, has been the focal point of life here for centuries and has stood at the heart of the Wednesday market. Right up until the late 1800s, a Statutes Fair, for the hiring of farm labourers and domestics, was held here at Michaelmas.

Parts of an Augustinian priory, founded in 1170, are incorporated in the buildings of **Repton College**, itself founded in 1557. Sir John Port had specifically intended the college to be a grammar school for the local poor children of Etwall, Repton and Burnaston. These intentions have somewhat deviated over the passing years and now Repton stands as one of the foremost public schools in the country. Interestingly, two of its headmasters, Dr Temple and Dr Fisher, went on to become Archbishops of Canterbury. A third archbishop, Dr Ramsey, was a pupil at the school under Dr Fisher's guiding light. Film buffs will recognise the 14th-century gatehouse and causeway, as they featured in both film versions of the popular story *Goodbye, Mr Chips*.

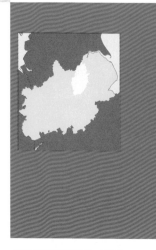

LOCATOR MAP

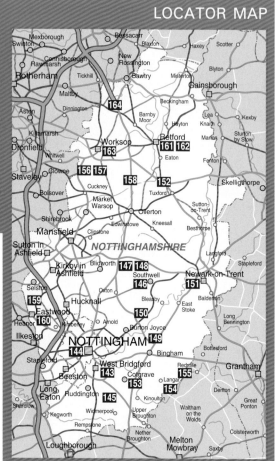

ADVERTISERS AND PLACES OF INTEREST

🏫 historic building   🏛 museum   🏚 historic site   🍃 scenic attraction   🌿 flora and fauna

6 Nottinghamshire

The county of Nottinghamshire, in the north Midlands, lies mainly on the low ground basin of the River Trent between the peaks of Derbyshire and South Yorkshire and the lowlands of Lincolnshire. It is a county of contrasts: it has plenty of industry, but it has also retained much of its rural heritage as well as the remains of the famous Forest of Sherwood.

As any local lad will be happy to tell you, Nottingham used to be called Snotingham after the unfortunately named Snot, chief of a 6th-century Anglo-Saxon tribe. But there was a settlement here long before then. In Celtic times it was known as Tigguocobauc, the house of caves, an appropriate name since this ancient people lived in the caves that occur naturally in the soft local sandstone. When the Vikings arrived in England in AD878, they recognised Nottingham's importance by making it one of the five boroughs of the Danelaw - the area of Middle England they controlled. There was more significant development in Norman times when the famous castle that features so prominently in the Robin Hood legends was built.

The glory of the central part of the county is Southwell Minster, a uniquely graceful building that is perhaps the least well-known cathedral in the country. Southwell itself is small, with a population under 7,000, but it is a delightful town with many fine buildings and a picturesque old coaching inn where Charles I spent his last night of freedom. Surrounding this appealing little town is a maze of country lanes and ancient villages.

With an historic castle, magnificent parish church and a host of fine buildings, Newark is an immensely likeable place. In medieval times, the town thrived as a centre for the wool trade, benefiting from its position on the Great North Road and beside the River Trent. The Civil War brought great suffering but, apart from the castle, surprisingly little damage to the town's buildings. South of Newark lies the Vale of Belvoir, an unspoilt pastoral landscape dotted with the spires of village churches and overlooked by the mighty

Green's Corn Mill, Sneinton

towers and turrets of Belvoir Castle, just across the border in Lincolnshire.

Sherwood Forest is known to old and young alike, all over the world, thanks to the tales of Robin Hood and the various stories, films and TV series' made about this legendary hero of the people. Sherwood, the shire wood of Nottinghamshire, was once part of a great mass of forest land that covered much of central England. Now officially designated as Robin Hood Country, the tract of land running north from Nottingham is an attractive mix of woodland and rolling hills.

To the north of the forest is the area known as The Dukeries, which is scenically one of the most attractive parts of the county. Here, in the 18th century, no fewer than four different Dukes acquired huge estates: Rufford, Welbeck, Clumber and Thoresby. All their great houses are now put to different uses but the glorious parks they created, especially at Clumber, make this a delightful area to visit.

The area around Mansfield was once the industrial heart of Nottinghamshire, its landscape dominated by pit-head wheels and chimneys, and the serried ranks of miners' terraced houses. This is Pilgrim Fathers' Country, since it was here that the unorthodox worship of Richard Clyfton inspired such men as William Brewster of Scrooby, and William Bradford of Austerfield, later Governor of New England. The best introduction to their story is to follow the Mayflower Trail, devised by Bassetlaw District Council, which follows a circular route starting from Worksop. Also in Worksop is the unusual National Trust property, Mr Straw's House, a time-capsule from the 1920s where nothing has altered in the subsequent 80 years. Retford and Blyth are both attractive old market towns: the former with some fine Georgian buildings, the latter boasting one of the most monumental Norman churches in the country.

Suspension Bridge over River Trent, Nottingham

Nottingham

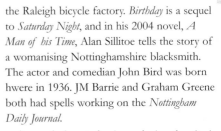

| 🏚 Trip to Jerusalem Inn | 🏚 Mortimer's Hole |
| 🏛 Museums | ⛏ Caves | 🦢 Goose Fair |
| 🏚 Castle |

A lively city of some 300,000 inhabitants, Nottingham offers a vast choice of shops, restaurants (more than 200 of them), cinemas, art galleries, two theatres, a world-class concert hall, and a host of other visitor attractions. The city also boasts a leading university, a major medical centre, and a legendary football team, Nottingham Forest. The self-proclaimed Queen of the Midlands, Nottingham is known worldwide because of the legendary Robin Hood and his persecutor, the villainous Sheriff of Nottingham. Others associate the city with Boots the Chemist, Players cigarettes (whose packets carry a picture of Nottingham Castle), Raleigh cycles and motor-cycles, and with the ice skaters Torvill and Dean - their world-beating performances led directly to the siting in Nottingham of the National Ice Centre. Alan Sillitoe, the author of *Saturday Night and Sunday Morning*, was born in Nottingham in 1928 and for a while worked at

the Raleigh bicycle factory. *Birthday* is a sequel to *Saturday Night*, and in his 2004 novel, *A Man of his Time*, Alan Sillitoe tells the story of a womanising Nottinghamshire blacksmith. The actor and comedian John Bird was born hwere in 1936. JM Barrie and Graham Greene both had spells working on the *Nottingham Daily Journal*.

A good place to begin exploring the city is in the Old Market Square, known to locals as Slab Square and believed to be largest market square in the country. Although no market has been held here since the 1920s, the vast expanse of the square still lies at the centre of Nottingham life. At its eastern end stands the dignified Council House with its porticoed frontage and a dome that is a replica of St Paul's in London. Part of the stately ground floor with its lofty ceilings and neo-classical architecture now houses some prestigious shops.

Until the Council House was built, the Market Square was the setting for the famous **Nottingham Goose Fair**, which began in medieval times and gained its name from the large flocks of geese that were sold here around Michaelmas. Mentioned in a charter dated 1284, the Goose Fair still takes place in early October, but has grown so much it is now held at Forest Fields on the edge of the city.

Nottingham Castle commands an imposing position on a rocky outcrop high above the city centre. However, those looking for the famous castle that features so frequently in the tales of Robin Hood will be sorely disappointed as the present buildings date from after the

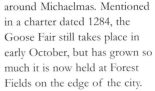
Nottingham Castle

Nottingham Castle

Castle Place, Nottingham, NottinghamshireNG1 6EL
Tel: 0115 915 3700
e-mail: castle@ncmh.org.uk
website: www.nottinghamcity.gov.uk

In 1067 William the Conquerer built the first **Nottingham Castle**, a wooden structure that was rebuilt over 100 years later in stone by Henry II, creating the principal royal fortress in the Midlands. In the most famous chapter of its history the Castle was reclaimed by returning crusader Richard the Lionheart from his brother Prince John in 1194 - the time of Robin Hood.

Most of the original medieval castle no longer exists, being demolished after the Civil War of 1651, but in its place stands a magnicent 17th century mansion, once home to the Dukes of Newcastle. Sited proudly above the city, the Castle South Terrace provides stunning views of Nottingham and beyond.

It incorporates a vibrant museum and art gallery housing collections of silver, glass, armour and paintings, plus fifteen centuries of Nottingham history. The galleries also bring the best regional, national and international artist's work to the city. Nottingham Castle is 10 minutes walk from Nottingham City centre, with easy access from train and bus stations. Parking is close by.

The Castle is a great place for children, with interactive displays and an activity - led gallery bringing paintings to life, specifically for the under 5s plus a medieval - style playground in the grounds with covered picnic area.

Underneath the Castle are many manmade caves and tunnels, some of which date back to medieval times. Visitors can take a guided tour to see Mortimer's Hole, King David's dungeon and the old wine cellar. The tour is strenuous and includes steep steps. Many visitors choose to descend through hundreds of years of history, learning on the way gruesome tales about Roger Mortimer and King David of Scotland.

There is also shop and cafe serving a wide range of refreshments with a panoramic view over the city. The castle is open every day except 24-26 December and 1 January.

🏛 historic building   🏛 museum   🏛 historic site   ⚘ scenic attraction   🌱 flora and fauna

GREENWOOD LODGE CITY GUEST HOUSE

5 Third Avenue, Sherwood Rise, Nottingham NG7 6JH
Tel: 0115 962 1206
e-mail: info@greenwoodlodgecityguesthouse.co.uk
website: www.greenwoodlodgecityguesthouse.co.uk

At **Greenwood Lodge** experienced hosts Sue and Doug Pearse offer high-quality accommodation combined with the warmest of welcomes and excellent personal service with notable attention to detail.

In a peaceful location a mile north of the city centre, just off the A60 Mansfield Road, the Lodge is perfectly placed as a quiet, civilised base for business people and for the many tourists who visit the city throughout the year.

The late Regency/early Victorian building set in a mature courtyard garden with immaculate tress and shrubs has six spacious, individually designed bedrooms in period style spread over the first and second floors, with en suite facilities, interesting pictures and antique furniture, TV, clock radio, trouser press, hairdryer and hot drinks tray. Three of the rooms boast four-poster beds. Guests can choose from an extensive breakfast choice served in the delightful conservatory, watching the birds and foxes and squirrels taking their own breakfasts in the leafy garden. The house also has a lovely drawing room where guests can relax and unwind and plan the day's activities. A frequent bus service runs from outside Greenwood Lodge into the city centre. Children of ten years and above welcome.

English Civil War and precious little remains of the original medieval fortification.

The original castle was built soon after the Battle of Hastings by William Peveril as part of William I's general fortification of many strategically important sites. Its elevated position, overlooking the city and the River Trent, made Nottingham Castle one of the foremost castles in Norman England and it played host to many important visitors. Of a typical Norman motte and bailey design, the stone walls are thought to have been added in the early 12th century and it was further fortified by Henry II. Nottingham Castle's heyday came in the 14th and 15th centuries however, when not only was King David II of Scotland held prisoner here for a while around 1346 but, in the mid 1400s, Edward IV proclaimed himself king from Nottingham

Castle. Later his brother, Richard III, rode out from here to the Battle of Bosworth field and his death.

For some reason, the Tudors shunned the castle, which gradually fell into disrepair until Charles I came to Nottingham in 1642 and raised his standard, marking the beginning of the Civil War. Unfortunately, the king found little support for his cause in the city (only 30 citizens joined his troops) so he moved on to Shrewsbury, leaving Nottingham and its castle in the hands of the Parliamentarians. During the course of the war, the Royalists made several attempts to recapture the castle but Cromwell's supporters held out. After the fighting was over the castle building was rendered uninhabitable and was finally demolished in 1674 by the Duke of Newcastle who then built his own palace on the site.

Today, that palace is home to the **Castle Museum and Art Gallery**. Some remains of the original castle still stand, most notably the 13th-century gatehouse, though much restored, and parts of the moat and outer bailey are visible. The museum, when it was opened by the Prince of Wales in 1878, was the first municipal art gallery in the country outside London. Today, the collection is particularly noted for its fine selection of Victorian paintings. The museum also has an outstanding collection of silverware and ceramics.

On the ground floor of the Castle Museum is the **Sherwood Foresters Regimental Museum**, which continues the castle's connections with the military. The regiment was first raised in 1741 and, among the many displays, there is an area dedicated to the Nottingham flying ace of World War I, Captain Albert Ball, VC. He died in 1917, at the age of 20, having shot down 43 enemy aircraft. A statue erected to his memory stands in the castle grounds.

At the base of Castle Rock lies the famous **Trip to Jerusalem Inn** where crusaders are said to have stopped for a pint before setting off on their long journey to the Holy Land. Dating back to around 1189, it claims to be the oldest pub in England, a claim hotly contested by other hostelries including another Nottingham one, Ye Olde Salutation Inn. Set back into the sandstone rock, the building was once the brewhouse for the castle and from here travellers to the Holy Land bought their ale. In the pub's cellars is **Mortimer's Hole**, a cave hewn out of the sandstone rock that leads to the castle. It is through this passageway that some two dozen conspirators crept to capture Roger de Mortimer, the lover of Queen Isabella. When her husband, Edward II was murdered,

Isabella had allowed Mortimer to effectively rule in place of her 18-year-old son, Edward III. De Mortimer's presumption was later punished by death. Edward III was in the castle at the time of Mortimer's capture and is believed to have known about, and encouraged, the plot.

Also at the base of Castle Rock and housed in a terrace of four 17th-century cottages, is the **Brewhouse Yard Museum**. Depicting the life of the people of the city, the museum has accurately furnished rooms as well as a series of reconstructions that includes a Victorian kitchen and shop window displays of the 1920s.

Just around the corner, the **Museum of Costume and Textiles** in Castle Gate contains a world-class collection of historical and contemporary dress displayed in period rooms. There are also many other exhibits on show including tapestries; knitted, woven and printed textiles; and fashion accessories through the ages. The museum is housed in a terrace of brick houses that was constructed in 1788 by Cornelius Launder, a former High Sheriff. Castle Gate is an interesting street in itself and well worth a second look. The entrance to the museum has one of the finest examples of an 18th-century doorcase and fanlight to be seen in the area.

Further down Castle Gate is Newdigate House, built in a refined fashion in 1680 and distinguished by a wrought iron screen and gates dating from the early 1700s. The house now forms part of the United Services Club, but between 1705 and 1711 it was the home of Marshal Tallard, commander of the defeated French army at the Battle of Blenheim in 1704.

The Lace Centre in Castle Road has now closed, but the famous Nottingham lace can be bought at the Tourist Information Centre.

Across the road from the Museum, in the impressive Shire Hall, the Galleries of Justice provides an unusual and interesting insight into justice 19th century style. Condemned, a major crime and punishment experience, allows visitors to put themselves in the place of an accused in the harsh days around 1833. Real trials are re-enacted in the imposing Courtroom where the hapless criminal faced the possibility of capital punishment or transportation to the New World. Their discomfort is made very real by the restored period settings.

Also in High Pavement is Nottingham's largest parish church, St Mary's, which is also probably the city's oldest as it appears to have been founded in Saxon times. However, today's church dates from the 15th century, though there are some 19th and early 20th century additions, which include windows by a series of renowned stained-glass makers. Also inside is a Bishop's Throne carved in 1890 when it was thought that the church would become the cathedral for the diocese of Southwell.

Another short walk brings visitors to the Caves of Nottingham, a popular attraction that lies beneath the Broadmarsh Centre, one of the city's major shopping precincts. The city is built on sandstone and throughout Nottingham's history the rock has been tunnelled to provide first shelter and then hiding places. More than 400 man-made caves run beneath the city streets. Now, thanks to local voluntary groups, these caves have been saved for future generations. The most spectacular cave in the system, the Pillar Cave, was carved out back in 1250 and contains remnants of the country's only underground tannery. The caves were commonly used as pub cellars: the constant temperature being ideal for the storage of beer and wine. More recently, they served as air raid shelters during the blitz of World War II, and one of the caves has been left as a memorial to those desperate times.

Around Nottingham

WOLLATON
2 miles W of Nottingham on the A609

🏛 Wollaton Hall   📷 Museum

Built in creamy white Ancaster stone, **Wollaton Hall** is one of the most attractive and elaborate Elizabethan mansions in the Midlands. Set in a spacious park, the house was built in the 1580s to the designs of Robert

Wollaton Hall

Smythson, who also designed Hardwick Hall in Derbyshire. His client was Francis Willoughby whose family had made a fortune from the local coal mines. The Elizabethan passion for symmetry is extravagantly displayed on the magnificent front façade with its matching classical columns, busts of philosophers and mythological characters, and flamboyant gables.

The building is also home to the **Natural History Museum** based on the collection of Francis Willoughby, a noted naturalist of the mid 1600s, while some of the Hall's outbuildings have been transformed into the Nottingham Industrial Museum where the city's major industries are all represented. The park surrounding the Hall is one of the city's great amenities. The 525 acres are contained within a seven-mile long wall, providing security for the herds of deer that roam here as they have for more than 400 years. The Museum and Park are open all year.

BULWELL
3 miles N of Nottingham on the B682

Originally the whole area surrounding the village was covered by forest and it is probable that the settlement took its name from a spring in the old woodland. However, a local legend tells the story of the naming of the village rather differently. Apparently, an enraged bull gored a rock here and released a stream of sparkling spring water.

BESTWOOD
6 miles N of Nottingham off the A60

🏃 Country Park

Bestwood was a favourite hunting ground of Charles II who often stayed here with Nell Gwynne. One local story tells of a wager the king struck with Nell, saying she could have all the land she could ride around before

breakfast. Nell, not known for being an early riser, made an exception on this occasion. The next morning, she rose at dawn and rode around the countryside dropping handkerchiefs along the way. Arriving back before breakfast, Nell claimed her winnings and Charles kept his side of the bargain. Whether or not the story is true, the king certainly gave Nell substantial landholdings in the area.

Part of the old royal hunting park is now **Bestwood Country Park**, whose 450 acres offer many differing landscapes. Here you'll also find the Bestwood Pumping Station, erected in the early 1870s. The Duke only gave his permission for it to be built after the architect solemnly promised that it would look nothing like a pumping station. With its 150ft tower, cooling pond disguised as an ornamental lake, and surrounded by beautifully maintained gardens, the station certainly lives up to the architect's promise.

SNEINTON
1 mile E of Nottingham on the A612

🏛 Windmill   🐦 William Booth Birthplace Museum

Sneinton's main claim to fame is as the birthplace, in 1829, of William Booth, the founder of the Salvation Army. The small terraced house where he and his family lived until 1831 is still standing in Notintone Place, fronted now by a statue of the great man. The family home has become the **William Booth Birthplace Museum**: entry to the house is by appointment only (0115 950 3927).

After his father's early death, Booth's mother was forced to move to Goosegate, Nottingham, where she ran a shop selling toys and sewing materials, and it was while growing up in this deprived area that Booth first became aware of the appalling conditions in which the urban working classes lived. He was only 16 when he gave his first sermon in a house in Kid.

In 1849, Booth left Nottingham for London where he became a Methodist minister. But, finding the church structures too constraining, he established, in 1865, the Christian Missions, which, in 1878, was renamed the Salvation Army. During the next 10 years, the movement spread to all corners of the world, including America, Australia and South Africa. The Army is still mobilised, with more than 1,000 local corps in the UK involved in both social and evangelistic work. Its missing persons bureau traces anything up to 5,000 people each year.

In Windmill Lane, Steinton, **Green's Windmill** is a Grade II listed working windmill that produces its own organic flour. It is the only inner city windmill in the UK and was once the home of the 19th-century mathematician George Green.

Green's Windmill, Sneinton

HOLME PIERREPONT
3 miles E of Nottingham off the A52

🏚 Holme Pierrepont Hall

🎿 National Water Sports Centre

Although Holme has been in the hands of the Pierrepont family since 1284, the present **Holme Pierrepont Hall** dates from the early 1500s and is regarded as one of the best examples of a brick-built house in the county. Opening times are restricted but the hall is well worth a visit. Some of the ground floor rooms have been restored to their original state and furnished in the style of the early 17th century, and the Upper Lodging still has superb ceiling timbers dating from the 1400s. There are two Victorian bedrooms with four-poster beds, one with its original William Morris fabrics. Refreshments are available in the Long Gallery with its walnut furniture and family portraits gazing down from the walls. Outside, the Charles II Grand Staircase leads down to a formal Courtyard Garden with an elaborate parterre, created around 1875, and, in the park, Jacob sheep graze peacefully.

These days, Holme Pierrepont is more widely known as the home of the **National Water Sports Centre**. Built to Olympic standards, the Centre boasts a full-size rowing course, a boating lake, a waterski cableway and a wild water slalom course, all man-made from the pasture and quarries that once dominated the area.

BEESTON
3 miles SW of Nottingham off the A52

🌿 Boots the Chemist

Lying on the southwest outskirts of Nottingham, Beeston is famous as the home of **Boots the Chemist**. Jesse Boot was born in 1850 and left school at the age of 13 to work in his mother's herbalist shop in the centre of Nottingham. She had started the business to supplement her husband's meagre income as a farm labourer. Following his

🎭 stories and anecdotes ⎯ 🌿 famous people ⎯ 🎨 art and craft ⎯ 🎿 entertainment and sport ⎯ 🥾 walks

death, when Jesse was only 10 years old, the shop became the mainstay of the family. Jesse quickly learnt the trade and in 1888 he set up the Boots Pure Drug Company.

In a business where quacks and charlatans abounded, Boot's emphasis on the purity of his drugs and medicines (and his competitive prices) attracted many customers, and by 1896 the company had a chain of over 60 shops. It was at his wife's suggestion that Jesse expanded the lines in the shops to include jewellery, stationery, books and art. In 1920 the business was sold to an American company, only to be bought back by Jesse's son during the depression in 1933. A great benefactor to the city and surrounding area, Jesse was knighted in 1903, created a baronet in 1917, and finally raised to the peerage as Lord Trent in 1929, two years before his death.

STAPLEFORD

4 miles SW of Nottingham off the A52

⬚ Hemlockstone

In Stapleford churchyard can be found the best preserved Saxon carving in the county in the form of a 10ft cross shaft. Dating from the late 11th century, the intricate carving depicts an eagle standing on a serpent - said to be the symbol of St Luke, the physician. The church, which dates mainly from the 13th and 14th centuries, has many war memorials to lost heroes. The village was once a thriving centre for framework knitting and terraced cottages built specifically for the workers can still be seen in Nottingham Road.

One other feature of Stapleford worthy of a look is the **Hemlockstone**, a massive redstone boulder standing 30 feet high and weighing around 200 tons, situated opposite Bramcote Park. Geologists believe the rock was probably deposited here by glacial action,

while wind erosion has contributed to its brooding appearance. Its geological make-up consists of sandstone cemented by the mineral barite, which is found in large quantities throughout the Stapleford and Bramcote Hills.

The village school was renamed the Arthur Mee Centre in memory of the writer who grew up in the town and was educated at the school. Born in 1875, Mee left school at 14 to work for the *Nottingham Evening Post* before moving to London and finding his niche writing for children. His works include the *Children's Bible*, the *Children's Encyclopaedia*, and the *Children's Shakespeare* but it is probably for *The King's England*, a series of guide books that ran to some 80 volumes, that Mee is best remembered.

CLIFTON

4 miles S of Nottingham on the A453

🜨 Clifton Grove

At first sight this village near the River Trent seems swamped by modern development, but the character of the old village can be found in and around the green. The manor of Clifton was held by the family of that name from the 13th century up until 1953 when they gave up the hall to what is now Nottingham Trent University.

Along the banks of the River Trent is **Clifton Grove**, a wooded cliff above the riverbank, where visitors can stroll in the footsteps of Paul Morel and Clare Dawes, characters in DH Lawrence's *Sons and Lovers*. This stretch of the River Trent was also the setting for a tragic love story. In 1471, a young squire called Henry Bateman went to the Crusades with his master. When he returned, he discovered that his sweetheart Margaret had fallen for another man and married him.

The heartbroken lover threw himself into the Trent from Clifton Grove. Some time later, Margaret herself took the same way out, presumably in remorse.

Ruddington

📷 Museums

This historic village, whose name is derived from the Saxon word Rudda - meaning headman - was once the home of many hosiery workers and several of their cottages still remain. In 1829, a factory and frameworkers cottages were built around a courtyard in Chapel Street. Later, a school was built and this is now occupied by the **Ruddington Framework Knitters' Museum**, which depicts community life through several reconstructed shops and an Edwardian schoolroom. Of the 25 hand frames seen here today, most are fully operational and there is an opportunity to buy samples made at the museum. This wonderful Victorian time capsule is open Easter to December from 11am to 4.30pm Wednesday to Saturday and Bank Holiday Mondays, also Sunday afternoons Easter to September.

The industry reached its height in 1880, with the staggering number of 20,000 frames operating in Nottingham, Derbyshire and Lincolnshire. As well as the knitting frames on show, the museum also has other machinery of specific importance to the village and to the hosiery industry. Regular demonstrations are given using the working exhibits. Visitors can try out their own weaving skills on one of the collection of circular sock machines.

Not far away is the **Ruddington Village Museum**, housed in the old village school building of 1852. Concentrating on the everyday life of the villagers, the museum has reconstructions of a cobblers, a chemist's, an Edwardian fish and chip shop, craftsmen's workshops and a telephone exchange. As well as having one of the school rooms restored to look as it once did, this volunteer-run museum also has a room devoted to a collection of farming implements.

Around Ruddington

GOTHAM
3 miles SW of Ruddington off the A453

The name is actually pronounced Goat'm and the village should not be confused with the home of the caped crusader, Batman. However, the village is remembered as the home of the Wise Men. King John had decreed that he wished to build a hunting lodge here in the village. Naturally displeased at having to give up their land to the king's whims, the villagers devised a plan. They decided that the best way to dissuade the royal presence was to feign madness. When the king's messengers entered the village, the inhabitants reacted in such a peculiar way that the men returned to His Majesty with the suggestion that the mad men of Gotham should be left well alone. Such were the odd tales of their bizarre acts that Dr Andrew Borde published the *Merrie Tales of the Mad Men of Gotham* in the 16th century. There are many bizarre stories, but one of the finest is kept alive in the name of the village pub - The Cuckoo Bush. A group of villagers, captivated by the song of a cuckoo, decided to capture the bird by encircling the bush in which it was sitting by a fence. Unfortunately, the men did not think to build a roof, so the cuckoo simply flew away.

RATCLIFFE ON SOAR
6 miles SW of Ruddington off the A453

The tiny village of Ratcliffe on Soar has a pretty little church with an eye-catching blackened spire, and a handsome manor farmhouse set picturesquely on the meadow banks of the River Soar. Although a massive power station looms over everything, and the railway clatters by, this charming village is still definitely worth a visit.

EAST LEAKE
4 miles S of Ruddington off the A60

Like its neighbour, West Leake, the village name is derived from the Anglo-Saxon word Leche, meaning water meadow, and both villages lie on the banks of a tributary of the River Soar. The village church, which was mentioned in the Domesday Survey of 1086, was extensively restored in the 19th century but has retained its prize possession, a Vamp Horn or shawm. This extraordinary instrument is some eight feet long and only five others are known to exist. Invented in 1670 by Samuel Morland, the horn was used by the bass singer to lead the choir from the gallery.

STANTON ON THE WOLDS
4 miles SE of Ruddington off the A606

This rural village, which was until the 1960s home to seven dairy farms, has few really old buildings though the village dates back to Norman times. In the late 18th century, Stanton was hit by a freak storm in which giant hailstones rained down on the cottages and smashed their roofs. The ancient village Church of All Saints did, however, survive and can be found standing alone in a field, reached by a footpath. Dating from the 11th century, the church, one of the smallest in south Nottinghamshire, is built mostly of

boulders some of which, undoubtedly, were purloined from the nearby Fosse Way.

BUNNY
2 miles S of Ruddington on the A60

This pretty village has a wealth of lovely architecture and owes much of its charm to the eccentricities of its one-time squire, Sir Thomas Parkyns (1663-1741). A man obsessed with the sport of wrestling, Sir Thomas employed two full-time professionals to spar with him at Bunny Hall. He also organised an annual tournament in the village to promote local wrestling talent and this event continued for nearly 70 years after his death. In St Mary's Church, which was designed by Sir Thomas, his memorial graphically illustrates his commitment to the sport. It depicts the squire standing victorious over his defeated opponent on a wrestling mat, while Old Father Time stands by, perhaps as referee.

Another of Sir Thomas' hobbies was collecting stone coffins, which he provided free to those of his tenants in need of one. During his long lifetime he rebuilt much of the village to his own designs, provided a school, gave his tenants free medical and legal advice and also found time to write a Latin Grammar and a book on wrestling, *Cornish Hugg Wrestling*.

KEYWORTH
3 miles E of Ruddington off the A606

In the heart of south Nottinghamshire's farming country this, until very recently, small village prides itself on having produced no fewer than 30 professional cricketers, one of whom went on to be capped for England.

The village has had its share of scandals, one local legend tells of a tenant farmer who

THREADS

2c Main Street, Keyworth, Nottinghamshire NG12 5AD
Tel: 0115 937 6010

Threads is located on the quaint village square of Keyworth, in the heart of Nottinghamshire's farming country. The village is known for the number of professional cricketers it has produced, but anyone with an interest in sewing and knitting will be bowled over by a visit to this very special place.

Owner Sheila Grudzinski and her assistants have created a very friendly, relaxed ambience in which customers shop for an amazing selection of threads and yarns and wools and cottons, zips and needles, ribbons, buttons and bows, patterns from across the world- everything, in short, for sewing and knitting. And if it's not in stock, they'll do their very best to order it as quickly as possible.

Threads also stocks a small boutique range of children's and ladies' clothes and kits for beading and jewellery. Shop hours are 9 to 5.30 Monday, Tuesday and Friday, 9 to 5 Wednesday, Thursday and Saturday. Once a fortnight, Sheila holds classes in the village hall - informal but informative sessions which she calls 'Knit, Stitch and Natter' evenings.

was visited by the rector who had a complaint to discuss. The farmer was not very agreeable to the criticism and soundly horse-whipped the clergyman before sending him on his way. This whip is still in existence though the nature of the complaint the rector was making is unknown.

Southwell

🏛 Minster and Chapter House 🏛 Vicar's Court

🏛 Workhouse 🏛 Norwood Park

🍏 Bramley Apple Exhibition

🚶 Farnsfield to Southwell Trail

Southwell is undoubtedly one of England's most beguiling towns, miraculously preserved from developers and with scarcely an ugly building to be seen. From whichever direction you approach, it is the twin towers of Southwell Minster that first catch the eye. With their pyramidal Rhenish Caps, these towers are unique in this country although they would look perfectly in place anywhere in the Rhineland.

James VI of Scotland was mightily impressed by Southwell when he passed through the town in 1603 en route to his coronation as James I: "By my blude," he is said to have exclaimed, "this kirk shall justle with York or Durham or any other kirk in Christendom."

Perhaps the least well-known of English cathedrals, Southwell's history goes back to AD956 when Oskytel, Archbishop of York, established a church here. The present building was erected in three phases. The nave, transept and western towers are the oldest parts, completed around 1150; the east end was built around 1240; and the superb

🎭 stories and anecdotes 🐦 famous people 🎨 art and craft 🎢 entertainment and sport 🚶 walks

Chapter House around 1290.

Octagonal in design, the Chapter House has been hailed as the pinnacle of the Decorated period of architecture - "among chapter houses as the rose among flowers". The architectural historian, Nikolaus Pevsner, devoted a whole book, *The Leaves of Southwell*, to the incredible wealth of stone carvings of foliage decorating the arcades above the Canons' seats.

The word most often applied to the cathedral is "serene" and, as one visitor put it, "Other churches may be older, a few may be larger, but none are more beautiful."

There is no space here to detail all the cathedral's other treasures, but the striking eagle lectern in the choir has an interesting story attached to it. The lectern was originally installed at Newstead Abbey. However, during the widespread looting at the time of the Dissolution of the Monasteries, the monks threw the lectern into the lake, intending to retrieve it later. Later turned out to be 200 years later, in 1750 in fact. Half a century after that, the 5th Lord Byron presented the lectern to the Minster.

The **Minster** (see panel below) stands in a delightful precinct, surrounded by attractive buildings. To the south stand the ruins of the palace of the archbishops of York built in the 14th and 15th centuries. Parts of the old palace, closest to the minster's south doorway, have been incorporated into the present Bishop's Palace.

At the east end of the Minster is **Vicar's Court**, a charming group of five Queen Anne houses built for the Vicars Choral around 1702. Just across the road from the Minster is a picturesque old coaching inn, the 16th-century Saracen's Head. Charles I spent his last hours of freedom before his final surrender in this delightful half-timbered building. At that time, the inn was known as the King's Head, the name was changed after Charles was beheaded.

Just to the north of the Saracen's Head is

Southwell Minster

Church Street, Southwell,
Nottinghamshire NG25 0HD
Tel 01636 817810
website: www.southwellminster.org.uk

Southwell Minster is a superb Cathedral and Minster Church with a Norman Nave which is one of the finest in Europe. Other features include the magnificent Angel window and the world-renowned stone carvings the 'Leaves of Southwell' in the Chapter House.

For children there is the popular search for the twelve wooden mice carved by 'Mousy' Thompson. The Visitors centre incorporates the Minster shop, refectory and audio visual centre.

Admission is free but donations are always welcome.
Open daily: Summer 8am – 7pm, Winter 8am – dusk.

🏠 historic building   🏛 museum   🏛 historic site   🦢 scenic attraction   🌱 flora and fauna

Burgage Manor, a handsome Georgian pile where the young Lord Byron stayed with his mother between 1803 and 1807 while on holiday from Harrow and Cambridge. He joined the local theatrical group and it was his friends in the town who encouraged him to publish his first set of poems. Under the title *Hours of Idleness*, the book was published by Ridges of Newark and brought great acclaim to the young poet. The **Workhouse** in Upton Road is the only 19th-century workhouse in existence offering visitors the opportunity to explore the building and its history, the segregated work yards, dayrooms, dormitories, master's quarters and cellars. There is also a Time Travel Tour and a Story Telling Club (01636 817251).

Southwell can also be credited as the birthplace of the Bramley apple. The story goes that in the early 19th century, two ladies planted some apple pips in their cottage garden in the nearby village of Easthorpe. Nature took its course and one of the seedlings grew into a tree. By this time, Matthew Bramley owned the cottage and the quality of the tree's fruit began to excite public interest.

Mr Henry Merryweather, a local nurseryman, persuaded Bramley to let him take a cutting, which he consequently propagated with enormous success. Permission had been granted on the condition that the apples took Mr Bramley's name and not that of the two ladies'. The **Bramley Apple Exhibition** in Halam Road explains the full history and development of this famous fruit. While in the town, visitors should also look out for a Southwell Galette, a scrumptious pastry confection of hazelnuts, sultanas, and, of course, Bramley apples.

The disused railway line from Southwell to Mansfield, opened in 1871, is now an attractive footpath known as the **Farnsfield to Southwell Trail**. As well as the varied plant and wildlife that can be found along the 4½ mile walk, there is also plenty of industrial archaeological interest including the Farnsfield Waterworks of 1910, a late 18th-century cotton mill, and Greet Lily Mill, a corn mill on the banks of the River Greet.

Norwood Park is the only one of the four original parks around Southwell that remains today. The property of the Archbishops of York, the park remained in the possession of the Church until 1778. A house was built here in Cromwell's day, but the present building dates from 1763. Open to visitors during the summer months, the house has a very lived-in feel. The surrounding parkland was laid out in the 18th century at the same time as the ice house and temple were built and the lime avenue planted. Southwell has a racecourse that stages racing throughout the year, most of it flat racing on an all-weather surface, but also with some meetings under National Hunt rules.

Around Southwell

KIRKLINGTON
3 miles NW of Southwell on the A617

Kirklington's church is partly Norman, and anyone venturing inside will see that the pulpit has some small holes in its side that have been plugged with more recent wood. The explanation for this odd feature is that in the early 1800s, Kirklington's sporting rector would use the pulpit as a portable screen when he went duck shooting. He would fire at the ducks through the holes in the pulpit's sides.

🎭 stories and anecdotes 🦢 famous people 🎨 art and craft 🎱 entertainment and sport 🚶 walks

THE WHITE POST FARM PARK

Mansfield Road (A614), Farnsfield, nr Newark,
Nottinghamshire NG22 8HL
Tel: 01623 882977 Fax: 01623 883499
e-mail: anthony@whitepostfarm.co.uk
website: www.whitepostfarm.co.uk

A great day out for the whole family is guaranteed at the **White Post Farm Park**, which has been attracting crowds and awards ever since it first opened its doors in 1988. The three young owners who took over in 2004, all with children of their own, provide visitors with an experience that is both exciting and educational. Twenty-five acres of picturesque farmland include pleasant walks through paddocks of farm animals both native and exotic, from sheep, cows, pigs, goats and ducks to llamas and wallabies. The Reptile House is home to an amazing collection of creatures large and small, including stick insects, crickets, locusts and leaf-cutter ants, boa constrictors and a Burmese python, tarantulas, turtles and terrapins, frogs, snails, axolotls, angel fish and clown fish. The site contains tea rooms and a burger barn and indoor and outdoor play areas.

THE WHITE POST FARM SHOP

Tel: 01623 882977

The Farm shop is full of lovely local produce. Fresh fruit and veg grown just minutes from the farm. Fresh break baked half a mile away and wonderful home-reared meat - it's delicious! With a great range of sheds and plants there is something for every garden.

The Centre stands on the A614 ten miles north of Nottingham in the heart of Robin Hood country.

CAUNTON

7 miles NE of Southwell off the A616

The village Church of St Andrew was rebuilt by the Normans at the beginning of the 13th century, but by the 1800s the building had fallen into such a state of disrepair that the altar, a wooden box, was only used as a resting place for the hat and gloves of visiting curates. Restored in 1869, the church contains many monuments to the Hole family, Lords of the Manor here since Elizabethan times.

The best-known member of the Hole family was Samuel Reynolds Hole who became known as the Rose King - a title bestowed on him by Tennyson. Before becoming Dean of Rochester, Hole lived at Caunton Manor as the squire and vicar and it was here that he began his extensive study of roses. By 1851, Samuel recorded that he possessed over 1,000 rose trees in more than 400 varieties, a collection that was to make him the most famous amateur rose grower of all.

UPTON

2 miles E of Southwell on the A612

🏛 British Horological Institute

Upton boasts a couple of very good pubs and its nine-pinnacled church is worthy of a visit too. A famous son of the village was James Tenant, the man who cut the world-renowned Koh-I-Noor diamond. But perhaps the most impressive building here is Upton Hall, a stylish Grecian villa with a central dome and elegant colonnade, built in the early 1800s. The hall is now the headquarters of the **British Horological Institute** and, inside,

🏛 historic building   🏛 museum   🏛 historic site   🍃 scenic attraction   🌱 flora and fauna

visitors can see a fascinating display of historic clocks and watches, as well as some 5,000 other items including the Post Office's original speaking clock. Open Saturdays, Sundays and Bank Holidays April to October. Call first on 01636 813795.

ROLLESTON
3 miles E of Southwell off the A617

🏛 Holy Trinity Church

Holy Trinity Church is certainly one of the county's finest churches and is also the source of a great treasure: a portion of the original paper register covering the years 1584 to 1615. An interesting and historic document completed by the vicar of the time, Robert Leband, it gives the local gossip as well as the price of corn and notes of local events. A curiosity in the church is a fragment of a Saxon cross, built into the wall and scratched with the words 'Radulfus Me Fe' (Radulfus made me). It is one of very few surviving Saxon works in England to bear its author's signature.

EAST BRIDGFORD
7 miles S of Southwell off the A6097

The village is situated on a ridge overlooking a crossing of the River Trent and the edge of Sherwood Forest beyond. The village Church of St Peter is believed to stand on one of the earliest Christian sites in Nottinghamshire.

EAST BRIDGFORD HILL

*4 Kirk Hills, East Bridgford,
Nottinghamshire NG13 8PE
Tel: 01949 20232 Fax: 01949 21124
e-mail: eastbridgfordhill@googlemail.com
website: www.eastbridgfordhill.com*

Genial hosts Patricia and Alfred Robens have lived at **East Bridgford Hill** for 30 years and since 2002 they have opened their house to Bed & Breakfast guests. Their lovely Georgian home enjoys stunning views from its hillside setting, and the beautiful grounds make it ideal for wedding receptions, private entertaining and corporate occasions. Patricia and Alfred have created an ambience of exceptional warmth and hospitality and pride themselves on providing personal service that larger establishments can't offer.

The guest bedrooms in the house and adjoining cottage, each individual in character, are particularly and comfortable, and the day starts with an excellent breakfast with prime local produce and eggs from the owners' hens. With a little notice resident chef Ronnie will cook a splendid evening meal for 4 or more. Guests have the use of a delightful conservatory and two drawing rooms period furniture and paintings and lots of books. Croquet and tennis are available in the grounds, and one of the favourite local walks is along the River Trent opposite Gunthorpe Lock and Weir. A pick-up service can be arranged from nearby stations and airports and a helicopter landing facility is available. The owners also offer a variety of holistic and beauty treatments and various retreats, courses and workshops. East Bridgford Hill lies a short drive east of Nottingham on the A6097, between the A46 and A612.

🏛 stories and anecdotes   🐦 famous people   🎨 art and craft   🎭 entertainment and sport   🚶 walks

GONALSTON FARM SHOP

Southwell Road, Gonalston,
Nottinghamshire NG14 7DR
Tel: 0115 9665 666
e-mail: info@gonalstonfarmshop.co.uk
website: www.gonalstonfarmshop.co.uk

A warm welcome and a feast of culinary delights await visitors to **Gonalston Farm Shop**, which stands between Lowdham and Gonalston on the A612 Nottingham-Southwell road. Opened in 2003 by Georgina (George) and Ross Mason, it is recognised as one of the finest in its field in the county. The majority of the produce on sale is local, and pride of place goes to the extended meat counter with its impressive selection of cuts and joints.

The farm is coupled with Riverlands Farm in Gunthorpe village, and both specialise in producing high-quality cattle from their own pastures in the Trent Valley. The beef off the farm is hung for a minimum of 21 days to develop the full flavour. Almost all the meat is sourced locally offering full traceability and keeping food miles to a minimum. Over 30 varieties of sausages are made on site, some of which have won Great Taste Awards Nationally.

The delicatessen offers over 100 handmade and farmhouse cheeses, local award winning hams, salamis, Parma ham, pork pies, game pies and many ready to eat delicacies. A wonderful selection of fresh seasonal local vegetables and fruit are available daily. Preserves, chutneys, condiments, herbs, spices and dry ingredients all add to the amazing shopping experience provided. Fresh handmade bread is delivered daily from Hambleton Bakery, Oakham and Atherly's bakery Farnsfield, superb cakes & pastries, beer, cider and wines complete your meal. Fresh cut Flowers, cards and gift wrap, Gift vouchers and hampers are available at any time of the year making this a great place to purchase a present for the person who has everything.

Awards and accolades cont....up until 2007, when a fresh wet fish counter was added offering fine quality day boat, line caught fish.

Customer loyalty is rewarded with a loyalty card and regular offers across all departments. Opening hours Tuesday-Saturday 9am to 6.30pm, Sunday 10am to 4pm. Open all summer bank holidays 10am to 4pm. Look at the excellent website for information on events and tastings and Christmas trading hours.

🏛 historic building　　🏯 museum　　🏚 historic site　　🜂 scenic attraction　　🌿 flora and fauna

There was already a church here in the 9th century, since it is known to have been plundered by the Danes when they came up the river to Nottingham.

SHELFORD
8 miles S of Southwell off the A6097

The name Shelford means the place of the shallow ford so, presumably, there was once a ford here across the River Trent, which flows in a horseshoe bend around the village. Though now a quiet and tranquil place, in the winter of 1644, Shelford was the site of a particularly fierce battle. Royalist soldiers, taking shelter in the church tower, were smoked out by the Parliamentarian army who set fire to straw at the tower's base. During the same weekend, some 140 men were slaughtered by Cromwell's men at the manor house that was subsequently burnt to the ground.

The Royalist troops were commanded by Shelford's Lord of the Manor, Philip Stanhope, a member of the illustrious family who later became Earls of Chesterfield. There are some fine memorials to the Stanhopes in the village church, including one by Nollekens.

OXTON
4 miles SW of Southwell on the B6386

🏛 Oldox Camp

A charming village near the edge of Sherwood Forest and surrounded by parkland, Oxton has a goodly number of 17th and 18th-century houses and cottages. The Sherbrooke family have been the lords of the manor here since the 16th century, and Oxton still retains the feel of an estate village even though the hall was demolished in 1957. An oddity is to be found in a yard opposite the Green Dragon Inn. Here stands the tomb of Robert Sherbrooke who died in 1710. The unusual location is explained by the fact that Sherbrooke was a Quaker and this was the site of their meeting house.

The uncovering of **Oldox Camp**, one of the largest and best preserved Iron Age hill forts in Nottinghamshire, to the north of the village suggests that this was the original site of Oxton. Extending over some three acres, the fort is surrounded by a single ditch and bank, except at the entrance to the fort where the defences are doubled.

CALVERTON
6 miles SW of Southwell off the B6386

🐾 Patchings

The charming cottages in this industrial village date back to the early 19th century and were once the homes of framework knitters. Carefully restored by the Nottinghamshire Building Preservation Trust, the cottages originally formed three sides of a rectangle, though one side is now missing. Unusually, the large windows that provided the light for the knitters are found on the ground floor instead of the more usual upper storey.

It was a curate of Calverton, William Lee, who invented the stocking knitting frame in 1589. According to an old story, his invention was the result of an unsuccessful love affair. Whenever William visited the girl he wanted to marry she "always took care to be busily employed in knitting...He vowed to devote his further leisure to devising an invention that should effectually supersede her favourite employment of knitting". Lee succeeded in creating an immensely complicated machine that could produce top quality work between 10 and 15 times as quickly as the fastest hand-knitters. To develop it further he sought the patronage of Elizabeth I, but the queen refused to encourage something that would

🏛 stories and anecdotes   🦜 famous people   🎨 art and craft   🏃 entertainment and sport   🚶 walks

mean great job losses for her loyal subjects.

After being refused a patent by Elizabeth I, Lee travelled to France and gained the promise of support from Henry of Navarre. Unfortunately, Henry was assassinated before any promises were made good and it is believed that Lee died in Paris in 1610. Lee's brother, James, brought the frame back to London where the hosiery industry first developed before it settled in the Midlands later in the 17th century.

Also at Calverton is **Patchings**, formerly known as Painters' Paradise, a series of gardens that have been designed with the artist in mind. Here, amongst the rolling hills of north Nottinghamshire, is a perfect reconstruction of Claude Monet's garden at Giverney, complete with the elegant little bridge and the pool of water lilies that he painted so often. Attractive gazebo studios are dotted around the 50 acres of grounds, each designed to provide a picturesque view. An impressive building of Norwegian spruce – one of the largest wooden structures in England – offers further facilities for artists and visitors: studios, workshop and dark room as well as a licensed restaurant.

Newark-on-Trent

🏛 White Hart Inn   🏛 Town Hall   🏛 Castle
🏛 Church   🏛 Henrietta Maria's Lodgings
🏛 Governor's House   🏛 Museum   🏛 Air Museum
🏛 Beacon Hill

John Wesley considered Newark one of the most elegant towns in England. More recently, the Council for British Archaeology included it in their list of the best 50 towns in the country, and in 1968 Newark town centre was designated as one of the first

Conservation Areas. Its medieval street plan remains intact, complete with a fine market square that is still busy every day of the week, except Tuesdays, with a market of one kind or another - plus a Farmers' Market once a month. Newark has become firmly established as one of the most important centres in Europe for the antiques trade and hosts the biggest European Antiques Fair every two months. The town also has long-standing musical connections. The composer John Blow, who was born in the town in 1649, taught Henry Purcell and held major positions at Westminster Abbey and St Paul's Cathedral. Newark College's International School of Violin Making is now one of the world's top violin schools and attracts students from all over the world.

The square is lined with handsome houses and inns. The most remarkable of them is the 14th-century former **White Hart Inn** (now a building society/estate agent), which has a magnificent frontage adorned with 24 plaster figures of angels and saints. Close by are the Saracen's Head where Sir Walter Scott often stayed, and the Clinton Arms, the preferred lodging of WE Gladstone during his 14 years as Newark's Member of Parliament.

Dominating one side of the square is the noble Georgian Town Hall, completed in 1777 and recently fully restored. It now houses the town's civic plate and regalia, and an art gallery displaying works by Stanley Spencer, William Nicholson and notable local artists.

The grandest building of all is the **Church of St Mary Magdalene**, by common consent the finest parish church in the county. Its slender, elegant spire soars above the town and serves as a landmark for miles along the Trent Valley. The church dates back

THE FRIENDLY FARMER RESTAURANT & FARM SHOP

A46/A17 Roundabout, Newark-on-Trent, Nottinghamshire NG24 2NY
Tel: 01636 612461
e-mail: info@friendlyfarmer.co.uk
website: www.friendlyfarmer.co.uk

The **Friendly Farmer Restaurant & Farm Shop** is part of a family-owned organic farm located off the eastbound A17 (direction Sleaford) just off the A1/A46/A17 roundabout complex. The bright, airy restaurant is a great place to seek out, to meet friends with plenty of choice for breakfast, lunch or afternoon tea. The farmhouse breakfasts include their own pork sausages, free-range eggs, traditionally cured bacon and freshly ground filter coffee and a variety of fair-trade teas. The lunch choice runs from sandwiches to pies to freshly cooked hot lunches and a carvery on Sundays, while carrot cake is just one of the many treats for afternoon tea. The Butchery sells the farm's own organic pork, lamb and Lincoln Red beef, along with sausages, pies, Scotch eggs and the superb 100% Lincoln Red burgers. The Farm Shop sells a range of seasonal vegetables fresh from the farm, locally produced cheeses, pickles, oils, honey, jams and chocolate, along with home-made or locally produced bread and cakes, some sugar-free and gluten-free items. Whether eating in the restaurant or shopping at the farm shop visitors know that they are supporting environmentally friendly local businesses and that the food is fresh, delicious and good value for money. Trading hours are 8 to 5 Mon - Sat, 9 to 5 Sunday.

to the early 12th century, though all that survives of that structure is the crypt, which now houses the treasury. Much of the building seen today dates from the 14th, 15th and 16th centuries and its exterior is a fascinating blend of carvings and tracery. The interior is spacious and airy, and the treasures on display include a huge brass commemorating Alan Fleming, a Newark merchant who died in 1373; a dazzling Comper reredos of 1937; a splendid east window depicting Mary Magdalene; a Victorian mosaic reproducing Van Eyck's *Adoration of the Lamb*; and fragments of a painted Dance of Death from around 1500.

Newark's recorded history goes back to Roman times when the legionaries established a base here to guard the first upstream crossing of the River Trent. One of their major arterial roads, Fosse Way,

passes close by on its way to Lincoln. Saxons and Danes continued the settlement, the latter leaving a legacy of street names ending in 'gate', from gata, the Danish word for street.

When the Normans arrived they upgraded the Saxon wooden fortification replacing it in AD1123 with a stone castle. The west facing curtain wall was rebuilt in the late 13th century. For over 300 years the castle was owned by the powerful Bishops of Lincoln. Then, in 1547, following the reformation, ownership of the castle was transferred to the Crown and leased out to a succession of noblemen.

The castle's most glorious days occurred during the Civil War. The people of Newark were fiercely loyal to Charles I and endured three separate sieges before finally surrendering to Cromwell's troops.

🎬 stories and anecdotes   🦅 famous people   🎨 art and craft   🎭 entertainment and sport   🚶 walks

Parliament ordered the 'slighting' of the castle, rendering it militarily useless, but following an outbreak of plague, left the demolition work to the townspeople. Understandably, they showed little enthusiasm for the task of demolishing the eight-foot-thick walls. As a result, the ruins are quite substantial, especially the mighty gateway that Pevsner called "the biggest and most elaborate of its period in England". It was here that King John, devastated by the loss of his treasure while crossing the Wash, came to die in 1216. The castle crypt and an intimidating beehive dungeon have also survived. Guided tours of the castle (and the town) are available and its history is colourfully interpreted at the Gilstrap Centre. This lies within the Castle Grounds, which, with its gardens and Victorian bandstand, is a popular venue for special events as well as a pleasant spot for a picnic.

Newark possesses several other reminders of the Civil War. As a defensive measure, two small forts were built to guard this strategic crossing over the River Trent. The King's Sconce, to the northeast, has since disappeared, but its twin, the Queen's Sconce, still lies to the southeast. Named after Queen Henrietta Maria, who brought supplies into the town after the first siege in 1643, this square earthwork has a bastion in each corner and a hollow in the middle.

In the town centre, on Kirk Gate, are **Henrietta Maria's Lodgings** where, according to tradition, the queen stayed in 1643. Travelling from Bridlington to the king's headquarters at Oxford, the queen was bringing with her men and arms from the continent. She had paid for them by selling off some of the Crown Jewels.

Nearby is the **Governor's House**, where the governors of Newark Castle lived during the Civil War and where Charles I quarrelled with Prince Rupert after the prince had lost Bristol to Parliament. This wonderful timber-framed building was restored in the late 19th century, and during the work a medieval wall and some beam paintings were revealed along with graffiti dating from 1757. Occupying a former oil seed mill on the banks of the Trent, the **Millgate Museum** concentrates on local life, with sections devoted to archaeology, social and natural history, art, photography, costume and civil and military war. The exhibits (more than 70,000) include an interesting array of shops and shop fronts, and there is also a reconstruction of an early 20th-century terraced house.

On the outskirts of the town, at **Beacon Hill**, one of the greatest victories over the Roundheads took place, in 1644, when Prince Rupert arrived to lift the second of Newark's sieges. Under Sir John Meldrum, the Parliamentarians lost more arms and equipment than during any other engagement of the Civil War.

Just northeast of the town, close to the A1, lies the **Newark Air Museum**, one of the largest privately managed collections in the country. Opened in the 1960s, the museum has more than 50 aircraft and cockpit sections on display. Visitors can see jet fighters, bombers and helicopters that span the history of aviation, as well as a great deal of aviation memorabilia, relics and uniforms on display in the Exhibition Hall. The museum shop has been described as "the best specialist aviation outlet in the Midlands". The many aircraft on show range from De Havilland Tiger Moths and Flying Fleas, to Vampires, Venoms, a Gloster Javelin and a mighty Avro Vulcan. Open daily.

🏛 historic building   🏛 museum   🏛 historic site   ⌂ scenic attraction   🌱 flora and fauna

Around Newark-on-Trent

CROMWELL
5 miles N of Newark off the A1

🏚 Museum of Dolls and Bygone Childhood

A 17th-century rectory and dower house is home to the **Vina Cooke Museum of Dolls and Bygone Childhood**. Appealing to adults and children alike, there are all manner of children's toys on display, but perhaps the most fascinating are the handmade dolls depicting royalty, stars of stage and screen, and famous historical characters (01636 821364).

SUTTON ON TRENT
7 miles N of Newark off the B1164

🏛 Mering Chapel

One of the largest Trentside villages, Sutton was once famous for basket-making, fishermen's baskets in particular. It has a fine church, first established in Saxon times and noted for its **Mering Chapel**. Dating from the early 1500s, the chapel was brought here from the village of Mering on the other side of the Trent - Mering has since vanished completely into the watery lowlands surrounding the Trent. The superb Mering Chapel, however, contains a distinguished memorial in Purbeck marble to Sir William Mering. The tomb is separated from the aisle by a very rare oak screen crafted around 1510. Sir William's family, like his village, is extinct.

SOUTH CLIFTON
9 miles N of Newark off the A1133

This pleasant village along the banks of the River Trent still has the remains of an old

wharf where the coal from Derbyshire and Yorkshire was unloaded before being distributed throughout the surrounding area. The river here is still much used, though the local fishermen now have to contend with water-skiers travelling up and down it. On the village green stands a young oak tree, planted in 1981, along with a plaque commemorating the achievements of a local farmer, Dusty Hare, who has lived in the parish all his life and scored the highest number (7,000) of points in Rugby Union Football and was honoured with an MBE in 1989.

NORTH CLIFTON
10 miles N of Newark off the A1133

🌱 Japanese Garden

The village, like its neighbour South Clifton, also lies on the east side of the Trent, close to the border with Lincolnshire. Although the two villages are quite separate, they share the same church, dedicated to St George the Martyr, which lies between them and has an imposing 15th century tower.

An unusual attraction here is the Pure Land Meditation Centre and **Japanese Garden**, which offers a haven of peace for all ages who wish to come and experience the benefits of relaxation and meditation. Buddha Maitreya, a former Zen monk from Japan, offers tuition in meditation to individuals and groups, and has devoted 25 years to creating the delightful Japanese garden with its large central pond, bridges and a small pagoda where visitors can relax and meditate amidst an abundance of flourishing plants and trees.

THORNEY
11 miles N of Newark off the A57

In 1805, this hitherto peaceful little village was the site of a dreadful murder. A local labourer, Thomas Temporell, also known as Tom Otter, was forced to marry a local girl whom, it was claimed, he had made pregnant. Tom was so upset by the accusations and the enforced marriage that, in a frenzy, he murdered his bride on their wedding night. The story goes that he then took her body and left it on the steps of a public house in Saxilby, Lincolnshire. Caught and tried, Tom was sentenced to death with the extra penalty of gibbeting (the practice of hanging the offender's body in chains at the scene of their crime).

Small though it is, Thorney possesses a huge and magnificent church, built in 1849 by the Nevile family of nearby Thorney Hall (now demolished). Constructed in the Norman style, the church contains a wealth of superb stone carvings, both inside and out. Among them are no fewer than 17 fearsome dragons' heads.

TUXFORD
12 miles NW of Newark off the A1

This pleasant little town used to have its own market and, because of its position on the Great North Road, prospered greatly during the days of stage coach travel. A devastating fire in 1702 destroyed most of the town, but the rebuilding produced some attractive Georgian buildings. Among the buildings that did survive are the pleasing little Grammar School with its hipped roof and dormer windows, founded in 1669, and the medieval Church of St Nicholas. The church contains some interesting memorials to the White family and a striking font of 1673 standing beneath a magnificent hanging canopy.

THE MUSSEL & CRAB

Sibthorpe, Tuxford, Nottinghamshire NG22 0PJ
Tel: 01777 870491 Fax: 01777 872302
website: www.musselandcrab.co.uk

Landlocked Nottinghamshire is not usually known for its seafood, but the passion of owners Bruce and Allison and the skills of head chef Philip and his team have made the **Mussel & Crab** a very notable exception. In their busy, lively country pub-restaurant they aim to provide the freshest fish, both native (much of it landed daily at Brixham) and from more exotic waters. Starters might include crab chowder, rock oysters from Mersea Island in Essex, King scallops from the Isle of Wight and mussels from the Isle of Shona in Scotland, while among main courses could be Atlantic cod, lemon sole, grilled tuna with pesto sauce, monkfish, red snapper, sea bass, barramundi and lobster Thermidor. There's also plenty of choice for meat-eaters, including steaks, duck, beef Wellington and seasonal game, and vegetarians always have a choice of main courses. The choice changes constantly, announced, along with the wines, on more than 20 blackboards spread around the various eating areas, which include the bar, the piazza room, the vibrant Mediterranean room, the traditional beamed restaurant, an alfresco are and a roof garden. There are quirky features and surprises at every turn, including wooden seats in the shape of cupped hands in the bar and live goldfish in the cisterns in the gents. The Mussel & Crab, which lies on the B1164 just moments from the A1/A57 junction at Markham Moor, is open every lunchtime and every evening.

🏛 historic building   🏛 museum   🏛 historic site   ⌕ scenic attraction   🌿 flora and fauna

KELHAM

3 miles W of Newark on the A617

Originally an estate village serving Kelham Hall, the village farms were among the first to grow sugar beet when it was introduced to England during World War I. A lane still leads from the village to the huge sugar beet factory a mile or so to the west. Kelham Hall, now council offices, is the third manor house to be built on the site. The first was the Kelum Hall where Charles I was briefly imprisoned. That building was destroyed by fire in 1690. Another mansion was built for the Sutton family, Lords of the Manor of Kelham. That too went up in flames in 1857. The present building was designed by George Gilbert Scott and opinions are sharply divided over the merits of its red-brick towers, pinnacles, gables and Gothic windows.

Like the Hall, Kelham's bridge over the Trent also suffered misfortune - during the frightful winter of 1881 ice packs floating down the river demolished the old wooden structure.

AVERHAM

4 miles W of Newark on the A617

🎭 Robin Hood Theatre

Pronounced locally as Airam, this pleasant town has a picturesque corner off the main road where the Norman church and Georgian rectory form an appealing little group on the edge of the Trent. In the rectory grounds stands the remarkable **Robin Hood Theatre**, established by a former Rector and built by a local carpenter. The Reverend Cyril Walker opened it in 1913 as a private theatre for opera lovers. It had a fully equipped stage and orchestra pit, and boasted the rare amenity of being lit by electricity. The late, great Sir Donald Wolfit, a local man born at nearby Balderton, gave his first performances here.

The theatre went through a rocky period in the 1960s and closed for several years, but it is now operating successfully again, offering a variety of shows and plays throughout the year, including a five-week production by the Robin Hood Theatre Group.

EAST STOKE

4 miles SW of Newark on the A46

🏛 Battle of Stoke Fields

The village is the site of the last great conflict of the War of the Roses, the **Battle of Stoke Fields** that took place here on 16 June 1487. The battle saw the army of Henry VII defeat the Yorkists and the pretender Lambert Simnel in a bloody conflict that lasted for three hours and left a toll of 7,000 deaths. The defeated army fled across the meadows to a ravine leading to the river, which is known locally to this day as the Red Gutter. Many of those who died in battle lie in Deadman's Field nearby, and local farmers have occasionally uncovered swords and other relics from the battle when ploughing their fields.

ELSTON

7 miles SW of Newark off the A46

🏛 Chapel

This rural village was once well-known for the local trade of skep-making, or basket-making, using specially grown willows, but the craft has all but died out. A curious building on the outskirts of the village is the deserted **Elston Chapel**, a quaint little building with a Norman doorway and many other Norman and medieval features. Its origins have been shrouded in mystery, but recent research has suggested that the building was the chapel to the hospital of St Leonard that once existed in this locality.

Sibthorpe Dovecote

SIBTHORPE
5 miles S of Newark off the A46

🏛 Dovecote

All that remains above ground of a priests' college, founded here in the 14th century, is the parish church and a **Dovecote** (NT). Standing in the middle of a field, and some 60 feet high, this circular stone building has a conical tiled roof and provided nesting places for more than 1,200 birds.

SCREVETON
7 miles S of Newark off the A46

🏛 Church of St Wilfrid

The ancient village, whose name means farm belonging to the sheriff, has a delightful, small 13th-century church that lies in a secluded position some way from the village. Reached by a footpath, the **Church of St Wilfrid** is home to a fine alabaster tomb of Richard

Whalley, who is depicted with his three wives and 25 children at his feet.

CAR COLSTON
8 miles S of Newark off the A46

Now a conservation area, this village is fortunate in that it has remained unspoiled by modern development. Of particular interest here are the village's two greens, both of which date from the reign of Elizabeth I. At that time individual strips of land were cultivated by the villagers and the typical ridge and furrow appearance can still be made out. In 1598, the parish was enclosed, the land being turned into the fenced fields that became the norm, but the land in the middle of the village was left open so that the villagers could graze their cattle. The Large Green, at 16.5 acres, is the largest in the county and, at the other end of the village lies Little Green (a mere 5.5 acres).

There are several interesting houses in the village, but Old Hall Farm, which dates from 1812, is probably the one that receives most attention. The interest is generated not so much by the building itself, but because it was the home of Robert Thoroton who, in 1677, published his *Antiquities of Nottinghamshire*. The first major history of the county, the work was updated in the late 18th century by John Throsby and remains today one of the prime sources for local historians.

SCARRINGTON
8 miles S of Newark-on-Trent off the A52

The main attraction of this small village is not a grand house or a splendid village church, but a remarkable man-made edifice. A pile of around 50,000 horseshoes towers 17 feet high and was built by the former blacksmith, Mr Flinders. Over the years, souvenir hunters have taken the odd shoe here and there, with the result that the monument is bending over very slightly at the top.

However, the obelisk that Mr Flinders began in 1945 stands rock solid, though all he used to bond the horseshoes was his skill and a great deal of luck! At one time it was coveted by an American visitor who wished to buy it and transport it to the United States.

ALVERTON
7 miles S of Newark-on-Trent off the A52

A small hamlet of just a handful of houses, Alverton's tiny population is occasionally augmented by two resident ghosts. The first has been seen in the old Church of England schoolhouse, which is now a private residence, and is believed to be the ghost of a teacher who was murdered at the school.

Alverton's second ghost, an elderly lady dressed in Victorian clothes, has been sighted at one of the hamlet's larger houses. The lady is believed to be Mary Brown, a sewing maid to Queen Victoria, who gave up her job after the death of her sister-in-law. Mary moved back to her brother's house to act as housekeeper to him and his four children and, by all accounts, she proved to be a formidable woman. She ruled the house with a rod of iron. In later years, when noises were heard on the upper floors, it was said that "Aunt Polly was on the warpath again".

Bingham

The unofficial capital of the Vale of Belvoir, Bingham is an ancient medieval market town that grew up around the church. After passing through a period of depression in the 20th century, the town is once again thriving. The area around the market square has been smartened up and the octagonal butter cross with its Victorian tiles and inscriptions provides an attractive focus here. Most of the buildings around the market place are also Victorian but All Saints' Church is medieval, dating from the 13th century though, again, there are many Victorian additions and decorations.

Bingham was the third Nottinghamshire town to provide an Archbishop of Canterbury. George Abbot's tenure of office was almost as unremarkable as that of Thomas Secker of Sibthorpe, except for one unfortunate accident in 1621. Abbot was out shooting deer with a crossbow when he missed and killed a gamekeeper instead.

Around Bingham

COTGRAVE
4 miles SW of Bingham off the A46

🏛 Mill Hill

The discovery of an Anglo-Saxon burial ground on **Mill Hill**, Cotgrave's highest point, confirms that there has been a settlement here for many centuries. The excavation team uncovered the skeletons of nearly 100 people including some 13 children and the remains have been dated to around the mid to late 6th century.

Close to the burial ground stood the village's old post mill, itself the site of an unsolved mystery. One of the millers disappeared without trace after having been accused of pilfering corn. Rumours in the 19th century suggested that a body had been discovered in the mill foundations and, despite believing that this could be the remains of the missing miller, the villagers kept quiet and the rumour was never investigated. During an excavation of the post mill site in the 1970s

BRUMPTON BUTCHERS LTD

3 Plumtree Road, Cotgrave,
nr Nottingham NG12 3HT
Tel: 0115 989 2220
website: www.cbrumptonbutchers.co.uk

Since 1896, four generations of the Brumpton
family have run this high-class family butchers.
Quality has always been paramount throughout the
range of meats, baked goods and accompaniments,
and Stephen and Judy work hard to ensure that **Brumpton Butchers** stays up-to-date, upholding
traditional values while keeping the shop fresh and contemporary with new ideas and new recipes.
Stephen sources his meat as locally as possible; he knows his farmers personally and his
knowledge of the rearing process ensures quality from start to finish – traditionally hung beef,
lamb joints, steaks and mince, succulent pork, bacon and sausages with both traditional and
special flavours. Judy's handmade pies, pasties, cakes and tartlets are treats not to be missed, and
other items include cheeses, preserves, pickles and sauces. Open from 7.30 to 5.30 (Monday to
12.30, Friday to 6, Saturday to 3).

the skeleton of a male was uncovered that
showed injuries suggesting that the
unfortunate man was killed by a blow to the
head. Whether or not this was all that
remained of the missing miller has never
been established.

Cotgrave is probably most well known as
the home of Cotgrave Colliery, which opened
in 1964 and was a showplace mine for a
number of years. The promise of work here
for the next 100 years brought many miners
from other coalfields to the village and also
generated a huge expansion and building
programme. Unfortunately, major geological
faults made it impossible to mine the huge
reserves and the colliery is now closed.

KINOULTON

6 miles S of Bingham off the A46

🏛 Church of St Luke

The village, on the edge of the wolds, stands
on high ground and from this vantage point
there are views over the Vale of Belvoir to
Belvoir Castle. Today, Kinoulton is a large
commuter village but it has a long and
interesting past. In the 12th century, there was
a castle here, its commanding position being
ideal since it was also close to the Fosse Way.
Archbishop Cranmer had a palace nearby and,
to the west of the village, lies the spring that
brought the village to prominence in Georgian
times as a spa with curative properties. Later,
the arrival of the Grantham Canal ushered in
a period of mild prosperity. (The canal still
passes through the village and provides some
pleasant walking.)

Standing beside the canal, Kinoulton's
Church of St Luke was a gift of the squire,
the Earl of Gainsborough, in the 1760s. The
earl felt the old church was too near what was
then a major thoroughfare, the Fosse Way. The
slate headstones in the old churchyard have
some fine inscriptions but not all of the
stones have survived. Some were 'borrowed'
by the local baker to line his oven, a piece of
recycling that was exposed when a customer
noticed that his loaf was imprinted with the
words "in loving memory".

🏛 historic building   📷 museum   🏛 historic site   🐟 scenic attraction   🦋 flora and fauna

HICKLING

7 miles S of Bingham off the A606

Lying on the western edge of the Vale of Belvoir, this agricultural village was the site of a busy basin on the Grantham Canal. Building work on the basin finished in 1797 and the canal, which carried coal, building materials, and agricultural goods, was in constant use until the 1930s when it began to fall into disrepair. Recently cleared, Hickling Basin is once again attracting people, this time visitors who come to see the resident flocks of wildfowl.

COLSTON BASSETT

4 miles S of Bingham off the A46

🏛 The Cross

For centuries this small village was the property of the Bassett family and later the Hackers and the Goldings. Between them they planted the many trees that shade the winding lanes, built a noble manor house, landscaped the gracious park, and in 1892 added a striking if rather over-elaborate church. The cumulative effect is to make Colston Bassett one of the most picturesque villages in the Vale of Belvoir.

At one time the village was large enough to sustain its own weekly market and the partly medieval **Market Cross** can still be seen. Since 1933, the Cross has been owned by the National Trust - the first property it acquired in Nottinghamshire. The Cross stands near the old post office, itself a picture postcard building that used to feature in GPO advertisements during the 1960s.

On the outskirts of the village stand the forlorn ruins of the former village church, which has been abandoned since 1892.

CROPWELL BISHOP

3 miles S of Bingham off the A46

🏛 St Giles' Church

Much of the furniture from Colston Bassett's old church was moved to Cropwell Bishop and installed in **St Giles' Church**. St Giles is the oldest building in this sizeable village and dates back to around 1215.

The village lies close to the old Roman road, the Fosse Way, now the A46. The coaching inns of Cropwell Bishop are said to have given shelter to highwayman Dick Turpin while he was plundering the coaches using the busy thoroughfare.

In modern times, the village has prospered from gypsum works. Two of the works' bottle kilns still stand alongside the Grantham Canal.

LANGAR

3 miles SE of Bingham off the A52

🏛 St Andrew's Church

🌿 Naturescape Wild Flower Farm Visitor Centre

"Really, the English do not deserve great men," declared George Bernard Shaw. "They allowed Butler to die practically unknown." He was referring to Samuel Butler, author of *The Way of All Flesh*, who was born in the elegant Georgian rectory at Langar on December 4, 1834. A trenchant satirist, Butler mocked the pomposity and exposed the hypocrisy of the Victorian middle classes. No wonder they didn't much care for him. Langar itself appears in his major work as Battersby-on-the-Hill and the portraits of its residents are far from flattering. The year 2002, the centenary of Butler's death, provided an opportunity to commemorate one of the village's most famous residents in some way but no one bothered. This small

LANGAR HALL RESTAURANT WITH ROOMS

Langar, Nottinghamshire NG13 9HG
Tel: 01949 860559 Fax: 01949 861045
e-mail: info@langarhall.co.uk website: www.langarhall.co.uk

'Once in a blue moon it is still possible to come across a
country house that makes one want to jump for joy.' These
are the words of someone who definitely knows his hotels,
and anyone who visits **Langar Hall** will agree with his praise.
Langar Hall is a house of charm in quiet seclusion
overlooking gardens, with sheep grazing under the ancient
trees in the park. Owned for over 25 years by Imogen
Shirving, this delightful home has gently evolved into a
lovely family hotel.

The en suite accommodation comprises eight double/twin
rooms, a four-poster room and a suite; most enjoy lovely
views, and all are quiet, very comfortable and well equipped
for both business and leisure stays. Among the day rooms are
the Study, for reading or small meetings; the White Sitting
Room for afternoon tea and pre-dinner drinks; the Indian
Room for private parties and conferences.

The popular neighbourhood restaurant serves fresh
seasonal food, including home-reared lamb, locally raised
pork, beef and poultry, fish from Brixham, game in winter
and home-grown vegetables and herbs, is the basis of the
menus. English country cooking with a twist, with the
emphasis on freshness and flavour provides memorable
signature dishes such as twice-baked cheese soufflé, a trio
of Langar lamb and scrumptious desserts.

rural village in the heart of the Vale was also the home of Admiral Richard, Earl Howe (1726-99), "Black Dick of Lanagar". Richard achieved national fame on the Glorious 1st of June, 1794, at the Battle of Ushant where his victory included the capture of seven French ships of the line. The Admiral himself merits only a modest plaque in **St Andrew's Church**, but other generations of the Howe family, their predecessors, the Scropes, as well as the Chaworths from nearby Wiverton Hall, are all celebrated by an extraordinary gathering of monuments. The most splendid is a four-poster free-standing alabaster monument to Thomas, Lord Scrope, who died in 1609, and his wife. According to Pevsner "the figures are good enough to be in Westminster Abbey".

To the south of Langar, the former airfield is surrounded by an unsightly industrial estate that nevertheless contains the **Naturescape Wild Flower Farm Visitors Centre**, part of a commercial nursery, where visitors are able to explore the 40 acres of wild flower meadows and see a wide variety of species in their natural habitat. Open from 11am to 5pm every day April to September.

GRANBY
4 miles SE of Bingham off the A52

This small, once self-sufficient village is still proud that its name was adopted by the Dukes of Rutland, of nearby Belvoir Castle, as the courtesy title of their eldest son. It was John, son of the 3rd Duke, who brought most lustre to the name as Commander in Chief of the British forces in Germany in the mid 1700s. The Marquis was immensely popular with his troops, many of whom followed an old tradition on leaving the Army and became publicans. Which explains why so many hostelries up and down the country are named The Marquis of Granby – including naturally the inn at Granby itself.

WHATTON
3 miles E of Bingham off the A52

The Norman St John's Church was restored in the 1860s under the direction of Thomas Butler, rector of Langar, and the stained-glass

---

THE PADDOCK AT PEACOCK FARM

Main Road, Redmile, Nottinghamshire NG13 0GR
Tel: 01949 84222475
e-mail: info@peacock-farm@.co.uk
website: www.peacock-farm.co.uk

The Paddock at Peacock Farm is a small, secluded B&B establishment where guests can look forward to style, comfort and friendly service from owner Nicky Need.
The setting in the Vale of Beauvoir is both beautiful and peaceful, adding to the Paddock's appeal as the perfect choice for business visitors, walkers, cyclists, riders and tourists. The three large en suite rooms are furnished and equipped to a very high standard, each having a double and a single bed and space for an extra bed or cot. Two of the three rooms are on the ground floor and have a kitchenette with fridge, microwave and dining area, a communal conservatory and a pretty garden with a children's play area. Well-behaved dogs are welcome. Nicky and her sister Mandy offer a number of massage and holistic treatments. "A relaxing retreat" the ideal place to meet up with friends or family.

[ᕕ] stories and anecdotes　🐦 famous people　🖌 art and craft　🖉 entertainment and sport　🏃 walks

windows, including some crafted by William Morris to the designs of Burne-Jones, were added later that century. The font, which is dated 1662, replaced one that had been damaged during the Commonwealth. This church was used by Thomas Cranmer and his family until he left the area to take up his studies at Cambridge. A memorial to his father, Thomas Cranmer senior, who died in 1502, can be found inside.

ASLOCKTON
2 miles E of Bingham off the A52

This village is now separated from its neighbour, Whatton, by the main Nottingham to Grantham railway line, though the footpaths linking the two can still be walked today. This was the village in which Thomas Cranmer was born and spent his early years. Born in 1489, he attended the parish church at Whatton and also a local grammar school, possibly at Southwell, before leaving at the age of 14 to continue his education at Cambridge. It was in 1533 that Henry VIII proposed this obscure theologian and academic as Archbishop of Canterbury, an appointment that had to be approved by the Pope – the last time Rome had any say over who should be Primate of All England.

One of Cranmer's first duties on gaining his appointment was to pronounce the marriage between Henry VIII and Catherine of Aragon null and void. During the course of his 23 years in office, Cranmer also pronounced invalid Henry's marriage to Anne Boleyn and granted him a divorce from Anne of Cleves. Loyal to his monarch throughout, Cranmer aided Henry in effecting the independence of the Church in England from Rome. He was also responsible for drafting much of the Common Prayer Book that was used right up until the 1970s when it was replaced by a modern language version. Following the death of Henry VIII, Cranmer was convicted of treason under Mary I and burnt at the stake in 1556.

Though not built until the late 19th century, Aslockton Church is appropriately dedicated to Thomas while the village school also bears the name of its most famous resident. Cranmer's Mound, to the east of the church, is a Norman motte some 15 feet high that is clearly visible from the footpath to Orston. Further along this same footpath can be seen the site of the manor house where Cranmer was born.

Sherwood Forest

It seems likely that it was William the Conqueror who designated Sherwood as a Royal Forest, an administrative term for the private hunting ground of the king. The land was not only thickly wooded, but also included areas of rough heathland as well as arable land, meadow land, small towns, and villages. The Norman kings were passionate about their hunting and, to guard their royal forests, there were a set of rigidly upheld laws to conserve the game (known as the venison) and vegetation (known as the vert). No one, even those with a private estate within the royal forest, was allowed to kill or hunt protected animals, graze domestic animals in the forest, fell trees or make clearings within the boundaries without the express permission of the king or one of his chief foresters. It is little wonder then, with such strict rules imposed upon them, that the people turned to the likes of Robin Hood and others who defied the laws in order to survive.

Edwinstowe

- 🌳 Major Oak
- 🎿 Vicar Water Country Park
- 🎦 Sherwood Forest Visitor Centre
- 🌳 Farm Park
- 🏛 Church of St Mary
- 🍃 Sherwood Forest Fun Park

Lying at the heart of Sherwood Forest, the life of the village is still dominated by the forest, as it has been since the 7th century. Edwin, King of Northumbria, who gave the village its name, died in the Battle of Hatfield in AD632. The village developed around the church built on the spot where he was slain. In 1912, a cross was erected by the Duke of Portland to mark the king's grave. From then on until the time of the Domesday Survey, Edwinstowe remained small. Following the Norman Conquest, the village found itself within the boundaries of the royal hunting forest of Sherwood and it became subject to the stringent laws of the verderers. Dating from the 12th century, the **Church of St Mary** was the first stone building in Edwinstowe and, according to legend, it was here that the marriage took place between Robin Hood and Maid Marian. Buried in the graveyard is Dr Cobham Brewer whose *Dictionary of Phrase & Fable*, first published in 1870 and still in print, is possibly the most readable reference book ever compiled.

A little way up the road leading northwards out of Edwinstowe is the **Sherwood Forest Visitor Centre**. The Visitor Centre (01623 823202) houses a display of characters from the Robin Hood stories, with appropriate scenes of merry making. This theme has also been successfully translated to the city of Nottingham in the Tales of Robin Hood exhibition.

Sherwood, the Shire Wood, was once a great woodland mass stretching from Nottingham to Worksop. Although only relatively small pockets of the original forest remain today, it is still possible to become lost among the trees. Whether or not Robin and his Merry Men ever did frolic in the greenshawe is, however, debatable. Arguments still rage as to which particular historical figure gave rise to the legend of the famous outlaw. Records from the 12th century suggest a number of possible candidates, including the Earl of Huntingdon.

During the 15th century, several references to the outlaw can be found in the writings of two Scottish historians. In 1521 a third Scotsman, John Major, wrote

About the time of King Richard I, according to my estimate, the famous English robbers Robert Hood and Little John were lurking in their woods, preying on the goods of the wealthy.

However, none of the historians gave any clues as to the sources of their writings. By the 16th century, there were two conflicting stories emerging as to the birthplace of Robin, one suggesting Kirklees, while the other suggested Locksley.

Tracing the stories of Robin Hood is a difficult task as the tales, which have been told for over 600 years, were spoken rather than written since few local people could read and write. One of the earliest known stories of the outlaw's exploits can be found on a piece of parchment that dates from the mid 15th century, but it was not until William Caxton set up his printing press in London in 1477 that cheaper books could be produced. From then on, the story of Robin Hood, his merry band of men, Guy of Gisborne, and the evil Sheriff of Nottingham has inspired countless books and at least a dozen major films. Among others, the medieval outlaw has been portrayed by Douglas Fairbanks, Kevin

---

🎦 stories and anecdotes   🐦 famous people   🖋 art and craft   🍃 entertainment and sport   🎿 walks

Costner and Sean Connery.

Undeterred by the vague foundations upon which the legend is built, visitors still flock to see the great hollow tree that the outlaws purportedly used as a meeting place and as a cache for their supplies. The **Major Oak** is located about 10 minutes walk along the main track in the heart of the forest and presents a rather forlorn appearance. Its 33ft girth and branches 260 feet in circumference are now supported by massive wooden crutches and iron corsets. There is no denying that the tree is at least 500 years old, and some sources claim its age to be nearer 1,000 years. Despite its decayed appearance the tree is still alive thanks to careful preservation. Recent tests have established that some parts of the tree have successfully taken to grafting and there are hopes that at some stage a whole colony of minor oaks may be produced.

Another impressive attraction in Edwinstowe is the **Sherwood Forest Fun Park**, which can be found to the north of the A6075 Mansfield to Ollerton road. This family-run funfair contains a variety of popular fairground rides including dodgems, a ghost train, and a giant Astroglide. The park is open daily from 10am to dusk between mid-March and mid-October; admission is free, pay as you go on the rides (01623 823536).

Not far from Edwinstowe, off the A6075, is the **Sherwood Forest Farm Park**, a naturalist and animal lover's delight, beautifully laid out, with picturesque water gardens and three wildfowl lakes. Enjoying a peaceful setting in a

The Major Oak, Sherwood Forest

secluded valley on the edge of Sherwood Forest, the Farm Park, open every day from April to the end of September, boasts no fewer than 30 of Britain's rarest breeds of farm animals and other endangered and protected species. A peaceful spot to relax can be found by visitors even on the busiest of days. The pets' corner with its goats and the exotic bird garden are just two of the delights, and among the many other attractions are the family of kune kune pigs, water buffalos, shire horses and Suffolk Punches, a group of wallabies, a tree house, tractor and trailer rides and the summer maize maze. A miniature steam railway meanders through the grounds.

A couple of miles southeast of Edwinstowe off the B6030 is **Vicar Water Country Park**. Open daily throughout the

---

🏛 historic building   🏛 museum   🏛 historic site   ♨ scenic attraction   🌱 flora and fauna year, from dawn to dusk, the Park covers 80 hectares of attractive countryside, complete with a large lake, and provides excellent walking, fishing, cycling and horse-riding. Footpaths and bridleways link the Park to the Sherwood Pines Forest Park, the Timberland Trail, the Maun Valley Way and the Robin Hood Way. The Visitor Centre has ample information about the area and also a café.

Around Edwinstowe

CUCKNEY
5 miles NW of Edwinstowe on the A60

Five main roads converge on this sizeable village, which in medieval times was a marshy island. A large mound in the churchyard is all that is left of Thomas de Cuckney's 12th-century castle. Because the nearby church was

built on the marshes it was necessary in the 1950s to shore it up by building a concrete platform underneath. In the course of this work the remains of hundreds of skeletons were uncovered. At first it was thought the bones were the grisly relics of some 12th-century battle. More recent research has revealed that the remains are much older. They have now been linked to the 7th century Battle of Heathfield between Edwin of Northumbria and Penda of Mercia.

An estate village to the country seat of the Dukes of Portland, Welbeck Abbey, Cuckney is made up of farm workers cottages. Along with Clumber House, Thoresby Hall and Rufford Abbey, Welbeck Abbey makes up the four large estates in this area of Nottinghamshire, all owned by Dukes. Naturally, the area became known as The Dukeries. It was the 5th Duke of Portland who began, in 1854, an extensive

THE SCHOOL OF ARTISAN FOOD
Lower Motor Yard, Welbeck, Nottinghamshire S80 3LR
Tel: 0845 520 1111
website: www.schoolofartisanfood.org

At The School of Artisan food we have passion, expertise and understanding - all under one roof. We specialise in providing a platform for non industrial food production methods to flourish once again. Our award winning team of practitioners guide students through the fascinating world of baking, dairy, butchery and brewing, as well as preserves and pickling, teaching the skills and techniques of each discipline.

Housed in an historic listed courtyard building in the heart of Sherwood Forest, our state of the art training rooms provide the perfect setting to master all aspects of artisan food and drink, from sourdough and specialist cheese, to sausage making and cider brewing.

Our courses range from half a day to five days in length and have been specially designed for all skill levels, whether you're an amateur cook or a critically acclaimed chef. More details and course structures are available on our website www.schoolofartisanfood.org

stories and anecdotes   famous people   art and craft   entertainment and sport   walks

THE COURTYARD AT WELBECK

A60 Mansfield Road, Welbeck, Worksop, Nottinghamshire, S80 3LW
The Farm Shop: 01909 478725   The Gallery: 01909 501700
website: www.harleygallery.co.uk or www.thewelbeckfarmshop.co.uk

The courtyard at Welbeck offers a unique mix of attractions set in the tranquil surroundings of rural North Nottinghamshire.

Spend a relaxed afternoon taking in an art exhibition at The Harley Gallery, enjoy a cream tea or light lunch at the Lime House Cafe, then sample some of the best foods produced North Nottinghamshire on sale at The Welbeck Farm Shop.

The award-winning **Harley Gallery** houses a unique mix of contemporary and historical art exhibitions, a craft shop selling work from fine jewellery to sculpture and an activity area for children. The Gallery was built in 1994 on the site of the original 19th century gasworks for Welbeck Estate and has won numerous awards including a Civic Trust Award for Architecture and a Heart of England Tourist Board Award for Excellence.

The **Welbeck Farm Shop**, voted one of the top 30 farm shops in the country by the Daily Telegraph, sells fantastic produce made on the Welbeck Estate, including Stichelton an organic blue unpasteurised cheese and traditional breads baked in wood fired ovens from the Welbeck Bakehouse. Welbeck reared game and meat alongside the finest seasonal vegetables is also always available.

The **Lime House Cafe** offers a stylish interior to enjoy its bistro style menu. A changing selection of freshly baked cakes, home made soups and open sandwiches are served alongside daily specials prepared by The Welbeck Farm Shop's resident chef which range from hearty stews to delicious light salads.

🏛 historic building   🏛 museum   🏛 historic site   ☘ scenic attraction   🌿 flora and fauna

building programme that turned Welbeck into what is seen today. Pedestrian access is confined to footpaths forming part of the Robin Hood Way. However, there is general public access to the Welbeck Farm shop and The Harley Gallery. This gallery, managed by the Harley Foundation trust, shows a combination of contemporary arts and crafts together with items from the Cavendish-Bentick art collections.

CLUMBER PARK
4 miles N of Edwinstowe off the A614

🏛 Chapel of St Mary the Virgin   🚶 Clumber Park

Clumber Park was created in 1707 when the 3rd Duke of Newcastle was granted permission by Queen Anne to enclose part of the Forest of Sherwood as a hunting ground. The building of Clumber House began in 1760, though it was much altered in the early 19th century. After a devastating fire in 1879, the house was rebuilt in an Italianate style but, due to the vast expense of its upkeep, Clumber House was demolished in 1938. All that remains today are the foundations.

However, any sense of disappointment is quickly dispelled by the charm of the buildings that remain in this lovely setting. The estate houses with their high pitched gables and massive chimneys are most picturesque. The redbrick stables are particularly fine as they are surmounted by a clock tower crowned by a domed cupola. The inset clock in the tower dates back to 1763 and the stables now house the café and visitor centre.

By far the most striking building on the estate, however, is the **Chapel of St Mary the Virgin**, built by GF Bodley in the 1880s. It was commissioned by the 7th Duke of Newcastle to commemorate his coming of age. A fervent Anglo-Catholic, he spent the

then colossal sum of £30,000 on its construction. The church has many elaborate features including some wonderful stone and woodwork and stained glass by Kempe.

The 3,800-acre **Clumber Park**, once the country estate of the Dukes of Newcastle, has been in the care of the National Trust since 1946. The man-made lake is particularly lovely and is crossed by a fine classical bridge. Five different roads enter the park and each entrance is marked by an impressive gateway. Most imposing of them all is the Apleyhead Gate, off the A614, which leads into the glorious Duke's Drive. Stretching for a distance of two miles, the drive is the longest double avenue of limes in Europe and contains some 1,300 trees. The house was demolished in 1938, but the Gothic Revival chapel still stands, along with some truly spectacular glasshouses. Produce from the organically managed Walled Kitchen Garden can be enjoyed in the smartly refurbished restaurant.

PERLETHORPE
4 miles NE of Edwinstowe off the A614

🎨 Thoresby Gallery

Situated in the valley of the River Meden, Perlethorpe lies within the estate of Thoresby Hall, at the eastern end of Thoresby Lake. The first hall was built in the late 17th century for the Earl of Kingston, but this was destroyed in 1745 and replaced by a Palladian-style mansion. The hall seen today is a Victorian mansion built by Anthony Salvin in 1864 for the Pierrepont family and is surrounded by the largest park in the county. The Hall itself is now a hotel.

The village church, which was completed in 1876, was built by Salvin at the same time as he was working on the hall. At the beginning of the 20th century, Countess Manvers of the

THAYMAR DAIRY ICE CREAM FARMSHOP & TEAROOM

Haughton Park Farm, nr Bothamsall, Retford, Nottinghamshire DN22 8DB
Tel: 01623 86232
e-mail: sales@thaymaricecream.co.uk
website: www.thaymaricecream.co.uk

Thaymar Dairy Ice Cream Farmshop and Tearoom has been delighting customers with its luxury ice cream and other delicacies since 1988. More than 35 delicious hand made flavours of ice cream and sorbets are now made on the farm, ranging from Apple &Cinnamon to Wild Cherry. They are made using fresh milk and double cream straight from the neighbouring dairy together with raw cane sugar. To this scrumptious base are then added delicious ingredients ranging from local fresh fruits to Belgian chocolate and Nottinghamshire honey to produce an unforgettable ice cream experience. Thelma, Thomas, Emily and Chris Cheetham are the family working together on the farm. They all make ice cream and love the fact that people travel from miles around to sample the delectable end product.

The tearoom offers a full menu of hot meals and sandwiches - and, of course, some wonderful ice cream desserts. All of the meals have been made on the farm by the tearoom team and if you have any special requirements they will do their best to accommodate you. Round off your visit with a browse through the farmshop which stocks a fantastic selection of local and homemade produce.

great hall took a keen interest in the welfare of the village children and was always informed of any who did not attend Sunday school. She would then visit them and scold those who had failed in their duty. But if a child had been absent because of sickness, she would ensure that hot soup was delivered until the child was well again. The **Thoresby Gallery** in Thoresby Park is an imaginative conversion with three well-lit exhibition areas featuring paintings, ceramics, glass, jewellery and textiles. There is a permanent exhibition of the works of Marie-Louise Pierrepont, Countess Manvers. Open 10.30am to 5pm daily.

OLD OLLERTON

2 miles E of Edwinstowe off the A614/A6075

🏛 Water Mill

Not to be confused with the more workaday town of New Ollerton, Old Ollerton is a delightfully preserved cluster of old houses, a charming Georgian coaching inn covered in creeper, and a church set beside the River Maun. Straddling the river is **Ollerton Water Mill**, more than 300 years old. Visitors are welcome to wander around the ancient building with its huge water wheel, browse in the Exhibition Area, watch a short video illustrating the age-old milling process, or sample the refreshments in the tearoom. The name of the village was originally Alreton, or Allerton, meaning farm among the alders, and the alders still grow here along the banks of the River Maun. The village lay on the road from London to York (though now it is bypassed) and also on the roads from Newark to Worksop and Lincoln to Mansfield. As a consequence, Ollerton

🏛 historic building   🏛 museum   🏛 historic site   🜨 scenic attraction   🌱 flora and fauna

developed as a meeting place for Sherwood Forest officials and the inns became staging posts during the coaching era.

WELLOW

2 miles SE of Ollerton on the A616

🏠 Maypole 🏠 Church of St Swithin

This pretty conservation village is located on the site of an early settlement and was once fortified by an earthwork and, on the western side, by Gorge Dyke. The remains of the earthwork can still be seen and villagers have retained the right to graze their cattle on enclosed land. On the village green stands the tallest permanent **Maypole** in England - 60 feet high, colourfully striped like a barber's pole, and with a cockerel perched on the top. Because earlier wooden poles rotted away, were stolen or got knocked down, this one is made of steel and firmly fixed in place. It was erected to commemorate Elizabeth II's Silver Jubilee in 1976 and forms the focus for the May Day festivities held on the Spring Bank Holiday Monday. The jollities include dancing around the Maypole and the crowning of a May Queen.

Other notable features of this surprising village include a Ducking Stool; part of the old stocks; and a 17th-century case clock in the 12th-century parish **Church of St Swithin**. The clock face was made locally to commemorate the coronation of Elizabeth II in 1953.

Each year on 19 September, the three church bells, which are between 300 and 400 years old, are rung in memory of a certain Lady Walden. Some 200 years ago she was paying a visit to Wellow and became lost in a local wood. Following the sound of the church bells, Lady Walden eventually found her way to the village and, such was her relief, that she left money for the bells to be rung each year on that day.

LAXTON

4 miles E of Ollerton off the A6075

🏠 Dovecote Inn 🏰 Castle Mound

Laxton is unique since it is one of a handful of places in the country that have managed to retain their open field farming system. Devised in the Middle Ages, this system was generally abandoned in the 18th and 19th centuries when the enclosure of agricultural land took place. The fields have been strip farmed here for about 1,200 years and the system ensured that farmers had an equal share of both good and poor land. A farmer could hold as many as 100 strips, representing about 30 acres. In the 1600s, the strips were, on average, about half an acre in size, but with the advent of more efficient means of ploughing, this increased to three-quarters of

Wellow Maypole

Egmanton and Laxton

Distance: *6.0 miles (9.6 kilometres)*

Typical time: *180 mins*

Height gain: *50 metres*

Map: *Explorer 271*

Walk: *www.walkingworld.com ID:1440*

Contributor: *David Berry*

ACCESS INFORMATION:

Egmanton lies between the A6075 (Ollerton to Tuxford road) and the A616 (Newark to Ollerton). It is only a short distance off the A1; northbound, leave at Tuxford, southbound at Markham Moor. There are bus services to Egmanton village from Tuxford, Newark, Ollerton and Retford.

DESCRIPTION:

This walk is set in the undulating Nottinghamshire countryside 10 miles to the northwest of Newark. The old coalmining area of Ollerton is five miles to the west but does not impinge on the scenery of this walk.

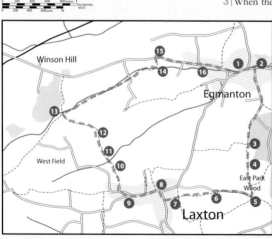

Egmanton is a typical, small, red-brick village of this area with church and pub. Laxton is a little bigger, again with church and pub. It is England's last open field farming village with an ancient strip field system. There is a visitors centre explaining this feudal scheme, and on the walk a couple of explanatory placards are passed. The majority of the walk is on farm tracks and field footpaths, but the last mile is along a quiet country road with little traffic.

FEATURES:

Pub, Toilets, Museum, Church, Wildlife, Great Views.

WALK DIRECTIONS:

1 | From The Old Plough Inn walk in an easterly direction. Shortly, take the right fork, Weston Road. Proceed along this road for 150 metres.

2 | Turn right up Wood Lane, which is between some expensive-looking new properties and a council-looking row of houses. The road becomes a stone track and climbs up, heading for the right-hand corner of Egmanton Wood. Ignore a turning left into the woods. Continue to the corner and stay on the track as it follows the edge of the wood.

3 | When the track ends, continue more or less straight ahead on a path across a field. In the middle of the field, there is a small tree on the path. In the distance, in line with the path, is a pylon. Walk to the hedge and turn left for 18m. Go through a gap in the hedge. Turn left and follow the edge of the field to your left.

4 | Turn right when you get to the footpath, which is identified by having an electricity pole and two large trees on it.

5 | Continue along the path to the far side of the field, which will lead you to a gateway (with no gate). Go through the gateway, turn sharp right

along a farm track. Over the brow of the hill you will see Laxton church tower.

6 | Having walked around 500 metres along this track, you will see a footpath off to the left. Follow this and you will now be heading slightly to the left of the church tower. The path enters a playing field. Keep left and walk the edge of the field. At the pavilion, continue on your heading to pass through the hedge. Turn immediately right for 30m.

7 | Turn left through the hedge and under a wooden bar at a footpath that once more heads towards the church. Go diagonally across the field to a footpath sign in the corner. Keep to the left edge of the next field to a stile. The next short footpath takes you down to a village road. Turn right and head for Laxton village centre. On the right you will pass one of the several placards explaining the open field system. Ahead is The Dovecote Inn. Beside it there is a visitors centre explaining the field system – and toilets. You might at this stage take in the centre and explore some of the fields. You might also choose to visit the pub.

8 | When all this is complete, the walk continues along the road to the left, signposted Boughton and Ollerton. Ignore a footpath by Cross Hill Farm and a bridleway sign by the information placard opposite the church. Pass the post office and a B&B at Lilac Farm.

9 | Take the right fork – 'No Through Road'. In 400m there is a public footpath sign to the right, just before a bungalow. Follow a well-defined footpath across the crop field to the left hedge, which the path then follows to the corner of the field.

10 | At the corner of the field, cross the stile and go through the gateway beyond. Walk down this narrow field to a stile on the left. Cross the stile and you will see, down to the left, a footbridge. Make for that by following the hedge to your right and then turning left on reaching a ditch. Cross the footbridge and the stile immediately beyond it.

11 | Continue straight ahead, along a well-defined path through the crop, keeping the hedge of the field to your right. As you reach higher ground, notice that you are heading towards a communications tower in the middle distance. To your right you can see your destination, Egmanton. It might seem that you are in the middle of nowhere, but beyond Egmanton you can see the A1 traffic and to the left and right, cooling towers. So, 'civilisation' is not that far away! The path is now diverging away from the hedge, but you are still heading towards the communications tower.

12 | The well-defined path ends at the corner of another field projecting into this one. Climb the mound at that corner and turn right along a track. A short way along that track there is a gateway (no gate) with a yellow arrow, the direction of which seems to indicate walking across the crop. It seems that previous walkers have not done this but have followed the track made by the wheels of a tractor. This runs parallel to the hedge, displaced into the field some 30m. As the hedge bends to the left and then curves right, so does the tractor-wheel track. As the track starts dropping down the hill, look for the line where previous walkers have turned left through the crop, which is the proper line of the footpath, towards a fingerpost in the far hedge. At the fingerpost over the stile, turn right and follow the fence, keeping it on your right.

13 | In the right-hand corner there is a wooden barrier, with a footpath sign. Go over the stile. Navigation is now simple – just follow a straight line keeping the hedge/ditch on your left. Look for quite an incredible amount of badger activity. Their paths for their nightly runs are long-established. It is almost a mile along this footpath. Reassurance that all is well is when you cross over a substantial private road up to a farm. You know you have reached the last field when you notice some strange mounds to your right. On the OS map they are labelled as an antiquity – Fish Ponds.

14 | At the corner of this field, the footpath ends and there is a rather dilapidated gate. Go through it onto a short track.

15 | The track leads to the road to Egmanton. Turn right.

16 | Entering Egmanton – the end is in sight!

an acre. The familiar three year crop rotation also ensured productive use of the land.

Another unique feature of this fascinating village is the magnificent **Dovecote Inn**, which is owned (but not run) by the Queen. Here, a form of manorial government that has survived from medieval times still continues. Each winter, villagers gather at the inn to appoint a jury that is then responsible for inspecting the fallow fields in the next cycle. The jurors tour the fields left fallow for the past year then adjourn for lunch back at the Dovecote. During the afternoon they discuss any offences committed by farmers. A week later comes the Court meeting.

The 18th century was a great time of rebuilding in Laxton and many of the houses display the patterned brickwork that was typical of this period. The still visible stonework around the bottom of some buildings suggests that the foundations were of much older timber-framed constructions.

Just north of the village, along a lane close to the church, is another fascinating aspect of Laxton's medieval history. This is the Norman motte, or **Castle Mound**, which lies almost hidden beneath the trees. At the beginning of the 12th century, the stewardship of Sherwood Forest moved to Laxton and the village became the administrative centre for the forest. As a consequence, the motte and bailey castle was one of the biggest in this part of the country. Although no ruined keep or crumbling walls exist today, the castle earthworks are still the largest and best preserved in the county.

EGMANTON
5 miles E of Ollerton off the A1

🏛 Shrine of Our Lady of Egmanton

Reached by quiet winding lanes, Egmanton is little visited these days, but during the Middle Ages it was very popular. A local woman claimed to have had a vision of the Virgin Mary and the **Shrine of Our Lady of Egmanton** became a major place of pilgrimage right up until the Reformation.

The cult was revived in 1896 by the 7th Duke of Newcastle who commissioned Sir Ninian Comper to completely restore and redecorate the church. The result is an exuberant re-creation of a medieval church with all its colour and graven images. The exterior is really quite modest, but the interior is resplendent and inspiring, with the light from many tapers and candles helping to create a mesmerising atmosphere.

RUFFORD
2 miles S of Ollerton off the A614

🏛 Abbey   🌳 Country Park   🎨 Craft Centre

Rufford Abbey was founded in 1148 by Gilbert de Gant as a daughter house to Rievaulx Abbey. During the Dissolution it suffered the fate of many religious houses and came into the hands of the 6th Earl of Shrewsbury, fourth husband of the redoubtable Bess of Hardwick. The Earl pulled down most of the abbey and built a grand Elizabethan mansion. All that remains of the abbey is a vaulted crypt, said to be haunted by the ghost of a giant monk with a skull-like face. According to the parish register for Edwinstowe, a man died of fright after catching sight of this unholy visitor.

The abbey's stable block now houses an impressive craft centre and a ceramics centre, and the restored 18th-century Orangery features a changing display of outdoor sculptures and large-scale ceramics. In the vaulted stone undercroft, and exhibition, Rufford the Cistercian Abbey, traces the varying functions of the Cistercian order in

England from the 12th century through to the Dissolution of the Monasteries in the reign of Henry VIII.

The grounds of the abbey, now the **Rufford Country Park** and **Craft Centre**, are well worth a visit. In addition to the variously themed formal gardens near the house, there are also some hides where birdwatchers can overlook a portion of the lake that has been designated a bird sanctuary. In the grounds, too, stands an 18th-century corn mill, now home to a display of Nottinghamshire history, and two icehouses dating from the mid 1800s. As well as the majestic Lime Avenue, there is also the Broad Ride, at the southern end of which are several animal graves. Most were pets belonging to the family at the house but one grave is that of the racehorse Cremorne, the 1872 Derby winner. Events throughout the year include the Earth & Fire Ceramic Fair in June (01623 822944).

Rufford Country Park

BILSTHORPE

4 miles S of Ollerton off the A614

The hall where, during the Civil War, Charles I is reputed to have hidden in a cupboard still exists, but is now incorporated into a farm that stands opposite the village church.

Bilsthorpe remained a quiet farming community, as it had been for many centuries, right up until 1922 when a coal mine was sunk in the village by Stanton Ironworks. An explosion at the mine with a subsequent loss of life brought the vicar and the mine manager into a dispute over compensation. The manager, unwilling to pay out, built a wooden church away from the main part of the village and near the temporary accommodation provided for the mine workers.

FARNSFIELD

7 miles S of Ollerton off the A614

🌱 Farm Centre 🐾 Wheelgate Adventure Park

Close to the crossroads of the A614/A617 near Farnsfield are two popular family attractions. **White Post Modern Farm Centre**, open daily from 10am, is a working farm with more than 4,000 animals, among them llamas, deer, owls, piglets, chicks and even mice. **Wheelgate Adventure Park** has a wealth of attractions for visitors of all ages: a large tropical house with exotic butterflies and birds, fish and insects, including a colony of leafcutter ants; a large indoor soft play area with a giant pirate ship and a Jungle Room; adventure play areas including a 54ft trawler in a giant sandpit; one of the largest hedges in the country; trails and woodland; a pet shed; a water fun fountain; a miniature railway; a garden centre and much more.

In Farnsfield village itself traces of a Roman camp can be found and the ghost of a Roman soldier is reputed to haunt one of the villages pubs. More recently, the village was the birthplace of the explorer, Augustus Charles Gregory. After emigrating to Australia, Gregory became the first person to explore the country's interior. The Royal Geographical Society commissioned an expedition led by him in 1855, a journey during which 5,000 miles of the country was mapped. Gregory's respect for the native culture earned him the unofficial title of Protector of the Aborigines.

RAINWORTH
7 miles SW of Ollerton off the A617

🏃 Rainworth Water

Pronounced Renoth locally, this is a mining village whose development was solely due to the now closed pits. There are, however, two very different places of interest within the village. **Rainworth Water**, a series of lakes and streams, which attracts walkers, naturalists, and fishermen, is also the site of a bird sanctuary founded by the naturalist Joseph Whitaker.

Rainworth's other claim to fame is its fish and chip shop, which found itself on the front pages of the national newspapers in the early 1980s as the place where the Black Panther was caught. A local shopkeeper had noticed a man loitering in the area and had contacted the police who kept a watch for the suspicious man on the main street of the village. Realising that he was being followed, the suspect began shooting at the police, injuring one, but the customers in the chip shop,

seeing what was going on, apprehended him. Though at the time the police did not know the identity of the gunman, he later turned out to be the notorious Black Panther who was later convicted of murder.

RAVENSHEAD
9 miles SW of Ollerton on the A60

🏛 Pumping Station   ⚒ Rural Craft Centre

Although the name Ravenshead appears in the Domesday Book, the village of Ravenshead is relatively new and dates from 1966 when the three hamlets of Fishpool, Larch Farm and Kighill merged. Situated by the side of the main road is the Bessie Shepherd Stone, which marks the spot where, in 1817, Bessie was murdered as she walked from Mansfield to Papplewick.

Longdale Lane Rural Craft Centre was established in the 1970s and it is the oldest such centre in the country. It's a re-creation of a 19th-century village, complete with flagstones and Victorian street lamps. Behind the decorative, period shop fronts a whole host of professional artists can be seen making both traditional and modern objects. **Papplewick Pumping Station** is Britain's finest Victorian water pumping station, superbly restored as a spectacular example of Victorian craftsmanship. Original features include an ornate engine house, an ornamental cooling pond and a boiler house with six Lancashire boilers. Open Sunday afternoons – call 0115 963 2938 for more details.

Mansfield

🏛 Bentinck Monument   🏛 Museum

The second largest town in the county, Mansfield stands at the heart of what were once the great North Nottinghamshire coalfields. That industry has now vanished, but Mansfield still has the atmosphere of an industrial town, although its economy is now based on a broader spread of varying businesses.

The most distinctive structure in Mansfield is undoubtedly the great railway viaduct that sweeps through and above the town, carried by 15 huge arches of rough-hewn stone. Built in 1875, it is one of the largest viaducts to be found in an English town and gives some dignity to a community that suffered badly from thoughtless development in the 1960s.

In the old market place stands the impressive Gothic **Bentinck Monument**. This was erected in 1848 in memory of Lord George Bentinck, the younger son of the Duke of Portland. Bentinck was a long serving Member of Parliament for the town and a great friend of Disraeli. The memorial was raised by public subscription but unfortunately funds ran out before the finishing touch, a statue of Bentinck himself, could be placed in the central space.

Standing just to the northwest of the market place, **Mansfield Museum** concentrates its collections largely on local interest and includes a model of a Roman villa that once stood at nearby Mansfield Woodhouse. The collection spans the centuries from that early occupation right up to more recent times, with pictures and artefacts relating to the industry of the town and surrounding villages. The adjoining art gallery also carries a local theme and features works by artists of the area including the water colourist AS Buxton, who is well-known for his paintings of Mansfield.

Around Mansfield

MANSFIELD WOODHOUSE
2 miles N of Mansfield on the A60

🏛 St Edmund's Church

Originally a settlement within Sherwood Forest, Mansfield Woodhouse is now virtually a suburb of Mansfield, but the core of the village remains remarkably intact and several interesting buildings have survived.

Opposite The Cross, in the heart of the town, stands one of these fine houses, the Georgian Burnaby House. Still retaining many of its original, elegant features, the house was obviously built for a prosperous family and, during the mid 1800s, it was occupied by the Duke of Portland's land agent. On the other side of the road stands a stump, which is all that remains of the Market Cross, erected here after a great fire in 1304. The village stocks stood close by and were once used to detain George Fox, the Quaker Movement founder, after he had preached the gospel to the villagers.

At the bottom of the street is the oldest building in Mansfield Woodhouse, **St Edmund's Church**. Most of the original church was lost, along with the parish records, when fire swept through the village in the early 14th century. The present church was built on the same site though it underwent some severe restoration in the 19th century. Standing not far from the church is a manor house known as Woodhouse Castle because of the battlements that were added to the building in the early 1800s. Dating from the 1600s, this was the home of the Digby family and, in particular, of General Sir John Digby, Sheriff of Nottingham, who distinguished himself during the Civil War.

🎬 stories and anecdotes 🐦 famous people 🎨 art and craft ♿ entertainment and sport 🚶 walks

Another building of note is the essentially 18th-century Wolfhunt House found just off the High Street. The unusual name is derived from a local tale that suggests that the land on which the house is built once belonged to a man who was employed to frighten away the wolves in Sherwood Forest by blowing a hunting horn.

SKEGBY
2 miles W of Mansfield off the A6075

Skegby's church had to be rebuilt in the 1870s because of mining subsidence, but some interesting features were salvaged from the old church: some monuments to the Lindley family; a fine east window; and two delightful effigies from the early 1300s showing a Sherwood Forester and his wife. She is dressed in a wimple and long gown; he carries a hunting horn.

The village is lucky in having a particularly fine example of a 14th-century cruck cottage though this was not discovered until restoration work was taking place on the building in the 1950s. The village's pinfold, the place where stray animals were held until their owner claimed them, has also been restored and can be found on the Mansfield road.

TEVERSAL
3 miles W of Mansfield off the B6014

A rural oasis in the heart of this former mining district, Teversal stands on a hill looking across to the lovely Elizabethan Hardwick Hall, which is actually just over the border in Derbyshire. Teversal village is the fictional home of Lady Chatterley and the woodlands of the Hardwick Hall estate were the meeting place for her and gamekeeper Mellors in DH Lawrence's *Lady Chatterley's Lover*.

The village also boasts, according to Pevsner, "one of the most rewarding village churches in the county". It has a Norman door, 12th-century arcades and a 15th-century tower, but eclipsing all these are the wonderful 17th-century fittings, all marvellously intact. A wealth of colourful hatchments, ornate monuments to the Molyneux and Carnavon families, Lords of the Manor, and original box pews all add to the interest. The Carnavons own family pew has embroidered cushions and is set apart from the lowlier seating by four spiral columns, which give it the appearance of a four-poster bed.

SUTTON IN ASHFIELD
2 miles SW of Mansfield on the A38

This once small village expanded over the years as a result of local coal mining and modern development has not been kind. However, a few of the original 17th and 18th-century cottages can be seen near the Church of St Mary Magdalene. The church contains some Norman work on the west wall, 13th-century arcades and a 14th-century spire. A tombstone lying beside the path leading to the porch commemorates a certain Ann Burton who achieved the remarkable feat of dying on the 30th of February 1836.

ANNESLEY WOODHOUSE
5 miles SW of Mansfield on the A608

All that remains of old Annesley is the roofless ruin of what DH Lawrence described as a "mouldering church standing high on a bank by the roadside…black and melancholy above the shrinking head of the traveller". Another great writer also knew the village well. Annesley Hall was the home of Mary Chaworth, a lady for whom Lord Byron formed an early affection. The poet and the beautiful heiress would often walk up to the breezy summit of Diadem Hill, 578ft high and visible for miles around. The liaison was a little odd since Mary had inherited her great fortune from William Chaworth: William had been killed in a duel by Byron's great uncle, the 5th Lord Byron. Perhaps because of this unfortunate event, Mary did not succumb to the poet's charms. Instead she married John Musters, the sporting squire of Colwick Hall near Nottingham. She died there in 1832 as the result of an attack on the Hall by Reform Bill rioters.

NEWSTEAD
5 miles S of Mansfield off the A608

🏛 Abbey

A magnificent 13th-century ruin attached to a Victorian reworking of a Tudor mansion provides one of the county's most historic houses. **Newstead Abbey** was founded by Henry II around 1170 as part of his atonement for the murder of Thomas à Becket, and sold at the Dissolution of the Monasteries to Sir John Byron who destroyed much of the Abbey and converted other buildings into a mansion. The Newstead estate remained in the Byron family for almost 300 years, its last owner being the celebrated poet George, Lord Byron.

He inherited the property from his great-uncle, the 5th Lord Byron, better known as Devil Byron (see previous entry). As mentioned earlier, the 5th Lord had killed an old family friend in a duel and although he was only convicted of manslaughter, he was obliged to pay huge punitive costs. Ostracised by London society, he retreated to Newstead in malevolent mood. To pay his debts he virtually denuded the estate of its great plantations of oaks. And just to spite his son and expected heir, he ordered the slaughter of the deer herd that had grazed the parkland for generations. As it happened, his son died before him and the estate passed to that "brat from Aberdeen", as he referred to his great-nephew who was living there in poverty with his mother.

When the poet arrived at Newstead in 1798, he found that the only room in this huge mansion without a leaking roof was the scullery. The estate was burdened with debts, and so was Byron. He managed to let the estate out for some years, but when he finally took up residence in 1808, he was still hard put to make the house even reasonably habitable. In 1817, he gave up the struggle, sold the estate to an old Harrow schoolmate,

Newstead Abbey

🎞 stories and anecdotes   🕊 famous people   ✐ art and craft   ✐ entertainment and sport   🚶 walks

Colonel Thomas Wildman, for £94,000, removed himself to Italy and never saw Newstead again.

Colonel Wildman spared no expense in refurbishing and extending the dilapidated house, an undertaking that took 12 years to complete. The house and grounds that visitors see today is essentially the creation of Thomas Wildman, but the presiding spirit of the house is undeniably that of the wayward poet.

Over the years, many Byron manuscripts, letters, books, pictures and personal relics have found their way back to the Abbey, and both the house and grounds are beautifully maintained by the present owners, the City of Nottingham, to whom the estate was bequeathed in 1931. The house is open every afternoon from April to September, and the grounds all year round. These include a secret garden; a beautifully carved fountain decorated with fantastic animals; the famous and elaborate memorial to Byron's dog Boatswain, and a large lake where the 5th Lord used to re-enact naval battles.

Byron died from a fever while travelling in Greece supporting the patriot's war of independence against the Turks. His body was returned to England, but his scandalous reputation for womanising made a proposed burial in Westminster Abbey unthinkable. Instead, he was interred at Hucknall, a couple of miles south of Newstead Abbey (see opposite).

LINBY
6 miles S of Mansfield on the B6011

"One of the prettiest villages on the north side of Nottingham," was Pevsner's rather cautious praise of this small village where a stream runs along the main street with its broad grass verges, and enough stone-built

houses to face down the unfortunate sprawl of 1930s red brick houses near the church.

The village is situated on the banks of the River Leen, which, during the late 18th century, was a busy, bustling place with six cotton mills being powered by the water. The mills were strictly functional but George Robinson, their owner, did not want to be outdone by his near neighbours at Newstead Abbey, so he added battlements and other ornate features and thus gave Castle Mill its name. Young apprentices were brought in from as far away as London to work in Castle Mill. Housed in small lodges nearby, the children worked long hours weaving cotton cloth in terrible conditions with minimal food and clothing provided. Brought to work in the mills from a young age (some were no more than 10 years old), many died early. In Linby churchyard the graves of 42 apprentice children bear witness to Robinson's callous pursuit of profit.

When the 5th Lord Byron dammed the River Leen upstream from Linby, in order to create a lake on his estate, he also played havoc with the water supply to the mills. With a reduction in power, Robinson had to find another reliable power source and in 1786 his sons were the first to apply steam power to a cotton mill when they installed a Boulton and Watt engine.

HUCKNALL
7 miles S of Mansfield off the A611

🏛 St Mary Magdalen Church

Hucknall attracts a constant stream of visitors to **St Mary Magdalen Church**, not so much for its 14th-century font or for the 27 attractive stained-glass windows by Kempe, but to gaze at a simple marble slab set in the floor of the chancel. It bears the inscription: BYRON, Born January 22nd, 1788, Died April 19th, 1824.

The inscription is surmounted by a laurel wreath, in classical times the only award to winners in the original Olympic Games. The memorial was presented to the church in 1881 by the King of the Hellenes in appreciation of Byron's support for the Greeks against their imperial masters, the Turks.

Byron died in Greece where his body was embalmed and transported back to England. For several days the body was exhibited at an inn in Nottingham before being buried in the Byron family crypt at Hucknall. Many years later, in 1938, the vicar of Hucknall entered the now closed crypt to challenge a tradition that the poet's body had been removed. He found the lid of the coffin loose and its lead lining cut open. "Very reverently, I raised the lid, and before my eyes lay the embalmed body of Byron in as perfect condition as when it was placed in the coffin 114 years ago…The serene, almost happy expression on his face made a profound impression on me. The feet and ankles were uncovered, and I was able to establish the fact that his lameness had been

that of his right foot." Another occupant of the family vault is Ada, Countess of Lovelace, Byron's only daughter. Ada was a friend and associate of Charles Babbage, inventor of the forerunner of the computer.

Hucknall boasts another famous son. Eric Coates, the son of a local doctor, was born here on 27 August 1886. He displayed musical talent at an early age (he demanded and got his first violin at the age of six), and became the most celebrated viola player of his generation. But Coates became even more famous as a composer of light music – his *Sleepy Lagoon* is immediately recognisable to millions as the signature music of BBC Radios' long-running programme *Desert Island Discs*.

SELSTON
9 miles SW of Mansfield on the B600

Mentioned in the Domesday Book as a place with a church and three acres of meadows, like many other village communities in this western area of Nottinghamshire, Selston was at that time very much a farming community. But beneath the fertile agricultural land lay coal, and leases for coal mining were granted

---

REDGATE'S FARM SHOP

Mansfield Road (A608), Brinsley, nr Eastwood, Nottinghamshire NG16 5AE
Tel: 01773 713403

The Redgate family have farmed here for many years and since 2007 David and Jean have sold produce from the farm at **Redgate's Farm Shop**, which stands on their farm off the A608 Mansfield Road just north of Eastwood. Customers come from many miles around to buy top-quality home-raised meat, including Limousin and Hereford beef, Lleyn and Dorset poll lamb and traditional cuts and joints of pork. The bacon is home-cured, sausages come in several tasty varieties and Jean's super pies are always in demand. The shop also sells game, poultry, eggs and dairy produce, locally grown fruit and vegetables and a selection of jams, preserves and pickles. Redgate's Farm Shop is open from 9 to 5 Tuesday to Saturday.

🎬 stories and anecdotes   🐦 famous people   🎨 art and craft   🌿 entertainment and sport   🚶 walks

as early as 1206. For centuries the coal mining operation remained small-scale, but by the 1850s Selston had taken on many of the aspects of a modern colliery village. The last coal pit in Selston closed in 1956, and more than half a century later, the village still has a lacklustre air to it.

From the churchyard of the partly-Norman Church of St Helen there are some splendid views across the neighbouring Derbyshire hills. The graveyard is the last resting place of Dan Boswell, king of the gypsies. For years newborn gypsy babies were brought to Boswell's gravestone to be baptised and many gypsies made special journeys to the church to pay their respects.

Eastwood

🏛 Heritage Centre

🏛 DH Lawrence Birthplace Museum

"I have always hated it," wrote DH Lawrence of the mining town where he was born in 1885. Reviling the "ugliness of my native village", he wished it could be pulled down "to the last brick". Local people reciprocated his dislike: "He were nowt but a big soft gel," said one of his contemporaries many years later when the gawky lad whose mum insisted he should never go down the pit had become a writer and painter of internatonal repute.

The Lawrence family home, a two-up, two-down, terrace house at 8a Victoria Street is now the **DH Lawrence Birthplace Museum** (see panel opposite). It has been furnished in a late 19th-century style with which the Lawrence family would have been familiar. There are some household items on display that belonged to the family and anyone visiting the museum will see that the

house's front window is larger than others in the same street. This is where Mrs Lawrence displayed children's clothes and other linen items that she made and sold to supplement the fluctuating wages brought home by her miner husband.

In 1887, the Lawrence family moved to a larger, end-of-terrace house in Eastwood, which today is known as the Sons and Lovers Cottage since it featured as the Morels' house, The Bottoms, in Lawrence's novel. This house too is open to the public, though by appointment only, and is also laid out with furnishings and artefacts appropriate to the time. Lawrence's father was a miner at the nearby Brinsley Pit and though the family moved house in Eastwood several times, the Lawrences remained short of money. Young Lawrence attended the local school and was the first Eastwood boy to gain a scholarship to Nottingham High School where he was a pupil until 1901. Lawrence started his working life as a clerk before undertaking a teacher-training course and moving to teach in a school in Croydon. The offices where as a boy DH Lawrence would pick up his father's wages are now the **Durban House Heritage Centre**, which houses a range of exhibitions.

Though Lawrence had already begun writing, his major novels were not written until after 1912, the year he eloped with his former professor's wife and left England. Drawing heavily on the influences of his upbringing in Eastwood, *Sons and Lovers*, first published in 1913, not only describes the countryside around Eastwood, but also portrays many local personalities. The unflattering descriptions of, among others, Lawrence senior, caused a great deal of local resentment, a resentment that astonishingly persists to this day in the village. Lawrence

D.H. Lawrence Birthplace Museum

Durban House Heritage Centre, Mansfield Road,
Eastwood, Nottinghamshire, NG16 3DZ
Tel: 01773 717 353 Fax: 01773 713 509
e-mail: culture@broxtowe.gov.uk
website: www.broxtowe.gov.uk

Whether you want to find out more about the son of a miner, who went on to become the infamous author of *Lady Chatterley's Lover*, or simply want to step back in time to domestic days gone by, then a trip to D.H. Lawrence Heritage is for you. Lawrence spent the first half of his life here in Eastwood, and describing the area in 1929, he wrote, "In this queer jumble of the old England and the new, I came into consciousness." Come and visit our two heritage sites to find out more. Although D.H. Lawrence is known primarily for his novels, such as Sons and Lovers and Women in Love, he also wrote short stories, poems, plays and was an exhibited artist. He was born in Eastwood, a small mining town in the industrial Midlands but against the odds escaped from this life to become one of the great writers of the twentieth century, travelling the world and challenging conventions at every step.

The Birthplace Museum is the house where Lawrence was born in 1885, and the first of the family's four Eastwood homes. Through a guided tour, you will be able to learn about his family life and the type of working class home and mining community that shaped his formative years.

The tour includes the parlour, kitchen and bedrooms as well as the outdoor washhouse. In the adjoining building there is the chance to watch a DVD on Lawrence and visit our exhibition space, which houses several original Lawrence paintings and personal items such as his travelling trunk.

and his wife, Frieda Weekley, returned to England during World War I, but they were unable to settle, and at one point were detained as suspected German spies. They were soon on their travels once again.

In the early 1920s, Lawrence published *Women in Love* and, a few years later, was diagnosed with tuberculosis, the disease from which he died in 1930. It was while he was in Florence, trying unsuccessfully to find a cure for his crippling condition, that Lawrence wrote his most famous novel, *Lady Chatterley's Lover*. First published in 1928, the full text of the controversial story was not printed until 1960 and, even then, it was the subject of a court case that is almost as famous as the book.

A place of pilgrimage for devotees of Lawrence, Eastwood also attracts those with an interest in railway history. It was at the Sun Inn in the Market Place that a group of Iron Masters and Coal Owners gathered on 16 August 1832 to discuss the construction of a railway that would eventually become the mighty Midland Railway. A plaque on the wall of the inn commemorates the seminal meeting.

The railway was formed to compete with

the Erewash Canal, completed in 1779 and effectively put out of business by the 1870s. Almost a century later, following years of neglect, the canal was cleared and made suitable for use by pleasure craft. The towpath was resurfaced and now provides a pleasant and interesting walk.

Around Eastwood

AWSWORTH
1 mile S of Eastwood on the A6096

In order to lay the tracks for the Great Northern Railway line from Derby to Nottingham, a viaduct was needed to carry the railway over the Erewash Canal, the River Erewash and the Nottingham Canal, which all lie close to Awsworth. The resulting construction, built in 1876-1877, is still an impressive sight though the line is now disused. One of only two viaducts in England to be made of wrought iron lattice girders, the Bennerley Viaduct has 16 spans, which are set on pillars 56 feet high.

KIMBERLEY
1 mile S of Eastwood off the A610

Kimberley - the name means a clearing in the forest - was first mentioned in the Domesday Book, and for many centuries it remained a small rural farming hamlet. The village church fell into ruin down the centuries, but with the arrival of industries such as brewing, mining and silk making, and the growth of the population, a new church, Holy Trinity, was built in 1847. A well-known landmark is the War Memorial, which commemorates the villagers who fell in the two World Wars. It is thought to be the only domed war memorial in the country. Most villages in Britain have their little eccentricities, and in Kimberley they

stage pram races on a day in July in support of local charities.

COSSALL
3 miles S of Eastwood off the A6096

Now a conservation area, this village draped across a low hill boasts some attractive buildings, notably the picturesque 17th-century Willoughby almshouses and a farmhouse that includes part of the original home of the Willoughby family. They were a branch of the Willoughbys of Wollaton, a dynasty that was founded by a wealthy 13th-century wool merchant from Nottingham named Ralph Bugge. This rather unfortunate name (which means hobgoblin) was understandably changed by his descendants to the more acceptable Willoughby; a name taken from the village of Willoughby-on-the-Wolds, on the border with Leicestershire, where Ralph owned a fair acreage of land.

Cossall was another of DH Lawrence's haunts and it featured in his novel *The Rainbow* as the village of Cossethay, home of the Brangwen family. The fictional character, William Brangwen, is said to have been based on Alfred Burrows, to whose daughter, Louise, Lawrence was engaged for some time. She duly appears as Ursula Brangwen. The Burrows family lived in a cottage, now marked by a plaque, near the charming village church, which contains a fine marble tomb of the Willoughbys.

Retford

🏛 Bassetlaw Museum

🏛 Percy Laws Memorial Gallery   🗽 Cannon Square

Retford is actually two communities, East and West Retford, set either side of the River Idle. West Retford is the older settlement; its twin grew up during the 1100s as a place where tolls could be collected from travellers making the river crossing. Retford has been a market town since 1246 and markets are still held here every Thursday and Saturday.

Retford received a major economic boost in 1766 when the Great North Road was diverted through the town. That was when the Market Square was redeveloped and some of the elegant Georgian buildings here, and in Grove Street, were erected. The grand and rather chateau-like Town Hall, however, dates from 1868 and replaced the Georgian hall. Outside the Town Hall can be found the Broad Stone, which is probably the base of an old parish boundary cross. Tradition has it that during the times of the plague in Retford, in the mid 16th and mid 17th centuries, coins were placed in a pool of vinegar in the hollow in the top of the stone to prevent the disease from spreading while trading was taking place at the market.

In the northwestern corner of the square is an archway that leads down to the River Idle. Bearing the inscription JP Esquire 1841, the archway once led to the gardens of John Parker who lived in a nearby house, now business premises. A close inspection of the garden wall will reveal that it has a hollow curve. This was in order to funnel hot air along the wall to warm the fruit trees grown in its shelter.

Cannon Square is home to one of Retford's more unusual attractions - a Russian cannon. Dating from 1855 and weighing over two tons, the cannon was captured by British soldiers at Sebastopol and brought to Retford at the end of the Crimean War. The townsfolk paid for its transportation and, in 1859, after arguments raged about its siting, the cannon was finally placed in the square and named the Earl of Aberdeen after the incumbent Prime Minister. During World War II, the cannon was threatened with being melted down to help the war effort and was only saved after a

Retford gentleman bought it and hid it until the war was over.

One of Retford's most infamous visitors was the highwayman Dick Turpin, and several historic inns still stand as a reminder of the romantic days of stage coach travel. Another man who stood and delivered here, though in a more respectable fashion, was John Wesley, who conducted many open-air meetings in East Retford.

While in Retford, it is well worth visiting the **Bassetlaw Museum** in Armcott House, Grove Street. This imposing late 18th-century town house was at one tome or another the home of the Whartons, the woollen drapers; Sir Wharton Armcott, MP for the Borough of East Retford; and the Peglers, local industrialists. It was extensively restored and opened as a museum for the District of Bassetlaw in 1983. The house is noted for its finely executed internal plasterwork and elegant wrought iron staircase, which the restoration has returned to their full Georgian splendour. The museum has a distinct local emphasis, with displays of local archaeology, civic, social and industrial history, and fine and decorative art. Occupying the former service wing of the house, the **Percy Laws Memorial Gallery** has a permanent display of historic Retford civic plate and also hosts short term exhibitions.

Around Retford

MATTERSEY
6 miles N of Retford off the B6045

🏛 Priory

From the eastern end of the village, a rubbly lane leads down to the sparse ruins of the romantically sited **Mattersey Priory**, founded in 1185 for the Gilbertine Order, the only

GOOD HEALTH

73 Carolgate, Retford, Nottinghamshire DN22 6EB
Tel: 01777 706384
e-mail: shop@goodhealthretford.co.uk
website: www.goodhealthretford.co.uk

Established over 30 years ago, Good Health is an independent health store in the Nottinghamshire market town of Retford. The friendly staff are on hand to offer information and advice for customers on all their products.

Good Health has a wide range of seeds, nuts, cereals and dried fruits, together with ranges of herbal teas, Japanese foods, preserves, honey and foods suitable for those who need special diets – gluten, wheat and sugar free. There are plenty of snack bars, seed mixes, healthy biscuits and drinks.

The main vitamin, mineral and herbal supplements stocked are Solgar, Bioforce, Lamberts, Higher Nature and Nature's Aid. Good Health also offers speciality supplements for a wide range of ailments and an Ayuvedic herbal range of remedies and great teas. Homeopathic remedies and creams are available by Helios and Weleda. Terranova is a truly holistic nutritional range of supplements, full of unadulterated superfoods for optimum nutrition.

For face, body and bath, choose from the holistic skincare ranges such as Dr Hauschka and Weleda. Barefoot Botanicals are great for those with sensitive skin conditions. Faith in Nature and Jason are good budget lines of natural, ethical bodycare. There are natural baby care ranges, dental products, make up and hair colours.

Good Health makes it easy for you to look after yourself inside and out as naturally as possible.

THE CRAFT SHOP & WORKSHOPS

Georgian House, 81a Carolgate, Retford, Nottinghamshire DN22 6EH
Tel: 01777 705433
e-mail: dianehemsley@sky.com website: www.the-craft-shop.biz

Diane Hemsley opened **The Craft Shop & Workshops** in September 2008, having converted the former coach house into an emporium of crafting and creativity. The shop stocks an extraordinary range of craft materials - as Diane says: "We opened our doors with only three shelves of wool and due to demand we now have an entire wool room!". Bursting with variety, the wool room is sure to provide inspiration. In addition to the beautiful wools, there are adult and children's knitting patterns, crochet patterns, knitting needles, crochet hooks and knitting kits. You'll find a similar wealth of embroidery materials, papercraft items and there is always a selection of handmade jewellery on display. New creations are constantly added as Diane develops new techniques and designs.

The shop also offers an extensive range of courses ranging from a couple of hours to a 7-week jewellery course. In addition to the large workshop area above the shop, there's also a gallery space which provides a perfect opportunity for upcoming artists and local groups to showcase their art to the public.

🏛 historic building   🏛 museum   🏛 historic site   ♧ scenic attraction   �_____ flora and fauna

monastic order to be established by an Englishman, Roger de Mattersey. When the Priory was founded, it had only six canons. Though the number of priests fluctuated over the years, Mattersey was never a wealthy institution, at the time of the Dissolution of the Monasteries only five canons had to be turned out onto the streets. The original priory buildings at Mattersey were destroyed by fire in 1279, so the remains seen today are of the 14th-century dormitory, refectory and the walls of the Chapel of St Helen. The site is rarely visited by tourists but, with the River Idle flowing nearby, it is a peaceful and picturesque hidden place, well worth seeking out.

GRINGLEY ON THE HILL
7 miles NE of Retford on the A631

Gringley commands some astonishingly wide views over Yorkshire, Lincolnshire, and Nottinghamshire. The best vantage point is Beacon Hill (235ft) on the east side of the village. As the name suggests, Beacon Hill was used as the site for beacon fires designed to warn of impending invasion.

The village Church of St Peter and St Paul dates from the 12th century and one of the church bells is, rather unusually, dated to the time of the Commonwealth. During that period, bells and other decorative items were considered frivolous and were generally dispensed with but, as the parish records show, the people of Gringley did not subscribe to such kill-joy ideas. They also celebrated Christmas in defiance of Puritan edicts forbidding the festival.

NORTH LEVERTON
5 miles E of Retford off the A620

🏚 Windmill 🐾 Adventureland

The correct name for this attractive village is North Leverton with Habblesthorpe, a mouthful that has been hailed in the Guinness Book of Records as the longest multiple place name in England.

The 12th-century village Church of St Martin is reached via a bridge over a stream and, with its 18th-century Dutch gables, looks rather like an import from Holland. So, too, does the splendid **North Leverton Windmill**, the only one in Nottinghamshire still grinding corn. When the mill was built in 1813, it was known as the North Leverton Subscription Mill in acknowledgement of the farmers from four surrounding parishes who subscribed to the cost. Three storeys high, the elegant structure has four sails, one of which was struck by lightning in 1958. Thanks to the efforts of local people, assisted by financial support from the County Council, the mill is now fully operational and visitors can follow the whole milling process in action. If they wish, they can also purchase some of the freshly ground flour.

About three miles south of the village, Sundown Kiddies **Adventureland** is a unique theme park designed especially for the under-10s. There's a pet shop where the animals join in and sing a musical chorus; a Witches' Kitchen where the kids are in charge of the gruesome cuisine; rides; an adventure play area; café and much more.

BABWORTH
1 mile W of Retford on the A620

Babworth has a fine Georgian Hall, a church with Pilgrim Father associations and a spacious park laid out by Humphrey Repton – but virtually no village. Its inhabitants were moved to the village of Ranby, two miles to the west, when the park was 'improved'. The old Great North Road used to pass through

Babworth and it was here, in 1503, that Margaret Tudor was entertained by the Alderman of Retford at a cost of £12.11s (£12.55p). She was on her way to marry James IV of Scotland.

Inside the porch of the small Church of All Saints, with its battlements and pinnacles, a plaque records that the Pilgrim Fathers William Brewster and William Bradford worshipped here before sailing on the Mayflower.

Worksop

🏛 Priory Gatehouse   🏛 Mr Straw's House

🏛 Chesterfield Canal

One of the major attractions of Worksop is the **Priory Gatehouse**, which is best approached from Potter Street where the full glory of the 14th-century building can be seen. Its great niches house large and beautifully carved statues and the immense entrance is rather reminiscent of a cave opening. Originally the portal to a large Augustinian monastery, the gatehouse together with the Church of St Mary and St Cuthbert, is all that remains. There is also a wayside shrine, which makes it a unique ecclesiastical attraction.

The first canal to be built in Nottinghamshire was the **Chesterfield Canal**, which runs from Chesterfield in Derbyshire to the River Trent. Some 46 miles long, work on the canal was begun in 1771 and took six years to complete under the supervision of John Varley, the deputy of the great canal engineer, James Brindley. In the mid 1800s, the canal was taken over by the Sheffield and Lincoln Junction Railway, which in 1863 decided to cease maintaining the waterway and allowed it to run down. The collapse of one of the canal's two tunnels, at Norwood in 1908, hastened its decline by effectively cutting off Chesterfield from the rest of the waterway.

During the canal's heyday, in the early 1800s, it was a busy waterway and many buildings lined its route, particularly through Worksop. Pickford's Depository, spanning the canal in the centre of the town, was typical of this time. The trap doors in the stone archway over the canal were used for the loading and unloading of the 'cuckoos', as the narrowboats on the Chesterfield Canal were called.

The National Trust's **Mr Straw's House** at 7 Blyth Grove, is a must for visitors to the area. The house, together with an endowment of one million pounds, was left to the Trust by William Straw in his will. The Trust's surveyors were surprised to find upon inspection of the Edwardian semi-detached house that they were actually stepping back in time. Inside, everything had remained untouched since the death in 1932 of William Straw senior, a grocer and seed merchant in Worksop. His wife, who died seven years later, neither altered nor added anything. Nor did her two sons, William and Walter, who lived a bachelor existence at the house. Walter, who took on the family business, died in 1976; his brother William in 1990. The parents' bedroom had been closed up and everything left as it was. A 1932 calendar was still hanging on the wall; William Senior's hats were still perched in the hall; his pipes and tobacco pouch lay ready by the fireside.

The Mayflower Trail starts at Scrooby church and guides visitors around the local sites connected with the Pilgrim Fathers, including William Brewster's Manor House at Scrooby and Gainsborough Old Hall, just across the Trent in Lincolnshire.

🏛 historic building   🏛 museum   🏛 historic site   🌿 scenic attraction   🍃 flora and fauna

THE HOUSE OF ELEGANCE

116 Bridge Street, Worksop,
Nottinghamshire S80 1HT
Tel: 01909 530201
website: www.house-of-elegance.co.uk

The **House of Elegance** is one of the largest ladies wear stockists in the area. It stands at the top end of the High Street, opposite Worksop Market, with car parking at the back. Owner Jayne Otter has many years' experience in the retail business and she knows her customers well. She regards customer service as key to the success of her enterprise, and she and her team of experienced sales staff are always ready with advice and assistance – a philosophy that regularly brings clients from as far as 50 miles away. The shop, catering for most ages and sizes mainly from 10 to 20, specialises in bridal, wedding guest and mother-of-the-bride outfits, prom dresses and tiaras, ball gowns and evening and cocktail wear, as well as a wide variety of casual, everyday, cruise and swim wear. Jayne also personally selects a range of hats and fascinators, shoes, handbags, jewellery and other accessories and new product ranges are introduced twice a year. Featured brands usually in stock include Dynasty – prom, cocktail and party dresses and ball gowns; After Six bridesmaids' dresses; Veni Infantino – Italian makers of wedding and occasion wear; wedding outfits by Tia and Whimsy; Unzo shoes; and Frandsen waterproof garments. The House of Elegance is open from 9.15 to 5 (Thursday 10 to 4; closed Sunday).

Around Worksop

CARLTON-IN-LINDRICK
3 miles N of Worksop on the A616

🏛 Old Mill Museum

This village's name has a delightful meaning – the freedmen's enclosure in the lime wood. In fact, it is not one, but two villages, North Carlton and South Carlton, the latter of which is the more ancient. Believed to have been a Saxon settlement, South Carlton, or Carlton Barron as it was also called, is home to the village church. With its massive Saxon tower, the church is quite awe-inspiring as it soars above the village. In Church Lane is the **Old Mill Museum**, housed in a converted 18th-century water mill. On display are some

unusual linen pictures, used by the Victorians as educational material, as well as farming implements and mill machinery.

BLYTH
5 miles NE of Worksop on the A634

⛪ Church of St Mary and St Martin

🌿 Hodsock Priory Gardens

A village on the old Great North Road, Blyth is distinguished by a fine church and, until the 1970s, also boasted a stately home, Blyth Hall. The latter was demolished and the site is now covered by executive homes. But the magnificent **Church of St Mary and St Martin** still stands, its great tower surmounted by eight lofty pinnacles soaring high above the village.

The original church was built around 1100

🎭 stories and anecdotes   🐦 famous people   ✒ art and craft   ✐ entertainment and sport   🚶 walks

HODSOCK PRIORY & GARDENS

Blyth, nr Bawtry,
Nottinghamshire S81 0TY
Tel: 01909 591204
e-mail: gb@hodsockpriory.com
website: www.hodsockpriory.com or website: www.snowdrops.co.uk

As seen on BBC One's The Big Day with Nick Knowles
& Gardeners' World with Alan Titchmarsh

Since 1765, **Hodsock Priory** has been the home of the Buchanan family, and the house is now in the excellent care of the ninth generation, George and Katharine. The major renovation programme they recently undertook has restored all the very best features of the house while adding stunning entertaining space for private events. The wonderful gardens, the style and elegance of the house and the owners' background in hospitality, entertainment, food and wine has given them the perfect qualifications to host weddings, family gatherings, anniversaries, birthdays and corporate functions, from an intimate dinner for six to sit-down meals for up to 120, evening parties for 250 and a major event for up to 500 in a marquee on the Italian Terrace. The archway of the Tudor gatehouse at the end of a mile-long private drive makes an impressive approach to the house, where the day rooms – the panelled hall, the library, the bar, the ante room – combine the grandeur of times past with a relaxing, inviting ambience.

The recently created Pavilion is a beautiful setting for ceremonies and receptions, and the superb gardens, with their lawns, lakes, ancient trees and terraces provide wonderful photographic opportunities for a wedding reception; the Priory is also licensed for civil ceremonies and partnerships. In February thousands of visitors come to see Snowdrops, with millions of snowdrops and many other early flowers, woodland walks, a bonfire, Victorian beehives, a shop, plant sales and a tea room. Hodsock Courtyard opens in 2010 offering B&B and 24 hour conferencing. Hodsock is signposted on the B6045 2 miles southwest of Blyth.

Revitalised!

and much of that Norman building has survived in all its sturdy strength. Pevsner thought that there was nothing like Blyth to get a feeling for early Norman grimness. Opinions differ on that, since the now bare and rough-hewn walls were originally brightly painted. However, most agree that the medieval Gothic additions to the church were eminently successful. The most treasured possession here is a 15th-century wall painting of the Last Judgment, one of the largest and most complete medieval murals in England. Restored in 1987, the mural has been described as "unsophisticated", "probably done by a travelling artist", but it is still mightily impressive.

There are many other buildings of note in the village, including a handsome stable block

🏛 historic building   🖼 museum   🏚 historic site   🏞 scenic attraction   🌿 flora and fauna

and the former rectory, surmounted by a cupola. Among the red brick Georgian houses there are also a number of coaching inns providing a reminder that Blyth was once an important staging post on the Great North Road.

Just to the southwest of the village lies **Hodsock Priory** (see panel opposite) and its beautiful Gardens surrounded by parkland and meadows. Although this would seem to be the perfect setting for a medieval monastery, no priory ever stood here. The present house was built in 1829 in the Tudor style to complement the marvellous 16th-century gatehouse. The gatehouse is approached across an ancient rectangular moat and, within this area, the gardens have been laid out. The southern arm of the moat was made into a small lake around 1880. The Snowdrop Garden and Snowdrop Woodland Walk are open to visitors for four weeks from early February. Hodstock Priory also briefly opens part of the grounds in Bluebell season and hosts occasional open-air theatrical productions.

Between Blyth and the nearby village of Styrrup, to the north, lies the Tournament Field. Dating back to the Middle Ages, the field was one of only five in the country to be granted a royal licence by Richard I.

CRESWELL
3 miles SW of Worksop on the A616

🏛 Creswell Crags

Creswell village is actually in Derbyshire, but its most famous feature lies just inside the Nottinghamshire border. **Creswell Crags** form a dramatic limestone gorge pitted with deep, dark and mysterious caves. Here the bones of prehistoric bison, bears, wolves, woolly rhinos and lions twice the size of their modern descendants have been found. Around 45,000BC, humans took over the caves, where today's visitors can see the only Ice Age cave art in Britain, carved some 13,000 years ago. One piece is a bone fragment engraved with a fine carving of a horse. Sir David Attenborough recently opened the new Creswell Crags complex, where in June 2009 the new museum became the UK's first National Centre for the Ice Age, bringing to life the human (and animal) story of Ice Age Britain. The exhibition spaces house state-of-the-art displays including temporary exhibitions from the British Museum and the Natural History Museum, and the new café has floor-to-ceiling windows that afford panoramic views over the limestone gorge below. Open every day February to October, weekends only November to January (01909 720378).

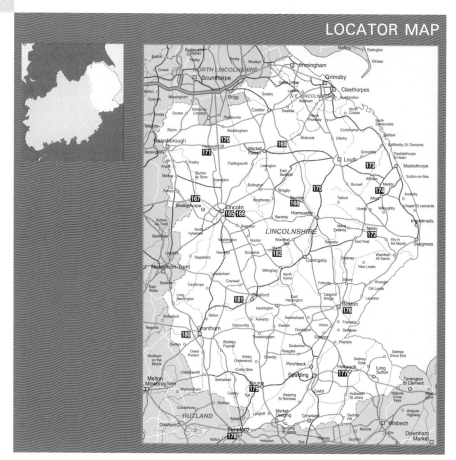

LOCATOR MAP

ADVERTISERS AND PLACES OF INTEREST

🏛 historic building　🏛 museum　🏛 historic site　🍃 scenic attraction　🌿 flora and fauna

7 | Lincolnshire

Known to the Romans as Lindum Colonia, Lincoln stood at the junction of two major Imperial thoroughfares, Fosse Way and Ermine Street. By the time of the Domesday Book, it had grown into a settlement of around 1,000 households. William the Conqueror won few friends here by peremptorily ordering 166 of these houses to be destroyed to make way for an imposing castle. Around the same time, he authorised the building of a cathedral and made Lincoln the ecclesiastical centre of a vast bishopric that extended from the Humber to the Thames.

The city reached its peak of prosperity during the Middle Ages, but when Henry VIII visited in 1541 the town fathers were reduced to begging relief from taxation or "they would be compelled in short time to forsake the city,

to its utter desolation". Henry rejected their plea. When Daniel Defoe passed through Lincoln in the 1770s he found "an ancient, ragged, decayed and still decaying city". Half a century later, another traveller dismissed the historic city as "an overgrown village".

Happily, improvements in roads and canals, and the arrival of the railway in the 1840s, returned the city to prosperity and Lincoln became a major centre for heavy engineering - steam engines, agricultural machinery, excavators, motor cars and other heavy duty items. But you only have to climb the hill to the old town to enter the serenity of the cathedral close, a tranquil enclave lying in the shadow of the noblest and most majestic of all English cathedrals.

The south bank of the River Humber is

Lincolnshire Wolds

indeed Lincolnshire's most industrial area but that is only part of the story. Rural north Lincolnshire is as peaceful and unspoilt as anywhere in the county, with scenery that ranges from the northern tip of the Wolds in the east, to the level plains of the Isle of Axholme in the west. The area also includes the largest town in the county, Grimsby (population 92,000), once one of the busiest fishing ports in the world and now an important centre of the food processing industry. A few miles up-river, and even more imposing, is the colossal Humber Bridge, the largest single span suspension bridge in Europe.

The Lincolnshire Wolds, a sweeping chalk downland stretching up the middle of the county, includes some of the most beautiful and largely undiscovered countryside in England. This is great walking and cycling country, but there are a few hills, too – Nab Hill and Tetford Hill both rise to over 400 feet. Picturesque villages and small towns such as Aby, Bag Enderby, Normanby-on-the-Wold, Somersby, Spilsby and Walesby are well worth exploring, as are the larger towns – Market Rasen on the western edge, Horncastle in the south and Louth in the east.

Stretching from Wainfleet and Skegness in the south, to Cleethorpes and the mouth of the Humber to the north, the Lindsey Coastal Plain runs for about 40 miles, north to south, and extends between five and 10 miles wide, east to west. The Plain offers a good range of animal sanctuaries and nature reserves. The area's other main attraction, the splendid sandy beaches running virtually the whole length of the coast, didn't come into their own until the railways arrived in the mid 1800s. The coastal villages of Skegness, Mablethorpe and Cleethorpes have grown steadily to become popular resorts for East Midlanders, each one offering a wide range of family entertainment.

The Elizabethan writer Michael Drayton must have deterred many of his contemporaries from visiting southeast Lincolnshire by his vivid word picture of the "foggy fens". It was, he wrote, "a land of foul, woosy marsh…with a vast queachy soil and hosts of wallowing waves". It can't have been quite that bad - the Romans farmed extensively here, for example. Since Drayton's day, various drainage schemes, from the 16th century onwards, have reclaimed many thousands of waterlogged acres. Spalding is known around the world for its annual Tulip and Spring Flower Festival when a procession of floats, adorned with millions of tulip heads, progresses through the town.

The Great North Road, now the A1, brought Grantham and Stamford a constant stream of travellers and trade, a traffic whose legacy includes some fine old coaching inns. One visitor during the early 1800s regarded this as "the only gentrified region" of Lincolnshire. Belton House, Belvoir Castle, Grimsthorpe Castle and the breathtaking Elizabethan splendour of Burghley House are four of the grandest stately homes in England.

Lincoln

🏛 Cathedral 🏛 Bishops Old Palace

🏛 Jews House 🏛 Castle 🏛 The Stonebow

🏛 Ellis Mill 🏛 Museum of Lincolnshire Life

🎨 Usher Gallery

Apart from Durham, **Lincoln Cathedral** is the only one in England to occupy a magnificent hilltop location, its towers soaring high above the Lincolnshire lowlands and visible for miles around. William the Conqueror ordered the first cathedral to be built here but that was almost entirely destroyed by an earthquake on 15 April 1185. The rebuilding that followed, under the energetic direction of Bishop Hugh of Avalon, resulted in the creation of one of the country's most inspiring churches. Among its many superb features are the magnificent open nave, stained-glass windows incorporating the 14th-century Bishop's Eye and Dean's Eye, and the glorious Angel Choir, whose carvings include the Lincoln Imp, the unofficial symbol of the city.

The imposing ruins of the **Bishops Old Palace** (English Heritage) in the shadow of the Cathedral, reveal the sumptuous lifestyle of the wealthy medieval bishops whose authority stretched from the Humber to the Thames. Visitors can wander through splendid apartments, banqueting halls and offices, explore the dramatic undercroft, gaze at the views from inside the Roman city walls, relax in the peaceful Contemporary Heritage Garden and see one of Europe's most northerly vineyards.

A good way to explore the city is to follow the Lincoln Heritage Trail, which takes in the city's Magnificent Seven tourist attractions. The cathedral, naturally, takes pride of place, but close by is **Lincoln Castle**, which dates from 1068. Visitors can climb to the ramparts, which include Observatory Tower, to savour some fine views of the city. Interesting features abound, notably the keep, known as Lucy Tower, Cobb Hall, where the public gallows were located, and the Victorian prison whose chapel has separate pews like upright coffins. The building also houses an original version of Magna Carta.

There are some fine Norman buildings on a lesser scale in Steep Hill and the Strait. **Jews House**, which dates from about 1170, is thought to be the oldest domestic building in England to survive intact. Its neighbour is Jews Court, a reminder of the time when there was a thriving Jewish community in Lincoln. Medieval splendour lives on in the black and white half-timbered houses on High Bridge and in the old city Gateways, while the residences in the Cathedral Close and Castle Square are models of Georgian elegance.

The most impressive survival of the old town walls is **The**

Jews House, Lincoln

🎬 stories and anecdotes 🐦 famous people 🎨 art and craft ✒ entertainment and sport 🥾 walks

Stonebowl, which spans the High Street pedestrianised shopping mall. The three-storey building houses the city's Guildhall, its civic insignia, royal charters and other historic artefacts. The Mote Bell on the roof, dated 1371, is still rung to summon the City Fathers to council meetings.

The Collection is a recently opened museum, standing next to the region's premier art gallery, the Usher. The archaeology collection contains over 2,000,000 artefacts from the Iron Age, Roman, Saxon, Viking and Medieval eras. The **Usher Gallery** was built in 1927 in the grounds of the temple Gardens with funds bequeathed by a Lincoln jeweller, James Ward Usher (1845-1921). It is a major centre for the arts, with collections of porcelain, glass, clocks and coins, and a display of memorabilia connected with the Lincolnshire-born Poet Laureate, Alfred Lord Tennyson. The gallery also houses an important collection of works by Peter de Wint and paintings by Turner, Lowry, Piper, Sickert and Ruskin Spear.

The Lawn, originally built in 1820 as a lunatic asylum and set in eight acres of beautiful grounds and gardens, is an elegant porticoed building whose attractions include a tropical conservatory with a display dedicated to the botanist Sir Joseph Banks, an aquarium, a specialist shopping mall and a fully licensed pub and restaurant.

Lincolnshire's largest social history museum is the **Museum of Lincolnshire Life**, which occupies an extensive barracks built for the Royal North Lincoln Militia in 1857. It is now a listed building and houses a fascinating series of displays depicting the commercial, domestic, agricultural, industrial and community aspects of Lincolnshire life. The

---

FORTY FOUR

44 Steep Hill, Lincoln LN2 1LU
Tel: 01522 527516
e-mail: fortyfoursteephill@btinternet.com
website: www.fortyfourshop.co.uk

Forty Four is a friendly independent gift shop, filled with cute, quirky and colourful things that are guaranteed to delight children and the young at heart. Originally trained in textile design, the owner created the shop in 2005, inspired by the shops she knew and loved in London and Brighton. Behind the cheerful turquoise door the shop has a homely feel, with a Victorian fireplace, Medieval beams and vintage furniture. It even has a large section of the Roman Southgate on display.

It is stocked with all sorts of retro homeware, letter sets, journals, notebooks, postcard books, party decorations, cake candles, tote bags, badges, photo frames, rubber stamp sets, melamine cups, great design ideas and much more. The unusual cards, stationery and gift wraps are sourced from all over the UK, Japan, Korea, Scandinavia and the USA, and feature illustrations by well-known artists and local talent. They are stockists of Lady Luck Rules OK, Artbox, Sukie and Rice, as well as the collectable Momiji dolls. Forty Four, located on an atmospheric street close to the Castle and Cathedral, is usually open from 10.30 to 5 Tuesday to Saturday and 11 to 4 Sunday.

🏛 historic building   🏚 museum   🏛 historic site   🔱 scenic attraction   🌱 flora and fauna

BELLES & BEAUX

38 Newport, Lincoln, Lincolnshire LN1 3DF
Tel: 01522 539602
e-mail: enquiries@bellesandbeaux.co.uk
website: www.bellesandbeaux.co.uk

Situated in the heart of historic Lincoln under the gaze of Lincoln Cathedral is the most delightful boutique run by Dorothy Griffiths and her daughter Rhianon Wilton.

Enjoy the warm and friendly advice offered by this family business – whether you are looking for that special mother of the bride outfit, a ball gown to die for or a stylish hat for the races, Belles & Beaux have a fabulous selection of outfits carefully hand picked from fashion designers around the world.

Dorothy has run Belles and Beaux in Lincoln for the past 20 years and has now been joined by her daughter Rhianon who will concentrate on Hattytude! - offering over 300 hats and fascinators to either hire or buy. With exciting new collections by Ispirato, Frank Usher, Chianti, Michaela Louisa, Peter Martin and Peruzzi there is an outfit for you. We stock sizes 8-24.

Belles & Beaux also have a specialized ballgown department with over 200 gowns all of which are available to hire or buy. Whether you are 16 and going to your school prom or 60 and going to a glamorous charity event, our hand picked collection of the very best gowns from Europe and the USA will ensure you look perfect for your event. Visit our shop in Lincoln – you are guaranteed a warm welcome.

Domestic Gallery turns the clock back to the beginning of the 20th century, showing what life was like in a middle-class home; settings include a nursery, bedroom, kitchen, parlour and wash house. The Transport Gallery shows the skills of the wheelwright and coachbuilder in such items as a carrier's cart and a horse-drawn charabier (hearse). It also contains a fully restored 1925 Bullnose Morris and a Lincoln Elk motorcycle. In the Agricultural and Industrial Gallery notable exhibits include Flirt, a World War I tank built by William Foster of Lincoln; a 20-ton steam ploughing engine; a steam traction engine and a number of tractors. Commercial Row features a builder's yard, a printing press, a village post office and several shops. All the above represent just part of the scope of this marvellous museum, where visitors can also pause for refreshment and perhaps a slice of the local speciality, plumbread, in the Hungry Yellowbelly café. (That peculiar name is applied to anyone born in Lincolnshire!)

Ellis Mill is the last survivor of a line of windmills that once ran along the Lincoln Edge, a limestone ridge stretching some 70 miles from Winteringham by the Humber to Stamford on the county's southern border. This four-sailed tower mill dates back to 1798 and is in full working order. For those interested in Lincoln's commercial past, the Lincoln Engineering Society has produced a leaflet detailing an Industrial Heritage Trail that guides visitors to a score of the city's manufacturing companies, past and present.

Lincoln stages several major annual events, including a flower festival in the Cathedral and the Lincolnshire Show at the Showground just north of the city. The Lincoln Waterfront Festival is a family-oriented street arts festival

PHILIPS & SONS IN LIGHTING

Unit 11 Riverside, Allens Business Park, Skellingthorpe
Road, Saxilby, Lincolnshire LN1 2LR
Tel: 01522 704400 Fax: 05601 167687
e-mail: info@philipsandsonsinlighting.com
website: www.philipsandsonsinlighting.com

Philips & Sons in Lighting is one of the largest stockists of old chandeliers and droppers in Europe. They have in stock around 30,000 chandeliers at any one time, with upwards of 3,000 on display in the showrooms. None are new or reproductions, all are genuine old items, in all shapes and sizes, ranging from 18 inches to 20 feet and covering a very wide price range. Items from across the range are perfect for adding a touch of class or luxury to hotel or office reception areas, to shopping centres and prestigious shops, to ballrooms and to family homes from pads to palaces. The firm exports all over the world, and customers near and far can be confident that their purchase is a genuine, beautifully crafted bespoke product.

The staff at Philips & Sons are all expert, experienced craftspeople, and clients can discuss their ideas with them before turning their chandelier dreams into chandelier realities. All the chandeliers are completely and painstakingly renovated, allowing clients to acquire an elegant original without the worry of old, sometimes potentially unsafe electrics (the bulb holders are new and always up to the highest British safety standards). This successful company grows day by day, enabling it to offer an ever wider range of stunning old chandeliers at amazing prices. The firm stocks literally millions of glass and crystal droppers to attach to the chandeliers, along with wall lights and lamps, candle holders and covers, cables, fittings and spares. They also offer a bespoke service from old parts when repairs are needed.

The trade and retail site is located in a rural business park off the A57 on the Lincoln side of Saxilby, a substantial village on the Foss Dyke Navigation Canal. The wheelchair-accessible showrooms are open from 9 to 5 Monday to Friday and at other times by appointment. There's ample riverside parking. For those who can't get to Saxilby the stock can be viewed and orders placed through the excellent, recently updated website.

based around the Brayford Waterfront in the bustling city centre. Each year a free programme combines exciting and innovative acts with well-established favourites such as the World Champion Jet Skiers, street theatre performers and a firework finale.

Around Lincoln

🏛 Lincolnshire Road Transport Museum

Just southeast of the city are the popular open spaces of Hartsholme Country Park and Swanholme Lakes Local Nature Reserve, 200 acres of woodland, lakes and meadows to explore. A little way further south is Whisby Nature Park, set on either side of the Lincoln-Newark railway line and home to great crested grebes, teal and tufted duck. Also on the southern outskirts of the city is the privately owned **Lincolnshire Road Transport Museum** where 100 vintage cars, commercial vehicles and buses span more than 70 years of road transport history. Also on display is a wide variety of old road signs, ticket machines and early bus timetables. Open Monday to Friday noon to 4pm, Sunday 10am to 4pm May to October; Sunday 1pm to 4pm November to April.

DODDINGTON
5 miles W of Lincoln off the B1190

🏠 Doddington Hall

About five miles west of Lincoln, **Doddington Hall**, is a very grand Elizabethan mansion completed in 1600 by the architect Robert Smythson, and standing now exactly as then, with wonderful formal gardens, a gatehouse and a family church. The interior contains a fascinating collection of pictures, textiles, porcelain and furniture

that reflect four centuries of unbroken family occupation.

BASSINGHAM
7 miles SW of Lincoln off the A46

🏠 Auburn

A pleasant little village with houses mostly of local warm red brick; an Elizabethan manor house (private) and, on one of the many little greens, an oak seat carved in the shape of a bull. This striking feature is part of an admirable enterprise masterminded by North Kesteven Arts to enhance both the natural and built-up areas of the District with all kinds of sculpture and art work. These imaginative pieces, many of them serving as public benches, range from the Dorrington Demons, based on a local legend, to the Scopwick Woman whose seat, in the lap of her skirt, has become a kind of letterbox with local people leaving tokens, messages or gifts for others to pick up. A booklet titled *In View*, which gives full details of these fascinating works, is available from TICs.

A couple of miles north of Bassingham, **Aubourn** is a charming Elizabethan and Jacobean manor house set in attractive gardens and notable for a finely carved oak staircase. Nearby, the tower of Aubourn's Victorian church stands alone, all that was left after the church was demolished in 1973 and parishioners reverted to worshipping in the chancel of the old church amidst the clutter of memorials to the Meres and Nevile families.

BARDNEY
10 miles E of Lincoln on the B1190/B1202

🏠 Abbey

The dominating feature of this little town beside the River Witham is the British Sugar Corporation's towering beet processing factory. In medieval times, a more elegant structure distinguished the town, and was just as important to its prosperity. **Bardney Abbey** was famous then because it housed the holy remains of St Oswald, an 8th-century King of Northumbria. Pilgrims flocked here in their thousands. The original Saxon abbey was demolished by Viking raiders in AD870 and its Norman successor fared little better at the Dissolution of the Monasteries. Only the ground plan is now distinguishable. Some fragments from the abbey were incorporated into Bardney's Church of St Lawrence, which is otherwise mostly 15th century. Features of interest here include a tomb slab of Abbot Richard Horncastle, who died in 1508, and two unusual Charity Boards dated 1603 and 1639. These list benefactors of the parish, complete with colour portraits of these generous souls.

Connoisseurs of unusual churches will be well rewarded by a short detour to Southrey, a remote hamlet set beside the River Witham. Built of timber by the parishioners themselves in 1898, St John the Divine is painted brilliant white outside and sky blue within. Resembling some Mission station in the Australian outback, this quaint little church stands on a plinth incorporating gravestones from Bardney Abbey.

MARKET RASEN
14 miles NE of Lincoln off the A46

🐾 Racecourse

This pleasing little market town stands between the great plain that spreads north of Lincoln and the sheltering Wolds to the east. Now happily bypassed, the town still has a market on Tuesdays and throughout the year there are regular National Hunt meetings at

---

BAUMBER PARK

Baumber, nr Horncastle, Lincolnshire LN9 5NE
Tel: 01507 578235 Mobile: 07977 722776
e-mail: mail@baumberpark.com
website: www.baumberpark.com or www.gathmanscottage.co.uk

Baumber Park is a spacious farmhouse of both Georgian and Victorian character, dating back to 1680. Situated in a tranquil location the farmhouse stands proud and elegant, surrounded by colourful gardens and beautiful parkland which is home to Lincoln Red cattle and Lincoln Longwool sheep. Clare Harrison welcomes bed and breakfast guests to Baumber Park and husband Michael runs the adjoining farm. Guest bedrooms (two doubles and a twin) are large with antique furniture and lovely views over extensive gardens and farm. Downstairs is a large guest lounge with open fire, piano and TV and a dining room with a big mahogany table and a collection of Lincolnshire books. Aga-cooked breakfasts use home-grown or locally-sourced produce.

Also on the farm is a thatched and Grade II listed self-catering property, Gathman's Cottage, which sleeps six. Lovingly restored to its original state, the cottage has all modern requirements whilst retaining its great character. Being in the centre of the County and close to the Lincolnshire Wolds, farmhouse and cottage are the perfect places to stay for an activity holiday with golf nearby, a little culture in historic Lincoln or simply relaxing in the peaceful countryside and pottering in interesting market towns.

🏛 historic building   🏛 museum   🏛 historic site   🏞 scenic attraction   🌿 flora and fauna

ATTICA DESIGN

37 Front Street, Tealby, nr Market
Rasen, Lincolnshire LN8 3XU
Tel: 01673 838241
e-mail: info@attica-design.co.uk

When Lisa Spivey drove past this
handsome 18th century ironstone
building she knew that she had found
the new location for her business. What had been Fishers the Butchers
became **Attica Design**, a treasure trove of beautiful things for you, your
home and garden and a source of lovely gifts that are certain to delight.
Since opening here in 2006 Lisa and business partner Sarah have gradually built up the business,
and with the stock constantly changing every visit is sure to reveal new surprises and delights.

Their own hand-poured scented vegetable wax candles are guaranteed best-sellers, and other
items in stock range from local handmade soaps and balms, pottery, scented fabric hearts,
cushions, Garden Trading home and gardenware, Thomas Kent clocks, Terrace and Garden Kew
Pots with locally grown herbs and True Grace home fragrances. There is also a lovely selection of
scarves and jewellery for every occasion and Emma Ball, Liz and Pip and Trumpers World Cards to
accompany the perfect gift. And if you don't find what you want the girls will do their best to find
– or to have it specially made. Lincolnshire producers are very much to the fore, and Lisa and
Sarah are prime movers in the Lincolnshire Living Fayre, an annual event devoted to beautiful and
exclusive rural crafts, showcasing some of the talented craft businesses that supply the shop.
Attica Design is open 9.30 - 3 Wednesday to Friday and 10 - 3 Saturday and Sunday, other times
by appointment.

EAST FARM FARMHOUSE

East Farm, Atterby, Lincolnshire LN8 2BJ
Tel: 01673 818917
e-mail: anneastfarm@hotmail.com
website: www.eastfarm.me.uk

Mick and Ann Drury are the friendly, welcoming hosts at
East Farm Farmhouse, where they rightly take pride in
creating a comfortable, home-from-home feel for their
guests. They took time to get things just right in the two
adjoining properties, investing care, thought and resources
into the creation of the guest accommodation, which
comprises double and twin en suite rooms and a double
with a private bathroom; all have TV with Freeview and a
hot beverage tray.

The day starts with a full English farmhouse breakfast
using the best Lincolnshire produce or a lighter
Continental version, and guests can plan their days in the
comfortable sitting room or enjoy a stroll in the quiet
garden. Guests feel instantly at ease in the relaxed,
serene surroundings of the farm, which lies a short drive
off the A15. Take the Atterby road off the A15 a couple of miles north of the A15/A631 junction.
Go over the first junction and follow the road to the last stone buildings on the right; look for the
stone pillars with lions on top – that's the entrance to the farm.

the **Market Rasen Racecourse**.

Taking its name from the little River Rase, Market Rasen was once described by Charles Dickens as being "the sleepiest town in England". Much of the central part is a conservation area.

GAINSBOROUGH

15 miles NW of Lincoln on the A156

🏠 Old Hall   🏠 All Saints Church

Britain's most inland port, Gainsborough is located at the highest navigable point on the River Trent for seagoing vessels. During the 17th and 18th centuries particularly, the town prospered greatly, and although many of the lofty warehouses lining the river bank have been demolished, enough remain to give some idea of its flourishing past.

The town's most famous building is the enchanting **Gainsborough Old Hall**, one of the most striking architectural gems in the county. The Hall was built in the 1470s by Sir Thomas Burgh, a Yorkist supporter in the Wars of the Roses. Sir Thomas later entertained Richard III in the Great Hall with its vast arched roof. The kitchens also remain virtually unchanged since those days. A century or so later, around 1597, a London merchant, William Hickman, extended the building in Elizabethan style. The Hall is generally considered one of the best preserved medieval manor houses in the country. Today, it is run jointly by Lincolnshire County Council and English Heritage, and is open most days throughout the year.

Gainsborough also boasts an outstanding church. Beautifully set in its own grounds in the centre of the town, **All Saints Church** is

ASTRA ANTIQUES CENTRE

Old RAF Hemswell, nr Caenby Corner,
Lincolnshire DN21 5TL
Tel/Fax: 01427 668312
e-mail: sales@astra-antiques.co.uk
website: www.astra-antiques.co.uk

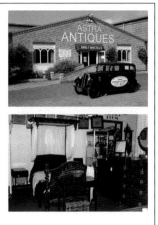

Astra Antiques Centre was opened in 1990 on the extensive site of the former RAF Hemswell, home of the Lancaster bomber. The base was closed in 1967, but many of the old buildings survive, and Astra is located in what was Campbell H Block, next to the Astra Cinema. One of seven antiques centres on the site, Astra is home to more than 100 dealers selling an amazing array of antiques and collectables, from period furniture of the finest craftsmanship to quirky items such as retro plastic lampshades. It is *the* place to come to spend many happy hours browsing and finding something a little bit different to enhance the home, to have fun with or to give as a present.

Categories include architectural and reclamation, fireplaces and ranges, books, maps and atlases, ceramics, glassware, furniture, pictures and prints, jewellery, militaria, toys, games and dolls, lighting and mirrors, rugs, linen and samplers, taxidermy, telephones, silver and pewter, tools, brewery memorabilia, arms and armour, kitchenalia, hunting, shooting and fishing....and a whole lot more. Astra also has perhaps the biggest costume department in the county, with everything from tie pins and braces to 40s clothing and accessories – much in demand for the stage, cinema and TV, parties or just having fun dressing up. The Centre is open from 10 to 5 seven days a week. For those who can't get to the Centre, a full range of what's on display can be viewed and bought online.

🏠 historic building   🏛 museum   🏛 historic site   ⚘ scenic attraction   ⚘ flora and fauna

a magnificent example of a Georgian classical city church. The interior, with its massive columns, box pews and gallery, is richly decorated in gold and turquoise. It is open during daylight hours, tours are available and there's even a cafeteria and gift shop.

Another notable building is Marshall's Britannia Works in Beaumont Street, a proud reminder of Gainsborough's once thriving engineering industry. Built around 1850, the quarter-of-a-mile long frontage bears an impressive figure of Britannia herself.

Gainsborough is believed to have provided material for George Eliot's *The Mill on the Floss*. The now-demolished Ashcroft Mill on the River Trent was the model for Tulliver's mill and the eagre, or tidal bore, that precipitates the tragic climax of the novel is clearly based on the surge that happens at Gainsborough. This usually takes place about 50 minutes after high tide at Grimsby and the bore can be anything between eight feet and 13 feet high.

Scunthorpe

🏛 Appleton Frodingham Railway Preservation Society

🏛 North Lincolnshire Museum

Up until the 1850s, the main activity around Scunthorpe was the maintaining of rabbit warrens - the local breed with their silvery coats being much in demand with furriers. Then a local landowner, Rowland Winn, discovered that the poor local soil lightly covered vast deposits of ironstone. Scunthorpe's rapid rise to becoming a major steel town was under way. Today, the Corus plant produces more than four million tonnes of liquid steel, from a 690-hectare site, which contains 90 miles of railways.

On selected summer weekends, the **Appleby Frodingham Railway Preservation Society**

runs two-hour rail tours around the plant. Pulled by a restored steam locomotive, the fully guided tour takes in all aspects of iron and steel making and includes a glimpse of red hot steel being rolled in the mills.

More of Scunthorpe's industrial and social heritage is on display at the **North Lincolnshire Museum**, with exhibits that include an ironmonger's cottage. The town has also created a Heritage Trail, which takes visitors through three of the parks created by Victorian benefactors - Scunthorpe is proud of its parks and gardens.

Around Scunthorpe

NORMANBY
4 miles N of Scunthorpe off the B1430

🏛 Normanby Hall   🏛 Farming Museum

Normanby Hall was built in 1825 for the Sheffield family and extended in 1906. The interior is decorated in Regency style, and displays include eight rooms that reflect the changes made down the years, as well as two costume galleries. The 300-acre Park has plenty to see and enjoy, including a deer park, duck ponds, an ice house in the middle of the miniature railway circuit, a Victorian laundry, a Victorian walled garden and a new children's play area. The Normanby Hall **Farming Museum** majors on rural life in the age of the heavy horse and, among the exhibits illuminating the workings of a 19th-century country estate are traditional agricultural equipment and transport and country crafts. Near the park gates, some picturesque estate cottages bear witness to the Sheffield family's reputation as good landlords. Rents were low and job security was good, so perhaps the only drawback was that the Sheffield family restricted the number of public houses they would allow on their lands.

A mile or so northwest of the Hall, St Andrew's Church in the agreeable village of Burton-on-Stather contains an impressive range of memorials to the Sheffield family, the oldest of which dates back to the 1300s.

ALKBOROUGH
11 miles N of Scunthorpe off the A1077

Julian's Bower

A scenic walk leads from Burton-upon-Stather to Alkborough, where the medieval maze known as **Julian's Bower** is a perplexing talking point. Not a maze made of hedges, but a pattern cut in the turf, it occupies a beautiful location on a clifftop overlooking the River Trent. The design of the maze is reproduced in the porch of the 11th-century village church, and again in a window high above the altar.

BARTON-UPON-HUMBER
10 miles NE of Scunthorpe off the A15

Baysgarth House   Barton Clay Pits

Water's Edge Country Park   Far Ings

Today, Barton is dominated by the colossal south tower of the Humber Bridge, connecting Lincolnshire with East Yorkshire. This has been a major crossing point for more than 1,000 years. The Domesday Book recorded a ferry here and the community was then the largest town in North Lincolnshire. In the 1770s, Daniel Defoe gave a vivid description of his passage across the Humber "in an open boat in which we had about 15 horses, and ten or 12 cows, mingled with about 17 or 18 passengers, we were about four hours tossing about on the Humber before we could get into the harbour at Hull". (The river at this point is about two-and-a-half miles wide.)

The heart of the town still has some pleasant streets - Fleetgate, Bargate, Beck Hill and Priestgate, all distinguished by mainly Georgian and early Victorian buildings. **Baysgarth House**, now a museum, is an 18th-century mansion with a collection of 18th and 19th-century English and Oriental pottery, a section on country crafts and an industrial museum in the stable block. The surrounding park has a picnic area, play area and various recreational facilities. Once an area of severe industrial contamination, **Water's Edge Country Park** is now home to an impressive number of species – bird, mammal, plant and insect – and its easy paths and tranquil surroundings make it a great place to unwind. Opened in April 2006, it is an environmentally-friendly visitor centre with displays on the wildlife of the Park, a coffee shop, and interactive cameras in nesting boxes (the first in the country).

Just to the north of Barton, on the banks of the Humber, is an observation area for viewing the mighty Humber Bridge. Opened in 1981, this is Europe's longest single-span suspension bridge with an overall length of 2,428 yards. This means that for more than a third of a mile only four concrete pillars, two on each bank, are preserving you from a watery death. From these huge pylons, 510 feet high, gossamer cables of thin-wired steel support a gently curving roadway. Both sets of pylons rise vertically, but because of the curvature of the earth they actually lean away from each other by several inches. The bridge is particularly striking when the vast structure is very occasionally floodlit at night.

Around the bridge are important nature reserves. **Barton Clay Pits** cover a five-mile area along the river bank and offer a haven for wildlife and recreation for sporty humans. **Far**

Humber Bridge

place is crammed with around 100 stalls. A farmers' market is also held on the fourth Saturday of each month, attracting producers of quality local produce and crowds of shoppers. A pedestrianised town centre, combined with ample parking nearby, has made Brigg's markets some of the busiest in North Lincolnshire.

Ings, with hides and waymarked trails, is home to more than 230 species of wild flowers, 50 nesting bird species and hundreds of different sorts of moths.

BRIGG
7 miles E of Scunthorpe on the A10

Brigg Fair

King John was not universally liked, but one of his more popular deeds was the granting of a charter (in 1205) that permitted this modest little town to hold an annual festivity on the fifth day of August. **Brigg Fair**, along with Widdecombe and Scarborough, joined the trio of 'Best Known Fairs in England', its celebrity enhanced by a traditional song (twice recorded by Percy Grainger), and the haunting tone poem, Brigg Fair, composed by Frederick Delius in 1907.

King John's son, Henry III, also showed favour to the town. He granted the loyal burghers of Brigg the right to hold a weekly market on Thursdays, a right they still exercise to the full. Each week, the market

Many visitors to Brigg, including the architecture guru Nikolaus Pevsner, have commented that some of the town's most interesting buildings are its pubs. Pevsner picked out for special mention the Lord Nelson, with its broad Regency bow window, the Dying Gladiator, remarkable for the "gory realism" of its pub sign, and the Black Bull, which boasts "a vigorous Edwardian pub front".

HAXEY
8 miles SW of Scunthorpe on the A161

Haxey Hood Game

Haxey is the site of a nature reserve, but is best known for the **Haxey Hood Game**, launched around 2.30 on the afternoon of Twelfth Night in front of the parish church. Three hundred men divided into four teams compete to push a leather tube or 'hood' into the pub of their team's choice. The game apparently started in the 12th or 13th century when Lady de Mowbray lost her hood and a number of village men scrambled to retrieve it. The strongest man caught the hood but was too shy to hand it back, and was labelled a fool by the lady, while the man who eventually handed it over was declared a lord. The lady suggested that the scene should be re-enacted each year, and gave a plot of land for the purpose. The scrum or 'sway' of men struggle across the fields working the hood towards the appropriate pubs and always staying within the sway - no open running. When the sway reaches the winning pub, the landlord touches the hood to declare the game over, and 'free' drinks paid for by a collection end the day in time-honoured style. Rather an elaborate build-up to a drinking session, but just one of the quaint traditions that make English country life so colourful.

EPWORTH
12 miles SW of Scunthorpe on the A161

🏛 Old Rectory   🏛 St Andrew's Church

This small town, the southern capital of the Isle of Axholme, is a hallowed place for Methodists from all over the world. From 1696 until his death in 1735, the Reverend Samuel Wesley was Rector here. John Wesley was born at the **Old Rectory** on 17 June 1703; his brother Charles on 18 December 1707. Two years later, inflamed by one of the Rector's outspoken sermons, local people set fire to the Rectory. The house was rebuilt incorporating ribs and keels from ships broken up in the nearby River Trent. It still stands today, a charming Queen Anne building. Several of its rooms have been refurnished in period style and some of the brothers' possessions are on display. There are also collections of portraits and prints.

St Andrew's Church, where Samuel

Wesley was minister, is a short walk from the town centre. His table tomb stands near the southeast door and it was from this vantage point that John would address his followers after he had been refused access to the church. Inside, the 12th-century font in which both John and Charles were baptised, can still be seen.

The best way to follow the footsteps of the Wesleys is to join the Wesley Trail, which has information boards placed at various locations connected with the family. A pamphlet giving full details of the Trail is available from various outlets in the town.

SANDTOFT
10 miles W of Scunthorpe off the A161 or Exit 2 of M180

🏛 Trolleybus Museum

On a wartime airfield on the Isle of Axholme, the **Trolleybus Museum** at Sandtoft is home to the world's largest single collection of trolleybuses and motorbuses. Started in 1969 by a small and enthusiastic group of volunteers, the collection includes vehicles dating from 1927 to 1985, including magnificent six-wheeled double-decker trolleybuses and a fascinating one-and-a-half decker from Aachen in Germany.

Skegness

🏛 Church Farm Museum   🐦 Seal Sanctuary

🐦 Gibraltar Point National Nature Reserve

🎞 The Jolly Fisherman

In the early 1800s, when the Tennyson family used to visit Skegness with the future Poet Laureate, Alfred, in tow, it was still a tiny fishing village but already famous for its miles of firm sandy beaches and its 'oh-so-bracing' sea air. As late as 1871, the resident population of Skegness was only 239, but two years later the railway arrived and three years after that the local landowner, the Earl of Scarborough, built a new town to the north of the railway station.

A huge pier, 1,843ft long, was erected. This survived for almost 100 years before a gale on the night of 11 January 1978 left it sadly truncated. Other amenities provided by the Earl of Scarborough for visitors included the Lumley Hotel, St Matthew's Church and a grand promenade. The Jubilee Clock Tower on the seafront was added in 1899 and, in 1908, the town fathers amazed even themselves by a stroke of advertising genius – their adoption of the Jolly Fisherman as the town's mascot.

The **Jolly Fisherman** has an interesting story behind him. In 1908 the Great Northern Railway purchased an oil painting of the plump and prancing fisherman for £12. After adding the famous slogan,

Skegness is so Bracing, they used the painting as a poster to advertise trips from London to Skegness (fare 3s 15p). Almost a century later, the same Jolly Fisherman is still busy promoting Skegness as a holiday resort. There are two statues of him in town, one at the railway station, another in Compass Gardens and, during the summer months, he can also be seen strolling around the town.

Naturally, the town is well-provided with funfairs – Bottons, Fantasy Island, and Butlin's, the latter two of which are actually in the contiguous town of Ingoldmells. It was in 1936 that Billy Butlin opened his very first holiday camp promising A Week's Holiday for a Week's Wage – about £2.50 in those days. The price included accommodation, meals and entertainment, and the holidays were understandably popular with workers – a new law had just guaranteed them a statutory week's leave with pay. Just three years later, World War II erupted and the holiday market imploded. But Billy Butlin still prospered. The government bought his camps to use as army barracks, appointed him Director-General of Hostels and, at the end of the war, sold the camps back to him at a knock-down price. The camp is still operating, now named the Butlin's Family Entertainment Resort, and day-visit tickets are available.

Alongside the obvious attractions of the beach and all the traditional seaside entertainment, Skegness and

Natureland Seal Sanctuary, Skegness

Gibraltar Point Nature Reserve

Distance: *1.9 miles (3.0 kilometres)*

Typical time: *80 mins*

Height gain: *0 metres*

Map: *Explorer 274*

Walk: *www.walkingworld.com ID:1833*

Contributor: *Sam Roebuck*

ACCESS INFORMATION:

The walk starts at the South Car Park, by the Visitor Centre of Gibraltar Point, though it is easy enough to pick up the walk from the North Car Park. Gibraltar Point itself is only accessible by car (or a good cycle track) via Skegness town centre, but is very well signposted and the South Car Park and Visitor Centre are at the very end of the access road.

ADDITIONAL INFORMATION:

The map does not represent the main paths too well, but don't despair - it is all but impossible to get lost. There are many bird hides accessible from this route and it is worth exploring at least one - don't forget your binoculars.

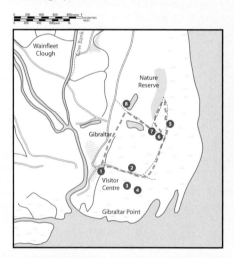

DESCRIPTION:

This is a gentle walk around one of England's best-known nature reserves, around the dunes of Gibraltar Point. Enjoy the peace and tranquillity, disturbed only by birdsong and the gentle rolling of the waves on the miles of quiet beach. An ideal walk for a summer's evening.

FEATURES:

Sea, Toilets, Wildlife, Birds, Gift Shop, Good for Kids, Mostly Flat, Nature Trail, Ancient Monument Description.

WALK DIRECTIONS:

1 | Look for the notice board in the corner of the car park and go through the gate on its right. Turn immediately right over a footbridge.

2 | In 400m, by a notice board and immediately before the wooden walkway continues over the dunes, turn right, keeping the dunes on your left.

3 | In 200m, at the bird observatory, turn left to ascend the steps that run to the right of the building.

4 | The path emerges on the edge of the beach, onto a sandy track that runs northwards with the dunes on the left. Follow this track for half a kilometre. There are many opportunities during this stretch to divert from the path towards the sea to explore the quiet, sandy beach.

5 | The dunes on the left give out as the track bends to the left, leaving you in front of a World War II pillbox. Walk up to the pillbox and turn left. Within 100m, pick up a vague, sandy track, then quickly another track that turns right into the dunes.

6 | At a high and distinctive dune, as the path bends left, climb the steps that ascend the dune, to the viewpoint. Continue over the dune and down the far side.

7 | At the junction of paths, fork right and follow this path for another 400m.

8 | As you reach the bird hide on your right, turn left and follow this path back to the car park.

Ingoldmells have other places of special interest. **Church Farm Museum**, a 1760s farmhouse and Lincolnshire's only open-air museum, is home to a collection of old farm implements and machinery, furnishings from the Edwardian period, re-created village workshops, a paddock of Lincoln Longwool sheep, and a fine example of a Lincolnshire 'mud and stud' thatched cottage brought here from the nearby village of Withern. Craft demonstrations can be viewed on most Sunday afternoons and a programme of special events - sheep shearing, steam threshing and so on - continues throughout the season. Open daily in summer.

Natureland Seal Sanctuary on North Parade provides interest and fun for all the family with its seals and baby seal rescue centre; penguins; aquarium; tropical house with crocodiles, snakes and tarantula; a pets corner and Floral Palace; and a large greenhouse teeming with plant, insect and bird life, including butterflies and flamingoes. Open daily from 10am.

Serious birdwatchers should head south along the coast to **Gibraltar Point National Nature Reserve**, a field station among the salt marshes and dunes with hides, waymarked routes and guided tours.

Around Skegness

WAINFLEET
5 miles SW of Skegness on the A52

🏛 Magdalen College School

Formerly a thriving port, Wainfleet now finds itself several miles from the sea. Narrow roads lead off the market place with its medieval stone cross, making this a place you really have to explore on foot. The most striking building

in the town is the former **Magdalen College School**, built in dark red brick in 1484 for William of Wayneflete, Bishop of Winchester and Lord Chancellor to Henry VI. William founded Magdalen College, Oxford, and later established the college school in the town of his birth. It continued as a school until 1933 but now houses the public library, a small museum, a tearoom and a walled tea garden.

This attractive little town has a Friday market, held in the unspoilt Market Place with its butter cross and Clock Tower, and among the variety of family-run shops there is one that offers an unusual culinary treat: - traditional fish and chips cooked on a coal range.

A curious feature lies about a mile south of the town, on the western side of the A52. Rows and rows of small, rounded mounds are all that remain of an important industry that flourished here from the Iron Age to the 1600s - the extraction of salt from sea water. Throughout these long centuries, salt was an expensive, but absolutely vital, commodity, both as a preservative and a condiment. During the Roman occupation of Britain, part of an Imperial soldier's remuneration was a pouch of salt, his salarium or salary. When the mounds at Wainfleet were excavated in the 1950s they were found to contain salterns - low hearths surrounded by brick in which fires were lit to evaporate pans of sea water and leave behind the precious salt.

BURGH LE MARSH
4 miles W of Skegness on the A158

🚶 Peddars Way   🏛 Gunby Hall

Pronounced Borough, this small town was once the terminus of a Roman road from Lincoln. Although Burgh is now several miles inland, it was from here, centuries ago, that travellers boarded a ferry to cross The Wash

🎬 stories and anecdotes   🦆 famous people   🎨 art and craft   🎭 entertainment and sport   🚶 walks

and join the **Peddars Way** in Norfolk.

About three miles northwest of Burgh, Gunby Hall (National Trust) is reputed to be the setting Tennyson had in mind when he wrote of:

an English home – gray twilight pour'd
On dewy pastures, dewy trees
Softer than sleep – all things in order stored,
A haunt of ancient peace.

Built in 1700 and extended in the 1870s, **Gunby Hall** is a delightful William and Mary house of plum-coloured brick surrounded by sweeping lawns and flower gardens. The Hall has long been associated with the Massingberd family whose portraits, including several by Reynolds, are on display, along with some very fine English furniture. The walled garden is particularly charming and beyond it the Church of St Peter contains some life-size brasses of early Massingberds.

WILLOUGHBY
11 miles NW of Skegness on the B1196

🕊 Captain John Smith

Willoughby is best known as the birthplace of **Captain John Smith**, founder of what is now the State of Virginia in the USA. A farmer's son, Smith was born in the village in 1580 and educated in nearby Louth. He left England as a young man and, after a spell as a mercenary in Europe, set sail with other optimistic colonists for Chesapeake Bay in 1607. A forceful character, Smith was elected Governor of the new settlement but his diplomatic skills proved unequal to the task of pacifying the local Native Americans. They took him captive and were intent on killing him until one of the chieftain's daughters, Pocahontas, interceded and saved his life. Pocahontas later married one of Smith's fellow colonists, John Rolfe, and returned with him to England. Beautiful and intelligent, the dark-skinned Pocahontas was welcomed as an exotic celebrity. King James I graciously allowed her to be presented at his Court but within a few months the lovely Indian princess died "of a fever". Four hundred years later, the romantic tale continues to provide the material for songs, stories, plays and musicals.

Willoughby village celebrates its most famous son with a fine memorial window in the church (a gift from American citizens), and at the Willoughby Arms pub, where a portrait painted on an outside wall may be seen and, inside, accounts of his adventures.

Horncastle

🏛 St Mary's Church

"Few towns of Horncastle's size can have so many Regency bow-windows", noted Nikolaus Pevsner. These attractive features, and the houses that went with them, were a direct result of the town's increased prosperity and the building boom that followed the opening of the Horncastle Navigation Canal in 1802. The town also has an unusual number of pubs; many of them were built to accommodate visitors to the annual Horse Fair, which started some time in the 1200s and continued until 1948. Its modern successor is the Summer Fayre, a popular event that takes place each June.

St Mary's Church has some interesting features, including a brass of Lionel Dymoke, dated 1519. The Dymokes were the hereditary King's Champions who, at the coronation feast of medieval monarchs, challenged anyone who disputed the validity of the king's succession to mortal combat. Above an arch in the Lady Chapel hang 13 scythe blades.

🏛 historic building   📷 museum   🏛 historic site   🍃 scenic attraction   🌿 flora and fauna

These agricultural tools were the only arms available to the local people who took part in the Pilgrimage of Grace of 1536. This was a mostly northern protest against Henry VIII's policy of closing down every monastery in the country. Their rebellion failed. The king graciously pardoned those who had taken part and the rebels returned peacefully to their homes. Once the crisis had been defused, Henry ordered the summary execution of the most prominent leaders and supporters of the uprising.

Around Horncastle

SOMERSBY
7 miles NE of Horncastle off the A158

🏛 Bag Enderby

For pilgrims on the Tennyson trail, a visit to Somersby is essential. The poet's father, Dr George Clayton Tennyson, was Rector of the village and the adjoining parish of **Bag Enderby**. Alfred was born here in 1809 and for most of the first 30 years of his life Somersby Rectory was his home. Many of his poems reflect his delight in the surrounding scenery of the Wolds, Fens and coast. When the family left Somersby in 1837, following the death of Dr Tennyson, Alfred wrote:

We leave the well-beloved place
Where first we gazed upon the sky;
The roofs, that heard our earliest cry,
Will shelter one of stranger race.

The Rectory, now Somersby House (private), still stands, complete with the many additions Dr Tennyson made to accommodate his family of 10 children. He is buried in the graveyard of the small church where he had been minister for more than 20 years and which now contains a fine bust of his famous son. Also in the graveyard, where a simple tombstone marks the Doctor's burial place, stands a remarkably well-preserved medieval cross.

The nearby village of Bag Enderby is associated with another celebrated figure, John Wesley. He preached here on the village green beneath a noble elm tree. The hollow trunk still stands. The church also has a special treasure: a beautifully carved 15th-century font "worth crossing Lincolnshire to see". The carvings include a tender Pietà, a hart licking the leaves of a tree growing from its back, and a seated figure playing what appears to be a lute.

SPILSBY
10 miles E of Horncastle on the A16

🏛 Church of St James

🐴 Northcote Heavy Horses Centre

A pleasant little market town with a population of about 2,000, Spilsby sits near the southern edge of the Wolds. Market day is Monday (with an open air auction as part of the fun), and there's an annual May Day Carnival with dancing round the maypole in the market square. The **Church of St James** has many interesting features, most notably the incredible array of tombs and memorials of the Willoughby family from the 1300s to the early 1600s. Perhaps the most striking of them, a 1580s memorial to the Duchess of Suffolk and Richard Bertie, fills the whole of the original chancel arch. Another monument honours Spilsby's most famous son, the navigator and explorer Captain Sir John Franklin, who lost his life while in charge of the expedition that discovered the North West Passage. A handsome bronze of the great man stands in the square facing the market hall of 1764.

THE CENTREPIECE

39 High Street, Spilsby,
Lincolnshire PE23 5JH
Tel/Fax: 01790 753807
e-mail: thecentrepiece@live.co.uk
website: www.thecentrepiece.com

The Centrepiece is a family run business situated in the centre of Spilsby, an historic market town on the Lincolnshire Wolds. The building, part of which dates back to the 17th century, houses a gift shop and tea room.

The gift shop is packed with a wonderful array of jewellery, ceramics, pewter, original paintings and prints, beauty products, essential oils, cards and gifts for all occasions. It also offers unique services such as passport photos, framing, trophies, engraving and digital developing.

The quaint, old fashioned tea room, with its open fire, serves freshly prepared, home cooked food and delicious home made cakes, scones, pastries and pies. Opening hours 9am - 5pm, Monday to Saturday.

About two miles east of Spilsby, on the B1195, the **Northcote Heavy Horses Centre**, opened in 1988 by Keith and Ruth Sanders, offers a unique hands-on experience with these gentle giants. Visitors have the options of participating in morning or all-day sessions during which they have close contact with the horses, including grooming them if they wish. The afternoon programme is for those who simply want to walk around on their own, explore the museum/vehicle workshop, watch the video display of the Centre's activities, enjoy a half-hour horse dray ride through country lanes, or settle down for tea and scones in the Hen's Nest Tea Room.

OLD BOLINGBROKE

8 miles SE of Horncastle off the A155 or B1195

🏚 Bolingbroke Castle

Old Bolingbroke is the site of **Bolingbroke Castle**, now in the care of English Heritage. Originally built in the reign of William I it later became the property of John of Gaunt whose son, afterwards Henry IV, was born at the castle in 1367. During the Civil War, Bolingbroke Castle was besieged by Parliamentary forces in 1643, fell into disuse soon after and very little now remains.

EAST KIRKBY

8 miles SE of Horncastle on the A155

🏛 Lincolnshire Aviation Heritage Centre

The airfield beside the A155 is the setting for the **Lincolnshire Aviation Heritage Centre**, based in the old control tower of a 1940s Lancaster bomber airfield. Displays include an Avro Lancaster bomber, a Shackleton, cockpits from Canberras, military vehicles and a wartime blast shelter.

🏚 historic building   🏛 museum   🏛 historic site   🍃 scenic attraction   🌿 flora and fauna

Louth

🏛 Church of St James   🏛 Museum   ✏ Art Trail

One of the county's most appealing towns, Louth is set beside the River Lud on the eastern edge of the Wolds in an Area of Outstanding Natural Beauty. Louth can make the unusual boast that it stands in both the eastern and western hemispheres, since the Greenwich Meridian line passes through the centre of the town.

There was a settlement here long before the Romans arrived. By the time of the Domesday Book in 1086, Louth was recorded as a prosperous market town. It still is. There's a cattle market on Thursdays; a general market on Wednesdays (with an open air auction), Fridays and Saturdays; and a Farmers' Market on the last Wednesday of each month.

The town is a pleasure to wander around, its narrow winding streets and alleys crammed with attractive architecture and bearing intriguing names such as Pawnshop Passage. Westgate in particular is distinguished by its Georgian houses and a 16th-century inn. A plaque in nearby Westgate Place marks the house where Tennyson lodged with his grandmother while attending the King Edward VI School. Founded in the 1200s, the school is still operating and among its other famous old boys are Sir John Franklin and Captain John Smith of Pocahontas fame. Broadbank, which now houses the **Louth Museum**, is an attractive little building with some interesting artifacts including some amazing locally-woven carpets that were displayed at the 1867 Paris Exhibition. And Tennyson fans will surely want to visit the shop in the market square that published *Poems by Two Brothers* and is still selling books.

But the town's pre-eminent architectural glory is the vast **Church of St James**, which boasts the tallest spire of any parish church in England. Nearly 300 feet high and built in gleaming Ancaster stone, this masterly example of the mason's art was constructed between 1501 and 1515. The interior is noted for its glorious starburst tower vault, beautifully restored Georgian pine roof, a wonderful collection of Decorated sedilia, and a fascinating array of old chests. On summer afternoons, visitors can climb to the base of the spire for a panoramic view that stretches from the Wolds to the North Sea.

An interesting recent addition to the town's attractions is the **Louth Art Trail** linking commissioned works of art, each of which will have some significant connection with the town's history. The trail incorporates a wide

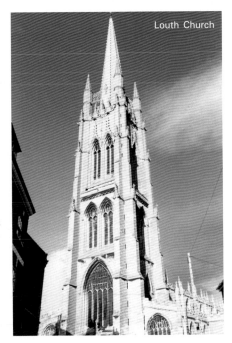

Louth Church

range of styles and media, including sculpture and street furniture. It starts at the Navigation Trust Warehouse on the west side of town and follows the River Lud into the centre and beyond. Call 01507 354364 for details of progress of the Trail. The Lud and the Louth Navigation Canal have both made important contributions to the town's prosperity, although the Lud has also brought disaster. In 1920 a flash flood destroyed hundreds of homes and killed 23 people. A plaque on the side of the town watermill shows how high the river rose during that disastrous inundation. Another Art Trail commission is based on the theme of the Greenwich Meridian, and there's a further sculpture located in Hubbards Hills, a picturesque public park lying in a 125ft-deep glacial valley to the west of the town.

Around Louth

LUDBOROUGH
6 miles N of Louth on the A16

🏛 Lincolnshire Wolds Railway

The only standard gauge steam railway in the county, the **Lincolnshire Wolds Railway** is a noble volunteer enterprise with the ambitious aim of extending its present half-mile track to a full 10 miles. The line is part of the original Great Northern Railway, which opened in 1848 and closed in 1980. The old Ludborough station has been restored, visitors can watch ongoing

restoration in the engine shed and, on steaming days, travel along the line. The former ticket office now houses a collection of railway memorabilia; there's a gift shop and a buffet car serving homemade light refreshments. Entrance to the site is free (01507 363881).

MABLETHORPE
13 miles E of Louth on the A52 & A1104

🐾 Seal Sanctuary   🏛 Museum

Mablethorpe is the northernmost and most senior of the three Lincolnshire holiday resorts that almost form a chain along this stretch of fragile coast, which has frequently been threatened by the waves, and whose contours have changed visibly over the years. Much of the original village of Mablethorpe has disappeared into the sea, including the medieval Church of St Peter. In the great North Sea flood of 31 January 1953, seven Mablethorpe residents were drowned.

Long popular with day-trippers and holidaymakers, Mablethorpe offers all that could be asked of a traditional seaside town, and a little more. One of the most popular attractions is the **Seal Sanctuary** at North

Lincolnshire Wolds Railway, Ludborough

🏛 historic building   🏛 museum   🏛 historic site   ⌕ scenic attraction   🐾 flora and fauna

End. This complex has rescued hundreds of injured or orphaned seals since 1974, releasing them after treatment or finding a permanent home here. The sanctuary has rescued many other creatures large and small, from an elephant hawk moth to hobbies, pigeons, barn owls, weasels, foxes and badgers. There are special wildcat and barn owl features, a seal and seabird hospital, and a nature centre with many fascinating displays. The lynx caves are particularly interesting, displaying three-dimensional scenes of Mablethorpe as it was 9,000 and 20,000 years ago, along with prehistoric tools and fossils.

A unique collection is on view at **Ye Olde Curiosity Museum** where Graham and Sue Allen have amassed an astonishing collection of more than 18,000 curios. One of the oddest is an 1890 'fat remover', which looks like a rolling pin with suction pads and was used in massage parlours. The Museum also houses the most complete collection of Pendelfin in the world.

ABY
10 miles SE of Louth on minor roads

🌱 Claythorpe Watermill & Wildfowl Gardens

Claythorpe Watermill & Wildfowl Gardens are a major draw for visitors of all ages to this small village at the tip of the Lincolnshire Wolds. A beautiful 18th century watermill provides the central feature, surrounded by attractive woodlands inhabited by hundreds of waterfowl and other animals. There are peacocks and pheasants, cockerels, wallabies, goats and even a miniature Shetland pony. Built in 1721, the mill is no longer working, but it provides a handsome setting for a restaurant, gift shop and Country Fayre shop. Open daily between March and October, the gardens also have a Bygone Exhibit Area.

ALFORD
12 miles SE of Louth on the A1114

🏠 Manor House 🏠 Windmill
🏠 Church of St Wilfrid 🎭 Alford Festival

Often described as Lincolnshire's Craft Centre, Alford is a flourishing little town with markets that were first established in 1238 still taking place on Tuesdays and Fridays. These are supplemented by a regular Craft Market every Friday throughout the summer.

Small though it is, Alford boasts some outstanding buildings. **Alford Manor House**, built around 1660, claims the distinction of being the largest thatched manor house in England. It's an attractive building with brick gabling and a beautifully maintained thatched roof. It serves now as a folk museum where visitors are invited to step back into the past and take a look at local life through time-warp shops, an old-fashioned veterinary surgery and a Victorian schoolroom. Reaching even further back into the past, the History Room contains a collection of interesting Roman finds and displays from the salt works that once prospered in this part of the county. Another exhibit explores the still-flourishing connections between Alford and the USA.

An even more tangible link with the past is provided by The **Five Sailed Windmill** on the eastern side of the town. It was built by a local millwright, Sam Oxley, in about 1837. Standing a majestic six floors high, it has five sails and four sets of grinding stones. This sturdy old mill came perilously close to total destruction in 1955. Thanks to the efforts of local enthusiasts it is now back in full commercial operation, complete with a vintage oven turning out bakery items with the full flavour that only the old-fashioned

WESTBROOK HOUSE B&B

Gayton-le-Marsh, Alford, Lincolnshire LN13 0NW
Tel: 01507 450624 Mob: 07818 854995
e-mail: info@bestbookwestbrook.co.uk
website: www.bestbookwestbrook.co.uk

Westbrook House, a contemporary home, stands in its own grounds in a tranquil village, just off the A157 and has been welcoming guests for 10 years. The guest bedrooms – two en suite doubles and a twin with a private bathroom – have been carefully designed and thoughtfully equipped to provide high standards of comfort and amenity; furnished mostly in pine, they all have controllable heating, hot drinks tray and radio alarm clock. Breakfast, featuring locally cured bacon, Lincolnshire sausages, free-range eggs and home-grown tomatoes, is served at a large table in the conservatory/dining area, where an optional evening meal (bring your own wine) is also available. Main courses might be local lamb chops with redcurrant wine sauce or salmon with lemon chive butter served with home-grown vegetables.

Guests have the use of a galleried sitting area as well as a patio garden, and the house has plenty of books, magazines, maps and local information. This is a good area for walking and cycling with a number of footpaths and bridleways nearby – bikes and route maps can be borrowed. Miles of sandy beaches are a short drive away in one direction, the beautiful Lincolnshire Wolds in the other, and the interesting old market towns of Alford and Louth are a few minutes' drive away.

COTTAGE NURSERIES

Thoresthorpe, Alford, Lincolnshire LN13 0HX
Tel: 01507 466968 Fax: 01507 463409
e-mail: bill@cottagenurseries.net website: www.cottagenurseries.net

Cottage Nurseries are stocked with well over 1,000 varieties of plants, some not widely available elsewhere and most of them grown on site. Developed from flat, uncultivated land, it has grown over the years into a delightful, well-regarded source of healthy plants, with alpines, perennials and tender plants the main specialities. Visitors are always welcome at this family-run enterprise, but if you can't get along to the nursery the plants, with full descriptions and prices, can be ordered by mail order through the comprehensive website. The nurseries lie on the edge of the Lincolnshire Wolds, a mile east of Alford on the A1104 Mablethorpe road. Opening times are 9 to 5 March to the third week in October, 10 to 3 end October to February. Closed 3 weeks Christmas/New Year.

methods seem able to produce. Other attractions here include a wholefood shop, tearoom and garden.

Alford's handsome medieval **Church of St Wilfrid** dates from the 14th-century and among its treasures are a curiously carved Jacobean pulpit, the marble tomb of the former Manor House residents, (the Christopher family), and an amazing collection of tapestry kneelers. With so many parish churches nowadays locked for most of the time, it's good to know that St Wilfrid's is

THE PADDOCK AT SCAMBLESBY

Old Main Road, Scamblesby, nr Louth,
Lincolnshire LN11 9XG
Tel: 07787 998906
e-mail: steve@thepaddockatscamblesby.co.uk
website: www.thepaddockatscamblesby.co.uk

Steve and Marion Cooney offer 'Bed & Breakfast with a hint of luxury' in their lovely home in a rural location midway between Louth and Horncastle. **The Paddock at Scamblesby** is a quiet, comfortable and very civilised base for business visitors, for walkers, for cyclists and for tourists. The two bedrooms – a double and a twin – are particularly well equipped, with bath and shower en suite, TV/DVD player, wireless internet access, hospitality tray, hairdryer and trouser press along with thoughtful touches such as fresh flowers, fruit and chocolates to welcome guests. A cooked-to-order breakfast is served in the pleasant conservatory overlooking the landscaped garden and the Lincolnshire Wolds beyond. No children under 5; no pets.

open daily from 9am - 4pm. In August, St Wilfrid's hosts a **Flower Festival**, part of the Alford Festival, which began in 1974 and over the years has attracted a growing variety of craftspeople, joined by dancers, singers, poets and actors.

DONINGTON-ON-BAIN

10 miles SW of Louth via A153/A157

🦃 Red Hill Nature Reserve   ⚹ Viking Way

Country roads lead westward into wonderful walking country at Donington-on-Bain, a peaceful Wolds village on the **Viking Way**. This well-trodden route, which was established in 1976 by Lincolnshire County Council, runs 147 miles from the Humber Bridge to Oakham in Rutland and is waymarked by Viking helmet symbols. While in Donington, have a look at the grand old water mill and the 13th-century church. There is a story that it was usual at weddings for old ladies to

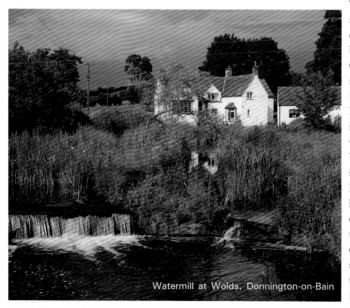
Watermill at Wolds, Donnington-on-Bain

🎬 stories and anecdotes   🐦 famous people   🎨 art and craft   🎭 entertainment and sport   ⚹ walks

throw hassocks at the bride as she walked up the aisle. This boisterous custom was ended in 1780 by the rector after he was hit by a badly aimed hassock!

To the east of Donington and south of Goulceby is the celebrated **Red Hill Nature Reserve**. The hill itself is an outcrop bearing a vein of spectacular red chalk that is rich in fossil finds. The small reserve is home to several species of butterflies and moths, the meadow pipit, common lizard and grass snake. From the clifftop there are some wonderful views across the Wolds. The hill also provides the setting for a Good Friday procession when the vicar of Asterby and three parishioners carrying crosses climb the steep lane. The three crosses are erected above a chalk pit and a short service takes place with music provided by the Horncastle Brass band.

Grimsby

🏛 Dock Tower 🏛 Fishing Heritage Centre

🏛 The Time Trap 🌿 People's Park

🏃 Freshney Park Way

According to tradition, it was a Dane called Grim who founded Grimsby. He had been ordered to drown the young Prince Havelock after the boy's father had been killed in battle. Grim could not bring himself to murder the child so he set sail for England. After a tempestuous crossing of the North Sea, Grim and the boy arrived at the Humber estuary where he used the timbers of their boat to build a house on the shore. They lived by selling fish and salt, thus establishing the foundations of an industry for which Grimsby would become known the world over.

But until 1848, Grimsby didn't even rank among Lincolnshire's 10 largest towns. That was the year the railway arrived, making it possible for fish to be swiftly transported to major centres of population inland. Only four years later, the town's most famous landmark, the elegant, Italianate **Dock Tower**, was built, soaring more than 300 feet above the busy docks. The Tower now enjoys Grade I listed building status, ranking it alongside such national treasures as Buckingham Palace and Chatsworth House. The tower's original function was purely utilitarian, the storage of 33,000 gallons of water to operate the hydraulic system that worked the lock gates. But shortly after it was built in 1852 it was discovered that water in a pressurised tube worked just as well so the tower became redundant. On open days, visitors can undertake the gruelling climb up the inside of the tower to enjoy the breathtaking views from the top.

The Tower stands beside Alexandra Dock, which enjoyed its heyday during the 1950s when Grimsby was the world's largest fishing port. The story of those boom days is told in vivid detail in the **Fishing Heritage Centre** in Alexandra Dock, where visitors are challenged to navigate the icy waters of the Arctic, experience freezing winds, black ice, and lashing rain as the trawler decks, literally, heave and moan beneath your feet. As well as re-creating the deep-sea fishing industry at the height of its importance, the Centre also explores the social setting of that period, with reconstructions of the twisting back streets and alleys of 1950s' Grimsby. **The Time Trap**, housed deep in old prison cells of the Town Hall, shows the seamier side of life on dry land and has proved a very popular annexe to the Heritage Centre. Visitors pass through dark, twisting

🏛 historic building 🏛 museum 🏛 historic site 🌾 scenic attraction 🍃 flora and fauna

corridors, explore mysterious nooks and crannies, discovering en route some unexpected facets of the town. The Town Hall itself, built in 1863, is a dignified building whose frontage has a series of busts depicting Queen Victoria, Prince Albert, local man John Whitgift (later Archbishop of Canterbury), Edward III (who granted the land around here to the Freemen of Grimsby), the Earl of Yarborough, (local landowner and High Steward of the borough at that time), and the historian Gervase Holles who was Mayor of Grimsby in 1640.

Many Victorian buildings were destroyed during World War II, but a surviving legacy from that era is the **People's Park** where the facilities include a heart-shaped lake, children's play area, bowling greens, croquet lawn, ornamental gardens and plenty of open space. The Floral Hall is vibrant with colour all year round and houses both tropical and temperate species, and a large variety of house and garden plants, shrubs and conifers are on sale. Away from the centre, by the banks of the River Freshney, is **Freshney Park Way**, 300 acres of open space that attracts walkers, cyclists, anglers and birdwatchers as well as picnickers.

Around Grimsby

IMMINGHAM
7 miles NW of Grimsby off the A180

🏛 Pilgrim Father Monument　📷 Museum

A small village until the early 1900s, Immingham's breakthrough came when a new port on the south bank of the Humber was proposed. Grimsby naturally thought that the honour should be hers, but consultants favoured Immingham because the deep water

channel of the river runs close to the shore here. The new Docks were opened by King George V in 1912, and rapidly grew in importance, especially when the Great Central Railway switched its passenger liner service from Grimsby. The Docks expanded yet further when the Humber was dredged in the late 1960s to accommodate the new generation of giant tankers and a huge refinery now stands to the west of the town. Not promising country for tourists, but the heart of the old village has survived with St Andrew's Church at its centre.

The **Immingham Museum** traces the links between the Docks and the railways and there is also an exhibit about the group of Puritans who, in 1607, set sail from Immingham to the New England. A memorial to this event, the **Pilgrim Father Monument**, was erected by the Anglo-American Society in 1925. It originally stood near the point of embarkation, but is now located near the church. Most of the 20ft-high column is made from local granite, but near the top is a block hewn from Plymouth Rock in New England where these religious refugees first landed.

CLEETHORPES
1 mile S of Grimsby on the A180

🏛 Ross Castle　📷 Cleethorpes Coast Light Railway
📷 Humber Estuary Discovery Centre

One of Cleethorpes' claims to fame is that it stands on zero longitude, ie on the Greenwich Meridian line. A signpost on the coastal path marks the Meridian line and points the way to London, the North Pole and other prominent places, an essential snap for the family album.

Just south of Grimsby and almost merged with it, Cleethorpes developed from a little village into a holiday resort when the railway line was built in the 1860s. The Manchester, Sheffield & Lincolnshire Railway Company developed much of the town and also built the splendid promenade, a mile long and 65ft wide, below the cliff. Above the promenade they built the sham ruin known as **Ross Castle**, named after the railway's general secretary, Edward Ross. Swathed in ivy, the folly marked the highest point of the cliffs, which the promenade now protects from erosion.

The railway company also funded the construction of a pier. This was opened on August Bank Holiday Monday 1873, when nearly 3,000 people paid the then princely sum of sixpence (2½p) for admission. The toll was reduced the next day to a much more reasonable penny (½p), and it is recorded that in the first five weeks 37,000 people visited. The pier, like many others, was breached during World War II as a defence measure to discourage enemy landings, and it was never restored to its full length. The pier now measures 355ft compared to its original 1,200ft, but the Edwardian pavilion of 1906 is still in place and is currently the largest nightclub in the area.

The town also boasts the last surviving seaside steam railway, the **Cleethorpes Coast Light Railway**. This narrow-gauge steam railway runs along the foreshore and lakeside every day from Easter to September, and on weekends throughout the year, from Kingsway Station to North Sea Lane Station at the mouth of Buck Beck. A recent addition to the town's attractions is the **Cleethorpes Humber Estuary Discovery Centre**. Here visitors can become time travellers, discover extinct creatures and submerged forests, and work off their aggression by participating in a

Viking raid. The Lincolnshire clockmaker, John Harrison, who solved the problem of finding longitude, is celebrated in one of the many exhibits and the complex also offers refreshments in the Boaters Tea Room.

NORTH SOMERCOTES
12 miles SE of Grimsby off the A1031

🌱 Donna Nook Nature Reserve

Olney's Shrove Tuesday pancake races may be better known, but those at North Somercotes are equally popular. Contestants run the length of this straggling village tossing their pancakes as they go. There are separate contests for adults and children.

To the east of the village is the **Donna Nook Nature Reserve**, which stretches six miles south along the coast to Saltfleet. In summer it's a favoured nesting site for many species of birds, among them dunnock, little grebe and meadow pipits. Large colonies of Brent geese, dunlin and other waders are attracted to the mudflats, while common and grey seals pup on the sandflats. As well as marram grass and sea buckthorn, the dunes also provide a support for the much rarer pyramidal orchids.

CAISTOR
10 miles SW of Grimsby on the A46

🏛 Church of St Peter & St Paul   🏛 Pelham's Pillar

Caistor's market place stands on the plain, looking across corn fields to the distant towers of Lincoln Cathedral; but its narrow streets wind their way up the western slopes of the Wolds. Caistor's name makes it clear that this agreeable little market town did indeed start life as a small Roman camp. Just a few hard-to-find fragments of the once massive walls remain. However, it's known that the camp measured just 300 yards by 100 yards and that the present

Church of St Peter & St Paul stands at the exact centre of the Roman enclosure. The church, whose oldest part is the Anglo-Saxon tower, contains a curiosity kept in a glass case. This is the famous Gad Whip, which until 1847 was "cracked over the head of the vicar on Palm Sunday by a man from Broughton in payment for certain parcels of land". Another version of the tradition claims that the whip, which had a purse containing two shillings tied to it, was simply waved over the head of the clergyman while the latter read the second lesson. Either way, Victorian opinion regarded the performance as not consistent with ecclesiastical decorum and it was suppressed.

A mile or so north of the town, **Pelham's Pillar** commemorates the planting of the surrounding woods by Charles Pelham, Earl of Yarborough. Between 1787 and 1828, the earl planted 12,552,700 trees – at least that is what the inscription claims. The lofty tower cost a staggering £2,395 to build and when it was completed in 1849, no less a personage than Prince Albert came to view it. The tower is locked, but if you want to climb up inside a key can be obtained within reasonable hours from the Keeper's Cottage, Pillar Lodge.

The 147-mile long Viking Way passes through Caistor and about five miles south of the town climbs to Normanby-on-the-Wold, the highest village in Lincolnshire. The path continues through Walesby, where All Saints Church is known as the Ramblers' Church because of its stained-glass window depicting Christ with ramblers and cyclists, and on to the delightful village of Tealby.

Boston

🏛 Boston Stump 🏛 Guildhall 🏛 Windmill

An important inland port on the River Witham, Boston's fortunes reached their peak during the Middle Ages when the town was second only to London in the amount of taxes it paid. Today, it's a prosperous market town of around 37,000 inhabitants and the administrative centre for the region. The market, more than 450 years old and the largest open air market in Lincolnshire, takes place every Wednesday and Saturday.

The town's most famous landmark is St Botolph's Church, much better known as the **Boston Stump**. 'Stump' is a real misnomer since the tower soars 272ft into the sky and is visible for 30 miles or more from land and sea. Building of the tower began around 1425 and was not completed for 100 years. The body of the church is older still - it dates back to 1309 and is built mainly in the graceful Decorated style of architecture. St Botolph's is the largest parish church in England (20,070 square feet in all) and its spacious interior is wonderfully light and airy. The church is noted for its abundance of often bizarre medieval carvings in wood and stone - a bear playing an organ, a man lassooing a lion, a fox in a bishop's cope taking a jug of water from a baboon.

One of Boston's most striking secular buildings is the 15th-century **Guildhall**, which for 300 years served as the Town Hall; it has recently re-opened after major refurbishment. Another impressive building is the **Maud Foster Windmill** (1819), the tallest working windmill in Britain and unusual in having five sails, or 'sweeps'. Visitors can climb to the top of the mill, see the machinery and millstones in action, and enjoy some fine views from the outside balcony. There's a tearoom and a Mill Shop that sells the mill's own stone-ground organic flour as well as local books and souvenirs.

If you enjoy seeking out architectural

🎭 stories and anecdotes 🍴 famous people 🎨 art and craft 🎵 entertainment and sport 🚶 walks

TIMOTHY GUY

12 Pen Street, Boston, Lincolnshire PE21 6TJ
Tel: 07855 310422
e-mail: jennybrewster@tiscali.co.uk

Jenny Brewster was a customer at **Timothy Guy** for many years before acquiring this high-class ladies clothes shop in 2005. The range of clothes she sells is aimed mainly at the over-35s, with sizes from 6 to 24 and clothes for any occasion, from casual to evening wear.

The stock on display on shelves and rails includes clothes made by Garella, Tutta Natura, the London-based Italian designer James Lakeland, Hebbeding from the Netherlands and Out of Xile – designed, cut, sewn, knitted, dyed and finished in England. The shop is one of very few European stockists of the Californian Mycra Pac range of lightweight all-weather jackets and coats. Jenny has the invaluable assistance of manageress Val, who has worked at the shop since the early 1980s. They make everyone welcome and are always ready with help and advice, and customers can relax with a cup of tea or coffee in the comfort of a Lloyd Loom chair while perusing their purchases.

Timothy Guy is located in a pleasant shopping street in a conservation area of Boston, with plenty of parking nearby. Shop hours are 9.30 to 5 Monday to Saturday.

---

curiosities, then there's a splendid one in a quiet back street of the town. The frontage of the Freemason's Hall represents a miniature Egyptian temple, complete with columns crowned by papyrus fronds. Half a century earlier, following Napoleon's Egyptian campaign, there had been a spate of such monumental buildings, but Boston's temple, built in the 1860s, presents a very late flowering of the style.

Around Boston

FISHTOFT
3 miles SE of Boston off the A52

This village has just one claim to fame. It was from an obscure creek near here that the Pilgrim Fathers made their first attempt to escape England's oppressive religious laws. A simple monument is inscribed with the words:

Near this place in September 1607
those later known as the Pilgrim Fathers
set sail on their first attempt to find
religious freedom across the seas.

DONINGTON
10 miles SW of Boston on the A52

A small market town, Donington boasts some elegant Georgian buildings, among them the former Grammar School, and a huge church that was bountifully re-endowed in the 14th century when Donington was flourishing as the centre of trade in flax and hemp. Like Deeping St James, the church has its own

---

🏛 historic building　🏛 museum　🏛 historic site　🍃 scenic attraction　🌿 flora and fauna

rather elegant hude, or movable hut. If inclement weather coincided with a burial, the hut would be moved to the graveside. Standing inside the shelter (complete with its own coat hook) the parson could smugly observe the mourners being drenched. Inside the church there are a number of memorials to the Flinders family. Their most famous son, Matthew, was born at Donington in 1774 and later became celebrated for his exploration of the Australian coastline. Returning from Australia to England via the Indian Ocean in a decrepit ship, Flinders put in at Mauritius for repairs. At that time, Mauritius was governed by the French who had watched British expansion in Australasia with alarm. They arrested Flinders as a spy and it was seven long years before they allowed him to continue his journey back to England and his home town of Donington.

Spalding

- 🏛 Gordon Boswell Romany Museum
- 🌷 Flower Parade 🌷 Springfields Festival Gardens
- 🏛 Ayscoughfee Hall Museum & Gardens

This small market town is known around the world for its annual **Flower Parade**, which attracts half a million visitors each year. Established in 1959, the Festival is held in early May when marching bands lead a succession of colourful floats, each adorned with thousands of tulip heads and spring flowers, through the town. The floats are then displayed at **Springfields Festival Gardens** whose 30 landscaped acres include marvellous show gardens, a carp lake, a shopping outlet, a play barn and Fenscape, a unique experience where you can discover how the landscape was created and what life is like for

those living on the Fens.

The two weeks around the Flower Parade coincide with the South Holland Arts Festival featuring open-air concerts, workshops, exhibitions and a host of other activities and performances. The festival is based on the South Holland Centre, a stylish venue that is active throughout the year and also has a café-bar on the first floor overlooking the Market Place.

Spalding itself is an interesting place to stroll around, with Georgian terraces lining the River Welland and many of the buildings revealing Dutch architectural influences. Before the days of mass car ownership, most visitors to the Tulip Festival arrived by excursion trains and a great mesh of sidings stretch to the north of the town. To cross them, the longest iron footbridge in

Butterfly & Wildlife Park, Spalding

Lincolnshire was built. Two, actually, because another equally impressive construction stands south of the station, spanning the main line and a now defunct branch line.

The jewel in Spalding's crown is undoubtedly **Ayscoughfee Hall Museum and Gardens**, a well-preserved medieval mansion standing in attractive gardens by the river and with some venerable yew tree walks. Pronounced Asscuffy, the Hall was built around 1429 for Sir Richard Aldwyn. It later became the home of Maurice Johnson (1688-1755), a member of the Royal Society and a leading figure in the intellectual life of his day. In 1710, he founded the Gentlemen's Society of Spalding, which still flourishes from its headquarters and small museum in Broad Street. Part of the Gentlemen's extensive collection of stuffed birds, dating back to 1800, is on display in Ayscoughfee Hall, which also has a prominent exhibit honouring the explorer and oceanographer Captain Matthew Flinders who has been mentioned earlier under his birthplace, Donington. Other galleries record Spalding's social and economic history.

Located in the lovely grounds of Ayscoughfee Hall is Spalding's War Memorial, which stands at one end of an ornamental pool that in winters past would freeze over. Blocks of ice were hewn from it and stored in the icehouse, which still survives, tucked away in a corner of the garden walls.

Connoisseurs of odd buildings should make their way down a lane off Cowbit Road to a red brick building that belongs to no recognisable school of architecture. Known as the Tower House, it was built in Victorian times but no one has any idea who built it, why or exactly when. It's a bizarre medley of medieval towers and crenellations, a random obelisk, Georgian-style windows and other bits and pieces. One writer described it as being "like a giant Lego construction". It is now a private house, but the exterior can be enjoyed from the lane.

A couple of miles south of Spalding, the **Gordon Boswell Romany Museum** has a colourful collection of Romany Vardos (caravans), carts and harnesses, along with an extensive display of Romany photographs and sketches covering the past 150 years. A slide show talk on the Romany way of life, and conducted tours and carriage rides are available and there's also a fortune-telling tent. Gordon Boswell and his wife Margaret also arrange Romany Days Out in a horse-drawn vardo, a trip that includes a meal cooked over a traditional Romany stick fire. Open Friday, Saturday, Sunday and Bank Holidays from Easter to the end of October (01775 710599).

Around Spalding

PINCHBECK
2 miles N of Spalding on the B1356

🏛 Pinchbeck Engine & Land Drainage Museum

🏛 Spalding Bulb Museum   🌿 Tropical Forest

For an interesting insight into how the South Holland Fen has been transformed by man, a visit to the **Pinchbeck Engine and Land Drainage Museum** is strongly recommended. The star exhibit here is the Pinchbeck Engine, a sturdy monster that was built way back in 1833. Each year for almost 120 years, up until 1952, the 20hp engine lifted an average of three million tons of water from the soggy fens at a rate of 7,500 gallons per minute.

In 1988, the Drainage Board and South Holland Council restored this superb piece of machinery and it now operates regularly. It is the centrepiece of the museum, which is open daily from April to October.

Also in Pinchbeck, in Birchgrove Garden, is the **Spalding Bulb Museum**, which follows the growth of the bulb-growing industry down the years with the aid of tableaux and artefacts, as well as audio-visual and seasonal working demonstrations. A third attraction is **Spalding Tropical Forest**, actually a water garden centre but promising "a tropical paradise full of plants, waterfalls, fountains and streams".

SURFLEET
4 miles N of Spalding off the A16

The River Glen provides an attractive feature in this popular village with its yachts on the water and holiday homes on the banks. Surfleet church has a tower that leans at an alarming angle, more than six feet out of true, the result of subsidence in the boggy ground. The north door is pockmarked with musket shot, a permanent reminder of an unwelcome visit from Cromwell's soldiers during the Civil War.

WESTON
3 miles NE of Spalding on the A151

🏠 St Mary's Church 🏠 Moulton Mill

This small village surrounded by tulip fields boasts a fine church, **St Mary's**, which is notable for having one of the most complete early Gothic interiors in the country. The superb arcades have been compared to those in Lincoln Cathedral and there's a wealth of carving known as Lincolnshire stiff-leaf. The 13th-century font is carved with huge flowers decorating each panel of the bowl, and the

Victorian pulpit has openwork panels somewhat Islamic in style. An eye-catching feature in the rather dimly-lit interior, is the display of colourful kneelers placed on the shelves of the pews.

Just to the southeast of Weston is **Moulton Mill**, the largest surviving windmill in the country. Open to the public after many years of use as a grain store, it offers a unique experience. A visitor centre, gift shop and The Granary tearoom will complete a visit.

HOLBEACH
10 miles E of Spalding on the A151/B1168

Located deep in the heart of the Fens, Holbeach stands at the centre of one of the largest parishes in the country. It extends some 15 miles from end to end and covers 21,000 acres.

Holbeach is a pleasing little town with a market on both Thursday and Saturday and also boasts an impressive church with a lofty spire visible for miles across the flat fields. The curious entrance porch, with its two round towers, is believed to have been 'borrowed' from the now vanished Moulton Castle, a few miles to the west.

When William Cobbett passed through Holbeach on his Rural Rides in the 1840s, he was delighted with the "neat little town, a most beautiful church, fruit trees in abundance and the land dark in colour and as fine in substance as flour". Surprisingly little has changed since William visited.

GEDNEY
13 miles E of Spalding off the A17

🏠 St Mary's Church

Of all the fine churches in this corner of the county, **St Mary's** at Gedney is perhaps the most spectacular. It is supernaturally light

THE WILLOWS

Old Main Road, Fleet Hargate,
Spalding, Lincolnshire PE12 8LL
Tel: 01406 423112
e-mail: sue.willows@btconnect.com

Located in the peaceful village of Fleet Hargate, **The Willows** is a charming B&B with licensed restaurant. Attention to detail is something owner Sue Harman delivers perfectly. The Willows is a quality establishment, run to a very high standard in all aspects. Dating back to the 17th century the building has been upgraded to give a contemporary feel inside and it is light and comfortable throughout. There are five modern and stylish guest en-suite bedrooms, all tastefully decorated and finished to a high standard. There is a king size, 2 double, family and twin/single room. All of the rooms have flat screen televisions with DVD players, tea and coffee making facilities, hairdryers, slippers, dressing gowns and ironing facilities on request. Wireless Internet access allows guests to continue business or keep in touch with family and friends.

Fine dining is what The Willows does best. In the restaurant there are some outstanding dishes to be tried, with the majority being cooked fresh and sourced locally when possible. There is an extensive new lunch menu, served from 12pm – 2.30pm, with goats cheese brochette, turkey, leek and bacon pie, just some of the fantastic dishes listed. On the evening meal there is plenty to choose from with starters including salmon & smoked haddock fishcakes and a vegetarian option of warm nicoise salad on baked mushroom. The main dishes really are delicious, with something for the fussiest of taste buds. Slow roast belly of pork or pan-fried red bream fillet (both served with new potatoes and seasonal vegetables) are among the options. Just reading the dessert menu will make your mouth water with blackberry brulee and chocolate pot among the favourites.

The Willows is an amazing find in the Lincolnshire countryside. It provides the ideal get-away and is close enough to all main roads. There are plenty of places to explore in the surrounding area, including the Fens and the Norfolk countryside. If you are after a good quality home from home experience, The Willows could be just what you are looking for. Popular with walkers and cyclists, there are many leisure activities to have a go at during your stay, including fishing and bird watching. With an airfield nearby, you can even learn to fly. The establishment is just two minutes from the A17, making it an ideal place to visit for travellers. There is ample parking at the rear of the property. Opening hours are Wed - Sat 9 - 4.30pm and Sun 12 - 3pm.

inside, an effect produced by its magnificent clerestory in which the medieval masons reduced the stonework to near-invisibility. The 24 three-light windows drench the interior with light, brilliantly illuminating the carvings and bosses of the roof, and the interesting collection of monuments. The best-known of these is a brass in the south aisle that depicts a lady, who died around 1400, with a puppy crouching in the folds of her gown.

LONG SUTTON
15 miles E of Spalding on B1359

🦋 Butterfly & Wildlife Park   🚶 Peter Scott Walk

🚶 King John's Lost Jewels Trail

Long Sutton is a very appropriate name for this straggling village. St Mary's Church has an unusual two-storeyed porch, the upper floor of which was once used as a school, and a rare, lead-covered spire 160 feet high.

The surrounding area borders The Wash and is a favourite place with walkers and naturalists, especially bird-watchers. One of the most popular routes is the **Peter Scott Walk** – during the 1930s the celebrated naturalist lived in one of the two lighthouses on the River Nene nearby. Another route, **King John's Lost Jewels Trail**, covers 23 miles of quiet country roads and is suitable for cyclists and motorists. It starts at Long Sutton market place and passes Sutton Bridge where the unfortunate king is believed to have lost all his treasure in the marsh. Sutton Bridge itself is notable for the swing bridge over the River Nene. Built in 1897 for the Midland & Great Northern Railway, it is one of very few examples still surviving of a working swing bridge.

The **Butterfly and Wildlife Park** has one of the country's largest walk-through tropical butterfly and bird houses. With its wallaby enclosure, reptiles, birds of prey flying displays and a host of other amenities, it makes the perfect family day out.

CROWLAND
10 miles S of Spalding on the A1073

🏛 Abbey   🏛 Trinity Bridge

It was in AD699 that a young Mercian nobleman named Guthlac became disillusioned with the world and took to a small boat. He rowed off into the Fens until he came to a remote muddy island (which is what the name Crowland means). Here he built himself a hut and a small chapel. Guthlac's reputation as a wise and holy man attracted a host of visitors in search of spiritual guidance. He died in AD714 and shortly afterwards his kinsman, King Ethelbald of Mercia, founded the monastery that became known as **Crowland Abbey**.

The abbey buildings have suffered an unusually troubled history. Nothing but some oak foundations remains of the first abbey - the rest was destroyed by Danish invaders. The monastery was rebuilt in Saxon style in about AD950 when the community began to live according to the rule of St Benedict. That abbey was also destroyed, on this occasion by a great fire in 1091. An earthquake in 1117 interrupted the rebuilding. Some 50 years later, the third abbey was completed, in the Norman style. Parts of this splendid building can still be seen, notably in the dogtooth west arch of the central tower. Another fire caused massive damage in 1143 and the restoration that followed provides most of the substantial ruins that we see today. They present an impressive sight as they loom forbiddingly over this small Fenland village. Happily, the abbey's former north aisle survived and now serves as the parish church.

Crowland is also noted for its extraordinary

Bridge without a River, also known locally as the Three Ways to Nowhere Bridge. When it was built in the 1300s, **Trinity Bridge** provided a dry crossing over the confluence of three small streams. Hence its unique triangular shape. But the streams dried up and the bridge now serves no purpose apart from being extremely decorative. At one end, there's a large seated figure, possibly of Christ and almost certainly pilfered from the West Front of the abbey where a surprising number of these 15th-century statues are still in place.

Stamford

🏛 St Leonard's Priory   🏛 Burghley House

🏛 Museum   🏛 Steam Brewery Museum

Proclaimed as "the finest stone town in England", Stamford was declared the country's first Conservation Area in 1967. Later, "England's most attractive town" (John Betjeman's words), became familiar to millions of TV viewers when its wonderfully unspoilt Georgian streets and squares provided an authentic backdrop for the BBC's dramatisation of George Eliot's *Middlemarch*. Stamford is a thriving little town with a wide variety of small shops (including a goodly number of antiques shops), and a bustling street market on Fridays.

A dubious local legend asserts that Stamford was founded in the 8th century BC by the Trojan king of Britain, Bladud, and continued as a seat of learning until the 14th century AD when it was supplanted by the upstart universities of Oxford and Cambridge. Whatever its past, what gives the present town its enchanting character is the handsome Georgian architecture, evidenced everywhere in private houses and elegant public buildings such as the Town Hall, the Assembly Rooms,

the theatre and the well-known George Hotel, whose gallows sign spans the main street.

Stamford's most ancient ecclesiastical building is **St Leonard's Priory**, founded by the Benedictines in the 11th century and a fine example of Norman architecture with an ornate west front and north side arcade.

Secular buildings of note include Browne's Hospital in Broad Street. It now houses the Museum of Almshouse Life - the ground floor presenting aspects of almshouse life, the upper hosting various exhibitions.

The town is well provided with museums. The **Stamford Museum** includes an exhibit celebrating one of the town's most famous visitors. Daniel Lambert earned a precarious living by exhibiting himself as the world's heaviest man. As an additional source of income he would challenge people to race along a course of his choosing. Daniel would then set off along the corridors of the inn, filling them wall to wall and preventing any challenger from passing. For most of his adult life he weighed well over 50 stones. When he died in the Waggon & Horses Inn at Stamford in 1809 the wall of his bedroom had to be demolished in order to remove his body.

Railway buffs will want to pay a visit to the Stamford East Railway Station. The station was built in 1855-1856 for the branch line of the Great North Railway. Because the land was owned by the Marquess of Exeter, of nearby **Burghley House,** the architect William Hurst was obliged to build in the classical style using the local honey-coloured stone. The result is surely one of the most elegant small stations in the country.

A rather more specialised museum is the **Stamford Steam Brewery Museum**, which has a collection of original 19th-century brewing equipment. The museum is housed in

T. & C. ROBINSON

4 St Marys Street, Stamford, Lincolnshire, PE9 2DE
Tel & Fax: 01780 755378
website: www.countrylifestyleonline.co.uk

T & C Robinson is one of the finest leathergoods shops in
Lincolnshire, owned by the Robinson Family since 1905,
granddaughter Anne Brown presently runs the business
from this beautiful Georgian grade II listed building, dating
back to 1780.

T & C Robinson specialise in leathergoods, county clothing
and gifts and the range of goods in this shop is simply
astounding with something for all ages.

There is an extensive selection of finely crafted leather
handbags, leather luggage and many unique gift ideas, with
top brand names such as Radley, Tula, Gianni Conti and La
Moda. Robinsons also sell country clothing from prestigious
names such as Dubarry, Barbour, Musto, Joules and Weird
Fish. There is also an attractive choice of chic gift ideas such
as small leathergoods, jewellery, cufflinks, traditional games
and childrens toys. You are guaranteed to find something you
like here, even if it's just the alluring smell of fine leather that
draws you in off the street to the perfect purchase. Priding
themselves on quality customer service T & C Robinson is a
must for anyone who visits Stamford.

the malt house and brewery, which was
established by William Burn in 1825 and
continued brewing right up until 1974. It was
restored in the late 1990s and is now open to
the public by prior arrangement.

Two more of Stamford's famous residents
should be mentioned. Buried in the town
cemetery is Sir Malcolm Sargent, the 'pin-up'
conductor of the Henry Wood
Promenade Concerts in the
1960s and 70s. The cross on his
grave is inscribed with the
Promenaders' Prayer. And in St
Martin's Church is the splendid
tomb of William Cecil, 1st Lord
Burghley, who was Elizabeth I's
Chief Secretary of State from
her accession until his death in
1598. Cecil's magnificent
residence, Burghley House, lies a
mile south of the town.

"The largest and grandest
house of the Elizabethan Age",

Burghley House, Stamford

Burghley House presents a dazzling spectacle with its domed towers, walls of cream coloured stone, and acres of windows. Clear glass was still ruinously expensive in the 1560s so Elizabethan grandees like Cecil flaunted their wealth by having windows that stretched almost from floor to ceiling. Burghley House also displays the Elizabethan obsession with symmetry - every tower, dome, pilaster and pinnacle has a corresponding partner.

Contemporaries called Burghley a 'prodigy house', a title shared at that time with only one other stately home in England – Longleat in Wiltshire. Both houses were indeed prodigious in size and in cost. At Burghley, Cecil commissioned the most celebrated interior decorator of the age, Antonio Verrio, to create rooms of unparalleled splendour. In his Heaven Room, Verrio excelled even himself, populating the lofty walls and ceiling with a dynamic gallery of mythological figures. The State rooms house the earliest inventoried collection of Japanese ceramics in the West, rare examples of European porcelain and wood carvings by Grinling Gibbons. Four magnificent state beds stand majestically against fine examples of Continental furniture and important tapestries and textiles.

In the 18th century, Cecil's descendants commissioned the ubiquitous Capability Brown to landscape the 160 acres of parkland surrounding the house. These enchanting grounds are open to visitors and are also home to a large herd of fallow deer which was first established in Cecil's time. Brown also designed the elegant Orangery, which is now a licensed restaurant overlooking rose beds and gardens.

Twelve acres of scrub woodland have been reclaimed and planted with specimen trees and shrubs and now provide a sylvan setting for the Sculpture Garden, featuring a number of dramatic artworks by contemporary sculptors.

Throughout the summer season, Burghley hosts a series of events of which the best known, the Burghley Horse Trials, takes place at the end of August.

Around Stamford

THE DEEPINGS
8 miles E of Stamford off the A16

🏛 Priory Church of St James

There are four Deepings in all and they lie alongside the River Welland, which here forms the county boundary with Cambridgeshire. The largest is Market Deeping, once an important stop on the London to Lincoln coaching route. The triangular town centre has some imposing Georgian buildings, a large antique and craft centre, and a church dating back to 1240.

Today, Deeping St James merges imperceptibly with its larger neighbour. The old village sits on the banks of the Welland where it is controlled by two locks. The **Priory Church of St James** is an impressively large structure and was originally built as a satellite cell of Thorney Abbey. Among its possessions is a hude - a small shelter rather like a sentry box which was designed to keep the Vicar dry when conducting burial services in the rain. Another interesting curiosity is the small square building in the centre of the village. It was originally the Market Cross, but was converted into a lock-up in 1819 to contain village drunks and other troublemakers. Three semi-circular stone seats with chains can still be seen through bars in the doors. Incongruously, the rather elegant little building is topped by a graceless modern street lamp.

BOURNE

10 miles N of Stamford on the A6121

🏛 Heritage Centre   🌳 Bowthorpe Oak

🌳 Bourne Wood

A small, attractive town, Bourne has a fine church, an impressive Town Hall of 1821 with an unusual staircase entry, delightful Memorial Gardens, and a variety of family shops, craft and antiques emporia, as well as modern shopping precincts. A colourful market takes place every Thursday and Saturday.

It was the springs of clear water that enticed the Romans to settle here. Today, the springs flow into St Peter's Pool from which a small stream known as the Bourne Eau runs into the town and Memorial Gardens. Here, willow trees border the crystal clear water, home to fish, wildfowl and small roosting houses. En route, the Bourne Eau passes Baldocks Mill, which functioned between 1800 and the 1920s, and now houses the **Bourne Heritage Centre**.

Notable sons of Bourne include Raymond Mays, who founded the BRM motor company in 1949 and built his cars in a workshop behind Eastgate House. In 1962, with Graham Hill at the wheel, a BRM became the first British car to win a world championship. Charles Frederick Worth, the couturier and founder of the House of Worth, was also born here. A mile west of the town, beside the A151, stands **Bourne Wood**, 400 acres of long-established woodland with an abundant and varied plant and animal life. Once part of the great Forest of Brunswald, it's a great place for walking or cycling, and has some interesting modern sculpture in wood and

CONCEPT

35b North Street, Bourne, Lincolnshire PE10 9AE
Tel: 01778 424878

Situated in the quiet market town of Bourne, Concept is a long established gift shop on North Street nestled a little way down from the town centre. Having been in its current location for the past 21 years, Dena Edis and her friendly staff are always on hand to offer advice on choosing that unique gift.

Concept prides itself on offering quality products at a range of prices in order to suit all budgets. As well as stocking a broad range of gifts for all ages and items for the home, Concept is also the proud stockists of Crabtree and Evelyn toiletries, Kit Heath's silver jewellery, Sia, Parlane, Gisela Graham and many more. Furthermore, Dena is also proud to stock handmade products, many that have been made locally.

For those that have a birthday or special occasion coming up Dena offers a wish list service so individuals can take pleasure in picking out what they would like! Or if you've already found that special present, a gift wrapping service is offered to help you finish off your shopping.

So whether you're after a kaloo soft toy for a newborn baby, a set of handmade star glass champagne flutes for an anniversary, or a Sixtrees photo frame for a friend's birthday, why not pop into Concept and see what they can offer you.

🎭 stories and anecdotes   🦜 famous people   🎨 art and craft   🎭 entertainment and sport   🚶 walks

stone. The waters around Bourne and the Deepings are credited with curative properties and the Blind Well, on the edge of the wood, is reputed to be particularly efficacious in healing eye complaints.

About four miles south of Bourne, near the village of Witham on the Hill, stands the **Bowthorpe Oak**, which is believed to be the largest in terms of its girth than any other tree in Britain. When last measured, the oak was just over 39 feet around. The tree is hollow and it's claimed that on one occasion 39 people stood inside it.

GRIMSTHORPE

5 miles NW of Bourne on the A151

🏛 Castle

Grimsthorpe Castle is definitely two-faced. Seen from the north, it's a stately 18th-century demi-palace. Viewed from the south, it's a homely Tudor dwelling. The Tudor part of the house was built at incredible speed in order to provide a convenient lodging place in Lincolnshire for Henry VIII on his way north to meet James V of Scotland in York. The royal visit to Grimsthorpe Castle duly took place in 1541, but the honour of the royal presence was tarnished by the adultery that allegedly took place here between Henry's fourth wife, Katherine Howard, and an attractive young courtier, Thomas Culpepper. In Tudor times, royal misbehaviour of this nature constituted an act of high treason. The errant queen and her ardent courtier paid a fatal price for their nights of passion at Grimsthorpe Castle. Both were condemned to the executioner's axe.

The imposing Georgian part of Grimsthorpe Castle was built in the early 1700s. The 16th Baron Grimsthorpe had just been elevated by George I to the topmost rank of the peerage as Duke of Ancaster. It was only natural that the new Duke should wish to improve his rather modest ancestral home. He commissioned Sir John Vanbrugh, the celebrated architect of Blenheim Palace and Castle Howard, to completely redesign the building. As it happened, only the north front and the courtyard were completed to Vanbrugh's designs, which is why the castle presents two such different faces.

There's no such confusion about the grounds of Grimsthorpe Castle. These could only be 18th century and were landscaped by who else but Capability Brown. His fee was £105, about £100,000 in our money. In return for this substantial consideration, Brown miraculously transformed the flat fields of south Lincolnshire into an Arcadian landscape of gently rolling hills, complete with an artificial lake and a sham bridge.

Seventeen generations of the Willoughby family have been Lords of the Manor of Grimsthorpe since they first arrived here in 1516. During that time they have borne a bewildering variety of other titles. All have held the Barony, but at different times have also been Earls of Lindsey, Dukes of Ancaster and, later, Earls of Ancaster. The Willoughby genealogy is further complicated by the fact that the Barony is one of the very few peerages in Britain that can descend through the female line. A marriage in 1533 between the 49-year-old Duke of Suffolk and the 14-year-old Margaret Willoughby added yet another title, Duchess of Suffolk, to the Barony's pedigree.

Grantham

🏛 The Conduit   🏛 St Wulfram's Church

🏛 Grantham House   🏛 Methodist Church

🏛 Museum   ♟ Arts Centre

A lively market town set beside the River

Witham. Turn a blind eye to the charmless environs that surround the town from whichever direction you approach and make your way to its centre, which boasts a pleasing core of old buildings. These cluster around the town's famous church, **St Wulfram's**, whose soaring spire, 282 feet high, has been described as "the finest steeple in England". When completed in 1300, it was the loftiest in England and is still the sixth highest. St Wulfram's interior is not quite so inspirational, dominated as it is by uncharacteristically drab Victorian stained glass, but the rare 16th-century chained library of 150 volumes is occasionally open to the public and well worth seeing.

Just across from the church, **Grantham House** in Castlegate is a handsome National Trust property, parts of which date back to around 1380. Additions were made in the 16th and 18th centuries. The house stands in 25 acres of garden and grounds sloping down to the River Witham. For opening arrangements

call the Regional Office on 01909 511041. Also in Castlegate, look out for the only living pub sign in the country. In a lime tree outside the Beehive Inn is a genuine bee hive whose bees produce some 30lb of honey each year. This unique advertisement for the pub has been in place since at least 1830.

After St Wulfram's Church, Grantham's most venerable building is that of the Angel and Royal Hotel in High Street. The attractive 15th-century façade still bears the weather-beaten sculptured heads of Edward III and Queen Philippa over its central archway. King John held his court here and it was in one of the inn's rooms that Richard III signed the death warrant of the 2nd Duke of Buckingham in 1483.

A hundred yards or so from the inn stands an unusual Grantham landmark. **The Conduit** is a miniature tower built by the Corporation in 1597 as the receiving point for the fresh water supply that flowed from springs in the nearby village of Barrowby. At the southern end of the High Street stands a monument to Sir Isaac Newton who was born nearby and educated at the town's King's School. It's an impressive memorial, cast in bronze from a Russian cannon captured during the Crimean War. Behind the statue is the ornate Victorian Guildhall (1869), which now houses the **Guildhall Arts**

Grantham Conduit

Centre. Originally, the building incorporated the town's prison cells but these now serve as a box office for the Arts Centre.

Next to the Conduit, the **Grantham Museum** provides a fascinating in-depth look at local history - social, agricultural, industrial - and has special exhibits devoted to Sir Isaac Newton, and to Margaret Thatcher, the town's most famous daughter. When elevated to the peerage she adopted the title Baroness Thatcher of Kesteven - the local authority area in which Grantham is located. She still retains close links with the town and once declared, "From this town I learned so much and am proud to be one of its citizens."

There is another connection with the former Prime Minister in Finkin Street **Methodist Church**, just off the High Street. Inside this imposing building with its pillared entrance and spacious balcony is a lectern dedicated to Alderman Alfred Roberts, a Methodist preacher, grocer, and father of Margaret Thatcher who worshipped here as a child.

The Thatcher family lived over Alderman Roberts' grocery shop in Broad Street. For a while this became The Premier Restaurant but is currently a natural therapies centre. Margaret Thatcher was Britain's first woman Prime Minister, but Grantham can also boast another distinguished lady who was the first in her profession. Just after World War I, Edith Smith was sworn in as the country's first woman police officer. Edith was reputed to be a no-nonsense lady who made the lives of the town's malefactors a misery.

Before leaving the town, do try to track down the local delicacy, Grantham Gingerbread. It was created in 1740 by a

---

THE CEDARS BED & BREAKFAST

Low Road, Barrowby, nr Grantham,
Lincolnshire NG32 1DL
Tel: 01476 563400
e-mail: pbcbennett@mac.com

Kinga and Peter Bennett offer top-quality Bed & Breakfast accommodation at **The Cedars**, a 17th century Grade II listed property in the attractive conservation area of Barrowby village, situated 2 miles west of Grantham. The hosts and their lovely dogs provide the warmest of welcomes, and some handsome original features add to the quiet, civilised feel that brings guest back to The Cedars year after year. The guest accommodation comprises two spacious but cosy bedrooms with en suite facilities and another with a shared bathroom. Amenities in the rooms include TV, radio and tea/coffee tray, and internet and fax facilities are available. The full English breakfast is definitely worth waking up for, with eggs from the resident free-range chickens and prime Lincolnshire bacon and sausages from the butcher just up the road. A one- or two-course evening meal can be provided by arrangement, with Italian cuisine a speciality, making fine use of home-grown vegetables and local meat and fish. Guests have the use of a quiet sitting room with an open log fire and a pretty walled garden.

🏠 historic building   🏛 museum   🏛 historic site   ⚜ scenic attraction   🌱 flora and fauna

local baker who mistakenly added the wrong ingredient to his gingerbread mix. The unusual result was a white crumbly biscuit, completely unlike the regular dark brown gingerbread. Traditionally, the sweetmeat was baked in walnut-sized balls and, until the 1990s, was always available at Catlin's Bakery and Restaurant whose baker possessed the secret recipe. Sadly, Catlin's Bakery is now closed and Grantham Gingerbread is no longer easy to find.

Around Grantham

BELTON
3 miles N of Grantham on the A607/A153

🏠 Belton House

"An English country-house at its proudest and most serene", **Belton House** stands in 1,000 acres of parkland surrounded by a boundary wall five miles long. Built in 1685 of honey-coloured Ancaster stone and in the then fashionable Anglo-Dutch style, Belton was the home of the Brownlow family for just under 300 years before being given to the National Trust in 1983. The Trust also acquired the important collections of pictures, porcelain, books and furniture accumulated by 12 generations of Brownlows. With its Dutch and Italian gardens, orangery, deer park, woodland adventure playground, indoor activity room and a Discovery Centre with various wildlife-themed activities. Belton provides a satisfying day out for the whole family.

Anyone interested in follies should make a short detour from Belton to the village of Londonthorpe. The original purpose of the "heavily rusticated stone arch with a horse on the top" has long since been forgotten, but it now serves as a bus shelter.

OSBOURNBY
8 miles E of Grantham on the A15

Set in rolling hill country, Ozemby is an attractive village with a pleasing mix of architectural styles from the 16th to the 19th centuries. The large church, unusually for Lincolnshire, has a tower rather than a spire and is also notable for its fine collection of medieval bench ends. Hanging on the wall of the nave are paintings of Moses and Aaron of which Pevsner enquires:

Are they the worst paintings in the county?
Anyway, one cannot help liking them.

ROPSLEY
6 miles E of Grantham off the A52

Described in Elizabethan times as "a considerable village remarkably situated as it were in a bason with hills all around", Ropsley was famous then as the birthplace of Richard Fox (1448-1528), a trusted advisor of Henry VII. Fox was appointed to a succession of bishoprics, two of which, Exeter and Wells, he never visited. But he did spend the last 12 years of his life in Winchester as its bishop. Fox founded Corpus Christi College at Oxford, and also established the King's School in Grantham where Sir Isaac Newton was later educated. The house in which Fox was born still stands on Ropsley High Street.

FOLKINGHAM
8 miles E of Grantham on the A15

Once a market town and an important coaching stop, Folkingham was also the venue until 1828 of the Kesteven Quarter Sessions, which were held in the former Greyhound Inn facing the Market Square. Convicted prisoners were confined in the nearby House of Correction of which only the forbidding gatehouse-cum-governor's house survives. This surprisingly roomy edifice is now available to rent as a holiday cottage through the Landmark Trust. Also recalling the penal provisions of the past are Folkingham's village stocks, which are preserved in St Andrew's Church.

WOOLSTHORPE BY COLSTERWORTH

7 miles S of Grantham off the A1 at Colsterworth

🏛 Woolsthorpe Manor

Voted Man of the Last Millennium, Isaac Newton was born in 1642 in the modest Jacobean farmhouse, **Woolsthorpe Manor**, which has scarcely changed since he lived here. It was at Woolsthorpe that the Father of Modern Science later made some of his greatest inventions and discoveries. The Manor is now owned by the National Trust, which has furnished the rooms to reflect the life of the period, and has converted a 17th-century barn into a Science Discovery Centre, which helps explain the achievements of one of the country's most famous men. Almost as famous is the legendary apple tree that helped clear Newton's thinking about the laws of gravity. The apple tree in the garden here is said to have been grafted from the original tree beneath which Newton was sitting when the apple fell on to his head. Newton's interests were wide and varied, from 1696 he was involved in reforming the nation's corrupt coinage system, and from 1699 until his death in 1727 he held the post of Master of the Mint.

A rather strange memento of the young Newton is preserved in the church at nearby Colsterworth. It's a sundial crafted by Newton when he was nine years old. It seems odd to place a sundial inside a church and even odder to install it upside down.

BELVOIR

8 miles SW of Grantham off A607

🏛 Castle

In Victorian times, the Dukes of Rutland could stand on the battlements of **Belvoir Castle** comfortable in the knowledge that, in whichever direction they looked along the pastoral Vale of Belvoir, everything in sight formed part of their estate, some 30,000 acres in all (plus large holdings in other parts of the country). William the Conqueror granted this spectacular site to his standard-bearer at the Battle of Hastings, Robert de Todeni and, more than 900 years later, his descendants, now the Dukes of Rutland, still live here. Perched on the hilltop, the present castle looks convincingly medieval with its great tower, turrets and castellations, but it was in fact built in the early 1800s and is the fourth to occupy the site. The opulent interior contains some excellent paintings, including works by Gainsborough, Reynolds and Poussin, and the familiar portrait of Henry VIII by Holbein. In the 130ft long Regent's Gallery are some remarkable Gobelin tapestries, while other magnificent rooms display elegant Regency furniture, a dazzling ceiling copied from the Church of Santa Maria Maggiore in Rome, a dramatic array of 18th-century weaponry and a monumental silver collection, which includes a wine cooler weighing more than 112lb. The castle also houses the Museum of the Queen's Royal Lancers. The grounds provide a marvellous setting for special events, among which the medieval jousting tournaments are undoubtedly the most colourful. (Incidentally, Belvoir Castle lies

🏛 historic building 📷 museum 🏛 historic site �´ scenic attraction 🌿 flora and fauna just across the county boundary, in Leicestershire, but has always been regarded as a Lincolnshire attraction.)

Sleaford

🏛 Cogglesford Mill   🏛 Church of St Denys

🎨 The Hub

The history of this busy market town stretches back to the Iron Age. In Roman times there was a massive mint here (730 coins were discovered in one dig), and when a railway was being constructed in Victorian times, a vast Anglo-Roman cemetery was uncovered. Later, the Normans built a sizeable castle of which only a small portion of a wall remains, but much of their other major contribution to the town, the **Church of St Denys**, still survives. Its tower, 144 feet high and dating from around 1200, stands separate from the main body of the church, and is among the oldest stone-built towers in England. The interior is notable for the superb 14th-century tracery in the north window, two magnificent monuments to the local Carre family, some stained glass by William Morris, and a striking rood loft restored by Ninian Comper in 1918.

Collectors of old inn signs will be interested in the Bull and Dog pub in Southgate. Set in the wall above its ground floor is a stone bearing the date 1689 and depicting a bull being baited by dogs. The scene is thought to be unique in the country and the stone itself the oldest surviving pub sign in England. **The Hub Centre** for contemporary craft is based in a restored seed warehouse by the Banks of the River Slea. Regularly changing exhibitions are held in the two galleries, as well as special events and craft courses, and the retail area, the

rooftop viewing area and the riverside café complete the visitor experience. On the eastern edge of the town, **Cogglesford Mill** has been restored to working order and is open to the public. Probably built around 1750, the Mill has an exhibition detailing its history.

Other features of interest in Sleaford include the 15th century vicarage near the church, the landmark Handley Monument, a memorial erected to the town's MP in 1846 and reminiscent of an Eleanor Cross, and the Old Playhouse, purpose-built as a theatre in 1824 and now home to the local theatre company.

Around Sleaford

NAVENBY
10 miles NW of Sleaford on the A607

🏛 Mrs Smith's Cottage

One of the county's most unexpected attractions is **Mrs Smith's Cottage**, just off the High Street of this village where Hilda Mary Craven was born on 28 October 1892. After spending her childhood in Navenby, Hilda moved out of the county but returned in the 1920s to live in a tiny cottage in East Road. At the age of 64 she married, becoming Mrs Smith, but her husband Joseph died less than four years later. Hilda stayed on in the cottage, resisting any change she thought unnecessary, until she was 103. During her 80 years of living here, she created a spellbinding time warp. The original ladder access to the first floor is still in place; Hilda's rocking chair and shawl still remain in her favourite place by the range; the original outside privy and washhouse can still be viewed. Opening times are restricted: for more details, call 01529 414294.

NORTH RAUCEBY

5 miles W of Sleaford off the A17

🏛 Cranwell Aviation Heritage Centre

Generations of RAF personnel have trained at the Royal Air Force College, Cranwell. When it opened on 5 February 1920, it was the first Military Air Academy in the world and it later chalked up another first when a jet plane designed by Frank Whittle, a Cranwell graduate, took off from the runway here in 1941. In the nearby village of North Rauceby the **Cranwell Aviation Heritage Centre** (see panel below) tells the Cranwell story and that of the other numerous RAF bases in the region, with the help of photographs, exhibits and film. The museum is open Wednesday, Thursday and Sunday from 10.30am - 4.30pm during the season.

HECKINGTON

5 miles E of Sleaford off the A17

🏛 Windmill   🏛 Church of St Andrew

There's plenty of variety and interest here, in particular the tall **Church of St Andrew**. The early 14th-century Church of St Andrew is famous for the wealth of stone carvings on its tower. Inside, there's an outstanding Easter Sepulchre on which medieval master masons depicted the events of Christ's Crucifixion and Resurrection. The same masons were also responsible for the sedilia (stone seats), beautifully carved with scenes from village life and figures of saints. At the back is an interesting display of the church's history. Other attractions are the Victorian almshouses and the magnificent eight-sailed **Heckington Windmill** by the railway

Cranwell Aviation Heritage Centre

Heath Farm, North Rauceby, Sleaford,
Lincolnshire NG34 8QR
Tel: 01529 488490
website: www.lincolnshire.gov.uk

The Royal Air Force College at Cranwell in Lincolnshire is probably the most famous landmark in R.A.F history. The Cranwell Aviation Heritage Centre portrays the history of this renowned Royal Air Force officer training establishment, from its early days as a Royal Naval Air Service balloon base to present day.

The attraction features photographs, exhibits and archive film. It also has a computerised flight simulator, outside courtyard area with Jet Provost aircraft, Vampire nose pod, an exhibition hall with interpretation panels, artefacts, and exhibits and video theatre, and an information and retail area which sells souvenirs and memorabilia.

For opening times, more information on the centre, or details of special events contact Sleaford Tourist Information Centre on 01529 414294, e-mail: tic@n-kesteven.gov.uk.

🏛 historic building   🏛 museum   🏛 historic site   🌄 scenic attraction   🌿 flora and fauna

station. When built in 1830, the mill's sails numbered a modest five, but after storms damaged the mill in 1890, eight sails were removed from another mill nearby and installed here. The only surviving eight-sailed mill in Britain rises to five floors and was in use up until 1942. It is now owned by Lincolnshire County Council and can be visited on weekend afternoons, Thursday and Friday afternoons in the season, and at other times by appointment.

DORRINGTON
5 miles N of Sleaford on the B1188

🏛 North Ings Farm Museum

Run entirely by volunteers, **North Ings Farm Museum** is a fascinating place where vintage tractors, commercial vehicles, stationary engines, a fairground organ, a narrow-gauge railway and a small foundry are among the attractions. The museum is open one Sunday a month (01526 833100).

SCOPWICK
8 miles N of Sleaford on the B1188/B1191

Stone cottages line the main street of this small village and a stream splashes alongside the road. In 1838, the Reverend George Oliver noted in his booklet, Scopwickiana, that the stream invariably overflowed in wet weather making progress along the street possible only by means of stepping stones. This inconvenience continued until fairly recent times. The Reverend Oliver also recorded that the village's only ale house was kept in good order by a formidable landlady who permitted her customers no more than a couple of pints before sending them home to their wives.

Just south of Scopwick is RAF Digby, which was the first Lincolnshire airfield to be attacked by the Luftwaffe in World War II. In the RAF Digby Operations Room Museum the wartime setting has been re-created, complete with plotting table, maps and personnel, and the airfield's story is told with the help of many exhibits, photographs and documents. Guided tours take place on summer Sundays. For further details call 01529 414294 (Sleaford TIC).

METHERINGHAM
9 miles N of Sleaford on B1189

🏛 Airfield Visitor Centre

Just outside this large, straggling village, on the B1189, is the **Metheringham Airfield Visitor Centre**, one of many Lincolnshire airfields established by the RAF during World War II. A leaflet available from local TICs gives details of the North Kesteven Airfield Trail, which includes Metheringham. Here, the Centre's exhibits, photographs and documents tell the story of the airfield and of 106 Squadron, Bomber Command, whose base it was. Open Wednesday, Saturday, Sunday and Bank Holidays from Easter to October.

Woodhall Spa

🏛 Cottage Museum   📖 Kinema in the Woods

Woodhall Spa is something of an anomaly – a chunk of the Home Counties transplanted to the heart of Lincolnshire. Surrounded by pine and birch woods, spacious Victorian and Edwardian villas are set back from tree-lined avenues, and it's said that not a single house in the town is older than the 1830s. Woodhall became a spa town by accident when a shaft sunk in search of coal found not coal but mineral-rich water. In 1838, a pump room and baths were built, to be joined later by

CHAPLIN HOUSE B&B

92 High Street, Martin, Lincolnshire LN4 3QT
Tel: 01526 378795
e-mail: info@chaplin-house.co.uk
website: www.chaplin-house.co.uk

Chaplin House is an award winning B & B which specialises in using the very best of local and organic produce. Built as an ale house in 1797, **Chaplin House** served the community as a public house until 1923. It was known throughout this time as Chaplin Arms, a name it retained until 2003. The building played an important role in village life, the first floor at the front being one large room used for parish meetings and other public gatherings. After life as a pub, it became a Post Office and a shop, but down the years it fell into disrepair. Successive owners have played a part in its revival, and that revival has been completed by the present owners David and Margaret Lockyer, who have created one of the most pleasant and friendly Bed & Breakfast establishments in the region.

In the main house itself is a double room, while the rest of the accommodation is in a recently renovated barn and adjacent outbuilding – a ground floor double with its own patio area (the Garden Room), a ground floor twin with disabled access including a wet room, and a first floor family room (a cot is available). All the bedrooms are spacious, stylish and very comfortable, with en suite accommodation, TV with DVD player, clock radio, hot drinks tray and hairdryer. Guests can relax in the peaceful garden or the barn lounge which is well supplied with a wide range of reading material. There is free wifi throughout the barn accommodation as well as internet access for looking up tourist or travel information. In the reception area in the main house (the owners' lounge) stands a beautiful cast-iron range made by C Duckering of Lincoln. It's no longer used for cooking but is still lit on winter evenings.

The day starts with an excellent breakfast served in the main house, with full English and a range of other options. Evening meals are available by arrangement. Guests are welcomed with tea or coffee and home-made cake, one of the many nice touches that make a stay here such a pleasure. Such attention to detail has been recognised by many awards including *East Midlands Enjoy England Excellence Gold Award; Visit Britain Silver Award; Lincolnshire Star Award Accommodation of the Year;* and *Taste of Lincolnshire Award.*

The village pub is just up the road. On the edge of the village is Car Dyke, a Roman waterway that commands splendid views. Woodhall Spa, Horncastle, Sleaford and Lincoln are all an easy drive away, and other attractions include the Viking Way (3 miles), golf (4 miles), fishing on the River Witham and aviation attractions at Coningsby, East Kirkby and Metheringham. Note that there are two Martins close to each other. This one lies on the B1191 southwest of Woodhall Spa, the other is northeast of Woodhall Spa also on the B1191.

hydro hotels. Here, real or imagined invalids soaked themselves in 'hypertonic saline waters' heated to 40 degrees centigrade (103 degrees fahrenheit). The arrival of the railway in 1855 accelerated Woodhall's popularity, but by the early 1900s the spa had fallen out of favour and the associated buildings disappeared one by one. But this beautifully maintained village has retained its decorous spa atmosphere, pleasantly relaxed and peaceful, and also boasting a championship golf course.

One interesting survivor of the good old days is a former farm building and tennis pavilion, now the **Kinema in the Woods**. When it was converted to a cinema during World War II, it inevitably became known as the Flicks in the Sticks. It's one of very few back projection cinemas in the country and the entertainment on offer includes classic and modern films and performances on an original Compton Organ. The **Cottage Museum** on Iddsleigh Road, also the Tourist Information Centre, tells the story of the establishment of the town as a spa resort.

Woodhall Spa had close connections with 617 Squadron, the Dambusters, during World War II. The squadron was based at nearby RAF Scampton and the Petwood Hotel was used as the officers' mess. Memorabilia of those days are displayed in the hotel's Squadron Bar, and outside is one of the few original Bouncing Bombs. In Royal Square a memorial to those intrepid airmen takes the form of a 20ft long model of a breached dam.

There are several sites of interest outside the town. To the north stand the ruins of a 15th-century hunting lodge called the Tower on the Moor, built for Ralph, Lord Cromwell of Tattershall Castle. And, standing all alone on Thimbleby Moor in the hamlet of Reeds

Beck, is a 36ft high memorial to the Duke of Wellington, erected in 1844 and topped by a bust of the Iron Duke. The column celebrates the successful cultivation of Waterloo Woods, an oak forest planted just after the battle in 1815.

At Kirkstead, off the B1191, stands a towering piece of brickwork, the only visible remains of a 12th-century Cistercian Abbey. Close by is the fine 13th-century Church of St Leonard, "a gem of early Gothic…with an interior like a cathedral aisle", according to Simon Jenkins. Originally built as a "chapel outside the gates" for visitors to the abbey, St Leonard's was closed in 1877, but restored in 1914 by the Society for the Protection of Ancient Buildings. Miraculously, its beautifully carved chancel screen has survived intact. Dating back to the 13th century, it is believed to be the second oldest such screen in England.

Around Woodhall Spa

CONINGSBY
4 miles S of Woodhall Spa on the A153

RAF Coningsby

The centre of this large village, which started life as a Danish settlement, is dominated by the church tower of St Michael, notable for its enormous single-handed clock; at over 16ft in diameter, this 17th-century clock claims to be the largest working example of its kind. South of the village is **RAF Coningsby**, whose mission is "to deliver the future, develop the present and commemorate the past of the RAF's combat air power". It is also the home of the Battle of Britain Memorial Flight, created in 1957 in memory of the gallant airmen who flew in that crucial battle. The Flight operates a Lancaster, five Spitfires, two Hurricanes, two Chipmunks and a Dakota. These historic World War II aircraft are not just museum pieces, they are all still flying and can be seen at a variety of air shows during the summer months. Over 7,000 Lancasters were built in the 1940s and Coningsby's veteran took to the air to celebrate the Memorial Flight's 50th anniversary in April 2007 after a full restoration in Coventry. Visiting these wonderful machines on their 'home territory' provides an added dimension, and knowledgeable guides provide informative tours. The Centre is open throughout the year, Monday to Friday, and at weekends for special events. For details call 01526 344041.

TATTERSHALL
4 miles S of Woodhall Spa on the A153

🏛 Castle   🏛 Holy Trinity Church

Tattershall lies on the opposite bank of the River Bain from Coningsby and is known all over the world for the astonishing keep of **Tattershall Castle**. Its six storeys rise 110ft, a huge rectangular slab built in local red brick. In the 1400s it must have appeared even more formidable than it does now. Construction began around 1445 on the orders of the Lord Chancellor, Ralph Cromwell, and it was clearly designed more as a statement of his power and wealth rather than for defence. Military fashion had moved on from such huge keeps

and in any case the peaceful heart of 15th-century Lincolnshire had no need for fortifications on this scale. Originally, the keep was surrounded by a large complex of other buildings, but these have almost entirely disappeared and the tower stands menacingly alone. Despite its magnificence, Tattershall had fallen into near ruin by the early 1900s. There was a very real possibility that it would be dismantled brick by brick, transported to the United States and re-erected there. Happily, the tower was rescued by Lord Curzon who

Tattershall Castle

bequeathed it to the National Trust on his death in 1925.

In the shadow of the castle is Tattershall Country Park, set in 365 acres of woods, parks and lakes and offering all sorts of sporting facilities.

As well as this superb castle, Tattershall boasts one of the county's finest churches. **Holy Trinity** was also commissioned by Ralph Cromwell. That was in the 1440s: the church was finally completed in 1480, long after Ralph's death. Constructed of Ancaster stone, this "glasshouse church" is dazzlingly light and airy inside, but because of its scale and the absence of all but a few adornments, more imposing than likeable. Among the items of note is a striking brass of Ralph himself, but sadly, his image is headless.

LOCATOR MAP

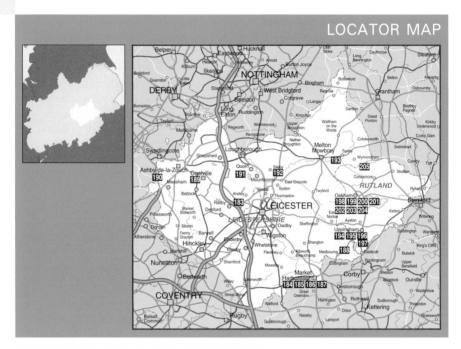

ADVERTISERS AND PLACES OF INTEREST

🏛 historic building   🏛 museum   🏛 historic site   🗠 scenic attraction   🌿 flora and fauna

8| Leicestershire & Rutland

Leicestershire's most attractive features are shy and quiet and have to be sought out, but they amply reward the explorer. The county is divided into two almost equal parts by the River Soar, which flows northward into the Trent. It separates the east and west by a broad valley, flowing like a silver ribbon through historic Leicester in the very heart of the county. This capital town was thriving in Roman days and is one of the oldest towns in England. It has managed to retain outstanding monuments of almost every age of English history. Red Leicester cheese was made in the southern part of the county in the 1700s, but now the only genuine product is made at Melton Mowbray, which also makes Stilton and, of course, the superlative

pork pies. And every schoolchild knows the name of Bosworth Field, one of the momentous battles that changed the course of English history.

Just 20 miles across and covering a mere 150 square miles, Rutland delights in its status as England's smallest county. Its 37,800 inhabitants were incensed when the Local Government changes of 1974 stripped the county of its identity and merged it with neighbouring Leicestershire. It took more than 20 years of ceaseless campaigning before bureaucracy relented and Rutland was reinstated as a county in its own right. Rutland has villages of thatch and ironstone, clustered around their churches, and the countryside is rich in pasture where once deer were hunted.

Its central feature is Rutland Water, whose 3,100 acres make it one of the largest man-made lakes in northern Europe. Started in 1971 to supply water to the East Midlands towns, it was created by damming the valley near Empingham.

Thornton Reservoir, National Forest

Leicester

🏛 Church of St Mary de Castro   🏛 Guildhall

🏛 Newarke Houses Museum   🏃 Castle Gardens

🏛 Jewry Wall & Museum   🏛 Gas Museum

🏛 National Space Centre   🏛 Abbey Pumping Station

🏛 New Walk Museum & Art Gallery

🏛 Guru Nanak Gurdwara

Designated Britain's first Environment City in recognition of its commitment to green issues and the environment, Leicester has numerous parks and open spaces, is one of the country's top 10 shopping destinations, has a buzzing nightlife and also boasts a rich architectural heritage with no fewer than 350 listed buildings.

When the Romans built a town here in the 1st century AD they called it Ratae Corielauvorum, and when they left 300 years later it survived in some form. It was the seat of a Christian bishop in the 7th century, and in the 9th century was conquered and settled by the Vikings along with Lincoln, Nottingham, Derby and Stamford. The city flourished in the Middle Ages when the cloth and wool trades became important, and the coming of the canals and the railways brought further prosperity. The development of road transport changed the face of the city, and modern Leicester is a thriving industrial and commercial city with superb shopping and recreational facilities, and a mixture of cultures and communities as rich and diverse as any in the land.

At the heart of Leicester's heritage is Castle Park, the old town, an area of gardens, churches, museums and other fine buildings. Here are concentrated many of the city's main

---

🏛 historic building   🏛 museum   🏛 historic site   🔱 scenic attraction   🌱 flora and fauna

visitor attractions. **Castle Gardens** was just an area of marshland by the River Soar until it was drained and opened as gardens to the public in 1926. In the gardens is a statue of Richard III who, on a sunny August day in 1485, rode out from the Blue Boar Inn to his death at the Battle of Bosworth Field. After the battle, his body was hung from the parapet of Bow Bridge before being buried at Greyfriars Church. After the Dissolution, his body was disinterred and thrown into the river, later to be recovered and buried near the bridge. Cardinal Wolsey died in Leicester after falling from his mule while on his way to London to face a treason charge. He was buried in the Lady Chapel of Leicester Abbey. The Abbey is now in ruins, and a simple memorial can be found in Abbey Park.

Castle Motte is a man-made mound built around 1070 by Leicester's first Norman lord. Like the gardens, it is open to the public during daylight hours, interpretation boards explain its history. Adjacent to the gardens is the **Church of St Mary de Castro**, founded in 1107 and still in use. The chancel, stained glass, carvings and tombstones are all well worth taking time to examine. Geoffrey Chaucer was married here and Henry VI was knighted in the church in 1426. Next to the church is the Great Hall of Leicester Castle. The Hall was built in the 12th century by Robert le Bossu and used by successive Earls of Leicester as their administrative headquarters; it is open to the public on special event days. Also in the same space is **Newarke Houses Museum**, showcasing information regarding Leicester in the 1930s/ 1940s, the old Leicestershire 'Tigers' regiment and the two world wars with an authentic trench as it would have been during World War I. The museum is also home to the Museum of the Royal Leicestershire

Regiment. Leicester's diverse cultural heritage is represented by the Jain Centre, the only one of its kind in the Western world, housed in a converted 19th-century Congregational chapel surmounted by a wondrously ornate facade; and the **Guru Nanak Gurdwara**, a Sikh temple and museum. Across the road from the Jain Centre is the **Jewry Wall and Museum**. It is not only the oldest surviving Roman civil building in Britain, but its wall is also the highest in the country and was part of the public baths, whose foundations are still visible. The museum chronicles the history and archaeology of the city and the county from Roman times to 1485. The adjacent St Nicholas Church dates back to Anglo-Saxon times and, despite later alterations, Saxon work and re-used Roman bricks can be seen in the

Guildhall, Leicester

🎪 stories and anecdotes   🦜 famous people   🎨 art and craft   🎭 entertainment and sport   🚶 walks

walls and tower. The Church of St Martin, which was in existence before 1086, was extended in the 14th and 15th centuries, restored in the 19th century and hallowed as the Cathedral of Leicester in 1927. Stained glass and carvings are impressive, and the memorial to Richard III is a highlight.

One of the very finest buildings in Leicester is the **Guildhall**, built around 1390 for the Guild of Corpus Christi and used as the Town Hall from the late 15th century to 1876. Concerts and theatrical performances are held regularly in the Great Hall. Across the road from the Cathedral is **Wygston's House**, a part timber-framed building, one of the oldest in the city, which now houses displays of fashion, textiles and crafts from around the world, along with a reconstruction of a 1920s draper's shop. This museum section also has an activity area where children are encouraged to dress up in replica historical costumes.

Leicester City Museums also include The **New Walk Museum and Art Gallery**, with displays including natural history, geology, ancient Egyptian mummies, a dinosaur skeleton more than 175 million years old, and a fine German Expressionist collection; Belgrave Hall and Gardens, a Queen Anne house whose rooms reflect Edwardian elegance and Victorian cosiness; the Abbey Pumping Station, an 1891 station with massive beam engines and several exhibitions; and the Gas Museum on Aylestone Road.

Over the past few years Leicester has had a major regeneration to transform the city. In 2008 the Highcross Shopping Centre opened with over 120 shops, bars and restaurants. The Curve Theatre, with state-of-the-art technology, also opened in 2008 and in 2009 the Phoenix Square Media Centre went live. The **National Space Centre**, opened in 2001

as part of the new millennium celebrations, is the UK's largest attraction dedicated to space. This multi-million pound project offers real rockets and satellites and capsules, interactive challenges and the most advanced space theatre in the world, transporting the audience on an awe-inspiring journey through the universe and beyond. The neighbouring **Abbey Pumping Station** is Leicester's Museum of Science and Technology, displaying Leicester's industrial, technical and scientific heritage. Between these two neighbours the story is told of nearly 200 years of science and technology, from the early days of steam to space exploration.

In 1485, King Richard III spent the night before the Battle of Bosworth Field at the Blue Boar Inn in Highcross Street. A plaque marks the site.

In Western Park, EcoHouse is an environment-friendly show home featuring energy efficiency, sustainable living and an organic garden. In Aylestone Road in the south of the city stands the **Gas Museum**, the largest of its kind in the world, with vintage heating and washing equipment, lighting, cookers, meters, an all-gas 1920s kitchen, model gas rig and many unusual items. Open afternoons, Tuesday to Thursday.

Around Leicester

KIRBY MUXLOE
2 miles W of Leicester off the B5380

🏠 Castle

Kirby Muxloe Castle is a picturesque ruined fortified manor house dating from 1480. Built of brick rather than the more usual stone, it was started by William, Lord Hastings, but not completed by him – he was executed by

Richard III. Only the great gatehouse and one of the four angle towers remain intact.

DESFORD
4 miles W of Leicester off the A47

🐦 Tropical Birdland

Tropical Birdland, which opened its doors to the public in 1987, is a breeding centre for rare and endangered species - birds of the rainforest, 85 species, walk-through aviaries, chick room, woodland walk, koi ponds, picnic gardens, bird shop, free parking – all this adds up to one of the county's most popular attractions. Open Easter to the end of October.

NEWTOWN LINFORD
5 miles NW of Leicester off the A50

🏚 Bradgate House   🚶 Bradgate Country Park

A picturesque village of thatched dwellings and timbered style buildings, Newtown Linford lies alongside the River Lin, which flows through the village and into **Bradgate Country Park**. This is the largest and most popular park in the county with well over a million visitors every year exploring its 850 acres. The park was created from Charnwood Forest 700 years ago as a hunting and deer park, and the scene is probably little changed since, a mixture of heath, bracken, grassy slopes, rocky outcrops and woodland – and the deer are still there. Man-made features of the park include a well-known folly called Old John Tower. Built in 1784 by the 5th Earl of Stamford in memory of a former member of his household, it stands nearly 700 feet above sea level and affords fine views.

Also here are the ruins of **Bradgate House**, built of brick at the beginning of the 16th century. This was the home of the Grey family and it was here that Lady Jane Grey was born in 1537. Her father was the scheming and ambitious Duke of Suffolk who forced her, at the age of 16, to marry the son of the Duke of Northumberland, Regent to Edward VI. With his own eye on power, Northumberland prevailed on the dying Edward to name Jane as heir to the throne. On hearing the news, Jane fell fainting to the ground. Public opinion recognised Mary Tudor as the rightful heir and within days both Jane's father and father-in-law had deserted her. Jane spent nine days as reluctant queen and a further seven months as a prisoner in the Tower of London – before a swift death on the executioner's block on 12 February 1554. Today, the lovely rose-red ruins of Bradgate House where Jane passed much of her brief life look too benign and inviting ever to have been involved in such a murderous tale of 16th-century politics. The story is that the foresters at Bradgate cut off the heads of the oaks in the park as a mark of respect to Lady Jane; pollard oaks can still be seen here.

ANSTEY
3 miles NW of Leicester off the A46

🏚 Packhorse Bridge

The 16th-century **Packhorse Bridge** that crosses Rothley Brook at Anstey is a particularly fine specimen: 5ft wide to give space for the horse's bulging panniers, 54ft long and supported by five low arches. In the late 18th century when the bridge was the only way to get to Leicester, some four miles distant, it would have been crossed many times by Ned Ludd, who was born in Anstey in 1811. He was apprenticed to a local weaver and one night broke two stocking frames. Groups of workers took this as a sign to rebel against the unemployment and hardship the new equipment was causing, and set about destroying other machines in the new textile milles. They gained the name of Luddites, a term now used to describe anyone opposed to modern technology. The government's response to the damage was to swoop on six of the leaders and hang them all at Nottingham.

REARSBY

5 miles NE of Leicester on the A607

According to meticulous accounts that have survived, the lovely old bridge in Rearsby was built by six men in just nine days during the summer of 1714. The village constable's accounts showed the total cost as £11 2s 2d (£11.11p) – with the largest expense, £2 12s 6d, being for 21 quarters of lime, the smallest, a payment of 5d (2p) "to George Skillington for Nailes". The bridge was paid for by a levy of ratepayers of 8d in the pound but, according to constable Richard Harrison, he ended up "£1 11s 0½d out of Pockett". A small consolation must have been to have the inscription on the sixth arch of his initials, RH, alongside the date 1714.

OADBY

3 miles SE of Leicester off the A6/A47

🌿 Botanical Gardens   🦆 James Hawker

🏃 Brocks Hill Country Park

Effectively a suburb of Leicester, Oadby nevertheless has three venues of interest to those who care for the environment. There's a treat for horticulturalists in the form of the University of Leicester's **Botanical Gardens**, which include an arboretum, herbaceous borders, water garden and glass houses that shelter tropical and temperate plants, alpines and succulents.

In Washbrook Lane, **Brocks Hill Country Park & Environment Centre** is a remarkable

building, completely self-sufficient and needing no electricity, gas or water supplies – not even a sewer. It was built to demonstrate wind and solar power, photovoltaics, rainwater re-cycling and sewage composting. The centre stands in 67 acres of recently planted Country Park with woodland, meadowland, community orchard and arboretum. There's an Exhibition Area, café and classroom facilities.

In Oadby graveyard is the tombstone of **James Hawker**, one of the most engaging rogues of all time. In his entertaining autobiography, *James Hawker's Journal*, he reveals that he found his vocation when he was 18 years old and poached his first bird. That was in 1844, and from then until his death in 1921, he honoured his declaration that "I will poach 'till I die". He was only caught once and on that charge, he indignantly claims, he was innocent – "They knew me and seized the occasion to punish my earlier misdemeanours". In later life James combined a respectable daytime career as a parish councillor and member of the school board with a nocturnal pastime of depleting his aristocratic neighbour's lands of their edible game. For 60 years his grave remained unmarked until EMMA Theatre Company, which had performed a play about his life, erected a simple monument bearing as epitaph his defiant, and true, claim:

"I will poach 'till I die".

WIGSTON

4 miles S of Leicester on the b582

🏛 Wigston Frameknitters Museum

Wigston Frameknitters Museum is an 18th-century Master hosier's house and 1890 workshop with eight original frames. Visitors can take a tour of the old machinery and have a go themselves. Call 0116 288 3396 for opening times.

WISTOW
6 miles SE of Leicester off the A6

Only two churches in the country are dedicated to St Wistan, a Christian prince of Mercia who was murdered by his wicked uncle Brifardus near this tiny hamlet in AD849. Wistow's Church of St Wistan was largely remodelled in 1746, so its interior has mainly Georgian fittings including box pews and ironwork communion rails. There are striking memorials to members of the Halford family of nearby Wistow Hall (private) where they lived continuously from 1603 to 1896. Their most distinguished visitor, albeit in some distress, was Charles I who stopped here briefly to change horses on his flight from the Battle of Naseby. In their haste, the king and his party left their battle horses with their saddles and other gear still in place. Charles even left his sword behind. Many years later it was given to George IV by Sir Henry Halford, physician to George III, George IV and William IV. The saddles and other equipment are now held by the New Walk Museum in Leicester. A popular family attraction is the Wistow Maze, comprising eight acres of maize and sunflowers, with a quiz trail amid the three miles of paths designed by the famous maze expert Adrian Fisher. It stands opposite Wistow Rural Centre.

KIBWORTH HARCOURT
8 miles SE of Leicester on the A6

The earliest type of windmill used in the county was the post mill, where the whole wooden body complete with the machinery was positioned on a post and could be turned so that the sails faced the wind. The only surviving one – dating from the early 18th century – is here.

Market Harborough

🏛 Church of St Dionysius   🏛 Old Grammar School
🏛 Museum

Halfway between Leicester and Northampton at a crossing point of the River Welland, Market Harborough was created as a planned market town in the mid 12th century. The booths that filled its market place were gradually replaced by permanent buildings, and many of these, along with the courts that led off the High Street, still stand. In 1645, Charles I made Market Harborough his headquarters and held a council of war here before the Battle of Naseby. The development

Old Grammar School, Market Harborough

🎞 stories and anecdotes   🦜 famous people   🎨 art and craft   🎭 entertainment and sport   🚶 walks

FARNDON FIELDS FARM SHOP

Farndon Fields Farm, Farndon Road,
Market Harborough, Leicestershire LE6 9NP
Tel: 01858 464838
e-mail: office@farndonfields.co.uk
website: www.farndonfieldsfarmshop.co.uk

The Farma National Awards recognise excellence in a number of categories related to farm retailing and direct sales. One of the main awards is Farm Retailer of the Year, which was won in 2008 by **Farndon Fields Farm Shop**. This particular award recognises outstanding farm retailers who combine vision with a passion for farming and a mind and feeling for retail. Kevin and Milly Stokes have been selling the produce of Farndon Fields to the public since 1983, initially from the farmhouse garage, then, from 1988, in purpose-built premises across the yard. Continued success has seen the rapid expansion of the business – and its premises – and farming has remained at the heart of the enterprise throughout its growth.

Farndon Fields Farm produces some 40 varieties of vegetables, including up to seven types of potato, as well as soft fruit. Visitors to the shop can be confident that the farm produce is as fresh as can be, with zero food miles an obvious bonus. Farming is Kevin's responsibility, while the shop is in the care of Milly, who puts her skills as a professional shop designer to excellent use.

The shop is bright, spacious and inviting, with a pleasing touch of rusticity, and the wow factor starts with the home-grown sunflowers and gladioli that adorn the glass-covered entrance in the summer months. In the butchery and the bakery, Kevin and Milly work closely with their butcher and a local baker to ensure that the homegrown element is present in every department of the shop. Meat comes from local farms – again guaranteeing minimum food miles. Among the butchery's specialities are a variety of superb sausages, while the bakers, whose premises are only a short walk away, have developed a range of recipes some of which incorporate the farm's produce.

That produce is the basis of much of the menu in the café, which specialises in farmhouse-style meals, snacks and cream teas. As well as its own produce, the meats and the baking, the shop sells a selection of top-quality goods from local sources, including chilled and frozen meals, red Leicester and Stilton cheese, milk, pies, wine, beer and juices. From outside the area come jams, pickles, oils, olives and Loch Fyne smoked goods. The quality of the produce and the passion of the owners and staff guarantee the ongoing success of this superb place, which lies a short drive south of Market Harborough centre on the road to East Farndon.

🏛 historic building   🏛 museum   🏛 historic site   ⚘ scenic attraction   🌱 flora and fauna

Bagel&Griff

6/7 Church Square, Market Harborough,
Leicestershire LE16 7NB
Tel: 01858 468764 Fax: 01858 535457
e-mail: shop@bagelandgriff.com
website: www.bagelandgriff.com

After a successful career in fashion, Helene Inchmore opened her own Interiors shop in 2005. Bagel&Griff is located close to the church in the centre of the historic old town of Market Harborough & offers an extensive range of natural products made from wood, slate, basket, stone and neutral ceramics. Black, white and naturals that would blend in with any home décor from a loft apartment to a cottage. You will find an excellent choice of bed linen, bathroom accessories, ceramics, glass, home items such as chairs, rugs, cushions, clocks, candles and lamps. There are also many unique pieces, statement pots and unusual framed prints and fabrics.

For the children, or their nostalgic parents, there's a choice of knitted and cotton soft toys, vintage sari animals, tin cars and beautifully packaged old fashioned games and gadgets.

The website www.bagelandgriff.com carries a similar range to the shop, clear product pictures and easy online ordering make this a great online one stop shop.

of turnpike roads - the motorways of their day - led to prosperity and the establishment of coaching inns in the town, many of them still in business. The canals and the railways transformed communications and manufacturing industry became established, the most notable company being RW & H Symington, creators of the liberty bodice.

The town trail takes in the major buildings, including the 14th-century parish **Church of St Dionysius** with its superb limestone broach. The church has no graveyard because it was, until the early 1900s, a daughter church of St Mary in Arden with the status of a chapel. The **Old Grammar School** is a timber-framed building with an open ground floor; built in 1614 to serve the weekly butter market and "to keepe the market people drye in time of fowle weather", it later became a school, a role that it sustained until 1892. The factory of the Symington Company, which grew from a cottage industry of staymakers to a considerable economic force in the town, now houses the Council offices, the library, the information centre and the **Harborough Museum**, which was relaunched in 2009 and contains some of the collection of the Hallaton Treasures.

Among the town's distinguished past residents are William Bragg, whose nephew and son shared the Nobel Prize for Physics in 1915; Jack Gardner, who was British Empire and European Heavyweight boxing champion between 1950 and 1952; and Thomas Cook, who spent 10 years of his life here and was married in the town. While travelling one day by road to Leicester he conceived the idea of an outing using the then newly opened railway. He organised the excursion from Leicester to Loughborough on 7 July 1841; the fare of a

🎞 stories and anecdotes   🦜 famous people   🎨 art and craft   🎵 entertainment and sport   🚶 walks

COUNTY CRAFTS

UNIQUE CARDS & GIFTS. GALLERY & FRAMERS

24/25 High Street, Market Harborough,
Leicestershire LE16 7NJ
Tel: 01858 432939

County Crafts situated on the corner of High Street and Abbey Street, this beautiful craft shop has been catering for a discerning clientele for 20 years with a reliable source of gifts and goods to grace the home. Products include Moorcroft pottery, the Border Fine Arts range of figures, toiletries by Crabtree & Evelyn, & Floris and unusual gifts for men, including the exclusive Dalvey range.

The Gallery caters for a wide range of originals and limited edition prints, and also offers a complete framing service. Shop hours are 10 to 5.30pm Monday to Saturday for both craft and jewellery shop.

COUNTY JEWELLERS

56 High Street, Market Harborough, Leicestershire LE16 7AF
Tel: 01858 462773

County Jewellers also sells a selection of hand-made jewellery in gold, silver and platinum, some pieces set with diamonds. The shop accepts commissions for bespoke pieces and undertakes repairs and restoration. Also stockist of large range of silver jewellery including Lovelinks, Petite and Blog.

---

shilling (5p) included afternoon tea. Cook later moved to Leicester, where he is buried at Welford Road cemetery.

Around Market Harborough

HALLATON

6 miles NE of Market Harborough off the B664

🐾 Hare-Pie Scrambling & Bottle-Kicking contest

🏛 Village Museum

On the village green of this picturesque village in the rich grazing lands of the Welland Valley stands an unusual conical butter cross. Hallaton is renowned for one of the country's many bizarre British folk customs, the **Hare-Pie Scrambling & Bottle-Kicking contest**. The contest is a free-for-all struggle between the neighbouring villages of Hallaton and Medbourne to get two out of three bottles of ale across the village boundary by whatever means possible. (The 'bottles' are actually small oak casks.) As many as 400 players may be milling around in the scrum

Hallaton

MEDBOURNE GRANGE

Nevill Holt, Market Harborough, Leicestershire LE16 8EF
Tel: 01858 565249 Fax: 01858 565257
e-mail: sallybeaty@googlemail.com
website: www.medbournegrange.co.uk

Medbourne Grange is a friendly farmhouse B&B establishment on a working farm off the B664, halfway between Market Harborough and Uppingham. The location, on the edge of the attractive village of Nevill Holt, is one of the most beautiful, unspoilt areas of Leicestershire, with glorious views in all directions. The house dates from the mid-19th century, and the décor and furnishings are in complete harmony with the age of the property. The guest accommodation offered by owner Sally Beaty comprises three rooms – two doubles and a twin – with en suite facilities, TV, radio, hot drinks tray and hairdryer. Central heating keeps things cosy at any time of year, and guests have ample off-road parking for their cars. A traditional farmhouse breakfast with local produce and home-made preserves starts the day, and the lounge is supplied with plenty of local information and maps for planning the day's activities.

The house is an ideal base for a walking, cycling or touring holiday. Rockingham Castle, Burghley House and Boughton House are within easy reach, as are the market towns of Market Harborough, Uppingham and Stamford. And Rutland Water, also an easy drive away, offers a wide variety of activities, including sailing, fishing and bird-watching.

and the battle has been known to continue for eight or nine hours. The day's events begin with a procession to Hare Pie Bank where pieces of a huge hare pie are thrown to the crowd. The antiquarian Charles Bilson believed the custom was a relic of a time when the hare was worshipped as a divine animal, but he has no explanation for the origins of the bottle-kicking contest. A display of this curious event is on show in the **Hallaton Village Museum**, along with relics from the motte and bailey castle, some unusual agricultural items and rituals, hoards and helmets, with coins and other artefacts making up the renowned Hallaton Treasure.

FOXTON
2 miles NW of Market Harborough off the A6

🏛 Locks & Canal Museum

The most famous site on the county's canals is

the **Flight of Ten Locks** on the Grand Union Canal, one of the great engineer Thomas Telford's most impressive constructions. Alongside the 10 locks are the remains of a remarkable inclined plane. This was built to bypass the locks by moving boats in steel tanks to a different level. Halfway down the flight is the **Canal Museum** in the rebuilt home of the incline plane boat lift. There are several other buildings and bridges of interest (including a swing-bridge) in this pretty village.

LUTTERWORTH
12 miles W of Market Harborough on the A4304

🏛 Stanford Hall   🏛 Museum

John Wycliffe was made Rector here under the tutelage of John of Gaunt as a reward for his diplomatic services. His instigation of an

🎞 stories and anecdotes   🦜 famous people   🎨 art and craft   🎫 entertainment and sport   🚶 walks

English translation of the Bible into English caused huge dissent. He died in 1384 and was buried in the church here, but when he was excommunicated in 1428 his body was exhumed and burned and his ashes scattered in the River Swift. Most of his Bibles were destroyed by the Church and the Latin versions continued to be used until William Tynedale produced an English Bible during the reign of Henry VIII. Close to the church, **Lutterworth Museum** and Historical Society contains a wealth of local history from Roman times to World War II.

About three miles southeast of Lutterworth and set in meadows beside the River Avon, **Stanford Hall** has been the home of the Cave family since 1430. The present house – pleasantly-proportioned, dignified and serene was built by the celebrated architect William Smith of Warwick in the 1690s. A superb staircase was added around 1730, one of very few structural alterations to the house in its 300-year history. One other was the Ballroom which contains paintings that once belonged to Bonnie Prince Charlie's younger brother, Henry Stuart. They include the last major portrait of the middle-aged Bonnie Prince Charlie, two of James III – the Old Pretender – and a particularly fine portrait of Charles II by Sir Peter Lely. The Cave family became Barons and it was the 6th Baron, Adrian, whose fascination with motor-cars is perpetuated in Stanford's collection of cycle-cars and motor cycles. Adrian was also closely associated with the pioneer aviator, Percy Pilcher who, in 1895, accomplished the first controlled flight in Britain.

Pilcher made several experimental flights in Stanford Park but a flight in his glider, The Hawk, on 30 September 1899 ended in disaster when a bamboo strut in the tail fractured, the machine turned on its back and crashed. In the stable block at Stanford there's a fascinating full-size replica of The Hawk "with its innumerable wires like the ribs of an umbrella". Lutterworth has another, more successful connection with aviation: it was the home of Sir Frank Whittle, inventor of the jet engine.

Hinckley

🏛 Museum

Few of the old timbered houses still stand in the town of Hinckley, whose Fair is mentioned in Shakespeare's *Henry IV*. Now a thriving industrial and market town, Hinckley was already an established community in Saxon times. When the Domesday Book was compiled, Hinckley had 60 families – four times as many as in contemporary Birmingham. The turning point in its fortunes came in 1640 when William Illife set up the first stocking frame in the town and so initiated the hosiery and knitwear industry that has made it known internationally. A surviving example of 17th-century cottages

Concordia Theatre, Hinckley

🏚 historic building 🏛 museum 🏛 historic site 🌳 scenic attraction 🌿 flora and fauna

once used for framework knitting still stand in Lower Bond Street and are home to **Hinckley & District Museum**. The Museum illustrates the history of town and district, and includes among its hosiery exhibits a stocking frame of 1740.

It was in 1727 that gossip across the county told of a tombstone in Hinckley churchyard that drips blood. Richard Smith, a young man of 20, was killed in Market Place by an army recruitment sergeant he had offended by some trifling joke. The tombstone, though moved from its original location when St Mary's Church was enlarged in the 19th century, is reputed to 'sweat blood' at midnight on the anniversary of his murder.

Ghostly visitations have been reported at several places around the town, including The Union Inn in the Borough, The Barley Sheaf in Lower Bond Street and the Concordia Theatre in Stockwell Head. The theatre, housed in the former Britannia Hosiery Works, hosts a wide variety of dramatic and musical entertainment.

In Regent Street, Joseph Hansom invented his cab and drove it along Watling Street.

Around Hinckley

BURBAGE
1 mile E of Hinckley on the B4668

🌿 Burbage Woods

The village was originally called Burbach, a name that came from the burr thistles that grew in profusion in the fields. The 9th Earl of Kent was an early incumbent, being rector here for 50 years at the Church of St Catherine, whose spire is a landmark for miles around. **Burbage Woods** are nationally important because of the spectacular ground flora, and Burbage Common is one the largest areas of natural grassland in the locality. For the visitor, there's a network of footpaths, bird observation hide, picnic tables and a visitor centre.

MARKET BOSWORTH
5 miles N of Hinckley off the A447

🚂 Battlefield Line Railway

🏊 Leisure & Water Park   🚶 Country Park

This market town is most famous as the battle site for the turning point in the Wars of the Roses - Richard III (Duke of York White Rose county) was routed here in 1485 by Red Rose forces (Henry Tudor, later Henry VII) and killed. This was the battle immortalised in Shakespeare's play *Richard III*, where the desperate king is heard to cry, "My kingdom for a horse". Richard's defeat led to the accession of the Tudor dynasty, Shakespeare's patrons and perhaps, therefore, the impetus behind his less-than-complimentary portrayal of Richard, which is disputed by historians to this day. The Visitor Centre gives a detailed insight into medieval times with the aid of models, replicas and a film theatre. Also on site are a picnic area, a country park and a battle trail - a self-guided trail of 1¾ miles that takes the visitor round the field of battle, passing the command posts of Richard and Henry. Huge flags are frequently flown from these sites, adding colour and poignancy to the scene. Visitors can see the well where Richard drank during the battle, and pause at the memorial stone on the spot where Richard died. Call 01455 290429 for details of visits, events, etc.

The Battlefield is on the route of the Ashby Canal, whose towpath offers delightful walks through beautiful countryside. Opened in 1804, this lock-free canal connects Hinckley,

Market Bosworth Country Park

Distance: *4.0 miles (6.4 kilometres)*

Typical time: *120 mins*

Height gain: *10 metres*

Map: *Explorer 232, Landranger 140*

Walk: *www.walkingworld.com ID:1505*

Contributor: *Roy Davenport*

ACCESS INFORMATION:

Served by buses from Leicester, Hinckley and Coalville. Car parking is in the Country Park situated on the B585 between Market Bosworth and the A447 Hinckley to Ashby Road.

ADDITIONAL INFORMATION:

Refreshments are available at several different places in Market Bosworth and also at the Royal Arms and Hercules public houses in Sutton Cheney and sometimes at the almshouses. Toilets are available in the Country Park and in the town. Gift shops and craft shops can be found in Market Bosworth. Almost flat throughout an easy walk. Good views across the Leicestershire borders into Warwickshire.

DESCRIPTION:

Market Bosworth is a small and pretty town in Leicestershire. This walk commences in the Bosworth Country Park a large area of parkland with a lake, and a variety of ducks, swans, moorhens and an abundance of wild birds.

The park also contains an Arboretum with many of the trees marked to show their individual species. The park is an ideal place for picnics and playing games with the children.

This walk leaves the park via fields and makes it way to Sutton Cheney, a small Leicestershire village. This village it close to the Bosworth Battlefield and contains the lovely little Battlefield church, where King Richard III heard mass on the morning of the battle. In the church there are battle emblems and a commemorative plaque.

Here too you will see the picturesque almshouses as you make your way up the church path. You will then return via more fields and an avenue of trees to pass through the arboretum and back to the lake in the park.

Depending on the height of crops, you may see three memorials. One is a giant stone pillar bearing the figure of Hercules, which may have been put up originally by the 4th or 5th Baronet of Bosworth Park and could be 200 years old. Also two memorial stones over a pit where three horses are buried. The sandstone plaques are now almost unreadable. The larger one refers to "Trumps", charger of Captain Norton Legge ARC. The smaller one reads "In memory of "Scots Grey" 10 seasons without a fall. Born 1876 died 1892. A trusty steed a faithful friend makes good the journey to the end". Sadly no public path actually allows access to the memorials.

FEATURES:

Lake/Loch, Pub, Toilets, Play Area, Church, Wildlife, Birds, Flowers, Great Views, Butterflies, Cafe, Gift Shop, Food Shop, Good for Kids, Mostly Flat, Public Transport, Restaurant, Tea Shop, Woodland, Ancient Monument.

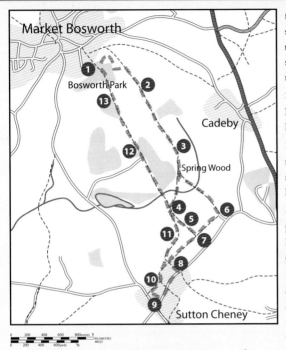

Market Bosworth

Bosworth Park

Cadeby

Spring Wood

Sutton Cheney

0   200   400   600   800metres   1
KILOMETRES
MILES
0   200   400   600yards   ½

forward between the hedge and a
storage barn to the next stile. The way
marker shows two footpaths one
straight ahead and one angling to the
right.

3 | The gate after this has a sign stating
No Dogs so dog walkers follow the
Divert Route and rejoin at waymark 7.

3 | **Divert Route** - Follow right hand
marker going close to corner of wood
and forward to stile in hedgerow, then
head for gap in hedgerow ahead.

4 | On reaching the gap, ignore the
path ahead and turn left to the
hedgerow. Follow this with the hedge
on your left.

5 | At the first corner turn right,
crossing the gap keeping to the right
of the hedge follow it to the end. At
the end of the hedge you are at
waymark 7. Turn right and follow the
main route.

3 | **Main route** - Through the gate and continue
forward with the hedge on your left, then through
the tree line and over the ditch. Bear slightly left
and head up towards the farmhouse. The path
passes between the farm on your left and a
hedgerow on your right and along the farm drive.
Just after the end of the farm garden and before
the metal gate go through the gate on your right.

6 | Head towards the large house and on reaching
the hedge turn right to follow the hedge round. At
the far end of the garden and end of the conifer
trees, go slightly right to the waymarker at the left
hand end of the hedgerow on the right. Divert
walkers rejoin at this point.

7 | The path now goes slightly left to a waymarker at
the end of a hedgerow on the left. Go forward over
the track and head towards the left hand telegraph

WALK DIRECTIONS:

1 | Walk across to the lake called Bow Pool, and
facing the lake turn left. Ignore the first footpath
right alongside the boathouse and find the next
footpath to the right on the edge of the wood
signposted Woodland Walk. Follow this path until
you reach a T junction with another footpath with a
wooden fence on the far side. Turn left and exit the
wood. Turn immediate right to pass a wooden
bench. Continue forward in almost a straight line
into and through a small plantation passing three
more benches on the way and exit into a clearing.

2 | Bear left to a marker post in front of a wood and
turn right going forward to the gate in the
hedgerow. From the gate make your way forward
keeping the hedgerow on your left. Continue along
the edge of a small wood, after that again continue

pole of the two that can be seen ahead of you. As you reach a path junction in the middle of the field opposite The Royal Arms, it's worth looking right to note the waymarker at the end of a hedgerow in front of an old tree.

8 | Through the gate and through the car park (or the bar!) to reach the road and turn right. Make your way through Sutton Cheney village to the church, passing The Square and The Old Bakery on the right and "The Hercules" pub on the left. (Pub so called because it stands in a direct line with Hercules Monument and Bosworth Park Hall.)

9 | Enter the churchyard on the right and as you pass through the second gate observe "The Old Alms Houses on the right. When you exit the church door turn right and leave the yard via the small gate next to a cottage. After the gate turn sharp right to pass between the cottages. Pass between Church Cottage and the very pretty Bumblebee Cottage. Continue forward past the gates at the entrance to the almshouses and down the grass lane ahead of you.

10 | At the next cottage (the opposite end of The Square passed earlier) go diagonally left across the corner of the field to the hedge corner between the two telegraph poles. Follow the hedge right to the next field. You will now see the paths ahead of you that you came along earlier and the Royal Arms over on the right. Ignore the direct path ahead and angle slightly left to reach the waymark at the end of the hedge you noted on your outward journey. On the photograph it's the smaller left hand path that can be seen, towards the right hand tree. Follow the hedgerow down to the right in the direction of The Leicester Round markers (black circle of arrows) to the bottom of the field.

11 | Go diagonally left across the corner of the field and head in the direction of the house that can be seen on the edge of the wood in the distance. At the bottom of the slope (divert walkers came to this point earlier on their outward journey) continue forward keeping the hedge on your left. At the end of the hedge go left and right over the stream (interesting old weir here) and with the wood on your right go up towards the house. Cross over the drive and continue forward to the stile

12 | Cross the stile and then turn left for about 50 yards and face right. Looking across to the right corner of the left wood on the brow of the slight hill you may see Hercules. Return to the stile and turn left to walk down the avenue of trees passing a pool on the left. As you approach the corner of the wood look to your right and again you may spot Hercules on his pedestal.

13 | Continuing forward at the end of the wood look through the hedgerow on your right to see the Horse Memorials in the field. Continue forward. As you approach the end of the avenue you may see:

Giant Hogweed - Do not touch
It can sting and some people are highly allergic to it.

Pass through the gate into the arboretum. After going through the gate ignore waymarkers ahead and turn left to follow the main pathway. Follow down to the bottom crossing the stream over the third bridge. Continue back up on the opposite side of the stream. At the junction of the paths continue forward, after visiting the Sensory Garden on the right continue over the bridge and back to Bow Pool. If you still have energy left why not finish with a final lap around the pool itself.

Bosworth Battlefield, Market Bosworth, Battlefield Railway, Measham Museum and Moira Furnace.

Market Bosworth Country Park is one of many beautiful open spaces in the area. Another is Bosworth Water Trust's **Leisure and Water Park** on the B585 west of town. This is a 50-acre leisure park with 20 acres of lakes for dinghy sailing, boardsailing and fishing. Railway nostalgia awaits at Shackerstone, three miles northwest of Market Bosworth, where the **Battlefield Line Railway** offers a steam-hauled nine-mile round trip from Shackerstone via Market Harborough to Shenton through the delightful scenery of southwest Leicestershire. The railway is the last remaining part of the former Ashby & Nuneaton Joint Railway, which opened in 1873. The steam locomotives include an ex-BR B1 4-6-0. At Shackerstone, the headquarters of the line, is an impressive museum of railway memorabilia, locomotives and rolling stock. Call 01827 880754 for timetable details.

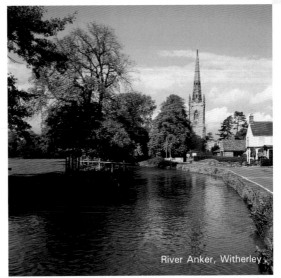

River Anker, Witherley

TWYCROSS
7 miles NW of Hinckley off the A444

🐾 Zoo

Five miles northwest of Market Bosworth, on the A444 Burton-Nuneaton road, **Twycross Zoo** is an ideal family attraction, home to a wide variety of animals including gorillas, chimps, orang-utans, gibbons, marmosets, elephants, lions, giraffes, flamingos and penguins. The zoo celebrated two notable new arrivals in 2009, a baby titi monkey and a rare tufted deer named Ying Xiong (hero in Chinese). Open daily throughout the year.

On a side road parallel to the A444, three miles north of Market Bosworth, lies a village with the wonderful name of Barton-in-the-Beans. The county was apparently once known as 'bean-belly' Leicestershire, on account of the large reliance on the bean crops that formed part of the staple diet in needy times. The beans were said to have been sweeter and more tender than anywhere else in the country.

Coalville

🏛 Snibston Discovery Park

Originally called Long Lane, the town sprang up on a bleak common when Whitwick Colliery was opened in 1824. The big name in the early days was George Stephenson, who not only established the railway here (in 1832) but also built the churches.

At Ashby Road, Coalville, **Snibston Discovery Park** (see panel on page 368) is

Snibston Discovery Park

Ashby Road, Coalville, Leicestershire LE67 3LN
Tel: 01530 278444   Fax:: 01530 813301
e-mail: snibston@leics.gov.uk

One of the largest and most dynamic museums in the Midlands, **Snibston** is Leicestershire's all-weather science and industry museum. Visitors can get their 'hands-on' loads of fun in the popular Science Alive! Gallery or explore the County's rich heritage in the Transport, Extractives, Engineering and Textiles and Fashion Galleries. Other attractions include guided colliery tours, outdoor science and water playgrounds, sculptures and Nature Reserve. Open daily 10am - 5pm

built on the 100-acre site of the former Snibston Colliery. Visitors can explore a unique mixture of nature, history, science and technology. Topics covered include the industrial heritage of Leicestershire, and former miners conduct a lively surface tour of the colliery. There are rides on board a diesel locomotive on the restored colliery line and the Extra Ordinary Gallery allows visitors to lift a Mini Cooper, beat a robot or make fire You can test your strength against a pulley system in the Engineering Gallery or relax in the Grange Nature Reserve and Victorian arboretum. The Fashion Gallery houses over 1,000 items from the 1750s to the present day, the largest such collection outside London. Call 01530 278444 for opening times.

Around Coalville

OAKS IN CHARNWOOD
2 miles NE of Coalville off the B587

🏛 Mount St Bernard Abbey

In a beautiful elevated position in Charnwood Forest, **Mount St Bernard Abbey** was the first Catholic abbey to be founded in England after the Reformation. It is a Cistercian Monastery of white monks founded in 1835 as a continuation of Garendon Abbey (1133-1538).

SWANNINGTON
1 mile NW of Coalville on the A511

The Leicester & Swannington Railway, which was opened in 1833 to bring coal to the city, was one of the first railway lines in Britain to use steam engines. The incline at Swannington is now part of one of the many heritage trails in the county. Traces of some of the many shallow 'bell pits' once common in this mining area can be seen in scrubland near the windmill on Swannington Common. Three floors of the restored Swannington Mill are open to the public on Sunday afternoons between April and September.

IBSTOCK
3 miles S of Coalville off the A447

🐦 Sense Valley Forest Park

🏛 Donington Le Heath Manor House

Sense Valley Forest Park, at Heather near Ibstock, is a 150-acre site that has been transformed from an opencast mine into a woodland and wildlife haven. The site includes several large lakes and areas of conservation grassland, and the number of species of birds recorded grows each year.

Also a little way south of Coalville is **Donington Le Heath Manor House**, an

🏛 historic building 📷 museum 🏛 historic site � scenic attraction 🐦 flora and fauna

attractive stone manor that is one of the few of its period (1280) to remain intact. It is now a museum.

Ashby-de-la-Zouch

🏰 Castle   🏰 St Helen's Church   🏛 Museum

🚶 National Forest

A historic market town whose name comes from the Saxon Aesc (ash) and Byr (habitation); the ending de la Zouch was added in 1160 when a Norman nobleman Alain de Parrhoet la Zouch became lord of the manor by marriage. In the 15th century, Edward IV granted Ashby Manor to his favourite counsellor, Lord Hastings, who converted the manor house into a castle and rebuilt the nearby St Helen's Church. During the Civil War **Ashby Castle** was besieged for over a year by the Parliamentarian Army until the Royalists surrendered in 1646. After the war the castle was partly destroyed to prevent its further use as a centre of resistance and almost wholly forgotten until the publication of Sir Walter Scott's *Ivanhoe* in 1820. He used the castle as the setting for the archery competition that Robin Hood won by splitting the shaft of his opponent's arrow in the bull's eye. The most striking feature of the imposing ruins is the 80ft Hastings Tower of 1464, which visitors can climb to enjoy the view. The earliest parts predate the conversion and include parts of the hall, buttery and pantry of the 12th-century manor house.

Hard by the castle ruins stands **St Helen's Church**, built by Lord Hastings in the 1400s on the site of an 11th-century church. Restored and enlarged in 1880, it contains much of interest, including some exceptionally fine stained glass depicting the life of Christ. There are several monuments to the Hastings family and an unusual relic in the shape of a finger pillory used to punish parishioners misbehaving in church. **Ashby-de-la-Zouch Museum** contains a permanent display of Ashby history, the highlight being a model of the castle during the Civil War siege.

Ashby was for a while in the 19th century promoted as a spa town; the Ivanhoe baths were designed in 1822 by Robert Chaplin in

Ashby Castle

🎭 stories and anecdotes   🦜 famous people   🎨 art and craft   🎵 entertainment and sport   🚶 walks

Grecian style and had a 150ft colonnaded front with 32 Doric columns. Nearby Georgian terraces, also by Chaplin, stand as testimony to the seriousness of the spa project, but a period of decline set in and the baths closed in the 1880s; the buildings were demolished in 1962. Yet another Chaplin building, the grand railway station, ceased to function as a station when the Leicester-Burton line was axed in the 1960s, but was restored in the 1980s for use as offices. The **National Forest** is Britain's boldest environmental project to create a new forest for the nation covering 200 square miles and spanning parts of Leicestershire, Staffordshire and Derbyshire. In its first 10 years more than seven million trees have been planted.

In the Ashby Tourist Information Centre (01530 411767) visitors can pick up a copy of the National Forest & Beyond Visitor Guide - Around Ashby de la Zouch.

MEASHAM
5 miles S of Ashby off the A42

🏛 Museum

Measham was a place of brick-making and coal-mining, with the Ashby Canal flowing past and the River Mease nearby. It was in his warehouse near the canal at Measham that Joseph Wilkes produced his double-size bricks, known as gobs or jumbies, to try to avoid the brick tax of 1784. Those bricks can still be seen in some of the buildings in the village. In the High Street, opposite St Lawrence's Church, **Measham Museum** is a small village museum with an interesting collection of artefacts, documents and illustrations preserved by a former village doctor and his father. They provide a unique personal history of a community over a period of almost 100 years. Look out for the

collection of colourful Measham Teapots, which were once very popular on canal boats. Many prehistoric artefacts have been found preserved in peat in the area, including stone hammerheads, solid wooden wheels and flint wedges bound in hazel (01530 273956).

MOIRA
2 miles SW of Ashby on the B586

🏛 Moira Furnace   🏃 Conkers

Conkers, an award-winning attraction in the centre of the National Forest (see under Ashby-de-la-Zouch), is located off the B5003 Ashby-Overseal road, five miles from the M42 (J11). It has 120 acres of themed trails, treetop walks, trains, two licensed lakeside restaurants, shop, garden and plants centre, amphitheatre and a number of craft workshops, as well as the Discovery & Waterside Centres with over 100 interactive exhibits and an all-year programme of events and activities. The site adjoins Sarah's Wood, a 25-acre farmland site transformed into a woodland and wildlife haven, with trails and paths suitable for wheelchairs and a children's play area.

Near Donisthope, two miles south of Ashby, Willesley Wood was one of the first National Forest planting sites and is now an attractive 100-acre area of mature woodland, a lake and meadows. One of the walks leads to Saltersford Valley, which features woodland sculptures, a lake and a picnic area.

The industrial heritage of the region is remembered in the **Moira Furnace**, an impressive, perfectly preserved blast furnace built in 1804 by the Earl of Moira. The site includes lime kilns, a casting shed and engine house, and a range of craft workshops, woodland walks, nature and industrial trails, country park and children's playground.

🏛 historic building   🏛 museum   🏛 historic site   🌢 scenic attraction   🌱 flora and fauna

FURNACE LANE POTTERY

Unit 7, Furnace Lane, Moira,
Swadlincote DE12 6AT
Tel: 01283 552218
e-mail: louiseroe@rocketmail.com

Louise Roe has always had a creative side to her personality and in particular a passion for pottery. Back in 1991 she decided to open her own pottery **Furnace Lane Pottery,** close to the historic Moira Furnace in the village of that name. A versatile artist, Louise creates a wide variety of pieces ranging from practical items such as jugs, mugs, cups, bowls, condiment sets, egg-cups and frost-proof garden ware, to striking decorative pieces that will enhance any interior décor. Everything on sale in the shop has been hand-made by Louise who fires all her pottery in a wood-burning kiln.

A visit to the pottery can easily be combined with a look around Moira Furnace, a spectacular brick building of 1806 which now houses a fascinating hands-on exhibit explaining the process of iron-making that took place here for many years.

STAUNTON HAROLD
4 miles N of Ashby off the B587

🐾 The Ferrers Centre   🏠 Calke Abbey

🚶 Reservoir

Another craft centre here, with 16 craft workshops within a magnificent Georgian courtyard. Crafts at **The Ferrers Centre** include contemporary furniture, ceramics, copper-smithing and forge, picture framing and sign studio, designer clothing and textiles, automata, stained glass, china restoration, stone carving and silver jewellery. Gift shop, gallery and tearoom on site. Staunton Harold Hall and Holy Trinity Church are surrounded by the beautiful parkland and lakes of the Staunton Estate. The Palladian-style hall is not open to the public, but the church is open for afternoon visits April to September, daily except Thursday and Friday. In the care of the National Trust, the church is one of the few to have been built during the Commonwealth period in 1653, designed by Sir Robert Shirley in defiance of Cromwell's Puritan regime. It retains the original pews, cushions and hangings, together with fine panelling and a painted ceiling.

Staunton Harold Reservoir, covering over 200 acres, has two nature reserves, fishing, sailing and a visitor centre with exhibitions and 3-D models. Footpaths and nature walks provide a link with the nearby 750-acre Calke Abbey park at Ticknall, near Melbourne. The National Trust's **Calke Abbey** is a baroque mansion built in 1701-1703 which has remained virtually unchanged since the death of the last baronet, Sir Vauncey Harpur-Crewe, in 1924.

Loughborough

🏛 Carillon 🏛 Museums 🏛 Great Central Railway

In Loughborough's Market Place is a statue of a seated man admiring his sock. Titled The Sock, this whimsical piece by sculptor Shona Kinlock celebrates the town's premier industry in times past, beginning with wool, then woollen stockings and progressing to knitwear and hosiery machinery and engineering.

Another major industry since mid-Victorian times is represented by the lofty **Carillon** in Queen's Park, which was opened in 1923 as an imaginative War Memorial to the dead of World War I. The 151ft carillon tower, the first to be built in Britain, contains a unique carillon of 47 bells, covering four chromatic octaves, under the care of the borough carilloner. Carillon recitals are given on Thursday and Sunday afternoons during the summer months. Visitors who climb the 138 steps to the viewing gallery are rewarded with magnificent views of the Charnwood scenery. The **Museum of Armed Forces** in Queen's Park has displays relating to the Great War and is open seven days a week.

Loughborough's connection with bells began in 1858 when the bell foundry of John Taylor moved here from Oxford. It is still producing and restoring bells for customers all over the world. Situated alongside the working factory, the **John Taylor Bellfoundry Museum** covers all aspects of bell-founding from early times and shows the craft techniques of moulding, casting, tuning and fitting up of bells. The foundry made Great Paul, which hangs in St Paul's Cathedral. It is the biggest bell in Britain, weighing 17 tons and standing nine feet high. Open Tuesday to Friday, also some Saturdays. (01509 212241).

The **Charnwood Museum** displays the natural and local history of Charnwood, the district around Loughborough that includes the majestic Charnwood Forest.

For many visitors to Loughborough, the most irresistible attraction is the **Great Central Railway**, Britain's only main line steam railway, established 30 years ago and run by a pool of up to 700 volunteers. Its headquarters are at Loughborough Central Station, where there is a museum, a working signal box and a collection of historic steam locomotives. The station, with its ornate canopy over the island platform, is worth a visit in its own right, and is in regular demand from film companies. It features in the film *Shadowlands* – other stars who have been filmed here include Nicole Kidman, Anthony Hopkins and Kate Winslet. The line runs eight miles from Loughborough to Birstall, just north of Leicester, crossing the Swithland Reservoir viaduct, and the service operates every weekend and Bank Holiday throughout the year, and weekdays from June to September. The line uses an impressive collection of ex-BR steam locomotives, from 4141, a GWR 2-6-2 Tank, to GWR 6990 *Witherslack Hall*, SR N15 30777 *Sir Lamiel*, Stanier Balck Fives, a Bulleid Light Pacific and Britannia 70013 *Oliver Cromwell*, as well as Diesel locomotives, multiple units and shunters. Call 01509 230726 for details of timetables and special events. In the Phantom & Firkin, Loughborough's only brew pub, visitors can see how traditional cask ales are made. Call 01509 262051 for details of free brewery tours.

Loughborough Market is one of the finest street markets in the country. Full of tradition and atmosphere, it is held in the market place and adjacent streets every Thursday and Saturday. November sees the annual Loughborough Fair, with stalls, shows, rides and other attractions.

🏛 historic building 🏛 museum 🏛 historic site 🔱 scenic attraction 🌿 flora and fauna

Around Loughborough

OLD WOODHOUSE

3 miles S of Loughborough on minor roads

🏛 Beaumanor Hall

The most impressive stained-glass window in Leicestershire is to be found not in any of the county's churches, but at **Beaumanor Hall**, the seat of the Herrick family from 1595 to the 1930s. The present Tudor-style mansion was built in 1848 and it was then that the extraordinary window, 15ft high and 25ft wide, was installed by William Perry Herrick. All his life William was obsessed with his family pedigree, so each of the 21 panels in the great window features the brilliantly coloured coat-of-arms of one of his ancestors. It's a breathtaking riot of heraldry. Sadly, for a man who took such pride in his ancestry, William died without a direct heir to succeed him.

Beaumanor Hall is now a Leicestershire County Council training centre, but the window may be viewed by prior arrangement by calling 01509 890119.

WOODHOUSE EAVES

3 miles S of Loughborough on minor roads

🌱 Long Close Gardens

🌳 Beacon Hill Country Park

The oldest house in this attractive village is Long Close, which is thought to have once been a royal hunting lodge. Secluded behind a high wall, the five acres of **Long Close Gardens** have become known as the Secret Garden. They've also been described as "a garden of exotic trees, luxuriant rhododendrons, shiny camellias, huge magnolias, terraced lawns, lily ponds and herbaceous borders". Call 01509 890376 for visiting times.

Woodhouse Eaves takes its name from being

GIFTED

53 Main Street, Woodhouse Eaves, Loughborough LE12 8RY
Tel: 01509 890666
e-mail: annie-84@hotmail.co.uk
website: www.giftedgb.co.uk

Stocked with contemporary, inspirational and luxury gifts, **Gifted** is a small boutique-style gift shop located on Main Street in the charming village of Woodhouse Eaves. The shop was lovingly prepared and is stocked by the mother and daughter team of Kate and Anne-Marie Walker both of whom have a passion for fashion and creativity. Their aim is to offer customers a diverse range of gifts and home-ware which will inspire customers and, as far as possible, be exclusive. For that reason they only hold limited stocks of each item, once they are gone, it is unlikely they will re-stock with the same item. Their advice, if you like it..buy it!

In the jewellery area you will find no shortage of sparkle or statement pieces and if you like to be completely different take a look at the individually designed and handmade pieces by Anne-Marie which are exclusive to Gifted.

Currently, the shop is only open on Friday and Saturday but you can also order on line.

🎭 stories and anecdotes   🦜 famous people   🎨 art and craft   🎟 entertainment and sport   🚶 walks

on the edges, or eaves, of Charnwood Forest. The views are superb, especially from the summit of **Beacon Hill Country Park**, one of the highest points in Leicestershire at 818ft.

SHEPSHED
4 miles W of Loughborough on the A512

The hosiery industry was once the principal employer here with some 900 stocking frames clattering away at the peak of the town's prosperity. Shepshed still offers factory outlet shopping for knitwear and clothing as well as traditional and farmers' markets. Around the medieval marketplace are some thatched cottages, homes to framework knitters in the 1800s.

CASTLE DONINGTON
7 miles NW of Loughborough off the A6

🏛 Donington Grand Prix Collection

Originally just Donington – the 'Castle' was added when the Norman castle was built to defend the River Trent crossing. It was demolished by King John to punish the owner for supporting Magna Carta and rebuilt in 1278.

The **Donington Grand Prix Collection**, in Donington Park, is the world's largest collection of single-seater racing cars. The five halls contain over 130 exhibits of motor racing. Donington is the new home of the British Formula 1 Grand Prix, taking over

---

VILLAGE CHIC

8 High Street, Sileby, Leicestershire LE12 7RX
Tel: 07971 597053
e-mail: sales@villagechic.co.uk
website: www.villagechic.co.uk

Furniture – Lighting – Accessories

Fine French furniture is the main stock in trade of Village Chic, which is located in the village of Sileby, north of Leicester between the A6 and A46. This unique enterprise is owned and run by Lucretia, who has years of experience in the world of interior design and decoration. She has grown the business into a major dealer in 18th and 19th century furniture, building up stock from a variety of sources. She always has a wide range of French armoires – single, 2-, 3- or 4-door, some mirrored – and other items on display include beds and bedside tables, dining room sets, gorgeous reproduction pieces, marbled and mirrored washstands, vintage/antique pieces in original condition and a wide variety of lighting and accessories.

Though a relatively small business, Village Chic can supply anything from a single item to a container load to furnish a room or a whole house. Styles include Old French Country, Vintage Boudoir, Louis XV, renaissance and specialist painted furniture. It also offers a paint service for customers' pieces, using water-based durable paint. One of the most popular styles is a 'shabby chic' effect, lightly or heavily distressed to bring out the details of carving then overwaxed. Lucretia is always interested in buying interesting, quality furniture and also offers an interior design service. She is constantly adding new items to the stock, a selection of which can be viewed (and purchased) online. Village Chic is open from Thursday to Sunday.

🏠 historic building   🏛 museum   🏚 historic site   🍃 scenic attraction   🌱 flora and fauna

from Silverstone for the 2010 renewal. Moving in the opposite direction is the British leg of Moto GP, which left Donington with a surprise winner in Andrea Dovizioso.

WYMESWOLD

5 miles N of Loughborough on the A6006

A large conservation village whose Georgian houses give it the air of an 18th-century market town – more than 30 of them are Grade II listed. The 14th-century parish church was restored by Pugin in 1844.

MOUNTSORREL

5 miles SE of Loughborough off the A6

🏠 Stonehurst Family Farm & Motor Museum

Peaceful since the A6 bypass was opened, Mountsorrel lies on the west bank of the Soar. Its elegant Butter Market, or Dome, lends distinction to an otherwise unremarkable little town. The Dome was built in 1793 by the eccentric Lord of the Manor, Sir John Danvers, and the town was surprised that he didn't have it painted red – almost everything else in Mountsorrel that could be painted was covered in brilliant red, a colour for which Sir John had an insatiable appetite. His clothes were predominantly red, set off by discreet touches of black: "being a broad-set man his appearance was like that of the Knave of Spades".

A great attraction in the village for the whole family is **Stonehurst Family Farm & Motor Museum**. Highlights range from baby rabbits and guinea pigs in Cuddle Corner, to all the familiar farm animals, pony rides, tractor and trailer rides, a working smithy and an impressive display of cars (Jim Clark's Lotus 25, the Flat 12 Ferrari 312B, the amazing 1936 Alfa Romeo Bimotore), motorcycles, other vehicles including Leicestershire's first motor bus, and a

fascinating collection of famous drivers' helmets. Also a restaurant, tea shop and farm shop selling home-grown organic produce.

Melton Mowbray

🏛 St Mary's Church 🏠 Ye Olde Pork Pie Shoppe

The very name of this bustling market town makes the mouth water, being home to the pork pie, one of the most traditional of English delicacies. The Melton Hunt Cake, a rich fruit cake spiced with Jamaican rum, is another local speciality, and Stilton, "king of English cheeses", is also made here. The cheese has a long history, dating back possibly as far as the 14th century and first made in the village of Little Dalby. It is only manufactured in Leicestershire, Nottinghamshire and Derbyshire. Of the six producers, four are in the Vale of Belvoir and one in Melton itself. The noble cheese became nationally popular in the 1740s when Frances Pawlett of Wymondham came to an arrangement with the landlord of The Bell Inn at Stilton to market the cheese. The inn was a coaching stop on the Great North Road and travellers who sampled the noble cheese soon spread its fame. Later, Melton Mowbray became the market centre for Stilton and from 1883 to 1914 three specialist fairs were held each year – 12,672 cheeses were sold at the first. A 16lb Stilton takes 17 gallons of milk to produce and a minimum of two months to mature. The town is also known for its Red Leicester cheese.

Hand-raised pork pies have been made here since 1831 and, since 1851, in the oldest surviving bakery, **Ye Olde Pork Pie Shoppe**, where visitors can watch the traditional hand-raising techniques and taste the pies.

Markets have long been a feature of life in

Melton Mowbray, and the Domesday Book of 1086 records the town's market as the only one in Leicestershire. Large street markets are held on Tuesdays and Saturdays in the Market Place, and butter and corn crosses still stand at two of the town's former market points. The town also has regular livestock auctions and a farmer's market.

St Mary's Church, considered the largest and stateliest parish church in the whole county, dates from 1170. It has a particularly imposing tower and impressive stained-glass windows.

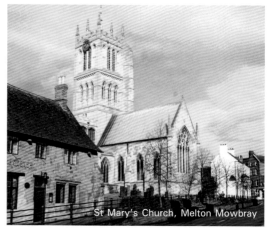

St Mary's Church, Melton Mowbray

Around Melton Mowbray

BURROUGH-ON-THE-HILL
5 miles S of Melton off the B6047

Burrough Hill is an Iron Age fort rising to almost 700ft overlooking the Wreake Valley. There are grand views from its flat summit that was used for horse racing in Victorian times.

TILTON-ON-THE-HILL
7 miles S of Melton on the B6047

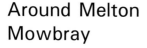 Owston Woods

The highest habitation in the county, some 700 feet above sea level, Tilton has a charming little church with some striking Norman gargoyles and stone carvings of human heads and animals, and some impressive monuments to members of the Digby family. About three miles east of the village there's pleasant walking in the Forestry Commission's **Owston Woods** – look out for the 800-year-old lime tree, which is still in remarkably good shape.

WYMONDHAM
6 miles E of Melton off the B676

🜚 Windmill and Craft Centre

A must for visitors here is the six-sailed **Windmill** dating from 1814 and currently being restored. It is one of only four of its kind in the country and most of its massive machinery is still intact. The mill's former outbuildings have been converted into a **Craft Centre** with workshops for wrought iron work, candle-making, pine furniture, hand-made kitchens, playhouses and architectural antiques. There's a tearoom serving light lunches and home-baked cakes, a free bouncy castle and play area. Bed & Breakfast accommodation is also available.

WALTHAM ON THE WOLDS
5 miles NE of Melton on the A607

Straddling the A607, high up on the Leicestershire Wolds, Waltham is an attractive village with an excellent hostelry and a tall-spired medieval church. Roman pavements and Saxon stone coffins have been discovered here, testifying to the antiquity of the

🏚 historic building 🏛 museum 🏛 historic site 🝔 scenic attraction �］ flora and fauna

STAPLEFORD PARK COUNTRY HOUSE HOTEL & SPORTING ESTATE

Stapleford, nr Melton Mowbray,
Leicestershire LE14 2EF
Tel: 01572 787000
Fax: 01572 787001
e-mail: reservations@stapleford.co.uk
website: www.staplefordpark.com

The approach to the house through the 500-acre estate offers the first glimpse of Georgian grandeur, confirmed when guests pass under the stone arch and into the welcome, warmth and grace of a bygone era. Most of the building is late 17th century, and the long history of hospitality is maintained by impeccable (but always approachable) hosts and staff. Oak floors, panelled walls, heavy drapes, fresh flowers, fine carvings and sumptuous armchairs and sofas set the scene in the day rooms, and the bedrooms are equally striking.

The 55 bedrooms have 55 unique designers, and the easy chairs, soft settees, beautiful beds and sumptuously appointed bathrooms put them in a class of their own. Most bedrooms enjoy glorious views of the grounds designed by Capability Brown.

Dining here is also a memorable experience, the finest and freshest seasonal ingredients used to create superb dishes complemented by a superb cellar. The private dining areas make a wonderful venue for a special celebration, and modern technology is available for meetings, conferences and events.

Stapleford also excels in its sporting and leisure facilities, which range from golf and tennis to riding, shooting, falconry, archery, croquet, boules and off-road driving. The Lifestyle Club in the converted stable block has a well equipped Technogym and six treatment rooms that offer a range of Clarins Gold Spa treatments. The main house features a swimming pool, sauna, steam room and Jacuzzi.

Stapleford Park
COUNTRY HOUSE HOTEL & SPORTING ESTATE

settlement. The country lane that leads from Waltham to Harby is unusually wide because, it is believed, it was an ancient drovers' road leading to Nottingham.

EASTWELL
5 miles N of Melton off the A607

🏛 Crossroads Farm Museum

Just outside the village, **Crossroads Farm Museum**, in a 17th-century barn, is a treasure trove of farming equipment and memorabilia from Victorian times to the present day.

STATHERN
7 miles N of Melton off the A607

A peaceful village nestling in the Vale of Belvoir, Stathern has a medieval church with a beautifully carved 13th-century doorway, an arcaded 14th-century font, and some fine modern glass. A one-time resident here was Colonel Hacker who acted as "master of ceremonies" at the execution of Charles I. After the Restoration he, too, was dispatched by the executioner's axe.

BELVOIR CASTLE
12 miles N of Melton off the A607

🏰 Castle   🏛 Queen's Royal Lancers Museum

The Leicestershire home of the Duke of Rutland is an imposing mock-medieval building in an equally imposing setting overlooking the pastoral Vale of Belvoir. The present **Belvoir Castle** was completed in the early 19th century after previous buildings had been destroyed during the Wars of the Roses, the Civil War and in the major fire of 1816. In the stunning interior are notable collections of furniture and porcelain, silks and tapestries, sculptures and paintings. There are works by Van Dyck, Reynolds, Hogarth and, most familiar of all, Holbein's imposing portrait of

Henry VIII. The **Queen's Royal Lancers Museum** has moved from the Castle to a new location – call 0115 957 3295 for information. The grounds are as splendid as the castle and are used for medieval jousting tournaments on certain days in the summer.

GRIMSTON
3 miles W of Melton off the A6006

Perhaps because of its unappealing name, Grimston tends to be overlooked by guide books. It is in fact one of the county's most appealing villages. At its centre is a lovely green where a set of ancient stocks stands beneath a chestnut tree. Overlooking the green are two venerable hostelries and the Church of St John the Evangelist. Here the curious custom of "bidding by candle" continued until the early 1900s.

A small stump of candle was lit and buyers would then make their bids for the item being auctioned. Whoever made the last bid before the candle guttered acquired the lot at that price.

Rutland

🌿 Rutland Water

The motto of the county is, appropriately, multum in parvo (much in little). It has two delightful market towns, Oakham and Uppingham, and 52 small, unspoilt villages of thatch and ironstone cottages clustered round their churches. The county's central feature is **Rutland Water**, which extends over 3,300 acres and is the largest man-made reservoir in Europe. Started in 1971 to supply water to East Midlands towns, it was created by damming the valley near Empingham. There's good walking and cycling around its 26-mile shoreline, some great bird-watching (including

🏛 historic building   🏛 museum   🏛 historic site   🌿 scenic attraction   🌿 flora and fauna wild ospreys), excellent trout and pike fishing, a wide variety of watersports and a rock climbing wall. St Matthews Church on the edge of the reservoir houses a museum.

The county boasts two leading public schools, Oakham and Uppingham; one of the most striking and best-preserved Norman churches in the country, at Tickencote; a grand 12th-century Great Hall and the home of the original Tom Thumb, both in Oakham.

Curiously for such a pastoral, peaceful county, it was Rutland men who were prime movers in two of the most dangerous conspiracies in England's history. In a room over the porch of Stoke Dry church, the Gunpowder Plot was hatched with the local lord of the manor, Sir Everard Digby, as one of the ringleaders. Some 75 years later, Titus Oates and his fellow conspirators hatched the anti-Catholic Popish Plot at his home in Oakham.

Uppingham

🏫 School

This picturesque stone-built town is the major community in the south part of the county. It has a long, handsome high street and a fine market place where traders have hawked their wares every Friday since 1280. The town is known for its bookshops and art galleries, but whereas other places are dominated by castles or cathedrals, in Uppingham it's the impressive **Uppingham School** that gives the town its special character. The school was founded in 1584 by Robert Johnson, Archdeacon of Leicester, who also founded Rutland's other celebrated public school at Oakham. For more than 250 years, Uppingham was just one of many such small grammar schools, giving rigorous instruction in classical languages to a

📖 stories and anecdotes 🐦 famous people 🎨 art and craft ✐ entertainment and sport 🚶 walks

SARAH HARDING INTERIORS LTD

27 High Street East, Uppingham,
Rutland LE15 9PY
Tel: 01572 823389 Fax: 01572 823772
e-mail: info@sarahhardinginteriors.co.uk
website: www.sarahhardinginteriors.co.uk

In the heart of historic Uppingham, Sarah Champion and her talented team offer a feast of inspirations to give their clients' homes a refreshing new look. **Sarah Harding Interiors** has been established in Uppingham for many years, starting in modest premises and moving into this prestigious High Street East location as the business expanded.

Two floors of showrooms occupy one of the oldest buildings in Uppingham (the site dates back to the Domesday Book) and beyond the handsome small-windowed stone façade every inch of space is filled with household goods large and small, including beautiful hand-finished curtains, new and interesting designs in curtain arrangements and wallpaper combinations and a terrific selection of fabulous fabrics. Sarah and her team invite customers to browse the latest designer fabrics through a vast range of fabric books, offering help and advice in relaxed, comfortable surroundings and tailoring orders to individual budgets and requirements.

All the leading brands of fabric suppliers and importers are to be found, including Colefax & Fowler, Zoffany, GP&J Baker, Parkertex, Osborne & Little, Nina Campbell, Designers' Guild, Jane Churchill, Lorca, Casamance, Manuel Canovas, Malabar, JAB, Sheila Coombes, Larsen, Vanessa Arbuthnott, Rubelli, Pierre Frey, James Brindley, James Hare and Mulberry. A large range of top-quality lamps and lighting caters for all budgets and settings, and an equally fine variety of beautiful accessories includes cushions and throws, vases and mugs, pottery and ceramics, aprons and tea towels, children's wear and other items from the likes of top designer-producers such as Emma Bridgewater, Cath Kidston and the Designers' Guild. The shop also stocks a range of exclusive gifts from Porta Romana, a UK-based firm established for and still committed to creating objects of beauty, drawing on the finest skills of glass blowers, metal workers, sculptors and furniture makers.

The furniture section features Victorian and Edwardian and some more recent pieces, lovingly restored and covered initially with blank calico, with customers choosing their own final covering. A full interior design and consultation service is available, either in the showroom or in the customer's home, and the firm undertakes re-upholstery of individual pieces and makes loose covers to order. They are specialists in restoring and re-covering antique chairs and settees.

🏠 historic building   🏛 museum   🏚 historic site   🐤 scenic attraction   🌱 flora and fauna

couple of dozen sons of the local gentry. Then, in 1853, the Rev Edward Thring was appointed headmaster. During his 43-year tenure the sleepy little school was transformed.

The Old School Building still stands in the churchyard, with trilingual inscriptions around the walls in Latin, Greek and Hebrew – 'Train up a child in the way he should go' is one of them. In its place rose a magnificent complex of neo-Gothic buildings: not just the traditional classrooms and a (splendid) chapel, but also a laboratory, workshops, museum, gymnasium and the most extensive school playing fields in the country.

Dr Thring wrote extensively on educational matters, championed education for girls and founded the Headmasters Conference. When he retired in 1897, he could look back with pride on the creation of one of the country's most successful public schools, both academically and financially. Call 01572 653026 for details of visits.

Around Uppingham

STOKE DRY
3 miles S of Uppingham on the A6003

There are some striking monuments in the church at Stoke Dry to the Digby family, particularly an engraved alabaster slab to Jaquetta Digby who died in 1496. One of her descendants, Sir Everard Digby born in the village in 1578, was to bring great shame on the family. When the Protestant James I ascended the throne, Sir Everard and his Catholic friends became involved in the conspiracy now known as the Gunpowder Plot. It was in the priest's room over the porch of St Andrew's Church that the conspirators met. After his conviction in 1609, Sir Everard endured the gruesome ordeal of death by hanging, drawing and quartering. The porch where the plotters met has another macabre story attached to it – it's said that one vicar locked a witch in the room and left her to die of starvation.

Stoke Dry overlooks Eyebrook Reservoir, a 300-acre trout fishery in an idyllic location in the Welland Valley, by the border with Leicestershire and Northamptonshire. Good bank and boat fishing from April to October.

LYDDINGTON
3 miles SE of Uppingham off the A6003

🏠 Bede House

A quiet village where English Heritage oversees **Bede House**, one of the finest examples of Tudor domestic architecture in the country. This house of prayer beside the church was once part of a retreat for the Bishops of Lincoln and was later converted to a hospital (bede house) for 12 poor men, two women and a warden. It remained in use right up until 1930. The fine 16th-century rooms can be visited daily from April to October. The small gardens contain a notable herb garden with over 60 herbs, both culinary and medicinal, and just outside the grounds lie the fish ponds that used to supply the bishop's kitchen.

WING

2 miles NE of Uppingham off the A6003

🕴 Maze

The little village of Wing is best known for a **Maze** in which it's impossible to get lost. The medieval Turf Maze is made of foot-high turf banks and measures 40 feet across. Its design is identical to the mosaic patterns in the floors of Chartres Cathedral and other French cathedrals. An old tradition asserts that penitents were required to crawl around the maze on their knees, stopping at various points to say prayers. Once a fairly common

Turf Maze, Wing

THE OLD WHITE HART

51 Main Street, Lyddington, nr Uppingham, Rutland LE15 9LR
Tel: 01572 821703 Fax: 01572 821965
e-mail: mail@oldwhitehart.co.uk
website: www.oldwhitehart.co.uk

The **Old White Hart** is a charming country inn set among sandstone cottages in the Rutland village of Lyddington. It lies off the A6003 just minutes from Uppingham and ten minutes from Corby. Stuart and Holly East's inn dates back to the 17th century, and small-paned windows, beams, stone walls, open fires, knick-knacks and prints of local interest all contribute to a delightful old-world atmosphere.

The inn has an excellent reputation for its food, with a variety of bar and restaurant menus providing plenty of choice every session except Sunday evening. The kitchen team show a combination of skill and imagination flair, highlighting prime produce in dishes such as crab & lobster terrine, salad of pigeon breast with pancetta, chard and sunblush tomatoes (starter or main), loin of lamb dauphinoise and rib-eye steak with tomato gratin and tarragon butter. Desserts like lemon meringue pie and sticky toffee pudding keep the enjoyment level high to the end, and the fine food is accompanied by real ales and a good choice of wines.

In cottages adjoining the inn are ten very well-appointed en suite bedrooms for B&B guests, one with a spiral staircase leading up from the bedroom to shower room and Jacuzzi. Pétanque is the favourite game at the Old White Hart, with regular events, tuition and convivial evenings of games followed by dinner. The Old White Hart appears in the Michelin Pub Guide, Good Pub Guide and Quality in Tourism four star.

🏛 historic building   📷 museum   🏚 historic site   ᇰ scenic attraction   🌱 flora and fauna

sight, only eight such turf mazes are known to still exist in England. They were already falling into disfavour by Shakespeare's time. In *A Midsummer Night's Dream* he wrote:

And the quaint mazes in the wanton green
For lack of tread, are indistinguishable.

Oakham

🏛 Castle   🏛 All Saints Church   🏛 Museum

🏛 Flore's House   🏛 School

Oakham is one of England's most appealing county towns, a friendly place with many old hostelries, a regular twice weekly market, a wide variety of family-owned shops, a fine church and a major public school.

Just off the Market Place with its charming market cross and stocks is **Oakham Castle**, a romantic, evocative fortified manor house built between 1180 and 1190, with the earliest surviving example of an aisled stone hall in the country. A unique feature is a collection of over 200 horseshoes hanging all around the walls of the hall. For centuries, any peer of the realm passing through the town has been required to present a horseshoe to the castle. When this custom started isn't clear, although one plausible story says that it began in the days of William the Conqueror when his farrier lived here. (The farrier's descendants, the Ferrers family, later built the Great Hall.) This unusual tax is still being imposed – amongst the hundreds of horseshoes of every size, some ornately gilded, others rusty, is one presented by Queen Elizabeth II.

All Saints Church is the spiritual centre of town, a fine parish church with a 14th-century tower. On the capitals in the nave are striking carvings of traditional subjects, including

---

ANGELS CAFÉ/BISTRO

2 Burley Road, Oakham,
Rutland LE15 6DH
Tel: 01572 755853
e-mail: gaynor-dean@hotmail.co.uk
website: www.angelsrestaurant.co.uk

Angels Café/Bistro occupies a double-fronted building just off the main street in Oakham, between the B640 and B668. Since opening hare in 2006, Dean and Gaynor poole have built up a loyal band of regulars with their authentic English cuisine with a personal twist. In stylish contemporary surroundings that include beams, carpets and a brick-fronted service counter, fresh ingredients are handled with skill and flair, with the layering of each constituent of main courses demonstrating cooking and presentation at a high level. It's a great place to visit at any time of day, whether it's for a snack and a cup of coffee, a sandwich, a pastry or a full meal.

The menu includes breakfast (all appetites catered for), sandwiches made to order on granary, farmhouse white or ciabatta bread, freshly made salads, stone-baked pizza, jacket potatoes, daily fish specials, scampi, burgers, scones, teacakes and always vegetarian main dishes like courgette and broccoli crumble. The re's a good choice of beer, wine, soft drinks, teas and coffees to accompany the excellent food.

🎭 stories and anecdotes   🦜 famous people   🎨 art and craft   🎭 entertainment and sport   🚶 walks

dragons, the Green Man, Adam and Eve, and Reynard the Fox.

Rutland County Museum, housed in a splendid 18th-century riding school in Catmose Street, has displays of farm equipment, machinery and wagons, domestic collections and local archaeology. The riding school belonged to the Rutland Fencibles, a volunteer cavalry regiment raised in 1794 and now remembered in a gallery in the museum.

Flore's House is one of the oldest buildings in the town. It dates from the late 1300s and was built by William Flore and his son Roger, who was a wealthy merchant and four times Speaker of the House of Commons.

Notable natives of Oakham include the infamous conspirator Titus Oates who was born here in 1649 and lived in Mill Street. A minor cleric, he played the leading role in fabricating the Popish Plot of 1678. Oates claimed to have uncovered a secret Jesuit plot to assassinate Charles II and return the Catholic Church to power. Many innocent Catholics were killed as a result of this alarm, but Oates, when the truth was discovered, did not escape lightly. He was sentenced to yearly whippings and was not freed until 1688; he died in obscurity in 1705.

Another Oakham man involved in Titus Oates' conspiracy was the famed midget Jeffery Hudson, "the smallest man from the smallest county in England". He lived in a thatched cottage that still stands on Melton Road opposite the White Lion pub. By the age of nine, Jeffery stood a mere 18 inches high and he never grew to more than 3ft 6in. His father, who was above average height, worked on the Duke of Buckingham's estate at nearby Burley on the Hill, a couple of miles northeast of Oakham. The duchess took a fancy to the

🏤 historic building 🏛 museum 🏚 historic site 🌣 scenic attraction 🌱 flora and fauna

HEIDI KJELDSEN

5 The Maltings, Mill Street, Oakham,
Rutland LE15 6EA
Tel: 01572 722666
e-mail: heidi@heidikjeldsen.com
website: www.heidikjeldsen.com

Amongst Oakham's charming boutiques, antique shops and haute couture shops in Mill Street sits fine jewellers **Heidi Kjeldsen**. In a quaint listed building Heidi Kjeldsen has been designing and making beautiful jewellery here since 1998, greatly influenced by her Danish connections and her love and extensive knowledge of Diamonds and coloured Gemstones and all varieties of pearls.

Heidi's collection includes rings, necklaces, pendants, earrings, bangles and bracelets, brooches, cufflinks, handmade silver gifts and loose Gemstones. Her designs are classical in concept but with a contemporary twist which makes their desirability truly timeless. Heidi Kjeldsen's collection ranges from the simplest of handmade sterling silver bangles to stunning Diamond-set jewellery, multi-coloured Sapphires, rare Emeralds, true pigeon's blood red Rubies and many other unusual Gemstones. The jewellery settings are handcrafted, to a very high standard, and all the Diamonds, Gemstones and Pearls are carefully selected for their exceptional quality. To the best of Heidi's knowledge, with written guarantees, the provenance of all the materials and Gemstones is conflict-free and ethically sourced. All pendants can be sold separately from their chains as the choice of chain lengths and designs is limitless and any ideas you have can be included in the final piece.

Heidi offers a model-making service and also a computer aided design process that allows all bespoke pieces to be viewed and if necessary altered prior to the final manufacturing process. Heidi's website-**www.heidikjeldsen.com** shows new pieces being added all the time and gives a snapshot of what stock is available to purchase online or in the shop. Apart from the pieces made here the website also includes the Picchiotti range of very exclusive handmade Italian jewellery which Heidi is privileged to stock.

Heidi and her team are always ready to help and advise, and they are happy to discuss designing and crafting individual pieces to your special requirements.

The charming county town of Oakham has much to attract the visitor and a visit to Heidi's shop should definitely be high on the agenda. Opening times are 9am to 5.30pm Monday to Saturday.

CAVELLS

16 Mill Street, Oakham, Rutland LE15 6EA
Tel: 01572 770372
e-mail: info@cavells.co.uk website: www.cavells.co.uk

Founded in 1993, **Cavells** has evolved into one of the most successful independent fashion stores in the UK providing stylish and select shopping for men and women outside London.

Located in the picturesque market town of Oakham and occupying 3,500 square feet Cavells is spacious, stylish and welcoming; a glorious retreat from everyday reality.

For ladies Cavells stock an unrivalled jeans selection including Armani, Seven and Citizens of Humanity; with formal collections from Ralph Lauren, Joseph and Marc Cain. For the more casual occasion; Oui Moments, Gant, Jackpot and Velvet. With shoes from Ash, Vic Matie and Geox and accessories from Mulberry, Paul Smith and Coccinelle.

Cavells Menswear offers an extensive range of Polo Ralph Lauren and Paul Smith including their accessories, plus heritage brands Fred Perry, Gloverall Duffle Coats and Baracuta Harrington jackets.

Cavells is renowned for a high level of service and the shop assistants are always on hand to provide unbiased advice. Cavells has a comfortable seating area with complimentary coffee, plasma screen TV, daily newspapers and magazines providing a perfect distraction for those non-shoppers.

CAVELLS OUTDOORS

The Old Mill, South Street, Oakham, Rutland LE15 6BG
Tel: 01572 772502
e-mail: info@cavellsoutdoors.co.uk
website: www.cavellsoutdoors.co.uk & www.cavellscountry.co.uk

Cavells Outdoors opened in August 2009 and stocks a fantastic selection of premium outdoor clothing and accessories. Cavells Outdoors is a new addition to the established and successful Cavells fashion store located just around the corner.

A contemporary feel with authentic outdoor materials and bespoke design Cavells Outdoors offers a unique shopping environment. Flooded with light and vibrant in colour you will be inspired by our collections whether travelling, walking in the countryside, trekking, skiing, climbing or just wanting to stay comfortable whatever the elements throw at you.

Cavells Outdoors brands include Icebreaker, 100% merino wool apparel from New Zealand, specialist clothing and equipment from Mountain Hardwear, Royal Robbins travel and adventure clothing and performance footwear from Keen and Brasher, to name just a few. Specialist advice is available from a team of dedicated outdoor enthusiasts.

Cavells Country is located on the first floor mezzanine of the Cavells Outdoors store and stocks an extensive selection of the finest, stylish and functional countrywear brands including Schöffel Countrywear, Barbour, Aigle, R M Williams, Really Wild Clothing, Dubarry with accessories by Marc Cain, Mulberry, Johnstons and Helen Kaminski plus many more.

THE CHOCOLATE BAR

49a High Street, Oakham, Rutland LE15 6AJ
Tel: 01572 724554
e-mail: enquiries@chocolatebar.co.uk
website: www.echocolatebar.co.uk

A very special shop on Oakham's High Street provides gifts to remember for Christmas, Easter, Mothers Day, Fathers Day, Valentines Day, weddings, birthdays.......for any occasion that calls for something special. The **Chocolate Bar** was opened in 2001 by two chocoholic friends Sharon and Lesley, who transformed a modest café and chocolate shop into a haven for chocolate lovers and a vibrant place to meet for coffee, hot chocolate and something delicious to eat.

The Chocolate Bar sells a wide range of the finest Belgian chocolates available in the region, and in addition to the mouthwatering display of individual chocolates there are bars, bags, boxes of 4, 8, 12, 18 or 24 chocolates and a selection of gluten-free, sugar-free and dairy-free chocs. In the Café, a treat not to be missed is the Choclate Bar Special – the finest hot chocolate laden with whipped cream, a smattering of marshmallows adorned with a flake and crowned with a dusting of cocoa powder. The menu also offers savoury snacks and meals as well as lots of lovely cakes. Customers can order their chocolates by phone or online for delivery anywhere in the UK.

---

minuscule lad, dressed him in costly silk and satin, and kept him by her as a kind of mascot. When Charles I and his Queen, Henrietta Maria, were guests at Burley, a huge cold pie was placed on the table before them and when the pie was cut open out popped Jeffery. The Queen was so delighted with the midget that she took him back to the royal court, where he became a popular figure, was knighted and had his portrait painted by Van Dyck. But Jeffery was an extremely quarrelsome character and on one occasion challenged Lord Crofts to a duel in which the latter was killed. Jeffery was banished for a time, but while travelling back to England was captured by Turkish pirates and sold as a slave. Ransomed by the Duke of Buckingham, he returned to Oakham and the house in the High Street. With his usual impetuosity he became involved in Titus Oates' Popish Plot and was imprisoned.

Oakham School was founded in 1584 by Archdeacon Robert Johnson, who also founded Uppingham School. As at Uppingham, the original single room school building still stands, its walls inscribed with Hebrew, Latin and Greek quotations. Both schools expanded greatly in the 19th century, but while the school buildings at Uppingham dominate the little town, at Oakham they are spread across the town centre, partly hidden away off the attractive market place where the ancient butter cross still provides shelter for the town stocks. Now co-educational, Oakham School has around 1,000 pupils.

On the outskirts of town, the road to Uppingham crosses Swooning Bridge, where condemned felons going on their last journey

---

📖 stories and anecdotes　🍃 famous people　🎨 art and craft　🎭 entertainment and sport　🚶 walks

Hambleton Peninsula

Distance: *3.7 miles (6.0 kilometres)*

Typical time: *90 mins*

Height gain: *0 metres*

Map: *Explorer 15 Rutland Water*

Walk: *www.walkingworld.com ID:29*

Contributor: *Nicholas Rudd-Jones*

Turning off on the A606, about 8 miles from the A1 Stamford turning. Park the car at the pub (if you intend to use it later) or in the road just outside.

ADDITIONAL INFORMATION:

Rutland Water is a created lake, supplying water to the East Midlands. It is basically a huge success story, attracting lots of active visitors.

DESCRIPTION:

A very pleasant walk around the edge of the Hambleton Peninsula, which looks out in all directions over Rutland Water, a man-made success. Rutland Water has many leisure pursuits, notably sailing and cycling. It's a very good place to come with the family.

The walk itself is simple, suitable for all ages with lots to distract youngsters. The Finch Arms at the end of the walk is an excellent place for (posh) snacks and refreshment and welcomes children. It can be very muddy; cyclists can be numerous on Bank Holidays.

FEATURES:

Lake/Loch, Pub, Wildlife, Birds, Flowers, Great Views.

WALK DIRECTIONS:

1 | Cross a cattle-grid at the end of the road, and strike out along a stony track that runs east along the side of the lake. Very shortly you should turn left, pass through another cattle-grid and continue on eastwards. The walk is very straightforward, flat and passing through interesting woods. There is always a lovely view of the lake to your right. Up on the hill, on your right, you will see a splendid Victorian hunting lodge – Hambleton Hall, now a famous restaurant. After about 2km the track takes a sharp left inland and then shortly afterwards, just before hitting the road, takes a sharp right.

2 | Go north from this point along the stone track (not down the road). The path soon reaches the other side of the promontory and swings back westwards. Stay on undulating path for about 3km, until you reach the road.

3 | When you reach the road, turn left – a short walk takes you back to the pub and the car.

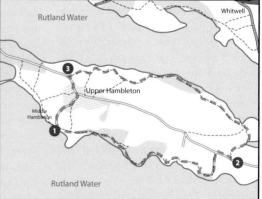

OAKHAM ORIENTAL RUGS

6-7 The Maltings, Mill Street, Oakham, Rutland LE15 6EA
Tel: 01572 724441
e-mail: mail@oakhamorientalrugs.co.uk
website: www.oakhamorientalrugs.co.uk

The prestigious shopping area of Mill Street in Oakham has been called the Knightsbridge of Rutland for its wealth of high-quality retail outlets. Among the many enterprises in the modern development of The Maltings is **Oakham Oriental Rugs**, a family business established in 1993 and owned and managed by Fiona and Christian Hawker. Soon after The Maltings was opened they took the opportunity to set up a business that has built up a fine reputation for offering the widest selection of hand-knotted traditional and contemporary rugs and carpets in the region.

Each piece, from small rugs to room-size carpets, is hand chosen by the owners, who offer expert knowledge, superb value for money and a money-back guarantee of satisfaction. The array includes Persian, Afghan and Indian rugs and carpets, world-renowned names such as Aubusson and Ziegler and an exclusive selection of antiques rugs. Oakham Oriental Rugs offers a cleaning and repair service, as well as bespoke commissions from a variety of styles, patterns, weaves and colours. 'Design Your Own Rug' is an offering unique to the business. Browsers are always welcome at this delightful place, where there are rugs on the floor, rugs on the walls, even rugs tent-style on the ceiling, in a setting complemented by appropriate décor and furniture. Shop hours are 10 to 5 Tuesday to Saturday.

from the town gaol first saw, on top of a small rise called Mount Pleasant, the gallows from which they were about to be hanged.

Around Oakham

EGLETON

1 mile E of Oakham on a minor road

🐦 Birdwatch Centre

Egleton is home to Anglian Water's **Birdwatch Centre**, located on two storeys on the west shore, with nature trails, bird hides and a Wildlife Trust shop (01572 770651).

EDITH WESTON

5 miles E of Oakham off the A6003

🏛 Normanton Church

This village takes its name from Edith, wife and then widow of King Edward the Confessor (1042-1066), who gave her this part of the county as a gift. A peaceful spot in the heart of really lovely countryside on the south shore of Rutland Water. Near the village, off the A606 and A6121, stands Rutland's best-known landmark. **Normanton Church**, on the very edge of Rutland Water, was formerly part of the Normanton Estate and now houses a display dedicated to the construction of the reservoir by Anglian Water and a history of the area. Open April to September. The estate was the property of the big local landowner Sir Gilbert Heathcote, sometime Lord Mayor of London, who pulled down the village of Normanton to enlarge his park and moved the villagers to nearby Empingham.

🎭 stories and anecdotes 🦜 famous people ✏ art and craft 🎫 entertainment and sport 🚶 walks

EMPINGHAM

5 miles E of Oakham on the A606

🏠 Dovecote

This pleasant little town is dominated by the tower and spire of St Peter's Church, whose interior features include fragments of ancient glass. In a field just outside the village stands a well-preserved **Dovecote** containing 700 nests. It could have been in this very field that one of the bloodiest slaughters of the Wars of the Roses took place, on 12 March 1470 – in all, some 10,000 men were killed. This gory clash of arms became known as the Battle of Losecoat Field because the defeated Lancastrians shed their uniforms as they fled in the hope of avoiding recognition, capture and certain death.

TICKENCOTE

8 miles E of Oakham off the A1

🏠 Church of St Peter

Apart from Canterbury Cathedral there is nothing in England to compare with the astonishing Norman sexpartite vaulting over the chancel of the parish **Church of St Peter** in the tiny village of Tickencote. Equally breathtaking is the chancel arch, a mighty six-layered portal leading to a miniscule nave beyond. Built around 1140, each of the overlapping six arches is carved with a different design – foliage, chevrons, double zigzags, beak-head ornament or just plain round mouldings. In addition to these masterpieces of Norman architecture, St Peter's also contains a remarkably fine 13th-century font and an unusual wooden life-size effigy of a 14th-century knight.

LITTLE CASTERTON

9 miles E of Oakham via the A606/A1

🏠 Tolethorpe Hall

Tolethorpe Hall, just off the A1 and close to the Lincolnshire border, is best known as the home of the Stamford Shakespeare Company, which each summer performs three different plays on an open-air stage in an idyllic woodland setting facing a 600-seat covered auditorium. 2009 sees its 33rd annual season. The old manor house has another claim to fame as the birthplace in 1550 of Robert Browne, one of the earliest congregationalists. His radical views led to his arrest and it was only through the intervention of his kinsman Lord Burghley that he was released. Browne's religious views mellowed with the passing of the years – his fiery temper did not. At the age of 80 Browne was consigned to Northampton for an assault on a constable and it was there that he died in 1633.

EXTON

5 miles NE of Oakham off the A606

🏠 Church of St Peter & St Paul

🌱 Barnsdale Gardens

A charming village in one of the largest ironstone extraction areas in the country with a church set in delightful parkland. The **Church of St Peter & St Paul** is remarkable for its wealth of fine monuments, a sumptuous series commemorating members of the Noel and Harington families interred here from the early 1500s to the late 1700s. This imposing collection is dominated by a colossal memorial to Baptist Noel, 3rd Viscount Campden, who died in 1683. Sculpted in black and white marble by Grinling Gibbons, it stands 22ft high and 14ft wide, almost filling one wall of the north transept. A lengthy inscription extols Viscount Campden's many fine qualities that had "justly rendered him the admiration of his contemporaries and the imitation of postery".

Barnsdale Gardens, in The Avenue, were

TABLE PLACE

FURNITURE RETAILER & BESPOKE CABINETMAKERS

*Thistleton Road, Market Overton, Oakham,
Rutland LE15 7PP
Tel: 01572 767636 Fax: 01572 767932
e-mail: oakham@tableplace.co.uk
website: www.table-place.co.uk*

Quality, reliability, service and value for money are watchwords at **Table Place**, which stands on a small industrial estate near Oakham. In Rutland for nearly 30 years, the business has built up an enviable reputation throughout the region under Managing Director Marietta King. Starting in a small way making tables for the trade, she has expanded the enterprise to direct selling of a wide range of classic English furniture – chairs, cabinets, desks, hall tables – in maple (the Mayflower range from Marietta is a great favourite), ash, beech, mahogany, oak and yew.

The expert cabinetmakers and polishers can be seen in the workshop, where no fewer than 327 different operations go into the making of a single piece of furniture, using traditional and modern methods as appropriate at each stage. The finished pieces can be viewed in the large showrooms around and above the workshop. Marietta and her team offer a variety of services, including restoration of antiques, re-polishing, upholstery work and room planning (fabrics and furniture). They are always happy to discuss commissions for bespoke pieces. Table Place is open Thursday to Monday from 10 to 4 (from 11 Sunday, closed Bank Holiday Mondays).

made familiar to millions by the late Geoff Hamilton, who designed the gardens, on TV's *Gardeners' World*. They are now run by his son and daughter-in-law and embrace many themes, including cottage, allotment and kitchen gardens, woodland, parterre and town and country paradises. Open all year.

PICKWORTH

9 miles NE of Oakham off the A1

Pickworth's most famous resident was John Clare, surely one of the saddest figures in the pantheon of English poets. Born in 1793 in a village near Peterborough, Clare came to Pickworth as a young man, finding work on a nearby farm. Over the course of a year he managed to save £1 from his meagre wages and used it to publish a prospectus of his poems. The poems were eventually published, in 1820, but did not sell. Poverty, poor health and incipient madness stalked him throughout his life. His happiest years may well have been spent at Pickworth for it was here that he met 18-year-old Patty Turner whom he immortalised in one of his most charming poems:

> *And I would go to Patty's cot,
> And Patty came to me,*

Each knew the other's every thought
Under the hawthorn tree.

And I'll be true for Patty's sake
And she'll be true for mine,
And I this little ballad make
To be her Valentine.

They married soon afterwards and eventually had seven children. But Clare was working beyond his strength and gradually his habitual melancholy deteriorated into madness. He spent the last 27 years of his life in asylums. His youngest son went to see him once; Patty could never bring herself to visit.

COTTESMORE
5 miles NE of Oakham on the B668

🏛 Railway Museum

The **Rutland Railway Museum** is the big attraction here. The working steam/diesel museum is based on local quarry and industrial railways, a living museum that recreates the heyday of quarrying in the 1950s and 1960s. The open-air steam centre is home to a large collection of steam and diesel locomotives, wagons, vans and coaches, together with many related items and artefacts and a mineral railway running from the quarry to the exchange sidings. Call 01572 813203 for details of steam days and gala days. A little further along the B668 is the village of Greetham on the Viking Way, one of the three long-distance walks that converge on Oakham.

CLIPSHAM
10 miles NE of Oakham off the B668

🌱 Yew Tree Avenue

Just to the east of this small village is one of the most extraordinary sights in the county, **Yew Tree Avenue**. In the 1870s, Amos Alexander, head forester to the Clipsham Hall

Rutland Railway Museum

🏛 historic building   🏛 museum   🏛 historic site   🌱 scenic attraction   🌱 flora and fauna

Estate, began clipping the yew trees around his lodge into chimerical shapes – a fantastic parade of animals, chess pieces and abstract forms. The Squire of Clipsham admired them greatly and gave Amos a free hand with the 150 yew trees lining the approach to the hall. Along the 700-yard avenue appeared a dream-like succession of figures, some commemorating local or national events, others recording family events.

Amos died in the early 1900s and the trees were left untended until, in 1955, the Forestry Commission assumed responsibility for the avenue and renewed the topiary tradition. Each of the trees is between 15 and 20ft high, and each is shaped individually. An elephant looks across to a ballerina; a Spitfire takes off towards a battleship, Diddy-men cavort near a windmill – there's even a Big Mac hamburger in there somewhere!

TEIGH
5 miles N of Oakham on a minor road

Teigh (pronounced tea) is one of the 31 Thankful Villages, those communities where all the men and women who served in World War I survived. A brass inscription in the church gives thanks for the safe return of the 11 men and two women from the village who went to war.

The Old Rectory, which stands next to the Strawberry Hill-style Gothic church, has a delightful partly-walled garden that was first laid out in the 1950s.

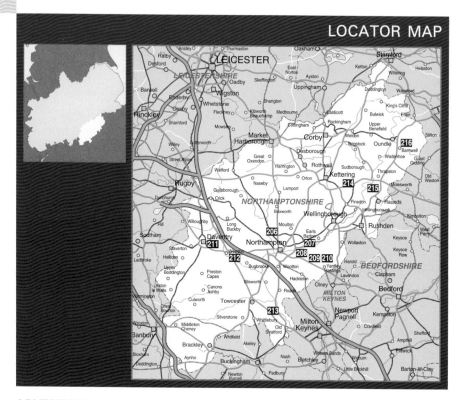

LOCATOR MAP

ADVERTISERS AND PLACES OF INTEREST

🏠 historic building   🏛 museum   🏛 historic site   🌳 scenic attraction   🌿 flora and fauna

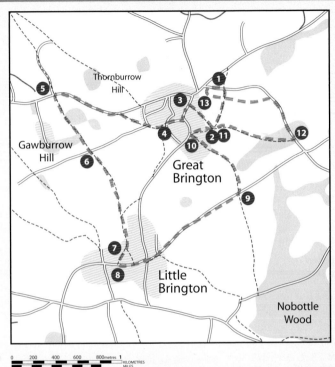

of the clump of trees. At the corner of the field go through the small gate and turn left onto the road. Follow the road for 500m.

11 | At the first footpath on the left, cross the stile and follow the right-hand edge of the field up to the edge of the woods. Go through the gate and follow the edge of the woods. As the edge of the wood turns to the left, head diagonally across the field, to the right of the telegraph pole in the distance. Following the marker-post, head uphill with the next section of woodland on the right. Cross the stile and take the footpath straight ahead, following the line of the telegraph poles.

12 | At the hedge field boundary, walk straight ahead with the hedge on your right. Follow the footpath straight ahead across three fields. At this point you join the Macmillan Way. Head across the field, aiming for the footpath to the right of the metal shed.

13 | Go through the gate to the right of the metal shed and walk straight ahead along the right-hand edge of the narrow field. Turn left to reach the car park.

8 | Go through the gate and follow the left-hand edge of the field, continuing through the next gate. Continue through the kissing-gate on the pathway between the houses.

9 | At the road turn left and follow it for 100m. Turn right at the next road and follow to its end (a further 100m).

10 | At the end of the road, continue straight ahead into the field. Then head slightly to the right, aiming for the left-hand end of the trees, to a gate. Go through the gate. Head diagonally across the field, slightly to the right

SMITH'S FARM SHOP

West View Farm, Brampton Lane, Chapel Brampton,
Northamptonshire NN6 8AA
Tel: 01604 843206 Fax: 01604 843299
e-mail: smithsfarmshop@btinternet.com
website: www.smithsfarmshop.co.uk

From small beginnings in 1958, selling strawberries from the farm gate, Smith's Farm Shop has grown into a retailer of a wide variety of quality produce, meeting the demand for one-stop grocery shopping. Much of the fruit and vegetables is home-grown, with natural fertilisers and organic manure and minimal use of chemicals to keep pests and disease at bay. The home-grown choice includes asparagus, potatoes and pumpkin squash. The shop also sells delicatessen items, dairy produce, preserves and honey, Mrs Smith's famous chutneys, health foods, cooking sauces, teas, coffees and juices, along with flowers and plants, garden and pet supplies and solid fuels. Another outlet is at Great Billing, Northamptonshire, Tel: 01604 412116.

CHAPEL BRAMPTON

4 miles NW of Northampton off the A508

🏛 Northampton & Lamport Railway

Steam train buffs will want to pay a visit to the **Northampton & Lamport Railway**, which is home to an interesting collection of railway-related vehicles. Visitors can enjoy a journey hauled by vintage locomotives such as ex-GWR 2-8-0 3862 and 5967 *Bickmarsh Hall*; there are heritage displays and special events throughout the year. For timetable details call 01604 820327.

HOLDENBY

7 miles NW of Northampton off the A428

🏛 Holdenby Hall

The Royal connections go back more than 400 years at **Holdenby Hall**, which was built by Elizabeth I's Lord Chancellor and favourite, Sir Christopher Hatton, for the purpose of entertaining the Queen. At the time, it was the largest Elizabethan house in England and, for the diarist John Evelyn, "one of the most pleasing sights that ever I saw". It was visited but once by Elizabeth; it later became the palace and eventually the prison of Charles I, who was kept under guard here for five months after his defeat in the Civil War. The house, which appeared as Limmeridge House in the BBC's *The Woman in White*, stands in magnificent grounds, which contain a falconry centre, a smaller scale reconstruction of Hatton's original garden, a fully working armoury and a 17th century farmstead that evokes the sights and smells of life in days gone by. There's a museum, a children's farm and a lakeside train ride together with tea in the Victorian Kitchen.

EAST HADDON

7 miles NW of Northampton off the A428

🌿 Haddonstone Showgardens

A village of thatched cottages, a village pump protected by a neat thatched cone, a 14th century church and an 18th century hall. It is best known for **Haddonstone Showgardens**, which has walled gardens on different levels and a huge stock of garden ornaments of every kind.

GUILSBOROUGH

9 miles NW of Northampton off the A5199

🌿 Coton Manor Garden

A handsome, dignified village where Wordsworth came to stay in the vicarage and, it is said, brought with him the yellow Cumberland poppy that is often seen here. The church has lovely windows by William Morris and Burne-Jones, and Guilsborough Grange has a wildlife park and areas for walking and picnicking. A short distance south of the village, in the tiny community of Coton,

Coton Manor Gardens, nr Guilsborough

Coton Manor Garden is a traditional garden originally laid out in 1925 and embracing several delightful smaller gardens. Beyond the garden are a wildflower meadow and a magical five-acre bluebell wood. The nursery propagates over 1,000 varieties of plant, and in the stable yard are a restaurant and tea room.

KINGSTHORPE
2 miles N of Northampton on the A508

Once a small riverside village, Kingsthorpe is now effectively a suburb of Northampton but its ancient church still looks across meadows to the River Nene. Inside, there are some massive Norman arches with varied ornamental carving.

PITSFORD
4 miles N of Northampton off the A508

Off the A508 just north of the village, Pitsford Water is an 800-acre reservoir with trout fishing and boats for hire, sailing, a picnic area, nature reserve and information centre. The reservoir is also accessible from the village of Holcot.

COTTESBROOKE
9 miles N of Northampton off the A5199

🏛 Cottesbrooke Hall

In secluded countryside near the site of the Battle of Naseby, **Cottesbrooke Hall** is one of the finest of all the grand houses in the county. The magnificent Queen Anne house, reputedly the model for Jane Austen's Mansfield Park, was begun in 1702 and is home to an impressive collection of pictures, porcelain and furniture. The grounds are quite superb, featuring the Statue Walk (statues from the Temple of Ancient Virtue, at Stowe), the Dilemma Garden with old roses and rare trees, the Dutch Garden, the Pine Court and many other charming gardens and courtyards. The hall and gardens are open to visitors on certain days in the summer.

EARLS BARTON
5 miles NE of Northampton off the A45

🏛 Church of All Saints

A great treasure here is the village **Church of All Saints**, with one of the most impressive Anglo-Saxon towers in the whole country, its

26-28 The Square, Earls Barton, Northamptonshire NN6 ONA
Tel/Fax: 01604 810289
e-mail: info@jeyesofearlsbarton.co.uk   website: www.jeyesofearlsbarton.co.uk

You'll be surprised what you will find behind the JEYES door.............

Whether you have an hour to spare or an afternoon to fill, Jeyes of Earls Barton is truly a special place to visit. Prominently situated on the village square you will find an unusual collection of shops all under one roof. The shop is full of surprises: with each corner you will find something new and exciting.

David and Georgina Jeyes established their traditional local pharmacy over 28 years ago – family roots go back to Philadephus Jeyes in The Drapery, Northampton and the well known Jeyes fluid, invented by John Jeyes in 1810 and still used throughout the world. Now their daughters, Philippa and Anna, have joined them and they all work together at **Jeyes of Earls Barton**. Marie, known to all as 'Nan' still works behind the scenes, and two new additions to the payroll are Philippa's toddler Maisie and baby Jack! A true family business.

Through the front door you will find; **The Keepsake Gift Shop**, located in the Old Natwest Bank, selling beautiful keepsakes and gifts; **Potty About Flowers Conservatory** where their love of flowers and floral gifts are displayed; **The Dolly Lodge**, a shop dedicated to dolls houses, furniture, books and much more for dolls house enthusiasts; **'The Fun of The Fair' Model Display** - as seen on *BBC Look East* -George Jennings Model funfair is on display free of charge for all the family. Also upstairs is **The Earls Barton Museum of Village Life** and a display of **Jeyes Pharmacy Memorabilia**. Relax and indulge in **The Apothocoffee Shop & The Walled Garden** with snacks, lunches and a delicious range of gateaux and ice creams.

"We hope you visit us here at JEYES soon – a warm welcome awaits you all".

Open Mon Fri 8.30 – 5.30, Sat 8.30 – 5pm

surface adorned with purely decorative masonry strips. The tower is 10th century, the south doorway is 12th, the aisles are 13th, the tower arch 14th, the south porch 19th but they all co-exist in great architectural harmony. Beyond the remarkably well-preserved Norman doorway the most amazing sight is the 15th century chancel screen, ablaze with hundreds of dazzling butterflies on the wing; next to it is a wonderful, heavily carved Jacobean pulpit in black oak.

CASTLE ASHBY

6 miles E of Northampton off the A428

🏚 Castle   ⚘ Craft Centre

Two major attractions for the visitor here.

Castle Ashby is a fine Elizabethan mansion, home of the Marquess of Northampton, standing in Capability Brown parkland with Victorian gardens and a lake. The building of Castle Ashby was started in 1574 on the site of a 13th century castle that had been demolished. The original plan of the building was in the shape of an 'E' in honour of Queen Elizabeth I, and is typical of many Elizabethan houses. About 60 years later the courtyard was enclosed by a screen designed by Inigo Jones. One of the features of Castle Ashby is the lettering around the house and terraces. The inscriptions, which are in Latin, read when translated "The Lord guard your coming in" and "The Lord guard your going out". Inside there is some

🏚 historic building   🏛 museum   🏚 historic site   🌊 scenic attraction   🌿 flora and fauna

CLASSIX DESIGN

Billing Wharf, Cogenhoe,
Northamptonshire NN7 1NH
Tel: 01604 891333
e-mail: sales@classix.co.uk
website: www.classix.co.uk

A striking modern brick building by the River Nene is home to **Classix Design**, which has earned its position at the top of the tree among Northamptonshire's interior design companies. In the early 1980s the firm's founder Matthew Rubython recognised that his discerning demanded and deserved the best, and that philosophy still holds good under the current management. The staff at Classix are always on hand to show customers a wide range of interior accessories and explain the services available to complement and enhance existing home styles, and the premises are among the few interior design companies in Northamptonshire to have both a showroom and a pattern book room. In the showroom is an inspiring range of furniture large and small, fabrics, wallpapers, trimmings, paints, curtains, lighting and lamps, flooring, carpets, rugs, upholstery and all manner of interior accessories.

In the pattern room clients can browse fabrics, wallpapers and paints from all the well-known sources, including Farrow & ball, Designers' Guild, Paint & Paper Library, Zoffany, Osborne & Little, William Yeoward, Andrew Martin, Romo and JAB. Another speciality is fitted carpets and rugs: there's a wide variety of rug samples, and the staff are always ready to accept commissions for bespoke rugs. The firm offers a complete curtain making and fitting service, the curtains interlined and hand-finished, with a vast choice of designs and style for curtains, pelmets and headings, poles and blinds. They also undertake upholstery and re-upholstery of chairs, footstools, sofas and chaises longues in modern or traditional style. Classix always has an impressive range of lighting and accessories, including lamps, wall lights, floor lights and chandeliers, as well as unusual designer mirrors to suit all interiors.

One of the most comprehensive range of home goods is regularly updated by the design team, offering an up-to-date style where classic meets contemporary. The design team, led by Ellie Dennis, has established an enviable reputation for innovative and inspirational design that attracts clients from far beyond its home county. Whatever the requirements, from dressing a window to furnishing and decorating a whole flat or house, they can inspire their clients to great design, providing advice and direction in all aspects of interior design and decoration. Classix regularly hosts designer collections, promotional events and exclusive presentations from some of the design industry's leading companies.

wonderful restoration furniture and paintings of the English and Renaissance schools.

On a much smaller scale the old Manor House makes a delightful picture by the church; it has a dungeon and there is a 13th century window with exquisite tracery set in the oldest part of the house near a blocked Norman arch. The poet, Cowper, loved to wander amongst the trees, some of which are said to have been planted by the Countess Judith herself. The tree that attracts the most visitors is called Cowper's Oak, the branches of which spread twice as far across as the tree is high. There is a tradition that it will never die because Cowper stood beneath it one day during a heavy thunderstorm and was inspired to write his famous hymn: "God moves in Mysterious Ways".

Castle Ashby **Craft Centre & Rural Shopping Yard** is set in an old farmyard and comprises a farm shop and delicatessen, craft shops, pottery, goldsmith's studio, art gallery and tea room.

HORTON

6 miles SE of Northampton on the B526

🌱 The Menagerie

A mile south of the village a gate leads off the road and across fields to **The Menagerie**, a fascinating garden surrounding the great house (pulled down in 1936) where Lord Halifax once had a private zoo. A lime avenue, water gardens, a rose garden and thatched arbours are among the delights of a garden that is still being developed. A distinguished son of Horton was Ralph Lane, the first Governor of Virginia.

SALCEY FOREST

8 miles S of Northampton off the B526

Reached from the A508 at Roade or the B526

between Horton and Stoke Goldington, the 1,250-acre Salcey Forest has been owned and managed by the Forestry Commission since the 1920s. Part of the chain of ancient Royal Hunting Forests that stretched from Stamford to Oxford, it produces quality timber while providing a home for a wide variety of animal and plant life, and recreational facilities for the public. There are three circular trails at Salcey, named after the three woodpeckers found there: the Lesser Spotted Trail of a leisurely hour; the Great Spotted Trail of about two miles; and, for the more energetic, the Green Woodpecker Trail of about 2½ hours. The forest is open to visitors all year round.

Daventry

🏛 Museum 🏛 Borough Hill 🚶 Country Park

Old and new blend intriguingly in this historic market town whose streets are shared by dignified Georgian houses and modern shops. A colourful market is held along the High Street every Tuesday and Friday, and in the Market Place stands the Moot Hall, built in 1769 of ironstone. Originally a private house, it became the moot hall, or town hall, in 1806 after the former town hall was demolished. It is now home to the Tourist Information Centre and to **Daventry Museum**, which illustrates the social history of the town and its environs. It also shows regularly changing arts and crafts exhibitions and contains archaeological finds from **Borough Hill** and some of the equipment used by the BBC when it had a transmitter station on the hill. The oval hill, which rises to 650 feet above sea level, is more than two miles round and covers an area of 150 acres. It was the third largest Iron Age hill fort in Britain and in more recent times was topped

PREZZENCE

1 Bishops Court, Daventry,
Northamptonshire NN11 4NP
Tel: 01327 872500 Fax: 01327 312524
website: www.prezzence-giftshop.co.uk

In 2005 Kim Moore took over the empty premises of what had been a dress shop and turned them into one of the most delightful shops in the area. **Prezzence** is located in a handsome modern brick building whose interior is filled with tables, shelves and cabinets overflowing with household goods and gift ideas, a one-stop shop for things for the home and presents for all occasions to suit all occasions, all pockets and all ages. Some are traditional, others unusual and quirky, all chosen by Kim for their interest. There are cuddly toys and a selection of games and puzzles for babies and children, silver jewellery in a variety of styles, china ornaments, candles, vases, cups and mugs, photo frames, wedding gifts, cards and gift wrap.

Prezzence also stocks gifts for men, including cuff links, wallets and those clever little 'toys' that men need to fiddle with while making life-changing decisions in the office. The stock changes all the time, so every visit to Prezzence is sure to reveal something new for a treat or a gift to remember. Shop hours are 9 to 5.30 Monday to Friday, 9 to 5 Saturday.

by the huge radio masts that transmitted the World Service of the BBC. This was the site of the world's first radar station, masterminded by Sir Robert Watson-Watt, a descendant of steam pioneer James Watt.

Daventry was once an important stop on the coaching routes, and it is said that King Charles I spent several days at the Wheatsheaf Inn before the Battle of Naseby, where he lost the battle and his kingdom. Shakespeare mentions the town in King Henry IV (Part 1), when Falstaff tells Bardolph the tale of a shirt stolen from a "red-nose innkeeper". During the coaching era the chief industry of Daventry was whip-making.

Daventry Country Park is a beautiful 133-acre site centred on the old Daventry Reservoir. Coarse fishing, a picnic area, adventure playground, nature trails, nature reserve and visitor centre are among the amenities. Open daily all year.

Around Daventry

CHARWELTON
4 miles SW of Daventry on the A361

The chief claim to fame of Charwelton is that it is the spot where the River Cherwell rises, in the cellar of Cherwell House. The river forms the county boundary as it travels south into Oxfordshire before joining the Thames. In the village is a lovely old packhorse bridge.

BYFIELD
5 miles SW of Daventry on the A361

⚐ Boddington Reservoir

The tall tower of the rich-stone 14th century church is one of the major local landmarks. A major leisure attraction just west of the village is **Boddington Reservoir**, a balancing reservoir for the Oxford Canal. A good place to start a walk, or to fish, sail or windsurf on the reservoir itself.

UPPER STOWE

5 miles SE of Daventry off the A5

A short drive up the A5 from Towcester brings the visitor to the village of Upper Stowe and the Old Dairy Farm Centre. The community of Stowe

Canons Ashby House

Nine Churches is very oddly named, particularly as there is only one church, late Anglo-Saxon. The story is that the builders tried eight times to build the church but each time the Devil took away the stones. At the ninth attempt they succeeded – hence the name.

CANONS ASHBY

7 miles S of Daventry off the A361

🏠 Canons Ashby House

This pretty village contains the Church of St Mary, once part of the Black Canons' Monastery church and much reduced in size at the time of the Dissolution of the Monasteries. **Canons Ashby House**, built from part of the ecclesiastical building after the Dissolution, is one of the finest of Northamptonshire's great houses. Home of the Dryden family since the 1550s and now in the care of the National Trust, it contains some marvellous Elizabethan wall paintings and sumptuous Jacobean plasterwork. The grounds are equally delightful, with yews, cedars and mulberry trees, terraces and parkland, and 2009 saw the start of restoring them to their Victorian splendour. Open Monday, Tuesday, Wednesday, Saturday and Sunday afternoons April to October.

FLORE

3 miles E of Daventry on the A45

🐦 Adams Cottage

Called Flora in the Domesday Book, the village has a wide green that slopes gently down to the River Nene. **Adams Cottage** was the home of the ancestors of John Adams (1797-1801), President of the United States, whose son was also President. In the 13th century church are several memorial windows, one of them dedicated to Bruce Capell, an artillery officer who was awarded the Military Cross at the age of 22 for courage and devotion to his wounded men. A simple wooden cross from Flanders hangs on the wall, and his window depicts the farewell between David and Jonathan.

ASHBY ST LEDGERS

3 miles N of Daventry on the A361

📖 Gunpowder Plot

From 1375 to 1605 the manor house at Ashby was the home of the Catesby family, and it was in a room above the gatehouse that Guy Fawkes is said to have met Robert Catesby to hatch the **Gunpowder Plot**. On the 5th of November, 1605, Catesby rode the 80 miles from London in seven hours with the news

ABRAXAS COOKSHOP

The Heart of the Shires Shopping Village, Top Floor, Barn Arcade,
A5 - 2 miles North of Weedon, Northamptonshire NN7 4LB
Tel: 01327 341080 Fax: 01327 341740
e-mail: info@abraxascookshop.com website: www.abraxascookshop.com

When Sarah George and Helen Sparrow met for coffee at The Heart of The Shires Shopping Village in 1996 and looked at an empty unit, they had little idea of what was to be the result. Eleven years later, and winners of no less than eight awards for Excellence in Housewares, including Cook & Housewares Retailer of The Year 2005, the flagship store has expanded into three local towns, Rugby, Banbury and Northampton.

Abraxas Cookshop, situated on the top floor of the Barn Arcade at The Heart of The Shires Shopping Village, is one of the finest of its kind and has been described as "an inspired shopping experience". The family run and owned business with the emphasis on quality goods and personal customer service together with the warm and convivial atmosphere created by the highly trained friendly staff makes this a magical journey not to be missed.

Abraxas Cookshop is an 'Aladdin's cave' of cookware for use by the everyday cook to the professional chef. The layout of the shop is in different sections for easy exploration by the customer. Begin at the Aga section carrying a varied selection of Aga cookware, bakeware and accessories then browse the many saucepan ranges on offer, brands include Mauviel French copper, Swift Supreme, Meyer-Prestige, Hahn, Fissler and Stellar. Moving on past butchers blocks and kitchen work stations, salt & pepper mills, pestle & mortars, chopping boards, steamers and frying pans customers arrive at the electrical section housing KitchenAid, Magimix, Cuisinart and Dualit food mixers, blenders, coffee machines and toasters in an array of eye-catching colours and finishes. Customers can then peruse the Nigella Lawson designer range and the complete range of Le Creuset cast-iron cookware together with textiles and accessories. Spend some time in our specialist bakeware section where everything from roasting pans, speciality cake tins and silicone bakeware is available. Abraxas Cookshop also stock a large range of knives; brands include Global, Sabatier, Wusthof, Henckels, I.O.Shen, Porsche and Victorinox. Tools, gadgets, textiles and jam making equipment are all housed in a large central area.

Extend this unique experience by visiting other shops on the site owned by the sisters, namely Abraxas China & Glass (stocking the entire Emma Bridgewater range), Dressage Outdoor Clothing and Ladies Fashions, The Garden Room and The Pickle Room, all on site at The Heart of The Shires Shopping Village.

For more information visit our website –
www.abraxascookshop.com

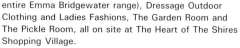

🏛 historic building   📷 museum   🏚 historic site   ⚜ scenic attraction   🌿 flora and fauna

that the plot had failed. He fled to Holbeach in Staffordshire, where he was shot dead after refusing to surrender. The Church of St Mary & St Leodegarious has much to interest the visitor, including Jacobean box pews, an elaborately carved rood screen, a Norman font, a number of Catesby brasses and, most notably, some medieval wall paintings depicting the Passion of Christ.

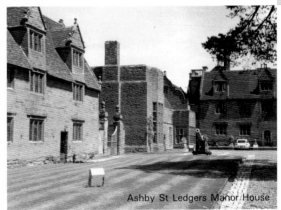

Ashby St Ledgers Manor House

Towcester

🏷 Racecourse

A busy little place, Towcester is popular with seekers of antiques – there are at least half a dozen different establishments selling antiques.

In Roman times the town was called Lactodorum and it stood on the major highway Watling Street (now the A5). The Romans improved the road and built a fort to guard their troop movements. During the Civil War it was the only Royalist stronghold in the area and in the following centuries it was an important stop on the coaching route between London and Holyhead. By the end of the 18th century there were 20 coaching inns in the town, servicing up to 40 coaches every day. Charles Dickens stayed at the Saracen's Head, then called the Pomfret Hotel, and immortalised it in The Pickwick Papers. The parish church of St Lawrence, built on the site of a substantial Roman building, is one of the loveliest in the county, with features from several centuries: the crypt, reached by a doorway from the sanctuary, is 13th century, the arcades 13th and 14th. On the arch of the south chapel is a carved jester's head probably from the 14th century, while the massive tower and the font are from the 1400s.

Close to the church is the Chantry House, formerly a school, founded by Archdeacon Sponne in 1447.

Towcester Racecourse is set in the beautiful parkland estate of Easton Neston, the family home of Lord Hesketh. The course, which has its entrance on the A5, came into being in 1876, when the Empress of Austria was staying at Easton Neston and attended an Easter steeplechase held in her honour. The course now stages about 16 National Hunt meetings a year, including a couple in the evening.

Around Towcester

BLISWORTH
3 miles NE of Towcester off the A43

🏛 Blisworth Tunnel

The building of the Grand Union and Oxford Canals brought trade and prosperity to the area and now provides miles of quiet, picturesque walks or boat trips. On the Grand Union Canal, the **Blisworth Tunnel** between Blisworth and Stoke Bruerne, opened in 1805, is the longest in England, at nearly two miles.

📖 stories and anecdotes   🐦 famous people   🎨 art and craft   🏷 entertainment and sport   🚶 walks

The pretty village of Blisworth is a mass of roses in summer, in the cottage gardens, in the Tudor and Jacobean houses and around the 13th century church. The most significant treasure in the church is a high screen of the 15th century complete with doors. Also of interest is a tablet near the altar that tells of the wife of a sergeant-at-arms to Queen Elizabeth I. The tablet records that she lived a maid for 18 years, was a wife for 20 years and a widow for 61, dying in her 99th year.

STOKE BRUERNE
3 miles NE of Towcester off the A508

🏛 Stoke Park   🏛 Canal Museum

A picturesque canalside village at the southern end of the famous Blisworth Tunnel. The canal provides the major attractions, with waterside walks, boat trips to the tunnel and a visit to the fascinating **Canal Museum**. Housed in a converted corn mill, the museum displays 200 years of canal history and life on the narrow boats (many of which are still in use for pleasure trips). The exhibits include working engines, old photographs, waterway wildlife and the tools used by canal workers and boatmen. The museum, which is open throughout the year, has a tea room and a souvenir shop. The canal has a series of locks at this point, and visitors can stop in the car park at the lower lock on the A508 and walk into the village along the towpath, passing seven locks en route. There are shops, pubs and restaurants at this popular place, which is the perfect location for a family day out and an ideal starting point for a canal holiday.

A private drive on the Stoke Bruerne to Shutlanger road leads to **Stoke Park**, a great

MAGNOLIA
Church Lane, Alderton, Northamptonshire NN12 7LP
Tel: 01327 811479
e-mail: bandb@magnolia.me.uk
website: www.magnolia.me.uk

Diana and Alan Redman own and run **Magnolia**, a delightful B&B establishment set amid beautiful countryside in the little village of Alderton. This pleasant spot lies between the A5 and A508 northwest of Milton Keynes and south of Northampton at the foot of an ancient castle mound overlooking the Tove valley. Their handsome modern brick-built house set in a secluded lawned garden has two letting rooms; both

have en suite shower rooms and a private balcony overlooking open countryside. A choice of breakfasts, with home-grown or local produce and home-made preserves is served in the elegant dining room, and there's a choice of lunch and dinner places in nearby Stoke Bruerne and Grafton Regis. The owners welcome business people, holidaymakers, tourists....and archaeologists. The TV Timeteam undertook a dig in the grounds, and digging in the village is an ongoing process. Also nearby is the site of a battle between Boudicca and the Roman invaders. Magnolia's garden attracts a variety of wildlife, including owls, kites, buzzards and badgers. A number of rural walks start from here, and Diana and Alan have a supply of maps and local information. Golf, riding and karting are available nearby as are Towcester Racecourse and Silverstone racetrack.

house standing in a 400-acre estate. Attributed to Inigo Jones, the house was built in Palladian style (the first in this country) around 1630 for Sir Francis Crane, head of the Mortlake Tapestry Works. The main house burnt down in 1886, and only the pavilions and a colonnade remain.

SILVERSTONE

4 miles SW of Towcester on the A43

Church

The home of British motor racing, located off the A43 in the village. Until 2009 the British Grand Prix has been the highlight of the year, but the circuit hosts a large number of other events, including rounds of the Auto Trader touring car championship and the International Historic Car Festival. The Grand Prix is due to relocate to Donington for 2010, with the Moto GP changing in the opposite direction.

Tucked away on country roads northwest of Silverstone are two of the many interesting churches for which Northamptonshire is famous. The **Church of St Mary** at Wappenham has a sculpture by Giles Gilbert Scott from the renowned family of architects, who had local connections; two fonts; a clock from the 17th century; and brass memorials to the Lovett family.

SLAPTON

4 miles SW of Towcester off the A43 or A45

Church   Weedon Lois

Slapton is little more than a hamlet but its tiny **St Botolph's Church**, set on the hillside above the River Tove, contains some of the finest medieval wall paintings in the county. Hidden under limewash for three centuries, the paintings were discovered in the mid-1800s and magnificently restored. Covering almost all of the interior walls, they colourfully depict Bible stories and scenes from the life and works of various saints. Slight variations in style suggest they belong to two separate periods, one in the late 1200s, the other in the mid-1300s.

The village of **Weedon Lois**, a mile or so to the west of Slapton, is the final resting place of Edith Sitwell (1887-1964). She often visited her brother Sacheverell at his home at nearby Weston. Her grave is marked with a restrained memorial by Henry Moore with a bronze of two intertwined hands depicting Youth and Age. It is inscribed with the last lines of her poem, The Wind of Early Spring.

BRACKLEY

10 miles SW of Towcester off the A43 or A422

School

A town of Saxon origins with houses clustered round a tangle of streets. A castle was built here in the early part of the 12th century, which some accounts claim as the meeting place for the rebel barons who drew up the first version of Magna Carta in 1215. King John did not approve of their proposals, and it took almost a year before he relented and signed. Wool brought prosperity in the Middle Ages, allowing the rebuilding of the Church of St Peter with a fine early English west tower and south aisle. A free hospital and chapel which had been built by Robert le Bossu for the benefit of the poor was sold to Magdalen College, Oxford, in 1484 and halfway through the following century a school was opened on the site. The buildings have been much altered down the years, but the school exists to this day, now known as **Magdalen College Comprehensive School**. A notable landmark on the High Street is the baroque town hall, with its handsome clock tower, built in 1706 at the instigation of the Duke of Bridgwater. During the 19th century, Brackley was served by two railway companies, the London & North Western and the Great Central, with stations at either end of town. Alas, the lines were axed in the 1960s.

AYNHO
16 miles SW of Towcester on the B4100

🏛 Aynho Park

A peaceful, picturesque limestone village of leafy lanes and lovely old cottages. The former manor house, **Aynho Park**, is a very grand 17th century country house in the care of the Country Houses Association. It was originally the property of the Cartwright family who, it is said, claimed the rents from their tenants in the form of apricots; some apricot trees can still be seen trained into fan shapes and growing on the walls of cottages. The house was burnt down by Royalist troops during the Civil war but was rebuilt by the Cartwrights, who at the same time rebuilt the village church with the same proportions as the house, so the church too has the appearance of a country villa. Later changes were made to the house by Archer and Soane. Public rooms and the grounds are open to the public on Wednesday and Thursday afternoons from May to September. The Wharf at Aynho on the Oxford Canal has holiday boats for hire and a canalside shop.

KING'S SUTTON
15 miles SW of Towcester off the A4260

🏛 Church

Located at the southernmost tip of the county, King's Sutton boasts one of Northamptonshire's finest church towers. The 15th century spire of the **Church of St Peter and St Paul** soars almost 200ft towards the

heavens and in a county famous for its elegant spires, King's Sutton is unmatched in its beauty. The interior, heavily restored by George Gilbert Scott in 1866, is less inspiring but is worth visiting to see the macabre memorial to Thomas Langton Freke who died in 1769. It represents Christ rising above His own skeleton which is depicted with gruesome realism and has a rib cage moulded in iron.

A famous son of the village was William Lisle Bowles, born in 1762. The poems written by this vicar's son so delighted Samuel Taylor Coleridge that he changed from studying theology to writing poetry himself.

SULGRAVE
10 miles W of Towcester off the B4525

🏛 Sulgrave Manor

The best-known attraction here is **Sulgrave Manor**, a Tudor manor house built by the ancestors of George Washington, first President of the United States of America. Lawrence Washington, sometime Mayor of Northampton, bought the manor from Henry VIII in 1539. In 1656, Lawrence Washington's great-great-grandson Colonel John Washington left England to take up land in Virginia, which later became Mount Vernon. This man was the great-grandfather of George. The Washington family arms, which are said to have inspired the stars and stripes design of the American flag, are prominent above the front door, and the house is a treasure trove of George Washington memorabilia, including documents, a velvet coat and even a lock of his hair. The house is Saturday and Sunday from April to October, then Saturday, Sunday, Tuesday, Wednesday and Thursday from May. A lottery grant has allowed the construction of a series of buildings in the grounds which are part of major educational programmes covering all aspects of Tudor history. The lovely gardens include yew hedges, topiary, herbaceous borders and a formal rose garden planted in 1999. There's a gift shop and a buttery serving light refreshments. Tel: 01295 760205

GREENS NORTON
1 mile NW of Towcester off the A5

🚶 Knightley Way

A village at the southern end of the 12-mile **Knightley Way**, one of several mapped walking routes in the county. At this point the Grafton Way takes over, continuing to Cosgrove in the very south of Northamptonshire. The church at Greens Norton is well worth a visit, with its Saxon stonework, Norman font and commemorative brasses of the Green family.

Kettering

🏛 Manor House Museum 🎨 Alfred East Gallery

An important town standing above the River Ise, Kettering gained fame as a producer of both clothing and shoes. It was in Kettering that the missionary William Carey and the preacher Andrew Fuller founded the Baptist Missionary Society in 1792, giving a new impetus to the cause of foreign missions all over the world. The parish church of St Peter and St Paul, with its elegant crocketed spire, is one of the finest in the country and a landmark for miles around. Much of the old town has been swallowed up in modern development, but there are still a few old houses in the narrow lanes, and the Heritage Quarter around the church gives a fascinating, hands-on insight into the town's past.

The **Manor House Museum**, housed in an

18th century manor house, has impressive collections of social and industrial history, archaeology and geology. Individual items range from a macabre mummified cat to an example of the Robinson car built in Kettering in 1907.

In the adjacent **Alfred East Gallery** a constantly changing programme of exhibitions of paintings, crafts, sculpture, photography and children's work ensures that there will be something new to see on every visit. Alfred East offered a selection of his works to the community on condition that a gallery was built to house them. The gallery was opened in 1913, in the year he was elected a member of the Royal Academy; he died later that year. The gallery is open from 9 to 6 Monday to Saturday. In between visits to the museum and gallery (both wheelchair-accessible) the Heritage Gardens are a pleasant place for a stroll or a picnic. The Tourist Information Centre is at the same location.

On the A6, on the outskirts of town, Wicksteed Park is a 148-acre site of leisure and pleasure, with 40 rides and attractions, including roller coaster, pirate ship, train ride, Mississippi river boat and pitch & putt. There are several catering outlets, shops, a pottery, a photographic studio and two playground areas. Open daily Easter-September, weekends to November.

Around Kettering

GEDDINGTON
3 miles NE of Kettering off the A43

🏛 Eleanor Cross 🏛 Boughton House

This attractive village, like many in the county, has known royal visitors: monarchs from the time of William the Conqueror used a summer palace as a base for hunting in the Royal Forest of Rockingham. In the centre of the village is an ornately carved stone cross almost 40 feet high. This is the best preserved of the three surviving **Eleanor Crosses** that marked the funeral procession of Queen Eleanor, who had died at Harby in Nottinghamshire in 1290. Her devoted husband, King Edward I, accompanied the body south to London, and he ordered the crosses to be erected to mark the places where the coffin rested. William Rishanger, a monk at St Albans, records the event: "The King gave orders that in every place where her bier had rested, a cross of the finest workmanship should be erected in her memory, so that passers-by might pray for her soul". Other crosses were raised at Lincoln (where the Queen's heart was buried), Grantham, Stamford, Hardingstone in Northampton (this still exists), Stony Stratford, Dunstable, St Albans, Waltham (this still exists), Cheapside and Charing Cross.

Boughton House, Geddington

Off the A43, on a minor road between Geddington and Grafton Underwood (where there is a monument to the crews of B17 bombers), stands one of the very finest houses in the country. The origins of **Boughton House**, the Northamptonshire home of the Duke of Buccleuch, go back 500 years to a small monastic building. Extended over the years, it was transformed into "a vision of Louis XIV's Versailles". In addition to the wonderful architecture, Boughton is noted for its French and English furniture, its paintings (El Greco, Murillo, 40 Van Dycks) and its collection of armoury and weaponry. The grounds, which include parkland, lakes, picnic areas and woodland play areas, are open May to September, the house in August only.

Large tracts of the ancient woodland of the region have survived, and in the fields by Boughton House are the remains of more recent planting. The 2nd Duke of Montagu, nicknamed John the Planter, had the notion of planting an avenue of trees all the way from the house to his London home. The plan hit immediate trouble when his neighbour, the Duke of Bedford, refused to let the trees cross his estate; instead, the Planter set down many avenues on his own estate, amounting to the 70 miles of the distance to London.

TWYWELL
4 miles E of Kettering off the A14

Twywell (the name means 'double spring') has a history that includes the Romans, the Saxons and the Normans, but the strongest, and most surprising connection is with Africa. Two African boys, Susi and Chuma, faithful servants and companions of David Livingstone, were with him when he died and carried his body hundreds of miles to the sea before accompanying it to Westminster Abbey. They had saved all Livingstone's papers and stayed at Twywell as guests of the explorer's friend Horace Waller while Livingstone's Journals were being prepared. In the church are three stones from Calvary in the window by the altar. They were sent by the rector's friend, General Gordon, who wrote a letter saying that he hoped to visit the Pope on his way back from Palestine. That letter is preserved in the church.

WOODFORD

6 miles E of Kettering off the A14

A bizarre story here. A human heart was found in one of the columns of the Norman church during restoration work in the 19th century. It is thought to belong to one of the Traillys, who died while fighting in the Crusades; his heart was brought back by his followers so that he could rest with the other Traillys, who were the local lords of the manor at the time. Also of note in the church are over 100 carved oak figures, some medieval brasses and a tablet commemorating John Cole, bookseller, schoolmaster and writer on antiquities. He lived from 1792 to 1848, dying in great poverty. Woodford was the home of a certain Josiah Eaton, a man of small stature (5'2") but great stamina. A prodigious walker, he set out in 1815 on a marathon walk around Blackheath, completing a mile every hour for six weeks, without ever stopping. At the end of this amazing feat of endurance he had covered 1,100 miles.

THRAPSTON

7 miles E of Kettering on the A605

The Medieval Bridge at Thrapston crosses the River Nene on one of its loveliest stretches. The town is surrounded by fine pastureland, created when the flood waters and rich mud subsided after the two Ice Ages. The main attraction in the church is a stone tablet carved

DAIRY FARM

Cranford St Andrew, nr Kettering, Northamptonshire NN14 4AQ
Tel: 01536 330273

At the centre of a 350-care mixed farm, **Dairy Farm** is a thatched Jacobean manor house opposite Cranford Hall, with outstanding views over open countryside. It's a place of great character, and the three guest rooms are tastefully appointed: one of the double rooms boasts a four-poster bed. Breakfast is based on farm and local produce, and with a little notice resident owner Audrey Clarke will also prepare a splendid evening meal.

In the garden are an imposing medieval stone dovecote and a charming summer house, and the 12th century village church is just beyond the garden wall. The area around the farm is perfect for pleasant country walks, and though peaceful and serene Dairy Farm is within easy reach of the local amenities. And with the A14 close by it is ideally suited for touring and sightseeing.

Open all year except Christmas.

🎬 stories and anecdotes   🐦 famous people   🎨 art and craft   🎭 entertainment and sport   🚶 walks

DODSON & HORRELL COUNTRY STORE

Ringstead, Kettering, Northamptonshire NN14 4BX
Tel: 01933 461539 Fax: 01832 737368
e-mail: rclark@dodsonandhorrell.com
website: www.dodsonandhorrellcountrystore.com

For more than 70 years the name of Dodson & Horrell has been synonymous with top-quality animal feed, and the complete range of feeds and supplements is sold in the **Dodson & Horrell Country Store**. The feeds include many varieties for horses and ponies, Chudleys complete dry diets for pets and working dogs, bird food for cage, aviary and wild birds and the Countryside range for cattle, goats, pigs, sheep, poultry, rabbits and game. The feed is produced not far from the shop at Islip, under the supervision of John and Richard Horrell, sons of the company's co-founder Claude Horrell. The company has always been committed to producing the highest-quality feeds, nutritionally sound and promoting the health of the animals. All the feeds are sourced from certified non-GM ingredients, from traceable raw materials, manufactured in D&H's own medication-free mill, tested for prohibited substances and all with a vegetarian formulation.

The store stocks everything for horse and rider, from grooming, hoof and skin care products to clothing (coats, jackets, tops, breeches, chaps, gloves, socks, hats and scarves), riding boots, jodhpurs, wellies, yard/country boots, tack, stable equipment, bedding, fleece and show rugs and blankets. All the top brands are kept in stock, including Harry Hall, Masta, Cottage Craft, Hac-Tac, Aerborn, Ultima, Korda, Hunter and Carr & day & Martin. Dodson & Horrell Country Store keeps an excellent range of fishing equipment – reels, nets, rods, hooks, floats and ready rigs and over 300 baits. Featured brands include Sensas, Belstane, Fox, Bait-Tech, Vision, Middy, Maverand Bag'em Matchbaits. Among other items in store are poultry feeders and drinkers, electric fencing and local produce including fresh cakes and pies, preserves, honey and Faringtons mellow yellow.

Friendly, professional staff are on hand with help and advice and as well as selling the vast range of stock they offer a number of services that include rug washing and repair, embroidery and fish smoking. Trading hours are 8.30 to 5.30 (Sunday and Bank Holidays 9 to 2); goods can also be ordered by phone, e-mail or online.

Dodson & Horrell has the highest market share of feeds for both the leisure and professional sectors of the industry. It holds Royal warrants of Appointment as horsefeed suppliers to the Queen Elizabeth II (1985) and for Chudleys Dog Food (2006). A full history of Dodson & Horrell can be viewed at www.dodsonandhorrell.com

---

with stars and stripes. It is thought by some that this motif was the inspiration for the American flag, being the coat of arms of Sir John Washington, who died in 1624. The church and nearby Montagu House, home of Sir John, are places of pilgrimage for many American tourists.

RAUNDS

7 miles SE of Kettering on the B663

A small town in the Nene Valley with a lofty (183ft) church spire. It was at the heart of the Northamptonshire shoemaking trade, specialising in army boots, and was also known for the manufacture of dolls. In May 1905 Raunds hit the headlines when 200 men marched to London to protest at the poor rates of pay for bootmakers. They were delighted to find on their arrival that a crowd of 10,000 supporters was waiting for them. After 10 days, the strikers won concessions and returned victorious.

IRTHLINGBOROUGH

7 miles SE of Kettering on the B571/A6

A small town noted for its leather and iron industries. It boasts two fine bridges across the Nene, one built in the 14th century, the other in the 20th. The medieval bridge has 10 ribbed arches, and the arms of an ancient monastery carved into one if its stones, suggesting perhaps that it was built by monks, perhaps from Peterborough. The modern one, running parallel to the old, is an impressive sight, its great arches stretching for half a mile over the low-lying land by the river. Irthlingborough is home to Rushden & Diamond Football Club, whose stadium is located in the magnificent Diamond Centre. Also in the centre is the Doc Shop, selling Dr Martens boots.

Market Cross, Higham Ferrers

HIGHAM FERRERS

10 miles SE of Kettering off the A45

🏛 Chichele College

Just off the Market Place in this delightful old town a narrow lane leads to a unique group of ecclesiastical buildings. These include the 13th century spired Church of St Mary the Virgin, a chantry and bede house, and a 13th century market cross. Also here is **Chichele College**, a college for secular canons founded in 1422, named in honour of a local worthy called Henry Chichele. Born here in 1362, he progressed from baker's boy to Archbishop of Canterbury, a position he filled for 30 years until his death in 1443.

PYTCHLEY

2 mile S of Kettering off the A509

🐎 Pytchley Hunt

The location of the old headquarters of the

Pytchley Hunt. One of the most famous Masters of the Hunt (1827-1834) was Squire Osbaldeston, a man of boundless energy and stamina, who once successfully wagered 1,000 guineas that he could ride 200 miles in 10 hours, changing horses as necessary. He used 32 horses and completed the 200 miles with more than an hour to spare. No one took up his offer of a vast sum of money if they could achieve the same feat with the same horses. The good squire was a crack shot, a talented underarm bowler and a fine boxer. He was evidently less accomplished at backing horses than riding them, for he ended his days in London in obscurity and comparative poverty.

WELLINGBOROUGH

8 miles S of Kettering off the A509 or A45

🏤 Church of St Mary 🏛 Croyland Abbey

🌿 Summer Leys Nature Reserve

This important market and industrial town, known for its iron mills, flour mills and tanneries, sits near the point where the River Ise joins the River Nene. The spire of the medieval All Hallows Church rises among trees in the centre of town, and the other church, whose great tower can be seen on the further bank of the Nene, is the **Church of St Mary**. It was built in the first decades of the 20th century and is regarded as Sir Ninian Comper's masterpiece. He declared St Mary's his favourite church and wished to be buried here with his wife but Comper's fame demanded interment in Westminster Abbey. Funded by two Anglo-Catholic spinster sisters, St Mary's has been described as "a sort of fantastical King's College, Cambridge", a sumptuous medley of extravagant Gothic features complete with gilded columns and golden angels. Not to be missed!

Wellingborough was granted its market charter in 1201 and markets are still held four days a week. In and around the market square are several interesting old buildings, including the gabled Hind Hotel. One of its rooms is called the Cromwell Room because it was being constructed while the Battle of Naseby was in progress.

Another fine building is **Croyland Abbey**, now a Heritage Centre with a wealth of local history, and near it is a splendidly restored old tithe barn originally used for storing the manorial tithes. Stone-walled and thatch-roofed, it is 70 feet long and 22 feet wide. It dates from the 1400s and has two great doorways at either side, one of them 13 feet in height. An attraction in the centre of town is the Millennium Rose Garden at Swanspool Gardens. The Embankment at Wellingborough is a great place for a family outing, where a thriving population of swans lives next to the outdoor paddling pool that dates from the 1930s. South of the town, **Summer Leys Nature Reserve** is a year-round haven for large numbers of birds. Each May, thousands of people visit the town for the International Waendel Weekend of walking, cycling and swimming.

IRCHESTER

2 miles SE of Wellingborough off the A45

🏕 Country Park

Originally a Roman settlement, a fortified town whose walls were eight feet thick. A Saxon cemetery was also discovered here, and Norman England is represented by the plinths in the church. The six-arched bridge that crosses the River Nene is 14th century and bears the crossed keys of Peterborough Abbey and the wheel of St Catherine. On the B570 is

Irchester Country Park, 200 acres of woodland walks, wayfaring course, nature trail, picnic meadows and ranger service in a former ironstone quarry.

PODINGTON
4 miles SE of Wellingborough off the A509

The noisiest place for miles around, this is the location of the Santa Pod Raceway, where the fastest motorsport on earth takes place on selected days between March and November. The Top Fuel Dragsters can accelerate from 0 to 100mph in under a second, so put in your ear plugs and don't blink!

LAMPORT
8 miles SW of Kettering off the A508

🏠 Lamport Hall

Lamport Hall is a fine 16th century house enlarged in the 17th century by John Webb. Home to the Isham family from 1560 to 1976, it features an outstanding collection of furniture, books, paintings and china. It has

gardens and parkland, including the first Alpine garden and the first garden gnomes in England, plus a shop and tea room and a farm museum. The gnomes were imported from Nuremberg by Sir Charles Isham and used, the story goes, as place-name holders at his dinner table. Proving unpopular with his guests, they were soon moved into the garden, where they found another first in the shape of bonsai trees for company.

NASEBY
10 miles W of Kettering off the A5199

🏛 Battle of Naseby

Two monuments and interpretation panels mark the site of the **Battle of Naseby**, where, in 1645, Oliver Cromwell's Parliamentarian forces defeated King Charles I and determined the outcome of the Civil War, thereby giving the English people the right to rule their own country. Cromwell and Fairfax with 14,000 Roundheads faced the Royalist forces, who advanced outnumbered two to one. The first attack came at 10 o'clock on the morning of June 14th and, after heavy fighting, Fairfax won a decisive victory, capturing all the King's baggage and a fortune in gold and silver. The King surrendered in Newark some months later and the Civil War was at an end. Naseby Battle and Farm Museum, in the village, contains a model layout of the battle, relics from the fight and a collection of bygone agricultural machinery.

Many of the defeated Royalists who fled after the battle were surrounded and killed at the village of Marston Trussell on the Leicestershire border. Their remains

Lamport Hall

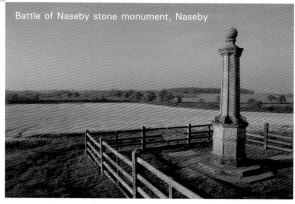

Battle of Naseby stone monument, Naseby

lie in the churchyard.

KELMARSH
6 miles W of Kettering on the A508

🏛 Kelmarsh Hall

Near Junction 2 of the A14, just outside the village of Kelmarsh, **Kelmarsh Hall** is an early 18th century house designed in Palladian style by an outstanding pupil of Sir Christopher Wren, James Gibbs (who is perhaps best known as the architect of the Church of St Martin in the Fields, London). One of only two surviving houses outside London by Gibbs in this style, it stands in 3,000 acres of farmland, with a lake, beautiful topiary and rose gardens and woodland walks. The Great Hall is the focal point of the house, with many of Gibbs' original features. One of the most attractive rooms is the Chinese Room, where the hand-painted wallpaper, from Kimberley Hall in Norfolk, dates from the 1840s. The church opposite the main

entrance to the Hall contains fine marble from Rome, some William Morris furnishings and the vaults of the families who have lived at the Hall – the Hanburys, the Naylors and the Lancasters.

RUSHTON
4 miles NW of Kettering off the A6

🏛 Rushton Triangular Lodge

One mile west of the village, on an unclassified road, stands the extraordinary **Rushton Triangular Lodge**, described as "the purest folly in the country". It was built by Sir Thomas Tresham in 1597 and symbolises the Holy Trinity, with three walls, each with three windows, three gables and three storeys, topped with a three-sided chimney. Thomas Tresham, known as Thomas the Builder, was brought up a Protestant but courageously returned to the Roman Catholic faith of his ancestors. At Rushton Hall, the Tresham family home since the 14th century, he was caught harbouring the renowned Jesuit Edmund Campion and was sentenced to

Kelmarsh Hall, Kelmarsh

seven years' imprisonment. Responsible for several intriguing buildings, he died soon after proclaiming the first Stuart king and just before his son Francis was arrested as a protagonist in the Gunpowder Plot.

Neighbouring Rushton Hall, also dating back 400 years, and described as a "dazzling example of Tudor and Stuart splendour", was built by Sir John Tresham, enlarged by Sir Thomas and completed by the Cockayne family. It is now a hotel, restaurant and conference centre.

DESBOROUGH
5 miles NW of Kettering on the A6

Desborough has the appearance of being a relatively modern town, but its history can be traced back to the Bronze Age. The oldest standing building is the Church of St Giles, built around AD1225, and other buildings of architectural interest include the 18th century Church House and the late 17th century Old Manor House coloured with the rich reds of Northamptonshire ironstone.

CORBY
6 miles N of Kettering off the A43

🌱 Top Lodge

A modern industrial town, but one with a history. Taking its name from a Scandinavian chieftain during the Danish occupation, it grew in significance in the mid-10th century, when King Edgar set up the Corby Hundred, with a local Moot Court governing the affairs of other villages in the area. True industry arrived at Corby in the later years of Queen Victoria's reign, with the building of the Kettering-Manton railway. Many of the bricks used in the building of the viaduct at Harringworth were made at Corby brickworks, which closed at the beginning of

the 20th century. But Corby was still essentially a small village until the 1930s, when Stewarts & Lloyds built a huge steel-making plant based on the area's known reserves of iron ore. That industry virtually stopped in 1980, but Corby remains a go-ahead modern town, with many cultural and leisure opportunities for young and old alike. It also treasures its heritage, both historic and geographic. 170 acres of woodland have been preserved intact at the very heart of the town, and there is much to interest the visitor in the surrounding villages that make up Corby Borough: Cottingham, East Carlton, Middleton, Rockingham, Stanion and Weldon. At **Top Lodge Visitor Centre**, two miles south of the roundabout at Duddington, The Barn enables visitors to watch live televised pictures of a family of red kites on their nest and offers the chance of seeing theses wonderful birds soaring above the barn and nearby woodland. Tel: 01536 407507

EAST CARLTON
1 mile W of Corby on the A427

🏃 Countryside Park

East Carlton Countryside Park comprises 100 acres of parkland with nature trails and a steel-making heritage centre with craft workshops, a forge and a cafeteria.

ROCKINGHAM
2 miles N of Corby on the A6003

🏰 Rockingham Castle

"450 Years a Royal Castle, 450 years a family home". Nine hundred years of history are contained within the walls of **Rockingham Castle**, built by William the Conqueror on the slopes of Rockingham Hill, overlooking the Welland Valley and the thatched and slate-

Rockingham Castle

in 1514 by Sir Robert Brudenell and has been occupied by the family ever since. One of the family's most distinguished members was James, 7th Earl of Cadogan, who led the Charge of the Light Brigade at the Battle of Balaclava. The Earl survived the slaughter but was killed four years later when he fell from the horse that had carried him safely at Balaklava. The horse's head is on display at Deene. Transformed from medieval manor to Tudor and Georgian mansion, Deene Park contains many fine examples of period furniture and some beautiful paintings. The oldest visible part is an arch of about 1300 in the east of the house; the Great Hall was completed in the late 1500s and has a magnificent sweet chestnut hammer-beam roof. The house is open on Bank Holiday Sunday and Monday afternoons from Easter to the end of August and all Sunday

roofed cottages of the village. The grand rooms are superbly furnished, and the armour in the Tudor Great Hall recalls the Civil War, when the castle was captured by the Roundheads. Owned and lived in since 1530 by the Watson family, the castle was put to atmospheric use by the BBC in the series By the Sword Divided, in which it was known as Arnescote Castle. Charles Dickens wrote much of Bleak House at Rockingham.

HARRINGWORTH
4 miles N of Corby off the B672

🏛 Viaduct

An impressive sight here is the great **Viaduct** carrying the railway from Kettering to Oakham a mile across the Welland Valley. Completed in 1879, it has 82 spans, each 40 feet wide. In the village are a notable village cross and the Church of St John the Baptist (12th to 14th centuries).

DEENE
4 miles NE of Corby off the A43

🏛 Deene Park 🏛 Kirby Hall

Surrounded by beautiful gardens and grounds filled with old-fashioned roses and rare trees and shrub stands **Deene Park**. Originally a medieval manor, it was acquired

Deene Park

🏛 historic building 📷 museum 🏚 historic site ⟐ scenic attraction 🌿 flora and fauna afternoons in June, July and August.

Also near Deene, in the parish of Gretton, is **Kirby Hall** (English Heritage), one of the loveliest Elizabethan ruins in England. Now only partly roofed, the hall dates from 1570 and was given by Elizabeth I to her Lord Chancellor and favourite courtier Sir Christopher Hatton. Alterations attributed to Inigo Jones were made in the 17th century. A version of Jane Austen's *Mansfield Park* was filmed here in 1998.

WELDON
2 miles E of Corby on the A427

This sizeable village is best known for the honey-coloured building stone quarried here. The stone was used to build nearby Rockingham Castle and Great St Mary's Church in distant Cambridge. An interesting house on the village green, is the windowless Round House, once used as a lock-up.

BRIGSTOCK
5 miles SE of Corby on the A6116

On the banks of a tributary of the River Nene called Harpers Brook, the Saxon village of Brigstock has many delightful old cottages, a 16th century manor house, and a church with an unusual circular extension to its tower. The village was once deep in Rockingham Forest, and the church bells were rung three times a day to guide travellers. By the little tree-covered village green a quaint Elizabethan cross topped by a ball weather vane stands on four steps.

EASTON-ON-THE-HILL
12 miles NE of Corby on the A43

🏠 Priest's House

An attraction here at the far northern tip of the county is the **Priest's House**, a pre-

Reformation priest's lodge which is of specialist architectural interest and is in the care of the National Trust. In the village church is a tablet commemorating one Lancelot Skynner, a rector's son, who died in 1799 when the ship La Lutine, laden with gold, sank off Holland. The ship's bell was recovered and now hangs in the London headquarters of Lloyd's who had insured the cargo.

Oundle

🏫 School   🎵 International Festival

Oundle is a beguiling little town with some fine stone buildings dating from the 17th and 18th centuries, ancient hostelries and a variety of specialist shops. The town is probably best known for its **Public School**, founded by Sir William Laxton in 1556. An inscription to his memory is written above the 17th century doorway in Greek, Latin and Hebrew. The medieval church, with its magnificent tower and 200-feet spire, is an impressive sight, and other notable buildings include three sets of almshouses. The museum, in the old courthouse, paints a picture of local life and the farming heritage down the years.

In mid-July, the town hosts the **Oundle International Festival** – 10 days devoted to a vibrant mix of classical music, theatre, jazz and film. The festivities include a hugely popular open-air jazz and firework spectacular.

Around Oundle

LYVEDEN NEW BIELD
4 miles SW of Oundle via the A427

🏠 Lyveden New Bield Lodge

Another of Sir Thomas Tresham's creations,

PLANTATION

Oundle Road, Polebrook, Peterborough, PE8 5LQ
Tel 01832 274755 www.plantation.co.uk
e-mail: info@plantation.co.uk

Plantation is a new, independent plant centre located just outside the beautiful and historic market town of Oundle. It was purpose built in 2006 and grows a broad range of plants and trees on its 4 acre site. With its all wooden shop and inspiration plant displays it offers a refreshing and different experience for both keen gardeners, looking for specific plants, and new gardeners who want help and ideas in developing their gardens. Other products include pots and containers, topiary, hedging, grow your own kits, composts, seeds and organic pest controls. Plantation also offers garden consultation and encourages customers to bring photos or drawing and will help in advising on suitable plants for space and use. Open days are held regularly with special events and courses running throughout the year. Please look at the website for details or call ahead.

In the shop you will find garden related gifts and tools. Refreshments and cream teas are available seasonably. Oundle hosts an international music festival, Festival of Literature, Farmers Market and has a wide range of independent shops and activities and is well worth a visit any time.

Lyveden New Bield is a cross-shaped Elizabethan garden lodge erected to symbolise the Passion. Begun around 1595 as a garden lodge for his main residence, the Old Bield, it remains virtually unaltered since work on it stopped with the death of Sir Thomas in 1605. An intriguing and haunting roofless shell, it features some interesting exterior frieze work and stands in beautiful open countryside, with the remains of late-Elizabethan water gardens adjoining the site. The new orchard contains many old varieties of apples, pears and plums.

ASHTON

1 mile E of Oundle off the A605

The village is the home of the World Conker Championships, which have taken place on the second Sunday in October since 1965.

For the 2009 renewal the event is moving from the tiny village green to a much larger site less than a mile away at the New Lodge Veterinary Centre.

FOTHERINGHAY

4 miles NE of Oundle off the A605

🏛 Church of St Mary & All Saints 🏛 Castle

🏛 Prebendal Manor Medieval Centre

The first **Fotheringhay Castle** was built around 1100 by the son-in-law of William the Conqueror; the second in the 14th century by Edmund of Langley, a son of Edward III. Richard III was born here; Henry VIII gave the castle to Catherine of Aragon and it later became the prison and place of execution of Mary, Queen of Scots, who was brought here in bands of steel and beheaded in the Banqueting Hall in 1587. Sir Christopher

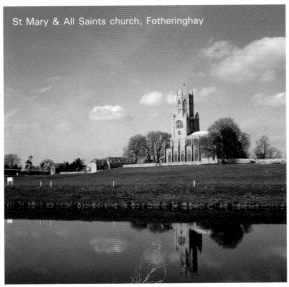

St Mary & All Saints church, Fotheringhay

village without seeing the **Church of St Mary and All Saints**, a 15th century former collegiate church in a prominent position overlooking the Nene Valley. Notable features include an unusual octagonal lantern tower.

The neighbouring village of Woodnewton has retained much of its historic character, and the many houses of limestone, thatch and Collyweston slate in Main Street have led to its designation as a Conservation area. In the graveyard of St Mary's Church is the grave of Nicolai Polakovs, better known

Hatton, a favourite of Elizabeth I, was one of the judges who sentenced Mary to death. Following her death, it is said that her jewellery was stolen and hidden in the woodlands around Corby. If so, it lies there still. The castle was pulled down in 1627 and 200 years later a gold ring was found with a lovers' knot entwined around the initials M and D - Mary and Darnley? Perhaps the ring fell from the Queen's finger as she was executed. The evocative site of the castles by the River Nene is rich in atmosphere, and visitors to Fotheringhay should not leave the

as Coco the Clown, who retired to Woodnewton in 1973 and died there shortly afterward. A short drive to the north, at Nassington, stands the **Prebendal Manor Medieval Centre**. At its heart is the manor, a 13th century Grade I listed building that for many centuries was home to Prebendaries, officials of the Church. The Centre provides an insight into the lives of these powerful men, including Simon of Sudbury, who later became Archbishop of Canterbury and was beheaded in the Tower during the Peasants Revolt of 1381.

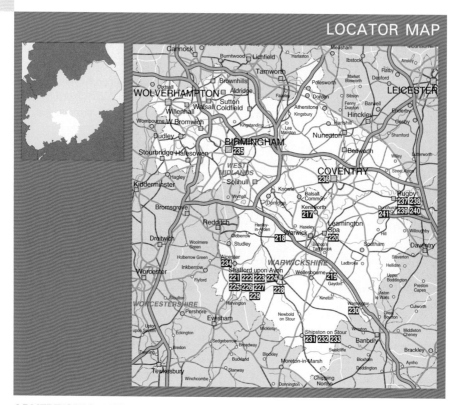

LOCATOR MAP

ADVERTISERS AND PLACES OF INTEREST

🏛 historic building   🏛 museum   🏛 historic site   🝔 scenic attraction   🌿 flora and fauna

10 | Warwickshire & West Midlands

A rich vein of medieval and Tudor history runs through Warwickshire and the romantic ruins of Kenilworth Castle, the grandeur of Warwick Castle and the elegance of Royal Leamington Spa set the tone for this most delightful of counties. However, it is Stratford-upon-Avon that is the focal point for most visitors. Known throughout the world as the birthplace of William Shakespeare, the old part of the town is completely dominated by this exceptional man who died nearly 400 years ago. Along with the various timber-framed houses that are linked with the Bard, Stratford is also the home of the Royal Shakespeare Company, which holds a regular programme of performances of his plays each year.

Another town that has found fame through one of its inhabitants is Rugby, as it was a pupil at the school there who, in the early 19th century, broke the rules of football during a match and, in so doing, founded the game that

bears the name of the town. Close by is the ancient village of Dunchurch that is often dubbed the Gunpowder Plot Village as it was here, in 1605, that the conspirators waited to hear if they had succeeded in blowing up the Houses of Parliament.

The West Midlands and the extreme north of the county of Warwickshire is dominated by the major cities of Birmingham and Coventry. It often gets overlooked by visitors but repays a visit. It is an area rich in natural beauty, with a wealth of beautiful gardens, some excellent museums and historic buildings, and a long and distinguished industrial and cultural heritage.

Kenilworth Castle

ADVERTISERS AND PLACES OF INTEREST

📖 stories and anecdotes   🦜 famous people   ✍ art and craft   ✒ entertainment and sport   🚶 walks

Warwick

🏛 Castle   🏛 Church of St Mary

🏛 Museums   🖌 Racecourse

Over the past 10 centuries **Warwick Castle** has witnessed some of the most turbulent times in English history. From the era of William the Conqueror to the grand reign of Queen Victoria, the Castle has left us a fascinating legacy to enjoy. Dominating the town, it is surely everyone's ideal of a medieval building, one of the country's most splendid castles and certainly one of the most visited. It still serves as a home, as well as retaining the greater part of its original masonry. Standing by the River Avon, Warwick is in a good defensive position and became part of Crown lands as recorded in the Domesday Book in 1086.

A tour of this palatial mansion takes you from the grim austerity of the original dungeons with their gruesome torture chambers, to the gloomy but sumptuous opulence of rooms later adapted for comfortable living. The castle's magnificent State Rooms, once used to entertain the highest members of the nobility, house some superb art treasures, including works by Holbein, Rubens and Velasquez. As the castle is owned by Madame Tussaud's, striking waxworks play their part in the displays. In the castle's Ghost Tower, visitors can learn of the dark and sinister secrets surrounding the fatal stabbing of Sir Fulke Greville who is said to haunt the premises to this day. In the Great Hall visitors come face to face with Oliver Cromwell's death mask. And the armoury houses one of the best private collections in the country.

The castle exterior is best viewed from Castle Bridge, where the 14th-century walls can be seen reflected in the waters of the River Avon. There is a walk along the ramparts, and much to explore within 60 acres of grounds, including a re-created Victorian formal rose garden, the Peacock Gardens and an expanse of open parkland designed by Capability Brown. Events throughout the year include Medieval Tournaments, open-air firework concerts and special entertainment days.

A strong link with the castle is found in the **Collegiate Church of St Mary** in Old Square, a splendid medieval church on the town's highest point. Of pre-Conquest origin, the church contains the magnificent fan-vaulted Beauchamp Chapel, built to house the monuments of Richard Beauchamp, Earl of Warwick, and his family. The chapel contains an outstanding collection of Warwickshire tombs, a chapter house and a Norman crypt (complete with a tumbrel, part of a medieval ducking stool). In summer, visitors can ascend the tower to enjoy the excellent views. The politician and scholar Enoch Powell is buried in his Brigadier's uniform in the churchyard of St Mary, the Church of his old regiment, the

Warwick Mill Street Bridge

Royal Warwickshire. (An earlier service for Enoch Powell was held at St Margaret's Church, Westminster, and included part of his own translation of the Gospel of St Matthew.)

The centre of Warwick was rebuilt after a fire in 1694, and though many older buildings survived, the centre is dominated by elegant Queen Anne buildings. A walk around High Street and Northgate Street takes in some of the finest buildings, including Court House and Landor House. Court House on Jury Street houses the Tourist Information Centre and the **Warwickshire Yeomanry Museum**, with displays of uniforms, arms, swords, sabres and selected silver. The Warwickshire Yeomanry existed from 1794 to 1956, when it was amalgamated with the Queens Own Worcestershire Hussars to become the Queens Own Warwickshire & Worcestershire Yeomanry. The Museum is open on Saturday and Sunday from Easter to October, also Fridays and Mondays of Bank Holidays.

Some of the town's oldest structures can be found around Mill Street, an attractive place for a stroll, with several antiques shops along the way. The Mill Garden at the end of Mill Street is home to a delightful series of plantings in a breathtaking setting on the Avon beside the castle. Here visitors will find a herb garden, raised beds, small trees, shrubs and cottage plants including some unusual varieties.

Warwickshire Museum in Market Place occupies an imposing 17th-century market hall housing collections that illustrate the geology, wildlife and history of the county. Notable exhibits include giant fossils, live bees, ancient jewellery and the historic Sheldon Tapestry map of Warwickshire. Changing programmes in the ground floor galleries offer exciting exhibitions of the work of acclaimed local and national artists.

One of the most important buildings in Warwick is St John's House, dating from 1666 and considered a very good example of the period. Today the building houses a museum where visitors can find out how people lived in the past. Upstairs is the Museum of the Royal Warwickshire Regiment.

Two of Warwick's medieval town gateways survive, complete with chapels. Of these, Westgate Chapel forms part of Lord Leycester's Hospital, a spectacularly tottering and beautiful collection of 15th-century half-timbered buildings enclosing a pretty galleried courtyard. The main interest is provided by the **Queen's Own Hussars Regimental Museum**. This 600-year-old medieval treasure has a unique chantry Chapel dating back to 1123, a magnificent Great Hall and Guildhall together with other timber-framed buildings, first established by the Earl of Leicester as an old soldiers' home in 1571. The historic Master's Garden, featuring a Norman arch and 2,000-year-old vase from the Nile, is a spectacular summer attraction.

In the heart of Warwick, just 400 yards from the castle, the Lord Leycester Hotel occupies Grade II listed buildings steeped in history: in 1694 they halted the Great Fire of Warwick; in the 1700s they housed the Three Tuns Inn; and by the 19th century, they were elegant townhouses.

Warwick Racecourse in Hampton Street offers flat and National Hunt racing throughout the year. This picturesque racecourse makes a good day out for all the family, with a programme of some 25 meetings throughout the year. The central grandstand incorporates the first stand built in 1809, among the oldest surviving in the country. On the city side of the racecourse stand the recently restored Hill Close Gardens.

Kenilworth Castle

Around Warwick

KENILWORTH
4 miles N of Warwick on the A452

🏛 Castle   🏛 Abbey

Although the town was here before the Domesday Book was compiled, Kenilworth's name is invariably linked with its castle. The remains of which stand today as England's finest and most extensive castle ruins, dramatically ensconced at the western edge of the town.

The red sandstone towers, keep and wall of **Kenilworth Castle** glow with an impressive richness in the sun, particularly at sunrise and sunset. Here you can learn about the great building's links with Henry V (who retired to Kenilworth after the Battle of Agincourt), King John, Edward II and John of Gaunt. The tales of this great fortress, immortalised (if enhanced) in Sir Walter Scott's novel *Kenilworth* written in 1821, are many and varied. The marvellous Norman keep, the oldest part of the ruins, was built between 1150 and 1175. John of Gaunt's Great Hall once rivalled London's Westminster Hall in palatial grandeur. After Simon de Montfort's death at the Battle of Evesham in 1265, Kenilworth was held by his son. At that time the castle was surrounded by the Kenilworth Great Pool, a lake covering about 120 acres.

An audio tour takes a revealing journey around the Castle, recounting stories of its turbulent past. There are fine views from the top of Saintlowe Tower, and lovely grounds for exploring and picnicking, as well as the beautifully reconstructed Elizabethan Garden with its bejeweled aviary, marble fountain and

🏛 historic building   🖼 museum   🏛 historic site   🌀 scenic attraction   🌿 flora and fauna

abundant colourful planting. The garden looks now as it did when it was designed by Robert Dudley, Earl of Leicester, for a visit in 1575 by Queen Elizabeth, whom he hoped to marry. The gatehouse he built has been fully restored and is open to the public. It was here that Dudley courted the Queen. It is said that she kept his last letter in a casket until the day she died. A copy of the latter is on display in the Elizabeth and Dudley exhibition. The remains of **Kenilworth Abbey** can be seen in the churchyard of the Norman parish church of St Nicholas in the High Street. Much of interest was discovered during excavations and there are many relics on display in the church, including a 'pig' of lead. It is said that this formed part of the roof at the time of the Dissolution but was then melted down and stamped by the Commissioners of Henry VIII. Special events throughout the year include a festival of Tudor Music, Saxon and Viking exhibitions, medieval pageantry, various re-enactments, plays and operas in the grounds.

ASHOW
4 miles NE of Warwick off the A46

Avon Cottage in Ashow, at the far end of this attractive village adjacent to the church, is a charming cottage garden surrounding a picturesque 18th-century Grade II listed building. It stretches for one-and-a-half acres with extensive River Avon frontage. Diverse and interesting plantings make for year-round interest. There is also an attractive orchard area with free-range domestic hens and waterfowl.

HATTON
2 miles NW of Warwick off the A41

🌿 Hatton Country World

Hatton Country World is a uniquely charming blend of family fun and country shopping. On this 100-acre farm, visitors will find the largest collection of rare breed farm animals in Britain and the largest craft village in England with some 25 workshops and shops lining the quaint streets of converted Victorian farm buildings. It's a great family attraction, with children's shows, pony rides, tractor & trailer rides, a guinea pig village and pumpkin patch. Known by many old boaters as the Stairway to Heaven, the Hatton Lock flight has 21 locks and lifts the Grand Union Canal 144 feet out of Warwick in two-and-a-half miles.

AUSTONS DOWN COUNTRYSIDE B&B

Saddlebow Lane, Claverdon, nr Stratford-upon-Avon, Warwickshire CV35 8PQ
Tel/Fax: 01926 842068
e-mail: info@austonsdown.com
website: www.austonsdown.com

Lucy and John Horner extend a warm welcome to **Austons Down Countryside B&B**, their imposing family home standing in 100 acres of grounds in the lovely Vale of Arden. They have three handsomely appointed double/twin letting bedrooms, all large enough for an extra bed, all with en suite bath/shower, sitting area, TV, radio and hospitality tray. With easy access from the M40 (J15 or 16), Austons Down is ideal for visitors to the Midlands, whether for business or leisure. Stratford, Warwick and Leamington Spa are all an easy drive away, and the NEC can be reached in less than half an hour.

📓 stories and anecdotes   🐦 famous people   🎨 art and craft   ✏ entertainment and sport   🚶 walks

BARFORD

3 miles S of Warwick on the A429

The name of Joseph Arch may not be known to many nowadays, but in his time he was one of the leading figures in the world of farming. Born in a tiny house in 1826 (the house still stands), he was a scare-crower, ploughboy, stable lad and champion hedge-cutter before his radical views led him to found the Warwickshire Agricultural Labourers Union, and later the National Union. He became the first truly working-class Member of Parliament (for North West Norfolk) and was a friend of the Prince of Wales, but he never forgot his roots and he died, at the grand old age of 93, in the little house where he was born. A much grander building is the Regency Barford House, notable for its giant Ionic columns. The Church of St Peter was mainly rebuilt in 1884 by RC Hussey.

SHERBOURNE

3 miles S of Warwick on the A46

�܀ Sherbourne Park

Set in lovely countryside with views over fields to the River Avon, **Sherbourne Park** is one of the very finest gardens in the county. Highlights of the gardens, which were designed by Lady Smith-Ryland in the 1950s, include a paved terrace covered by clematis, wisteria and a magnolia; an 'orchard' of sorbus trees; a box-edged, rose-filled parterre; and the White Garden surrounded by yew hedges. The red brick house of the Park is early Georgian, and the view is dominated by the parish church, built in 1863 by Sir George Gilbert Scott. Open on certain afternoons and by appointment (01926 624255).

Royal Leamington Spa

🏛 Pump Rooms   🏛 Art Gallery & Museum

This attractive town boasts a handsome mixture of smart shops and Regency buildings, and The Parade is undoubtedly one of the finest streets in Warwickshire. At the beginning of the 19th century very few people knew of the existence of Leamington, but by 1838 all this had changed. By this time the famous waters were cascading expensively over the many 'patients' and the increasingly fashionable spa was given the title 'Royal' by permission of the new Queen, Victoria. The

---

CHURCH HILL FARM B&B

Lighthorne, nr Warwick, Warwickshire CV35 0AR
Tel: 01926 651251 Fax: 01926 650339
e-mail:sue@churchhillfarm.co.uk website:www.churchhillfarm.co.uk

An early-16th century timber-framed farmhouse provides a delightful base for visitors to this attractive part of the world. The three rooms all en-suite in the main building at Church Hill Farm are very cosy and comfortable, and two equally pleasant annexe rooms with deep mattresses on king-size beds can be booked on B&B or self-catering terms. The drawing room, with its log fire and paintings of horses and country scenes, is a charming spot to unwind after a day's sightseeing and plan the next day's activities. A super Aga-cooked breakfast with local sausages, bacon and eggs from owner Sue Sabin's hens makes a fine start to the day. The farm is located in the village of Lighthorne just off the B4100 (M40 J12 or 13) south of Warwick and Leamington Spa.

🏛 historic building   🏛 museum   🏛 historic site   🌊 scenic attraction   🌿 flora and fauna

EPISODE HOTEL

Upper Holly Walk, Leamington Spa, Warwickshire CV32 4JL
Tel: 01926 883777
e-mail: leamington@episodehotels.co.uk
website: www.episodehotels.co.uk

Episode Hotel, a handsome Regency townhouse centrally located in Royal Leamington Spa, provides top-notch accommodation and facilities for both business and leisure visitors. The 32 individually decorated and furnished en suite bedrooms – standard, superior and executive – are superbly appointed, with TV, direct-dial phone, free internet access, tea/coffee tray, hairdryer, ironing facilities, top-quality toiletries and lovely soft towels. Room service is available 24 hours a day.

An excellent breakfast starts the day, and various menus offer bar snacks and meals – classics and more inventive choices – and an evening à la carte that combines modern British cooking with a sprinkling of Continental style and technique. The 1-, 2- or 3- course traditional Sunday lunch is always a popular occasion. The interesting wine list features both Old and New World wines, and the terrace is a lovely spot for pushing the boat out with cocktails and champagne.

The hotel is also well set up for meetings, conferences, corporate events and celebrations and holds a licence for civil ceremonies. Ladies Night, with various special offers, is the first Thursday of the month, and Friday nights are music nights. The George Hotel in Shipston-on-Stour (qv) is in the same ownership.

Pump Rooms were opened in 1814 by Henry Jephson, a local doctor who was largely responsible for promoting the Spa's medicinal properties. This elegant spa resort was soon popularised by the rich, who came to take the waters in the 18th and 19th centuries. A converted swimming pool and Turkish Bath houses the **Art Gallery & Museum**, which contains paintings by British and European artists, a Cabinet of Curiosities with activities and trails for children, the story of Leamington and its people, a Hammam - part of the Victorian Turkish Baths - and changing exhibitions and regular events. Immediately opposite the Spa itself are Jephson's Gardens containing a Corinthian temple that houses a statue of him. Acclaimed as one of the country's finest ornamental gardens, it has many unusual trees and plants and a glasshouse

with a range of habitats from desert to tropical.

UFTON FIELDS
5 miles E of Leamington Spa off the A425

🌱 Ufton Fields Nature Reserve

Ufton Fields Nature Reserve is a 100-acre haven with an all-weather footpath and a wealth of wildlife, including butterflies, dragonflies and wild flowers, as well as birds and a bird hide.

HARBURY
5 miles SE of Leamington Spa off the B4452

The history of this area goes back many years – dinosaur fossils have been found in the local quarries and the Fosse Way, a major Roman road, passes close by. Just outside the village lies Chesterton Windmill, an unusual mill built in 1632.

🎭 stories and anecdotes   🦜 famous people   🎨 art and craft   🎟 entertainment and sport   🚶 walks

Stratford-upon-Avon

🏚 Hall's Croft   🏚 Holy Trinity Church

🏚 Nash's House   🌱 Butterfly Farm

🏚 Shakespeare's Birthplace

🏛 Harvard House   🏛 Museum of British Pewter

🖋 Royal Shakespeare Company & Theatre

After London, many visitors to England put Stratford-upon-Avon next on the itinerary, and all because of one man. William Shakespeare was born here in 1564, found fame in London and then retired here, dying in 1616. Needless to say, the places connected with his life and work have become Meccas for anyone interested in the cultural history, not just of these islands, but of the entire world.

Each of the houses associated with the Bard has its own fascinating story to tell, and staff at the houses are happy to guide visitors on a journey encompassing what life might have been like in Stratford-upon-Avon during Shakespeare's day. The half-timbered house that is **Shakespeare's Birthplace** has been returned to the way it would have looked in his day. Household inventories, books and pictures have been assembled, and a room thought to have been his father John's workshop was been re-created with the help of the Worshipful Company of Glovers. The garden is planted with flowers and herbs mentioned in the plays. An adjoining exhibition charts Shakespeare's life and features many rare local artefacts and an edition of the collected plays published in 1623.

Further along, on Chapel Street, stands **Nash's House**. This half-timbered building was inherited by Shakespeare's granddaughter, Elizabeth Hall, from her first husband, Thomas Nash. It now contains an exceptional

---

IDEAL CLOTHES

38 Sheep Street, Stratford-upon-Avon,
Warwickshire CV37 6EE
Tel: 01789 263859

Ideal Clothes stands right opposite Basler No 20 in fashionable Sheep Street in the historic heart of Stratford-upon-Avon. In the same ownership, with the same comfortable, air-conditioned surroundings and the same high standards of personal service, Ideal Clothes stocks a wide range of ladies' fashion clothes and accessories featuring the seasonally changing collections of some of the most respected European brands, aimed primarily at the discerning, style-conscious over-20s market.

The shop is the main stockist in the region of Oska, whose two annual collections combine high quality with distinctive design. Annette Gortz blends comfort with ingenious cuts, focusing on natural materials and the highest quality to produce interesting knitwear and creative casual wear. The Dutch firm Hebbeding produces clothes designed by women for women, aimed at the self-assured woman who seeks exclusive, original and timeless design. Equally stylish accessories stocked at Ideal Clothes include formal and casual shoes by the Italian firm Gardenia and eye-catching costume jewellery from Gabby. Shop hours are 9.30 to 5.30 Monday to Saturday.

🏚 historic building   🏛 museum   🏛 historic site   🏞 scenic attraction   🌱 flora and fauna

Shakespeare's Birthplace

collection of Elizabethan furniture and tapestries, as well as displays, upstairs, on the history of Stratford. The spectacular Elizabethan-style knot garden is an added attraction. Next door, in New Place, Shakespeare bought a house where he spent his retirement years, from 1611 to 1616. Today all that can be seen are the gardens and foundations of where the house once stood. An exhibit in Nash's House explains why this, Shakespeare's final home in Stratford, was destroyed in the 18th century. Opposite New Place is the Guild Chapel, and beyond this is the Grammar School, where it is believed that Shakespeare was educated.

Hall's Croft in Old Town is one of the best examples of a half-timbered gabled house in Stratford. It was named after Dr John Hall, who married Shakespeare's daughter Susanna in 1607. This impressive house contains outstanding 16th and 17th-century furniture and paintings. There is also a reconstruction of Dr Hall's consulting room, accompanied by an exhibition detailing medical practices during Shakespeare's time. Outside, the beautiful walled garden features a large herb bed; visitors can take tea near the 200-year-old mulberry tree or have lunch in the restaurant here.

Hall's Croft is near **Holy Trinity Church**, an inspiration for many poets and artists because of its beautiful setting beside the River Avon. It is here that Shakespeare is buried. Dating partly from the 13th century, it is approached down an attractive avenue of limes. The north door has a sanctuary knocker, used in the past to ensure any fugitive who reached it 37 days grace. Shakespeare's wife, Anne Hathaway, and their daughter Susanna and her husband John Hall are also buried here.

THE WEST END

9 Bull Street, Stratford-upon-Avon,
Warwickshire CV37 6DT
Tel: 01789 268832
website: www.thewestendstratford.co.uk

Roger and Helen Hatch are the hosts at the **West End**, an established favourite with the locals and now sought out by growing numbers of visitors to this marvellous town. Smartly updated behind its period frontage in the Old Town, the inn always has three cask ales on tap and a choice of house wines to enjoy in the bar or outside in the suntrap patio garden. The main menu offers something for everyone, with chicken liver or smoked mackerel pâté, crab & coriander linguine, pork & cider stew and Thai green chicken curry among typical choices. Lighter options include soup, panini and jacket potatoes. Booking is recommended at the weekend.

---

stories and anecdotes · famous people · art and craft · entertainment and sport · walks

BASLER AT NO 20

20 Sheep Street,
Stratford-upon-Avon,
Warwickshire CV37 6EF
Tel: 01789 266850

Basler is a familiar and well respected name in the world of ladies fashion.

From Goldbach to Germany, Basler reaches out to shops with international appeal around the world.

Basler at No 20 is a privately owned exclusive Basler shop in Sheep Street. Based in the heart of Stratford-upon-Avon, close to the Royal Shakespeare Theatre. Basler is noted for quality and wearability in sizes 10 - 22. The clothes are supported by stylish accesories.

Basler produces two collections a year, Spring/Summer and Autumn/Winter. The shop invites customers to regular promotions with Basler's house model showing the latest collections.

A warm friendly welcome, with a one to one service and a comfortable ambience brings customers back time after time.
Shop hours are 9.30 - 5.30 Monday to Saturday.

Shakespeare is not the only illustrious name to have associations with the town. **Harvard House** in the High Street, dating from 1596, was the childhood home of Katherine Rogers. Her son, John Harvard, went to the American Colonies in the early 1600s and founded the university named after him in 1636. In 1909 Harvard House was restored and presented to Harvard University. It boasts the most ornately carved timbered frontage in the town. Cared for by the Shakespeare Birthplace Trust, it houses the **Museum of British Pewter**, based on the nationally important Neish Collection.

There are many other fascinating old buildings in Stratford. The old market site in Rother Street has a history dating from 1196, when a weekly market was granted by King John. In the square is an ornate fountain-cum-clock tower, a gift from GW Childs of Philadelphia in the jubilee year of Queen Victoria. It was unveiled by the actor Sir Henry Irving who, in 1895, became the first Knight of the Stage.

Stratford has become a shrine for theatre-lovers, who flock to enjoy an evening at one of the town's three theatres. The first commemoration of Shakespeare's passing was organised by the actor David Garrick (of Garrick Theatre and the Garrick Club fame), 150 years after the Bard's death. People have been celebrating this illustrious poet and playwright's life and times ever since. The **Royal Shakespeare Company** has an unrivalled reputation both in the UK and worldwide, and wherever the RSC perform, the audience is certain to enjoy performances of the highest standard. The **Royal Shakespeare Theatre** opened in 1879 with a performance of *Much Ado About Nothing* starring Ellen Terry and Beerbohm Tree. The season was limited to one week as part of a

CORNUCOPIA HOME INTERIORS & GIFTS

10 Bards Walk, off Wood Street, Stratford-upon-Avon,
Warwickshire CV37 6EY
Tel: 01789 299494
e-mail: goldby.cornucopia@googlemail.com

Cornucopia Home Interiors & Gifts is located in a smart modern shopping mall close to Shakespeare's birthplace. Owners Caren and Tony Goldby, who took over this excellent emporium in 2007, have filled its shelves and cabinets and walls and tables with an impressive array of homeware and giftware large and small, from dining tables and chairs and garden furniture to chinaware and glassware, candles and burners, jewellery, soft toys and greetings cards. Among the featured brands are SIA – furniture, home fittings, lamps and candles, beautiful silk flowers; Emma Bridgewater – English crockery (Cornucopia the main stockist in the region); Parlane glassware, furniture and frames; Cœur de Lion jewellery from Germany; Lampe Berger bacteria-busting fragrance burners; Dartington glass and crystal; Gisella Graham giftware; John Hine handmade raku (crackle-glaze) sculptures of hares and other animals; Winstanley china cats; Jelly Cat toys; and Woodmansterne greetings cards. Cornucopia is open from 9.30 to 5.30 (Sunday 11.30 to 3.30).

BROADLANDS GUEST HOUSE ★ ★

23 Evesham Place, Stratford-upon-Avon,
Warwickshire CV37 6HT
Tel: 01789 299181 Fax: 01789 551382
e-mail: philandjohn@broadlandsguesthouse.co.uk
website: www.broadlandsguesthouse.co.uk

The guest always comes first at **Broadlands Guest House**, where resident proprietors Phil Gray and John Worboys are the most welcoming and attentive of hosts. The bay-windowed house in a quiet road was completely refurbished a couple of years ago, and the six guest bedrooms offer a peaceful, civilised and very comfortable base for a break in historic Stratford. The three doubles, one twin and two singles, each with its own individual charm, all have en suite facilities, television, hairdryer, good toiletries, bottle water and hairdryer, and some of the bathrooms feature attractive tiles fitted by the owners.

Excellent freshly cooked breakfasts start the day, and guests can browse through a supply of magazines spread out on a chaise longue on the stairs. The house has a pretty little front garden, and private car parking is available. Situated in the Old Town conservation area, Broadlands is well placed for visiting Shakespeare's birthplace, the theatres, the River Avon and the town's many other attractions. Children over 12 are welcome, but not dogs.

THE CREAKY CAULDRON MAGIC SHOP & LIVING MUSEUM

21 Henley Street, Stratford-upon-Avon, Warwickshire CV37 6QW
Tel: 01789 290969
e-mail: davematthews@drbombay.co.uk
website: www.seekthemagic.org
website: www.drbombay.co.uk

To step inside the **Creaky Cauldron Magic Shop & Living Museum** is to enter a world of magic and mystery, sorcery and spookery, witchcraft and wizardry. This amazing place is the creation of Dave Matthews, also known as Dr Thaddeus Bombay, whose merchandise is among many magical products on sale in the shop, along with the very best of the most renowned and longest established makers and purveyors of magical wares. Spread over three floors in a historic building next to the site of Shakespeare's birth, the Museum – 'a living museum we're dying to show you!' – is filled with exciting and informative magical settings and scenes. The Creaky Cauldron is the setting for magical birthday parties – 'fun-filled magical evenings at magic school with the wizards of Henley Street' – and of spooky birthday parties, trying to solve the mystery of the Bombay family curse. Both parties include personalised wax-sealed invitations, themed entertainment and activities, party buffet and birthday cake and personalised goodie bags and certificates. Creaky Cauldron by night invites brave souls (grown-ups and older children) to scary happenings based on grisly events that took place here in the late 18th century – spine-tingling tales and ghosts walks and an adults-only night-long ghost hunt.

STRATFORD-UPON-AVON

Butterfly Farm
& Gift Shop

The UK's largest tropical butterfly paradise!
Rain or shine, discover many of the world's most beautiful butterflies in an exotic environment of tropical blossom with splashing waterfalls and fish-filled pools. Watch in awe as hundreds of spectacular and vibrantly coloured butterflies fly and feed around you.
Open every day (except Christmas Day).

Swans Nest lane, Stratford-upon-Avon, Warwickshire, CV37 7LS
Tel **01789 299288**, e-mail sales@butterflyfarm.co.uk, or
visit our website at www.butterflyfarm.co.uk

🏠 historic building   🏛 museum   🏛 historic site   ⚜ scenic attraction   🌿 flora and fauna

summer festival. It was so successful that, under the direction of FR Benson, it grew to spring and summer seasons, touring the nation in between. In 1925, because of the excellence of the performances and direction, the company was granted a Royal Charter. Sadly, a year later the theatre was destroyed by fire. At the time, playwright George Bernard Shaw sent a one-word telegram: Congratulations! Apparently the building was a bit of an eyesore, but there are few such buildings in today's Stratford. The company, undeterred, continued by giving performances in cinemas while a worldwide fundraising campaign was launched to build a new theatre, which was opened on 23 April 1932, the 368th anniversary of the Bard's birth.

Quite apart from the industry that has grown around Shakespeare and his life and times, Stratford boasts a number of other world-class attractions. The **Butterfly Farm**

(see panel opposite) provides a specially designed and constructed habitat for Europe's largest collection of butterflies. There is also a Caterpillar Room, Insect City – leaf-cutter ants, giant millipedes, and, for the brave of heart, Arachnoland where the world's largest spider, rain forest scorpion colonies and other 'spinners' can be seen in perfect safety. The farm is open every day from 10am to 6pm (till dusk in winter).

The Royal Shakespeare Theatre Summer House on Avonbank Gardens is home to the Stratford Brass Rubbing Centre, which contains a large collection of exact replicas of brasses of knights and ladies, scholars, merchants and priests of the past.

Around Stratford-upon-Avon

SHOTTERY
1 mile W of Stratford off the A422

🍃 Anne Hathaway's Cottage

This was the birthplace of Anne Hathaway, Shakespeare's wife. Here visitors will find the Elizabethan farmhouse now known as **Anne Hathaway's Cottage**, and can retrace the steps that the courting couple, who married in 1582, might have taken. The epitome of the traditional thatched cottage, this delightful spot was home to Hathaways since the 15th century, up until some 70 years ago when the Shakespeare Birthplace Trust decided it was time to open up the home to the public. The Hathaway bed, settle and other pieces of furniture owned by the family remain, and there is a traditional English cottage garden and orchard – plants and herbs grown by the Shakespeare Trusts' gardeners can be

Stratford Brass Rubbing Centre

STRATFORD GARDEN CENTRE

Campden Road, Clifford Chambers, nr
Stratford-upon-Avon,
Warwickshire CV37 8LW
Tel: 01789 205745
e-mail: mail@stratfordgardencentre.co.uk
website: www.stratfordgardencentre.co.uk

Situated on the B4632 south of Stratford-upon-Avon, **Stratford Garden Centre** is an independent family-owned garden centre and is Warwickshire's premier centre for horticulture, with a mix of flowers, plants, trees, gifts and fine foods that represent the best the county has to offer. The range of outdoor plants changes with the seasons and a wide selection of garden accessories and sundries is always available. The centre also sells a wide range of stylish outdoor furniture, along with gas and charcoal barbecues and patio heaters. Smaller items run from seasonal decorations to gifts, gift wrap and cards, books, candles and home fragrances.

Tasty light lunches, freshly made teas, coffee and soft drinks are served in the bright, modern 80-seater café, and the deli section tempts with a wide choice of cheeses, cold meats, fresh bread and cakes.

The centre has many concessions which enhance the centre including Arctic Spa's hot tubs, Maidenhead Aquatics, Prior Products, Cotton Traders, Pownalls Fine Foods, Childsplay Toy Shop and Ceramic Studio.

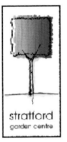

stratford
garden centre

Opening hours are 9am to 6pm Monday to Saturday, 10.30am to 4.30pm Sunday.

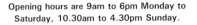

Anne Hatherway's Cottage, Shottery

it aluminium was used for its replacement. Every June pupils of Welford Primary School dance round the pole.

LONG MARSTON
10 miles SW of Stratford off the A46

🚶 The Greenway

Charles I stayed at a house in Long Marston after his flight from the Battle of Worcester. The village's 14th-century church has a half-timbered turret and porch. From Long Marston there's access to **The Greenway**, a converted railway line ideal for cycling or walking. This open public greensward boasts two-and-a-half miles of surfaced paths amid beautiful scenery, with picnic areas and a tranquil atmosphere of rural calm.

purchased. Other attractions of this handsome village are the Shakespeare Tree Garden, the tranquil Shottery Brook, a sculpture garden and an Elizabethan-style yew maze planted in 2001. A growing willow cabin inspired by *Twelfth Night* allows visitors to hear reading of the Sonnets by well-known actors.

WELFORD-ON-AVON
4 miles WSW of Stratford off the B439

Welford is a beautifully kept village of timbered and thatched cottages situated on the south bank of a bend of the River Avon. It is famous for its maypole, at 65 feet the tallest in the country. The original was made of wood, but after a lightning strike destroyed

ILMINGTON
10 miles S of Stratford off the A3400

🏚 Ilmington Manor   🌳 Ilmington Downs

🏛 Meon Hill

Along the northeastern Cotswolds, at the foot of the Wilmington Downs, you'll come to the village of Ilmington. This eye-catching place has several lovely old houses. Its part-Norman

---

COLIN SMITH FAMILY BUTCHER

Chapel Street, Welford-on-Avon, Warwickshire CV37 8PX
Tel: 01789 750213

Once a year they dance round the famous maypole in the pretty village of Welford-on-Avon, four miles upstream from Stratford. But every day of the year the locals dance with delight at having such an excellent butcher on the doorstep. Colin Smith, head of **Colin Smith Family Butcher**, has been in the business for nearly 40 years, and in that time he has built up a loyal clientele that extends far beyond the village bounds. He sources his beef, lamb and pork from the best local farmers, and uses their prime produce for his home-made sausages, pies and faggots. Seasonal game is another speciality, and this super little shop also sells cooked and cured meats, dairy products, fruit and vegetables, jams, chutneys and home-baked cakes.

📷 stories and anecdotes   🐦 famous people   ✎ art and craft   🌿 entertainment and sport   🚶 walks

church, which features oak furnishings by Robert Thompson of Yorkshire, is approached through a Norman arch. This is truly a hidden place and one of the most picturesque one could hope to find. Lying in the valley between the Campden and Foxcote hills, it is surrounded by green fields and Cotswold countryside. Here there are fine old stone cottages with roses round the doors, and gardens full of colour. The village's name means the elm grown hill. It was made famous on Christmas Day 1934, when the first radio broadcast by George V was introduced by Walton Handy, the village shepherd, and relayed to the world from **Ilmington Manor**, the fine Elizabethan house once owned by the de Montfort family. The remains of a tramway, once the main form of transport to the village, can still be seen.

The nearby **Ilmington Downs** are, at 850 feet, the highest point in the county, commanding fine views of the surrounding country. Across the B4632 you will pass **Meon Hill**, where an Iron Age fort stood dominating the valley.

WILMCOTE
3 miles NW of Stratford off the A34

🏠 Palmers Farm   🪶 Mary Arden's House

Another notable house connected with Shakespeare is that of his mother, situated here in the village of Wilmcote, slightly off the well-beaten tourist track. **Palmers Farm** is a striking Tudor farmhouse, now home to the Shakespeare Countryside Museum of farming and rural life. **Mary Arden's House** is next to the farmhouse. Note in particular the bread oven doors, which are made of bog oak, which never burns, and are seen only very rarely now in England. Special events and demonstrations of traditional sheep shearing,

weaving and spinning, crook making and other country crafts are held throughout the year, as well as celebrations and entertainments based on accounts from Shakespeare's plays, in particular *A Winter's Tale*. Best of all, however, is the dovecote of the house. Robert Arden, who was lord of the manor, was in this capacity the only villager allowed to have one. It has over 600 pigeonholes and, at nesting time, would house about 3,000 birds.

Wilmcote is also one of the few small villages left that retains its Victorian Gothic railway station.

CHARLECOTE
3 miles E of Stratford off the B4086

🏛 Charlecote Park   🏛 Mill

The National Trust's **Charlecote Park** is a magnificent stately home occupying extensive grounds overlooking the River Avon. Home of the Lucy family since 1247, the present house was built in the mid 1500s. Thomas Lucy was knighted here by Robert Dudley, Earl of Leicester, deputising for Elizabeth I, who spent two nights here in 1572. The house was comprehensively modernised during the 1700s, but when George Hamilton Lucy inherited it in 1823, he took the decision to 'turn the clock back' and create interiors according to rich Victorian 'Romantic' ideals of the Elizabethan era. The house, apart from the family wing, which is still used by descendants of these early Lucys, has not been changed since. The lavish furnishings include important pieces from William Beckford's Fonthill Abbey sale in 1823. A treasure trove of historic works of sculpture and painting, no visitor can fail to be impressed by the house's sheer magnitude, grace and beauty. In 2009 a project using special events and interpretation to encourage visitors to get involved and experience the hidden history of the place was introduced. The park was landscaped by Capability Brown and reflects his use of natural and man-made features complementing each other. The park supports herds of red and fallow deer (in about 1583 the young William Shakespeare is alleged to have been caught poaching Sir Thomas' deer; years later he is said to have taken his revenge by using Sir Thomas as his inspiration for the fussy Justice Shallow in *The Merry Wives of Windsor*), as well as a flock of Jacobs sheep, first introduced here in 1756.

Charlecote Mill is situated on the site of an earlier mill mentioned in the Domesday Book, at which time it was valued at six shillings, eight pence (33p). In 1978, this 18th-century building was restored with the help of volunteers from Birmingham, and the west waterwheel was repaired at the expense of the BBC for their film of George Eliot's novel, *The Mill on the Floss*.

MORETON MORRELL
7 miles E of Stratford off the B4455

🏠 Church

In the **Church of the Holy Cross** (Norman with 14th and 15th-century rebuilding) is an effigy of Richard Murden, High Sheriff of Warwickshire in 1635. The village has an American connection. Richard Randolph had seven children baptised in the church, and his third son, William, went to Virginia in 1672. William was an ancestor of Thomas Jefferson, the third President of the USA and the man chiefly responsible for the drafting of the Declaration of Independence. In the same family were John Marshall, America's first Chief Justice, and General Robert E Lee, whose surrender to General Grant in 1865

brought the American Civil War to an end.

WELLESBOURNE
4 miles E of Stratford off the A429

🏠 Wartime Museum 🏠 Watermill

Wellesbourne Wartime Museum is located on the site of a wartime airfield. On display are tools, ration books and an exhibit in the style of a contemporary battle operations control room. Open Sundays and Bank Holidays from 10am to 4pm. **Wellesbourne Watermill** (due to reopen in 2010) is a genuine brick-built working flour mill dating back to 1834. This restored mill on the River Dene, a tributary of the River Avon, is one of the few in the country that visitors can see working as it did when new. A video presentation prepares visitors for the mill itself, providing an insight into this heritage site. Demonstrations of the art and skill of milling stoneground flour are enacted and explained by the miller, and visitors are encouraged to take part. Apart from the working demonstrations, there are guided walks alongside the river and two ponds, tree trails, and coracle boats along the river. There is also a display of antique farm implements, a craft shop, and a tearoom in the wonderful 18th-century timber-framed barn where teas and lunches are served.

COMPTON VERNEY
6 miles E of Stratford off the B4086

🏠 Manor House

Before crossing the Fosse Way, the Roman road that runs from Exeter to Lincoln passes **Compton Verney Manor House**. For many years closed to the public, this magnificent manor has been renovated and is now open to visitors. An exquisite collection of works of art has been assembled, including British portraiture, European Old Masters and modern works, along with a unique collection of British Folk Art. Workshops, evening talks, lectures and special events bring to life the processes and inspiration behind some of these great works. The manor house stands in 40 acres of parkland landscaped by Capability Brown and rich in flora and fauna, with a lake, arbour, stirring stone obelisk, Victorian watercress bed, Cedar of Lebanon, and Adam Bridge. The handsome avenue of Wellingtonias line what was once the entrance to the estate.

KINETON
8 miles E of Stratford on the B4086

🏛 Battle of Edgehill

This pleasant old market town is a peaceful retreat with an old courthouse and several 17th and 18th century houses. To the south-east of the town is the site of the **Battle of Edgehill**, fought here in October 1642. For the Royalists this was the first and one of the

most devastating clashes of the Civil War. A year after the battle, Charles I was again in Kineton to meet his wife, Henrietta Maria, who had spent the previous night in Shakespeare's house as the guest of the poet's daughter Susanna.

GAYDON
8 miles E of Stratford off the B4100

🏛 Heritage Motor Centre

The **Heritage Motor Centre** in Gaydon hosts a most impressive collection of historic British cars, and also offers a variety of outdoor activities for the whole family. This fascinating Centre tells the story of the British motor industry from 1896 to the present day, including a 50 Years of the Mini exhibition. It boasts about 200 exclusively British vehicles from the world-famous makes of Aston Martin, Rover, Austin (the rare A35 convertible is a great favourite), Morris, Wolseley, Riley, Standard, Triumph, MG and Austin Healey. Open 10am - 5pm

The National Herb Centre

Banbury Road, Warmington,
Warwickshire OX17 1DF
Tel: 01295 690999 Fax: 01295 690034
website: www.herbcentre.co.uk

Visitors to the **National Herb Centre** an expect a warm welcome with a host of attractions for all the family. The philosophy behind the whole growing policy is to ensure that herb production works in harmony with nature.

The plant centre has hundreds of varieties of herb plants, which will delight the chef, intrigue the gardener and fascinate anyone with an interest in alternative medicine. Access to the plant centre has been made as easy as possible for disabled and wheelchair-bound visitors. You will find many of the plants in raised beds.

There is a plant centre & gift shop, herb bistro & deli shop as well as herb display gardens, children's activity area and workshops and demonstrations.

🏛 historic building   📷 museum   🏛 historic site   🌾 scenic attraction   🌿 flora and fauna

daily. The 65-acre site also features a 4 x 4 off-road demonstration circuit.

FENNY COMPTON
11 miles E of Stratford off the A423

🚶 Country Park

This charming village close to **Burton Dassett Hills Country Park** and just half a mile from the Oxford Canal provides endless opportunities for scenic walks along the edge of the Cotswold Scarp. Burton Dassett Park itself is distinguished by rugged open hilltops topped by a 14th-century beacon with marvellous views in all directions.

FARNBOROUGH
11 miles SE of Stratford off the B4086

🏛 Farnborough Hall

The National Trust's **Farnborough Hall** is a lovely honey-coloured stone house built in the mid 1700s and the home of the Holbech family for over 300 years. The interior features some superb plasterwork, and the delightful grounds include a terrace walk, 18th-century temples and an obelisk.

WARMINGTON
10 miles SE of Stratford on the B4100

🌿 National Herb Centre

The **National Herb Centre** (see panel opposite) enjoys a great location on the northern edge of the Cotswolds on the B4100 close to the Warwickshire-Oxfordshire border. A centre for research and development work for the UK herb industry, the site has been developed with an eye towards providing visitors with a fascinating range of activities and sights. The Plant Centre has one of the widest selections of plants, trees and shrubs with herbal uses in the country. The Herb Shop stocks a range

of herbs, health foods and gifts, many produced on site. The Centre hosts regular art and craft exhibitions.

OXHILL
8 miles SE of Stratford off the A422

A charming village of brown and red brick cottages on a tributary of the Stour. The Church of St Laurence is mainly Norman with a unique 12th-century font lavishly sculpted and depicting Adam and Eve at the Tree of Life, and an impressive Norman doorway decorated with strange faces peering through foliage.

UPTON HOUSE
11 miles SE of Stratford off the A422

🏛 Upton House

Here on the border with Oxfordshire, **Upton House** is a late 17th-century National Trust property built of the mellow local stone. The house was remodelled in 1927-9 for the second Viscount Bearsted to house his growing art collection and also to modernise the premises. The collections in the house are the chief attractions, featuring paintings by English and Continental Old Masters including El Greco, Brueghel, Bosch, Hogarth and Stubbs. Brussels tapestries, Sèvres porcelain, Chelsea figures and 18th-century furnishings are also on display. In the fine gardens, in summer, there can be seen the typically English scene of white-clad cricketers; in winter, the Warwickshire Hunt holds its meet here.

UPPER TYSOE
8 miles SE of Stratford off the A422

🚶 Windmill Hill   🚶 Compton Wynyates Park

From Upper Tysoe there is a lovely walk south over **Windmill Hill** (which actually does have a windmill on it), taking you to the church on the edge of **Compton Wynyates Park**, with views of the attractive Tudor manor below - a refreshing bit of brick building in this Cotswold-edge stone country.

SHIPSTON-ON-STOUR
9 miles SE of Stratford off the A3400

For centuries, Shipston-on-Stour was an important agricultural centre, in the heart of a rural district known as Feldon. From the

---

TAYLORS OF SHIPSTON –
BUTCHER & DELICATESSEN

Market Place, Shipston-on-Stour, Warwickshire CV36 4AB
Tel: 01608 661429
website: www.taylorsofshipston.co.uk

High standards of quality and service keep the customers returning to **Taylors of Shipston**, a high-class family butcher in a prime location on the Market Place. They come for the locally sourced meat – 28-day matured beef, Cotswold lamb, Gloucester Old Spot pork, offal, game, poultry – and for the dry-cured bacon, the superb sausages (up to 18 varieties), the barbecue supplies and the various accompaniments and condiments. In August 2008 owner Darren Taylor opened the **Deli & Bakery** a few doors away at 29 high Street, Tel: 01608 662472. Customers here will find a fine selection of home-cooked meats, ready meals, cheeses, specialist deli fare, daily-delivered bread and cakes, hot and cold baps, panini, jacket potatoes and hot and cold drinks.

SHIPSTON ON STOUR NEEDLECRAFT

24-26 Sheep Street, Shipston-on-Stour,
Warwickshire CV36 4AF
Tel: 01608 661616
e-mail: info@needlework.co.uk
website: www.needlework.co.uk

Whatever your needlecraft requirements, it's no exaggeration to say that you will almost certainly find all of them at Jan and David Cohen's colourful **Shipston on Stour Needlecraft** shop. There's a huge range of threads from leading manufacturers, including threads for gold work; a comprehensive selection of accessories including beads, embroidery ribbons and presentation cards. There are cross stitch kits from various suppliers, amongst them the shop's own Burford Collection; crewel and embroidery kits, and much, much more. The shop also stocks 100s of books and charts and offers a canvas stretching service, a cushion making-up service and picture framing. They will also make to measure foot stools, fender stools, widescreens, pole screens, work and key boxes. The shop runs workshops for hardanger, gold work, stump work, crewel embroidery, trammed needlepoint and non-specific - that is, what you want to do. For all courses except the non-specific, a small kit is included in the price. The shop is open from 9am to 5pm, Monday to Saturday, and there is a convenient car park at the rear of the premises.

THE GEORGE

High Street, Shipston-on-Stour, Warwickshire CV36 4AJ
Tel: 01608 661453
e-mail: info@thefabulousgeorge.com
website: www.thefabulousgeorgehotel.co.uk

In a prime position on the High Street, **The George** is a comfortable, superbly appointed base for both business and leisure visitors. The accommodation comprises 16 individually styled en suite bedrooms named after favourite foods like asparagus, popcorn, lobster and chilli pepper. They vary in size, shape and price, but all have king-size beds with immaculate linen, luxurious fabrics and bespoke furniture, wall-mounted TV, DVD/CD player, free wi-fi, hot drinks tray, bottled water, Molton Brown toiletries and pampering soft towels.

Food is an important part of The George's business, starting with breakfast, locally sourced traditional English or lighter Continental options served from 7.30 to 10.30. Sandwiches and hot snacks are served from noon to 6pm, and the choice for lunch and dinner runs from pub-style classics like burgers, fish & chips and sausage & mash to the main à la carte menu of modern British dishes. Interesting wines are available by glass or bottle and beers include cask ales from a local micro-brewery. The main bar is an informal, relaxed spot for meeting or making friends, and the Library Bar can be booked for canapés and drinks parties. A stylish private dining room is a popular choice for parties, get-togethers and meetings and for entertaining clients.

Episode Hotel in Leamington Spa (qv) is in the same ownership.

1200s, tradesmen and craftsmen helped shape the town, which remains to this day a centre for fascinating shops, galleries and antiques shops.

The hills that surround the town are perfect for gentle strolls and cycling. This small town has quite a busy shopping centre, but is rewarding to stroll through, with a nice church and many handsome old stone buildings.

HONINGTON

8 miles SE of Stratford off the A3400

Honington Hall

Honington Hall encapsulates the architectural and decorative styles popular in the late 17th and 18th centuries. Opening times are limited, but the Hall is well worth a visit, presenting many delightful examples of Regency tastes and refinements.

LONG COMPTON

12 miles SE of Stratford off the A3400

Whichford Wood   Rollright Stones

Just a short distance from the Oxfordshire border, this handsome village lies close to the local beauty spot known as **Whichford Wood**. It is a pleasant Cotswold village of thatched stone houses and some antiques shops. A mile or so to the south of Long Compton, straddling the Oxfordshire border, are the **Rollright Stones**, made up of the King Stone on one side of the lane, with the other two stone groupings – known as the King's Men and the Whispering Knights – on the other. Legend has it that this well-preserved stone circle is a king and his men, tricked by a sorceress into falling under her spell and then petrified.

---

stories and anecdotes   famous people   art and craft   entertainment and sport   walks

Solihull

🏛 National Motorcycle Museum

Solihull began life as a sparsely populated village in a relatively under-populated part of the country. It did not begin to grow in size and importance until the 1930s. Its motto – Urbs in Rure (town in country) – is well deserved. Its cottages and houses have since medieval times always blended well with the greenery that covers a large swathe of the surrounding region. Today, Solihull's 17th and 18th-century houses clearly demonstrate the good planning that has always been a hallmark of the town's social and architectural design. The chief glory of Solihull's Church of St Alphege is some fine glass by Kempe. At nearby Bickenhill, the **National Motorcycle Museum** is a tribute to, and a priceless record of, the once-great British motorcycle industry. (0121 704 6130).

Around Solihull

KNOWLE
1 mile SE of Solihull off the A4141

🏛 Grimshaw Hall   🏛 Chester House

The Elizabethan **Grimshaw Hall** in Knowle is a fine example of a carefully restored building of great historic significance (but is not open to the public). Nearby **Chester House** was built in the mid 1300s; it has been successfully refurbished and is today used as a library, thus offering a practical service to the current population.

LAPWORTH
5 miles S of Solihull off the A3400

🏛 Baddesley Clinton   🏛 Packwood House

Here, where the Grand Union and Stratford Canals meet, handsome Lapworth boasts some characterful old buildings. At Chadwick End, a mile west of the A4141, **Baddesley Clinton** is a romantic, medieval moated manor house that has changed little since 1633. Set against the backdrop of the Forest of Arden, this National Trust-owned property has had strong Catholic connections throughout its history. There is a tiny chapel in the house, and secret priests' holes, used to hide holy fathers when Catholic, during the reign of Charles I, were persecuted. The grounds feature a lovely walled garden and herbaceous borders, natural areas and lakeside walks. Lunches and teas are available. Nearby **Packwood House**, also in the care of the National Trust, is a Jacobean country mansion with a beautiful interior filled with rare furniture, tapestries, stained glass and ornaments. The recently restored Carolean garden features an unusual topiary – a series of yew trees created to represent The Sermon on the Mount.

HENLEY-IN-ARDEN
7 miles S of Solihull off the A3400

🏛 Beaudesert Castle

🏛 Church of St John the Baptist

Possibly the finest old market town in Warwickshire, its mile-long High Street brimming with examples of almost every kind of English architecture from the 15th century onwards, including many old timber-framed houses built with Arden oak. Little remains today of the Forest of Arden, the setting adopted by William Shakespeare for his *As You Like It*, as its stocks were diminished in the 1700s by the navy's demand for timber, but nothing could diminish the beauty of Henley itself.

The town emerged initially under the protection of Thurston de Montfort, Lord of the Manor in 1140. **Beaudesert Castle**, home to the de Montfort family, lies behind the churches of St John and St Nicholas, where remains of the castle mound can still be seen. Famous visitors of the past to this delightful town have included Dr Johnson, his friend James Boswell, and the poet Shenstone.

The 15th-century **Church of St John the Baptist** has a tower that dominates the High Street where it narrows near the ancient Guildhall. The roof of the Guildhall is supported by oak beams, which were growing at the time of the Norman invasion, and a wooden candelabra hangs from the ceiling. At one end of the hall is a huge dresser displaying a set of pewter plates dating back to 1677. The charter granted to the town has a royal seal embossed in green wax, kept in its own glass case in the Guildhall.

The town's Court Leet still meets yearly with the lord of the manor at its head, as it has for centuries. Members of this distinguished grouping have included the High Bailiff, Low Bailiff, Ale-taster, Butter-weigher, Mace bearer, Town Crier, Town Constable, Two Affearers and Two Brook Lockers. Just outside Henley lies Beaudesert, a village even older than its near neighbour, with a good few timber-framed cottages and the beautifully restored Norman church of St Nicholas.

WOOTTON WAWEN

9 miles S of Solihull off the A3400

🏛 St Peter's Church   🏛 Wotton Hall

🏛 Saxon Sanctuary

Handy for walks on nearby Stratford Canal, Wootton Wawen also contains some fine timber-framed buildings and Warwickshire's oldest church – **St Peter's**, an impressive structure that still has its Saxon tower, now more than 1,000 years old. The main building is actually three churches in one; there are three completely separate chapels tacked on to each other with a refreshing disregard for architectural design which does not in any way detract from the church's charm. One of these chapels, the barn-roofed Lady Chapel, is now the **Saxon Sanctuary**, a colourful exhibition that traces the history of 'Wagen's' woodland village in the Forest of Arden. It reveals how this small village conceals a Roman road, two monasteries, an ancient fort, mysterious underground passages, a river that changes with fashion, a disappearing pond and an aqueduct.

St Peter's stands within a picturesque churchyard, which has won the Diocesan Best Kept award several times. Next to the church stands **Wotton Hall**, dating from 1637. Maria Fitzherbert, wife of George IV, spent her childhood here and is thought now to return in ghostly form as the Grey Lady who has been seen wandering about the Hall.

COUGHTON

12 miles S of Solihull off the A435

🏛 Coughton Court   🏛 Dovecote

The parish church of this very pretty village was built by Sir Robert Throckmorton between 1486 and 1518. It has six bells, which were restored in 1976 but are still carried in their original wooden frame. Inside, there are some interesting oddments: a faceless clock, fish weather vanes and a dole cupboard from which wheaten loaves were distributed to the needy.

The crowning glory of the village is one of the great Tudor houses, **Coughton Court**, home of the Throckmorton family since 1409. The family were very prominent in Tudor times and were instigators of Catholic emancipation, playing a part in the Gunpowder Plot – the wives of some of the

Ullenhall and Henley-in-Arden

Distance: *4.5 miles (7.2 kilometres)*

Typical time: *120 mins*

Height gain: *69 metres*

Map: *Explorer 220*

Walk: *www.walkingworld.com ID:2920*

Contributor: *Richard and Kathy Wood*

ACCESS INFORMATION:

Take the A4189 from Henley in Arden. Take a right turn, along Ullenhall Lane signposted to Ullenhall. When you arrive in the village of Ullenhall, before reaching the pub, turn left up Church Hill. Park along the roadside before the church.

DESCRIPTION:

This beautiful circular walk begins in the picturesque Warwickshire village of Ullenhall. It starts from the church, slowly crossing fields and lanes towards Hallend, which follows the Arden Way. Before crossing Henley in Arden Golf & Country Club there are a couple of benches, ideal for that well-earned rest and bite to eat. The walk then follows the perimeter of the golf course for a while before returning to Ullenhall across farmland.

FEATURES:

Pub, Church, Wildlife, Birds, Flowers, Great Views, Mostly Flat.

WALK DIRECTIONS:

1 | After leaving the attractive Ullenhall church, walk down Church Hill to the main Ullenhall road in the village. Cross the main road and head up Watery Lane. Walk to the right of the white railings and then go through the gate. Turn right to follow the footpath behind the house.

2 | Cross the road and go straight through the gate. Continue straight on over the hill and down the other side to the gateway by the road junction. Continue straight on along Chapel lane for 200 metres.

3 | At the road junction, turn right up towards a small church. Go through the church yard to the left of the church and through the gate. Go down the hill following the hedge eventually leading to a road. Turn right on to the road.

4 | Follow the road until you meet the entrance to Hallend farm. Go

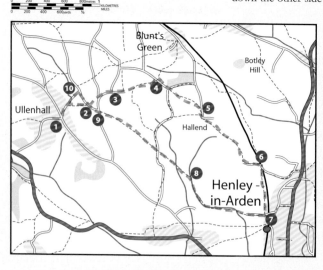

through the gate to the farm. On passing through the gate turn left into the field. Go straight across the field towards a small group of trees at the top of the hill. Go down the other side to a stile by a lane. Turn right on to lane.

5 | Continue along the lane passing a couple of cottages on a left hand bend. Immediately after this bend turn right by a barn to follow the Arden Way. Keeping on the Arden Way the path crosses the golf course before running between the Tennis courts and a couple of houses, finally emerging at the Golf Club House.

6 | Turn left at the club house to go across the car park. Do not go over the railway bridge, follow the footpath to the right of the bridge, also signed up for the first golf tee. Follow the footpath along side the railway line and edge of the golf course. Cross over the stile by the railway bridge and down the steps to the road.

7 | Turning right on the road, head up towards a gate. Go through the gate and follow the edge of the golf course until arriving at a stile.

8 | Cross the stile and go straight across the field to arrive at a small wooden bridge. After crossing the bridge, cross the fields keeping the farm house on your left. Carry on up the hill crossing three further stiles. Keeping the hedge to your left, carry on up the hill to another stile. Cross the next field to a gateway on the lane. Turn right on to the lane.

9 | Immediately turn left down Perry Mill Lane. Follow the lane down until you reach the junction of Watery Lane.

10 | Turn left and continue down Watery Lane until you meet the main road. Cross the road, then go up Church Hill back to your starting point by Ullenhall church.

Coughton Court

Gunpowder Plotters awaited the outcome of the Plot in the imposing central gatehouse. This, and the half-timbered courtyard, are particularly noteworthy, while inside there are important collections of paintings, furniture, porcelain and other family items from Tudor times to the present day. Treasured possessions include the chemise of Mary, Queen of Scots, and the Throckmorton Coat; the former was worn by Queen Mary at her execution in 1587. The Coat was the subject of a 1,000 guinea wager in 1811. The priest's hole found in the house was constructed by one of the most famous builders of hiding places, Nicholas Owen. A Gunpowder Plot children's trail and a Top Ten Highlights Trail for adults was introduced in 2009 and a special events programme celebrates 600 years of the Throckmorton family at the Court.

This National Trust property has extensive gardens and grounds, a lake, a riverside walk and two churches to add to the interest. The fountain pool in the courtyard leads out to formal paths of lime trees. Spring heralds a magnificent display of over 100,000 daffodils and other spring blooms. The grounds also boast a walk planted with willows and native shrubs and trees beside the River Arrow, a new bog garden, a formal orchard and a walled garden project opened in 1996 and maturing into a splendid example of garden rooms set with their own particular plant themes. One herbaceous border is planted with cool blues and yellows, the other with hot reds and orange. Also on site there is the Tudor Restaurant serving coffee, lunches and teas, an attractive gift shop and a plant centre.

A little way east of Coughton, at Kinwarton just south of the B4089, there stands another National Trust property - **Kinwarton Dovecote**. This circular 14th century dovecote still houses doves and retains its 'potence', a pivoted ladder by which access is possible to the nesting boxes. Open every day from April to October. The Dovecote is the only survivor of a moated grange that belonged to Evesham Abbey.

ALCESTER
15 miles S of Solihull off the A435

🏛 Roman Heritage Centre   🏠 Ragley Hall

Alcester is an ancient Roman market town built on the Icknield Street Encampment. **Roman Alcester Heritage Centre** explores everyday life in and around Roman Alcester. The museum houses an interactive exhibition of discoveries from the town and surrounding area. Local excavations have made Alcester one of the most understood small Roman towns in the country. There are many interesting properties in the medieval streets, including the Church of St Nicholas with its 14th-century tower and the early 17th-century town hall. Alcester is popular for good local walks along the confluence of the Rivers Alne and Arrow. The town has been regional winner of a Britain in Bloom award. Alcester has many interesting buildings, including the 13th-century Church of St Nicholas. One of its treasures is a painted alabaster effigy of

Lord of the Manor Sir Fulke Greville, his wife and his 15 children (two of the children died in infancy and are represented by swaddling).

The adjacent village of Arrow is interesting to stroll around (despite some development), as is the pretty stream that divides Arrow and Alcester.

Nearby **Ragley Hall** is a genuine 17th-century treasure. The Warwickshire home of the Marquess and Marchioness of Hertford, it is a perfectly symmetrical Palladian house set in 400 acres of parkland and gardens landscaped by Capability Brown. One of England's great Palladian country houses, it was inherited by the 8th Marquess in 1940 when he was only nine. During World War II the house was used as a hospital, and thereafter became almost completely derelict. In 1956, the Marquess married, and he and his wife set about making the Hall their home. All the main rooms have been redecorated in colours similar to the original ones that would have been used, and the process of restoring and improving continues. This magnificent stately home boasts James Gibb's elegant

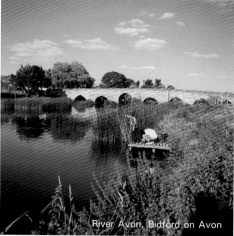

River Avon, Bidford on Avon

HUMPHRIES SHOES

23 High Street, Alcester, Warwickshire B49 5AE
Tel: 01789 764986
e-mail: sales@humphriesshoes.co.uk
website: www.humphriesshoes.co.uk

Humphries Shoes is a traditional family business established in 1862 by Walter Humphries and run today by the fourth and fifth generations of the family. Walter began the business by handcrafting individually measured boots which were fitted for each of his customers. He was able to make three pairs of boots every two days.

Over the years the small business became a first-class shoe store, stocking a wide range of styles from all the top British manufacturers together with some overseas brands. The emphasis has always been on fitting, quality and value for money and it was one of the very first shoe stores to offer fitted shoes for children. Humphries Shoes has been in Alcester for over 10 years on the High Street. The listed building suits the friendly atmosphere of a family business while still boasting a wide range of styles. *Ranges for men include:* Clarks, Rieker, Padders, Loake, Grenson, Barker, Anatomic Gel, Ecco, Merrell and Timberland. *Ranges for women include:* Lotus, Rieker, Hotter, Clarks, Gabor, Van Dal, Tamaris, Caprice, Rohde, Ecco, Josef Seibel, Riva, Padders and Equity.

The shop also offers a professional fitting service for children's shoes on an extensive range from Clarks, Geox, Timberland and Lelli Kelly. Shop hours are 9 to 5.30 Monday to Saturday. Other Humphries Shoes shops are in Redditch, Worcestershire and Stow-on-the-Wold, Gloucestershire.

Baroque plasterwork in the Great Hall, as well as Graham Rust's stunning 20th-century mural, The Temptation. A tour takes in Ragley Hall's fabulous collection of treasures from a bygone age, featuring paintings (including some modern art), china, furniture and a goodly assortment of Victorian and Edwardian dolls and toys. The Stables house an impressive carriage collection.

The main formal garden, to the west of the Hall, descends in a series of wide terraces, now entirely occupied by roses. The rest of the garden, covering 24 acres, consists of shrubs and trees interspersed with spacious lawns providing vistas across the 400-acre park. The lake, created in 1625, is now used for fishing, sailing, swimming and water skiing; there is also a lakeside picnic area. The cricket pitch is in regular use. A country trail of about two miles wends its way through the park and the woods, to end at a very popular adventure playground. The Hall also boasts licensed terrace tearooms. Special events such as craft fairs, gardeners' weekends, dog trials and outdoor concerts are held throughout the year.

Birmingham

- Sarehole Mill
- Soho House
- Birmingham Back to Backs
- Museum & Art Gallery
- Botanical Gardens
- Science Museum
- Nature Centre
- Barber Institute

Birmingham rewards a visit many times over with its wealth of museums, marvellous public spaces, historic buildings and myriad other sights, sounds and attractions. It is a city with a rich and varied industrial history taking in everything from the first steam engine to button, buckles, clocks and chocolate.

Peter de Bermingham obtained rights of trading in a Market Charter granted in 1166 by King Henry II. By the mid 16th century there were some 1,500 people living in 200 homes, as well as one main street and a number of side-streets, markets for grain and livestock, and mills for tanning. Already the smiths were selling their knives and all manner of tools throughout England. This growth was helped along by the demands of the Parliamentarians who, during the Civil War, needed a virtually endless supply of swords, pikes and armour. So it was that Birmingham emerged with a strong reputation as a metal centre.

Castle Bromwich Hall Gardens, Birmingham

By the 1750s, the population had swelled to over 20,000 and, by the time of the Industrial Revolution, Birmingham had become the industrial, commercial and cultural capital of the Midlands. This was due in large part to the industriousness of the native Brummies. Today this tradition continues, enhanced by the influx of peoples of differing nationalities and cultures, each adding their own unique gifts and talents to the mix.

The Birmingham Symphony Orchestra, recognised as one of the finest in the world, performs a regular season in the classical Roman-inspired Town Hall, built by Joseph Hansom, of hansom cab fame.

There are no fewer than 6,000 acres of parkland and open space in Birmingham. Cannon Hill Park in Edgbaston is one particular highlight. It has 80 acres of flower and ornamental gardens. Also in Edgbaston, on Westbourne Road, the **Botanical Gardens** (see panel opposite) comprise 15 acres and boast a Tropical House with lily pond, banana and cocoa trees, the Palm House, Orangery, National Bonsai Collection, Cactus House and the gardens themselves, filled with rhododendrons, azaleas and a good collection of trees. **Birmingham Nature Centre**, not far away on Pershore Road, has British and European wildlife – including wallaby, fallow deer, otters and reptiles – in indoor and outdoor enclosures resembling as closely as possible the creatures' native habitats.

The focus for shopping is the area bounded by New Street and Corporation Street; away from these areas there are some very attractive Victorian arcades that house the smaller speciality shops, including jewellers. Birmingham is traditionally a centre of jewellery, indeed there is an 18th-century church in St Paul's Square known simply as

The Jewellers Church. The Jewellery Quarter Discovery Centre is a good place to start if you'd like to learn more about both past and present in the Birmingham jewellery trade. It is located on Vyse Street, centred round the preserved workshops of Smith & Pepper, still much as they were at the end of the 19th century.

The **Museum and Art Gallery** in Chamberlain Square represents the 17th, 18th and 19th centuries, including the world's finest collection of works by the Pre-Raphaelites. The contemporary art of sculpture is also well represented. As are costume, silver, textiles and ceramics, as well as works of ethnography from around the world, among which is a large and rare copper Buddha from Sultangani.

The **Barber Institute** at Birmingham University houses an excellent collection of paintings and sculptures. There is a wealth of Impressionist pieces, as well as the work of European masters.

Soho House is a handsome Georgian building that has been carefully restored to its original elegance. Former home of the pioneering industrialist Matthew Boulton,

The Birmingham Botanical Gardens and Glasshouses

Westbourne Road, Edgbaston, Birmingham B15 3TR
Tel: 0121 454 1860
e-mail: admin@birminghambotanicalgardens.org.uk
website: www.birminghambotanicalgardens.org.uk

The lush rainforest vegetation in the Tropical House includes many economic plants. Palms, tree ferns, orchids and insectivorous plants are displayed in the Subtropical House. The Mediterranean House features a wide variety of citrus plants, a pelargonium collection and seasonal displays of conservatory plants. A desert scene, with its giant agaves and opuntias, fills the Arid House.

Outside there is colourful bedding on the Terrace and a tour of the Gardens includes rhododendrons and azaleas, herbaceous borders, an impressive Rock Garden and a collection of over 200 trees. There are Herb and Cottage Gardens, a Water Garden, Alpine Yard, Historic Gardens, Organic Garden and the National Bonsai Collection. Ferns, grasses and sensory plants all have their own areas.

A magnificent Lawn Aviary stands at the far side of the main lawn, in front of which is a formal sunken Rose Garden. From a deep red centre the roses shade to pale pink and cream. A collection of shrub roses continues the rose theme behind the aviaries. A Sculpture Trail takes you to every corner of the Garden. The Children's Adventure Playground and Children's Discovery Garden provide excitement for our younger visitors who are also enthralled by our bird collection. The Gallery has different exhibitions each month. The 'Shop at the Gardens' stocks a wide range of gifts and plants. Refreshments are available in the Pavilion. Bands play every Sunday afternoon throughout the summer. Open daily from 9 am (10 am. Sunday) until dusk (7 pm Latest).

stories and anecdotes 	famous people 	art and craft 	entertainment and sport 	walks

James Watt's business partner and founder of the Soho Mint, who lived here from 1766 to 1809, it contains some of his original furnishings. Displays relate the story of the man and his times, and offer a chance to see some of the fruits of Boulton's nearby factory - buttons and buckles, ormolu clocks and vases, silver and Sheffield plate tableware - where he and Watt developed the steam engine.

There are some 2,000 listed buildings in Birmingham, dating from the Elizabethan, Jacobean, Georgian and Victorian periods. The 1879 neo-Renaissance Council House is an impressive testament to the city's success and achievements. The Curzon Street Goods Station is a colonnaded building dating from 1838. Built by Philip Hardwick, its Ionic portico celebrates the wonder of the then-new railway industry. Also on Curzon Street is a **Science Museum and Planetarium**. In 2004, the National Trust took over the **Birmingham Back to Backs**, the city's last surviving court of back-to-back housing, now fully restored by the National Trust and the Birmingham Conservation Trust. Guided tours take visitors through four different periods, from 1840 to the 1970s, the design of each interior reflecting the varied cultures, religions and professions of the families who lived there. Booking recommended, call 0121 666 7671.

Sarehole Mill in Cole Bank Road in Hall Green is Birmingham's only working water mill. The former childhood haunt of JRR Tolkien (author of *The Hobbit* and *Lord of the Rings*), it was used as a flour mill and also to roll and smooth metal needed during the Industrial Revolution. The present buildings are mainly Georgian, having been rebuilt in the 1760s, and were in commercial use right up to 1919. The mill then fell into disrepair, though it was later carefully restored to working order. Another nearby attraction well worth a visit is Castle Bromwich Hall Gardens, on Chester Road, about four miles east of the city centre. This boasts a collection of plants grown here in the 18th century, including historic herbs and vegetable species, shrubs and border plants, in a classic formal layout popular in the 1700s. Guided tours available.

Around Birmingham

ASTON
2 miles N of Birmingham off the A34

🏛 Aston Hall

Aston Hall was one of the last great Jacobean country houses to be built in England. Like Hatfield House and Blickling Hall, it has a highly intricate plan and a dramatic skyline of turrets, gables and chimneys. It is also administered by Birmingham Museum and Art Gallery, who have done much to make it a memorable place to visit. The house was built between 1618 and 1635 by Sir Thomas Holte, and remained the seat of the Holte family until it was sold off in 1817. King Charles I came to Aston Hall in 1642, at the beginning of the Civil War, and it was later besieged and sacked by Parliamentarian soldiers.

KINGSBURY
7 miles NE of Birmingham off the A4097

🏕 Water Park   🐾 Children's Farm

Kingsbury Water Park boasts of over 600 acres of country park, with loads to see and do, including birdwatching, picnic sites, nature trails, fishing and a good information centre. There is also a cosy café and special unit housing the park's shop and exhibition hall. Also with the park, **Broomey Croft**

Children's Farm makes for an enjoyable and educational day out for all the family, with a wealth of animals housed in renovated early 19th-century farm buildings.

YARDLEY
2 miles E of Birmingham off the A45/A4040

🏛 Blakesley Hall

Blakesley Hall is Birmingham's finest Elizabethan building. Built in 1590, it is an extremely attractive timber-framed farmhouse that has been carefully restored. Its rich, decorative framing and jettied first and second floors reflect the wealth of its Elizabethan owner and builder, Richard Smallbroke, one of the leading merchants of the time. A diminutive and rare Long Gallery survives, while in Smallbroke's bedroom the original wall paintings were uncovered in 1950. Some of the 12 rooms are furnished to look as they did in 1684, when an inventory of the house's contents was drawn up.

Old Yardley village is one of Birmingham's outstanding conservation areas. Within walking distance of Blakesley Hall, it is truly remarkable for its medieval church and Trust School. Of particular note are the pretty Georgian cottages.

BOURNVILLE
4 miles S of Birmingham off the A4040

🏛 Cadbury World

This planned village built by the Cadbury family, which moved its factory from the city centre in 1879, is a testament to good labour relations. **Cadbury World** is located in the heart of the famous Bournville factory. Here visitors can follow the story of chocolate, from tropical rain forests to 16th-century Spain and on to Georgian London and, finally, Victorian Birmingham. Of course, a highlight of any tour here is the chance to sample the modern day product!

Coventry

🏛 Cathedral 　 🏛 St Mary's Guildhall

🏛 Phoenix Initiative 　 🏛 Priory Visitor Centre

🎣 Canal Basin 　 🐎 Lady Godiva

🏛 Transport Museum

Although on the fringe of the West Midlands conurbation, Coventry is surrounded by some of the finest scenery and places of historic interest in the country. It claims among many of its famous sons and daughters the novelist George Eliot, who attended school in Warwick Row and lived with her father on Foleshill Road between 1841 and 1849, and the poet Philip Larkin, son of Coventry's city treasurer and born in the city in 1922.

The famous three medieval spires of Coventry - Christchurch, Holy Trinity and St Michael's - are still prominent on the city skyline. During the terrible bombing inflicted on the city during World War II, St Michael's, a former parish church

Blakesley Hall, Yardley

🎞 stories and anecdotes 　 🍃 famous people 　 🎨 art and craft 　 ✍ entertainment and sport 　 🚶 walks

elevated to Coventry's cathedral in 1918, suffered direct hits. Its spire and outer walls are all that remain, evoking both the horror and the spirit of reconciliation that arose from those times. Standing in the ruins of this 14th-century church can be a strange and moving experience. The altar is made of broken stones gathered from the destruction on the night of 14 November 1940. It is surmounted by a cross of charred roof beams and a cross of medieval nails, behind which are inscribed the words, Father Forgive.

The new **Cathedral**, designed by Basil Spence, stands at right angles to the old, and together they symbolise sacrifice and resurrection. The cathedral's worldwide ministry of peace and reconciliation has been echoed by the city fathers in Coventry, who in the years since World War II have aquired 26

Ford's Almhouses Hospital, Coventry

twin towns and cities around the world, many of the links forged from a shared experience of war. Though unashamedly modern, the vast and striking interior of Spence's cathedral conveys a powerful sense of the past. It is also an unrivalled gallery of post-war British art, with Jacob Epstein, Elizabeth Frink, John Piper and Graham Sutherland among those artists represented. In a national poll conducted by English Heritage and Channel Four in 1999, it was voted Britain's most popular 20th-century building.

Coventry has ancient links with the myth of St George the dragon-slayer, but its most famous legend is, of course, that of **Lady Godiva**, who rode the streets naked to protest against taxation on the 11th-century town-dwellers. A bronze statue in Broadgate stands to her memory. It was Godiva's husband Leofric who started commerce and industry in Coventry as early as 1043, when he chose the small Saxon township as the site for a Benedictine priory. He gave the monks land on which to raise sheep, laying the basis for the wool trade that by 1400, had turned Coventry into the fourth biggest and most powerful city in England. Leofric and Godiva's church, dating from the 1040s, was later turned by the Benedictines into the **Cathedral Church of St Mary**, and was fated to become the only English cathedral to be destroyed on the orders of Henry VIII.

The site of the city's lost first cathedral has in recent years become the focus of the **Phoenix Initiative**, a Millennium project that has blended archaeology and the restoration of historic buildings with the creation of new public spaces and cutting edge architecture. Among the new buildings is the **Priory Visitor Centre**, which tells the story of the great lost cathedral and displays artefacts from archaeological excavations. Beneath another

🏠 historic building   🏛 museum   🏛 historic site   🌳 scenic attraction   🌱 flora and fauna

Museum of British Road Transport

Hales Street, Coventry CV1 1PN
Tel: 02476832425
e-mail: museum@mbrt.co.uk
website: www.mbrt.co.uk

Coventry is the home of British road transport, and the
Museum offers the largest display of British cars, cycles
and motorcycles anywhere in the world. Step back in
time to pioneering cycles and motorcars and the beginning of mass production.
Experience the recreated Coventry Blitz and share in the City's spirit of optimism as it
rebuilt after the war. Find out about Coventry's *Boomtime* in the 50s, 60s and 70s
and reflect on past and future designs in the *Icons* Gallery. Includes the land speed
record cars 'Thrust 2' and 'ThrustSSC', the Coventry Blitz Experience, and the world
famous Tiatsa model collection.

new building nearby are the Priory
Undercrofts, standing archaeology that allows
visitors to take conducted tours of the cellars
where monks once lived.

Despite its roller-coaster history, modern
Coventry still has many ancient treasures:
Bond's Hospital in Hill Street is a beautiful
timber-framed almshouse, founded in the 16th
century and restored by the Victorians. It
forms one side of a courtyard, open to the
public, that also includes the 16th-century
Bablake School and the 14th-century Church
of St John the Baptist, used as a prison for
Royalist soldiers during the Civil War and
almost certainly the origin of the expression
Sent to Coventry. Ford's Hospital in
Greyfriar's Lane is another half-timbered
Tudor almshouse, founded in 1509 by
Coventry merchant William Ford as a home
for elderly women and still in use as that today.

Nearby, in New Union Street, is the
gatehouse to Cheylesmore Manor, once
owned by the Black Prince and the only
unfortified royal palace in England. This
attractive half-timbered building is Coventry's
Register Office, the oldest building in the

country to be used for such a purpose. Not far
away stands Whitefriars, a Carmelite friary
established in the 1340s. Coventry's main civic
museum, the Herbert Art Gallery and
Museum, houses a permanent exhibition of
the city's history. A few yards away stands the
jewel in Coventry's medieval crown, **St Mary's
Guildhall**, where kings and queens have been
entertained and the city's mayors appointed to
their office since the middle of the 14th
century. Its tower once imprisoned Mary,
Queen of Scots, and it has a restored 600-
year-old crypt. One of England's finest
guildhalls, St Mary's Hall also features a superb
Arras tapestry made for its north wall in 1500,
and a window above that portrays nine
English kings, including a rare representation
of the legendary King Arthur. The building is
a treasure house of oak carving, suits of
armour and stained glass, and has associations
with many famous people, including George
Eliot and Oliver Cromwell.

At Holy Trinity, just along the street,
experts have recently restored and uncovered
the Coventry Doom, a 15th-century
Judgement Day wall painting that is regarded

as one of the finest works of medieval art to have survived in this country.

Coventry's industrial history since the Middle Ages has been one of boom and slump, with staple industries like silk-weaving and watch-making falling victim to foreign competition in the 19th century. It was cycle manufacture and then automotive engineering that laid the foundations for the city's 20th-century prosperity and growth. Back in 1885, the first modern bicycle was invented and manufactured in Coventry. A decade later Daimler opened a factory in a disused Coventry cotton mill – and the British motor industry was in business.

The **Coventry Transport Museum** (see panel on page 459) in Hales Street examines the enormous contribution made by the city to the transport industry, spanning more than a century, from the first cycles to the latest in automotive technology. Its collection of more than 240 British-made cars, 94 motorcycles and 200 bicycles is the largest in the world and is backed up by 25,000 models and a million archive and ephemera items (024 768 2425).

The engineering boom made Coventry a magnet for skilled engineers from all over Britain, among them the father of Coventry-born Frank Whittle, inventor of the jet engine. But there is a surviving relic too from an earlier period of the city's industrial history: on the edge of the city centre, a few minutes walk from the main shopping areas, is **Coventry Canal Basin**, the only canal terminus in the country to be located in the centre of a city. Its warehouses, some dating from the 18th century, are now home to artists' studios and specialist craft workshops, and the basin has been the focus in recent years of a new development of offices, apartments and shops. The five-mile canal towpath to the boundary of the city features around 40 works of art – the longest art trail in the country.

For an industrial city, Coventry also boasts many 'green' credentials, with acres of protected ancient woodland, outstanding parkland and public spaces.

Lady Herbert's Garden, restored as part of the Phoenix Initiative, lies between the last two surviving medieval city gates. Incorporating part of the old city wall, it forms a link between a new public square, Millennium Place, and the new Garden of International Friendship.

Greyfriars Green close to the city's railway station, is a conservation area with attractive gardens and two terraces of fine buildings. The War Memorial Park in Kenilworth Road is Coventry's premier park, with tree-lined walkways, a giant children's water feature and a cenotaph.

Coombe Country Park, close to the city's eastern boundary, comprises almost 400 acres of historic Capability Brown landscapes surrounding a luxury hotel in what was the medieval Cistercian abbey of Coombe.

And what of the expression 'sending to Coventry'? There are many possible explanations, the most likely being that already mentioned of the garrison once based here that was so unpopular with the locals they shunned the soldiers. Another, less likely, theory is that the name of Coventry derived from the covin-tree, an oak that stood in front of the castle. It was used as the gallows.

Around Coventry

BAGINTON
5 miles S of Coventry off the A444

🏛 Midland Air Museum

The **Midland Air Museum** at Coventry Airport in Baginton houses a unique

---

🏠 historic building 　🏛 museum 　🏛 historic site 　⚘ scenic attraction 　🌿 flora and fauna

collection of aircraft, engines and exhibits telling the story of the jet engine (it incorporates the Sir Frank Whittle Jet Heritage Centre). In this hands-on museum, which is open daily, visitors can sit in the cockpit of a Vulcan Bomber or Meteor and, with over 35 aircraft on display, there is something to interest everyone. This very relaxed and informal museum features local aviation history, with a Wings Over Coventry gallery and a wealth of Coventry-produced aircraft and other exhibits, dominated by the giant Armstrong Whitworth Argosy freighter of 1959. The airport was the base of 308 (Polish) Squadron in 1940 and 1941.

STONELEIGH
6 miles S of Coventry off the A444

🏛 Abbey

This attractive village has a sandstone Norman church, several timber-framed houses and, nearby, the headquarters of the Royal Agricultural Society of England, and the Showground famed for its annual Royal Show (the last show took place in 2009). The history of **Stoneleigh Abbey** began in 1154 when Henry II granted the lands to a community of Cistercian monks, who built their abbey on the site. Visitors can view the superb interior only on guided tours (01926 858535) but are welcome to stroll through the grounds, which were landscaped by Humphry Repton in 1809. They contain many beautiful trees, including a 1,000-year-old oak.

BUBBENHALL
7 miles SE of Coventry off the A445

🚶 Country Park

Between Bubbenhall and Ryton-on-Dunsmore, off the A445, **Ryton Pools Country Park** is a 100-acre country park with an exciting range of facilities, including a Visitors Centre, picnic areas, bird hide, numerous footpaths, model railway, fishing site and two adventure playgrounds.

Rugby

🏛 School   📷 Webb Ellis Museum

🌳 Cock Robin Wood   🚶 Pathway of Fame

🚶 Great Central Walk

The only town of any great size in north-eastern Warwickshire, Rugby has a Market Place surrounded by handsome buildings and the striking Church of St Andrew, built by the Rokeby family after their castle had been destroyed by Henry II. The old tower dates from the 1400s. With its fireplace and three foot-thick walls, it looks more like a fortress and was, indeed, a place of refuge.

Rugby is probably most famous for its **School**, founded in 1567. Originally situated near the Clock Tower in the town, it moved to its present site in 1750. There are many fine buildings, splendid examples of their period, the highlight being the school chapel, designed by William Butterfield. These buildings house treasures such as stained glass believed to be the work of Albrecht Dürer, the 15th-century German artist and engraver.

There are few places in the world where you can gaze with any certainty over the birthplace of a sport that gives pleasure to millions. The game of Rugby originated here at the school when William Webb Ellis broke the rules during a football match in 1823 by picking up and running with the ball. Opposite the School, in the original building where the first rugby football balls were made by James Gilbert in 1842, the **Webb Ellis Rugby Football Museum** is open from 9am - 5pm

VANILLA (INDEPENDENT STORE)

16 Albert Street, Rugby, Warwickshire CV21 2RS
Tel: *01788 573303*
e-mail: vanillalifestyle@yahoo.co.uk

Next to the main post office in the heart of Rugby. **Vanilla** is a store with something for everyone, it has an inviting ambience that makes every visit a real pleasure. Spread over 2 floors its departments are 'V boutique' - clothes to covet. 'Present Time' - contemporary giftware inc Alessi, Joseph Joseph, Momoji dolls and much more. 'Somthing for the Girls' - accessories and gorgeous giftware inc bombay duck, burts bees, nougat body lotions, lampe berger perfumed bottles,. 'Jewellery Quarter' - makers inc. coeur de lion, tracy davidson, and carrie elspeth whose Welsh beaded jewellery is always in demand. 'Cardmix' - a huge choice of cards and stationery inc. five dollar shake and woodmansterne. 'Ellie and Me' - faboulous childrens giftware inc. moulin roty, trousselier, and no added sugar. 'Home Time' - 1st floor homewares inc amazing clocks by karlesson, contemporary lighting by leitmotiv and think gadgets, and not forgetting ' Upstairs at vanilla' the coffee shop, serving hand roasted coffee , delectable sandwiches and the now ledgendary homemade cupcakes. Vanilla the store also sells gift vouchers and the opening hours are 9 - 5.30.

SHOOBIZ FASHION ACCESSORIES

Churchside Arcade, Little Church Street, Rugby,
Warwickshire CV21 3AW
Tel: *01788 570220*
Fax: *01788 813997*

Shoobiz is a stylish boutique in a beautifully restored Victorian arcade behind one of the town's main shopping streets. In this gem of a setting, owner Pam Garaghty has stocked her smart, contemporary shop with a wide selection of fashion accessories and lifestyle products. Among the brands prominently featured are Jump luggage and bags made of durable synthetic suede with leather trim; Lupo – stylish, sophisticated handbags in leather, belts and scarves designed and produced in Barcelona; Smith & Canova British-designed leather bags, handbags and purses; Fashionable bags, purses and accessories from Lulu Australia; and bags, belts and gloves by Dents, synonymous with quality and durability since 1777. Shoobiz also stocks Cocowai cardigans, shawls and pashminas, French Sole ballet-style pumps and flats designed by Jane Winkworth, Italian umbrellas, jewellery, candles, home fragrances and body care products by Bath House. Gift vouchers are also available. Shoobiz is open from 10.30 to 5.00 Monday, Tuesday and Wednesday, 10.30 to 5.30 Thursday, Friday and Saturday.

🏛 historic building   🏛 museum   🏛 historic site   ♧ scenic attraction   ☙ flora and fauna

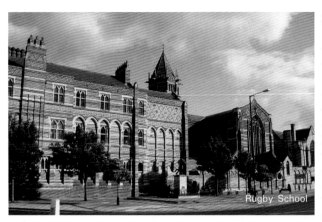
Rugby School

Monday to Wednesday.

Rugby Town Trail is a two-hour walk that brings to life the town's history from its Saxon beginnings to the present day. The walk begins and ends at the Clock Tower in Market Place. This edifice was intended to commemorate the Golden Jubilee of Queen Victoria in 1887, yet it was not completed until 1889

Monday to Saturday, and the **Rugby Pathway of Fame** begins at the Visitor Centre and follows a series of bronze plaques, each dedicated to a famous player or a historic moment in the development of the game. Demonstrations of ball-making can be seen

because over-indulgent citizens had dipped too deep into the Tower funds to feast and drink at the Jubilee. The Trail takes in many of the town's main tourist attractions, including the house where Rupert Brooke was born, and his statue in Regent Place.

ETCETERA DISTINCTIVE GIFTS

31 Regent Street, Rugby, Warwickshire CV21 2PE
Tel: 01788 570444 Fax: 01788 697299
e-mail: enquiries@etceterarugby.co.uk
website: www.etceterarugby.co.uk

Established in 2003, **Etcetera** really lives up to its name, stocking an eclectic range of gifts for all the family. Major brands on offer include Radley handbags and accessories, Kipling bags and luggage, Fiorelli bags and Nica bags. Other enticing items include Crabtree & Evelyn toiletries, Spaceform glass; Kit Heath jewellery; Simon Drew mens gifts; Stubbs mugs; Metal Planet and Terramundi money pots, and delightful soft toys from Jelly cat.

ETCETERA STYLE

20 Regent Street, Rugby, Warwickshire CV21 2PE
Tel: 01788 552400

Only recently opened, **Etcetera Style** specialises in "Fashion for real women", offering stylish clothing from a number of designers. You'll find beautiful clothes from Olsen, Jackpot and Masai, all from Denmark; Steilman, All Is Beautiful, Tivoli Knitwear and more. To complement the clothes, Etcetera Style also stocks an extensive selection of smart and elegant accessories such as scarves, jewellery, gloves and more.

Napton Windmill

Distance: *4.5 miles (7.2 kilometres)*

Typical time: *150 mins*

Height gain: *60 metres*

Map: *Explorer 222*

Walk: *www.walkingworld.com ID:350*

Contributor: *Ron and Jenny Glynn*

ACCESS INFORMATION:

By car: parking at village green.

ADDITIONAL INFORMATION:

Stout footwear is needed for this walk.

DESCRIPTION:

From the peaceful village green, surrounded by attractive houses and cottages, the route climbs the High Street, then drops to pastureland below the village. It leads to the Oxford Canal on its descent from the summit via the locks. Following the towpath past the Folly Pub, famous for its pies, the canal then follows the twisting, winding route round the contours of the land, eventually leaving it to start the ascent back to the village.

The walk passes the huge crater where once clay was quarried to make bricks. The climb to a height of 500ft provides distant views across the wide vista of seven counties. The windmill at the top is a fine feature of Napton, and the Church of St Lawrence nearby also occupies a lofty position. It is but a short distance down to the village green.

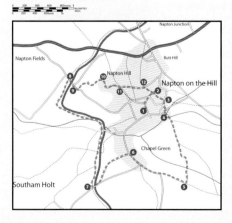

WALK DIRECTIONS:

1 | With the Crown Pub on the left, walk uphill along High Street into Hackwell Street and on.

2 | Turn right opposite Vicarage Road sign, by side of The Granary, down steps to take a stile. Follow line of two telegraph poles and on, to cross a stile and down a bank.

3 | Turn right along a narrow lane to come out on to a road and follow round to Dog Lane.

4 | Turn left just before school, into bridleway. Ignore footpath on left and continue straight ahead to go through middle metal gate, continue out into another field in same direction. At third gateway turn left to another gate. Go through and turn right. Pass a pond and go through a walkers' gate over stream.

5 | At the next gate turn right, with hedge and fence on right. Go through gate at end of field and out on to road. Continue at junction along Chapel Green and past 'Pondarosa' on left.

6 | Turn left at 'Eureka' along private drive and through gate, right along back of garage and tight to hedge on right to cross a stile. Walk diagonally left and head for dip in westerly direction. Look for concrete footbridge downhill. Cross and head diagonally left (aim for collapsed pylon) and, once past, look for the gate that leads out on to the road. Turn right and walk over canal bridge.

7 | Turn left down on to towpath by a lock, then left under the bridge. Notice the windmill on the hill as you walk down to the bottom lock. Pass the Folly Pub on left and walk on. Enjoy now the tranquillity of still waters, wild life, domestic animals and far distant views, along the winding Oxford Canal in this glorious setting.

8 | At Bridge 112 turn left and walk over it to pass buildings on left.

9 | Turn left over stile and walk on over uneven land, keeping close to fence overlooking old disused quarry. Walk uphill where Jacob sheep and donkeys roam. Follow line of fencing round to left, past huge rock boulders, then uphill with hedge on left. Pause for breath (several times) on the steep ascent and take in the panoramic views across seven counties.

10 | The line of the hedge bends to the right, to take a narrow path along to a stile that leads out on to the driveway of Napton Windmill. Turn left and continue.

11 | Take left fork, to pass Leys Farm and then the parish church of St Lawrence.

12 | Turn right a few yards on, into enclosed downhill path. Come out on road opposite The Granary and retrace steps to start point.

THE RUGBY MEAT COMPANY

11 Clifton Road, Rugby, Warwickshire CV21 3PY
Tel: 01788 541143
e-mail: therugbymeatcompany@yahoo.co.uk

Regular customers come from many miles around to shop at the **Rugby Meat Company**. Located in the very centre of Rugby, with plenty of free parking nearby, Eddie Fallon's high-class butchers has established a firm reputation for quality, reliability and value for money throughout the range of premium beef, lamb, pork, poultry, game, gammon, bacon, top-notch home-made sausages and home-cooked meats. The shop also sells locally made pork pies, cheese and a selection of accompaniments and condiments. The Rugby Meat Company sells a variety of hampers for the Christmas season.

Caldecott Park, in the centre of town, has beautiful floral displays, trees and a herb garden. Picnicking areas and a play area are two more of the highlights of this lovely park, and there are also facilities for bowls, putting, tennis and boules.

Rugby is bounded by two of the greatest Roman roads, Fosse Way and Watling Street, which meet just northwest of Rugby at High Cross, one of the landmarks of the area.

The town is as far inland as it is possible to get in the British Isles, yet Rugby is an excellent centre for all kinds of water sports and aquatic activities. The Oxford Canal winds its way through the borough, and the Rivers Avon, Leam and Swift provide good angling, pleasant walks and places to picnic.

Cock Robin Wood is a nature reserve on Dunchurch Road, near the junction with Ashlawn Road. Here the visitor will find extensive areas of oak, ash, rowan, cherry and field maples, as well as grassy areas and a central pond, a haven for insects, frogs and butterflies.

The **Great Central Walk** is a four-mile ramble through Rugby. Along the way visitors will encounter an abundance of wildlife, plants and shrubs, as well as conservation areas and picnic sites.

Around Rugby

ASHBY ST LEDGERS
4 miles SE of Rugby off the A361

The Gunpowder Plot conspirators took refuge here in the manor house owned by Robert Catesby. Though not open to visitors, the manor house is close to the road and worth seeing, as it is very evocative of the times. This charming village also rewards a stroll, with some cottages designed by Lutyens. Parts of the handsome village church date back to the early 1500s.

NAPTON ON THE HILL
9 miles S of Rugby off the A425

This attractive village on a rounded hill above a curve in the Oxford Canal - one of the prettiest in this part of the world, with pleasant towpath walks. There are views of seven counties from the hilltop.

DUNCHURCH
1 mile S of Rugby off the A426

⟡ Guy Fawkes

The gunpowder plot village: on 5 November 1605, the Gunpowder Plot conspirators met at

THE OLD THATCHED COTTAGE HOTEL & RESTAURANT

Southam Road, Dunchurch, nr Rugby,
Warwickshire CV22 6NG
Tel: 01788 810417
website: www.englishcountryinns.co.uk

Starting life in the 15th century as a row of
four artisans' dwellings, the **Old Thatched Cottage** is now a
delightful family-run hotel and restaurant. Seven en suite
bedrooms (six with bath and shower) provide a quiet, comfortable base for a relaxing break, for
touring or for people with business in the area. Individual in style, they combine period furnishings
with home comforts including TV, radio-alarm, hairdryer, hot drinks tray and central heating. A
very good breakfast with 'full English' kippers and haddock among the options starts the day. The
Old Thatched Cottage also has an excellent restaurant with a good-value midweek lunchtime
menu, lounge and bar menus Monday to Thursday evenings and an interesting à la carte menu
Monday to Saturday evenings.

the Red Lion Inn, Dunchurch, to await the
news of Guy Fawkes' attempt to blow up the
English Houses of Parliament. The Red Lion
still exists today, as a private residence known
as **Guy Fawkes House**.

This attractive village with its rows of
thatched cottages has a 14th-century church
built by the monks of Pipewell Abbey, with
one of the oldest parish registers in England.

Such was the considerable trade in looking
after travellers who stopped over in
Dunchurch during the great coaching days (up
to 40 coaches a day stopped here), it is said
that every property in the centre of the village
was at some time an inn or ale house. For
centuries Dunchurch has been a popular
stopover point for travellers on the main
Holyhead-London road. A coaching stop to
take on fresh horses, Dunchurch was also the
staging post for pupils, masters, parents and
visitors travelling to Rugby School. Many
famous and important people have stayed in
the village over the centuries, including
Princess Victoria, Longfellow, the Duke of
Wellington and William Webb Ellis of Rugby
Football fame. Today, the village is in a
designated conservation area with a lovely

village green complete with village stocks and
maypole, charming 16th, 17th and 18th-
century buildings, many of which retain the
traditional Warwickshire thatched roofs. The
Old Smithy, which stands on the Rugby Road,
is believed to have been the inspiration for
Henry Wadsworth Longfellow's poem *Under
the Spreading Chestnut Tree*.

DRAYCOTE
4 miles SW of Rugby off the A426

🦆 Draycote Water   🏕 Country Park

Draycote Water is a centre of watersports,
fishing, sailing, birdwatching and attractive
walks around the reservoir. Fly fishing permits
are available from the Fishing Lodge.
Draycote Country Park, next to Draycote
Water, boasts 21 acres for walks, kite flying,
picnicking by the lake, and magnificent hilltop
views over Draycote Water, one of the largest
reservoirs in the region.

LONG ITCHINGTON
8 miles SW of Rugby off the A423

🏛 Church of the Holy Trinity

The picturesque village of Long Itchington

🏛 historic building   🏛 museum   🏛 historic site   🍃 scenic attraction   🌿 flora and fauna

straddles the lovely Grand Union Canal. The Anglo-Saxon 'Farm by the River Itchen' boasted a population greater than that of Coventry at the time of the Domesday Book. The village **Church of the Holy Trinity** dates in part from 1190. The tower has only the remains of its original spire, which collapsed when struck by lightning during a Sunday morning service in 1762. The carvings in the chancel bear a closer look: one depicts a monkey with her young, another the head and shoulders of what is believed to be a jester.

SOUTHAM
9 miles SW of Rugby off the A426

Southam is an attractive town along the River Itchen. It is first mentioned in a charter of King Ethelred in AD998, but there was probably an Anglo-Saxon village here before this, and Roman coins found within the parish hint at an earlier community. It repays a visit for the lovely rural scenery surrounding the town, and the wealth of good walking in the area. The Battle of Southam in 1642 was the first skirmish of the Civil War, and it was here in Southam that Charles I spent the night before the battle of Edge Hill. In the main street is the surprisingly named Old Mint Inn, a 14th-century stone building taking its name from an occurrence following the Battle of Edge Hill. Charles I commanded his local noblemen to bring him their silver treasure, which was then melted down and minted into coins with which he paid his army.

WOLSTON
5 miles W of Rugby off the A428

The Church of St Margaret is Norman in origin, but was substantially rebuilt after the steeple collapsed into the chancel in 1759. A stone in the churchyard poses the simple question: 'Tell me which is best, the toilsome

journey or the traveller's rest?' Near the 1837 railway bridge are the earthworks of Brandon Castle, which was destroyed not very long after it was built in the 13th century.

RYTON-ON-DUNSMORE
6 miles W of Rugby off the A45

🌱 Henry Doubleday Research Association

🌱 Ryton Pools Country Park   🌱 Pagets Pool

This village is home to the **Henry Doubleday Research Association** at Ryton Gardens. Started in 1970 by a group of gardeners, smallholders and farmers committed to going organic, this organic farming and gardening organisation leads the way in research and advances in horticulture. The grounds are landscaped with thousands of plants and trees, all organically grown. Also on site are a herb garden, rose garden, garden for the blind, shrub borders and free-roaming animals. **Ryton Pools Country Park** is a 100-acre country park opened in 1996. The 10-acre Ryton Pool is home to great crested grebes, swans, moorhens and Canada geese. There is also an attractive meadow area for strolling or picnicking, a Visitor Centre, shop and exhibition area. **Pagets Pool** near the northeastern end of the park is one of the most important sites in Warwickshire for dragonflies, with 17 species including the common blue, emperor dragonfly and black-tailed skimmer. Other highlights include guided walks and a model railway run by Coventry Model Engineering Society.

BRANDON
6 miles W of Rugby off the A428

🌱 Nature Reserve

Brandon Marsh Nature Centre is 200 acres of lakes, marshes, woodland and grassland, providing a home and haven for many species of wildlife. There are bird hides, an informative Visitor Centre and a nature trail, as well as guided walks, pond-dipping and changing exhibitions.

STRETTON UNDER FOSSE
5 miles NW of Rugby off the B4112

🏛 Prison Museum

For a slightly unusual day out visit **HM Prison Services Museum** at Newbold Revel. It has displays on the history of imprisonment from medieval times to the present. Visits are strictly by appointment; contact the Curator on 01788 834168.

NEWBOLD-ON-AVON
1 mile N of Rugby off the B4112

🚶 Quarry Park

Newbold Quarry Park affords visitors the opportunity for a country walk just north of Rugby town, with hilly woodland and

extensive waterside paths. This bit of countryside is a haven for birds and wildlife.

NUNEATON
8 miles N of Coventry on the A444

🏛 Museum & Art Gallery

Originally a Saxon town known as Etone, Nuneaton is mentioned in the Domesday Book of 1086. The Nun was added when a wealthy Benedictine priory was founded here in 1290. The Priory ruins left standing are adjacent to the church of St Nicholas, a Victorian edifice occupying a Norman site, which has a beautiful carved ceiling dating back to 1485.

The town has a history as a centre for coal-mining, which began in Nuneaton as early as the 14th century. Other industries for which the town has been famous include brick and tile manufacture and ribbon making on hand looms. As the textile and hatting industries boomed, the town began to prosper. Today's Nuneaton is a centre of precision engineering, printing, car components and other important trades.

Nuneaton Museum and Art Gallery, located in Riversley Park, features displays of archaeological interest ranging from prehistoric to medieval times, and items from the local earthenware industry. There is also a permanent exhibition of the town's most illustrious daughter, the novelist and thinker George Eliot. Born to a prosperous land agent at Arbury Hall in 1819, Eliot

Seeswood Pool, Nuneaton

🏛 historic building   🏛 museum   🏛 historic site   🝆 scenic attraction   🌿 flora and fauna

(whose real name was Mary Ann Evans) was an intellectual giant and free thinker. She left Warwickshire for London in adulthood, and met George Henry Lewes, a writer and actor who was to become her lifelong companion. Lewes, married with three children, left his family so that he and Eliot, very bravely for the time, could set up house together. Eliot's novels return again and again to the scenes and social conventions of her youth, and are among the greatest works of English literature – in particular her masterpiece, *Middlemarch*. For more information call 024 7638 4027 or 024 7634 7006.

MONKS KIRBY
9 miles SE of Nuneaton off the A427

🏛 Denmark Field

The Saxons were the first people to build a church in this ancient settlement, probably a wooden structure originally, being replaced by a stone building later. The Danes arrived about AD864 as part of their conquest of this part of the country. The field at the rear of the church is still known as **Denmark Field**.

After the Norman Conquest, a Benedictine Priory was established and a church rebuilt on the old site. Most of the present building dates from the 14th century. The tall spire, built above the tower in the 15th century, could be seen by travellers for many miles around until it was blown down by a great storm on Christmas night in 1701. From its earliest days Monks Kirby grew in size and importance, eventually taking on the full status of a market town. Pilgrims and merchants were accommodated in the Priory's guest house, which probably stood on the site of the current Denbigh Arms public house. This rural, quiet village, dominated by the ancient church, also boasts many pretty cottages along its main streets.

BEDWORTH
3 miles S of Nuneaton off the B4029

🌿 Miners' Welfare Park

This small town was once part of the North Warwickshire coalfield established at the end of the 1600s. Local people were largely responsible for the building of the Coventry Canal, running from Coventry to Fradley near Lichfield and completed in 1790, 22 years after work on it began. It was constructed to connect the fast-growing town with the great new trade route, the Grand Trunk – and to provide Coventry with cheap coal from the Bedworth coal field.

French Protestant families fleeing persecution sought refuge here, bringing with them their skill in silk and ribbon weaving.

The Old Meeting church dates from 1726 and is one of the earliest nonconformist chapels in the region. Bedworth's award-winning **Miners' Welfare Park** contains some of the finest spring and summer bedding layouts in the region, as well as areas devoted to tennis, bowls, pitch and putt, roller skating and cricket.

ARBURY HALL
3 miles SW of Nuneaton off the B4102

A visit to Arbury Hall fits another piece in the jigsaw of George Eliot's life and times. She was born on the estate, where her father was land agent; in *Mr Gifgil's Love Story* she portrays Arbury as Cheverel Manor, and gives detailed descriptions of many of the rooms in the house, including the Salon and the Dining Room – comparing the latter, unsurprisingly given its grandeur, to a cathedral. The Hall's grounds include a delightful tranquil 10-acre garden.

ANSLEY

5 miles W of Nuneaton off the B4112

Ansley is best known for adjacent Hoar Park, which dates back to the 1430s. The existing house and buildings date from 1730, and now form the centrepiece of the 143-acre park, which contains a handsome Craft Village. The Park, as well as being a craft, antiques and garden centre, is still a working farm.

MANCETTER

5 miles NW of Nuneaton off the A5

🏛 Church of St Peter

This former Roman camp is situated on a rocky outcrop overlooking the valley of the River Anker. This camp was once one of a line of forts built by the Romans as they advanced northwards. The village is chiefly associated with the Mancetter Martyrs, Robert Glover and Joyce Lewis, both of whom were burnt at the stake for their religious beliefs. The martyrs are commemorated on wooden tablets in the fine **Church of St Peter**, which dates back to the early 1200s. The glory of this church is its rich glass in the east window of the chancel, most of which is 14th century in origin and thought to have been created by John Thornton, builder of the great east window of York Minster. Between the manor and the church are two noteworthy rows of almshouses dating from 1728 to 1822.

ATHERSTONE

5 miles W of Nuneaton off the A5

🏛 St Mary's Church

Atherstone is a small market town situated on the Roman Watling Street at the eastern edge of the Warwickshire Forest of Arden, off the A5 between Nuneaton and Tamworth. Set against the wooded hills of the Merevale Estate, the picturesque town centre dates from medieval times and is unspoiled by modern development. Atherstone's history predates medieval times to the Anglo-Saxons; at the time of the Norman Conquest it belonged to the Countess of Mercia, Lady Godiva. The Domesday Book of 1086 records 14 residents: 11 villagers, two smallholders and one slave. Its importance as a trading centre grew and grew over the ensuing years, so that by 1724 Daniel Defoe could describe it as "a town famous for a great cheese fair on the 8th September".

Atherstone's **St Mary's Church** was founded in 1365 as a chapel-of-ease, becoming a parish church in 1835, when Atherstone separated from Mancetter to become a parish in its own right. The tower was rebuilt in 1782

Oldbury, nr Nuneaton

🏛 historic building   📷 museum   🏛 historic site   🏞 scenic attraction   🌿 flora and fauna

in modern Gothic style. To the rear of the building, the 12th-century Baddesley Porch, brought from Baddesley Ensor church when the latter was demolished in 1842, boasts lovely decorative detail.

GRENDON
3 miles NW of Atherstone off the A5

Grendon once boasted its own mint, owned by Sir George Chetwynd of Grendon Hall. It was this same Sir George who fell in love with the actress Lillie Langtry, and who fought Lord Lonsdale in a fist fight to win her favour. He led an extravagant life, spending a lot of time at race meetings and entertaining the Prince of Wales, with the result that his beloved Lillie began a liaison with the Prince, and Sir George lost so much money that Grendon Hall had to be sold off; it was pulled down in 1933.

NEWTON REGIS
6 miles NW of Atherstone off the B5493

One of the most unspoilt villages in Warwickshire, Newton Regis has been voted Best Kept Small Village on numerous occasions. Near the Staffordshire border and between the M42 and B5453, this lovely village is built around an attractive duck pond, which was once a quarry pit. The village's name is thought to derive from its former royal ownership, having once been

the property of King Henry II. It has in its day also been known as King's Newton and Newton-in-the-Thistles – the latter perhaps referring to the abundance of thistles or specially grown teasels that were used in the carding of flax fibre. Linen looms were worked in the house, which is now the Queens Head Inn.

ALVECOTE
6 miles NW of Atherstone off the M42

🏛 Priory   🧍 Priory Picnic Area

Alvecote Priory, just on the border with Staffordshire, was founded by William Burnett in 1159, who built it as a penance after having (mistakenly) believed that his wife had been unfaithful during his pilgrimage to the Holy Land. This small Benedictine Priory was founded as a cell to the Great Malvern Priory in Worcestershire. As with many others, it was dissolved in 1536, when the buildings were converted into a house, which was pulled down in about 1700 when another house was constructed using some of the old materials. The 14th-century remains include a fine moulded doorway and dovecote. **Alvecote Priory Picnic Area** boasts canalside picnic spots and a nearby nature reserve. There is also an interesting circular walk that takes in lakes, wildlife, many unusual plants, the old North Warwicks Colliery tip, and handsome canal bridges.

TOURIST INFORMATION CENTRES

Derbyshire

ASHBOURNE

13 Market Place, Ashbourne, Derbyshire, DE6 1EU
e-mail: ashbourneinfo@derbyshiredales.gov.uk
Tel: 01335 343666

BUXTON

The Crescent, Buxton, Derbyshire, SK17 6BQ
e-mail: tourism@highpeak.gov.uk
Tel: 01298 25106

CASTLETON

Buxton Road, Castleton, Hope Valley,
Derbyshire, S33 8WN
e-mail: castleton@peakdistrict.gov.uk
Tel: 01629 816572

DERBY

Assembly Rooms, Market Place, Derby,
Derbyshire, DE1 3AH
e-mail: tourism@derby.gov.uk
Tel: 01332 255802

MATLOCK

Address:Crown Square, Matlock, Derbyshire, DE4 3AT
e-mail: matlockinfo@derbyshiredales.gov.uk
Tel: 01629 583388

SWADLINCOTE

Sharpe's Pottery Museum, West Street, Swadlincote,
Derbyshire, DE11 9DG
e-mail: tic@sharpespotterymuseum.org.uk
Tel: 01283 222848

Herefordshire

BROMYARD

The Bromyard Centre, Cruxwell Street, Bromyard,
Herefordshire, HR7 4EB
e-mail: tic-bromyard@herefordshire.gov.uk
Tel: 01432 260280

HEREFORD

1 King Street, Hereford, Herefordshire, HR4 9BW
e-mail: tic-hereford@herefordshire.gov.uk
Tel: 01432 268430

LEDBURY

The Master's House, St Katherine's, Ledbury,
Herefordshire, HR8 1EA
e-mail: tic-ledbury@herefordshire.gov.uk
Tel: 01531 636147

LEOMINSTER

1 Corn Square, Leominster, Herefordshire, HR6 8LR
Tel: 01568 616460

QUEENSWOOD

Queenswood Country Park, Dinmore Hill, Leominster,
Herefordshire, HR6 0PY
Tel: 01568 797842

ROSS-ON-WYE

Swan House, Edde Cross Street, Ross-on-Wye,
Herefordshire, HR9 7BZ
e-mail: tic-ross@herefordshire.gov.uk
Tel: 01989 562768

Leicestershire

ASHBY-DE-LA-ZOUCH

North Street, Ashby-de-la-Zouch,
Leicestershire, LE65 1HU
e-mail: ashby.tic@nwleices.gov.uk
Tel: 01530 411767

HINCKLEY

Hinckley Library, Lancaster Road, Hinckley,
Leicestershire, LE10 0AT
e-mail: hinckleytic@leics.gov.uk
Tel: 01455 635106

LEICESTER

7/9 Every Street, Town Hall Square, Leicester,
Leicestershire, LE1 6AG
e-mail: info@goleicestershire.com
Tel: 0844 888 5181

LOUGHBOROUGH

Loughborough Town Hall, Market Place, Loughborough,
Leicestershire, LE11 3EB
e-mail: tic@charnwoodbc.gov.uk
Tel: 01509 218113

MELTON MOWBRAY

7 King Street, Melton Mowbray,
Leicestershire, LE13 1XA
e-mail: tic@melton.gov.uk
Tel: 01664 480992

Lincolnshire

BOSTON

Market Place, Boston, Lincolnshire, PE21 6NN
e-mail: ticboston@boston.gov.uk
Tel: 01205 356656

GRANTHAM

The Guildhall Centre, Council Offices, St Peter's Hill,
Grantham, Lincolnshire, NG31 6PZ
e-mail: granthamtic@southkesteven.gov.uk
Tel: 01476 406166

HORNCASTLE

14 Bull Ring, Horncastle, Lincolnshire, LN9 5HU
e-mail: horncastleinfo@e-lindsey.gov.uk
Tel: 01507 526636

LINCOLN CORNHILL

21 Cornhill, Lincoln, Lincolnshire, LN5 7HB
e-mail: tourism@lincoln.gov.uk
Tel: 01522 873256

LOUTH (CUSTOMER ACCESS POINT)

Cannon Street, Louth, Lincolnshire, LN11 9NW
e-mail: louthinfo@e-lindsey.gov.uk
Tel: 01507 609289

MABLETHORPE

Louth Hotel, Unit 5, High Street, Mablethorpe,
Lincolnshire, LN12 1AF
e-mail: mablethorpeinfo@e-lindsey.gov.uk
Tel: 01507 474939

SKEGNESS

Tower Gardens, Grand Parade, Skegness,
Lincolnshire, PE25 2UG
e-mail: skegnessinfo@e-lindsey.gov.uk
Tel: 01754 899887

SLEAFORD

Advice Centre, Money's Yard, Carre Street, Sleaford,
Lincolnshire, NG34 7TW
e-mail: tic@n-kesteven.gov.uk
Tel: 01529 414294

SPALDING

South Holland Centre, Market Place, Spalding,
Lincolnshire, PE11 1SS
e-mail: tic@sholland.gov.uk
Tel: 01775 725468

STAMFORD

Stamford Arts Centre, 27 St Mary's Street, Stamford,
Lincolnshire, PE9 2DL
e-mail: g.burley@southkesteven.gov.uk
Tel: 01780 755611

WOODHALL SPA

The Cottage Museum, Iddesleigh Road, Woodhall Spa,
Lincolnshire, LN10 6SH
e-mail: woodhallspainfo@e-lindsey.gov.uk
Tel: 01526 353775

Northamptonshire

NORTHAMPTON

(www.explorenorthamptonshire.co.uk)
Northamptonshire Enterprise Ltd, Royal & Derngate
Theatre (Foyer), Guildhall Road,
Northampton NN1 1DP
e-mail: northampton.tic@northamptonshireenterprise.ltd.uk
Tel: 01604 838800

CORBY

Willows Arts, George Street, Corby,
Northamptonshire, NN17 1QB
e-mail: tic@corby.gov.uk
Tel: 01536 407507

TOURIST INFORMATION CENTRES

KETTERING
The Coach House, Sheep Street, Kettering,
Northamptonshire, NN16 0AN
e-mail: tic@kettering.gov.uk
Tel: 01536 410266

OUNDLE
(www.east-northamptonshire.gov.uk)
14 West Street, Oundle, Northamptonshire, PE8 4EF
e-mail: oundletic@east-northamptonshire.gov.uk
Tel: 01832 274333

Nottinghamshire

NEWARK
The Gilstrap Centre, Castlegate, Newark,
Nottinghamshire, NG24 1BG
e-mail: newarktic@nsdc.info
Tel: 01636 655765

NOTTINGHAM CITY
1-4 Smithy Row, Nottingham,
Nottinghamshire, NG1 2BY
e-mail: tourist.information@nottinghamcity.gov.uk
Tel: 08444 775678

OLLERTON
Sherwood Heath, Ollerton Roundabout, Ollerton,
Nr Newark, Nottinghamshire, NG22 9DR
e-mail: ollertontic@nsdc.info
Tel: 01623 824545

RETFORD
40 Grove Street, Retford, Nottinghamshire, DN22 6LD
e-mail: retford.tourist@bassetlaw.gov.uk
Tel: 01777 860780

WORKSOP
Worksop Library, Memorial Avenue, Worksop,
Nottinghamshire, S80 2BP
e-mail: worksop.tourist@bassetlaw.gov.uk
Tel: 01909 501148

Rutland

OAKHAM
Rutland County Museum & Visitor Centre,
Catmose Street, Oakham, Rutland, LE15
e-mail: museum@rutland.gov.uk
Tel: 01572 758 441

RUTLAND WATER
Sykes Lane, Empingham, Nr. Oakham,
Rutland, LE15 8PX
e-mail: tic@anglianwater.co.uk
Tel: 01572 653026

Shropshire

BRIDGNORTH
The Library, Listley Street, Bridgnorth,
Shropshire, WV16 4AW
e-mail: bridgnorth.tourism@shropshire.gov.uk
Tel: 01746 763257

CHURCH STRETTON
Church Street, Church Stretton, Shropshire, SY6 6DQ
e-mail: churchstretton.scf@shropshire.gov.uk
Tel: 01694 723133

ELLESMERE SHROPSHIRE
The Meres' Visitor Centre, Mereside, Ellesmere,
Shropshire, SY12 0PA
e-mail: ellesmere.tourism@shropshire-cc.gov.uk
Tel: 01691 622981

IRONBRIDGE
Ironbridge Gorge Museum Trust, Coalbrookdale, Telford,
Shropshire, TF8 7DQ
e-mail: tic@ironbridge.org.uk
Tel: 01952 884391

LUDLOW
Castle Street, Ludlow, Shropshire, SY8 1AS
e-mail: ludlow.tourism@shropshire.gov.uk
Tel: 01584 875053

MARKET DRAYTON

49 Cheshire Street, Market Drayton,
Shropshire, TF9 1PH
e-mail: marketdrayton.scf@shropshire-cc.gov.uk
Tel: 01630 653114

MUCH WENLOCK

The Museum, High Street, Much Wenlock,
Shropshire, TF13 6HR
e-mail: muchwenlock.tourism@shropshire.gov.uk
Tel: 01952 727679

OSWESTERY (MILE END)

Mile End, Oswestry, Shropshire, SY11 4JA
e-mail: oswestrytourism@shropshire.gov.uk
Tel: 01691 662488

OSWESTRY TOWN (HERITAGE CENTRE)

The Heritage Centre, 2 Church Terrace, Oswestry,
Shropshire, SY11 2TE
e-mail: ot@oswestry-welshborders.org.uk
Tel: 01691 662753

SHREWSBURY

Music Hall, The Square, Shrewsbury,
Shropshire, SY1 1LH
e-mail: tic@shrewsburytourism.co.uk
Tel: 01743 281200

TELFORD

The Telford Centre, Management Suite, Telford,
Shropshire, TF3 4BX
e-mail: tourist-info@telfordshopping.co.uk
Tel: 01952 238008

Staffordshire

LEEK

Stockwell Street, Leek, Staffordshire, ST13 5HH
e-mail: tourism.services@staffsmoorlands.gov.uk
Tel: 01538 483741

LICHFIELD

Lichfield Garrick, Castle Dyke, Lichfield,
Staffordshire, WS13 6HR
e-mail: info@visitlichfield.com
Tel: 01543 412121

NEWCASTLE-UNDER-LYME

Newcastle Library, Ironmarket, Newcastle-under-Lyme,
Staffordshire, ST5 1AT
e-mail: tic.newcastle@staffordshire.gov.uk
Tel: 01782 297313

STAFFORD

Stafford Gatehouse Theatre, Eastgate Street,
Stafford, Staffordshire, ST16 2LT
e-mail: tic@staffordbc.gov.uk
Tel: 01785 619619

STOKE-ON-TRENT

Victoria Hall, Bagnall Street, Hanley, Stoke-on-Trent,
Staffordshire, ST1 3AD
e-mail: stoke.tic@stoke.gov.uk
Tel: 01782 236000

TAMWORTH

Tamworth Information Centre, 29 Market Street,
Tamworth, Staffordshire, B79 7LR
e-mail: tic@tamworth.gov.uk
Tel: 01827 709581

Warwickshire

KENILWORTH

Kenilworth Library, 11 Smalley Place, Kenilworth,
Warwickshire, CV8 1QG
e-mail: kenilworthlibrary@warwickshire.gov.uk
Tel: 01926 748900

LEAMINGTON SPA

The Royal Pump Rooms, The Parade, Leamington Spa,
Warwickshire, CV32 4AB
e-mail: leamington@shakespeare-country.co.uk
Tel: 0870 160 7930

TOURIST INFORMATION CENTRES

NUNEATON

Nuneaton Library, Church Street, Nuneaton,
Warwickshire, CV11 4DR
e-mail: nuneatonlibrary@warwickshire.gov.uk
Tel: 024 7634 7006

RUGBY

Rugby Visitor Centre, Rugby Art Gallery Museum &
Library, Little Elborow Street, Rugby,
Warwickshire, CV21 3BZ
e-mail: visitor.centre@rugby.gov.uk
Tel: 01788 533217

STRATFORD-UPON-AVON

Bridgefoot, Stratford-upon-Avon,
Warwickshire, CV37 6GW
e-mail: stratfordtic@shakespeare-country.co.uk
Tel: 0870 160 7930

WARWICK

The Court House, Jury Street, Warwick,
Warwickshire, CV34 4EW
e-mail: touristinfo@warwick-uk.co.uk
Tel: 01926 492212

West Midlands

BIRMINGHAM

The Rotunda, Tourism Centre & Ticketshop,
150 New Street, Birmingham, West Midlands, B2 4PA
e-mail:callcentre@marketingbirmingham.com
Tel: 0844 888 3883

COVENTRY TRANSPORT MUSEUM

Millennium Place, Coventry, West Midlands, CV1 1PN
e-mail: tic@cvone.co.uk
Tel: 024 7622 5616

MERRY HILL

Merry Hill, Brierley Hill, West Midlands, DY5 1SR
Tel: 01384 487900

SOLIHULL

Central Library, Homer Road, Solihull,
West Midlands, B91 3RG Email: ckelly@solihull.gov.uk
Tel: 0121 704 6130

WOLVERHAMPTON

18 Queen Square, Wolverhampton,
West Midlands, WV1 1TQ
e-mail: visitorinfo@wolverhampton.gov.uk
Tel: 01902 556110

Worcestershire

BEWDLEY

Load Street, Bewdley, Worcestershire, DY12 2AE
e-mail: bewdleytic@wyreforestdc.gov.uk
Tel: 01299 404740

BROMSGROVE

Bromsgrove Museum, 26 Birmingham Road, Bromsgrove,
Worcestershire, B61 0DD
Tel: 01527 831809

DROITWICH SPA

St Richard's House, Victoria Square, Droitwich Spa,
Worcestershire, WR9 8DS
e-mail: heritage@droitwichspa.gov.uk
Tel: 01905 774312

MALVERN

21 Church Street, Malvern, Worcestershire, WR14 2AA
e-mail: malvern.tic@malvernhills.gov.uk
Tel: 01684 892289

REDDITCH

Palace Theatre, Alcester Street, Redditch,
Worcestershire, B98 8AE
e-mail: info.centre@redditchbc.gov.uk
Tel: 01527 60806

UPTON UPON SEVERN

4 High Street, Upton Upon Severn,
Worcestershire, WR8 0HB
e-mail: upton.tic@malvernhills.gov.uk
Tel: 01684 594200

INDEX OF ADVERTISERS

INDEX OF ADVERTISERS

JEWELLERY

PLACES OF INTEREST

INDEX OF ADVERTISERS

SPECIALIST FOOD AND DRINK SHOPS

Looking for more walks?

The walks in this book have been gleaned from Britain's largest online walking guide, to be found at *www.walkingworld.com*.

The site contains over 2000 walks from all over England, Scotland and Wales so there are plenty more to choose from in this book's region as well as further afield - ideal if you are taking a short break as you can plan your walks in advance. There are walks of every length and type to suit all tastes.

Want more detail for the walks in this book? Next to every walk in this book you will see a Walk ID. You can enter this ID number on Walkingworld's 'Find a Walk' page and you will be taken straight to the details of that walk.

- Over **2000** walks across Britain

- Print routes out as you need them

- No bulky guidebook to carry

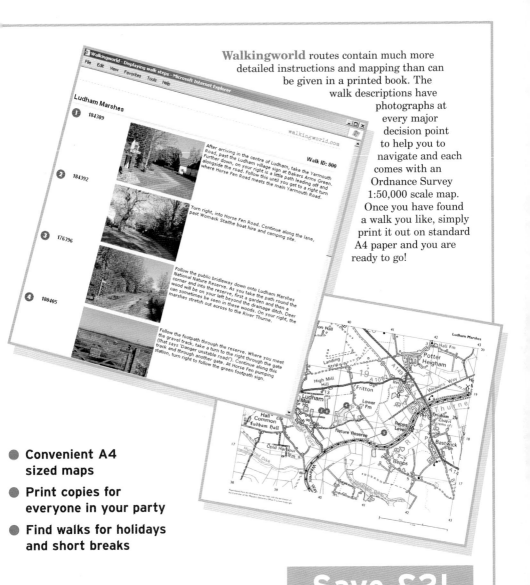

Walkingworld routes contain much more detailed instructions and mapping than can be given in a printed book. The walk descriptions have photographs at every major decision point to help you to navigate and each comes with an Ordnance Survey 1:50,000 scale map. Once you have found a walk you like, simply print it out on standard A4 paper and you are ready to go!

- Convenient A4 sized maps
- Print copies for everyone in your party
- Find walks for holidays and short breaks

A modest annual subscription gives you access to over 2000 walks, all in Walkingworld's easy to follow format. The database of walks is growing all the time and as a subscriber you gain access to new routes as soon as they are published.

Visit the Walkingworld website at *www.walkingworld.com*

INDEX OF WALKS

ORDER FORM

To order any of our publications just fill in the payment details below and complete the order form. For orders of less than 4 copies please add £1 per book for postage and packing. Orders over 4 copies are P & P free.

Please Complete Either:

I enclose a cheque for £ [   ] made payable to Travel Publishing Ltd

Or:

CARD NO: [   ] EXPIRY DATE: [   ]

SIGNATURE: [   ]

NAME: [   ]

ADDRESS: [   ]

TEL NO: [   ]

Please either send, telephone, fax or e-mail your order to:

Travel Publishing Ltd, Airport Business Centre, 10 Thornbury Road, Estover, Plymouth PL6 7PP
Tel: 01752 697280   Fax: 01752 697299   e-mail: info@travelpublishing.co.uk

	PRICE	QUANTITY		PRICE	QUANTITY
HIDDEN PLACES REGIONAL TITLES			**COUNTRY LIVING RURAL GUIDES**		
Cornwall	£8.99	....	East Anglia	£10.99	....
Devon	£8.99	....	Heart of England	£10.99	....
Dorset, Hants & Isle of Wight	£8.99	....	Ireland	£11.99	....
East Anglia	£8.99	....	North East of England	£10.99	....
Lake District & Cumbria	£8.99	....	North West of England	£10.99	....
Lancashire & Cheshire	£8.99	....	Scotland	£11.99	....
Northumberland & Durham	£8.99	....	South of England	£10.99	....
Peak District and Derbyshire	£8.99	....	South East of England	£10.99	....
Yorkshire	£8.99	....	Wales	£11.99	....
HIDDEN PLACES NATIONAL TITLES			West Country	£10.99	....
England	£11.99	....			
Ireland	£11.99	....			
Scotland	£11.99	....			
Wales	£11.99	....			
OTHER TITLES			**TOTAL QUANTITY**	[ ]	
Off The Motorway	£11.99	....	**TOTAL VALUE**	[ ]	
Garden Centres and Nurseries of Britain	£11.99	....			

READER REACTION FORM

The **Travel Publishing** *research team would like to receive readers' comments on any visitor attractions or places reviewed in the book and also recommendations for suitable entries to be included in the next edition. This will help ensure that the* **Country Living series of Rural Guides** *continues to provide its readers with useful information on the more interesting, unusual or unique features of each attraction or place ensuring that their visit to the local area is an enjoyable and stimulating experience. To provide your comments or recommendations would you please complete the forms below and overleaf as indicated and send to:*

The Research Department, Travel Publishing Ltd, Airport Business Centre, 10 Thornbury Road, Estover, Plymouth PL6 7PP

YOUR NAME:

YOUR ADDRESS:

YOUR TEL NO:

Please tick as appropriate: COMMENTS ☐   RECOMMENDATION ☐

ESTABLISHMENT:

ADDRESS:

TEL NO:

CONTACT NAME:

PLEASE COMPLETE FORM OVERLEAF

READER REACTION FORM

COMMENT OR REASON FOR RECOMMENDATION:

....

....

....

....

....

....

....

....

....

....

....

READER REACTION FORM

The **Travel Publishing** *research team would like to receive readers' comments on any visitor attractions or places reviewed in the book and also recommendations for suitable entries to be included in the next edition. This will help ensure that the* **Country Living series of Rural Guides** *continues to provide its readers with useful information on the more interesting, unusual or unique features of each attraction or place ensuring that their visit to the local area is an enjoyable and stimulating experience. To provide your comments or recommendations would you please complete the forms below and overleaf as indicated and send to:*

The Research Department, Travel Publishing Ltd, Airport Business Centre,
10 Thornbury Road, Estover, Plymouth PL6 7PP

YOUR NAME:

YOUR ADDRESS:

YOUR TEL NO:

Please tick as appropriate: COMMENTS ☐   RECOMMENDATION ☐

ESTABLISHMENT:

ADDRESS:

TEL NO:

CONTACT NAME:

PLEASE COMPLETE FORM OVERLEAF

READER REACTION FORM

COMMENT OR REASON FOR RECOMMENDATION:

....

....

....

....

....

....

....

....

....

....

....

TOWNS, VILLAGES AND PLACES OF INTEREST

TOWNS, VILLAGES AND PLACES OF INTEREST

TOWNS, VILLAGES AND PLACES OF INTEREST

TOWNS, VILLAGES AND PLACES OF INTEREST

TOWNS, VILLAGES AND PLACES OF INTEREST

TOWNS, VILLAGES AND PLACES OF INTEREST

TOWNS, VILLAGES AND PLACES OF INTEREST

TOWNS, VILLAGES AND PLACES OF INTEREST

TOWNS, VILLAGES AND PLACES OF INTEREST

TOWNS, VILLAGES AND PLACES OF INTEREST

TOWNS, VILLAGES AND PLACES OF INTEREST

TOWNS, VILLAGES AND PLACES OF INTEREST

TOWNS, VILLAGES AND PLACES OF INTEREST

TOWNS, VILLAGES AND PLACES OF INTEREST